FUTILE DIPLOMACY

Volume 4

OPERATION ALPHA AND THE
FAILURE OF ANGLO–AMERICAN
COERCIVE DIPLOMACY IN THE
ARAB–ISRAELI CONFLICT, 1954–1956

FUTILE DIPLOMACY

Volume Four

Operation Alpha and the Failure of Anglo–American Coercive Diplomacy in the Arab–Israeli Conflict, 1954–1956

NEIL CAPLAN

Routledge
Taylor & Francis Group
LONDON AND NEW YORK

First published in 1997 by FRANK CASS PUBLISHERS

This edition first published in 2015
by Routledge
4 Park Square, Milton Park, Abingdon, Oxon OX14 4RN
605 Third Avenue, New York, NY 10017

Routledge is an imprint of the Taylor & Francis Group, an informa business

© 1997 Neil Caplan

All rights reserved. No part of this book may be reprinted or reproduced or utilised in any form or by any electronic, mechanical, or other means, now known or hereafter invented, including photocopying and recording, or in any information storage or retrieval system, without permission in writing from the publishers.

Trademark notice: Product or corporate names may be trademarks or registered trademarks, and are used only for identification and explanation without intent to infringe.

British Library Cataloguing in Publication Data
A catalogue record for this book is available from the British Library

ISBN: 978-1-138-90521-4 (Set)
ISBN: 978-1-315-69594-5 (ebk)(Set)
ISBN: 978-1-138-90525-2 (hbk)(Volume 4)
ISBN: 978-1-315-69508-2 (ebk)(Volume 4)
ISBN: 978-1-138-90755-3 (pbk)(Volume 4)

Publisher's Note
The publisher has gone to great lengths to ensure the quality of this reprint but points out that some imperfections in the original copies may be apparent.

Disclaimer
The publisher has made every effort to trace copyright holders and would welcome correspondence from those they have been unable to trace.

FUTILE DIPLOMACY

VOLUME FOUR

OPERATION ALPHA AND THE FAILURE OF ANGLO–AMERICAN COERCIVE DIPLOMACY IN THE ARAB–ISRAELI CONFLICT, 1954–1956

NEIL CAPLAN

FRANK CASS
LONDON • PORTLAND, OR

First published in 1997 in Great Britain by
FRANK CASS PUBLISHERS
Newbury House, 900 Eastern Avenue
London IG2 7HH

and in the United States of America by
FRANK CASS PUBLISHERS
c/o ISBS, 5804 N.E. Hassalo Street
Portland, Oregon 97213-3644

Website: http://www.frankcass.com

Copyright © 1997 Neil Caplan

British Library Cataloguing in Publication Data:

Caplan, Neil, 1945–
  Futile diplomacy
  Vol. 4: Operation Alpha and the failure of Anglo–American coercive diplomacy in the Arab–Israeli conflict, 1954–1956
  1. Israel-Arab conflicts 2. Jewish-Arab relations – 1949–1967
  3. Diplomatic negotiations in international disputes
  I. Title
  327.5'694'0174927

ISBN 0-7146-4757-8 (cloth)

Library of Congress Cataloging-in-Publication Data

Caplan, Neil, 1945–
  Operation Alpha and the failure of Anglo-American coercive diplomacy in the Arab–Israeli conflict, 1954–1956 / Neil Caplan
    p. cm. — (Futile diplomacy ; v. 4)
  Includes bibliographical references (p.) and index.
  ISBN 0-7146-4757-8 (cloth)
  1. Jewish–Arab relations—1949–1967. 2. Jewish–Arab relations—1949–1967—Sources. 3. United Nations—Palestine. 4. World politics—1945–1955. I. Title. II. Series: Caplan, Neil, 1945– Futile diplomacy ; v. 4.
  DS119.7.C319
  956.04'2—dc21   82-213007

All rights reserved. No part of this publication may be reproduced in any form or by any means, electronic, mechanical, photocopying, recording or otherwise, without the prior permission of Frank Cass & Company Limited.

Typeset by
Vitaset, Paddock Wood, Kent
Printed in Great Britain by
Bookcraft (Bath) Ltd, Midsomer Norton, Avon

Contents

Documents   viii
Preface   ix
Abbreviations   xi
Illustrations   xiii
Introduction   xv

Part One: The Background of Anglo–American Co-operation, 1948–54

I Anglo–American Support for Bilateral and United Nations Peace Efforts   3

Dynamics of Anglo–American Co-operation
Support for Bilateral Negotiations
Support for United Nations Initiatives

II The Two-Pronged Approach   14

'A Gradual Process of Education' of the Arabs to Accept Israel
Pressure on Israel for Gestures and Concessions

III Nibbling at the Edges: The Failure of Conflict Management   27

The Tripartite Declaration
Diplomatic Representations in Support of UNTSO
Anglo–American Proposals for Reducing Frontier Tensions
Starting a Chain of Confidence-Building Measures
From the 'Edges' Back to the Core Issues

IV Attempts at Conflict Resolution   49

Calls for a 'Positive Policy' – A Settlement by Compulsion?
American and British Plans for a Comprehensive Settlement
Convergence of British and American Thinking

Part Two: The Best Laid Plans

V Preparing Alpha — 73
British Good Offices Offered
Looking for an Arab Opening; Keeping the Israelis Reassured
From Co-operation to Collaboration: Formulation of Anglo–American Terms of Settlement

VI First Approaches — 96
Eden and Nasir: First Hints of Alpha
Setbacks: Baghdad pact and Gaza Raid
Byroade, Fawzi and Nasir: Early Probings
London and Paris Meetings: Fine-Tuning the Negev Proposals
Factoring in Israel: Security Treaty versus Arab–Israeli Settlement

Part Three: Stumbling from Obstacle to Obstacle

VII From Secret Sounding to Public Pronouncements: The Dulles Statement, August 1955 — 123
The Waiting Game, April – August 1955
Dulles' Decision to Go Public
The Dulles Statement
Aftermath

VIII Arms and Alpha: The Arab Connection — 152
Western Arms and Aid for the Arabs
Soviet Arms for Egypt: The End of the Tripartite Monopoly
Sharett's Hat-in-Hand Diplomacy: Paris and Geneva
Fears of an Israeli Pre-emptive Strike
New Moves to Court Nasir

IX Eden's Guildhall Speech, November 1955 — 175
Guildhall Speech: Seeking a Compromise between 1947 and the Status Quo
Arab Reactions
The Israeli Reaction
Mahmud Fawzi: Principles behind the Egyptian Position

X Showdown with Sharett — 187
Build-Up to a Confrontation between the US and Israel
Dulles' 'Bombshell Surprise', 21 November 1955
Not Another Munich: Israel Sets Out its Position
A New Israeli 'Peace Offensive?
Finessing US–Israeli Differences
Between Optimism and Pessimism

CONTENTS   vii

XI   Arms and Alpha: The Israeli Connection   204
      Hesitations Regarding Israel's Arms Requests
      Lake Kinneret Raid
      Arms as Carrots for Negotiations
      Arms and the Anderson Mission
      A Brief Assessment

XII   Alpha's Last Chance: The Anderson Mission   220
      Preparing for American Mediation
      Anderson's Mission: Mandate and Expectations
      First Meetings in Cairo
      First Meetings in Israel
      Return to Cairo
      Return to Jerusalem
      Interlude: Washington, Cairo, Jerusalem

Conclusions

XIII Alpha and Gamma: Post-Scripts and Post-Mortems   245
      'Last Shot' at a Meeting between Nasir and Ben-Gurion
      Anderson's Final Visit
      From 'Alpha' to 'Omega'
      The Principal Players: Nasir and Israel

XIV Carrots and Sticks: The Limits of Anglo–American
      Coercive Diplomacy   262
      Militant Protagonists and International Opinion
      The Context: British and American Interests
      Carrots and Sticks: An Inventory
      Anglo–American Co-operation
      American and British Presumptions
      The Limits of Coercive Diplomacy
      'Arms and the Dam'

Documents   290

Notes   319

Bibliography   392

Index   407

Documents

1. Tripartite Declaration, 25 May 1950 — 290
2. F.O. Conditions for Settlement, 29 July 1952 — 291
3. F.O. Possible Terms of a Palestine Settlement, 2 December 1953 — 292
4. C.A.E. Shuckburgh, the Elements of a Settlement, 15 December 1954 — 294
5. Points of Agreement in London Discussions of Arab–Israeli Settlement, 10 March 1955 — 296
6. Proposals by Secretary of State Dulles for a Settlement in the Arab–Israel Zone, 26 August 1955 — 304
7. Sir Ivone Kirkpatrick Minute: The Middle East, 30 October 1955 — 307
8. Anthony Eden's Guildhall (Mansion House) Speech, 9 November 1955 — 309
9. Draft of Proposed Agreed Position between US and UK on Middle East Policy, 9 November 1955 — 311
10. Aide-Mémoire from the Israeli Embassy, Washington, to the Department of State, 6 December 1955 — 315
11. Statement of General Principles which would provide a satisfactory basis for the resolution of the several points at issue between the Arab States and Israel, authorized by Gamal Abd al-Nasir, 4 February 1956 — 317

Preface

This book grew out of a misguided attempt to present, in a single volume, an overview documentary history of the period between the first and second Arab–Israeli wars. Given the level of analysis and the complexity of the manoeuvring of the main protagonists, a full volume (Volume III in this series) was required to cover the futile attempts before 1954 to convert the shaky 1949 armistice agreements into stable peace accords, mainly through conference-style diplomacy. The current volume focuses on the Anglo-American co-operation which began during the relatively uneventful years 1953 and 1954, and which led to a covert operation, code-named 'Alpha', which aimed – unsuccessfully – at convincing Egyptian and Israeli leaders to consider a settlement through secret negotiations.

This study would not have been possible without the financial assistance of the Government of Québec's FCAR Programme, the Canadian Institute for International Peace and Security (Ottawa), and the Memorial Foundation for Jewish Culture (New York). Research was conducted in England as a Visiting Scholar of the Oxford Centre for Postgraduate Hebrew Studies, which provided me its idyllic base of operations at Yarnton Manor. Much of the work in Israel was done as a Fellow of the Moshe Dayan Center for Middle Eastern and African Studies of Tel Aviv University, to which I am deeply indebted not only for financial support but also for warm hospitality and unparalleled opportunities for research and discussion with colleagues. During my time at Tel Aviv University, I was most fortunate to have met with Professor Shimon Shamir (who has also served as Israel's Ambassador to Egypt and Jordan). His pioneering research on the subject has earned him the honorary presidency of a select circle known as the 'Alpha Club'. His extensive article on the collapse of Project Alpha serves as an inspiration and model to be emulated, and I was very grateful for his advice, which was always offered with great kindness and patience.

For their helpfulness in dealing with my many requests, I wish to thank the staffs and directors of the following institutions: Ben-Gurion Archive, Sede Boqer; Central Zionist Archives, Jerusalem; Documentation Center, Library and Press Archives, Moshe Dayan Center, Tel Aviv University; Foreign Affairs Oral History Collection, Georgetown University Library; Institute for Palestine Studies, Washington; Israel State Archives, Jerusalem; Kressel Collection and Library, Yarnton, Oxford; Public Record Office, Kew, England; St Antony's College, Middle East Centre Library, Oxford; United Nations Archives, New York; United States National Archives, Washington DC; and Washington National Records Center, Suitland MD.

Among the fine people upon whom I have imposed in search of their valued advice or services, I wish to thank Laura Eisenberg, Yehoshua Freundlich, Mordechai Gazit, Philip Mattar, Moshe Mossek, Itamar Rabinovich, Gideon Rafael, Yemima Rosenthal, Avraham Sela, Shimon Shamir, Avi Shlaim and Shabtai Teveth. Special thanks go to Kamal Abdel-Malek, Dina Cohen and Fawaz Gerges for their assistance in handling Arabic materials, and to Bryna Bogoch and Ben Caplan for their excellent work in the assembling of research materials.

Neil Caplan
Humanities Department
Vanier College, Montréal, Québec, Canada   *January 1997*

Abbreviations

airg	airgram
AL	Arab League (= League of Arab States)
BMEO	British Middle East Office
BrComDiv	British Commonwealth Division, Israel Ministry of Foreign Affairs
CIA	Central Intelligence Agency
CZA	Central Zionist Archives, Jerusalem*
Del	Delegation
desp	despatch
DMZ	Demilitarized Zone
DSB	United States, *Department of State Bulletin*
EIGAA	Egypt–Israel General Armistice Agreement
EIMAC	Egypt–Israel Mixed Armistice Commission
Emb	Embassy
EnDept	Eastern Department, (British) Foreign Office
ESM	Economic Survey Mission (1949)
FD	*Futile Diplomacy**
FO	Foreign Office, London
FRUS	*Foreign Relations of the United States**
GAA	General Armistice Agreement (1949)
HMG	His (Her) Majesty's Government, United Kingdom
ID	*Documents on the Foreign Policy of Israel**
IDF	Israel Defence Forces
IJGAA	Israel–Jordan General Armistice Agreement
IJMAC	Israel–Jordan Mixed Armistice Commission
IMFA	Israel Ministry of Foreign Affairs
ISA	Israel State Archives, Jerusalem*
JTA	Jewish Telegraphic Agency
LCA	Local Commanders' Agreement
Leg	Legation
LevDept	Levant Department, (British) Foreign Office

MAC	Mixed Armistice Commission
MEC	Private Papers Collection, Middle East Centre, St Antony's College, Oxford, England*
MFA	Ministry of Foreign Affairs; Minister for Foreign Affairs
Mis	Mission
NATO	North Atlantic Treaty Organization
NEA	Bureau of Near Eastern, South Asian and African Affairs (US Department of State)
NIE	National Intelligence Estimate
NSC	National Security Council
PCC	Palestine Conciliation Commission (= United Nations Conciliation Commission for Palestine)
PGI	Provisional Government of Israel (May 1948 – January 1949)
PMO	Prime Minister's Office
PPSG	*Public Papers of the Secretary-General of the United Nations**
PRO	Public Record Office, Kew, England*
PSC	Provisional State Council (= Cabinet of the PGI)
RCC	Revolutionary Command Council, Egypt
ResDiv	Research Division, Israel Ministry of Foreign Affairs
SNIE	Special National Intelligence Estimate
tgm	telegram
UN	United Nations
UNA	United Nations Archives, New York*
UNGA	United Nations General Assembly
UNRWA	United Nations Relief and Works Agency
UNSC	United Nations Security Council
UNTSO	United Nations Truce Supervisory Organization
USDiv	US Division, Israel Ministry of Foreign Affairs
USNA	National Archives, Washington DC*
USSD	United States, Department of State
WEurDiv	Western Europe Division, Israel Ministry of Foreign Affairs
WNRC	Washington National Records Center, Suitland MD*

* see Bibliography

Illustrations

MAP: 'Recent Incidents', *The New York Times*, 6 November 1955 — 137

Cartoon: 'Poor Cure for Volcanoes', *The Christian Science Monitor*, 1 November 1955 — 160

MAP: 'Southwestern Israel, Gaza, and Auja, 1949–1956' — 167

Cartoon and text: 'March of Events: Goliath's Grudge Fight' [1955] — 206

Photocopy of letter: Gamal Abdel Nasser to President Dwight D. Eisenhower, 6 February 1956 — 240

Introduction

The Arab-Israeli conflict is today a matter of general public interest as well as a special concern of policy analysts and strategic studies experts. In recent decades, those committed to the study of war and peace have often focused their attention on this particular conflict because of its intractable nature and its potential for destruction and superpower confrontation. It has had global implications during various crises in the past, most notably the nuclear alert declared by the United States during the October 1973 war and the oil supply and price crisis of 1973–75. Egypt and Israel surprised most observers by concluding a peace treaty between 1977 and 1979, but a more comprehensive settlement involving other Arab states and the Palestinian Arabs remained elusive. In December 1987, the core Palestinian–Israeli impasse, for decades entangled in the regional conflict between Israel and the Arab states, reasserted itself in the form of a popular uprising known as the *intifada*. Only after the peace process began publicly at Madrid October 1991 and secretly in Oslo during 1993 did there appear to be any promise of a breakthrough.

While the extent of international involvement has waxed and waned over the years, the conflict's local and regional dimensions have been more constant. This bitter and persisting dispute has exploded into serious regional wars seven times during 40 years. Even the relatively peaceful periods between these eruptions were often marred by a pattern of 'terrorism' and 'reprisal', inflicting death, suffering and trauma upon generations of Arabs and Israelis.

Not surprisingly, much of the writing on this subject continues to be focused on the origins or consequences of one or more of these wars. The rarer episodes of attempts at peacemaking have also been studied, but too often in polemical presentations which blame one party or another for a missed opportunity. The present study focuses on the period leading up to the second Arab–Israeli war (the Suez–Sinai war of October–November 1956), and offers the anatomy of a joint Anglo–American operation code-named 'Alpha', a little-known diplomatic exercise in promoting peace between Egypt and Israel during 1955 and the early part of 1956.

In the years following the first Arab–Israeli war of 1947–1949,[1] both Arabs and Israelis were sinking deeper and deeper into a conflict over which the United Nations (UN) and the two major Western powers were losing control. A number of initiatives by the UN aimed at persuading the Arab states and Israel to make the compromises necessary to move from an inherently shaky armistice to a more durable peace proved futile, despite parallel efforts and unofficial sponsorship from both the United Kingdom (UK) and the United States (US).

Between 1948 and 1954, the UN, US and UK were involved in five major efforts aimed at bringing about Arab–Israeli negotiations towards a definitive settlement of their dispute:

- the unsuccessful attempts of UN mediator Count Folke Bernadotte to move the warring parties from truce to armistice negotiations and a political settlement;
- the Egyptian–Israeli armistice negotiations conducted by Acting Mediator Ralph S. Bunche at Rhodes in early 1949, which produced the first of four similar General Armistice Agreements (GAAs);
- a 'peace conference' in Lausanne, Switzerland, under the auspices of the United Nations Conciliation Commission for Palestine (or Palestine Conciliation Commission, PCC), from April to September 1949;
- a second PCC conference, held in Paris, from September to November 1951; and
- the unsuccessful attempts by the UN to promote direct negotiations (late 1952), and particularly the efforts by its Secretary-General to convene a conference between Israel and Jordan (November 1953 to April 1954).[2]

Neither the moral authority of the United Nations nor the incentives or pressures available to Great Britain and the United States seemed capable of budging the parties from the irreconcilable stances to which they became committed after 1948. By the autumn of 1954, policy makers in London and Washington were reaching similar conclusions regarding the deteriorating situation in the Middle East. Making matters worse were growing Western fears of Soviet penetration into the area. Officials in Great Britain and the United States came to regard the building of a pro-Western regional defence system as imperative, but they found that plans for such defence arrangements were thwarted, in part, by the continuing increase in tensions and frontier skirmishes between Israel and its Arab neighbours.

A solution to the Arab–Israeli conflict thus became a priority foreign policy interest of both Britain and the United States. Along with the perceived increased risk of the outbreak of a new war came the decline, in both London and Washington, of hopes of dealing successfully with the Arab–Israeli dispute *via* the UN and its available organs. The cumulative experience of their futile efforts between 1948 and 1954 led British and American policy makers to conclude that, rather than continuing to work through (and behind the scenes of) the UN, they would have to embark on a bold initiative and assume responsibility for proposing their own peace plan. Realizing the impossibility of either a truly voluntary or a truly imposed solution, they believed that they could provide sufficient incentives and pressures on both parties to make them accept, however reluctantly, a settlement which could then be underwritten by the United Nations and guaranteed by Britain and America.

Such a diplomatic initiative required a highly co-ordinated Anglo–American effort requiring two sets of pressures to be applied simultaneously

- on the Arabs (mainly by the UK) to accept Israel's existence and end the state of declared and undeclared hostility, and
- on Israel (mainly by the US) to convince the Jewish state to make significant concessions on territory and the return of Palestinian refugees.

During December 1954 and January 1955, the first steps were taken in preparation for Operation Alpha, which soon developed into a major top-secret Anglo–American exercise in 'coercive diplomacy'.[3] During high-level consultations in Washington and London, British and American officials, led by Evelyn Shuckburgh and Francis Russell, hammered out the outlines of a detailed joint proposal, along with lists of incentives to be used to win the co-operation of the prospective negotiating parties.

The persistent efforts of Alpha's planners to interest Egypt and Israel in a settlement proved to be a frustrating and futile exercise. The process of disclosing certain aspects of the Anglo–American peace plan to the main protagonists unfolded in fits and starts during unpropitious times. In the end, the entire episode never went beyond the stage of 'prenegotiation'.[4] After initial behind-the-scenes efforts failed to win a sufficient commitment to Alpha from Egypt's Prime Minister, Gamal Abd al-Nasir, both American Secretary of State John Foster Dulles and British Prime Minister Anthony Eden attempted to create momentum for peace by issuing public statements which urged the parties to consider a settlement. Operation Alpha also involved strong, but ultimately unsuccessful, secret American pressure on Israel to make territorial concessions in the Negev desert so as to create contiguity between Egypt and Jordan.

After a series of setbacks, Alpha was given one last chance in early 1956 when President Eisenhower sent special emissary Robert Anderson to try to arrange a secret meeting between Gamal Abd al-Nasir and Israel's Prime Minister, David Ben-Gurion. Anderson's mediation attempt, also known under the code-name 'Gamma', involved the close co-operation of the American Central Intelligence Agency (CIA). The collapse of the Anderson mission in March 1956 became one of the key turning-points in London's and Washington's stiffening attitude towards an increasingly defiant Abd al-Nasir.

The onus of blame for the failure of this last-ditch mediation attempt fell upon the Egyptian leader for having maintained his refusal to enter into direct talks with Israeli representatives. The State Department thereupon moved quietly from Alpha to a new plan, code-named 'Omega', designed to undermine and isolate Nasir's pro-Soviet régime. Omega was one of several crucial steps in the 'descent' to Suez,[5] leading, in late October of that year, to the second major Arab–Israeli war.

SOURCES AND APPROACH

The Anglo–Franco–Israeli 'collusion' in launching the Suez War of 1956 was denounced almost immediately by the international community and has since been well documented and discussed by

INTRODUCTION xix

scholars.[6] By contrast, the earlier Anglo–American 'collusion' in pursuing Operation Alpha remained unknown, until recently, outside a tight circle of diplomats and undercover agents. Until the release of British and American documents, which are kept closed under a 30-year rule, our knowledge of this episode in coercive diplomacy was speculative and fragmentary at best. Prior to the opening of Foreign Office and State Department files, scholars had to rely only on the public record and selected disclosures in published memoirs.

Thus, students of the history of the Arab–Israeli conflict identified John Foster Dulles' and Anthony Eden's speeches of August and November of 1955 as important calls for peace[7] – but no one recognized them as co-ordinated steps in a joint Anglo–American plan. In his first memoirs, published in 1977, Abba Eban, former Israeli Ambassador in Washington, recalled his discussions with Francis Russell (then Special Assistant to Secretary of State Dulles) about American suggestions for a territorial compromise with Egypt and Jordan by which Israel was asked to cede two triangles of the Negev Desert.[8] A further element of Alpha was disclosed – again, in isolation from the other pieces of the puzzle – with the 1971 publication of David Ben-Gurion's records of his early-1956 conversations with President Eisenhower's personal emissary, although without revealing Anderson's name.[9] The identity of 'the emissary' did not remain secret for long, however, as Mohamed Heikal, a close confidant of Gamal Abd al-Nasir, gave his own version of Anderson's talks with the Egyptian leader, along with the American intersecting-triangles proposal, in *The Cairo Documents*.[10] Yaacov Herzog, a senior Israeli adviser who took part in the talks, left a brief oral memoir of the Anderson mission which appeared in a 1975 posthumous collection of speeches and writings.[11] In 1978, Yaacov Sharett published the revealing *Personal Diary* of his father Moshe, former Israeli Foreign Minister (1948–56) and Prime Minister (1954–55), in eight volumes, containing additional clues to the story. In the same year, Teddy Kollek, then mayor of Jerusalem and Ben-Gurion's *chef de cabinet* during the mid-1950s, included his own brief account of the Anderson mission in a memoir published with his son.[12]

Making skilful use of the available diaries, memoirs and other sources, political scientist Saadia Touval produced an excellent chapter on the Anderson mission, one of nine case-studies in his seminal work on mediators in the Arab–Israeli conflict.[13] But, even after the story of the Anderson mission was reconstructed, the existence of Alpha remained a well-kept secret even to those who had had first-hand experience with individual components of the more comprehensive and ambitious plan. Only in the 1980s did scholars and analysts begin to discern that the various peace efforts of 1955–56 were parts of a co-ordinated operation.

Alpha was first mentioned by name in the published memoirs of former CIA agent Wilbur Crane Eveland in 1980.[14] One of the peculiar features of the operation was the overshadowing, in late 1955 and early 1956, of normal US State Department [USSD] diplomacy by the 'crypto-diplomacy' of CIA operatives, who were able to boast more intimate and reliable channels to Colonel Nasir and his confidants than the American Embassy in Cairo.[15] Interestingly, both Israelis and Egyptians at this time had cause to believe that CIA personnel gave them a more sympathetic hearing than did State Department officials.[16] The USSD–CIA collaboration in the final stages of Operation Alpha was greatly facilitated by the coincidence that the two US organs were headed at the time by the Dulles brothers: John Foster at State, and Allen W. at the Agency.

During the 1980s more details about Alpha became known with the publication of the revealing memoirs of the chief British architect of the plan, Evelyn Shuckburgh.[17] Most importantly, the mid-1980s also saw the opening of British and American archive materials on the period. The authoritative, but edited, documentation of the American side of the story has recently become available with the appearance of relevant volumes in the invaluable USSD series, *Foreign Relations of the United States (FRUS)*.[18] Making use of available British, American and Arabic primary sources, Shimon Shamir, professor at Tel Aviv University and former Israeli Ambassador to Egypt, produced a pioneering analysis of Operation Alpha which stands as a model of careful and balanced scholarship.[19] A 1991 revisionist study of Anglo–American relations during the Suez crisis was among the first full-length books to incorporate newly-available evidence on Operation Alpha.[20] W. Scott Lucas' *Divided We Stand* was followed by two doctoral dissertations containing valuable chapters on Alpha based on original archival research: a study of Egyptian–Israeli relations by the American–Israeli scholar, Michael (Bornstein) Oren, and a detailed analysis of Israeli defence and foreign policy by

Mordechai Bar-On, who also served as private secretary and *chef de bureau* to Israeli Chief of Staff Moshe Dayan during the period under discussion.[21]

The treatment of the Operation Alpha offered in these pages places the episode within the framework of British and American policymaking and peacemaking in the Middle East between the first and second Arab–Israeli wars. The present study is the fourth in the author's series of documentary histories which began with the pre-1948 Arab–Israeli conflict.[22] Like its predecessors, this book is based principally on documents: archival sources in London, Washington and Jerusalem, as well as secondary sources in English, Hebrew and Arabic.[23]

By examining these documents, one has the possibility of delving below the surface of the *declared* motives or intentions of the various protagonists, whether in their contemporary public statements or in their retrospective (but usually more self-serving than revealing) memoirs. Diaries, correspondence and internal memoranda written at the time of the events as they occurred are the primary sources which are given most credence in the reconstruction of events offered in these pages. These documents shed more light on the true preoccupations which affected policy-makers, along with the calculations they made when away from the glare of public scrutiny. Seen through archival documents, both the principal adversaries and would-be mediators and conciliators can be credited, in retrospect, with having had a keen sense of timing and a rather sophisticated approach to tactical manoeuvring.

Given the many-sided and intractable nature of the Arab–Israeli dispute, the availability of parallel documentary sources which offer several different perspectives can help today's readers achieve a better understanding of the complexities not only of the Alpha episode, but also of the very nature of the conflict, demonstrating that there are often *more* than the proverbial 'two sides to every story'. By examining a multiplicity of primary documents, I hope that I have succeeded in achieving an accurate, but 'imaginative', understanding of each of the various parties involved in Alpha, without appearing to endorse any of the protagonists and without falling victim to what E.H. Carr has called a 'fetishism of documents'.[24]

Part One

The Background of Anglo–American
Co-operation, 1948–54

CHAPTER I

Anglo–American Support for Bilateral and United Nations Peace Efforts

Those who were to become the American and British planners of Operation Alpha at the end of 1954 embarked upon their joint peace project not in a void but against the background of a decade of Anglo–American experience at co-operating on the Palestine question. The first formal instance of an effort at such co-operation regarding Palestine dates back to 1945, with the work of the Anglo–American Committee of Inquiry. Six Americans and six Britons surprised all observers by producing a unanimous report, but a number of their recommendations proved unworkable. Revised Anglo–American proposals were drawn up during the subsequent Morrison–Grady talks, but these too fell by the wayside when the United Nations appointed, and acted upon, the report of its own Special Committee on Palestine in 1947.[1]

Throughout 1948, State Department officials seemed intent on pursuing a 'joint strategic approach with Britain'.[2] Attempts at joint action continued after the creation of the state of Israel. From the aborted Bernadotte plan of 1948 until Anglo–American efforts to 'nibble at the edges' of Arab–Israeli frontier disputes in 1954, there were almost a dozen episodes which required co-operation between the two Western powers. Our examination of the evolution of Anglo–American co-operation will focus on the following areas:

- dynamics and mutual perceptions; support for bilateral and UN peace efforts (Chapter I);

- the development of a two-pronged approach, pressing both Arabs and Israelis to consider concessions (Chapter II);
- efforts at conflict *management* and the prevention of explosions of military action (Chapter III); and
- efforts at conflict *resolution*, or attempts to persuade or coerce the parties into negotiating a settlement (Chapter IV).

The cumulative Anglo–American experience of 1948–54 was fairly extensive, but not always encouraging. As we shall see below, the Western powers found themselves relatively ineffective in restraining the parties from provocations or retaliations along the armistice lines, but merely attempting to manage the conflict, without taking risks in an effort to resolve it, gradually became an untenable position for the Western powers. By late 1954, both Britain and the United States were reaching disturbing conclusions about the potential explosiveness of the Arab–Israeli stand-off. Given the Cold War and fears of the expansion of Soviet influence in the region, both the US and the UK were concluding that, without more active intervention on their part in pursuit of a definitive peace accord, the situation would only grow worse. They were also forced to recognize that, to realize the goal of an Arab–Israeli settlement, a greater degree of Anglo–American co-ordination and co-operation was essential.

DYNAMICS OF ANGLO–AMERICAN CO-OPERATION

In the years leading up to Operation Alpha, the two Western powers, whether singly or in tandem, reacted to situations in an *ad hoc* manner. Neither country acted in pursuit of a preconceived policy. The pattern which developed was one in which danger signals periodically led to calls for co-ordinated action or a joint Anglo–American plan for resolving the Arab–Israeli conflict. During six years of cumulative trial-and-error experience, American and British approaches to a possible resolution of the dispute came to share several basic assumptions:

- The non-resolution of the Arab–Israeli conflict was progressively threatening to undermine Western interests in the Middle East. These interests, largely strategic location and the uninterrupted supply of oil, required the maintenance of stability in, and the exclusion of Soviet influence from, the region.

- Despite Israeli protestations to the contrary, there was no real hope of the parties arriving at a settlement voluntarily and through direct negotiations.
- United Nations mediation and conciliation efforts were proving unequal to the challenge of resolving the festering dispute. Even the UN machinery for conflict management was increasingly losing its ability to prevent an escalation of frontier incidents.

Although these presumptions were never put together coherently as a basis for policy-making, by late 1954 they seemed axiomatic to officials at the State Department and the Foreign Office.

Mutual perceptions

Seen from the perspective of each of the protagonists, neither Britain nor America ever did enough to achieve a proper settlement of the post-1948 Arab–Israeli conflict. Each party, at various times, has accused one or both of the Western powers of being unwilling (or unable) to apply sufficient pressure to the *other party* to adopt the reasonable and conciliatory attitude that might have made a settlement possible. One academic has even speculated that

> [i]n 1953 ... it was not too late realistically to envision both repatriation of Palestinians to Israel and changes in the 1949 armistice lines to allow for an independent state.... The opportunity for the resolution of the Question of Palestine – never really desired by the Eisenhower administration – was lost.[3]

The presentation offered in Part One of this study, based on a careful analysis of archival sources, thoroughly contradicts such a hindsight-driven appraisal as a facile and polemical misreading of the policies and possibilities of the period.

Both powers, in pursuit of their respective national interests, had strong reasons for wanting to see a resolution of the conflict; as a consequence, they invested serious efforts in attempting to prepare the main protagonists for possible concessions. But, at every turn, British and American policy-makers confronted growing evidence of just how *limited* was their ability to influence the Arab states and Israel in the direction of a settlement. The former's price for their consent to enter into negotiations remained a revision of boundaries in accordance with the 1947 partition lines and the return of the

Palestinian refugees, while the latter continued to seek peace based on the *status quo* and was prepared to consider only minor concessions regarding refugees and territory.[4]

Efforts at co-operation between the two Western powers also had to overcome some mutual perceptions which were not always flattering. As former CIA operative Miles Copeland recalled, the 'international gameboard we thought we were playing on differed in important respects from the gameboard the British thought we were playing on'.

> [W]hile the words of Winston Churchill about the empire were still ringing in British ears, we had become openly sympathetic to nationalist movements, and our Secretary of State had publicly admitted that he believed the US to be handicapped by Britain's 'colonialist' policies and that he was trying to dissociate our government from them.

Justifications for British attitudes and policies were often explained 'so patronizingly to Americans as though we were a lot of backward children'.[5] Echoing Israeli complaints, some US officials also tended to believe that the British did not do as much as they could have done to influence the Arab states in the direction of agreeing to deal with Israel.

Counterbalancing these views were British perceptions of the Americans. The more experienced British 'senior partners' often had cause to regard the 'junior' Americans as naïve, impatient and well-meaning, but dangerously misguided in their overall approach which displayed romanticized sympathies with emerging Third World anti-colonialism and nationalism. Bemoaning the 'misunderstandings and unfounded prejudices' which spoiled Anglo–American relations during the 1950s, Sir John Bagot Glubb noted:

> Some people would have us believe that American Big Business is deliberately endeavouring to oust Britain from all Asia and Africa, in order itself to be able to exploit these countries without a competitor. It is certainly striking how often the USA seems to lead the attack on Britain's position in some Eastern country.

Glubb was therefore slow to accept expressions of American suspicions of 'British "colonial methods"' as completely disinterested.[6]

With regard to the Arab–Israeli conflict, American officials often appeared to behave irresponsibly by distributing harmful advice and too often taking an embarrassingly pro-Israeli line. Like the Arabs, many British officials believed that the US government was under the nefarious influence of 'the Jewish vote' in domestic politics; as a result, American leaders seemed to lack the resolve to back UN decisions consistently in the face of alleged Israeli defiance. Seeing this American attitude as partially contributing to Israel's intransigence, many British envoys and civil servants felt that the task of maintaining British (and Western) influence in the Middle East was made that much more difficult because of the largely tacit, but unquestioned, American support for Israeli policies.

These mutual perceptions operated mostly between the lines and did not seriously jeopardize the development of a co-ordinated Anglo–American approach to an Arab–Israeli settlement during the early 1950s. In the course of their dealings over the conflict, an informal 'division of labour' evolved between the two powers whereby London would exploit its privileged links with Arab leaders while Washington capitalized on its warmer relations with Tel Aviv. Yet, from the earliest days, policy-makers sought to avoid an undesirable situation in which the UK was too closely identified as advocate of the Arab cause, with the US relegated to the role of Israel's protector.[7] While Britain's decades of experience in the region made it the senior of the two partners, the growing influence and prestige of an economically powerful USA in world affairs gave considerable clout to the 'junior partner'.

SUPPORT FOR BILATERAL NEGOTIATIONS

On a number of occasions between 1948 and 1951, Egyptians, Syrians, Jordanians and Israelis found themselves either contemplating or actually engaging in secret bilateral talks.[8] The parties frequently turned to either Britain or the US to serve as channels of communication, usually in order to sound out the other side or to request intervention to break a deadlock in ongoing negotiations. For example, an approach by Mustafa Nusrat, Egyptian Minister of War and Marine, to the British Embassy in Cairo in early 1950 sought British help in sounding out the Israelis regarding their willingness to concede the Southern Negev and Aqaba coastline. The British reaction, then as later, was to avoid being thrust into the role of go-between. As Sir Geoffrey Furlonge noted at the Foreign Office, 'We can do no more than express to the Egyptians at any suitable opportunity our view that they will sooner or later have to negotiate with Israel.' Until leading Egyptians themselves became 'convinced of the desirability of negotiating' directly with the Israelis, the British declined to take the responsibility of transmitting such feelers.[9]

The various phases of the secret Israeli–Jordanian talks between 1949 and 1951 offered more opportunities for the powers to be dragged into bilateral negotiations. Britain and the US were frequently the target of entreaties by one side or the other to intervene in order to break recurring deadlocks allegedly caused by the other party – whether by offering 'encouragement' to King Abdullah, or by exerting pressure for greater Israeli 'flexibility'.[10] Both Washington and London always expressed their general encouragement of any efforts that might produce a settlement between Israel and its neighbours, but were reluctant to become too actively involved. This reluctance often resulted in criticism from one quarter or another – including American diplomats – of the powers' failure to capitalize on a 'golden opportunity' for Israeli–Jordanian peace.[11]

The powers especially wished to avoid being manoeuvred into the position of acting as the advocate of one of the parties against the other. Third-party diplomats quickly learned that their involvement carried unwritten responsibilities and was seldom confined to merely passing along neutral information. They knew that the receiving party was bound to attach more weight to an overture transmitted in this way than one coming through less august channels. Furthermore, serving as postman carried the disadvantage of allowing Arab politicians to perpetuate their avoidance of direct dealings with the Jewish state. In any event, the use of third parties automatically aroused suspicion and begged the question: why could secret, informal but *direct* channels not have been used instead to transmit or elicit the same information?

In the case of Israeli–Jordanian peace negotiations, Britain and the US reached the similar conclusion that, despite their genuine desire to see a durable accord succeed, it was pointless to make any strenuous representations in Amman or Tel Aviv, especially against the increasingly hostile domestic and regional public opinion which mounted against what Mordechai Gazit has called Abdullah's 'lonely effort'. During 1950 and the first half of 1951, the British were occasionally subjected to Israeli and international criticism for unwisely putting a 'brake' on Abdullah's eagerness to conclude a treaty with the Israelis, or for failing to provide the Jordanian ruler with sufficient moral and political support. In reply, the Foreign Office (following the advice of Sir Alec Kirkbride, its powerful and experienced Minister in Amman) was concerned about 'the danger of pressing [the Jordanians] too hard in view of the pressure of public opinion against negotiations with Israel'. This British reluctance was reinforced by the Foreign Office's belief that the US State Department was 'even more disinclined than we are to exert pressure on the two sides to negotiate'.[12]

SUPPORT FOR UNITED NATIONS INITIATIVES

In all the activities of UN bodies from 1948 onwards – United Nations Truce Supervisory Organisation (UNTSO) monitoring and reporting of the armistice lines, UNGA debates, UNSC hearings of complaints, PCC conciliation or conferences – the Western powers (and particularly the United States) played a prominent behind-the-scenes role. As we have argued elsewhere, the support of either the US or the UK was a crucial factor in maximizing the chances of all peacekeeping or peacemaking activities undertaken under the official banner of the United Nations. But the two Western powers were not always pulling in the same direction, or with equal vigour.

The first real test of Anglo–American co-operation was a British initiative to help direct Count Bernadotte's mediation efforts, and co-ordination between the powers got off to a very good start.[13] In late August 1948, London and Washington despatched special envoys to Rhodes in a top-secret attempt to influence Bernadotte's report to the UNGA. The Foreign Office had formulated detailed proposals which it hoped would be endorsed by, and promoted jointly with, the United States.

The two powers appeared ready to co-operate in backing the passage of the Bernadotte plan through the UNGA, even in the face of strenuous objections from the parties themselves. Although both Arab and Israeli spokesmen were firm in rejecting the Bernadotte plan, for several weeks British and American envoys lobbied Arabs and Israelis respectively in an energetic two-pronged campaign to get them to consider the proposals as a basis for discussion.

But an about-face by the US during October and November 1948 left the UK alone in promoting the Bernadotte plan. Not surprisingly, many British officials were left with the impression that the Americans were unreliable and fickle allies, too vulnerable to pro-Israeli opinion and arguments, especially during a Presidential election period.[14]

A second post-war opportunity for Anglo–American co-operation was the backing offered to Acting Mediator Ralph Bunche in convening the early 1949 Rhodes talks and in seeing them to their fruitful conclusion. Both London and Washington were caught in the cross fire of Israeli and Egyptian appeals for intervention to break various stalemates at Rhodes. While the British tended to follow a non-interventionist course, the Americans did make representations to the parties at selected moments.[15] While the Rhodes talks concentrated on concluding an Egyptian–Israeli armistice, the British again attempted to enlist American support for joint action on a more comprehensive Palestine settlement. Several British observers saw the US, and its alleged power to persuade the Israelis 'to observe international decencies', as the 'key' to any breakthrough.[16] Foreign Secretary Ernest Bevin himself pressed for a 'clearcut statement [of] US views on [a] Palestine territorial settlement' and for the two governments to 'do something' about the Palestine situation, including perhaps issuing a joint public statement embodying a common policy regarding the Middle East.[17]

Setting a pattern that would be repeated over the coming years, Acting Secretary of State Robert Lovett turned aside these British requests for both US pressure on the Israelis and, generally, greater American involvement. Lovett invoked the USSD's 'general line of policy ... to operate through the United Nations', and felt that the Americans were already doing 'a great deal' towards resolving the Palestine conflict – adding that 'perhaps [the] UK had been doing too much in a non-constructive sense'. The Acting Secretary believed that the 'proper means' for achieving a final political settlement was 'by negotiations bet[ween] the parties either directly or through UN auspices'.[18]

Not for the first or last time, British officials were dismayed by America's inability or unwillingness to act more decisively in putting pressure upon Israel. Many suspected that the good intentions of the State Department were being subverted by pro-Israeli influences at work in the White House. The Foreign Office's perception in early 1949 was that American motivation regarding the

Palestine issue was anything but high-minded or principled. 'We must', wrote Sir Orme Sargent

> in spite of the disappointments, rebuffs and tergiversations to which we have been exposed, still try to pin the US Government to a policy which we can work out together and which will safeguard our common interests in the Middle East. But meanwhile we must do our best to hold the position single-handed until President Truman begins to see straight and to free himself from the Jewish pressure to which he has succumbed.[19]

During and after the 1949 Lausanne Conference, the United States played an intricate and intensive role which, in effect, relegated the British to the sidelines, except for the Foreign Office's formulation of an ambitious eight-point peace plan, which we shall discuss below (Chapter IV, pages 61–3). American dominance over the activities of the PCC continued, throughout 1950 and 1951, to exclude the British and to create strains in Anglo–American co-operation on the Palestine question. Upon learning of the plans for the 1951 Paris conference, the Foreign Office was 'surprised that a matter of this importance should have been decided upon with such apparent precipitation and without our being given an opportunity to consider it and to express our views'. The grounds for the British expecting to be consulted included their 'known interest in all matters discussed', their signature on the May 1950 Tripartite Declaration (cf. below, Chapter III), and the Anglo–Jordanian Treaty of Alliance.[20]

Reacting to repeated pleas from the French to support the proposed Paris talks, one official at the FO minuted that Britain simply could not support 'what [was] obviously a misconceived and ill-digested proposal, no matter how strongly we favour any prospects of reaching an Arab–Israel settlement'.[21] A senior official went further, regarding the PCC Paris conference as 'clumsy and ill-advised'. Not only did Sir Geoffrey Furlonge doubt its chances of success, but he felt it was 'desirable that we should as far as possible dissociate ourselves from any odium which the PCC, or the governments represented on it[,] may have brought upon themselves by making it'.[22] 'It seems a great pity', Furlonge later wrote to the British Embassy in Washington that the Americans should have charged ahead in this way. The initiative now taken on their impulse appears to us entirely misconceived; moreover the way in which it was done puts us in the embarrassing position of having to choose between supporting a proposal with which we were not in agreement and of risking giving the impression of a divergence of policy from the Americans, French, and Turks. We felt on balance bound to accept the latter risk as the lesser evil.[23]

The utter failure of the Paris conference could only have left the British in a classic 'I-told-you-so' frame of mind.[24]

During 1952, as well, the Americans and British did not quite see eye-to-eye on how to approach the lingering Arab–Israeli impasse. A late-1952 UNGA draft resolution calling for direct Arab–Israeli negotiations saw the Americans, for the first time, taking an active lead in lobbying at the UN and in conveying firm instructions to their Middle East envoys. British support for the resolution was, by comparison, reserved and discreet. None the less, both powers soon felt the backlash of hostile press commentary and diplomatic notes in Arab capitals, reminding them about the limits of their political intervention on this still-sensitive issue.[25]

Geoffrey Furlonge, after leaving the Foreign Office to become British Ambassador in Amman, reported that the direct negotiations episode had been a setback for both Britain's overall position in the region and the prospects for an Arab–Israeli settlement. In his view, all previous thinking about the possibility of imposing a peace settlement on the Arabs had 'over-estimate[d] the degree of influence which we retain in the Middle East'. The only way to maintain British interests in the region, he argued, was by 'retaining or creating Arab goodwill' through a policy of 'say[ing] as little as possible in public on the subject [of Arab–Israeli relations] while doing anything we can to convince the Arabs in private.'[26] For other British diplomatic personnel in the Middle East, the direct negotiations resolution episode served as a depressing reminder of 'the strength of feeling that this question still arouse[d]' among the Arabs. There was 'no sign ... of their cooling and no reason to expect it on the basis of present Western or Israeli policy.'[27]

One year later, when Israel invoked Article XII of the Israel–Jordan General Armistice Agreement (IJGAA) calling upon the Secretary-General to convene a conference with Jordan, both the

US and UK offered their strong support, largely for the sake of maintaining the prestige and authority of the UN, but the Foreign Office's backing of the UNSG's efforts was given at the cost of damaging Anglo–Jordanian relations and against the best advice of most British representatives stationed in Arab capitals. Throughout this episode, British officials regarded the apparent American enthusiasm for a conference between Israel and Jordan as naively over-estimating the powers' ability 'to force the Arabs to do what they are strongly opposed to doing'. Such a course could not be pursued, they argued, without 'creat[ing] violent resentment in all the Arab states and ... risk[ing] impairing Western influence, and probably damaging Western interests, in those states.'[28]

Thus, from 1948 to 1954 the UK and the US were regularly drawn into dealing with the Palestine problem by having to react to calls for their intervention from either the main protagonists or the United Nations. There were also, as we shall see below (Chapters II–IV), numerous occasions on which the Western powers took steps, on their own initiative, to defuse tensions and foster *rapprochement* between the Arab states and Israel.

CHAPTER II

The Two-Pronged Approach

In Chapter I we referred to the informal 'division of labour' that evolved between the two powers whereby London and Washington attempted to influence Arab and Israeli decision-makers respectively. As the post-1948 deadlock persisted, British and American efforts at reconciling the conflicting parties took the form of a two-pronged approach: trying to get the Arabs to accept the *fait accompli* of the creation of Israel, and to persuade the Israelis that concessions on their part over refugees (repatriation or compensation) and territory were essential ingredients without which there could be no stable peace in the region. In the following pages we trace the evolution of this dual approach in British and American thinking, and its less-than-successful application in practice.

'A GRADUAL PROCESS OF EDUCATION' OF THE ARABS TO ACCEPT ISRAEL

Despite frequent Israeli accusations that the British did nothing to encourage 'realism' among the Arabs, or – worse still – that London actually stimulated Arab 'rejectionism' and animosity, British diplomats in the Arab world were under specific instructions, from late summer 1951 until 1954, to use opportune moments to advance the cause of Arab–Israeli reconciliation in what became known, somewhat paternalistically, as 'a gradual process of education' of the Arabs to accept Israel. While this campaign brought no visible results, investigating the assumptions behind it and the various reactions to it can help us to understand better the depth of Arab animosity to Israel, as well as the obstacles to Anglo–American intervention in favour of a settlement.

Foreign Office instructions, 1951

The impetus for a more active British effort towards bringing the Arab states 'into a peace frame of mind' came from Sir Alexander Knox Helm, British Ambassador to Tel Aviv.[1] One of Helm's despatches of late June 1951 provoked a chain-reaction in the Foreign Office and among British missions in Arab capitals. Like most other officials at the FO, P.R. Oliver was critical of the Israelis for not appearing to realize that their survival depended on concessions which could 'only come from the victor' and which 'need not be regarded as evidence of weakness'. Nevertheless, he did agree with Helm that Britain should seek to 'disabuse' the Arabs of the notion that Israel would collapse, and to 'persuade them that Israel has come to stay and that it is in their own interests to come to some working agreement with her'.[2]

In an August 1951 Foreign Office minute, entitled 'The Effect of Arab Israel Relations on the Defence of the Middle East', J.C. Wardrop dealt with the strategic question of Western fears of Soviet penetration of the region. Wardrop's 'inescapable conclusion' was that 'The defence of the Middle East will never really be organised on a sound footing unless peace is concluded between Israel and the Arab States.' Admitting that the British had, to date, 'certainly ... not put any pressure on [the Arabs] to reach a settlement' with Israel, Wardrop was 'afraid that our attitude may have been interpreted as indifference, or reluctance to urge an unpopular course, or fear of a rebuff, or weakness, or vacillation'. He felt strongly that a serious attempt had to be made 'to correct such misapprehensions without further delay', and proposed several lines of argument which might be used with the Arabs to urge the advantages of an early settlement with Israel.[3]

Wardrop appreciated that this recommended course of action would be 'a bitter pill for the Arabs to swallow'; but that, he went on, was 'no reason why we should not administer it'. Moreover, Wardrop argued, the powers 'could and should attempt to sweeten it in various ways by extracting concessions from Israel'. Even if such attempts were to be rejected once, twice or three times, he insisted that the British ought to persevere:

> If we hastily withdraw at the first sign of disagreement we shall only encourage the view which has unfortunately already gained far too much currency, namely that there is no strength in our convictions.

Impressed by the reasoning in Wardrop's minute, Sir Geoffrey Furlonge recommended that the Foreign Office 'adopt a more positive line in inducing the Arab States to modify their attitude towards Israel'. British diplomatic personnel in Arab capitals should now be sent 'more positive instructions than they have so far received', with corresponding efforts being directed at the Israelis.[4]

On 24 August 1951, the Foreign Office sent new instructions to all Middle East posts. R.J. Bowker's despatch to Arab capitals began by referring to ongoing planning for Middle East defence, and by admitting that hitherto the British had refrained from urging the Arab states to make peace with Israel 'because we believed that we should not succeed and that our efforts would merely alienate' the Arabs. Bowker now informed British envoys of the Foreign Office's second-thoughts as to whether 'we have done enough to inculcate in the Arabs the realisation that they are gaining nothing, and losing something, by persisting in their present attitude towards Israel'. Among the risks and losses to which the Arabs were exposing themselves by continuing to reject a settlement, the Foreign Office letter listed:

- the encouragement of an 'expansionist mentality' among the Israelis;
- potentially explosive frontier incidents;
- alienation of Western opinion and potential loss of Western assistance;
- prolonging the misery of the Arab refugees; and
- 'in the last resort, jeopardising the stability and economic prosperity of the area as a whole.'[5]

While fully familiar with 'Arab feelings about Israel, and about the responsibility of the Western Powers for the present situation in Palestine', the Foreign Office letter noted that

> the logical conclusion of the present attitude of too many of the Arab leaders must be that they would like us and the Americans to assist them in pushing Israel into the sea. We

> cannot believe that the Arabs are so blind as to imagine that this is practical politics or would be in anybody's interest.

Despite the bluntness of the message, British diplomats were asked not to make 'a frontal attack' on the governments to which they were accredited, but rather to 'take any suitable opportunity that may present itself', with the object of convincing the Arabs – 'by a gradual process of education' – that they were 'gaining nothing, and losing something important, by persistence in their present attitude'.

In a parallel letter to Tel Aviv, Bowker advised Chargé d'Affaires J.E. Chadwick of the steps being taken 'to bring home to the Arabs the unwisdom of their present mentality', but added that, if 'the process of education on which we now wish to embark with the Arabs is to bear any fruit, a change of attitude on the part of the Israelis is no less necessary'. Chadwick was asked to urge Israelis 'to take full advantage of any opening or advance from the Arab side', and (like his colleagues in Arab capitals) to report to London 'any specific concession which might reasonably be asked of Israel or of any of her neighbours which might help to promote a settlement'.[6] The Foreign Office also asked for supportive action by the US and France in this campaign of 'gradual education', but the State Department seems to have given no special instructions in this direction to its envoys.[7]

In September, replies began to be received from Middle Eastern posts, and these included a formidable array of political and psychological obstacles to the Foreign Office's hopes of fostering an Arab–Israeli *rapprochement*. A lively correspondence developed around the subject, as ministers in the various Middle Eastern postings had opportunities to comment on each other's analyses. One of the most forceful assessments came from Alexandria, where Sir Ralph Stevenson doubted whether any change could be brought about 'by the use of arguments based on pure reason and strict utilitarian principles'. This was, in his view, largely because there was, 'to the Egyptian mind, a moral or ethical element in the problem'.

> [T]he Egyptians think that notwithstanding the material advantages they might gain from a peace settlement, it would be *wrong* [he underlined] to make peace ... [E]xasperating as it may be to us, the Egyptian refuses to believe that the good cause, as he sees it, is lost. Right has been temporarily defeated because wrong had more guns, that is all.

But even if the British 'education' of the Egyptians could be advanced through 'utilitarian' arguments and without reference to right and wrong, Stevenson listed, point by point, the ready counter-arguments which the Egyptians would offer in response to each of the lines of approach suggested by the Foreign Office. The Ambassador felt unable to offer any practical suggestions, except to conclude bleakly that 'time' would be 'the only healer' – adding that he 'fear[ed] it w[ould] be a long time.'[8]

Stevenson's arguments were vigorously supported by his colleagues in other capitals. The British Minister in Damascus, for example, wrote that the arguments listed in the FO despatch did 'not carry any weight here, and ... if this is all that we are going to have to go on, we shall have to wait a long time before the situation appreciably improves.'[9] Although he had already contributed a number of responses on the subject, Sir John Troutbeck in Baghdad reported separately on the views of his American counterpart in Baghdad, who believed that an 'indirect approach was the one likely to lead to results'. The approach envisaged by Edward Crocker was one in which 'the real frightening danger of Communism and Russia' would be brought home to the Arabs who would, as a result, 'begin to think more realistically about Israel'. In the opinion of the American diplomat, the direct approach of pressing the Arabs to make peace with Israel 'would do more harm than good' and would only result in making 'the Arabs dig their toes in still more firmly'.[10]

Despite the strongly pessimistic streak in all the responses to the August instructions, P.R. Oliver at the Foreign Office refused to succumb to despair, believing that 'circumstances make strange bedfellows'.[11] Although the August 1951 guidelines had been rather unenthusiastically received, British representatives were still nominally expected to be following the instructions 'On all possible occasions to impress upon the Arabs, if not the advantages of making peace with Israel, at any rate the disadvantages of not doing so.'[12]

New State Department instructions, 1952

Although the burden of the efforts at softening Arab attitudes to Israel rested on the British, there were occasional signs from American quarters that an initiative in the same direction might be useful. By late 1952, for example, there was a growing feeling that the time might be propitious for the powers to try to foster an

Israeli–Arab *rapprochement*.[13] Although the US government had been following a cautious course of avoiding any overly active role aimed at reconciling Arabs and Israelis, its Ambassador in Tel Aviv pointed to a favourable mood among Israelis that ought to be exploited through an American 'endeavor [to] convince [the] Arabs of [the] desirability [to] reach agreements before another period of discouragement and defeatism sets in in Israel'.[14] In November, the Egyptian daily *Al-Ahram* reflected a widespread expectation and optimism in the Arab world that the incoming US President, Dwight D. Eisenhower, would be proposing an Arab–Israeli peace settlement based on a less pro-Israeli attitude than the previous Truman administration.[15]

Indeed, State Department officials, impressed by apparent changes over the previous six months, began advocating what they termed a 'positive and constructive approach' toward the problem – 'however difficult and apparently unproductive this may seem at time[s]'. In a circular telegram to all Middle East missions, Henry Byroade, newly appointed Assistant Secretary of State for Near Eastern, South Asian and African Affairs, stressed that

> Arab leaders must not be encouraged [to] entertain views that if sufficient American opinion can be mobilized on their side[,] Arabs may be given weapons and [an] opportunity to crush Israel or that American aid to Israel might be terminated. In this connection [it is] particularly important [that] American officials should not adopt [an] apologetic attitude toward US policy since this serves to encourage Arab intransigence and render more difficult [the] positive US action which I now feel can be initiated.

Byroade asked diplomatic personnel posted to Arab countries to enlist American private citizens abroad in a campaign to discourage both the '*mea culpa* attitude' toward US Middle East policy and support for 'Arab recriminations'. Rather, envoys were to encourage all Americans 'to think and speak of [the] need for all N[ear] E[ast] states [to] face realities and build political, economic and social strength to reach proper statute in [the] world community.'[16] In a public address several weeks later, the Assistant Secretary stressed that 'the United States must, in its own interests, devote a major effort toward easing the tensions that have sprung from' the Arab–Israeli impasse.[17]

Within six months, however, the visit of the new Secretary of State and his staff to the region convinced American policy-makers of the virtues of not pressing Arabs or Israelis too hard. In private conversations with Arab leaders, John Foster Dulles heard repeated expressions of Arab disappointment with US policy on the Palestine question and calls for American pressure on Israel to comply with UN resolutions, especially General Assembly resolution 194 of December 1948. Upon his return, the Secretary announced in a radio broadcast that the 'parties concerned' continued to have 'the primary responsibility of bringing peace to the area', and that the US would 'use its influence to promote a step-by-step reduction of tension in the area and the conclusion of ultimate peace'.[18]

The need to curb Soviet influence and to win Arab participation in a proposed Middle East Defence Organization helped to consolidate the Secretary's preference for a piecemeal or step-by-step approach. 'Any move on our part for immediate and total peace would be unrealistic', he wrote upon his return.[19] This disappointed some regional leaders and foreign observers who had been hoping that the Secretary's newly acquired familiarity with the region's problems might lead to dramatic new proposals for an initiative towards a comprehensive Arab–Israeli settlement.[20] In private diplomatic conversations, State Department officials admitted that neither the United States nor any of its Western allies was 'in a position to exert much influence on the Arab world today'.[21] 'Until [the] Arabs have confidence in our impartiality,' explained the American Chargé d'Affaires in Tel Aviv to a senior Israeli official, 'we can do very little.'[22] Any official suggestions for the powers to become actively involved in promoting a settlement between Israel and the Arabs would have to come, it appeared, from London rather than from Washington.

'Asking the impossible'

In January 1954, the British Ambassador to Lebanon reported a conversation with Prime Minister Abdullah al-Yafi regarding the Arab–Israeli dispute. Such periodic reports by Western diplomats to London and Washington were not uncommon, and served to provide policy-makers with 'snap-shots' of the mood among Middle Eastern politicians. This time, al-Yafi spoke at length about the inability of the Arab leaders to deal with Israel as a normal state in

THE TWO-PRONGED APPROACH

the region. While fully aware of Western criticism of the Arabs' 'ostrich-like attitude' and lack of 'realism', the Lebanese Prime Minister believed that

> for the time being and perhaps for many years to come even moderate Arab leaders would not be prepared or allowed by the Arab peoples to go further than to treat Israel as though it existed in some remote region.... [al-Yafi] maintained that the West would simply have to accept this attitude as being a moderate one. The more extreme one was easy to discern in the pronouncements of certain Arab leaders describing Israel as a canker or cancer that would have to be removed by surgical operation and similar statements.[23]

Continuing his report to the Foreign Office, E.A. Chapman-Andrews gave his own assessment of the damage which the continuing Palestine dispute was causing to Western interests. The Arabs, he admitted, were 'unfortunately unrealistic people', but there were 'forty million of them sprawling over a region which is to-day even more than in the past vital to the West both for oil and as a vast area of manoeuvre in war.' There could be little doubt that Palestine was 'a festering sore in our relations with the peoples of this region'. Given the weakness of the Arab governments to deal with serious internal social and political problems, Arab leaders could all too easily create a distraction by attacking Britain and America 'for being responsible for the Palestine tragedy. They know that by so doing they can be sure of popular support.' Hence, the British envoy in Beirut felt it was 'asking the impossible of Arab statesmen' to tell them that, as a condition for improved relations with the West, 'they must accept the fact of Israel's existence and treat her as a neighbour, good or bad, whether they like it or not.'

This snap-shot of the existing state of 'moderation' in the Arab world in early 1954 was an indication of the disappointing lack of success of five years of not only British, but also American and United Nations' attempts at promoting a 'realistic' attitude among the defeated Arabs, in the hope of influencing them in the direction of a settlement with Israel. It also helps us understand why Britain and the US found themselves continuing to opt for a piecemeal, or 'nibbling-at-the-edges', approach to the conflict (below, Chapter

III). It was the least ambitious but also the least risky option, and it made eminent good sense in view of patently unsuccessful attempts at 'gradual education of the Arabs'.

PRESSURE ON ISRAEL FOR GESTURES AND CONCESSIONS

In embarking upon its 'gradual education' of the Arabs, the Foreign Office had left no doubt that the campaign required a vital Israeli component in order to have any chance of success. In his August 1951 letter to Tel Aviv, R.J. Bowker admitted that Israel had legitimate grievances on at least two issues: the blockade of Israeli shipping through the Suez Canal and the Iraqi closure of the oil pipeline to Haifa. But he went on to list half a dozen episodes in which Israeli actions had been either the cause of, or the pretext for, Arab hostility. Bowker realized that he was delegating to Chargé Chadwick in Tel Aviv the 'extremely difficult task' of convincing the Israelis 'that their self-righteous attitude [was] not above reproach'. He instructed Chadwick, whenever suitable opportunities arose,

> to impress upon prominent Israelis our feeling that Israel's attitude is at least largely contributory to the present situation, and that more response from her is needed if she is to have any hope of achieving the settlement which she professes to desire.[24]

In their responses to the Foreign Office instructions on the 'gradual education' of the Arabs, British envoys in the Arab world included a discussion of Israeli attitudes and behaviour. Several pointed to the lack of American pressure for Israeli concessions on refugees or territory as a serious obstacle to peace. From Beirut, Chapman-Andrews felt that an Arab–Israeli settlement would not become 'practical politics' unless 'much greater pressure [were] brought to bear upon Israel'. While a settlement implied 'concessions by both sides', Chapman-Andrews pointed out that it was 'the Arabs who [had] lost most and [were] suffering most today as a result of the existence of Israel', while it was 'the Jews who [had] gained most'. Referring to Jewish influence on American electoral politics in previous years, the British Minister felt it was 'now high time the United States Government reversed the heat and turned some of it on Israel'.[25] From Damascus, Britain's Minister John

Gardener suggested a shift of emphasis towards 'educating' the Israelis on the need to demonstrate 'good neighbourliness' if there was to be any hope of peace. In concrete terms, Gardener suggested compensation for the Palestinian refugees and the unfreezing of blocked Arab bank accounts. He specifically proposed that the Israelis might 'devote a proportion of the aid they receive from Germany [in reparations payments] for this purpose'.[26]

Even when not dealing explicitly with the 'gradual education' campaign, British and American officials never really abandoned their efforts since 1948 at persuading Israeli diplomats that a 'goodwill gesture' on their part would help to reverse the deterioration of Israeli–Arab relations. On two points there seemed to be unanimous agreement among British diplomats and policy-makers, including Britain's Ambassador to Tel Aviv:

- in order to win Arab co-operation for any settlement promoted by the powers, concessions on refugees and territory would have to be extracted from Israel; and
- such significant concessions could not be obtained without strong American political support.

Over the years, most of the working documents and position papers drawn up by the Foreign Office for improvements or for a possible Arab–Israeli settlement also presupposed the reallocation of parts of Israeli-held territory to Jordan, Syria or Egypt. The notion that Israel, as the victor in 1948–49, had to make the first move became almost an axiom in both British and American thinking.[27]

Viewing themselves as the victims of Arab aggression during and after the first Arab–Israeli war, most Israelis resented and resisted such third party requests for gestures and concessions. During 1948 and 1949, they were subjected to mounting criticism and pressure from UN Mediator Count Bernadotte and the first chief US delegate to the PCC, Mark Ethridge. During the early years of statehood, they also had to deal with the friendlier admonitions of Acting Mediator Ralph Bunche, President Truman himself, Secretary of State Dean Acheson, and Ethridge's successors on the PCC, Paul Porter and Ely Palmer.[28]

For Israel's Ambassador in Washington, Aubrey (Abba) Eban, the PCC Paris conference marked an important turning-point in American attitudes. In sharp contrast with the Lausanne experience of 1949, Eban interpreted the late 1951 mood at the State

Department as indicating that there was no point in the US 'demanding any substantive gesture from Israel', given the intransigence of the Arab side. The absence of American pressure at Paris, he wrote to his counterpart in the French capital, was especially fortuitous, 'since there [had] never been a moment in the life of the State of Israel when it was more sensitively vulnerable' to suffering a major economic and political crisis. Nevertheless, he warned, 'American policy remain[ed] obsessed by the necessity of what it calls an Israeli "gesture"', and his government's ongoing tactical objective had to be 'to assess the minimal Israel concession which would have the result of diverting the pressures of American mediation away from us and towards the Arab states.'[29]

Thus, for almost two years after September 1951, the Americans and British applied relatively little pressure on the Israelis for major gestures or concessions. To the relief of the Israelis and the corresponding consternation of the Arabs, the US was reluctant to confront the Israelis directly with respect to their position on the return of refugees and territorial adjustments. In October 1951, for example, one State Department position paper considered repatriation of Arab refugees to Israel 'a dead issue' and 'substantial territorial readjustments ... entirely unlikely' – although it did feel that 'Israel must give concrete indications to the neighboring Arab countries of its willingness to pay substantial compensation to Arab refugees.'[30] This, with variations in tone and terminology, remained a fair guideline to the American stance for several years, even though pressure for a more forceful and openly critical attitude to Israel continued to emanate from a variety of quarters: not unexpectedly from Arab spokesmen, but also from American officials both inside and outside the State Department and, ever so discreetly, from British officials.

In the realm of conflict management, the powers continued to support UNTSO peacekeeping efforts by admonishing and preaching to both sides. Although they attempted to mete out official criticism for truce violations in equal measure, many at the State Department and the Foreign Office took a grim view of Israel's practice of launching tough reprisal raids for what they considered to be relatively minor provocations.[31] At the same time, American members of the PCC continued to press for Israeli gestures and flexibility on the issues of refugee compensation and the unblocking of frozen Arab assets. James Barco and others made special efforts to convince Israelis to abandon their 'orthodox' approach to peace under which their agreement to pay compensation was a 'trump card' to be played in overall peace negotiations. Instead, PCC members and State Department officials argued that an Israeli gesture on compensation without requiring anything in return might enable the Commissioners to be in a 'much more persuasive position ... [to] have greater success in urging [the] Arabs [to] come to terms.'[32] Such guarded gestures on refugee compensation as the Israelis did agree to make did nothing, however, to provide the psychological or political breakthrough for which the PCC was hoping.

The situation regarding American pressure on Israel began to change in 1953, with the advent of the Eisenhower administration and its declared intention of pursuing an even-handed policy in the Middle East. As the frontier situation continued to deteriorate under the impact of Arab incursions and Israeli retaliations, and as Western interests in the region became less secure in the face of Soviet rivalry, the State Department gradually reverted to its position of demanding more from Israel. In the spring of 1953, Assistant Secretary Byroade began probing Israeli attitudes towards territorial concessions and a token repatriation of Arab refugees, hinting broadly that sooner or later the US might have to come up with a compromise peace plan that might not please either side.[33] During informal conversations in Tel Aviv in early 1954, the US Chargé d'Affaires indicated to Israeli officials that his government believed that Israel would advance the cause of peace if it were prepared to pay compensation and to accept the return of between 40,000 and 70,000 refugees.[34] In July 1954, a major NSC Policy Paper included clauses recommending the use of 'US influence to secure Arab–Israel boundary settlements, which may include some concessions by Israel' and the continued urging of Israel not only to settle the blocked-accounts and compensation issues, but also 'to accept a limited number of refugees'.[35]

By late 1954, the men who would lay out the plans for Operation Alpha could look back upon the following results of their two-pronged approach to preparing the parties for peacemaking:

- the British campaign of 'gradual education' of the Arabs had not brought Arab leaders any closer to the idea of accepting Israel as a normal state in the region; and
- American diplomatic pressures had been insufficient to cause Israel to contemplate making gestures regarding concessions on refugees or territorial adjustments.

As the Alpha planners approached their task in the context of the need to win the co-operation of the Arab states in a pro-Western regional defence plan, it seemed inevitable that any progress towards a breakthrough would require increased efforts on the latter, rather than the former, front.

CHAPTER III

Nibbling at the Edges:
The Failure of Conflict Management

One of the approaches to resolving protracted conflicts whose basic issues appear particularly impervious to compromise and negotiation is to single out peripheral issues in the hope that success in resolving these lower-intensity disputes at the 'edges' will generate some momentum towards solving the more difficult issues at the 'core' of the conflict. As the months and years went by without the expected transition from war to armistice to peace, British and American policy analyses frequently made the distinction between the edges and the core of the post-1948 Arab–Israeli conflict. Pessimism and cynicism grew quickly regarding the chances of attacking the core of the conflict – corresponding roughly to conflict *resolution* – while more hopes were attached to working along its periphery – which went hand-in-hand with efforts at conflict *management*.

THE TRIPARTITE DECLARATION

As early as 1950, one can detect a shift away from seeking a definitive resolution of the conflict to a more modest concern for keeping it within manageable proportions. One of the earliest signs that the powers were abandoning hope that the UN would succeed in its efforts at converting the 1949 armistices into more stable peace arrangements was the decision by the US, UK and France to issue jointly what became known as the Tripartite Declaration of 25 May

1950 (Document 1).¹ As a way of managing, rather than resolving, Arab–Israeli differences, the Declaration sought to guarantee regional stability by controlling the flow of arms and by setting limits beyond which the countries of the region could not go without risking concerted intervention by the three Western powers.

A major impetus to Anglo–American co-operation at this time was an increase in the number of requests for arms from all Middle Eastern governments. Both the US State Department and the British Foreign Office began to realize that co-ordination of their policies was essential. The powers had to consider Arab and Israeli requests for armaments not only on their local political and military merits, but also while considering their own global and regional strategic interests. In the hopes of avoiding an arms race, US policy since mid-1949 had been to permit only the exportation 'of such arms as it considered necessary for internal security and legitimate self-defense'. Complicating these ambiguous guidelines was the powers' conviction that Egypt, in particular, had to be provided with adequate forces to help protect the region from a feared 'major Soviet thrust'.² The Western powers also wished to avoid creating 'a most undesirable situation' in which the UK 'would supply arms to the Arabs only and that the US would supply arms to the Israelis'.³

The simple but potentially far-reaching Declaration of 25 May 1950 contained three paragraphs, the first of which attempted to clarify the principles according to which the US, Britain and France would consider arms requests from the Arab states and Israel. Secondly, purchasing states would be required to offer assurances that they did 'not intend to undertake any act of aggression against any other state'. Finally, the three powers declared that, in the interests of maintaining peace and stability in the area, they 'would, consistently with their obligations as members of the United Nations, immediately take action, both within and outside the United Nations, to prevent' any violation of the frontiers or armistice lines contemplated by any of the states in the region.

The effectiveness of the Tripartite Declaration hinged on the deterrent effect of the powers' pledge to 'immediately take action' in the event of a threat to the peace. From the start, there was reason to suspect that the signatories' announced firmness was largely bluff. The paternalistic thinking behind American involvement at the time is colourfully reconstructed in a paragraph from George McGhee's memoirs:

[T]he three powers can, if we are firm and get together, enforce our views on the states of the area. We are the 'big boys'. The Middle East states are the 'little boys'. All we have to do is to set the rules and say, 'Look here, you little boys, you behave yourselves or we are going to take care of you.' We don't have to say precisely how or under what conditions. If we are really 'big boys' we don't need to. They will mind us. Moreover, they are all so concerned just now about what might happen that they will welcome our assuring them that we won't permit a bully, from whatever quarter, to threaten them.[3a]

Despite the ambiguous threat of the use of troops in the final section of the Tripartite Declaration, it was clearly intended by the original American drafters that the 'action' referred to would not involve the use of US military forces.[4] Internal British working documents likewise indicate that the tripartite statement, hedged as it was with mental reservations and legalistic disclaimers, was not intended to be more than declaratory.[5] This did not, however, prevent American and British officials, in conversations with Israeli or Arab representatives, from exaggerating the extent of their intentions to act against aggression in the area.[6]

Most leaders in the region had no trouble welcoming the powers' stand against a Middle Eastern arms race.[7] During the first year after its issuance, the State Department considered that the Tripartite Declaration was 'help[ing] to give both the Arab states and Israel a sense of confidence in future security', thereby 'hasten[ing] the progress being made toward peace in the Near East'. The powers periodically congratulated themselves on the effectiveness of the Declaration 'in lessening tension in the area' and in 'stabiliz[ing] the situation'.[8] In addition to being credited with some early success at managing the conflict, the Declaration also served as a satisfactory instrument for consultations and voluntary arms-control among the signatories, for whom it represented a 'major attempt at collective self-restraint'.[9]

The first attempts by local protagonists to test the resolve of the powers under the Tripartite Declaration came in September 1950, when Jordan raised a complaint about an Israeli incursion into its territory near Naharayyim; during the same month, Egypt protested against Israel's expulsion of Beduin of the Azazmeh tribe.[10] More serious cross-border clashes between Syria and Israel in early April 1951 provided a second opportunity where recourse to the Tripartite

Declaration was considered. Behind-the-scenes consultations between American, British and French representatives in New York resulted in the drafting of a Security Council resolution calling for observance of the armistice and the suspension of Israeli drainage works in the DMZ.[11] Likewise, the devastating Israeli raid on Qibya in Jordan, in October 1953, led the powers to more forceful diplomatic action in the spirit of the Tripartite Declaration – namely, joint sponsorship of a UNSC resolution condemning the Israeli action.[12]

Although the Declaration was largely intended to dissuade the parties from resorting to force, there were also isolated cases when the US and France sought to use it actively in an attempt to promote a resolution of the wider conflict. In early 1951, for example, the State Department seized upon a suggestion by Mahmud Fawzi, Egypt's Permanent Representative to the UN, that

> while it was impossible at present for [the] Arab states to enter into peace settlements with Israel[,] they were prepared to consider [a] treaty system based upon the Tripartite Declaration which would give every possible assurance of protection for Israel.

But the sounding-out of opinion in Arab capitals revealed little support for the 'premature ... trial balloon' launched by Dr Fawzi in New York.[13] In response to persisting Syrian–Israeli frontier tensions during the summer of 1951, the French Foreign Ministry attempted in vain to enlist British and American backing under the Declaration for an approach to the parties, urging them either to conclude peace settlements, or – at the least – to undertake negotiations with a view to revising the faltering GAAs,[14] but such attempts at using the Tripartite Declaration to encourage Arab–Israeli talks remained non-starters, given the deepening deadlock of Arab–Israeli relations during and after 1951.

Despite the persistent optimism and expectations of its makers during the early 1950s, the Tripartite Declaration was a glaring example of the three powers' inability to impose peace on the Middle East. Both Arabs and Israelis came to view the powers' reluctance to act under the Declaration as unfair partisanship: the former's view of the Western powers as being incorrigibly 'soft' on Israel was reinforced, as was the latter's perception that their security was being jeopardized by the West's interest in wooing the Arab states into co-operating with anti-Soviet regional defence arrangements.[15] Within

18 months of its issue, there were few leaders in the Middle East who really believed in the Western powers' determination to take effective action under the Declaration, which was seen as a pious statement without teeth.[16] This experience of the limited effectiveness of a simple conflict management device was a good indicator of the difficulties the powers would face when circumstances would later lead them to make plans to impose a *political* settlement on Arabs and Israelis.

DIPLOMATIC REPRESENTATIONS IN SUPPORT OF UNTSO

In 1949, four Mixed Armistice Commissions (MACs) were established pursuant to the GAAs signed between Israel on the one hand and Egypt, Lebanon, Jordan and Syria, on the other. Each commission was composed of an equal number of Israeli and Arab military or police representatives who met under the chairmanship of a UN official serving with the UNTSO. In 1950, a pattern of cross-frontier incursions and reprisals began which involved local investigations and reports by these MACs.[17] The escalation of border violence and the deterioration of the armistice also led to many debates among Israelis (and between Israelis, Americans, and British) as to the wisdom of their country's retaliation policy. Whether it was an *effective* form of deterrence is a question which social psychologists, strategic studies analysts and historians are still investigating and debating.[18]

It soon became commonplace for British and American posts in the Middle East to report Arab, Israeli and UN observers' versions of every incident, great and small, to the Foreign Office and the State Department. This, in turn, produced a steady flow of representations and exhortations from London and Washington to Foreign Ministers and Prime Ministers in the area, preaching statesmanlike behaviour and restraint in the face of continuing mutual provocation. British and American officials in the region not only passed along these messages, but also did their best to lend the weight of their home governments to UN personnel in their investigation of incidents and the arrangement of ceasefires. The attitude of the two Western powers has recently been summarized as follows:

> Britain and the United States believed that the retaliatory policy was immoral (the innocent were punished in place of the guilty), ineffective (it did not stop infiltration) and counter-

productive (it sparked more Arab terrorism). But, despite suasion, threats and occasional sanctions, they were unable to reverse it; they never applied sufficient pressure to make Ben-Gurion and his protégés sit up and listen. In part, this was because the West felt that Israel did have a case (the Arab states were belligerent; there were terrorist infiltrator attacks; and the Arab states had proved incapable of stopping them); ...[19]

The cycle of incursion-reprisal-admonition became a tedious routine which underscored the disintegration of the armistice régimes. Some observers grew dissatisfied with the role played by the MACs, which was merely to report on and react to the destructive spiral of ever more frequent incidents. A few hoped to see the commissions develop a more preventive orientation, such as the early American suggestion that the MAC be utilized as an avenue for launching broader political talks.[20] During 1951, the Syrians used the MAC as a forum to extend an invitation to the Israelis to open discussions on dividing their disputed DMZ.[21] But these manoeuvres were futile, leaving left no doubt that the usefulness of the MACs remained limited to localized border policing. Any attempt to utilize them as vehicles for conflict resolution was doomed to fail, as the Israelis themselves discovered when they invoked Article XII of the IJGAA seeking to force Jordan, during late 1953 and early 1954, into higher-level discussions with inevitable political implications.[22]

After several years, the effectiveness of the MAC even as a limited instrument of conflict management became seriously doubtful because of its 'lack of teeth to enforce decisions'. As the US envoy in Amman recommended, one of the only ways to make the UNTSO machinery work would have been for the tripartite powers to become involved by 'follow[ing] up every MAC decision by bringing immediate pressure to bear on the offending state'.[23] Unfortunately, there were few occasions on which all three Western powers felt compelled to take such action.

ANGLO–AMERICAN PROPOSALS FOR REDUCING FRONTIER TENSIONS

In the wake of the Qibya raid, and at the height of the campaign to convene a conference between Israel and Jordan under Article XII of the IJGAA, the deterioration of the Israeli–Jordanian frontier situation reached the point where both the UK and the US began considering the need for new and more effective ways to defuse an explosive atmosphere. The Foreign Office felt especially concerned, as a major Israeli attack would probably have involved active British participation in the defence of Jordan under their treaty of alliance.[24]

At the Foreign Office, Roger Allen weighed the available options, including a major initiative to convene a round-table conference. In the end, however, he recommended the more modest course of pursuing 'a policy of "nibbling at the edges" of the problem as [the] opportunity arises' – an approach recently proposed by the US State Department.[25] British officials then sought to co-ordinate their efforts with the Americans and the French for a tripartite approach to the parties. While British and American officials began exploring this option in earnest, France's hesitations ultimately relegated it to the sidelines of what became largely an Anglo–American initiative.[26]

During an April 1954 meeting with John Foster Dulles in London, British Foreign Secretary Anthony Eden suggested that the powers proceed to make systematic approaches to Israel and the Arab states regarding 'effective frontier control', applying the same procedure that the British and Americans had recently used successfully in mediating the Trieste dispute between Italy and Yugoslavia.[27]

The evolution of American thinking during this period dovetailed neatly with that of the British. No less than their British counterparts, the Americans feared that increasing tension on the Arab–Israeli frontiers could lead to a situation which the 'Soviet Union might be able to turn ... to its advantage'. The American Chiefs of Mission meeting in Istanbul in May 1954 concluded that, while a 'clear-cut peace between the Arab states and Israel would be in the American interest', such a goal was 'unrealistic' in the foreseeable future. The participants recommended, instead, that 'the most practical approach would be to seek progress under a *modus vivendi* ... to alleviate present tensions.' The Istanbul conference also 'recognized the importance of reaching understanding and working in collaboration with the British in the implementation of such a policy.'[28] Several months later, a National Security Council paper echoed the general conclusions of the Istanbul conference, recommending that the US 'approach should be gradual and practical' and citing the 'reduction of border tension and effective assurances to both sides against aggression' as 'prerequisites to progress towards a peaceful settlement.'[29]

Initial Anglo–American co-ordination regarding their planned *démarche* for reducing border tension went very smoothly.[30] The Foreign Office and State Department began by consulting their respective posts in the Middle East and compiled a list of practical suggestions for improving the Israeli–Jordanian frontier situation. The consultation process provided not only the requested list of practical proposals but also an opportunity for some respondents to go beyond the narrow frontier question to discuss a variety of broader political issues relating to the Arab–Israeli impasse.[31]

Critique from the field

Given the accumulated evidence of the difficulties inherent in an initiative for a comprehensive settlement, policy-makers in London and Washington must have been surprised to receive a number of elaborate criticisms of the proposed piecemeal approach of 'nibbling at the edges'. Several British diplomats warned that dealing with the issue of border controls would not be enough. From Beirut, Edwin Chapman-Andrews urged the Foreign Office to be more ambitious in tackling 'all aspects of the Palestine problem ... with the determined object of deciding what we both [UK and US] consider to be a fair and politically feasible settlement.'[32] From Tel Aviv, Francis Evans warned that unless Britain could demonstrate to the Israelis

> that we intend to exercise effective influence on the Arab States to adopt a more cooperative attitude towards Israel ... over the whole range of Israel–Arab relations, the effect of our *démarche* will be at best short lived.

Evans feared that treating the border problem in isolation would have the effect of ramming a lid on a boiling pot, merely increasing the build-up of steam.[33]

Similarly, the American Ambassador in Beirut criticized the narrow focus of the State Department questionnaire that had been sent to him. '[U]nless and until we and our major allies, working both within and outside the UN, can come forward with substantial plans which could be made [the] basis for effective General Assembly action', wrote veteran diplomat Raymond Hare, it was 'pointless to seek [to] maintain [a] policy of seeking "peace" in some other way.'[34] After listing some practical suggestions for improving the border situation based on the Israeli–Syrian experience, Ambassador Moose in Damascus added that 'of greater importance' to a solution of the Palestine problem were the 'basic attitudes of Near East governments', which he identified as:

- Israel's '"tough" policy toward its Arab neighbors';
- the Arabs' 'lack of confidence in [the] policy of [the] UN and western powers'; and
- the 'emotional spite' of the Arabs which 'render[ed] them unable to regard [the] relationship with Israel rationally'.[35]

Also in response to the State Department questionnaire, the American Consul in Jerusalem focused on the need to 'confront Israel' with the apparent contradictions between her calls for the easing of border tensions, on the one hand, and what he termed her 'hostile acts of reprisal raids and sabotaging [of] local commanders agreements [LCAs] and rules of [the] MAC', on the other.[36]

Likewise, the American Chargé d'Affaires in Tel Aviv, Francis Russell, urged that Israel be told to show more sensitivity to the damaging effects of such policies as reprisal raids, 'unlimited immigration into Israel', and her 'unilateral and *fait accompli* approach on such problems as Jerusalem and Banat Yaacov'.[37] Russell – who would later be appointed as chief American liaison with the British under Operation Alpha – also underlined the need to attack what he felt was the root cause of the problem, namely the hundreds of thousands of Palestinian refugees in need of resettlement. Russell went on to recommend the 'reaffirmation, strengthening and spelling out of [the May 1950] tripartite guarantee of [the] present Israel–Arab border.' This, he felt, would not only reduce the perceived need for military measures on both sides of the border, but would also lessen the Israeli Government's

> compulsion [to] take measures to counteract Israel's public nervousness resulting from hostile declarations of Arab leaders and [the] prospective change in [the] balance [of] military power in [the] area from Egyptian control [of the]

Suez base and [the] US program of arms aid [to the Arab states].³⁸

Despite such far-reaching suggestions from the field, the thinking at the State Department and the Foreign Office remained narrowly focused on modest, short-term improvements. In an address to the anti-Zionist American Council for Judaism, Assistant Secretary of State Henry Byroade declared that his experience had taught him that one of the 'fundamentals' of the Arab–Israeli conflict was that 'the possibility of an early and formal peace treaty type of settlement between Israel and the Arab States just d[id] not exist.' One of the first lessons to be drawn, he believed, was that 'all concerned should abandon a will-of-the-wisp search for an all embracing formula and concentrate on what can be done – within the limits of practicability.'³⁹

For their part, officials at the FO in London acknowledged that 'measures to reduce border tension [were] of course only palliative', and conceived of the need for a broader strategy 'directed towards checking Israeli aggressiveness, while doing our best to induce the Arabs to refrain from bellicose attitudes and to make terms with Israel.'⁴⁰ In the short term, however, no such action was taken upon such broad policy orientations.

A joint Anglo–American meeting in Washington on 26 April produced an agreed draft list of 13 practical suggestions for frontier improvements. The list was then circulated to British and American Middle East postings for further comment.⁴¹ The scope of the suggestions was deliberately restricted to practical matters – such as increasing the number of UNTSO observers, assigning UN translators and 'politico-legal advisers' to MACs, providing improved equipment for observers, and making clearer delineation of armistice lines – and did not deal with any of the broader political issues that were the object of many British and American officials' comments. The wisdom of limiting the proposals seemed to be validated by a report from the most experienced British officer in Jordan, who advised that for any approach to be successful, the suggested frontier improvements should not

> be regarded as preliminary to a final settlement with Israel. It would be impossible at this stage [General Glubb was reported as saying] for any Jordanian Government to give an appearance of preparing for a peace conference.⁴²

Jordanian and Israeli responses

The Foreign Office then instructed its representative in Amman to put the revised list of suggestions 'tentatively' to the Jordanian Government, while the Americans would be asked to make a similar approach to Israel once a 'fruitful' response was received from Amman. With minor reservations, the State Department and the Quai d'Orsay agreed with the plan.[43] British officials in New York informed UN Secretary-General Dag Hammarskjöld about the proposed tripartite *démarche* and received his comments on the list of suggestions.[44]

On 22 May 1954, the British Embassy in Amman presented the Jordanian Prime Minister with an *aide-mémoire* listing 11 practical suggestions for improving the frontier situation.[45] The timing of the approach was particularly unpropitious, given the recent international pressures on Jordan to co-operate with the call for a conference under Article XII. The new British Ambassador, Charles Duke, reported that, during his meeting with the Prime Minister, Tawfiq Abul-Huda dwelt at length on his apprehension at agreeing 'to anything that could be represented as leading towards peace talks with Israel'.[46] After several weeks of deliberations, the Jordanian Foreign Ministry announced its acceptance of five of the Anglo–American proposals for improving the situation on the frontier, rejected two of the suggestions, and withheld comment on three as being reserved for UN consideration.[47]

The powers then co-ordinated plans for a formal approach to be made to the Israeli Government. But, as the Americans would soon discover, the timing was hardly more auspicious. During the preceding months, Israeli officials had been demonstrating considerable scepticism about proposals for piecemeal efforts at improving or expanding UN supervisory machinery.[48] Israeli spokesmen had recently been lobbying for an expansion of the Tripartite Declaration of May 1950 to include not merely guarantees against forcible changes in frontiers but also all acts and threats of hostility.[49] Still, Israel was in no position to appear unco-operative when, on 19 June 1954, Francis Russell, on behalf of the three powers, delivered an *aide-mémoire* listing the same 11 'suggestions of possible practical measures for reduction of frontier incidents' as had been submitted to the Jordanian Prime Minister.[50]

Subsequent events did not augur well for a favourable or useful

Israeli reply to the tripartite suggestions. The semi-official *Jerusalem Post* immediately published a story based on what it claimed was the text of the *aide-mémoire* delivered earlier to Jordan, in an apparent attempt to sabotage the tripartite initiative by compromising its secrecy.[51] The situation along the frontier deteriorated even further, leading some British observers to suspect that an all-out Israeli attack on Jordan was in preparation.[52] In anticipation of a joint meeting with American officials in Washington in late June, pessimistic FO officials felt the need to consider suggestions 'for keeping Israel in line', and hoped to sound out Secretary Dulles on the possibility of American economic sanctions being brought to bear 'in the event of a deterioration of the Israeli attitude'.[53] Meanwhile, behind closed doors, Israeli Foreign Ministry officials held consultations on whether to

- reject the tripartite list, for its unacceptable clauses, its omissions (especially on preventive measures), and its origins (especially the British involvement);
- endorse the document; or
- use stalling tactics to keep the matter open for continued discussion and clarification.[54]

More than a month elapsed before the IMFA transmitted its comments on the tripartite suggestions for improving the frontier situation. The Israeli note of 29 July expressed appreciation for the powers' concern about border incidents, but sought to obtain maximum political mileage from the situation. Israel advised the powers that efforts needed to be directed at 'removing [the] root of [the] trouble', which was defined as being the 'determination of [the] Arab world to maintain a state of war, and its relentless campaign of economic warfare and hostile propaganda and incitement, breaking out in acts of violence.' The Israelis further prefaced their comments on the proposals by criticizing Jordan's 'practice of selective implementation' of the armistice agreements, as evidenced by its failure to honour Articles VIII and XII, as well as the recent refusal to pledge itself publicly to the 'settlement [of] its disputes with Israel by peaceful means' as enjoined by Article 35(2) of the UN Charter. If the suggested improvements amounted to a revision of the Armistice Agreement, why, Israel asked, should this tripartite effort be any more productive than the UNSG's efforts to convene a conference under Article XII – efforts which had met with a flat Jordanian refusal to attend?[55]

As for the proposals themselves, the Israeli note expressed disappointment 'that not many of them [were] in fact preventive in character'. Equally serious, in Israeli eyes, was the contemplated 'radical change in [the] status and function of UN machinery'.

Reverting to its longstanding preference for direct bilateral talks with each of its neighbours, Israel argued that,

> [i]n any case, detailed consideration of specific proposals could usefully be conducted only between the parties directly concerned, who must see themselves jointly responsible for [the] conclusions reached.

After welcoming two of the proposals and expressing conditional approval of a third, the note spoke disingenuously of the possibility

> that consultation and discussion between [the] parties to [the] armistice agreements would lead to agreement on additional preventive measures which could be carried into effect by co-operation between them.

The note concluded with an appeal to the US government to

> use its influence with [the] Kingdom of Jordan to impress on it [the] imperative necessity of restoring [the] full effective validity of the General Armistice Agreement to which it is [a] signatory and of proceeding faithfully to discharge its obligations under it.

Forced to regard this as a 'negative response', the US Chargé d'Affaires in Tel Aviv reported that more pressure would have to be applied to convince the Israelis of the need to co-operate with Anglo–American plans.[56]

For his part, the British Ambassador called the note 'unhelpful, discouraging and disappointing', and concluded that it held out 'no hope for the early application of any of our border proposals'. After his talk with the IMFA Director-General, Sir Francis Evans was convinced that Israel would not budge from its insistence on a prior reaffirmation by Jordan of the Armistice Agreements, which would have meant yet another manoeuvre along the lines of the Article XII *démarche*. Given the demonstrated inability of the Western powers to convince Jordan to comply, he felt that the net result was 'a rejection by Israel of the concept of mediation between her and the Arab states.' Evans noted further that Israel

> would oppose any intervention which might prejudice the chance of obtaining direct negotiations, or which might encourage the Arab States to persist in their refusal to discharge all their obligations under the Armistice Agreements.

He then drew the disturbing conclusion that Israel was expecting and hoping that 'tension will eventually become so extreme that the Western Powers will be compelled to step in to prevent a general outbreak, and to enforce a lasting settlement.'[57] From Amman, Charles Duke added his own warnings to what Evans had been predicting: namely, that Israel could not be expected to remain passive while the powers avoided any initiative towards a peace settlement on the grounds that they could not afford to alienate Arab opinion. Israel's 'frontier raiding' was, according to Duke, producing a new and dangerous climate.[58]

When the British took stock of the responses to the tripartite initiative to reduce border tensions in late August, there seemed to be little hope for any Jordanian–Israeli agreement on any of the proposed practical steps.[59] At the same time, the Foreign Office continued to look for 'a suitable opportunity of saying in public or telling the Israelis that in our view reprisal raids [were] the ugliest feature of the border situation.'[60] This course of action was strongly recommended by HMG's Ambassadors in both Amman *and* Tel Aviv – the latter adding the suggestion that the warning be accompanied by a genuine threat of economic sanctions.[61] For its part, the US continued to offer its criticism of Israeli reprisals. But this criticism lost much of its effectiveness, since it was usually given in the context of the broader American aims of deterring Israel from embarking on 'aggression as a preventive measure', while at the same time allaying Israeli fears about the possibility of Arab attack following a programme of US arms aid to the Arab states.[62]

Throughout August, the State Department and the US Embassies in Cairo and Tel Aviv embarked on a parallel but separate effort to 'nibble at the edges' by discussing with Egyptians and Israelis steps aimed at improving and expanding the scope of the Local Commanders' Agreements. These efforts collapsed owing largely to Egyptian suspicions that the Israeli interest in direct communication between local commanders was a means of side-stepping

FAILURE OF CONFLICT MANAGEMENT   41

United Nations personnel and also an attempt to 'broaden [the] agenda to [the] point where Egyptians feared "peace talks".'[63]

Although British and American policy-makers continued to pay lip-service to the pursuit of proposals for frontier tranquillization, by September the Americans were disappointed by a 'notable lack of [British and French] enthusiasm' for reactivating steps to implement the eleven points.[64] A number of factors in the fall of 1954 led American envoys in the Middle East to recommend that the timing was not right for renewed pursuit of the various initiatives for improving the situation on the frontiers.[65] As we shall see below, the marked deterioration of the Gaza frontier would become a backdrop for the powers' promotion of the more ambitious scheme for a comprehensive Egyptian–Israeli settlement under Operation Alpha.

STARTING A CHAIN OF CONFIDENCE-BUILDING MEASURES

Included among Anglo–American efforts at managing the Arab–Israeli conflict were attempts to start a chain-reaction of moves to reduce tension and build mutual confidence. A number of these initiatives, which often incorporated ingredients for conflict resolution as well, were offshoots of the 'nibbling at the edges' activity described above. The powers on several occasions attempted to elicit a quasi-political gesture from one side in the hope that it would, with some behind-the-scenes fostering, be reciprocated by a conciliatory gesture from the other party. Three such episodes in 1954 involved:

- non-aggression statements associated with the Tripartite Declaration;
- freedom of shipping through the Suez Canal; and
- free port facilities for Jordan in Haifa.

In the fall of 1954, given the impossibility of bringing Arabs and Israelis together for direct talks and amid growing fears of a desperate Israel lashing out with a preemptive strike, a Foreign Office official speculated on the possibility of approaching the Arab states to 'repeat publicly the assurances which they gave in 1950 to the signatories of the Tripartite Declaration to the effect that arms supplied by the Western powers would not be used aggressively.'[66] The State Department's first reaction was to doubt the feasibility of a public disclosure of such assurances, which had been given in confidence. But the Americans still wished to consider persuading the Arabs to make some gesture which would have the appearance of reciprocating recent press reports of Israel's decision to release blocked Arab bank accounts in Israel. British Ambassador Sir Roger Makins reported Washington's hopes that such action might lead the Israelis to 'draw the conclusion that conciliatory tactics gave better results than the policy of intimidation[,] in the efficacy of which they have hitherto appeared to believe.'[67] A month later, however, this line of approach was abandoned by the British, owing largely to lack of American and French enthusiasm.[68]

* * *

A second issue around which the powers attempted to encourage confidence-building gestures was the continuing dispute over Israeli passage through the Suez Canal. Since the adoption of UNSC resolution 619 (VII) of 1 September 1951, Israelis had been seeking, in vain, to mobilize international pressure on Egypt to terminate restrictions on the passage of Israeli shipping through the canal.[69] In addition to the economic aspect, such freedom of passage would have been interpreted as an Egyptian acknowledgement of an end to the state of belligerency with Israel.

During their London talks in early October 1954, John Foster Dulles and Anthony Eden considered the possibility of a joint *démarche* by the powers to persuade Egypt to abandon its interference with Israeli shipping.[70] Eden asked Anthony Nutting, Parliamentary Under-Secretary of State who was then visiting Egypt, to approach Gamal Abd al-Nasir at a propitious moment after the signing of the Anglo–Egyptian accord. Nutting attempted, in vain, to elicit an Egyptian goodwill gesture towards Israel: namely, releasing its ship, the *Bat Galim*, which had been seized while testing the blockade against Israeli transit.[71] Even after Nutting's return to London, British 'quiet diplomacy' continued, with the British Chargé d'Affaires being instructed to point out to the Egyptian leadership that 'nothing would do more to create a favourable impression in the Western world, and help to produce the necessary atmosphere for a settlement of the Arab–Israel dispute, than the lifting of restrictions on Suez Canal traffic.'[72]

But the atmosphere was already too poisoned to permit such a gesture. The American Ambassador in Cairo reported that the previous Egyptian willingness (privately) to contemplate the 'possibility of [an] eventual agreement with Israel' was being eroded by 'what Egyptians consider[ed] to be recent Israeli aggressive tactics.'

> As matters now stand [wrote Jefferson Caffery in October 1954], if publicly pushed into [a] corner [the] Egyptians will, in [the] face of Egyptian and Arab public opinion, have no alternative but to reaffirm their previous position with respect to [the] 1951 [UN]SC resolution.

Egypt was, in the Ambassador's analysis, 'buying time' and it was 'an impossible moment for Egypt to make the slightest friendly gesture toward Israel.' He felt that the Egyptians might be induced to lift their blockade of Israeli shipping only 'in return for some *quid pro quo*', such as Israeli compensation payments to refugees.[73]

The next day, at the State Department, outgoing Assistant Secretary Henry Byroade (soon to be named American Ambassador to Egypt) raised this very idea with Ambassador Eban. In Byroade's view, 'the best approach for lasting reassurances to Israel was to chip away at the differences between Israel and her neighbors'. But, while Eban 'indicated Israel's readiness to take measures looking toward peace', he was more concerned about obtaining broader American reassurances regarding arms sales and the regional balance of power.[74] While Israel was again tempted to provoke a showdown in the UN Security Council to press its demands for Egyptian compliance with the resolution on freedom of shipping, the State Department sought ways to avoid 'exacerbat[ing the] situation' by such confrontations, and quietly searched for middle ground between the stubborn and legalistic stands of Egypt and Israel.[75]

Anglo–American optimism about fostering confidence-building measures on the Suez issue was ill founded, as the initiative turned out to be very poorly timed, taking place during a serious (and irreversible) downturn in Egyptian–Israeli relations. After July 1954, a crisis in relations between the two countries set in with Egypt's detention and trial of Israeli operatives who had attempted to damage Egypt's relations with the US and UK by a bombing campaign in Cairo. Subsequently known as 'The Mishap' or the 'Lavon Affair', the domestic political fallout of this intelligence fiasco remains until today a *cause célèbre* in Israel. Even the activation of direct, secret Egyptian–Israeli contacts aimed at reducing the sentences of the accused (and preventing the imposition of the death penalty) were to no avail.[76]

* * *

A third potential matching of reciprocal goodwill gestures involved Israel and Jordan in the latter part of 1954. During the autumn, Israeli spokesmen had been floating new hints of a willingness to accord Jordan free port facilities at Haifa in exchange for a relaxation of Jordan's adherence to the Arab League boycott on trade with the Jewish state.[77] These public overtures were followed up in private conversation at the Foreign Office with an appeal for British influence to be exerted on Jordan to consider capitalizing on its 'economic interest in improved relations with Israel'. Israel was aiming at having the Jordanians make 'some limited move towards relaxation of the trade ban', and the Foreign Office agreed to test the waters in Amman.[78]

After considering the matter, the British Chargé d'Affaires in Jordan reported that there was 'no prospect of Jordan agreeing to a relaxation, however limited, of the trade ban with Israel'. Given the pan-Arab consensus on maintaining the total boycott as an 'all-out effort ... at strangling Israeli economic life', J.C.B. Richmond warned that any approach to the Jordan Government 'would be of no effect, and would succeed only in damaging our own position here'.[79] Despite this discouraging assessment, Assistant Secretary Evelyn Shuckburgh was about to visit Amman and was hoping to 'soften up the Jordanians' by emphasizing that Israel could not be destroyed by the Arab blockade, 'that the world around must live with her, and that one of the most serious effects of the blockade [was] to cripple not the Israeli but the Jordanian economy'. A Foreign Office minute on 'Israel–Jordan Relations: Port Facilities at Haifa' went on to list the advantages to Jordan of access to Haifa. While sensitive to the delicate 'political aspects', the Foreign Office nevertheless recommended that Shuckburgh attempt to persuade the Jordanians by invoking the wider considerations of continued development, progress and the return of regional stability:

> the keynote should not be fear of Israel but a realistic assessment of how to live with the new state ... Jordanian interests should clearly not be sacrificed indefinitely to what even thoughtful Arabs cannot regard as the common good.[80]

FAILURE OF CONFLICT MANAGEMENT 45

Whatever quiet efforts were undertaken, no further results were obtained by advancing the idea of a thaw in Israeli–Jordanian relations based on the economic *quid pro quo* involving Jordanian access to the port of Haifa.[81] Like the other Anglo–American attempts of this period, it did not create the desired momentum for a chain reaction of mutually reinforcing confidence building measures. The lack of success of such efforts at improving the tense and hostile atmosphere was yet another indication of the powers' underestimation of the deep mistrust and psychological barriers which separated Arabs and Israelis.

FROM THE 'EDGES' BACK TO THE CORE ISSUES

By September 1954, the Western powers' piecemeal approaches towards managing the Arab–Israeli conflict were showing serious signs of strain. Repeated diplomatic representations in which Britain and the US expressed their concern to Tel Aviv and Amman about the cycle of cross-border raids and reprisals had done little to prevent their escalation. New rumours of a planned Israeli attack on Jordan increased tensions during August and September. The British felt the need to initiate consultations with France and the US as co-signatories of the May 1950 Declaration regarding the possibility of an official tripartite warning to be addressed to Israel's leaders.[82]

The untenability of a policy which aimed merely at practical remedies to limited issues was highlighted, as we have already seen, by warnings from several British and American diplomats in the field. There were also a number of telling signals that a policy which concentrated on 'nibbling at the edges' was doomed to fail. One area which displayed abundant evidence of this was the acrimonious Anglo–Jordanian discussions over the deterioration of the frontier situation during the summer and autumn of 1954. On several occasions the British Ambassador in Amman found himself lecturing Jordanian leaders on the wisdom of a policy of restraint in the face of continuing reprisal raids. The British were keen to convince the Jordanians of the need to avoid giving the Israelis a pretext for a full-scale attack on the Arab Legion or a possible conquest of the West Bank. Charles Duke also gently but persistently hinted that secret direct meetings with Israelis might be the only way to defuse the crisis.[83]

At one point, the Foreign Office also offered the Jordanians an opportunity, via the British Ambassadors in Amman and Tel Aviv, to provide Israel 'in confidence' with a message of reassurance that the government was doing everything possible to prevent cross-border raids. The Jordanians were evasive, however, and declined on the grounds that 'Israel propaganda might represent this as a sign that Jordan was breaking with the Arab League['s] united front in regard to Israel.'[84]

A second indication of the failure of the 'nibbling at the edges' approach came from the British Consulate-General in Jerusalem, Britain's main channel to the UNTSO machinery, whose effectiveness at conflict management was now seriously in doubt. In his appreciation the dangers of the current 'cold war' being subjected to 'a dangerous if gradual increase in temperature', Bill Wilson wrote of the Israelis' long-standing dissatisfaction with the truce régime and their frustration at the UN's inability 'to promote peace by enforcing discussions'. Wilson warned that the powers could 'avoid disaster' only by (a) strengthening UNTSO so that it could 'compel' Israel to 'accept for a bit longer' the admittedly unsatisfactory armistice, while at the same time (b) actively promoting a peaceful settlement, even though the prospects of such an effort were 'sadly dim'. Wilson argued that the Western powers had a strong interest in bringing about a settlement, and should use their influence – '[e]ven at financial cost to themselves' – to get Israel and the Arab states to accept a far-reaching regional solution to integrate the Palestinian refugees. Underscoring the inadequacy of the 'nibbling at the edges' approach, Wilson recognized that Israel would 'not help us to make the truce work unless some effort to promote peace has been made'.[85]

A number of signals at this time seemed to validate Wilson's last point. The Israeli Prime Minister had recently been critical about UN peacekeeping and the responsibility of the great powers in an interview in *US News & World Report*:

> The Arabs' 'antipeace' attitude should be unmasked and condemned, not condoned and pandered to. They should know that if they take up their stand on the policy of no peace, they will incur the odium of world opinion for it and not get away with that obstructionist and negative policy. ... [W]hile Israel views the armistice agreements as a bridge to peace, the Arab states try to use them as cover from behind which they can carry on their warfare against Israel by all possible means short of a full-scale war.[86]

FAILURE OF CONFLICT MANAGEMENT 47

Seen from an Egyptian perspective, however, the situation took on a different complexion. The problem was caused by what Egyptians saw as Israel's tactical aim of 'maintain[ing] Arab–Israel tensions in [an] effort to compel [the] UN and [the] West to force [the] Arabs [to] meet with Israel.'[87] Regardless of which of the two arguments was the more persuasive, the net result was a severe drop in the parties' confidence in the conflict-management capability of the five-year-old armistice and truce-supervisory machinery.

In late August 1954, the US State Department seemed to have concluded that addressing only the 'edges' rather than the 'core' of the problem was an untenable policy for dealing with the Arab–Israeli conflict. The Department began to sound out its Middle East postings regarding the advisability of taking steps which might

- 'deter Israel from rash action on [the] theory that growing Arab strength calls for "preventive" war';
- relieve Israel's 'feeling [of] isolation'; and
- 'encourage her acquiesence in our policies' regarding 'co-operation with Arab states in area defense arrangements' or 'at least mitigate [the] extent [of] her opposition.'[88]

The British, too, were receiving worrisome reports of heightened Israeli fears in the wake of the Anglo–Egyptian agreement for evacuation of British troops from Suez, an increase in Arab bellicose rhetoric, and a worsening of Israeli–American relations.[89] Since the planned arms sales to the Arab states in pursuit of a pro-Western regional defence network would drastically upset the existing military balance within the region, Acting Secretary Bedell Smith consulted all Middle East missions, urgently requesting their comments on a draft policy statement to be issued in the hopes of reassuring an apprehensive Israel.[90]

Replies from the field were quite critical, often including suggestions that the emphasis on reassuring Israel ought to be balanced by a call for Israeli 'restraint' in pursuing its reprisals policy.[91] Other American diplomats felt that such assurances aimed at Israel

> would negate ... the thoughtful and constructive efforts of [the] past 18 months to restore confidence in [the] US as being as genuinely interested in [the] friendship of 40 million Arabs as of 1½ million Israelis.[92]

James Wadsworth replied from Jidda that the Arabs would find the proposed statement 'distressingly inadequate' and a 'mockery of self-contradiction', and reminded Assistant Secretary Byroade of a comment made earlier that the 'road to [the] Palestine disaster was paved with palliatives'.[93]

In view of the difficulties and criticisms raised, the State Department's plan to issue such a statement of reassurance to Israel was quietly abandoned. Nevertheless, by the fall of 1954 both Britain and the United States concluded from experience that their efforts at conflict management would be inadequate, and that more ambitious attempts at conflict resolution were called for – even if the chances of agreement between Israel and the Arabs were not bright.

CHAPTER IV

Attempts at Conflict Resolution

CALLS FOR A 'POSITIVE POLICY' – A SETTLEMENT BY COMPULSION?

From 1948 onwards, British and American policies towards a settlement between Israel and the Arab states were neither consistent nor co-ordinated. Among the obstacles to the formulation of an agreed approach were, as we have shown in Chapter I, contrasting mutual perceptions of the two powers' biases: alleged British unwillingness to push uncompromising Arabs too far, and alleged American softness *vis-à-vis* a defiant and aggressive Israel. By mid-1954, however, American expectations of Israel were stiffening and moving closer to those entertained by the British.

Throughout the early 1950s the two powers had to harmonize their positions on another question: whether the time was 'ripe' for an active intervention in the search for an Arab–Israeli settlement.[1] The two most frequent patterns set during this period were:

- some envoys in the field pleading for active intervention (pressing either Arabs or Israelis, or both), but being overruled by a cautious and reluctant Foreign Office or State Department bureaucracy; and
- a guardedly activist Foreign Office attempting to enlist the support of a largely non-interventionist State Department.

In this and the following sections, we shall examine several examples of these patterns.

The case for non-involvement

Towards the end of October 1951, a Foreign Office minute summarized the replies received from Arab capitals to the August instructions regarding the 'gradual education of the Arabs' (above, Chapter II). Examining the possible courses of action open to the British government, P.R. Oliver found there were but three, namely:

- 'to do, in fact, nothing beyond seeking to prevent a deterioration of Arab/Israel relations, in the hope that time will eventually work a cure';
- 'to continue our present policy of trying to effect amenagements and resolve minor disputes' – presumably as part of the 'gradual process of education'; or
- 'to adopt a more vigorous policy in seeking to bring Israel and the Arab States to a peace settlement, in the hopes that such a settlement will bring in its train a gradual improvement in relations'.

Surprisingly perhaps, Oliver dismissed the first two, and felt the time was right for trying the third course. He recommended that Britain – with the 'active cooperation of the United States, without which the scheme cannot succeed' – proceed to promote a settlement between Israel and the Arab states. He recognized the risk that such a policy might 'achieve nothing and ... leave us, if anything, worse off, in that we shall have incurred the bad feeling of one or both parties'. Nevertheless, he believed it was 'a risk worth taking if we accept the premiss that a stable Middle East is an essential'.[2]

Oliver was in favour of exerting 'maximum pressure' on both sides in what he called a 'process of knocking heads together'. The ultimate result, he felt

> may well be a clearer and more favourable atmosphere. If one party agrees to our suggestions and not the other, we should at least know where the blame lies and should let our views be widely known. If both refuse we are back roughly where we started. If, however, both can be induced to agree, real progress will at last have been made after three years of stagnation.[3]

But Oliver was almost alone in his enthusiasm for trying this third, activist, option. The prevailing Foreign Office view was expressed by J.C. Wardrop, who recognised 'the disadvantages inherent in the prolongation of the present deadlock' but nonetheless raised 'serious doubts' as to 'whether a combined effort by ourselves and the Americans ... would stand any chance of success'. He pointed to the unlikelihood of being able to 'bring Israel to heel' in getting her to agree to territorial concessions, as well as the difficulty of persuading the Arabs:

> [E]ven the considerable sacrifice we might demand of Israel would not go anything like far enough to satisfy the Arabs. ... At best they want the collapse of Israel: at the very least something on the lines of the 1947 Partition Plan. The inescapable conclusion seems to be that the only solution acceptable to the Arabs is one which they know to be unacceptable to Israel.

Apart from these fundamental contradictions, Wardrop also disagreed with Oliver on the timing of such an initiative. Among other factors, he cited reports from Washington which indicated that there was little chance of receiving the necessary US backing at this time. State Department officials reportedly considered that 'the chances of an Arab–Israel settlement [were] virtually non-existent at present and that no individual however eminent or gifted will produce a settlement where no will for peace exists'.[4]

During 1951 and 1952 British policy towards the conflict was based on the assumption that, until circumstances changed, no dramatic initiative would be called for. The FO appreciated that 'only time and events [would] produce any result'.[5] This non-interventionist line was maintained in the face of periodic proposals for a more forceful British role in promoting a settlement, such as the late-1952 suggestion that Britain become involved in facilitating possible Israeli–Jordanian negotiations over Mount Scopus and free-port facilities at Haifa. The conclusion reached at the FO was that there was nothing to warrant 'an effort on the part of HMG to take an active part in bringing the two sides together. The initiative must come from the parties themselves.'[6] Officials reasoned that, just as it had been during the Mandate period, it was now

> beyond our means, or the means of anyone else, to reconcile the two viewpoints. ... Only when forces, economic, strategic or social, outside the two parties have free play and introduce

new elements does it seem likely that an agreement between them may be reached. ... It is possible that we press the two sides too much to reconcile their differences, and that time alone will produce a solution.[7]

A challenge to this prevailing non-interventionist orientation came in late 1953, with US Presidential envoy Eric Johnston's call for concerted Anglo–American pressure upon the Arabs and Israelis to co-operate in developing the Jordan waters (see below, page 58). The British reaction remained cool, essentially leaving Johnston to promote a uniquely American proposal. Responding to the news of Johnston's forthcoming visit to promote his plan for sharing the Jordan waters, Sir Geoffrey Furlonge in Amman reminded the FO of the consensus that British officials had reached on the inadvisability of the Western powers attempting to force the Arabs to make peace with Israel. In the circumstances, he argued

> persuasion or exhortations to the Arabs to act as we should like will have no effect. The Americans [he continued] seem to imagine that they might succeed, if backed by inducements such as the TVA [Tennessee Valley Authority, i.e., Johnston] scheme plus a slight territorial readjustment in favour of the Arabs.

This he described as a 'fallacy'.[8]

Furlonge's lengthy despatch went on to scrutinize the available means of pressure – actual or future economic and military aid – in the hands of the Western powers. He found them 'a great deal smaller, and less likely to be effective, than they may appear, at least, in Washington'. He was forced to conclude that 'such position as we or the other Western Powers can maintain must be based on goodwill'.

> Some goodwill we still possess, especially in Jordan and Iraq, but it will not [he predicted] survive the adoption on our part of a policy which brings us into a head-on clash with the innermost convictions of the Arabs. These convictions cannot in present circumstances be changed either by the carrot of appeals to economic self-interest, or by the stick of 'pressure'.

Furlonge concluded by arguing that there was

no action open to the Western Powers which would not be ineffective and which, by alienating Arab sympathies and thus reducing still further our influence in the Arab countries, would not risk aggravating the situation.

He could only suggest several palliative, short-term measures to manage the conflict – which would 'remain uncomfortable, but need not be too dangerous' – without assuming the risks of striving for a solution with what some were calling a 'positive policy', i.e., for Britain to initiate or even try to force a solution upon the reluctant protagonists. Furlonge claimed to be 'all for such a policy, provided that it succeeds. As seen from here, however, no new policy is at our disposal which will not make a bad situation worse.' Sir Geoffrey's pessimistic views regarding a 'positive policy' were endorsed by Britain's envoys in Damascus and Baghdad, the latter offering his own 'very strong advice' to 'keep as quiet as we can over Palestine for the present and not gratuitously to stir up a hornet's nest'.[9]

Forestalling Israeli pre-emptive action

An eloquent challenge to this *non possumus* line of thinking came in early December 1953 from the British Ambassador to Tel Aviv, who offered some new, Israel-based, reasons in favour of resuming British efforts at winning Arab acceptance of the post-1948 realities. Sir Francis Evans' main argument was that 'we cannot long count on ... the comparative passivity of Israel' in deciding whether or not to work actively for a Middle East settlement. With great empathy, the Ambassador described to Foreign Secretary Anthony Eden Israel's feelings of smallness, isolation and military insecurity, and warned that prolongation of the unresolved conflict held the risk of an Israeli military attack on one or more of its neighbours. There was no guarantee that the UK and international public opinion would, in such a scenario, succeed in restraining Israel or in forcing an Israeli retreat from newly conquered territories. Without visible progress towards a final settlement, he warned, 'moderates' (led by Moshe Sharett) currently leading the Israeli government might be replaced by 'extremists' (led by David Ben-Gurion).[10]

While Sir Francis appreciated the risks to British strategic and economic interests of attempting to pursue a Palestine policy unpopular with the Arab world, he nevertheless recommended that

British representatives in Arab capitals be given the task of persuading the Arabs to accept a solution along the lines of the 'conditions for a settlement' drafted eighteen months earlier (Document 2; see below, pages 63–6):

> If HMG and the United States Government were to make it plain that these conditions were the best that the Arabs could hope for; that if they were accepted the frontiers of the Arab States with Israel would be permanent[l]y and irrevocably guaranteed, but that otherwise the Tripartite Declaration would be withdrawn, and the Arabs left face to face with Israel; if the conditions, by careful presentation, could be made to appear as embodying substantial concessions by Israel, and in particular if compensation to the refugees could be on a most generous scale, then one might expect that commonsense and the normal rules of bargaining would lead the Arab States, after suitable manoeuvring, to accept.

As for Israeli compliance with this imposed settlement, Evans felt the Jewish state 'could almost certainly be compelled' to go along with such a proposed settlement 'if the US Government were determined'.

From Baghdad, Sir John Troutbeck disputed Evans' analysis in a lengthy and vigorously argued despatch, while Sir Geoffrey Furlonge in Amman reacted by proposing a simple New Year's resolution for 1954: 'In our dealings with the Arabs we will refrain from beating our heads against brick walls.'[11] From Damascus, Ambassador John Gardener likewise reported 'not the slight[est] hope of success in enforcing' a Palestine settlement; nor did he think the British 'could bribe the Syrians into friendship with Israel, ... even if we have the means to do it'.[12]

Reviewing the correspondence of the previous two months in January 1954, G.H. Baker at the Foreign Office evaluated Sir Francis Evans' challenge to the current non-interventionist line of British policy and concluded that the risks of unsuccessful intervention still predominated:

> [B]efore we embark on a 'positive policy' or using sanctions to compel the Arabs to make peace with Israel, we should be sure that the advantages of such action would outweigh the damage done to the UK and the West.[13]

At the end of March 1954, Sir Francis repeated his arguments in favour of a 'positive policy' directed at the Arab states as an urgent measure needed to forestall provocative or pre-emptive action by an Israel dominated increasingly by 'feelings of frustration, isolation and growing alarm'. Despite the force of the arguments advanced by his colleagues Troutbeck, Furlonge and Gardener, Evans reported that the events of the last four months had 'served only to confirm' his opinion that some heed had to be paid to Israel's contention 'that the Western Powers should, in the interests of peace in the region, take a decisive initiative to persuade the Arab States to make peace'.[14]

Within 12 months, similar fears of an Israeli pre-emptive strike against Egypt would dominate Anglo–American strategic thinking. Evans' successor, Jack Nicholls, would write eloquently about the need to reassure Israel of Western commitment to the security of the Jewish state in order to preclude 'suicidal' risks of a military adventure.[15] By that time, the powers would be looking to Operation Alpha to bring about a political settlement to avert the danger of an Israeli–Egyptian war.

Waiting for the right moment

Another response to the deterioration of Arab–Israeli relations in late 1953 was a suggestion by Selwyn Lloyd, the Minister of State, that Britain attempt to convene 'a conference of all parties concerned in the Palestine dispute' in early 1954. On 2 December 1953, Roger Allen circulated a memorandum at the Foreign Office 'to consider whether there [were] any additional steps which Her Majesty's Government might take, in concert with the United States and French Governments, towards a settlement of the Palestine problem'.[16]

Allen's list of disadvantages of allowing the unstable Arab–Israeli impasse to persist was a long one. In the absence of a settlement, it would be impossible to organize 'any coherent system of defence in the Middle East', while Western supplies of arms to both sides 'amount[ed] ... to encouragement of an arms race'. But his list of possible courses of action was short:

- to pursue 'a policy of "nibbling at the edges" of the problem as opportunity arises' (cf. Chapter III, above);

- to undertake a joint initiative backing the Johnston scheme for shared use of the Jordan waters, 'in the hope that political relations will eventually be eased by co-operation in the economic field'; or
- '[t]he three Western Powers could make a major effort, either directly or through the United Nations (or both) to induce the Arabs and Israelis to negotiate a general settlement on the issue[s] between them.'

Allen concluded that '[o]n balance, it would be premature to take any initiative in calling a conference'. Instead, he recommended high-level consultations with the US and France with a view to 'soften[ing] up the parties' by proceeding with the first two options.

Allen's analysis pointed to the unfavourable timing for a peace initiative, and also raised serious doubts regarding the powers' ability to 'bring heavy pressure to bear on the Arabs and Israelis ... by threatening to withdraw their economic and military support'. The execution of such threats, he warned, 'might well be disastrous to the political, strategic and economic interests of the Western Powers'. Britain's impotence to apply sanctions in pursuit of an Arab–Israeli settlement could also be seen in a Foreign Office reply to a suggestion from a Member of Parliament. Under-Secretary Dodds-Parker warned against threatening to cut off subsidies to Jordan as a means of pressing the Hashemite Kingdom to accept the UN Secretary-General's invitation to meet with Israeli representatives. It was 'not by hitting the Arabs over the head', he wrote, 'that you will get them to see reason on the Palestine problem'. The British would be 'achieving no useful purpose' by such threats, he argued, but would actually be 'jeopardis[ing] the strategic and economic benefits which we enjoy in the Arab countries by attempting to dragoon them into a settlement with Israel'.[17]

These remarks, it should be recalled, came during the Article XII affair – an episode in which the inability of Western powers and the UNSG to persuade the Arab states to meet directly with Israel was made plain for all to see. The British – who ostensibly controlled more 'carrots' and 'sticks' to influence Jordanian behaviour than anyone else – had been visibly powerless to do anything to ensure the success of proposed Israeli–Jordanian meetings, whether in Jerusalem, in London under the 'good offices' of Selwyn Lloyd, or in New York through a sub-committee of the UN Security Council.[18]

In February 1954, a Foreign Office review of the options found that the arguments against a major initiative by the powers still prevailed.[19] One fear expressed at this time was that an attempt to coerce the Arab states to negotiate with Israel might endanger the security of Britain's supply of Middle Eastern oil.[20] In late March 1954, another review of the situation concluded that piecemeal efforts at exerting a moderating influence over Israeli and Arab policies were the best option – 'until such time as the political climate in the Middle East becomes favourable for [a] major effort to induce the Arabs and Israelis to negotiate a general settlement between them'.[21]

As events would unfold during the next 18 months, policy-makers in London and Washington would never have the luxury of seeing the advent of a favourable political climate. What would determine their decision to proceed with an ambitious political initiative such as Operation Alpha would not be a range of equally promising options, but rather the unhappy choice between 'bad' and 'worse': intervening at an admittedly bad moment, or *not* intervening, and witnessing a worse situation develop.

AMERICAN AND BRITISH PLANS FOR A COMPREHENSIVE SETTLEMENT

As we have seen, the emerging Anglo–American partnership for approaching the Arab–Israeli impasse usually had the British taking the lead in considering initiatives for resolving the conflict. British policy-makers often found themselves working against a latent US inertia against too much intervention. Not surprisingly, the actual drafting of possible *terms* for a settlement was almost always done in the Foreign Office. In the following pages we shall examine these British efforts at a comprehensive settlement, but first we shall highlight briefly the rare American contributions to conflict resolution prior to 1954.

American initiatives

There were only two specifically American efforts at an Arab–Israeli peace settlement during the early 1950s. The first was the 'Pattern of Proposals' submitted, with much difficulty, by the PCC to the parties assembled for a conference in Paris during the autumn of 1951. The original drafting of the Proposals had taken place between

US Representative on the PCC, Ely Palmer, and members of the State Department during the summer preceding the conference. The Israeli delegation in Paris successfully engaged in all kinds of procedural manoeuvres to delay the official submission of the peace plan, which was discussed during one final meeting and subsequently forgotten.[22]

The only other major initiative undertaken by the US government prior to its decision to co-operate with Britain in Operation Alpha was the Johnston mission. In October 1953, President Eisenhower despatched Eric Johnston, head of the International Advisory Board of the Technical Cooperation Administration and president of the American Motion Pictures Association, as his personal emissary to enlist the co-operation of the governments of Syria, Lebanon, Jordan and Israel in an agreed plan for sharing the waters of the Jordan River. Johnston's arduous brand of shuttle diplomacy stretched intermittently over the next two years. Although his mediation produced a workable, *de facto*, unsigned understanding regarding the sharing of water resources, it demonstrated how unreal were expectations that the promotion of economic development for shared benefits could diminish existing political antagonisms.[23] Not only did Ambassador Johnston have to overcome a number of psychological and political obstacles in dealing with Arab and Israeli politicians but he also found his mission impeded by the incomplete and somewhat grudging support offered by British diplomatic personnel in the region.[24]

Backing for Bernadotte, 1948

In formulating specific peace proposals prior to Operation Alpha, the Foreign Office had far more practical experience than the State Department. Despite the prevailing Foreign Office view that conditions were not yet ripe for conflict resolution, there were four occasions between 1948 and late 1953 on which officials prepared and discussed detailed peace plans with an eye to obtaining American endorsement:

- August 1948, during the drafting of the Bernadotte report;
- July 1949, during the PCC Lausanne conference;
- June 1952, in response to concerns expressed by the head of the British Middle East Office (BMEO); and
- December 1953, when a revision of the June 1952 paper was made.

In our survey of these four episodes, we shall be focusing more on aspects of *process* – the circumstances in which they emerged, the assumptions that lay behind them, the efforts at Anglo–American cooperation – than on the *contents* of these hypothetical peace plans.

During 1948 and 1949, London entertained high hopes of enlisting the US government in the formulation of a joint policy for a definitive settlement to the Palestine question. A certain degree of high-level co-operation was achieved in attempts to influence the preparation of Count Bernadotte's report to the UNGA's meeting in mid-September. In the course of co-ordinating efforts with the US State Department, the British Foreign Office formulated its first post-war plan for a Palestine settlement. The outline of the British proposals was transmitted to Washington on 27 August 1948, along with a working paper entitled 'Tactics for Putting into Effect the Mediator's Recommendations'.[25]

It is not clear to what extent the recommendations that Count Bernadotte finalized on 16 September 1948 (shortly before his assassination in Jerusalem) were influenced by the secret visits of senior British and American envoys to Rhodes.[26] Nevertheless, most of the proposals were bound to please the powers, especially Britain. They included placing Jerusalem under United Nations control and the merger of the Palestinian West Bank and Transjordan to the east. The mediator also advocated the reallocation of the Negev to Arab, and Western Galilee to Jewish, sovereignty, along with a call for the declaration of a free port in Haifa, whose terminal for the all-important pipeline carrying Iraqi oil to the Mediterranean had been closed in the early stages of the fighting. Bernadotte further recommended that 'the right of the Arab refugees to return to their homes in Jewish-controlled territory at the earliest possible date should be affirmed by the United Nations'. His final proposal was for the establishment of a conciliation commission to continue working for 'the peaceful adjustment of the situation in Palestine'.[27]

Not surprisingly, the British were impressed by the plan's potential to ensure their strategic interests in a vital region from which their forces were partially withdrawing. In particular, Bernadotte's proposals (like subsequent plans) reflected Britain's preference for an Arab-controlled Negev. These territorial provisions were, however, soon overtaken by events on the ground as Israeli military action during late 1948 and early 1949 resulted in more favourable and secure frontiers for the Jewish state. Several weeks prior to the IDF's final push to extend Israel's southernmost frontier to the Gulf of Aqaba (Operation *Uvda* (meaning *fait accompli*)), Michael Wright explained in a brief for his Minister, Ernest Bevin, the Foreign Office's view that

> the settlement to be reached must take account of the realities of the international strategic picture. It is essential that British forces, which form the stiffening of the Middle East against communist aggression, should be able to move freely throughout the area in case of emergency. We cannot rely on the Jews to let us do this if they control the communications. Therefore there must be good communications in Arab lands west of the Dead Sea, i.e. the Gaza–Beersheba and Auja–Beersheba roads.[28]

One of the main presumptions behind British support for the Bernadotte plan, on the tactical-procedural level, was that it was not a proposal for *negotiation with* the two parties, but rather one to be *imposed on* them with the expected full weight of the United Nations. The mediator's report at first benefited from firm Anglo–American support in principle, with both London and Washington making strong representations to Arab and Israeli leaders, urging them to acquiesce in allowing the Bernadotte plan to serve as a basis for discussion – even if they found the various provisions difficult to accept.[29] They were joined in this effort by the Count's successor, Ralph J. Bunche, who engaged in extensive personal diplomacy aimed at softening the unco-operative stances adopted by both parties, who repeatedly stressed that they found the proposals unacceptable.[30]

During October and November, however, American support for such joint diplomatic activity steadily eroded, partly in response to an Israeli diplomatic campaign aimed at rallying presidential candidates and American public opinion against forcing the Israelis to retreat from the Negev. By mid-November, the British were left alone to press for UNGA endorsement and implementation of the Bernadotte proposals and their territorial provisions.[31] While parts of Bernadotte's final report were transformed into the landmark UNGA resolution 194 of 11 December 1948,[32] in the end, nothing further came of the plan itself.

The 'eight points', 1949

Even as Anglo–American co-operation on the Palestine issue increased throughout 1949, there remained a marked American reluctance to join the British in formulating a formal joint plan for a settlement. During the first months of activity of the PCC, some American diplomats suggested that the issuing of a public statement defining a common Anglo–American stand on the questions of boundaries, refugees and the internationalization of Jerusalem would greatly assist the Commission in its task. From his experience in the field, America's first PCC delegate, Mark Ethridge, also argued for greater co-ordination between the State Department and the British Foreign Office so that the PCC could derive maximum benefit from the expertise and influence of British diplomats in Middle Eastern capitals.[33] The State Department, however, took a firm line urging the Commission to search for 'common ground for agreement among [the] parties without regard to preconceived ideas of our own about [a] final settlement' and without any attempts to hammer out a common position with the British.[34]

During Foreign Secretary Ernest Bevin's visit to Washington in early April 1949, the need to avoid alienating the Arab and Muslim world was discussed, along with ideas for economic development and refugee rehabilitation. Bevin invited his American colleagues to look upon the UK as 'the best window towards this area'.[35] In Paris in late May, Bevin and Acheson met again and discussed the water-resources and refugee aspects of the Arab–Israeli problem, as well as the need to maintain a 'common front' on the question of resuming arms shipments to the region.[36] Well aware of American reluctance to intervene too prominently in the efforts of the PCC, Bevin chose to wait for 'the earliest convenient time' before making any new overtures to the State Department regarding a joint approach to an overall Palestine settlement.[37]

Such an opportunity for Anglo–American co-operation arose in early July 1949. The frustrating experience of two months of talks at Lausanne helped to create an apparent openness, among certain State Department officials, to the idea of the US playing a more active role in concert with the British government. On 9 July, the Foreign Office prepared a 'Suggested Basis for a New Approach by the Conciliation Commission to the Parties on their Resumption of Work on the 18th July'.[38] The eight-point plan included provisions for:

- acceptance by both sides of refugees 'in proportions to be determined';
- suggestions of areas considered 'politically and geographically suitable' to be offered by Israel for territorial compensation, including 'a land-bridge in the southern Negev between Egypt and Jordan';
- free port facilities for the Arab states in Haifa, including an arrangement for the resumption of the flow of Iraqi oil through that port;
- incorporation of Arab Palestine into Jordan; and
- an Israeli–Arab agreement for sharing the waters of the Jordan and Yarmuk Rivers.

On 12 July, a slightly revised version of the eight-point outline was forwarded to Washington for comments. Discussions in Washington and telegrams from London during the following weeks sought to clarify the proposals but the British soon grew impatient with the State Department's inability to go beyond the expression of its 'tentative thinking' on most of the points.[39] Secretary Acheson questioned the need for a 'formal' US endorsement of the British plan and considered it 'preferable to maintain flexibility at this stage rather than to adopt [a] rigid position'.[40] The State Department's change of orientation in August 1949, preferring to proceed with an 'economic' (rather than a 'political') approach to solving the refugee issue, further restrained American enthusiasm for the British initiative. Nevertheless, the British Foreign Office proceeded to instruct its Ambassadors in Paris and Ankara to approach the French and Turkish governments with the details of the latest draft of the eight-point plan. Despite favourable reactions to the Eight Points from French and Turkish authorities,[41] the plan did not, in the end, become integrated into the workings of the PCC, largely because of American reservations.

The British Eight Points thereafter served as a rough guide for evolving British policy on a Palestine settlement, and also as a basis of continuing efforts to work jointly with the US towards a more activist approach to the Palestine issue.[42] While State Department officials continued to pay lip-service to the necessity for 'careful and continuous study and a high degree of coordination ... between the US and the UK' regarding the economic, political and military situation in the Middle East,[43] Assistant Secretary of State George

McGhee distanced himself from the British approach by announcing that the US government

> had decided that it was neither desirable nor possible for the United States itself to propose any overall solution. It was not considered that the United States had sufficient influence on the countries concerned to persuade them to accept such a solution, and the result would only be to create bad relations and impair the position of the United States in assisting the United Nations or the states concerned in arriving at an agreement.

While agreeing with the British that 'private' advice and 'informal action' by the powers 'could facilitate a settlement', the Americans 'emphasized that the parties must themselves come to grips with the problem'.[44]

'Conditions of Arab/Israel Settlement', 1952

The next opportunity resulting in the preparation and discussion of a Foreign Office peace plan came two-and-a-half years later. Invoking what he considered the inherent dangers of allowing the uncertainties of the Arab–Israeli stand-off to fester unresolved, Sir Thomas Rapp, head of the BMEO, argued that 'short of actual hostilities, nothing [could] break [the Arab–Israeli deadlock] but an imposed settlement – and one imposed equally on both sides'. The 'key' to the situation, as Rapp saw it, was the attitude to be taken by the United States 'politically and financially'. Several days later Rapp submitted a list of ten 'Suggested Conditions of Arab/Israel Settlement',[45] and that list subsequently became the subject of discussions at a Foreign Office conference of British Middle East representatives.

Against Rapp's emphasis on the need for an imposed settlement stood the Foreign Office view that, 'since there was no hope at present of either side agreeing, all we could do for the present was to watch the situation closely, and take advantage of any openings that occurred'. In contrast to Rapp's assumption that both Western powers 'might exercise strong influence ... and make aid to either party dependent' on its co-operation, some diplomats expressed their doubts whether Britain and the US could really induce the Arabs and the Israelis to comply. The envoys attending the meeting saw no real prospect of an 'opening', but agreed on the usefulness of pursuing discussions with the Americans.[46]

Accordingly, the British Embassy in Washington was instructed to communicate to the State Department the results of the Foreign Office conference, as well as a revised version of Rapp's suggested 'Conditions for an Arab/Israel Settlement' (Document 2).[47] The FO plan contained several territorial provisions, including rectifications along disputed stretches of the Israeli–Syrian and Israeli–Jordanian frontiers to be guaranteed by the UN. Departing from the UNGA position, the proposal called for resettling 'of all Arab refugees on Arab soil', with Israel paying compensation for loss of both movable and immovable property. Envisaging a possible voluntary exchange of populations, one of the four 'ethnographic' suggestions called for the lifting of discriminatory legislation in the Arab states and Israel and for the encouragement of freedom for minorities to emigrate 'if they so desire[d]'. The British list also included a scheme for developing and sharing the Jordan waters, the establishment of free ports at Haifa and in the Aqaba-Eilat zone, and 'free transit rights across Israel and Jordan territory between Saudi Arabia and Egypt'. The latter point was a common thread running from the Bernadotte plan of 1948 through to the Alpha proposals of 1955, but there was already some doubt in British political circles during 1952 as to the practicality of asking Israel to concede territory in the Negev.[48]

While this tentative list incorporated conditions that the FO considered 'desirable and necessary for a settlement', Archie Ross of the Foreign Office confided to the British Embassy in Washington that 'we have no illusions as regards their acceptability to either side or, consequently, the chances of realising them'. This admittedly 'academic exercise' was considered valuable none the less in order to 'keep the problem in the fore-front of our minds, to temper the pessimism it induces in us, and to prevent us from relapsing into complete lethargy'. Ross asked Bernard Burrows at the Washington Embassy to invite comments and suggestions for amendments from the State Department.

There does not seem to have been any response from Washington to the British list of conditions for a settlement. Several months later, Sir Thomas Rapp again pressed the Foreign Office to involve the United States in jointly working out a settlement which would have to be 'virtually imposed' on both parties. The United States, he argued, had to cease evading its responsibilities, and to apply sufficient economic pressure to secure concessions from Israel. In promoting the 'tentative suggestions' which he had advanced in June, Rapp called for 'an agreement with the Americans on what we consider is an equitable settlement' as a first step. The powers would then be ready to implement such a plan when 'circumstances eventually produce[d] a more favourable atmosphere'.[49]

In late November 1952, the Foreign Office again rejected Rapp's call, despite the well-known 'difficulties which the continued existence of the Palestine problem put in the way of any effective plan for the defence of the Middle East'. R.J. Bowker conceded that, at some future date it might be possible for the British and Americans to 'take an active part' in resolving the Arab–Israeli dispute, and the two powers should 'keep under constant review the proper ingredients of a just and fair compromise'. But the Foreign Office was convinced that 'a settlement by compulsion could not succeed, at any rate in present circumstances'. Bowker's analysis dwelt on the far-reaching nature of the concessions that would be required not only from Israel but also from the Arabs. The powers would, after all, be attempting to compel the latter not merely to 'to recognise and make peace with Israel', but with an Israel 'as at present constituted and, with certain small exceptions, [he underlined,] *within her present boundaries*'.

> During the past four years the concrete poured into the mould of Israel's boundaries has pretty well solidified, and it is unrealistic to think of chipping off large slabs of it. Nothing could be better calculated to arouse Jewish and pro-Israeli opinion, more especially in the United States, and we should have thought it impossible for any United States Government in the face of this to exercise the necessary pressure on Israel.[50]

The prospects, for Bowker and others in London, were no rosier on the other side. Any attempt to enforce 'an unpopular settlement' on the Arabs would 'seriously jeopardize' chances of winning Arab co-operation in area defence plans. 'The sort of settlement the Arabs at present seem prepared to consider', Bowker noted, 'would be quite impossible to achieve.' Thus, there was no point in pressing the State Department to study or react to the tentative FO list of conditions at this time.

Interestingly, at this time, opinion was shifting in US State

Department circles. By late 1952, several memoranda circulating in Washington began to argue independently in favour of a more interventionist US role in seeking a Palestine settlement. A number of analyses left the impression that, since June 1952, Israeli attitudes to peace were becoming more amenable to compromise and that the USSD's relations with the IMFA had 'improved to a degree where we are in a position to press the Israelis to make concessions necessary for a peace or at least a *modus vivendi* with the Arab States'.[51] Interestingly, perhaps, these internal American drafts made no mention about the need to coordinate efforts with the UK.

'Possible Terms of Settlement', 1953

Roger Allen's memorandum which weighed various options for British intervention in quest of a Palestine settlement in late 1953 (above, pages 55–6) included two important annexes: 'Possible Terms of Settlement' (Document 3) and 'Means of Pressure Available to the Three Powers'. A brief look at these documents provides us with yet another snap-shot of British thinking and intentions. The 13 points of the 'Possible Terms' were a revision of the FO's 1952 Conditions, incorporating new territorial provisions which took into account the Johnston proposals for sharing the Jordan waters, and elaborating further the role of the United Nations in refugee rehabilitation.

In a second annex Allen listed the military and economic means of pressure available to the powers, and went on to assess the 'effectiveness of great power pressure'. Citing the consistent and bitter opposition of the Arab states 'to any peace settlement' as the prime obstacle, Allen concluded that

> it would be dangerous to embark on the suggested means of pressure, since their full application would involve, on the one hand, the collapse of Israel – which US public opinion at least would not tolerate – and on the other, grave damage to our strategic and economic position in the Middle East.

The working paper concluded with a list of six likely examples of the latter, beginning with 'an explosion of popular feeling in the Arab States against the West', including the loss of expected military contributions from Iraq and Jordan 'for resistance to a Soviet attack', and ending with the likelihood that 'supplies of oil from the Middle East would be lost to the West in war and made more precarious in peace'.[52]

CONVERGENCE OF BRITISH AND AMERICAN THINKING

Having traced the evolution of FO and USSD thinking in the early 1950s, we can see that, by 1954, the differences between British and American approaches were narrowing. While the British tendency towards active intervention became increasingly shrouded in doubts as to the feasibility of exercising influence over Arabs and Israelis, the cautious thinking of the State Department was moving in the opposite direction. In contrast with the non-involvement practised since 1948, the American Chiefs of Mission meeting in May 1954 concluded that,

> although the parties must play an important role in seeking ... solutions, the full task was beyond their power of negotiation and that the US Government, in association with other powers, would have to assume responsibility for developing solutions and for enforcing their implementation.[53]

Several months later, the National Security Council's list of long-term objectives included several which presumed a greater interventionist role than in the past, namely:

- the use of American influence 'to secure Arab–Israel boundary settlements, wh[i]ch may include some concessions from Israel';
- working 'for the eventual elimination of the Arab economic boycott of Israel';

and (as we noted in Chapter II):

- making it 'clear to the Arabs that we cannot accept their negative attitude toward proposals involving recognition of the existence of Israel and their refusal to consider the possibility of an eventual settlement'.[54]

Later that year, Britain and the United States would begin co-operating on a full-fledged exercise in 'coercive diplomacy' aimed at dislodging the stubborn protagonists from their unstable deadlock.

If one assumes that the makers of foreign policy are capable of learning from cumulative experience, then British and American officials engaged in the quest for an Arab–Israeli settlement in the early 1950s might have deduced the following 'lessons' from several years of their dual efforts at the 'gradual education of the Arabs' and pressure for Israeli gestures and concessions:

- the depth of Arab feeling on the Palestine issue was deeper than most outsiders had expected and constituted a real obstacle to a negotiated settlement;
- the extent of British influence over Arab leaders was growing progressively weaker;
- any British efforts directed at the Arab side of the equation had no hope of succeeding without equivalent American pressure exerted on the Israelis to offer concessions on territory and refugees; and
- the UN and its various organs and officials had proven themselves incapable of making any real headway towards an Arab–Israeli settlement, leaving responsibility for that task squarely on the shoulders of the two Western powers.[55]

The question of achieving a settlement of the Arab–Israeli dispute was, furthermore, not viewed in isolation or for its own sake. It was delicately intertwined with the problems of maintaining the Western powers' strategic and security interests in the region. Isaac Alteras has described well the American position in his recent study of US–Israeli relations during the 1950s:

> In its attempt to block Soviet penetration into the Middle East, the Eisenhower administration soon realized that the Arab–Israeli conflict had given the Soviet Union its greatest opportunity to exploit Arab grievances and win Arab favour. How could Arab cooperation against the Soviet Union be won if Arab eyes were fixed on the 'loss' of Palestine and the 'menace' of Israel? Furthermore, Arabs viewed the United States as closely associated with those twin problems.

Thus, 'finding a way of stopping Soviet penetration in the Arab world became the main motivating force' that shaped Dulles' and Eisenhower's attitudes towards the Arab–Israeli dispute. In the hopes of 'rally[ing] the Arab states against the Soviet Union', the two men promoted an American policy of 'friendly impartiality' and 'deliberate duality' in pursuit of a settlement of the conflict.[56]

By late 1954 it was clear to both the Foreign Office and the State Department that the only way the parties would budge from their irreconcilable stances would be by a settlement *imposed* by the powers. Any settlement beyond the shaky *status quo* required that the Arabs be persuaded to abandon their rejection, in principle, of the legitimacy and existence of the Jewish state of Israel in place of Palestine. Only the British had any prospect of 'delivering' the Arabs' acceptance of the reality of Israel in exchange for Israeli concessions.

It was also clear to the powers that Arab recognition of, and peace treaties with, Israel could not be obtained without Israeli agreement to territorial adjustments and to concessions on the Palestinian refugees. If there was any hope of influencing the Israelis to accept such conditions, it would have to be under heavy pressure exerted by the United States.

Although doubts existed as to the means of coercion available to the powers and their ability to influence their Middle Eastern client states in the direction of an overall settlement, decisions were taken in late 1954 to harness British and American efforts in an ambitious joint attempt at Middle East peacemaking. In the following chapters, we shall trace in detail the unfolding of a sustained Anglo–American effort at coercive diplomacy to be known as Operation Alpha. The weakest link in the operation would be the gross overestimation of the powers' ability to 'deliver' Arabs and Israelis to the negotiating table. Not only would the UK and the US prove unable to extract concessions from the reluctant adversaries but the entire operation would remain stymied at the stage of manoeuvring and prenegotiation.

Part Two

The Best Laid Plans

CHAPTER V

Preparing Alpha

BRITISH GOOD OFFICES OFFERED

In mid-September 1954, a group of eight Arab ambassadors in London called on Selwyn Lloyd, the Minister of State for Foreign Affairs, and presented him with an *aide-mémoire* urging British pressure on Israel to comply with United Nations resolutions regarding Palestinian refugees and Jerusalem. In presenting his own prearranged statement, Lloyd expressed his concern regarding the 'explosive' situation in the region and stressed that

> Her Majesty's Government believed that discussion of the differences between the parties would help. This could be either direct or through third parties. There could be either a preliminary discussion designed to create more peaceful conditions on the borders, which could lead to a wider discussion of all the outstanding differences, or a more general discussion straight away. In either case Her Majesty's Government for their part were willing to offer their good offices. The timing of such discussions would be important; the best preliminary would be the reduction of tension by the cessation of incidents and a more conciliatory attitude on both sides.

In his meeting with the Arab ambassadors, as well as in a subsequent private talk with Iraq's Prime Minister, Nuri Sa'id, Lloyd expressed the hope that there could be some room for manoeuvre on territorial adjustments between the present Israeli borders and the Arab demand for a return to the 1947 partition lines.[1]

News of the British encouragement of discussions and the offer of good offices was welcomed by Israeli spokesmen, although this positive reaction came amid an Israeli campaign criticizing the impending signature of an Anglo–Egyptian agreement for the evacuation of British bases in the Suez Canal zone. The approaching expiration of the Anglo–Egyptian Treaty in 1956 would mean the withdrawal of some 38,000 British soldiers from the Suez Canal zone. Fearing the 'accretion ... of strategic and military strength' to Egypt, which constituted 'a plain menace to the security of Israel',[2] Israeli diplomats became engaged in a vain attempt to have the British make their withdrawal conditional, *inter alia*, on an Egyptian commitment to allow complete freedom of passage through the Canal.[3]

In a conversation with Ambassador Eliahu Elath, Foreign Secretary Anthony Eden sought to reassure the Israelis that the impending Anglo–Egyptian treaty would help reduce tensions in the area, and felt that the best approach would be to try 'to make progress by slow degrees' – what we have described in Chapter III as 'nibbling at the edges'. Eden recognized Israel's preference for direct, one-on-one negotiations with Arab states and offered to encourage such contacts. But on the basis of recent FO contacts with Arab representatives, the Foreign Secretary was 'frankly sceptical as to the possibility of such meetings'. In the circumstances, Ambassador Elath indicated that Israel would be 'very ready' for the British to use their good offices.[4]

Arab reaction to Lloyd's offer of British good offices was hostile and, at times, shrill. One Damascus editorialist recalled the Article XII episode to point out that 'the Western Powers [were] still wanting to force peace on the Arabs'. Such efforts, he warned, would

> make the Arab peoples lose all hope and seek other means to solve this problem. ...[T]he Arab peoples will ... consider any official who calls for peace to be a traitor and to be killed. There will be no peace with Israel. This is the Arab wish which stops short all Western efforts. They [the Arabs] want to find ways of regaining Palestine.[5]

The next day, Ahmad Shuqayri, Assistant Secretary-General of the Arab League, issued a statement accusing Britain of avoiding the true facts of the Palestine question, which (he maintained) had little to do with promoting negotiations between Arabs and Jews. The real issue, for Shuqayri, was the return of the Palestinian refugees to their country, and he called upon Britain and the US to co-operate in forcing Israel to comply with UN resolutions to that effect.[6]

These Arab reactions were clear enough to cause the British Foreign Secretary to revert to his earlier suggestion 'to employ the Trieste technique in trying to reach a wider settlement between the Jews and the Arabs'. During the Eden–Dulles London meeting of early October, the American Secretary of State promised to consider the idea on his return to Washington.[7] As Dulles would later explain it to American diplomatic missions, the aspects of the Trieste technique which appeared pertinent to the Arab–Israeli conflict were:

> (1) presentation to the parties by third powers of suggestions for a settlement; (2) no direct meetings between the parties; (3) subsequently[,] efforts by the third powers to reconcile the conflicting positions.[8]

But opinion still seemed divided over whether the time was right for any initiative beyond 'keep[ing] things quiet, prevent[ing] incidents if we can, [and] get[ting] small improvements on the frontier'. Evelyn Shuckburgh, Eden's closest diplomatic assistant for the previous three years and now Under–Secretary in charge of Middle East affairs at the Foreign Office, felt that 'no real progress [was] possible' towards an overall settlement 'until *after* the [conclusion of the] Anglo–Egyptian agreement, the Jordan elections, etc.'[9] In the United States, the congressional election campaign also dictated a certain caution against high-profile foreign-policy statements or ventures at this time.[10] The new British Ambassador in Amman suggested that it would not 'be possible for some time to come for any Government in Jordan to adopt an attitude ... which departed from the intransigence of the Arab League' and that there was 'no possibility at present ... of successful mediation by Her Majesty's Government between Israelis and Arabs'.[11]

LOOKING FOR AN ARAB OPENING; KEEPING THE ISRAELIS REASSURED

Even before the Anglo–American decision to work jointly in promoting Operation Alpha, a two-pronged pattern was already becoming discernible in the Anglo–American approach to the region:

- soundings about the prospect of a peaceful gesture towards Israel (mainly in Egypt, regarding freedom of passage through the Suez Canal), as a step towards relieving tensions and removing obstacles which seemed to be hindering plans for area defence; and
- reassurances to an increasingly anxious Israel that the Western powers were not, in the course of seeking friendship and military alliances with the Arab states, abandoning the Jewish state to the danger of future Arab attack.

One prelude to Alpha which displayed this two-pronged pattern occurred immediately after the signing of the Anglo–Egyptian accord on British evacuation of the Suez Canal base. Before the conclusion of Anthony Nutting's visit to Egypt in late October 1954, the Minister of State had a 'lively discussion' with members of the Revolutionary Command Council [RCC] on 'the Israel problem'. Nutting began by urging the Egyptians, and the Arabs as a whole, 'to view the problem more broadly than they had done so far' – to appreciate that a resolution of the Arab–Israeli impasse would lead to an improvement in Arab–Western 'practical co-operation'.[12]

In his reply to the visiting British envoy, Colonel Gamal Abd al-Nasir was reported to have stated that

> there could be no peace in the Middle East until the frontiers of the Arab States and Israel had been settled ... as defined in the United Nations resolution. ... The present situation, leaving the Negev as a wedge in Jewish hands, dividing the Arab world in two, was no basis for peace.[13]

The Egyptian Premier renounced any territorial ambitions on either Gaza or the southern Negev, which could conceivably go to Jordan so long as 'a common frontier between the Arab States would be restored'. Nasir went on to say that he believed the other Arab states might follow an Egyptian lead – 'although he made it plain that in his estimation no opportunity was yet in sight'. He repeatedly pointed to UN resolutions as the only available basis for embarking on a negotiated peace. Major Salah Salem added that 'no settlement which did not bring a solution of [the refugees'] problems would be workable', while Foreign Minister Mahmud Fawzi defined Egypt's view as: 'a little smaller Israel, with the Arab countries reconciled'.

This, in Dr Fawzi's view, would 'pave the way for closer and more fruitful co-operation with the West'.

Reporting on the conversation to London, the British Chargé d'Affaires commented that the discussion contained evidence of the existence of 'a general disposition of the Egyptian Government ... to pursue a practical rather than a purely political line with regard to Israel'. He urged the FO to consider 'how we give gradual encouragement to these traces of growing realism in the mind of the Egyptian Government'.

> The elimination of the Arab–Israeli conflict would certainly represent a substantial accretion of strength to Western interests in the Middle East, and this Government may prove indeed to have the will, though they have not yet the power, eventually to take a statesmanlike lead.

Reaction at the Foreign Office was cautious. One official saw nothing in the Egyptian proposals that 'would provide a basis for any fresh initiative by us to try to reconcile the Arabs and Israel at present'.[14] Indeed, this was not the first time since 1949 that the British picked up signals from Egyptian leaders that they might be prepared to conclude a settlement with Israel in exchange for part of the Negev.[15] Nasir's and Fawzi's latest references to territorial changes in the Negev elicited FO counter-suggestions for more modest or feasible proposals which might be considered in an eventual settlement. J.P. Tripp also suggested that the Chargé in Cairo should

> tell Nasser that, while we appreciate Egypt's inability to work for a settlement with Israel at present, he should realise that anti-Israel propaganda not only made the eventual settlement more unlikely, but also tended to justify Israel's pleas for increased arms in the face of hostile Arab intentions.

This, he added, was 'surely not to the Arab advantage, since it inevitably leads to an increased supply of arms to Israel'.[16]

Reacting to the same report of Nutting's talks, the newly arrived British Ambassador in Israel found parts of the Egyptian leaders' position 'encouraging', but warned that it would be 'unwise to encourage the Egyptian Government to hope for any substantial cession of the Negev by Israel'. Yet Jack Nicholls seemed to think there might be some reason to hope that an Israeli offer 'to negotiate for some kind of corridor to provide land communication between

Egypt and Jordan' might be worth exploring.[17] This advice was incorporated into Foreign Office instructions to Cairo in late November. P.S. Falla added that the British Chargé should, at his discretion, advance the additional argument that it was 'unrealistic to insist on the Israelis accepting as a basis of settlement the 1947 partition resolution, which the Arabs themselves repudiated at the time'. Falla concluded by asking the Chargé to remind the Egyptians of Selwyn Lloyd's recent offer of HMG's 'good offices at any time to bring about discussions between the parties, either on border conditions or on all outstanding differences'.[18]

Meanwhile, an escalation of tension on the Israeli–Egyptian Gaza frontier (including sabotage to water pipelines in the northern Negev) was accompanied by a chorus of particularly threatening speeches by Syria's Prime Minister, Faris al-Khouri, Saudi Arabia's King Sa'ud and Jordan's King Husain.[19] Against this background, Israeli leaders at home and representatives abroad multiplied their expressions of fear of being isolated amid continuing Western plans to arm Iraq and Egypt. Moshe Sharett hinted broadly to the British Ambassador that several months of Israeli restraint were now turning to his country's disadvantage[20] – indeed, his own political leadership was under attack from those seeking a more 'activist' defence policy.[21]

During a private meeting at the UN, Anthony Nutting sought to reassure Israeli representatives that their apprehensions were unfounded, and mentioned that his government 'would do all in their power to bring both parties nearer to a settlement' using the model of the Trieste mediation. Nutting pointed optimistically to an increase in British influence with the Arabs since the signing of the Anglo–Egyptian accord: 'That influence would be used to the utmost to improve Israeli–Arab relations; the dispute between them was the most disturbing issue in the Middle East.'[22] Likewise, Anthony Eden assured Ambassador Elath 'That the Anglo–Egyptian Agreement ... will result in a general lessening of tension in the Middle East. By increasing confidence between the Arab States and the West it should facilitate the solution of major problems in the area.'[23]

British policy-makers would take a year or more to realize that such hopes for better relations between Egypt and the West were nothing more than wishful thinking. In the meanwhile, tension in the area continued to mount, with Israel feeling increasingly embattled and abandoned. No British official was more concerned about the need to keep Israel reassured than the Ambassador to Tel Aviv. While not fearing any '*deliberate* [Israeli] policy of provoking war with the Arab States', Jack Nicholls did see the possible dangers of (a) a series of frontier incidents leading to a war which neither side wanted, or (b) the replacement of the 'moderate' Sharett government by 'a more extreme one'

> if the conviction gained ground that the present policy of restraint was resulting merely in the multiplication of frontier incidents and an increasing tendency on the part of the Western Powers to put all their eggs in the Arab basket.

Nicholls argued strongly in favour of Britain reducing Israeli suspicions and misconceptions by issuing

> a firm and authoritative statement that in our view Israel was not only a permanent but a desirable feature of the Middle East; or by a stiff public rebuke of the next Arab leader who indulges in irresponsible and dangerous talk about a second round.

The 'important thing' was 'to get it into the heads of the Israelis that, though we may be paying the piper in the Arab world, we are not leaving it to the Arabs to call the tune'.[24] Otherwise, Nicholls feared that Israel was

> likely to embark on an apparently suicidal policy in a state of national exaltation, based on a compound of mystical conviction that somehow Jehovah would intervene to save his people and shrewd calculation that United States Jewry might turn out to be his chosen instrument. We cannot, I believe, count on these people remaining inactive simply because the odds against action being successful appear to be overwhelming.[25]

The problem of reducing Israeli apprehensions was felt even more keenly in the United States than in London. With one exception, prior to 1962 'the United States adhered to a policy of not selling major military items to Israel'.[26] Yet, when the Americans announced their plans to sell arms to Iraq in the spring of 1954 (as part of the establishment of the 'northern tier' of an anti-Soviet regional defence system), the Eisenhower–Dulles administration encountered much domestic controversy as Israel's supporters energetically highlighted the perceived threat of American weapons being turned against the Jewish state.[27] In September 1954, Acting Secretary Bedell Smith sent a circular telegram to all Middle East missions (above, Chapter III) urgently requesting comments on a draft policy statement which the State Department wished to issue in response to Israel's continuing expressions of concern.

The draft statement sought to reassure Israel that America's 'traditional friendship ... remain[ed] firm and ha[d] in no way been diminished by its friendship also for the various Arab states'. The 'increasingly serious threat posed by Soviet Communist imperialism' was cited as the reason for the US 'to assist immediately [the] efforts of states in [the] area to increase their ability to resist outside attempts at overt or covert aggression'. Significantly, the statement went on to affirm that '[t]his course of action cannot await [a] solution [of] Arab–Israel differences'. Equally important was the comment that the US did 'not exclude an eventual program of arms assistance to Israel'. The US continued to hope for Israeli and Arab co-operation in the quest to 'abate [the] causes of Arab–Israel tension', and announced that it would 'take measures to ensure that armed strength developed for defense of [the] area as a whole [was] not misused and misdirected toward aggressive purposes within [the] area itself'. Finally, the draft statement reaffirmed US determination, in the event of an armed attack by an Arab state on Israel or vice versa, to 'take appropriate action' under the Tripartite Declaration 'to cut off aid to [the] aggressor and to seek to thwart such aggression'.[28]

Replies from Arab capitals included warnings that the sentence about potential arms assistance to Israel would provoke a strong Arab backlash.[29] From Tel Aviv, Chargé d'Affaires Francis Russell predicted Israel's likely arguments regarding the inadequacies of the proposed reassurances, but he fully appreciated that the draft statement went as far as his government could go 'in view of constitutional limitations, military considerations, and our area objectives'.[30]

In the end, the various difficulties and objections raised were enough to cancel the idea of issuing a far-reaching statement of reassurance to Israel. John Jernegan at the State Department succinctly captured the basic differences between American and Israeli assessments of the impact of American arms sales to Iraq and Egypt as follows:

> Israel was opposing US arms aid to the Arabs primarily on the grounds of the psychological effects of such action – Israel

maintained that such US action would only stiffen Arab resistance to the idea of coming to terms with Israel. We, however, were convinced that our policies were necessary to produce an improved atmosphere in the Arab states and that such an improvement was essential to the future of Israel.[31]

FROM CO-OPERATION TO COLLABORATION: FORMULATION OF ANGLO–AMERICAN TERMS OF SETTLEMENT

Repeating a familiar pattern of the previous five years, the Foreign Office turned to the State Department in early November 1954 with a new suggestion for an Anglo–American initiative to resolve the Arab–Israeli conflict.[32] Following up on the Dulles–Eden talks in London a month earlier, the British now formally suggested activating the 'Trieste method' of mediation. Although there appeared 'no immediate danger of a fresh outbreak of hostilities', the Foreign Office feared that 'if nothing [were] done to improve matters during the next few months, the danger may well recur'. Secretary of State Anthony Eden believed that 'the situation offer[ed] a challenge to American and British statesmanship and diplomatic skill'. Evelyn Shuckburgh had just been despatched to the Middle East 'in search of ideas'. The State Department was invited to send someone to discuss the situation with him upon his return to London 'and to work out with him the main ingredients to a solution of all these problems for consideration by our two Governments'. The powers could then 'determine how to proceed with the Arabs and the Israelis with a view to their accepting our solution'.[33]

In a marked departure from the State Department practice of avoiding such entanglements over the previous six years, Secretary of State Dulles now welcomed the invitation. Against the backdrop of the recent mid-term congressional elections, Dulles had just survived a showdown with American Zionist leaders over the US decision to supply Iraq with arms. He was now prepared to envisage collaboration with the British for a sustained effort spread over 'one or two years'. Pinning his hopes on Eric Johnston's mission, Dulles felt the new initiative might focus first on water development.[34] The British Ambassador in Washington reported to London that the American Secretary appeared 'interested and pleased' with, and 'extremely sympathetic to', Eden's initiative.[35]

Alpha launched: American consultations

The British overture came at a time when some American advisers were pushing the State Department to take a more energetic part in promoting an Arab–Israeli settlement. The persistence of the Arab–Israeli conflict was increasingly perceived as a key obstacle to the development of a sound programme of US military and economic aid to Egypt. On 17 November 1954, the State Department officially welcomed Eden's proposal and suggested joint consultations to begin in mid-January 1955, after completion of a departmental review of the situation.[36]

Operation Alpha was now under way. For the next 16 months, the two Western powers would co-operate in promoting an ambitious attempt at 'coercive diplomacy'. Alpha would encounter many temporary setbacks before its ultimate collapse. Frequently faced with obstacles which threatened either to stall or crash the operation, Alpha's planners somehow found a way to take another small step – if not directly forward, then at least sideways, keeping up hopes and the appearance of some momentum. At the end of the day, however, it would prove impossible not only to extract concessions from the reluctant adversaries, but even to move the operation beyond the stage of manoeuvring and prenegotiation.

The main element in the State Department's late-1954 preparation for Alpha was a circular despatch to all Middle East posts, seeking advice regarding 'the elements of a final settlement' and 'the most effective tactics to this end, including timing'. With regard to the latter, the despatch stated that 'An ideal time to seek a comprehensive settlement will probably never arrive and the present appear[ed] ... as propitious a moment as [was] likely to occur in the foreseeable future.' The goal was the conversion of the armistice agreements into formal peace treaties within two years, but without 'unduly jeopardizing other US area objectives (notably area defense arrangements) and without the employment of unusual measures (i.e., economic sanctions or armed force).'[37]

The State Department despatch also outlined possible 'inducements' which the US might extend to obtain the co-operation of Arabs and Israelis. The plan was to combine the present 'step-by-step approach with an across-the-board effort directed originally at securing an Egyptian–Israel[i] agreement and then a Jordan[ian]–Israel[i] agreement, utilizing the Trieste technique.' Egypt was the preferred starting-point for several reasons, including the hope that 'Her example, as in the case of Bunche's negotiations of the armistice agreements at Rhodes, would help induce the other Arab states to act.'

The State Department suggested a tentative timetable for successive approaches to Egypt and Israel, spread over the period January–April 1955. The US would be prepared to offer a guarantee including the 'use [of] force if necessary to prevent alterations by force of the boundaries established and to preserve the security of Israel and the Arab states against each other.'

Between 10 December 1954 and 10 January 1955, seven eloquent and elaborate analyses from American Middle East envoys were received in Washington. A common thread running through most of the despatches from the field was a doubt as to both the achievability of a peace accord at this time and the attractiveness of the suggested inducements to the Arab states.[38] Similarly, the in-house studies prepared for Operation Alpha were far from unanimous in endorsing the project's basic assumptions. For example, the Division of Research of Near East Affairs produced a special report which concluded that

> while the present truce [could] be maintained as long as the Western powers [were] prepared to maintain it by force, no Arab leader [was] likely in the foreseeable future to sponsor peace with Israel since in doing so he would risk almost certain assassination or would at least alienate all his domestic support and be regarded in other Arab countries as a traitor to the Arab world.

The most that could be expected, in this analysis, was that 'in the course of time' the Arabs might 'become reconciled to the fact of Israel' and might

> achieve sufficient stability and strength in their own countries to give them a sense of confidence and a feeling that they would be negotiating with Israel from positions of strength rather than of inferiority.

But this, the report noted, 'would be a matter of many years'.[39]

Policy choices were made to disregard this sort of advice, and during December various other 'talking papers' and background summaries of current US thinking were drafted in the State

Department for use during the upcoming joint meetings with the British. Secrecy was an 'essential element' in the proposed approach.[40] Francis H. Russell, Counsellor at the US Embassy in Israel, was soon named as the Department's choice for the key job of liaison with the British.

British preparations: Shuckburgh's tour of the Middle East

Parallel to this American consultation process, the task of outlining a British contribution to proposals for an Arab–Israeli settlement was left largely in the hands of one man, Evelyn Shuckburgh, who toured Middle Eastern capitals between late October and early December. The Under-Secretary held a conference with British Middle East envoys in Beirut, where the topics of discussion included timing and the need to provide reassurances for an increasingly anxious Israel. The assembled British diplomats recognized that keeping the Arabs 'on-side' for regional defence plans was as a major factor which inhibited the powers' ability to promote an Arab–Israeli settlement. Most of the participants at the conference felt it would be impossible for the powers to use arms supplies as leverage to induce the Arabs to contemplate a settlement with Israel. Most had doubts as to the timeliness of any move by Britain.[41]

Upon his return to London, Shuckburgh reported that there was a certain 'weariness' and a 'desire for a relaxation of tension' in the Arab countries, but without 'much disposition to compromise'. Most leaders in the region said 'privately' that they would like a settlement, although publicly they were 'committed to oppose it except on terms known to be unobtainable'. Shuckburgh singled out the attitude of Egypt as different from that of the other Arab states: the Egyptian government, he felt, was 'less emotional on the subject and less subject to public opinion'. Egypt would 'probably like a settlement if [it] could play a part in obtaining it and if it led to increased Egyptian influence in the Arab world'. Nasir was described as 'a man of courage[,] capable of leading rather than following public opinion'.[42]

During one of Shuckburgh's meetings with senior Israeli officials, Gideon Rafael of the IMFA outlined his country's ideas for the first steps towards a settlement. These he listed as six 'don'ts' that would be required of the Arab states:

- Don't cross the border.
- Don't impose a boycott.
- Don't adopt measures to weaken the Israeli economy.
- Don't make declarations on the existence of a state of war.
- Don't continue the inciteful propaganda.
- Don't continue the policy of undermining the plans which the refugees will develop.

In exchange for the Arabs following such a policy, Israel would be ready 'to match it with positive contributions' in three ways:

- Implementation of a compensation plan.
- A free zone in Haifa port.
- An international guarantee of the territorial *status quo*.

In Rafael's opinion, the powers could help peacemaking

> above all if they would openly commit themselves to the territorial integrity of Israel and as an additional contribution would exert all their influence on the Arab states to adapt themselves to the existing reality of Israel, and to open contacts with it even for only a partial settlement of [specific] problems.[43]

During an after-dinner chat several days later, Shuckburgh and Ambassador Nicholls provoked well-rehearsed counter-arguments when they spoke to IMFA Director-General Walter Eytan about the need for Israel 'to make some gesture of friendship or good will towards the Arabs'. The British officials then launched into a discussion of the differences between Arabs and Israelis: the former's alleged irrational 'mentality' was compared to the latter's alleged rationality. In the view of these British officials, Israel's 'superiority in intellect and resources' was a factor contributing to the difficulties of reconciliation – provoking the sarcastic comment from Eytan, 'If only Israel would allow herself to be thoroughly levantinized, all would be well between her and her neighbours!'[44] The informal meetings with Shuckburgh reinforced the Israelis' apprehensions about Britain's intentions to promote a Middle East peace accord largely at their expense.[45]

Shuckburgh's report

Upon his return to London, Shuckburgh prepared a lengthy report on his tour and on the suggested lines of an approach for resolving the Arab–Israeli conflict. The nine-page 'Notes on Arab–Israel Dispute' dealt with most of the topics that had been commented on by British and American policy-makers over the preceding years, under the following sub-headings:[46]

1. *State of the Arab world*: Shuckburgh's opening sentences read: 'A deteriorating picture. Weakness, instability and fanaticism of the Arabs.' Communists were exploiting 'the sense of humiliation and injustice under which the Arabs [were] suffering as a result of their defeat by Israel.' In such a 'dangerous and excitable state of opinion no Arab statesman dare[d] to speak loudly in favour of co-operation with the West or of peace with Israel.'

2. *Weakness of the Western position*: Shuckburgh described Western influence in the Arab world as 'very precarious'. The Arabs considered both the British and American policy to be 'dominated by Jewish opinion' and the UN was not respected. Western military strength was seen to be declining. 'We are thought to be trying to force the Arabs to make peace with Israel on "unjust" terms, i.e. on less than full Arab terms.'

3. *State of Israel*: Shuckburgh found the Israelis 'obsessed with their own national struggle. They see it in apocalyptic terms and are always in the right.' The 'moderates' under Sharett were 'for the moment in the ascendant'. But Ben-Gurion was 'always in the background and could be returned to power if the policy of patience and restraint brings no improvement in the prospects of a settlement.' Shuckburgh believed that the Israelis 'need[ed] a settlement because there [was] no future for them without one', but that they did not 'go the right way about getting a settlement':

> Their actions [were] calculated to discredit and weaken the Arab governments and to anger Arab opinion. They [were] more concerned to score debating successes at the United Nations and to avenge minor insolences on the frontier than to help the Arab governments to make a settlement with them.

He therefore saw Britain's first task as being to show the Israelis 'how to make it possible for Arab governments to talk to them'. The second would be 'to leave them no room for doubt as to our

intention to defend Jordan against aggression'. Thirdly, Israelis must be reassured that 'the security of the State of Israel will be fully guaranteed under any settlement'.
4. *Immediate dangers*: Communist penetration ranked first. The frontiers also provided a 'constant risk of incidents'.
5. *The case for some initiative by the Western powers*: Although aware of the repeated warnings expressed by British diplomatic personnel against undertaking a risky initiative, Shuckburgh felt the powers 'ought to try something in the next few months, with great care and under strict conditions'. Time, Shuckburgh believed, was running against a settlement and against co-operation between the Arab world and the west. The 'Israeli issue' stood in the way of regional defence plans and

> poison[ed] our relations to such an extent that we are impotent to counter the Communist advance. It intensifie[d] hostility to Western economic 'exploitation' and will increase the difficulties of our position in the Persian Gulf and in all matters relating to oil in the Middle East.

6. *Methods to be used*: Shuckburgh proposed to proceed by 'secret soundings', beginning with Israel and followed by Egypt. The proposals should 'cover the whole field and offer a balance of advantage for each side'. Contrary to current Anglo–American practice in the region, he saw no point in pressing either side for 'gestures'. The aim should be 'an over-all settlement', but the word 'peace' should be avoided in deference to Arab opinion.[47] Other requirements for success included strictest secrecy, close Anglo–American co-operation, détente on the frontiers, and moderation in public statements from both sides. Shuckburgh's proposed method involved taking the Israelis 'into our confidence to a certain extent'.
7. *Anglo–American machinery required*: Shuckburgh proposed that 'working groups' be set up to study the following subjects: (a) a territorial settlement; (b) 'the refugees and how to get them moving'; (c) Jordan waters; (d) economic aspects of a settlement; (e) political guarantees; and (f) policy on the supply of arms to Israel and the Arabs.
8. *Action required in the meantime*: During the proposed period of soundings, Shuckburgh recommended six steps:

- UN truce supervisory machinery should be strengthened;
- steps should be taken to speed up calculations of the compensation to be paid by Israel to the refugees;
- the US and UK should make no further concessions to either side, and especially should 'avoid public statements liable to increase Arab suspicion of our motives';
- harmony between US and UK should be maximized to make the most of Western strength 'so as to establish confidence in our ability to guarantee whatever settlement is reached and to offset Communist influence';
- Arab and Israeli 'consciousness of the outside Communist danger' should be increased through Western propaganda; and
- the powers should try to 'turn the economic factor to account in solving the refugee problem'.

The Arabs, in Shuckburgh's peace scenario, would have to be persuaded that 'the Israel which they are asked to accept' was '(a) final in its extent, and (b) based upon a just and internationally recognised agreement and not upon their defeat in war.' As for the other side, he felt that it ought to be possible 'to persuade Israel to make visible concessions (including some territory) in return for a settlement, provided they can be given guarantees of security by the Great Powers ... in more specific terms than have hitherto been contemplated.'

Although its elements and detailed contents would be subject to frequent revision in the course of co-ordination with the Americans, the Annex to Shuckburgh's report – 'The Elements of a Settlement' – may be considered the basic working document of Operation Alpha (Document 4).[48] These elements were:

(a) *Territorial* – a number of minor rectifications along Israel's eastern frontier, and the granting of 'direct access between Egypt and Jordan on the Gulf of Aqaba', balanced possibly by Egyptian cession of the Gaza strip to Israel.
(b) *The refugees* – (i) repatriation of small numbers under existing programmes, given Israel's firm rejection of the right of return; and (ii) implementation of a compensation plan once the Arabs agreed to relax their blockade restrictions on Israel.
(c) *Economic* – Lifting of the Arab blockade, accompanied by making Haifa into a free port giving access to Jordanian trade.

(d) *Jordan waters* – Provisions for a fair distribution of the Jordan waters, making use of Eric Johnston's latest proposals.
(e) *Political* – The need to reinforce any settlement 'by the strongest possible British and US political support'. However, elaboration of the May 1950 Tripartite Declaration was not recommended.

Shuckburgh then distributed his report to various ambassadors and officials, stressing its tentative nature and the need to modify it in light of further discussions.[49] The British Under-Secretary also summarized his findings orally, first to the American Embassy in London, and then to a meeting between Eden and Dulles in Paris on 16 December. During the Paris talks, Shuckburgh provided the Americans with the text of his report. A follow-up meeting at the American Embassy in London brought together Shuckburgh and George V. Allen, incoming Assistant Secretary of State (replacing Henry Byroade, who was to become America's next Ambassador to Egypt).[50]

The need to maintain 'absolute secrecy' required the invention of a 'cover story' to deflect curiosity and to camouflage the planned movements of high-ranking British and American officials during the coming months.[51] After 21 December, all American communications on the proposed Anglo–American initiative were classified 'Top Secret – Alpha' and given extremely restricted distribution.[52] Innocuous half-truths were formulated to respond to 'fishing expeditions' by suspicious journalists and foreign diplomats.[53]

Washington Meetings, January–February 1955

Practical arrangements were made for Anglo–American working groups to begin meeting in mid-January. Originally London was the suggested venue, but this was later changed to Washington in the hopes of arousing less attention and suspicion. The question of timing was an immediate concern in Francis Russell's first communication to Shuckburgh. Since Eric Johnston was planning to resume his meetings with Middle Eastern officials regarding sharing of the Jordan waters, Russell was concerned that 'nothing be done which [would] endanger' his planned visit between 23 January and 26 February 1955.[54] Previous rough spots in Anglo–American co-operation with regard to the Johnston mission were smoothed out during the early preparations for Alpha. Shuckburgh was soon won over to the view that if Johnston 'were able to bring about a Jordan waters agreement he would be halfway to achieving the reduction of tension we all aim for'.[55]

The next step was the creation of an agenda for the scheduled joint meetings, with Russell providing a first draft.[56] Although sticking to the chosen 'Trieste approach' by which the powers would perform most of the communication between the principal parties, Russell's formulation brought up three options, one of which included efforts at 'bringing about direct talks and leaving it to [the] parties to initiate [the] terms of settlement'. Shuckburgh then offered a revised agenda which sought to clarify certain confusing phrases, reorganized some headings and sub-headings 'in a way which seem[ed] ... more logical', and tried to be more precise about the proposed 'inducements', in particular, adding a heading: 'Possibility of pressure to coerce the parties'.[57]

As the date for Anglo–American talks in Washington approached, the State Department produced a major working paper, 'Suggested Main Points of Approach Toward Israel–Arab Settlement', which was the product of consultations involving Russell, his immediate assistant, Raymond Hare, and Acting Under-Secretary John Jernegan. Parts of the American draft document resembled Shuckburgh's report of 15 December, but differences in emphasis between the two powers could be seen in several areas. For example, the Americans suggested the use of 'direct talks where possible ... in lieu of a strict following of the Trieste approach'. Secondly, the American proposal for 'a free route across Israel linking Egypt with Jordan' fell short of the British call for 'direct access between Egypt and Jordan on the Gulf of Aqaba'; in many minds, the latter was equivalent to asking Israel to cede part of its territory in the Negev, even including the port of Eilat. The American document also included five separate and elaborate scenarios entitled 'Inducements and Psychological Factors in Securing Cooperation' for each of the Middle Eastern countries targeted by the peace initiative.[58]

The first round of Anglo–American talks on Alpha opened in Washington on the morning of 21 January 1955.[59] Five high-level meetings chaired by Russell and Shuckburgh were held over the next twelve days. Secrecy was still considered so essential that many of those taking part in Anglo–American discussions on the Jordan waters scheme later that day – including chief trouble-shooter Eric Johnston himself – were not told of Alpha or the morning's meeting.[60]

Three Britons and nine Americans began by reviewing the desirability of a settlement and the risks of taking the initiative. Despite the risks, the consensus was that 'an attempt should be made at the present time to obtain a settlement'. The dilemmas of trying to promote area defence arrangements while pushing for an Arab–Israeli settlement were once more brought to the fore. The discussants weighed the relative merits of 'piecemeal' attempts and a 'general' settlement, and agreed to combine the former (with regard to border security measures and the Johnston mission) with the latter (on all other matters). Participants also agreed that the 'exact Trieste approach [was] not applicable' and that some combination of third party mediation and direct Arab–Israeli talks would be attempted.

During the second session on the following morning, participants discussed a number of items, including the possible form of guarantees which the powers would offer to back up any signed agreements. None of the participants was satisfied with arrangements resembling the May 1950 Tripartite Declaration. Shuckburgh was delighted at the American proposal for a series of parallel, bilateral treaties to be submitted to the US Congress. Another item discussed was the point at which French, Turkish and UN involvement should be sought.[61]

The first two days of meetings left the principal co-ordinators satisfied with the joint efforts. Shuckburgh appreciated working with Russell, noting that his American counterpart's experience in Tel Aviv made him able to see the Israeli point of view clearly, yet without being pro-Israeli.[62] Predictably, there were differences in the assessments of the two delegations regarding how much sacrifice Israel could be expected to make.

The third and fourth meetings of the Alpha group took place on 26 January.[63] In the morning session, planners agreed upon a list of 'inducements' to be offered to Egypt. Some of these, as later reported to Under-Secretary Herbert Hoover, were:

- the 'flattery implied in the fact that we have chosen to consult Nasser first and cannot get on without him';[64]
- help to the RCC to stay in power;
- support for Egypt to enable her to 'play her rightful role in the area and in the world';
- military aid in the framework of a peace settlement;
- assistance towards construction of the High Aswan Dam.

The last item was considered by some to be the 'biggest inducement'.[65] The practical question of how to approach the Egyptians had also been the subject of one of the earliest background papers which the State Department prepared for Operation Alpha: a six-page draft instruction for the American Ambassador-designate to Egypt.[66] The American tendency to court and flatter Egypt had to overcome some resistance from the UK delegation.

Under the heading 'Timing and Tactics', US and UK officials agreed to wait until late February before discussing the matter further, mainly in order to await the results of Eric Johnston's mission. A key question was whether to begin Operation Alpha with an overture to Egypt or to Israel. After some discussion, the British representatives put aside the anti-Egypt feeling rampant in England and deferred to the American suggestion to make the initial Alpha overture – a general request for co-operation – to Egypt. If Nasir's response was encouraging, the next step would be an approach to Israel, divulging, for the first time, the broad outlines of the proposed settlement. Sir Anthony Eden, who was scheduled to stop over in Cairo on 20 February, was 'to endeavor to establish the right psychological climate' in his talks with Nasir, but to 'avoid revealing the present plan'.

The decision to begin first with Egypt and then turn to Israel was a crucial one for setting the tone and dynamics of Operation Alpha. The unfolding of Alpha would thus be based on the presumption (sometimes challenged by Dulles) that Israel was the petitioner wanting peace, while Egypt was the reluctant party being courted.

The 26 January discussions also went over some of the requirements for the successful *début* of Alpha, chief among which was that the frontiers remain quiet during the coming months. The American Secretary of State would have to continue to be evasive with regard to the persistent Israeli campaign for a US security guarantee. The afternoon session established working groups on refugee compensation and territorial adjustments. The results of the four sessions were then reported to Under-Secretary Hoover and Secretary Dulles on 27 January.[67]

The planners of Operation Alpha addressed the anticipated difficulties in satisfying both Egypt and Israel with regard to the Negev and came up with an ingenious proposal to allow Egypt a small 'wedge', or triangle, of the Negev just north of Eilat, that would touch a similar Jordanian triangle without cutting the Israeli road to Eilat. A bridge and underpass at this junction-point would allow freedom of movement in both directions, with a possibility of 'some form of international supervision and control'.[68] Although they would later be forced to realize that this 'kissing triangles' proposal was not acceptable to the Egyptians or the Israelis, policy-makers were impressed by this clever 'combination of diplomacy and engineering', regarding it as 'a novel, but perhaps decisive, feature in the settlement proposed'.[69] Secretary Dulles would later be quoted as comparing the triangles idea to 'the judgment of Solomon'.[70]

Towards the close of the Washington talks, the onus of all the Alpha efforts appeared to be on finding inducements for the Arabs while convincing the Israelis to make the appropriate sacrifices. As Shuckburgh pointed out during the 26 January meeting, 'we want to build up something to look as if Israel is retreating' on territorial concessions and compensation for the refugees. 'For her part, Israel will receive peace and security and an improved trading position.'[71] Jumping ahead to speculate on the *second* stage of Alpha's unfolding (the approach which would be made to Israel after the expected 'green light' was given by Nasir), Shuckburgh argued that

> it should be made very plain to the Israelis at that stage that this is their big chance and that, if they reject the proposed basis for discussion, the responsibility for failure of our effort will lie on them ... It would be pointed out to them that the prospects of their obtaining security guarantees (on which it seems they have been pressing the United States Government very hard), and of receiving military and economic aid from the United States, will be gravely prejudiced in that event.[72]

Secretary of State Dulles' contribution to the Alpha discussions included a cross-examination of the Anglo–American working group during which he introduced domestic political considerations. These, he felt, had to be factored into decisions about the timing and content of the operation. Dulles stressed the importance of launching the project before the start of campaigning for the 1956 elections, so as to obtain maximum leverage over Israel without interference from US Jewry.[73] The Secretary was also concerned that a mere 'settlement', rather than a full 'peace', would be more difficult to sell to Congress, whose support would be necessary to underwrite the proposed firm treaty guarantees.[74]

The Washington round of Anglo–American discussions on Alpha ended with a fifth meeting on 1 February. The participants reached a consensus on the mechanics of co-ordination and on restricting the flow of information. The Alpha planners also agreed on the desirability of Secretary Dulles sending a 'private message' to Prime Minister Sharett, reassuring him that Israel's problems continued to receive the Secretary's 'personal attention'. The message would also stress the US's 'appreciation for the relative quiet now existing on the borders' and emphasize 'the importance of continued calm'. The question was, as Russell put it, 'How far we can go in talking to Israel without revealing enough to wreck the plan?' He also appreciated that, domestically, Sharett was currently experiencing a 'low moment' and that a message of reassurance should be sent 'the sooner the better'.[75]

All in all, the British and American planners of Alpha felt the chances of success were 'only moderate'. In particular, some were not convinced that they had included 'enough in the plan for the Arabs to make it worth-while going ahead'.[76] As Evelyn Shuckburgh reported to the Foreign Office, '[W]e have emerged with no great optimism as to the chance of success, but we agree that the attempt should be made.'[77] There was also some lingering ambiguity with regard to the ultimate goal of the operation: was it to be 'outright peace', or the more achievable aim of 'an end to the state of belligerency'? In deference to 'the state of Arab public opinion', Francis Russell argued that

> [w]e should endeavor to bring about to the maximum extent possible permanent arrangements which would provide the substance, as distinguished from the form, of peace. It should be our objective to obtain the termination of the state of belligerency between the countries ... to remove the basis for the Suez Canal blockade and the secondary boycott.[78]

However, Russell also realized that 'we do not want to lower our sights too much and give away all our cards merely for a prolongation of the present situation'.[79]

Another clear policy choice was the Alpha planners' decision to proceed on the basis of having a prepared plan ('Elements of a Settlement') to present to the parties. In so choosing, the American participants were breaking the taboo on advancing specific proposals

– a self-imposed taboo which the State Department had respected fairly consistently since 1948.

Other preparations

The huge volume of paperwork produced on behalf of Operation Alpha in Washington and London is one measurement of the seriousness of its American and British sponsors. In addition to the frequent redrafting of 'Agreed Points' and 'Elements of a Settlement', background papers of various lengths were produced on specific topics. One such memorandum dealt with the linkage between the granting of military aid to Egypt and expectations of Egypt's co-operation in advancing Operation Alpha.[80] During February, the State Department produced lengthy background papers on compensation, repatriation and resettlement of refugees, as well as a draft treaty to embody the proposed Great Power guarantees of a settlement.[81] The British Foreign Office produced its own research papers on territorial recommendations: division of DMZs, Israeli–Jordanian frontier adjustments, the proposed cession of Mount Scopus to Jordan, cession of the Gaza Strip to Israel, and a Negev land-link between Egypt and Jordan.[82]

Another part of the preparations involved the State Department making limited inquiries of the American Embassy in Tel Aviv regarding the anticipated Israeli reaction – under both the current Sharett government or a possible new government under Ben-Gurion – to various proposals for refugee repatriation, compensation and resettlement.[83] While officials were quietly engaged in their research and report-writing, Anthony Eden would approach Prime Minister Nasir. Following this opening move, Francis Russell and his colleagues were scheduled to visit London for a further round of Anglo–American consultations.

CHAPTER VI

First Approaches

EDEN AND NASIR: FIRST HINTS OF ALPHA

At the conclusion of the Washington talks on Alpha it had been agreed that the first approach should be made to Gamal Abd al-Nasir by British Foreign Secretary Sir Anthony Eden on his way through Cairo *en route* to the Far East. It would be left to Eden's discretion 'to determine how fully he would develop the subject. If Nasser's reaction warrant[ed], he could give him a general idea of US–UK thinking, but not reveal the existence of a plan'.[1]

On 15 February, Shuckburgh wrote to Sir Ralph Stevenson about Eden's forthcoming visit, making the Ambassador in Cairo one of the first men in the region to learn about the proposed Alpha operation. Noting that 'we have cast Colonel Nasser for a leading role', Shuckburgh hoped that Eden would be able to convey to the Egyptian leader 'that the present [was] a favourable time to work for a settlement of the Palestine affair, ... and to discover whether Nasser [was] prepared to help towards a settlement'.[2] Shuckburgh also drew up a detailed brief for the Secretary of State's talk with the Egyptian leader, and, in accordance with Alpha collaboration arrangements, this brief was passed to the State Department for comment.[3] The same FO brief would later be used by the newly appointed American Ambassador, Henry Byroade, in preparation for his own approaches to Nasir.

The historic first and only meeting between Anthony Eden and Gamal Abd al-Nasir at the British Embassy in Cairo on 20 February 1955 has been the subject of much interpretation, since the two went on to become 'the two primary contestants in the [1956] Suez conflict'.⁴ The meeting was particularly important for Anglo–Egyptian relations and allowed the Egyptian leader an opportunity to express his unhappiness about the imminent signing of the Turco–Iraqi or Baghdad Pact (see below).

The subject of a settlement with Israel was mentioned, but did not receive special prominence. First reports on the Alpha aspects of the Nasir–Eden meeting from Ambassador Stevenson indicated that although the Egyptian Prime Minister 'was not entirely negative, we got practically nowhere'. The best that could be said of the Egyptian attitude was that Nasir 'showed no disposition to create a diversion by frontier incidents'. But the chances of further progress, Stevenson wrote, were 'nil (repeat nil) until we are out of the mess caused by the Turco–Iraqi issue'.⁵

When Eden met Foster Dulles in Bangkok several days later and reported on Nasir's reluctance to proceed at this time, the American Secretary of State reacted with some impatience, reminding Sir Anthony that the 1956 US elections constituted a serious deadline and a very real constraint on America's ability 'to continue with [the] policy of strict impartiality' required by Alpha.⁶ Despite the vague nature of the Eden–Nasir discussions, the Egyptian leader 'did advance [the] thesis that territorial contiguity with other Arab states was important to Egypt and he indicated that [the] idea of [a Negev] corridor was unsatisfactory'.⁷ This was to be the first of many indications that, despite all the clever formulations of Alpha planners' triangles, Egyptian demands for an Israeli cession of the southern Negev would remain a serious stumbling block to any chance of an accord.

SETBACKS: BAGHDAD PACT AND GAZA RAID

Two turning-points – one political, one military – made February 1955 a particularly difficult month for Anglo–American peace-making efforts centred on Egypt. Eden's report to Dulles highlighted Nasir's preoccupation with an Iraqi–Turkish treaty that was to become known as the Baghdad Pact. While Americans had originally hoped that this pact might provide a catalyst and a 'backlash' which would help them in promoting Alpha with Egypt,⁸ the result was just the opposite. The signing of the Baghdad Pact on 24 February 1955 quickly inflamed the simmering, decades-old Egyptian–Iraqi rivalry for regional leadership.⁹

During the coming weeks, Egyptians unleashed a propaganda campaign against the Baghdad Pact. Cairo accused Iraq and the Western powers of being engaged in nothing less than a conspiracy to reduce Egypt's importance and to put 'pressure on a divided Arab world to come to an agreement with Israel'.[10] Thus, almost from the outset, the planners of Operation Alpha encountered a contradiction which they would never manage to finesse. Their secret plans to promote Egypt as the leading player for reaching an Alpha settlement with Israel would prove incompatible with British (and, to a lesser extent, American) support for Iraq under the ageing Nuri Sa'id and a 'Northern Tier' defence arrangement which necessarily excluded Egypt.

The signing of the Baghdad Pact was the first of two setbacks which simultaneously undermined the promotion of Operation Alpha. The second was the Israeli raid on Gaza. Not for the first or the last time in the history of the Arab–Israeli conflict, an unexpected military action occurred to work against careful plans for a political settlement. A year later, in the twilight stages of Alpha (below, Chapter XII), Nasir would still be citing 'Gaza and Baghdad' as the two main reasons inhibiting his freedom of manoeuvre and openness to negotiating a settlement with Israel.[11]

On the night of 28 February – 1 March, a heavy Israeli raid on a military camp near Gaza left 36 Egyptian soldiers and two civilians dead, with another 29 soldiers and two civilians wounded – the most serious clash since the signing of the Israeli–Egyptian armistice in January 1949.[12] Although the devastating extent of the Israeli raid seems to have been the result of unexpected developments rather than an operational plan,[13] its impact on the Egyptian military junta was none the less traumatic. In the words of one of Abd al-Nasir's confidants, the raid was seen

> as a message from Ben-Gurion to Nasser, and Nasser understood the message. This was that building hospitals and schools and steel mills was not going to protect Egypt from a ruthless neighbour who was set on ensuring that it should not be allowed to prosper.[14]

In the following months, the RCC leadership acted with single-minded determination to build up an army that could be a match for the IDF – moves which involved a massive arms deal with the

Soviet Union which would be finalized in September (see below, Chapter VIII). At the same time, the Egyptian authorities began to train and organize units of *fidayyin* (commandos, 'self-sacrificers') to undertake commando operations across the Gaza frontier inside Israel.[15]

In the political sphere, Prime Minister Nasir seized upon the incident and began repeating to Western observers and officials that, prior to the Gaza attack, he might have considered the possibility of a settlement with Israel but that the attack had now extinguished this prospect. Surprisingly, perhaps, the Egyptian leader even disclosed, on at least one occasion, some details of his previous secret contacts with Sharett's emissaries in Paris.[16] Nasir's disillusionment with those earlier secret peace feelers was also transmitted to the Israeli leadership through various channels.[17] A year later, during the Anderson mission (below, Chapter XII), the American President's emissary suggested that the Israelis display some confidence-building measures to help convince Nasir that they had not, as the Egyptian leader was claiming, initiated direct secret contacts in December 1954 merely 'for the purpose of working a deception on him' while planning the attack which had 'caught [him] with [his] pants down' at Gaza.[18]

The Gaza raid quickly became an important landmark in the continuing deterioration of Egyptian–Israeli relations, with many analyses considering it the event 'which started the real countdown to the Suez war'.[19] The evidence certainly justifies revisionist historian Benny Morris's conclusion that

> [t]he Gaza Raid proved to be a turning-point in Israeli–Egyptian relations and in the history of the Middle East. In effect, the two states stopped toying with the possibility of a settlement and plunged headlong down the road to war.[20]

Yet it remains open to interpretation whether Gamal Abd al-Nasir's protestations should be taken at face value, making Gaza into a decisive 'missed opportunity' for peace, lost because of a gratuitously aggressive IDF attack. Within the region, the Egyptian leader certainly boosted his leadership profile by denouncing the raid as further proof of an 'imperialist-Zionist conspiracy' related to the Baghdad Pact.[21] Indeed, analyst Jonathan Shimshoni has argued that 'Egypt had positive strategic interests in escalation *unrelated to*

Israeli actions' at Gaza or elsewhere; chief among these interests was its fight against the expansion of the Baghdad Pact.[22]

Countering Nasir's professions that *rapprochement* with Israel was made impossible largely because of the Gaza raid, many Israelis believed – both at the time and since – that such talk from the Egyptian leader was merely self-serving and a convenient excuse for his real unwillingness, or inability, to move towards reconciliation during and after March 1955. IMFA and PMO files contain numerous monitoring reports – both before and after the Gaza raid – of calls for a 'second round' against Israel in the region's Arabic press and radio broadcasts.[23] As we shall see in the coming chapters, the view that Nasir was interested merely in creating an *appearance* of seeking peace while pursuing his genuine aim of preparing for war was strongly held by David Ben-Gurion and others.[24]

Most American observers at first found it 'difficult to fathom' Israel's motives and timing for the attack.[25] The raid took place shortly after David Ben-Gurion came out of retirement to replace Pinhas Lavon as Minister of Defence. Both his return and the raid signalled the ascent proponents of 'direct action' against those who emphasized moderation and international diplomacy.

In late March Henry Byroade, overestimating Israeli intelligence capabilities, felt 'certain' that the Israelis knew 'more about Alpha than we suspect,' and he speculated that '[s]uch knowledge ... could even have been one of the motives for the Gaza raid'.[26] One CIA agent considered the raid a classic 'game plan stratagem' known as 'the Prod'; Miles Copeland suggested that the operation was designed to provoke Nasir into showing himself to be 'unequivocally anti-Israeli', rather than appearing 'so mildly anti-Israeli that he might [have] sway[ed] us Americans with his reasonableness'.[27]

While Copeland's speculation seems more correct with regard to IDF tactics after October 1955,[28] there is no internal Israeli evidence which indicates that the February raid on Gaza was conceived with such sophisticated political goals in mind. All available archival sources do demonstrate clearly, however, that Israel's attack on Gaza – whatever its *intentions* – together with the signing of the Baghdad Pact several days earlier, did have the *results* of

- contributing heavily to alienating Nasir from the West;
- ensuring his organizational support for *fidayyin* raids; and
- speeding-up Soviet–Egyptian co-operation and arms sales.

Impact on launching Alpha

A further result of the Gaza raid was its undermining of the opening *démarches* of Alpha. While it may be an overstatement to claim that 'the main "peace" victim of the raid' was Operation Alpha, or that '[t]he raid certainly delayed the launching of the initiative', Benny Morris is right to note that 'There can be no doubt that Gaza at the very least put a spoke in the wheels of Alpha – and may have decisively put an end to any real interest by Nasser in the initiative.'[29] On 4 March, Ambassador Byroade reported Egyptian complaints about the lack of any public US condemnation of Israel for the raid, and pointed out that 'all this bodes ill for operation Alpha'. At the very least, he felt, the timetable would have to be readjusted,[30] and so it would be – but not as drastically as some might have expected.

In response to Egypt's complaint, the UN Security Council discussed the Gaza raid, escalating the cycle of denunciations and counter-arguments and ending with a condemnatory resolution, perhaps 'the first time the United States and the Soviet Union had voted together in the Council [against] Israel'.[31] The State Department had advised against giving in to Israel's attempts to broaden the terms of reference of the Gaza debate at the UN, hoping to avoid a repetition of the pointless UN wrangling which had followed Israel's invocation of Article XII in the wake of the October 1953 Qibya raid.[32] When the Gaza tensions persisted, the powers were forced to look beyond the United Nations and to contemplate possible steps under the Tripartite Declaration of May 1950. Since regular UN peacekeeping machinery was proving incapable of bringing the situation under control, the US and the UK started to debate the merits of various ways of warning the parties against full-scale military attacks, with the Americans initially favouring economic sanctions and the British proposing gunboat diplomacy.[33]

Despite the obvious untimely setbacks caused by signing of the Baghdad Pact and Israel's raid on Gaza, Russell, Shuckburgh and the Alpha planners were still keen to proceed at the earliest opportune moment. Ten days of consultations in London in early March produced a full blueprint for a settlement.[34] The plan[35] – a revision and synthesis of earlier drafts dating back to 15 December 1954 – was now, in Evelyn Shuckburgh's opinion, 'As complete as it could reasonably be made without discussion with the parties, and there was entire accord between the British and American officials concerned.' The planners were pleased that the existence of the Anglo–American discussions had so far been kept out of the newspapers, 'though there was some evidence that the Israelis were aware that something was going on'.[36]

The most difficult questions remained the timing and tone of the approaches to be made, especially in the light of frontier tensions and Israel's resumption of its earlier lobbying for a US security guarantee.[37] At first the Gaza raid caused some planners to consider postponing Alpha for six to eight weeks, but Russell and Shuckburgh sought to make a virtue out of necessity by trying to transform the setback into an inducement. If they could 'make use of [the] Gaza raid as symptomatic of [a] situation which weaken[ed] Egypt's position at home and abroad', they might then present Operation Alpha to Nasir 'as a remedial measure for his present troubles'. Shuckburgh was not, however, optimistic that these arguments would convince Nasir.[38]

The Alpha planners thus decided in London to proceed with their original plan and timetable largely unaltered. If Nasir reacted favourably to the proposed approach, signed letters from the two Secretaries of State, 'setting out the Alpha proposals in broad detail', would be conveyed to Prime Minister Sharett following secret Anglo–American consultations on Cyprus. If the Egyptian and Israeli leaders agreed, their Ambassadors in London could eventually be mandated to continue discussions with British representatives. 'The object would be in due course to get the two parties into the same room.'[39]

Towards the conclusion of the London meetings in the second week of March 1955, UK and US participants agreed to consult Ambassadors Stevenson and Byroade about 'whether ... an approach could safely be made [to Nasir] at the present time'. If their advice was favourable, the Ambassadors would be allowed some discretion to test the ground, with Byroade making the first move.[40] Shuckburgh and Russell agreed that they would now be doing 'something more than the casting of another fly over Nasser', as had been done recently by Anthony Eden. Henry Byroade would be expected to go 'thoroughly and fully into the advantages which Nasser might expect to derive from participating in an attempt of this kind to reach a settlement'. Without entering into details or committing the US or UK, the Ambassador would be instructed to 'outline the broad features in general terms and he would make it clear that our two Governments had gone seriously into the problem and were ready to put their weight behind the effort.'[41]

On 16 March, Stevenson informed the Foreign Office of his and Byroade's joint assessment of the proposals to approach Nasir. The shadow of the Baghdad Pact still loomed large in the Ambassadors' shared conclusion that it would be 'useless' to approach Nasir at this time:

> If Nasser forms his group [an Arab security pact to rival the Baghdad Pact] and thus salves his hurt pride and then goes off to the Afro–Asian Conference in Bandung [in April,] attention may be diverted from this irritating squabble and the general temperature may drop. We are therefore in favour of leaving the matter for a few weeks in the hope that the sky will become clearer.[42]

One week later, both Ambassadors repeated this advice in identical cables in response to formal instructions from London and Washington. Byroade supplemented the Ambassadors' joint opinion with a further cable containing the argument that a premature approach would appear to justify Egyptian propaganda claims that 'the real motive of [the] US behind [the] northern tier and Turk–Iraqi pact matter was [an] indirect method of forcing [a] settlement and [the] integration of Israel into [area] defense [plans].' Both Ambassadors recommended that their governments 'should do what they can to restore Nasser[']s confidence in us and in himself as he remains the best hope of promoting [an] eventual settlement'.[43]

Although disappointed, Shuckburgh and Russell had little choice but to accept the Ambassadors' advice. Russell's reappraisal of the situation led to considerations of how to 'rehabilitate Egypt's prestige and self-esteem', as well as to devise an approach to Jordan as a back-up plan.[44] When Dulles returned to Washington from meetings in Ottawa and was updated on the London talks and subsequent steps, he saw 'no leader in the Arab world through whom it [could] be initiated besides Nasser'. The Secretary favoured policies that would help 'build up Nasser and ... give us the opportunity to say to him that we are prepared to co-operate with him in strengthening his position but that it must be accompanied by his co-operation in Alpha.'[45]

During the same conversation, Secretary Dulles also expressed his concern that 'the UK had grabbed the ball on the northern-tier policy and was running away with it in a direction which would have the ... unfortunate consequences' of alienating Nasir and jeopardizing Operation Alpha. Indeed, Dulles had put his finger on the Egyptian–Iraqi rivalry which would also prove to be the source of the most serious of several Anglo–American differences in an otherwise harmonious joint operation. If the British persisted in their idea of promoting the expansion of the Baghdad Pact beyond the northern tier (to include Jordan, Syria and Lebanon), this would invariably undermine Nasir's ability to play a leading role in Alpha. To win Nasir's confidence, Russell and Dulles planned to tell him that the US was prepared to discourage the adherence of additional Arab states to the Baghdad Pact, while helping the Egyptian leader to promote an all-inclusive Arab defence organization.[46] By 'permit[ting Nasir] to gain new prestige and influence in [the] Middle East', the Americans were hoping to 'enable him to take [the] initiative in launching Alpha'.[47]

Gaza frontier tensions: UN attempts at conflict management

Although concern about Nasir's annoyance with the Baghdad Pact gradually abated, the situation on the Gaza front in the wake of the Israeli attack of 28 February was not so quickly stabilized. Cross-border shooting, mining and raiding persisted during the following months.[48] From late March until early June, the escalation of sabre-rattling rhetoric included 'leaked' news of high-level Israeli discussions on whether to conquer and occupy the Gaza Strip if incidents could not otherwise be controlled.[49] These events kept the atmosphere tense and unpropitious for the American Ambassador in Cairo to approach Nasir in pursuit of Operation Alpha.

While Alpha planners waited impatiently for the right moment to proceed, British officials were attempting to tranquillize the Egyptian–Israeli frontier situation by various means.[50] American envoys in Cairo, Tel Aviv and Jerusalem lent their backing to the efforts of General E.L.M. Burns, head of the UNTSO, to defuse the crisis. For more than three months Burns became engaged in a two-pronged initiative:

- to have both sides endorse a four-point pacification plan which he had devised; and
- to arrange a high-level meeting between Egyptian and Israeli

representatives – a suggestion which he adopted as his own after it was first made by Moshe Sharett.[51]

Although the UNTSO chief attempted to promote both proposals simultaneously, most of his energies at this time were devoted to trying to win Egyptian agreement to hold talks with Israeli representatives. American officials lent their support for high-level talks to deal with the specific border situation, but drew the line at any attempt to 'broaden [the] basis [of the] discussions', which some observers feared was a possible 'prelude to [a] formal Israeli request ... for talks under Article 12' of the Israel–Egypt GAA.[52] Indeed, Egyptian reluctance to co-operate stemmed from fears that General Burns would advance Israel's interests by using such talks as the thin edge of a wedge leading to an 'overall review of Egyptian–Israeli relations' and to 'political discussions'.[53] The American Embassy in Cairo sympathized with the Egyptian position that agreement to high-level talks constituted a 'major move in [the] direction of [the] Israelis' and that it would be 'extremely difficult' for the government to make such a move. As the tension persisted, the British and American Ambassadors were reluctant to press the Egyptians regarding the proposed direct high-level talks.[54] Burns, too, grew wary of Israel's general approach (attributed to Chief of Staff, Moshe Dayan) which he termed 'a slightly indirect method of using military power to force the Arab states (primarily Egypt) to accept the Israeli terms of peace.'[55]

None of the efforts at pacification bore fruit, but raids and reprisals continued and tensions mounted. On the level of polemics, both sides cleverly placed the burden of responsibility for the lack of progress on the other party. Inside Israel, the worsening Gaza situation discredited Sharett's 'diplomatic' approach which was continuing to lose ground to Ben-Gurion's 'direct action' option.[56] In reply to an exploding mine which killed three Israelis near Kissufim, a reprisal raid across the Gaza frontier on 18 May seemed to torpedo whatever slim hopes existed of securing Egyptian consent to high-level talks – and also helped to set back hopes of advancing Operation Alpha.[57]

During May and June 1955, General Burns persisted in his efforts to convince the Egyptians of the advantages of agreeing to a high-level meeting with Israeli representatives. In early June, he undertook some 'shuttle diplomacy' between Cairo and Tel Aviv, where matters became further complicated by two counter-proposals made by Nasir[58] and by Israel's release of a new set of four proposals for relieving frontier tension. By this time, American diplomats, along with Burns himself, were growing weary of constantly having to eliminate 'smokescreens' being erected by Egyptian and Israeli 'amendments, reservations or emasculations', and abandoned their attempts to bring into sharper focus the 'real intentions [of] both parties'.[59]

During this period, the effect of Israel's retaliation policy could be clearly seen on Arab diplomatic manoeuvring, recalling the situation in late 1953 and early 1954, when the Qibya and Nahhalin raids had served only to stiffen the Arabs' refusal to agree to meet with the Israelis. During a talk with the British Ambassador in early June, Prime Minister Nasir contended that if Egypt agreed to the proposed high-level meeting, 'Ben-Gurion would take this as proof of the rightness of his aggressive policy'.[60]

In a similar vein, Henry Byroade reported that the whole Arab world was 'familiar with [the] tactics of [the] Israelis over [the] past several years to attempt to shoot their way into such talks.' Nasir, Byroade reported, 'would not place himself in [the] eyes of his army, Egypt and [the] Arab world in [the] light of having been forced to accept such talks by [the] threat of force.'[61] For his part, the American Ambassador in Tel Aviv responded to Byroade's report and challenged Nasir's logic and arguments by reviewing the origins and motives behind the direct-talks proposal. In his estimation, there was no 'convincing evidence' that the Israel government was 'in fact trying "to shoot its way into high level talks"'.[62]

BYROADE, FAWZI AND NASIR: EARLY PROBINGS

In this strained atmosphere between March and June 1955, and amid the intensive but unavailing efforts of General Burns to calm the Gaza frontier, the planners of Operation Alpha were forced to look for an opportune moment to approach Nasir. Having decided reluctantly to hold off until the Egyptian leader's return from Bandung in late April, Operation Alpha received a welcome boost when, on 26 March, the Egyptian Foreign Minister invited Ambassador Byroade for a talk which unexpectedly turned into a wide-ranging discussion of the need to resolve the Arab–Israeli conflict.

Taking the American Ambassador by surprise, Dr Mahmud Fawzi spoke in considerable detail about the lines of a refugee and territorial settlement which would be acceptable to Egypt. On the latter issue, the Foreign Minister 'felt it imperative that a land link be re-established between Egypt and the rest of the Arab world'. A mere 'corridor' would not be sufficient. What he envisaged was a strip of land 'swing[ing] up in an arc to include Gaza which could be ceded to Jordan. Gaza was only a liability to Egypt', Byroade reported him as saying, 'and she would be glad to get rid of it'.[63] Byroade was joined by Ambassador Stevenson and Evelyn Shuckburgh in welcoming Dr Fawzi's approach, which they believe represented a development 'of great interest', especially when the Egyptian Foreign Minister indicated 'that Nasser would be kept completely in the picture if the talks proceeded'.[64]

Several days later, Dr Fawzi met again with Ambassador Byroade to receive a State Department message regarding the Gaza situation. When Fawzi asked for the Ambassador's reactions to their previous discussion regarding an overall settlement, Byroade was faced with the choice between backing away from the subject or going ahead. He chose the latter, and proceeded along the lines of the February brief prepared by the Foreign Office. Among the points made during a two-hour conversation, the Ambassador praised Egypt's 'realism' as recently demonstrated by the 'positive attitude' it had taken in support of the Johnston mission on regional water development, and he hoped 'that Nasser and Fawzi [would] be disposed [to] accept [a] practical realistic settlement and [would] help us to work for it.' Byroade also outlined the 'tough policy' which he claimed the US had been following with regard to Israel's requests for arms and security guarantees. 'We believed', the Ambassador informed the Egyptian Foreign Minister, that the

> net result was to inject realism into Israeli thinking. This policy had, however, made Israel feel frustrated and insecure. One must judge with great care how far it [was] profitable [to] carry such a course. ... All in all, this seemed [the] best time to try for [a] settlement.

What the Americans had in mind, he said, was a 'slightly smaller Israel' – nothing like a 'radical frontier change along [the] lines [of the] 1947 UN resolution' – with security guarantees from the Western nations.[65]

Dr Fawzi was reported in 'complete agreement' regarding both the general approach and the timing. He suggested, further, that a 'solution must be found which both sides [could] advertise as a victory but that secretly both sides would consider equally unsatisfactory. This [was] the best that could be hoped for.'

The two men were forced to acknowledge that bridging the gap between the Egyptian and Israeli positions regarding the Negev might prove to be an 'impossible problem'. Byroade ended his report by cautioning the State Department that he was 'unable as yet to weigh the significance of what appears on [the] surface to be [an] extremely encouraging development.' A talk with Nasir, scheduled for the next night, would continue the discussion.[66]

On the evening of 4 April, Gamal Abd al-Nasir came to dinner at Ambassador Byroade's residence and their discussions went on until 03h00 the next morning. Byroade's presentation sought to build up Nasir's confidence by offering to 'help him out of his present dilemma' and by describing America's hopes for the new Egypt. These included a long list of 'wishes', including the wish for Egypt to become a

> prosperous, healthy, forward looking, non communist, modern state ready to cooperate in [the] foreign field in [the] achievement of UN objectives. We wished to see an Egypt alert to [the] dangers of Commie subversion and the impossibility of neutralism.

The United States also wished for

> an Egypt that would recognize that collective security arrangements [would] bring strength to the Middle East and were in fact in her own interest. We also hoped to see an Egypt willing to deal realistically on the Arab–Israeli situation which was only serving to perpetuate weakness and insecurity.

After the Ambassador repeated the substance of his Alpha presentation, he found the Egyptian Premier 'less forthcoming' than Foreign Minister Fawzi had been, suggesting that the 'matter should be developed further after Bandung'. Nasir had difficulty seeing how he could take an initiative in the current state of inter-Arab dissension without being accused of 'falling into [a] deliberate plot to further weaken Egypt's position in [the] Arab world'. One thing was clear, however: Nasir 'desperately wished land connections from Egypt to other Arab states.'[67]

Thus was Operation Alpha launched – its timing determined not by a calculated Anglo–American move but by an unexpected Egyptian overture. Despite the unabated regional tensions which undermined Alpha's chances of success, neither Byroade nor Stevenson expressed any misgivings about having taken the first step in this way and at this time.[68] The Foreign Office reinforced Byroade's approach with a message to Nasir in support of the 'search of a solution of the Palestine question', while the State Department sent Ambassador Byroade a personal message of admiration and appreciation for the success of his first approaches to the Egyptian leadership.[69] Shuckburgh felt that Byroade's conversations had yielded 'quite promising results. If the Jews will just keep quiet for another four or five weeks', he added, 'we might get some sort of negotiation going. ...' At the same time, London appreciated that Nasir had been 'a good deal more cautious (and perhaps more realistic) than Fawzi and that we shall have to wait and see how far he is willing to go when he gets back from Bandoeng.'[70]

On 7 April, Mahmud Fawzi invited the British Ambassador to call and reiterated Nasir's willingness 'to go ahead and do his best to play the part which the United States and United Kingdom Governments wished him to play in restoring peace' in the area. The Foreign Minister suggested that the powers develop their ideas in more detail so that they could be discussed with Nasir after his return from Bandung. In the interim, however, Fawzi was categorical in stating that Egypt was 'not willing to bargain' regarding a corridor across the Southern Negev: 'Israel's southern boundary', he declared, 'should be Beer[s]heba'. When Stevenson asked

> whether he seriously considered that any Israeli Government could abandon the whole of the Southern Negev[, h]e retorted by asking me whether I seriously considered the Arab States could make peace with Israel unless the latter were prepared to give way on this.[71]

Fawzi's and Nasir's insistence on 'no corridors' would prove categorical and consistent over the coming months, as would the corresponding Israeli rejection of the idea of ceding any of the Negev Desert to Egypt or Jordan. While it appears easy, in hindsight, to comment that '[f]rom this moment onwards Alpha was doomed',[72]

Anglo–American assessments at the time were far from being so dramatic or clear-cut. The planners of Alpha were able to maintain sufficient optimism to justify proceeding with their ambitious hopes for an Egyptian–Israeli settlement thanks, in part, to the erroneous assumption, fostered particularly by Secretary Dulles, that this 'greatly exaggerated' Egyptian stance was little more than 'an initial statement of [a] trading position'.[73] A parallel assumption shared by both American and British policy-makers was that, despite their eloquent protestations, the Israelis would in the end 'have to' make territorial concessions in the Negev – ceding perhaps 'one third of the total area'.[74]

LONDON AND PARIS MEETINGS: FINE-TUNING THE NEGEV PROPOSALS

While awaiting the next developments after Nasir's return from Bandung, several Cabinet ministers began to query the wisdom of Britain being drawn into heavy financial commitments earmarked to assist Israel in the future compensation of Palestinian refugees.[75] At the same time, the British and American Ambassadors in Cairo were very concerned about the possibilities of Operation Alpha breaking down over irreconcilable differences over Gaza and the Negev.[76] Indeed, as early as May 1953, John Foster Dulles had personally encountered mutually contradictory Egyptian and Israeli attitudes towards redrawing the Israeli map south of Beersheba.[77] Anticipating an Egyptian rejection of the current Alpha territorial plan, Evelyn Shuckburgh realized that some fine-tuning of the original proposals would be necessary. He invited Francis Russell to visit London for further consultations, including a consideration of Shuckburgh's new ideas for a Gaza–Negev frontier settlement.

In response to Fawzi's insistence on Egyptian demands for a line near Beersheba, Shuckburgh's new proposals for a territorial settlement replaced the idea of relatively small 'kissing triangles' in the south with larger triangles in the northern Negev.[78] He expected that the attractiveness of the revised plan for Egypt would be that it followed some of the lines of the 1947 partition resolution, and that it involved a fairly large cession of territory, making it 'easier for Nasser to defend to his own people and the other Arab states'.[79] Yet, while promoting the northern triangles scheme, Shuckburgh had to 'agree that it would be very difficult to sell to the Israelis' –

even though it avoided taking from Israel any irrigable land or known mineral deposits, and left the Israelis 'in full control of the port of [Eilat] and its hinterland'. As unattractive as the plan might be to Israel, Shuckburgh felt that 'something like it' might well be Nasir's 'minimum price for a settlement'.[80] 'We shall not achieve Alpha', Shuckburgh had to remind his Foreign Office colleagues, 'without painful concessions from Israel.'[81]

At the end of his consultations in London, Russell reported that 'our hopes at the moment are slightly higher than they were a month ago'.[82] But on the point of the Negev territorial settlement, the British and American planners of Alpha had not really reached agreement. While not denying the 'intrinsic merits' of the appeal of the 'northern triangles' scheme to the Egyptians and the fact that it 'did not really deprive Israel of any valuable territory', the Americans remained hesitant because 'on a map it would look like a serious dismemberment of Israel territory and would[,] if leaked[,] have [an] enormous and adverse psychological impact on Israel and world Jewry.'[83] In the end, Secretary Dulles approved 'the whole approach except for the proposal for the northern triangles'.[84] Shuckburgh had no choice but to work around this American reluctance, although he feared that valuable time would be lost, 'And if we are not careful we may be manoeuvred into a position in which the Israelis can claim that Nasser is to blame for the lack of progress.'[85]

FACTORING IN ISRAEL: SECURITY TREATY VERSUS ARAB–ISRAELI SETTLEMENT

On 15 April, the Foreign Office and State Department decided to disclose the existence of Operation Alpha to their Middle East envoys for the first time. Once progress was reached in conversations with Nasir and the envoys were informed, an approach to Israeli Prime Minister Sharett would be scheduled for the end of May, at the earliest, in accordance with the original plan of sending parallel letters signed by John Foster Dulles and Harold Macmillan, the new British Foreign Secretary (replacing Anthony Eden who became Prime Minister). The Secretaries' letters were to be followed by the despatch of special Israeli envoys to meet Shuckburgh and Russell secretly on Cyprus or Malta. Byroade was to undertake further soundings of Nasir in early May.[86]

After devoting so much attention and calculation to their initial discussions with Nasir, it was now time for the planners to take their first steps in the direction of winning Israeli confidence in Operation Alpha. This task was made even more difficult by developments during the months following the Gaza raid. The raid itself was seen by the US Embassy in Tel Aviv as a sign that the 'sands of time ran out on Israel['s] moderation policy' before the atmosphere of détente on the borders, necessary for Alpha, could be created. The problem now, as seen from Tel Aviv, was the 'much more formidable one of obtaining [a] reversal [of the] new activist trends' among the Israeli leadership. Ambassador Edward B. Lawson reported, with some concern, that the Prime Minister had just put on the public record, in addition to Israel's existing call for stronger security guarantees, an appeal for help to 'increase our defensive potential'. This phrase was interpreted to mean the acquisition of arms in order to maintain a balance with the Arab states. Lawson did not believe that the Government of Israel would be prepared to give serious consideration to proposals on refugees or territorial adjustments 'unless [the] US [was] prepared simultaneously to discuss Israel['s] security requirements' in this new light.[87]

Ben-Gurion's latest moves were part of an important shift in Israel's foreign and defence policy in late 1954 and early 1955, involving a concerted campaign not only for arms, but also for a bilateral security pact with the US. Following the April 1954 precedent of a US military aid programme for Iraq and the conclusion, three months later, of Anglo–Egyptian negotiations for the evacuation of British bases from Egypt, Israelis felt particularly vulnerable and isolated. This enhanced vulnerability and isolation led to a reassessment of Israel's previously negative attitude to the idea of seeking a formal and public American guarantee of the Jewish state's security. The first formal expression of what one scholar has called a 'revolutionary shift in Israel's policy' came in September 1954, with efforts for a bilateral security treaty were redoubled in early 1955.[88]

During their March 1955 consultations in London, Russell and Shuckburgh were well aware of Israel's growing security anxieties, but they felt that the powers could consider satisfying its requests for a guarantee and for arms only *after* successful implementation of plans for regional defence. Those plans necessarily involved arms sales to the Arabs and the formation of a regional defence organization from which Israel would, at least in the initial stages, be excluded. Realizing the inevitability of strong Israeli objections, Russell proposed that Eden and Dulles send personal messages to Sharett assuring him of their good intentions – but deferring any security guarantee to Israel (or Israeli participation in a regional defence pact) until after 'conditions of stability and calm' were restored and the Middle East, as a whole, was strengthened against 'outside aggression'.[89]

During April 1955, both in Washington and via the US Embassy in Tel Aviv, Israeli representatives launched a full-fledged campaign on behalf of 'a defence treaty between the United States and ourselves, such as would guarantee the territorial integrity of Israel and assure us an arms supply corresponding to that offered to the Arab States.'[90] Prime Minister Sharett found himself cornered by a combination of severe Egyptian provocations along the border and internal pressure for stern retaliation. Israel's feeling of vulnerability and isolation was further enhanced by anti-Israeli statements issued by Third World leaders in the wake of the Bandung conference of non-aligned nations.[91]

In a lengthy reply to two earlier personal messages from Secretary Dulles urging restraint and reassuring Israel that its concerns were being giving serious attention, Sharett expressed his appreciation but gave reasons why 'the sense of isolation prevalent amongst our people [was] deepening'. Among other things, the Middle East was 'beginning [to] be a network of pacts from which Israel [was] excluded'.

> All the Arab States concerned are active enemies of Israel. They profess a fierce desire [to] see Israel obliterated. Their 'peace terms' spell Israel's doom. Their association in a western defence system without a prior change in their attitude inevitably hardens their intransigence. Their arming is a direct threat to Israel's survival.

The Prime Minister appealed to the Secretary of State to be taken into his confidence 'as to the action the United States intends taking in the near future for the Middle East and in particular as to the exact steps contemplated regarding Israel'. In one of several contemporary documents that suggest – between the lines – that the Israelis suspected the existence of Operation Alpha, Sharett went on: 'Advance knowledge might be helpful in achieving a common policy or would eliminate unnecessary misunderstanding.'[92]

The next day, Ambassador Abba Eban met with the American Secretary of State to discuss and amplify Sharett's message. Dulles informed the Israeli Ambassador, in less vague terms than previously, that the US had been examining the possibility of arranging a settlement on several outstanding Arab–Israeli issues. During this meeting, Eban became the first Israeli to receive hints from an authoritative source about the existence of Operation Alpha. Although the settlement envisaged by the Americans might not be 'wholly acceptable to either side', the Secretary indicated that the State Department had now reached the stage of deciding on timing and procedure. The 'Gaza incident' and Nasir's trip to Bandung had 'upset [the] time-table' somewhat, he confessed, but the Americans were contemplating an approach to Nasir on his return, 'presupposing quiet along the Israeli–Egyptian border for the next two or three weeks'. The Secretary described the contemplated moves as necessary 'in order to get the kind of treaty [of security] Israel wanted', and indicated that the US government was anticipating an effort to reach a settlement within one year. In the course of his reply, Eban urged that the 'present agreed frontiers be guaranteed'.[93]

The following day, Eban tried in vain to extract further details from Assistant Secretary George Allen, inquiring 'as to what the Secretary had meant by such terms as "agreed border adjustments", "satisfaction of refugee claims", and "water adjustments in addition to those envisaged in the Johnston negotiations".' The Ambassador pointed out that 'there would be a tendency in Israel to speculate as to the nature of the concessions which Israel might have to make', adding that the 'capacity of Israel to make such concessions was limited by her legitimate concern for her sovereignty and security.' Allen made light of Israel's apprehensions, suggesting that '[p]erhaps what we were seeking was a mutually unsatisfactory solution'. The two men also discussed the advantages of beginning with Egypt and working with one Arab state at a time, following the 'Rhodes model', on the logic that a 'settlement with one country would start momentum for settlement with other countries'.[94]

Dulles had mentioned neither Anglo–American collaboration nor the existence of specific proposals for a settlement, but his partial disclosure of Alpha to Eban was welcomed by Shuckburgh in London as something which he hoped would help 'quieten the Israelis'.[95] Indeed, the disclosures had been specifically intended by the American Secretary to convince the Government of Israel that it could 'obtain

[a] security guarantee if it will cooperate in maintaining calm in [the] area and work toward [a] settlement of some basic Israel–Arab issues.'[96] In his formal reply to Sharett regarding the requested security arrangements, Secretary Dulles underlined the difficulties of concluding a US treaty guarantee during an ongoing 'highly inflammatory dispute', but suggested that Senate approval could be more easily forthcoming if 'the major issues between Israel and her neighbors' were to be 'brought measurably nearer [a] solution'. The US government was, he declared, 'ready to exert every effort to achieve' the desired 'settlement of the major outstanding issues'.[97]

The linkage between a security guarantee for Israel and an Arab–Israeli settlement contained a built-in 'horse-and-cart' dilemma which made it impossible for the Israelis to find Dulles' arguments either attractive or convincing. Several days later, Prime Minister Sharett invited IMFA officials to his home for consultations regarding the approach to be taken with Dulles and the State Department. 'You are putting the cart before the horse', was what Sharett proposed should be said to the American Secretary of State. 'What interest', he asked, 'would the Arabs have in making a settlement in order that we should receive a [security] treaty? On the contrary, ... [b]y making the treaty dependent on a settlement [Dulles] was postponing peace.' Sharett also urged his advisers to warn the Americans against 'submitting plans that were likely to arouse great anger in Israel without giving rise to a will for peace among the Arabs.'[98]

The opposite viewpoint on the 'horse-and-cart' dilemma was well expressed by Shuckburgh in a late-April brief for Clement Attlee. The 'prospect of a new guarantee from the US and ourselves' was the 'one great inducement we have to offer Israel to make concessions. ... This is our trump card and to throw it away in advance of a settlement would gravely if not fatally endanger the prospects of getting a settlement at all.'[99] During Francis Russell's visit to London, this 'trump card' was refined, taking the form of a secret 'Draft of Treaty between the United Kingdom, United States and Israel' which might be utilized at the appropriate moment.[100]

Israeli reactions

The harshness of the Israeli response to Dulles' intended reassurances of 16 April came as a surprise to the American and

British planners of Alpha. Moshe Sharett's lengthy official reply of 4 May repeated his request for a security treaty and reviewed the reasons for Israel's feelings of vulnerability in 'a security situation thrown markedly out of balance against Israel and aggravating the state of siege to which she is anyhow subjected by her neighbours.'

> By proving conclusively that the US is determined not to leave Israel in the lurch, but on the contrary to make the most of Israel's association, the treaty would give Israel a sense of poise and stability. It would at the same time[, Sharett argued,] promote a more realistic spirit within the Arab States and bring them nearer to peace.[101]

Sharett was most emphatic in responding to Dulles' hints to Eban about forthcoming US proposals for an Arab–Israeli settlement. The Israeli leader began by warning against any attempt by the US to 'indicate the specific lines along which a settlement is to be sought' – a position which recalled Israel's adamant stance during the activities of the Palestine Conciliation Commission between 1949 and 1951.[102] Sharett was by no means reassured by Dulles' remarks that Israel would not like some of the proposals while the Arabs would not like others. This prediction, he said, had 'filled our hearts with an anxiety not less serious than the one you are so earnestly endeavouring to allay.'

> Should proposals of this nature be presented, the following results will ensue. Israel will have no alternative but to reject them. The Arab States will regard them as a premium upon their intransigence in which they will persist hoping to extract larger concessions.

As for the linkage between a security treaty and an Arab–Israeli settlement, Sharett issued a warning: 'If the treaty is made contingent upon a prior settlement, there will be no treaty; and if the settlement is predicated upon one-sided concessions, there will be no settlement. A double vicious circle may well be created.' The Prime Minister appealed 'in all earnestness' to Dulles 'to give further urgent thought' to proceeding with the security treaty which would 'itself pave the way for ... progress' on an overall settlement.

In the part of his letter which concerned Alpha planners most directly, Sharett went on to 'make it clear beyond any possibility of misunderstanding' that there could be no question for us of cession of territory or the return of Arab refugees. The United Nations compromise of 1947 was annulled by Arab aggression which deserves no reward. Any reversion in that direction is now a political and physical impossibility.

'Minor and mutual adjustments' of the frontiers would, however, be possible within the terms of a peace settlement.[103] Israel hoped that 'an agreed solution' to the Jordan waters question was within reach, and announced that it was ready to proceed with payment of compensation for refugee lands – 'provided Egypt lifted the Suez Canal blockade and the Arab States discontinued their threats and reprisals against foreign firms, aviation companies, etc., operating in Israel.' While welcoming American help in pursuit of a settlement, Sharett ended by repeating arguments that he had made earlier:

> Such assistance, to be successful, need not be accompanied by the formulation of definite proposals for a peace settlement, either complete or partial. Indeed, ... the prior enunciation by the USA or by any other third power, of specific terms is liable to wreck the chances of a settlement. ... In the case of such decisive problems as territory and population, the setting forth by a third party of concrete terms in advance may lead to fatal results and should at all costs be avoided.[104]

Thus Israel was again resisting outside *mediation* (i.e., with proposals), as it had done consistently since 1948, and was willing to accept only limited third-party *conciliation*.

Sharett's tough letter to Dulles was followed the next day by an *aide-mémoire* read to the British Ambassador in Tel Aviv, in reply to a recent personal message from British Foreign Secretary Harold Macmillan.[105] British officials immediately recognized the message as similar to, if not identical with, the one sent by Sharett to Dulles. While Ambassador Nicholls found the tone of the message to HMG 'distinctly tarter', G.G. Arthur at the Foreign Office did not 'find much to choose between the two: both [were] very uncompromising'. Arthur's recommendation was to defer a reply until after receiving clarification of Nasir's attitude to the Alpha proposals.[106] Evelyn Shuckburgh's personal reactions were less sober; he found it 'impossible to read Mr Sharett's memorandum without indignation at the arrogance and logic-chopping of the Israelis'.[107]

In Paris, with Dulles and Macmillan for the NATO meetings, Shuckburgh advised the two leaders to co-ordinate their reactions to the Israeli Prime Minister's defiant letters and to 'make it plain to Mr Sharett at once, ... that neither the US Government nor HM Government can contemplate a security treaty with Israel except in connexion with a settlement'.[108] Shuckburgh was no doubt relieved when Secretary Dulles informed Harold Macmillan that he 'felt strongly that [a] territorial guarantee was [the] biggest carrot we had and that it would be folly to give this away until we had a general settlement agreed between [the] Arabs and Israel'. When he replied to Sharett, Dulles intended to make it 'clear that we could not give [a] guarantee in advance'.[109]

Neither the Foreign Office nor the State Department had any intention of allowing Sharett's notes to deflect them from proceeding with the next step of Alpha, namely, the follow-up soundings with Colonel Nasir. It was 'only to be expected', Shuckburgh wrote, 'that the Israelis would at some stage take up an uncompromising position on any proposals which they thought we were on the point of making.' He recommended that Ambassador Nicholls make only two points, informally, to the Israeli Prime Minister:

- that a security treaty 'must come after a settlement', and
- that the British 'had no intention of coming out with a ready-made plan involving sacrifices by Israel'.

While the second assurance was definitely misleading, Shuckburgh felt it would be beneficial because 'Mr Sharett probably expects that the concessions which we are likely to ask of Israel ... will be much greater than is in fact the case.'[110]

Downplaying the tone of outrage and defiance displayed by his Prime Minister, the head of the British Commonwealth desk at the IMFA advised Ambassador Elath in London to argue that Israel's objections were primarily against being stuck with a prefabricated British solution. With this reservation, Elath was instructed to express appreciation for British efforts at 'preparing the ground for direct talks with Nasir', but to oppose 'their mediation regarding the contents of a settlement'.[111] Following consultations in Tel Aviv, the Israeli Ambassador returned to the Foreign Office to argue on behalf of Israel's need for a security treaty *prior to* a settlement with the Arabs. In defining Israel's attitude to the prospect of talks with the Arabs, Elath's argument was received loud and clear, both at the Foreign Office and at the US State Department. The Israelis

> were not ready to start discussions on the basis of any previously thought-out programme involving changes in the territorial *status quo* or acceptance of refugees into Israel. They were ready to talk to the Arabs unconditionally any time and if such talks took place concessions would no doubt be made on both sides. But Israel would not accept any *a priori* conditions.[112]

In his first follow-up to Sharett's letter at the State Department, Abba Eban had also softened its confrontational edge but stressed the crucial differences between the two countries on the linkage between a security guarantee and an Arab–Israeli settlement. George Allen seemed pleased to learn that Israel was willing to discuss the two matters simultaneously.[113] Following his return from consultations in Tel Aviv one month later, Eban attempted to convince Assistant Secretary Allen of the merits of a 'formal security association' between the US and Israel, beginning with the claim that 'it would convince the Arabs that Israel was there to stay'. The Ambassador argued against considering 'frontier adjustments ... as a condition precedent to a security guarantee'. On this last point, Eban advanced an ingenuous line of argument consistent with Israel's desire to avoid territorial concessions. 'The armistice lines themselves were not, in fact, sources of border tension. Indeed', he stated

> they represented one of the few aspects of Arab–Israel relations which were covered by formal agreement between the two parties. It could hardly be said that Ralph Bunche had received the Nobel Prize for creating tension in the area. If changes were needed, the machinery for making such changes existed in the armistice agreements themselves.[114]

Turning to the US role, Eban claimed that it was 'contrary to usual practice for third parties to mediate questions of frontiers between two countries'. The Ambassador summarized his presentation by stressing that Israel wanted to 'get on with' (a) a draft security treaty, (b) the question of compensation of refugees, and (c) elimination of the Arab secondary boycott of firms and countries dealing with Israel. As the clock was ticking away against the timetable of Operation Alpha during the summer of 1955, Israel continued to seek an American commitment to proceed with these three items.[115] Preoccupied with its campaign for a security guarantee from the US, Israel's leadership was not ripe for receiving proposals from the powers for a far-reaching settlement with Egypt. Alpha's planners still had much work ahead of them in their uphill struggle to create a more receptive Israeli attitude.

Part Three

Stumbling from Obstacle to Obstacle

CHAPTER VII

From Secret Soundings to Public Pronouncements: The Dulles Statement, August 1955

During the spring and summer of 1955, the promoters of Operation Alpha found themselves locked into an uncomfortable holding pattern. For a number of reasons they were unable to take any steps to advance the project with the Egyptians or the Israelis. State Department and Foreign Office officials continued to produce elaborate background papers on various aspects of an eventual Alpha settlement.[1] During this period several Anglo–American differences also emerged to complicate an otherwise smooth collaborative effort. Most importantly, circumstances during this period forced a fundamental change in approach from the use of highly secret diplomacy to public pronouncements.

THE WAITING GAME, APRIL – AUGUST 1955

The cycle of raids and reprisals along the Gaza frontier was one of several factors which contributed to an atmosphere that was not propitious for a resumption of talks with Prime Minister Nasir. One incentive for keeping up Egyptian pressure on Israel's frontier near Gaza was the information received from a friendly American source that border incidents would obstruct Ben-Gurion's plans to bring more Jews to settle the Negev and expand the port at Eilat.[2] The deterioration of Egyptian–Israeli relations was reflected in a *Newsweek* feature layout producing a head-on clash between Nasir and Sharett.³ Having incited his troops to 'hate the Israelis' before leaving for Bandung, 'how', Nasir asked Ambassador Stevenson rhetorically after his return, 'could [I] now turn round and work with the Israelis to restore peace?'⁴

State Department instructions continued to leave it to Ambassador Byroade's discretion to choose the best available opportunity for an approach regarding Operation Alpha. During most of May, however, various reasons – mostly relating to Nasir's 'difficult mood' – were adduced for waiting a while longer and 'play[ing] it by ear'.⁵ The Gaza tension was not diminishing, and there were internal political problems which made this 'on the whole a bad time for [Nasir] to show himself publicly "soft" on Israel.'⁶ The 'right moment' for broaching the subject always seemed just out of reach. Although the bitterness aroused specifically by the signing of the Baghdad Pact seemed to be abating, Nasir returned to Cairo from Bandung as the new champion of Third World neutralism. Believing that American agents were at work discrediting and destabilizing his régime, his attitude to the Western powers displayed new levels of militancy and mistrust.⁷

While waiting for an opportune moment to approach Nasir, American and British officials continued their consultations over tactics. Differences remained between Shuckburgh's wish to propose larger northern triangles to Nasir on the one hand and the Americans' preference for the original smaller southern triangles on the other.⁸ Reflecting the declining optimism about winning Nasir's co-operation for Operation Alpha, Francis Russell mapped out several contingency plans containing enhanced inducements. Notably, he recommended that Ambassador Byroade, when he finally succeeded in broaching Alpha with Nasir, should be authorized to mention the possibility of a US contribution of $100 million to the High Aswan Dam project.⁹ Wishing to avoid further delays, Russell also prepared a draft letter for President Eisenhower's signature, to be used if needed 'as a basis for soliciting Nasser's co-operation in Alpha'. Failing that, he again suggested turning to Jordan. Finally, if all else failed, Russell recommended a public announcement by the powers, stating 'their conviction that an equitable settlement of the Israel–Arab dispute [was] possible' and making clear 'the contribution which the US and the UK [were] prepared to make to assist in such a settlement'.¹⁰

Throughout June, the combination of an explosive Gaza frontier and Israeli lobbying for a security guarantee increased State Department pressures on Byroade and Stevenson in Cairo to make their next approach to Nasir. The fear was also growing that 'the Israel Government may try to forestall [the Alpha] action', and so the British Cabinet was warned that 'decisions may have to be taken at short notice'.[11] In Washington, Russell wrote to Dulles that the time was 'growing short', and suggested allowing three or four weeks before abandoning Nasir and embarking on an approach to Jordan and Lebanon.[12] Evelyn Shuckburgh 'agree[d] whole-heartedly' to instruct the Cairo Ambassadors to 'follow up their discussions with Nasser immediately', but was clearly unenthusiastic about approaching Jordan or Lebanon.[13]

Still, Byroade and Stevenson could not seem to find the appropriate moment to broach the subject in Cairo. On 9 June, Byroade did attempt to engage Nasir in a discussion about Operation Alpha – even though he 'realized [the] atmosphere was bad'. But it was 'very clear from [the] discussion', he reported, 'that in [the] present state of tension at Gaza [one] cannot expect serious talks regarding Alpha'. Byroade did not consider it 'wise ... to raise [the] issue with him again until [the] present tenseness over Gaza abated'.[14] In early July, London and Washington repeated their standing instructions to Ambassadors Stevenson and Byroade to approach Nasir if 'any favourable opportunity' presented itself. Reflecting his growing scepticism, Dulles reportedly told Byroade, in effect, 'every month that you make me wait will make my eventual position less favourable to the Arabs'.[15]

Meanwhile, a new development came to sour American–Egyptian relations: Egypt's frustrations with the State Department's lack of generosity in response to its arms-procurement requests, coupled with an intensification of Soviet–Egyptian contacts.[16] In early August, the US government agreed to sell Egypt $27.5 million worth of military equipment. But Egypt's inability to pay in foreign currency and the standard American requirement for on-site administration by US military personnel became obstacles to the deal.[17] It was quickly becoming clear that arms-sales would become a source of bitterness and resentment, rather than an effective political lever enabling Washington to generate Egyptian gratitude and co-operation.

DULLES' DECISION TO GO PUBLIC

As originally conceived, Alpha was to have remained a top-secret operation within a tight circle of participants at the highest levels, but after several months of attempting to take the first steps, Alpha's American partners began considering a departure from the 'secret-diplomacy' route in favour of a public pronouncement. This development was caused by four independent sets of considerations:

- the prospect that Nasir's co-operation would not be forthcoming merely through informal soundings;
- the growing pressures of domestic US politics, particularly the fear that pro-Israeli sentiment during the forthcoming election campaign would deprive the State Department of sufficient leverage to insist on Israeli concessions;
- the desire to take the initiative in order to outmanoeuvre the Soviets, who were engaged in arms negotiations with the Egyptians; and
- the planners' fear that the Israelis might have penetrated Alpha's secrecy and were about to torpedo the plan, either by disclosing Anglo–American collusion (to embarrass Nasir) or by launching a peace initiative of their own (to contaminate Anglo–American efforts in Arab eyes).[18]

The original inspiration for maintaining maximum secrecy had included the need to avoid the possibility that unco-operative Israelis – who were seen by some officials as 'given to devious ways of achieving their ends' – might choose to publicize the operation as a means of sabotaging it.[19] As the project progressed, the circle of those 'in the know' naturally had to be widened.[20] By the time of Secretary Dulles' partial disclosure of Alpha to Ambassador Eban on 13 April 1955 (above, pages 113–14), Israeli suspicions were already maturing into a feeling of near-certainty that the UK and the US were actively planning to impose an undesirable settlement on the Jewish state.[21] An article in *The Times* of London, entitled 'Strategic and Economic Value of Negev – Israelis' Devotion to an Arid Land', was clipped for the Foreign Office files with the marginal comment: 'All this is, I suppose, part of the defensive build-up against Alpha.'[22] After the meeting between Dulles and Eban, Russell expected the Israelis to 'make an all-out effort to obtain as much information about the ALPHA proposals as it can ... through ingenious and persistent questioning.' In early May, he warned that 'the information that the I[srael] G[overnment] might thus gain could be used to embarrass seriously the efforts of Ambassador Byroade during the next few weeks.'[23]

After 18 May, the extent to which Israeli intelligence was penetrating the secrecy of Alpha became a matter of serious concern at the American Embassy in Tel Aviv. Teddy Kollek, Director-General of the Prime Minister's office, returned from a visit to Washington and his comments to the American Chargé d'Affaires, Ivan White, displayed such a 'strong element of accuracy' about US Middle East policy that Ambassador Lawson surmised that there had been a serious breach of secrecy – one which might

> account for the 'crystal globe' which Sharett seemed to possess when he last wrote to the Secretary [on 4 May; above, pages 115–17] and set down Israel's position with regard to the territorial concessions and the refugee problem in such firm terms.[24]

American and British suspicions were further aroused when the Israeli Ambassadors to Washington, London and Paris were recalled to Tel Aviv for consultations. (In fact, these consultations focused not directly on Alpha, but on how to conduct a concerted campaign for a security treaty, detached as much as possible from considerations of a peace settlement with the Arabs.)[25]

Inside the State Department, officials were convinced (as William Burdett recalls) that Israel had

> obtained word of our plans (Israeli intelligence on our planning was 'remarkable' indicating inside leaks), found them distasteful, and deliberately adopted policies including aggressive borders raids, to make it politically difficult for Nasser to move towards an accommodation.[26]

By late May some in the State Department believed that Israel was on the verge of making a public statement 'to the effect that the time had now come for a settlement of the problem and giving its own proposals of the possible terms of such a settlement'. Ambassador Sir Roger Makins in Washington informed the Foreign Office that, in order to 'forestall the expected Israeli move and retain the initiative', the Department was about to consult US Ambassadors in Amman, Beirut and Cairo on the 'possible issue of a joint United States–United Kingdom statement setting out the advantages of

Alpha to both the Arabs and the Israelis' – including mention of the proposed $100-million contribution to the High Aswan Dam.[27]

The State Department's assessment was based, Makins reported to London

> on their knowledge of Israeli psychology. They say that it would be characteristic of the Israelis to open a flank attack of this kind, the effect of which would be to kill any chance of Alpha succeeding for some time to come, in that it would brand the whole idea of a settlement as a purely Israeli scheme.[28]

The Americans believed that a statement coming from the Israelis 'would of course seriously damage [the] ability [of the] US and UK [to] influence [the] Arabs [to] move toward [a] settlement as we would appear [to] be acting on I[srael] G[overnment] initiative.'[29] The State Department's reasoning, as Makins described it, was that, despite the risk that it might lead to Arab rejection of Alpha, a joint public statement would

> at least let the world know what the United States and United Kingdom were prepared to do and would leave the idea of a settlement in a more favourable state than if it had been wrecked through the Israelis getting their statement in first.[30]

Replies from US envoys in the region ranged from mild to strong opposition to the idea of a public declaration. Some, including Edward Lawson in Tel Aviv, doubted that the Israelis were about to issue their own statement.[31] The American Ambassadors in Beirut and Amman both pointed to the setback which an Anglo–American announcement would cause to the 'more or less successful agreement' which Eric Johnston seemed to be on the point of concluding in his Jordan Valley negotiations.[32] From Cairo, Ambassador Byroade regarded a joint statement as 'tantamount to announcing [the] failure [of] our good offices [to] bring about [a] settlement'. He further predicted that 'such influence as I may have here would be drastically reduced'. Both he and Stevenson were especially keen not to see anything published regarding the financial inducements, so as to avoid 'an outcry against dollar diplomacy and bribery and make it much more difficult for Nasser in particular to proceed any further in the matter'.[33]

In London, the Foreign Office's first reaction was to warn that this 'sudden change [of] direction' was a 'very dangerous' move which 'would prejudice [the] success [of] the enterprise'; the British requested more time and called for joint high-level consultations.[34] Foreign Secretary Macmillan preferred to forestall the Israeli move by 'quicken[ing] up our own plan', i.e., to 'tell our Ambassadors to go and talk to Nasser right away and open up the whole matter to him'.[35] The advice received from both London and the Middle East caused Dulles to retreat – but only temporarily – from the idea of a public announcement.[36]

One week after the 'panic' reaction to the feared Israeli peace plan (which did not materialize), domestic political considerations led John Foster Dulles to revive his idea of issuing a public announcement. As he became increasingly convinced that the original approach was leading nowhere with Nasir, the Secretary was having difficulty sidestepping the Israelis' mounting campaign for a US security guarantee. During a weekend visit to South Carolina in early June, Dulles composed his own draft of a possible public announcement disclosing the main lines of Operation Alpha. That draft was followed by several versions of varying length prepared in the State Department over the coming weeks.[37]

Overriding the continued hesitations of his staff, and despite criticism from British officials,[38] the US Secretary of State continued to argue that a public statement would 'appeal to the good judgment of all concerned' after the expected first unfavourable reactions. Arab and Israeli objections, Dulles believed, 'were so weak that they could be overcome'.[39] The need to keep pro-Israeli voters from falling under the sway of Democratic Party candidates was now becoming a factor influencing the Secretary's timing. As Russell later explained to Harold Macmillan,

> the longer Mr Dulles waits the more difficult it will be for him to make a balanced statement on the subject of Palestine. As the elections approach so the pressure for a statement favourable to Israel will increase.[40]

The proposed policy statement would be directed both towards 'reassuring Israel' and responding to the criticism that the Eisenhower administration had 'no policy' regarding an Arab–Israeli settlement.[41]

During their New York meeting in mid-June, Dulles informed Harold Macmillan that 'he would have to make a policy statement ... on the general lines of Alpha without, of course, compromising the plan itself.' In reply to the British Foreign Secretary's fears of jeopardizing Alpha, Dulles claimed that 'such a statement would help the Alpha Plan in the long run'. The timing and tactics of issuing the statement remained to be determined (with elections in Israel scheduled for 26 July) but Dulles hoped that its publication would 'act as a magnet which would draw into a constructive channel the more decent elements and forces on both sides'. Macmillan remained unconvinced, pointing out that the proposed declaration would still leave the Israelis unhappy, as their real goal was something more: a security *treaty*.[42]

These 'new thoughts' about Alpha by the Secretary caused some concern to officials in London. Evelyn Shuckburgh began to worry about America's ability to withstand pro-Israeli pressures, adding that it would 'be fatal if the operation develop[ed] into an attempt to force the Arabs to make peace with Israel on Israel's terms'. The British Under-Secretary listed his reasons against Dulles' plans for going public with Alpha. The proposed statement would 'be violently rejected by both sides' and 'would heighten the already dangerous tension' on the Gaza frontier. Like Byroade and Stevenson, Shuckburgh also feared that abandoning secret diplomacy in favour of a public declaration would undermine the effectiveness of one of the powers' best 'carrots' – namely, the financial 'inducements outside the settlement itself' which 'could not be held out in a public statement'.

> [T]he resulting outcry against Western bribery would make it more difficult than ever for any Arab statesman to accept our ideas. Yet without such inducements the Alpha proposals would be branded by the Arabs as an 'imperialist' trick to force them into peace with the usurpers of their rights. Alpha would be damned forever.[43]

Only after discussions with Russell in early July were Macmillan and Shuckburgh somewhat reassured.[44] Minister of State Anthony Nutting even became convinced that, from a strictly British point of view, the statement should be issued sooner rather than later. If it were made close to the presidential elections scheduled for 1956, he reasoned, Secretary Dulles would find it almost impossible 'to resist making a declaration which [would] be effectively little less than a declaration of love for Israel'.

THE DULLES STATEMENT

> [W]e should then have to choose between two equally awkward and unpleasant alternatives, i.e. either to dissociate ourselves publicly from the Americans or allow ourselves to be tarred with the same brush, thereby losing all our influence with the Arabs.

At the same time, Nutting could not hold back his frustrations in dealing with the Americans: 'It is maddening', he wrote, 'that we should be pushed around by the requirements of American politics in this way. But it is not the first time this has happened nor will it be the last!'[45] On balance, the Minister of State recommended that 'We must reluctantly accept that the least objectionable course is to acquiesce in an early and impartial account of Alpha being given publicly by the US Government.'[46]

Several days later, Foreign Secretary Macmillan made the same recommendation to the British Cabinet.[47] Once the British had acquiesced in the proposed statement as 'the least objectionable course', officials at the Foreign Office were left hoping at least to be able to influence the text of Dulles' proposed statement in a way that would help the American Secretary hold his ground about insisting on concessions from Israel on a peace settlement prior to granting the requested security guarantee.[48]

THE DULLES STATEMENT

Timing and preparation of the statement

During July 1955, John Foster Dulles was faced with having to choose the best moment for the delivery of his statement. Ambassador Eric Johnston's ongoing negotiations for a Jordan waters agreement were in a particularly delicate phase and officials warned the Secretary of State that poor timing of his proposed public announcement might lead the Arabs to renounce their tentative understanding regarding the sharing of the Jordan waters 'on the grounds that they were tricked into taking a political step which they were not prepared to face'.[49] Johnston travelled to Washington to meet Dulles and 'urged forcefully' that the Secretary postpone any statement until after his next round of talks. Johnston's appeal resulted in several modifications of the target date for the speech.[50] But once it became clear that Arab endorsement of the Johnston scheme was not as imminent as expected, Secretary Dulles decided that the timing of his Alpha statement could not be made dependent on the prior conclusion of a Jordan waters agreement.[51]

The Alpha planners then turned their attention to the precise wording of the statement, and practical questions such as the forewarning that needed to be given to Nasir, Sharett and other world leaders. Key decisions were made concerning the level of detail to be disclosed, and how to reflect accurately (in summary form) the total Alpha package with the proper balance among the various ingredients that might prove unpalatable to the Arabs and to the Israelis. Plans were also made for feeding supportive articles to the American and British press, and for following up the statement in private talks with Middle Eastern leaders.[52] After considering various methods by which the UK could associate itself with the proposed Dulles statement without revealing the full extent of Alpha collaboration, the FO decided that Harold Macmillan would issue a brief supporting statement shortly after Dulles' speech.[53]

On 22 July Russell and Shuckburgh despatched parallel instructions to selected ambassadors, enclosing the latest version of the proposed Alpha terms of settlement and a draft of the public statement to be made by Secretary Dulles. The envoys were requested to comment on the best way of presenting the proposals and the likely reactions in the countries to which they were accredited.[54] British postings especially underlined the unfavourable impact such a statement would have, and some questioned whether HMG really needed to be associated with a step 'which might be connected with American politics'.[55] One of the dilemmas raised by both American and British Ambassadors in Tel Aviv was whether the Secretary's statement should make specific mention of territorial concessions in the Negev: if the Negev were mentioned by name, Edward Lawson believed the Israelis would refuse to enter into discussions; if, on the other hand, it were omitted, Jack Nicholls doubted whether the Egyptians would agree to come to the table.[56]

In the Soviet shadow

Meanwhile, relations between the US and Egypt continued to deteriorate, despite the bridge-building efforts of Foreign Minister Mahmud Fawzi and Egypt's Ambassador to Washington, Ahmad Hussein. During a talk between Dulles and Fawzi in early July,

American financing for the High Aswan Dam – originally seen by Russell and others as the chief 'carrot' for winning Egyptian co-operation with Operation Alpha – was linked with progress towards an Arab–Israeli settlement,[57] but such linkage, rather than serving as an inducement to a settlement, actually contributed to Egyptian suspicions of American Middle East policy and added to other motives favouring increased Soviet–Egyptian co-operation.[58]

Against the backdrop of imminent Soviet aid to Egypt, both Hussein and Fawzi turned to the US with appeals for ideas on how to 'force' a 'quick' Arab–Israeli settlement. In their mid-August talks, Fawzi and Byroade again focused on the Negev as the prime obstacle. The Foreign Minister was now willing to contemplate – off the record[59] – trading away Egypt's insistence on the refugees' right to return in exchange for Egyptian–Jordanian territorial contiguity in large parts of the Negev. For his part, Henry Byroade

> [could] not conceive of being able [to] convince Israel [to] accept this type of solution[,] yet when one weigh[ed] the consequences of continued controversy against the value of this worthless spot of desert it [was] difficult not to reach [the] conclusion [that] maybe we should try to sound out what is [the] furthest Israel could accept under real pressure from [the] US for [a] quick settlement.[60]

Signals from Ambassador Byroade in Cairo regarding the likelihood of active Soviet involvement in the Middle East 'on [the] Arab side of [the] Arab–Israeli conflict' added their weight to Secretary Dulles' decision to 'expedite the Alpha matter and to telescope somewhat the preparatory plans'.[61] This necessarily disappointed the British, who had wanted more time to consider Dulles' proposed public disclosure of Alpha.[62] The date finally chosen was 26 August, and the venue was to be the meeting of the American Council for Foreign Relations in New York. The British were given one final opportunity to comment on the text. While Foreign Secretary Harold Macmillan offered some last-minute suggestions which were duly incorporated, the Prime Minister was reported to be more uncertain than ever about the Dulles statement. Anthony Eden even considered, for a brief moment, an eleventh-hour appeal to President Eisenhower, asking 'for the operation to be called off'.[63] In the end, however, the British offered their full co-operation. Even though London may have been disappointed with the 'watered down' version of Alpha that was to become public in the Dulles speech, Anglo–American disagreements regarding the statement were soon papered over.[64]

Meanwhile, American embassies in Tel Aviv, Cairo and other capitals were instructed to prepare the ground by requesting interviews with Nasir, Sharett and other leaders 48 hours prior to the delivery of the speech. The Ambassadors were also provided with background notes for follow-up discussions of the speech with Middle Eastern leaders.[65] The British Foreign Office sent out similar instructions to help prepare Arab and Israeli Prime Ministers and Foreign Ministers to 'receive Mr Dulles' statement in a constructive spirit and with willingness to look seriously for common ground'.[66] One line of argument which British envoys were requested to advance in Arab capitals was the following:

> We have no intention of forcing the Arabs into an unreasonable settlement; but we feel we have the right to expect from our Arab friends something better than a completely negative attitude towards the problem.[67]

The UN Secretary-General, the French government, and the Israeli and Arab Ambassadors in Washington were also given advance notice of the Secretary's speech in confidence. Deflecting Ambassador Eban's arguments against the issuing of a public statement, Assistant Secretary George Allen stressed the 'constructive' character of the proposed speech as a 'springboard' for peace in the area; Allen 'was convinced that in the light of history it would be considered a state paper of the first order'.[68]

Bad omens on the eve

As the date of the speech approached, a number of omens were not good. In the course of moving from secret diplomacy to a public pronouncement, new strains had occurred in the Anglo–American partnership. Even after reluctantly accepting the necessity for an *American* announcement, officials in London were most concerned about possible attacks against *British* interests in the region. With advance warning of the proposed American statement, British embassies in Damascus and Amman were 'giving serious thought to the physical safety of British subjects'.[69]

London also feared that Dulles' speech might be a catalyst leading to the overthrow of Nuri Sa'id's government in Iraq, sparking 'a wave of indignation against his policy of co-operating with the Western Powers' in the Baghdad Pact. The worried British requested that their American allies assist them in bolstering Nuri's position by agreeing to supply (British-made) tanks to Iraq and by the US offering to join the Baghdad Pact. This two-part request began as 'conditions' or the 'price' for issuing a statement of support for Dulles' public announcement, but the British were forced ultimately to settle for less on both counts.[70]

After much deliberation, Secretary Dulles informed Ambassador Makins of US agreement to supply ten tanks if the UK agreed to supply two – a far cry from British hopes for an American contribution of 70 tanks as against 10 by the UK.[71] The British Prime Minister and Foreign Secretary both found the American decision 'most disappointing', with Eden informing the Foreign Office that he thought the Americans were 'behaving outrageously' and was personally prepared, if necessary, 'for us to have a row with the Americans about all this'.[72] It must have been with bitter irony that Harold Macmillan read Dulles' 25 August letter which praised 'the close cooperation' achieved by the two governments on the eve of launching Alpha's first public statement. Only six days earlier, the British Foreign Secretary had pleaded (in vain) for Francis Russell to be sent to London 'at once', and a postponement of the statement for at least a week in order to arrange adequate briefing of UK missions.[73]

Preliminary meetings with Nasir and Fawzi in Cairo with regard to the forthcoming policy statement went smoothly enough. Ambassador Byroade asked Washington to provide the text of the speech to Nasir far enough in advance to help him prepare a controlled press reaction in Egypt,[74] but Secretary Dulles was unable to accommodate last-minute suggestions from Byroade regarding the phrasing about territorial adjustments and the timing of an expected US announcement on arms sales to Egypt.[75]

From Tel Aviv, the British Ambassador informed the Foreign Office that 'the moment [of the American statement] could ... be hardly worse chosen', both from the viewpoint of Israeli post-election coalition-building and the success of the Johnston mission.[76] Jack Nicholls also reported on Prime Minister Sharett's 'deep apprehension' about what he felt was a serious lack of symmetry in Dulles' approach. 'The Arabs', Sharett argued, 'could only be asked to abandon pretensions: the Israelis would be asked to abandon positions (e.g. territorial or in regard to refugees) which she actually held.' American Ambassador Lawson also met with Sharett and found him in 'a state of gloom', 'deeply apprehensive' about the policy statement which he presumed would require concessions that Israel would be unable to offer.[77]

To make matters worse, tensions along the Gaza frontier rose dramatically on the eve of the scheduled policy statement. An armed clash between Israeli and Egyptian forces near Kibbutz Mefalsim on 22 August led Nasir to break off the still-inconclusive talks with Israelis regarding General Burns' proposals for border pacification.[78] Following a tip-off from British intelligence, the Americans learned on 25 August that the Egyptians were about to launch a series of attacks along the frontier with Israel.[79] Ambassador Byroade attempted to avert the military operations by warning his Egyptian friends that Israeli intelligence might be trying to draw Egypt into a 'trap' on the eve of the Secretary's speech, since that statement promised to be 'an extremely good development for [the] Arab side'.[80]

Byroade's efforts were in vain, however. During 25–26 August, three separate incidents of Egyptian ambush and sabotage took place on Israel's side of the Gaza border. These terrorist attacks were part of a series of more than twenty co-ordinated Palestinian *fidayyin* operations launched over a seven-day period which caused 11 Israeli deaths and wounded nine. The raids from bases in Gaza, directed by the Egyptian authorities, were also connected to a more elaborate, long-term plan involving diversionary operations from Syrian, Jordanian and Lebanese soil.[81] Captured Egyptian documents, along with recently available archival sources, indicate that directives from Cairo had actually been aimed at *restraining* Palestinian cross-border raiding prior to February 1955, but that this caution had changed to official encouragement following the Gaza raid.[82] A number of Egyptian spokesmen again recalled Israel's pivotal raid on Gaza as the original source of the current troubles.[83] According to Jordan's military attaché in Cairo, the purpose of the new Egyptian-backed raids was to

> create an intensive [sic] atmosphere of fear and the loss of security within Israel which would lead to the shaking of the confidence of the inhabitants in the Israeli government and

THE DULLES STATEMENT

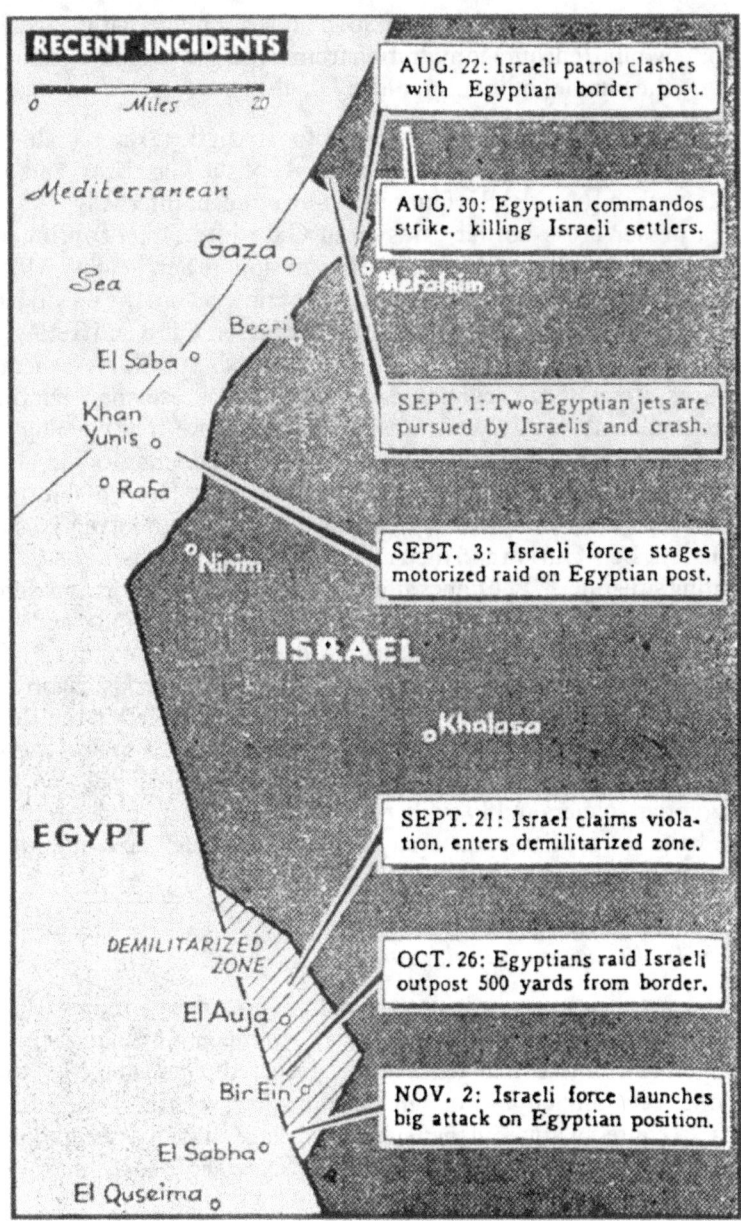

Map: 'Recent Incidents', 6 November 1955
Map copyright © 1955 The New York Times Co. Reprinted by permission.

army. ... The creation of such an atmosphere within Israel w[ould] encourage migration from Israel and w[ould] decrease the number of immigrants to Israel.

Such operations were also expected to 'strengthen the morale of the Egyptian army as well as the morale of the Gaza area' and to 'strengthen [Nasir's] Revolutionary Government internally'.[84]

Further cross-border raids from Gaza into Israel continued during the last days of August, raising tensions to new heights. Most observers felt that it was only a matter of time before the inevitable Israeli reprisal. The American Ambassadors in Cairo and Tel Aviv counselled restraint on both sides, while UNTSO Chief, General Burns, attempted to negotiate a fresh cease fire agreement,[85] but the accumulated mistrust was most difficult to remove. The opening of a third, informal Egyptian–Israeli channel of communication – in which American Quaker representative Elmore Jackson shuttled between Cairo and Tel Aviv, conveying messages between Nasir, Sharett, Ben-Gurion and their aides – had no impact on the deteriorating situation.[86] The hopes attached to the Jackson mediation were offset, for the Israelis, by the unabated *fidayyin* activity and by intelligence reports that Nasir had informed leaders of other Arab countries that henceforth he 'intend[ed] to engage in most vigorous measures against Israel'.[87] The expected Israeli retaliation came on 31 August in the form of an attack on Khan Yunis in the southern Gaza Strip. This was a large-scale reprisal which left 25 *fidayyin*, 10 Egyptian soldiers and 19 civilians dead and had the immediate effect of halting Egyptian-sponsored *fidayyin* raids from Gaza, although not from third countries.[88]

The Dulles statement, 26 August 1955

The day chosen for the major US policy announcement thus fell at a most unpropitious time. On Friday afternoon, 26 August 1955, John Foster Dulles read his carefully prepared statement before the American Council for Foreign Relations in New York (Document 6). In contemplating further steps to advance 'stability, tranquillity, and progress in the Middle East', the Secretary focused on three problems:

- 'the tragic plight of the 900,000 refugees who formerly lived in the territory that is now occupied by Israel';

THE DULLES STATEMENT   139

- the 'pall of fear' hovering over Arabs and Israelis regarding the intentions of the other side; and
- 'the lack of fixed permanent boundaries between Israel and its Arab neighbors.'

Since the area 'may not, itself, possess all the ingredients for the full and early building of a condition of security and well-being', the United States wished to enunciate 'certain conclusions' which it had reached after 'deep and anxious thought'. As 'a friend of both Israelis and Arabs', the US hoped that the statement would 'help men of good will within the area to fresh constructive efforts'.

In the hopes of resolving the refugee problem 'through resettlement and – to such an extent as may be possible – repatriation', the US was prepared to offer a loan to Israel to help cover compensation payments, as well as investment in regional water development projects. To reduce the level of mutual fears, the US was willing to enter into 'formal treaty engagements to prevent or thwart any effort by either side to alter by force the boundaries between Israel and its Arab neighbors.' Turning to the task of drawing permanent, agreed boundaries, Dulles recognized the difficulties involved. Alluding to the Negev but without mentioning it by name, he added that these difficulties were 'increased by the fact that even territory which is barren has acquired a sentimental significance'. Without specifying any particular approach to resolving frontier disputes, he hoped that the overall advantages of a settlement as outlined would help Middle East leaders find the wisdom to reconcile their differences so as to 'convert armistice lines of danger into boundary lines of safety'. The thorny Jerusalem question could become the subject of a United Nations review.

In a short, five-paragraph statement, the British Foreign Office on 27 August welcomed and endorsed Secretary Dulles' speech as 'An important contribution towards the solution of the most critical outstanding problem in the Middle East.'[89] The Foreign Office instructed each of its Middle Eastern envoys to approach the government to which he was accredited with a request 'to use its influence ... in favour of an urgent move towards a settlement'. Upon the publication of the British communiqué of support, envoys were to speak of 'Her Majesty's Government's hopes that the [Dulles] statement will lead the parties to discuss, either between themselves or with third parties, the possibility of moving towards a settlement.'[90]

While partially disclosing the existence of Operation Alpha for the first time, the Dulles statement was deceptive in two important ways:

- it deliberately hid the fact of nine months of extensive Anglo–American collaboration on Operation Alpha (including the drafting of the speech itself); and
- it misleadingly omitted any indication that the US (and Britain) had been considering very specific proposals for a settlement of the territorial and refugee issues.

In fact, during follow-up consultations with Israeli and Arab leaders the US would explicitly deny that it had any preconceived plan for an Arab–Israeli settlement.[91] Only in November 1955 did some press reports speculate that Britain and the US had been working together 'since last summer on a plan for an over-all settlement'.[92]

AFTERMATH

Harold Macmillan understood one of the merits of Dulles' public pronouncement to be its generality, 'on the lines of a helpful recommendation', so as to leave

> a great deal ... for subsequent negotiation. It would be our purpose [he had informed his Cabinet colleagues], after administering the jolt of public statements, to draw the interested parties back into the process of secret, 'Trieste-type' negotiation from which eventual agreement might be achieved.[93]

But, while the 'jolt' did much to elicit unhelpful public reactions from politicians and editorialists in the Middle East, it was met with calculated posturing and evasiveness on the part of the intended negotiating partners.

Early reactions

The level of generality of the Dulles speech may well have contributed to the guarded and muted reactions it received in Middle Eastern capitals. In particular, Nasir's reaction was reported to be 'somewhat less satisfactory than had [been] hoped'. Ambassador Byroade had the feeling that the Egyptian Prime Minister was 'somewhat confused by the general nature of [the] approach and really did not understand [the] significance of some passages'.[94] Over the coming weeks and months, Nasir would be studiously evasive regarding Dulles' speech, although Ambassador Byroade claimed that 'privately' the Egyptian leader remained interested in working for a settlement with Israel.[95] In London, Prime Minister Eden, still somewhat peeved by the American decision to forge ahead with the Dulles statement, informed the Foreign Office that 'The responsibility for whatever result may follow ... must rest with the American Government and ... we ought not to pull their chestnuts out of the fire for them.' He was reported 'Very much averse to any approach to Nasser being made by the United Kingdom representative alone.'[96]

Earlier fears that the public announcement might harm Ambassador Eric Johnston's delicate negotiations seemed at first to be borne out. The Jordanian Prime Minister informed the US Ambassador that the Hashemite Kingdom 'would have to reject [the] Johnston proposals which [were] now tied to [a] political settlement'.[97] In the wake of the 26 August speech, Johnston fought an uphill battle trying to convince Arabs, and especially Jordanians, to view his water-sharing negotiations as something separate from Dulles' statement of high policy. Although the Ambassador did make some headway in this task, a number of Arabs remained suspicious that

> the Johnston project by its nature represent[ed] a bridge which leads to the execution of the Dulles Project and which results in presenting the Arabs with a fait accompli. ... [I]f the project is put into effect, it will mean that the Arabs have admitted the right of Israel to water of the Jordan River and, thereby admitted the sovereignty of Israel.

The 'harmful secret' linking the two projects, *Al-Bilad as-Saudiyya* went on to warn, was that the Negev – irrigated with diverted Jordan waters – would thereby be ready for settlement by 'hundreds of thousands of Jewish immigrants, foreigners'.[98] By mid-September, key Jordanian support for the project seemed to be eroding, leaving Eric Johnston in the position of hoping for 'forceful' British pressure to be applied on the Hashemite kingdom.[99] As one scholar has recently summarized it, Alpha had 'overloaded the political circuits of the Arabs, who could no longer be persuaded to separate the functional and political dimensions of the Unified Plan'.[100]

Critical press coverage came as no surprise. Officials at the State Department and the Foreign Office had been expecting a certain amount of *pro forma* protests, and were relieved when the Secretary's speech sparked less strident denunciation than anticipated. Secretary Dulles, pleased that his statement had not met with any outright official rejection, described preliminary reactions as 'in [the] main ... gratifyingly thoughtful, sober and responsible'.[101] Yet ultimately the State Department had to be disappointed as time passed without any leader coming forward to embrace any part of the statement as a good starting-point for discussions leading to a settlement.

During the first weeks of September, articles, speeches and interviews in the Arabic press grew increasingly hostile.[102] A frequent criticism was Dulles' omission of any mention of United Nations resolutions, including the 1947 partition resolution. The American emphasis on solving problems by throwing money at them was also attacked by a number of spokesmen, including former Jordanian Minister of Foreign Affairs, Dr Husain Fakhri al-Khalidi, whose Palestinian origins came to the fore:

> America forgets it cannot purchase people and their friendship with its dollars. ... Secretary Dulles and his government want us refugees to forget Palestine and accept the *fait accompli*; they want us to forget Haifa, Jaffa, Nazareth ... to exchange the beautiful coastal area with the Sinai desert and burning valley of the Jordan River. ... This is the fate which Secretary Dulles and his government want us to accept for the love of the Jews and their influence.[103]

The British Embassy in Damascus reported 'a hardening of opposition to the idea of reaching a settlement with Israel which would recognise Israel's existence and prepare the way for more normal relations between her and the Arab states'; the press depicted an American–Israeli 'collusion' to launch a 'war of nerves against the Arab states with the aim of forcing the latter to enter negotiations with Israel on the basis of Mr Dulles's proposals'.[104] In Saudi Arabia, the semi-official *al-Bilad as-Saudiyya* expressed Arab fears that the Americans intended to enter into a security treaty with Israel. 'As long', the editorialist wrote, as Dulles' proposals 'concentrate[d] wholly on [the] preservation of Israel – which contradict[ed the]

THE DULLES STATEMENT

Arab policy of liberating Palestine – there [was a] basic contradiction [of the] historical facts of [the] Palestine problem.'[105] The call for a careful study of the Dulles proposals by the Chairman of Iraq's Foreign Affairs Committee was seen by the American Embassy in Baghdad as the only bright spot 'in the wilderness of often irresponsible press criticism'.[106]

In clarifications with Arab spokesmen, British and American officials were at pains to stress that the statement did not represent an attempt to coerce any parties into a peace treaty. They argued further that the Arabs ought to be pleased that the US would not be offering Israel a security guarantee 'except as part of an overall agreed settlement'.[107]

In their contacts with American officials, Israeli spokesmen were careful to praise Mr Dulles for his 'serious act of public statesmanship', even though privately they may have felt that the Secretary 'was trying to forestall the Soviet arms transaction by sending out signals to Egypt of American support for territorial concessions by Israel'. In a conversation at the State Department, Ambassador Eban complained to Assistant Secretary of State George Allen that it was

> unfortunate that a US security guarantee had apparently been linked to changes in the frontiers. This contingency was so remote as not to come within the bounds of feasibility. The statement might therefore contain a 'built-in deadlock'.

While Eban pressed the case for the maintaining the existing boundaries, Allen pointed to the desirability of 'agreed frontiers', but added that 'Israel should not assume that all adjustments would have to be at her expense'. The Ambassador also expressed Israel's appreciation of Dulles' loan offer for resolving the refugee problem, and especially his stress on resettlement (ahead of repatriation) of refugees.[108]

Israeli and Jewish public reaction to the Dulles statement followed closely the outline of remarks made by Eban behind closed doors: namely, a stress on its positive features was combined with expressions of concern regarding such matters as an American security guarantee for Israel.[109] In fact, both Prime Minister Sharett and Defence Minister Ben-Gurion were 'deeply apprehensive' about the American suggestions for frontier changes. Privately, Sharett also viewed the speech as the death-knell for Israel's hopes for a security treaty. 'The entire issue', he wrote to Eban, had been 'postponed until the coming of Elijah the Prophet' because it had now become 'dependent on agreed border changes, which today stand no chance at all.' In sum, Sharett felt the speech had been designed 'to tell the Jews of America what they wanted to hear ... while at the same time removing [the security guarantee] from the agenda indefinitely'.[110]

Naming the starting price: Israeli and Egyptian manoeuvring

The Secretary's speech soon led to new, intricate patterns of manoeuvring among the powers, Egyptians and Israelis. During September, the Americans wanted Middle Eastern leaders to commit themselves to continue studying the proposals, and were prepared to deal with general requests for clarifications of the Secretary's speech. Arab and Israeli spokesmen tried to offer minimum commitment while extracting maximum information regarding Dulles' ultimate intentions, details of his proposals, and the reactions of the other party. For their part, Alpha planners preferred to flush out Arab and Israeli indications of what concessions they were prepared to make before disclosing too many details of their own prepared package of proposals.[111]

One of the many episodes in the process of the parties' feeling each other out in the wake of the Dulles speech was Prime Minister Sharett's invitation to Ambassador Lawson to his Jerusalem home for 'an oral examination of some of [the] points' raised by the 26 August statement. After praising the lofty aims of the speech, Sharett sought clarifications on a number of issues, beginning with a request to know whether Dulles' remarks against an arms race in the region 'meant "an end to [the] one[-]sided arming" policy of [the] United States'. The Israeli leader reiterated Ambassador Eban's critical remarks about the proposed link between a security guarantee and a settlement of the frontiers, and also explained that Israel's interest in retaining the Negev and the southern port of Eilat was more than 'sentimental'. In connection with the latter, Sharett also disputed Egypt's and Jordan's historical or legal rights to territorial contiguity. The Prime Minister confessed that the mention of proposed territorial adjustments had 'aroused considerable apprehension' in his government, and asked for either a public statement or a 'confidential message' to allay this apprehension:

> [W]hat category of ... adjustments to [the] boundary is involved in US thinking? ... [W]hat procedures with regard to revision of armistice lines are contemplated? ... If Arabs will not agree ... will [the] question of [a] defense pact between [the] US and Israel be put off indefinitely?

While Israel had 'always stood ready for mutual adjustments of boundaries', Sharett 'repeated rather forcefully "there is no question of concession of land by Israel"'.[112]

While, as we have seen, some Arabs perceived the statement as primarily designed to bolster Israel's security, for his part, Reuven Shiloah of the Israeli Embassy in Washington suspected that Dulles' references to guaranteed borders were inserted 'mainly for electoral purposes' in the United States. What he feared most was intense American pressure on Israel for impossible concessions, and he quoted Moshe Sharett's 4 May warning to Secretary Dulles against specific proposals emanating from third-parties[113] as prophetic and most pertinent in the wake of the 26 August statement. Shiloah did not accept at face value the Americans' claims that they had no preconceived detailed plan for a settlement and that they would back any arrangement agreed to by the parties: 'Indeed, I am aware that they don't always tell the truth, and that there are undoubtedly among them schemers and planners.' He recommended that, in response to the Dulles initiative, Israel should formulate and submit proposals on compensation for refugees, holy places, the Arab boycott, and a free port at Haifa, in such a way as to steer the discussion away from territorial concessions and along lines more favourable to Israel.[114]

Manoeuvring on the Arab side was complicated by a certain ambivalence, with most official responses remaining guarded. Only Syria took an openly harsh stand against the Dulles statement. Most other Arab leaders at this time seemed determined 'to avoid the *appearance* of being negative', even if there was little 'promise of positive action'. In the opinion of a Counsellor at the American Embassy in Amman, Jordanian leaders were 'Slowly acquiring a certain amount of political sophistication though they [were] at least a quarter-century behind the Israelis in this respect.'[115]

While the reactions of individual Arab leaders were, *in private*, mildly encouraging, the *public* attitudes they adopted became entangled in the dynamics of inter-Arab politics, recalling a phenomenon which Itamar Rabinovich has called 'the mechanism of political overbidding':

> Arab politicians sought to raise their political stock by portraying themselves as advocates of a political position more radical and pure than that of their competitors. The practical outcome of these dynamics was a radicalization of the Arab side's position and conduct.[116]

This time, however, the dynamic *vis-à-vis* the Dulles statement might better be described as 'underbidding', with no leader wishing to risk appearing too pro-Western. Iraqi, Lebanese and Jordanian leaders looked to the Arab League or to Egypt to set the tone. In Baghdad, Nuri Sa'id informed the British Ambassador that, while he personally believed that the American and British statements 'constitute[d] a good and helpful contribution to [resolving] the problem of Palestine', the Iraqi government 'would hold back and say as little as possible ... if the reactions of Egypt, and to a lesser degree of other Arab countries, were unfavourable'.[117]

Gradually the Egyptian press became openly hostile. Ahmad Hussein, Egypt's Ambassador to Washington, indicated during a visit to Cairo that Nasir feared that 'His own position would suffer if Egypt's reaction were to appear soft in comparison [with] that [of the] other Arab States.'[118] Most Arab leaders were reserving their final judgment until after an attempt to reach a consensus at a meeting of the Arab League Political Committee scheduled for 3 September to discuss the situation in North Africa. American officials hoped that the Cairo meeting 'would avoid taking a negative attitude towards the Secretary's statement' and that Arab leaders, but especially Nasir, 'would continue to wish to explore its significance'.[119]

But, owing partly to more pressing business, the scheduled Arab League discussion of the Secretary's statement was postponed indefinitely. This outcome was greeted with a sense of relief by American and British policy-makers, who seemed happy to be redirecting their attention to Egypt and Israel separately through secret diplomacy.[120] This left the Americans and British, throughout September, in the same 'waiting and wondering' situation that they had experienced in the spring: waiting for an appropriate moment to approach the Egyptian Prime Minister, and wondering how much detail of the proposed Alpha settlement should be revealed to him should an overture be made.[121]

On 3 September, the recently appointed British Ambassador to Egypt, Sir Humphrey Trevelyan, recommended that 'It would be inadvisable to press matters now, and that we should give the Egyptian Government a reasonable time to make the next move.'[122] But the fact that by mid-September the Israelis had responded to (and were making inquiries regarding the intentions behind) the Dulles statement left the Foreign Office wondering whether 'we may soon have to make determined attempts to talk to Nasser, in spite of our Ambassadors' advice against forcing the pace with him.' American policy-makers shared British fears of seeing their room for manoeuvre eroded, and Francis Russell was despatched to London for another round of consultations (see below).[123]

Meanwhile, tensions continued to mount along the Gaza frontier. South of the Gaza Strip, in the al-Auja/Nitzana demilitarized zone along the Sinai–Negev frontier, new incidents led to Egyptian and Israeli redeployments.[124] The increased border friction led to tripartite consultations under the Declaration of May 1950 and became one of the obstacles cited for hesitating to follow up the Dulles statement with Colonel Nasir. The need to avoid arousing 'undesirable speculation' in the public eye led the American and British Ambassadors to recommend against making any direct overture to the Egyptian Prime Minister at this time.[125]

Foreign Minister Mahmud Fawzi resumed his earlier Alpha role as informal consultant about the next steps to be taken. On the eve of his departure for New York, Dr Fawzi met separately with the American and British Ambassadors and they repeated their previous impressions that a settlement had to be reached before the issue became entangled in US electoral politics in 1956. Again, Fawzi reminded his listeners that the frontier question would be 'much more difficult' to resolve than the refugee or Jerusalem issues. Trevelyan reported the Egyptian Foreign Minister as stating that the Egyptians

> would not agree to either an Arab corridor through Israeli territory or an Israeli corridor through Arab territory, or adjustments which amounted only to frontier rectifications, but insisted on a re-establishment of territorial continuity, by which he meant the Negev up to (and I understood him to say

including) Beersheba. ... He was not taking up a bargaining position. These were the minimum term[s upon] which the Egyptian Government could politically justify a settlement with Israel. ... If they could not get their terms, the matter would have to wait for perhaps a long time.

As a result of Dr Fawzi's tough stand, both ambassadors recommended that the original Alpha procedure be altered to make soundings of the Israeli position earlier than planned, i.e., before achieving a fuller harmony of views among Egypt, the US and the UK.[126]

Back to the drawing-board: London consultations, September 1955

The Alpha planning team was now faced with the question of how to get negotiations started given Israel's position of no territorial concessions and Egypt's categorical claim to all of the Negev.[127] Francis Russell travelled to London for a new round of Anglo–American meetings which opened on 20 September. Evelyn Shuckburgh proposed that the next step should be an overture to the Israelis in the hope of eliciting some kind of counter-offer on the Negev. He argued that Nasir would be unwilling to discuss other items unless 'he was convinced that he could get some satisfaction on the Negev'.[128]

On this point the Americans adopted the opposite approach: namely, to try to 'get negotiations started and create an atmosphere of progress on other issues' *before* tackling the Negev, which was seen as 'the most difficult problem'. Russell also felt that the powers should first seek a more definite commitment to 'the idea of negotiations unconditionally' from Nasir and Fawzi, while addressing a set of specific questions regarding refugee compensation to Tel Aviv as a stalling tactic 'to engage the Israelis' attention for some time'.

American and British ideas on the next moves were now pulling in different directions. Shuckburgh was insistent that Nasir would be reluctant to make any move towards a settlement

> unless he received something in return, that is to say an assurance that Israel would be ready to make some concession on the Negev during the negotiations. Only if we could show

him that he would get something out of Israel could we expect him to move from that position.

The problem for the Alpha planners was thus how to move Nasir's position 'that the acquisition of the Negev was a *condition* for negotiations at least to the point at which his claim would appear as *part of* negotiations which he had already accepted in principle'.

Francis Russell took a different approach, hoping to win Nasir's co-operation by offering the inducement of long-term credits for acquiring American arms supplies – 'if he was ready to commit himself formally to negotiations with Israel through an intermediary'. Shuckburgh, on the other hand, felt this would be better done by first obtaining an Israeli concession which they could use as a 'lever to shift Nasser' from his present position. Both British and American policy-makers recognized the difficulty that

> neither the Egyptians nor the Israelis wanted to be first in the field with concessions. The situation resembled an oriental bazaar bargain in which neither vendor nor purchaser would name the starting price.

Even though Russell tended to view Fawzi's suggestion as an evasive manoeuvre aimed at 'transferring the onus of starting concrete negotiations to the Israelis', State Department instructions for Ambassador Lawson's reply to Prime Minister Sharett's queries did aim at putting the ball back into Israel's court.[129] At the same time, the Alpha planners would seek Nasir's agreement to an agenda for negotiations which incorporated his demand for the Negev.

At a joint meeting held the following day, British and American officials received reports of a disappointing interview between Ambassador Trevelyan and Gamal Abd al-Nasir. The Egyptian Prime Minister was reported to be less optimistic regarding a settlement than his Foreign Minister Mahmud Fawzi had been. Invoking Israel's major raid on Gaza once again, Nasir claimed that

> [b]efore February 1955 people were beginning to forget the Palestine war and to feel secure. Since that date tension had greatly increased and Egyptian public opinion was badly affected by fear and a feeling of insecurity. This feeling had been increased by the Israeli elections and by the speeches of Ben Gurion and Beigin [*sic*] during the campaign. His own thinking also was dominated by this feeling of fear. This,

therefore, was not the time for a settlement of the Palestine question.

Nasir also claimed to be worried that 'other Arab States would conduct a political attack on Egypt if Egypt took the lead' in trying to achieve a settlement at this time. The Egyptian leader repeated that 'A settlement now was impossible and emphasised the great strategic importance of the Negev to Egypt.' In view of Nasir's determined reluctance to proceed, Trevelyan now recommended against any approach to Israel.[130] Foreign Office officials were further discouraged (and surprised) to receive signals that even Nasir's chief rival, Nuri Sa'id, had declared himself in favour of a land link between Egypt and Jordan, thus elevating this already difficult Egyptian–Israeli issue into a 'general Arab demand'.[131]

Francis Russell looked askance at Nasir's 'not-now' posture as being 'simply an excuse for further postponement', possibly hiding 'a deep and enduring reluctance to make any move towards a settlement'. Russell was clearly impatient, and wished to capitalize on the Alpha 'momentum' achieved to date, even if it meant meeting Nasir 'head on'. He felt inclined to respond to Nasir's remarks by scolding him for 'the first negative response we had had from any government to Mr Dulles's statement', and to inform him that

> if this continued to be Nasser's position the United States Government, who had not expected this of Egypt, were seriously disturbed and might be forced to reconsider their whole policy in the Middle East.[132]

Evelyn Shuckburgh, confronted with 'a number of rather drastic suggestions' from his American colleague, counselled patience and restraint. It seemed wise, he felt, to wait a few weeks to see how strongly Egypt's leadership role would be affirmed during the Arab League discussions of the Jordan waters scheme. If Johnston's plan were accepted, 'it would be a most important achievement in itself and have a favourable effect on the prospects for Alpha'. Only after that meeting should they press Nasir to consider the draft agenda which had been prepared. Shuckburgh also realized it was 'dangerous to threaten a reappraisal of our policies in the Middle East', since there was no question of Britain and America simply 'transfer[ring] our support to the Israelis'. While Russell agreed, he still kept open the option of 'withdraw[ing] support from Egypt alone'.[133]

The Alpha consultations were thus at a difficult crossroads. To make matters worse, all of the careful calculations were abruptly overtaken by the news, which reached London on 22 September, of an Egyptian deal to purchase Soviet arms via Czechoslovakia.[134] The already limited abilities of the Western powers to influence Egyptian policy towards a settlement of the Arab–Israeli conflict were now diminished even further.

CHAPTER VIII

Arms and Alpha: The Arab Connection

The Soviet–Egyptian arms agreement of September 1955 – also known officially as the Czech–Egyptian arms agreement[1] – was a watershed in the international and regional politics of the Middle East.[2] In this chapter, we shall see how the consummation of this deal rudely upset so many Western (and Israeli) calculations, including the Anglo–American operation known as Alpha.

WESTERN ARMS AND AID FOR THE ARABS

Prior to September 1955, the record of American military assistance to Nasir's Egypt had been paltry. In the concluding words of one former State Department official, 'The complicated story of America's attempts to use military aid as a political lever in Egypt in the period 1952–55 remains a tale of lost opportunities.'[3] The August 1954 offer of US military assistance had been disappointingly only a fraction of what Nasir had been led to expect, and during the early part of 1955 'Egyptian doubts about the desirability of relying on the United States as an arms supplier' had deepened in the wake of the signing of the Baghdad Pact, the Israeli raid on Gaza, and Nasir's participation at the Bandung Conference.[4] During the summer, American diplomatic and intelligence officials in Cairo had worked hard, but in vain, to elicit a generous State Department response to Egyptian requests for arms and financial aid, partly in order to avert Nasir's imminent turn towards the Kremlin.[5] Given the higher costs and the overt conditions and restrictions attached to American aid, a leader of an Afro–Asian country like Egypt would have found rival offers from Moscow at this time quite enticing.[6]

From the first Anglo–American Washington meetings in January until the latest consultations in London, arms and other inducements to Egypt had been a major preoccupation of the planners of Operation Alpha. State Department officials were slow to learn the severe limitations of attempting to hold out the prospect of Western military assistance as a means of influencing Arab political positions, especially with regard to the Arab–Israeli conflict. Difficulties became evident in the basic difference of opinion which emerged between Henry Byroade and John Foster Dulles over the political use of promised arms aid for Egypt. On the eve of the Secretary's August 1955 statement, Byroade had argued that it was 'extremely important' that Nasir did not gain the impression that the Dulles speech 'requir[ed] prior cooperation on his part before [the arms] purchase c[ould] be consummated'.[7]

But that was *precisely* the impression the State Department (and especially Under-Secretary Herbert J. Hoover, Jr.) wanted to leave: namely, that the government's decision on arms supplies would 'necessarily be affected by [the] attitude Nasser adopts toward [the 26 August] statement'.[8] In early September, Byroade wrote that '[t]he sale of some equipment would not in my opinion reduce our bargaining power but in fact enhance it.' Against State Department hesitations, Byroade also urged Washington to be more forthcoming with steps to help Nasir enhance his prestige (such as an invitation to visit the US)[9], and to offer Egypt a more central role in plans for Middle East defence. As his impatience with Washington grew, Byroade advised the Department that it was wrong to 'wince' under the impression that Egypt's co-operation with the Soviets was 'blackmail'. The Ambassador warned that

> by our unwillingness [to] manipulate a few million dollars we are permitting [the] situation [to] deteriorate to [the] point where [a] chain reaction of [a] nature that will constitute a major defeat for US policy in [the] Middle East, as contrasted to that of [the] Soviet bloc, is highly probable.[10]

Unmoved by such arguments from the field, the State Department continued to insist on having a sign that Nasir would indeed be willing to co-operate in advancing Operation Alpha. After outlining the technical difficulties of obtaining financial assistance for Nasir's arms purchases, Acting Secretary Hoover zeroed in on the real political calculations involved. While recognizing the 'disadvantages [of] delaying [an] answer to Nasser for [a] protracted period', '[p]ositive steps by him such as [a] start in exploring [the] Secretary's statement would bolster greatly [the] case for accommodating Egypt on financing.' Both the question of arms financing and the timing of an official invitation for Nasir to visit the US should, the State Department affirmed, 'tie in with demonstrable progress on Alpha'.[11]

SOVIET ARMS FOR EGYPT: THE END OF THE TRIPARTITE MONOPOLY

On 19 September 1955, the US State Department received reports that an Egyptian mission in Moscow was on the point of concluding an arms deal seen by the Americans as 'almost embarrassing in size'.[12] IDF intelligence estimated that the Egyptian order from the USSR included between 90 and 120 MIG-15 jet fighters, around 50 Illyushin-28 bombers, between 14 and 20 Illyushin-14 transport planes, 60 half-tracks with 122 mm guns, 200 armoured troop carriers, between 230 and 275 T-34 and Stalin-III tanks, 56 130 mm multiple rocket launchers, 100 self-propelled SU-100 tank destroyers, several hundred field guns, two destroyers, four to 15 minesweepers, 12 torpedo boats, two to six submarines, and 150 heavy field vehicles, radar systems and recoilless guns.[13]

Unaware of this dramatic development, Alpha planners began their London consultations by basing their next moves on the erroneous presumption that Nasir's interest in Soviet arms purchases was merely bluff. British officials warned that American 'talk about arms may provoke Nasser into another attempt to frighten the Americans with the prospect of Soviet assistance'. Another British concern at this time was that, by offering Egypt 'substantial bribes in the form of capital for the High Aswan Dam and free arms on a large scale in return for her willingness to start negotiations with Israel', the Americans might be giving away too much, too soon, in exchange for too little.[14]

All these calculations quickly went by the boards once American and British officials learned of the signing of the Soviet–Egyptian arms agreement. It would take Western policy-makers several more months to reach the simple, but stark, realization that Egypt's basic aims simply

> did not accord with those of the West. The latter sought to maintain an informal Western hegemony in the region, barring the Soviet Union. The Egyptian leadership sought to escape this Western security network. Equally, the Western desire to settle the Arab–Israeli confrontation and turn the attention of the Middle Eastern states toward joint defense against the Soviet Union totally reversed Egyptian strategic priorities.[15]

The weeks following disclosure of the arms deal were filled with much posturing. Explaining his decision to ignore Ambassador Byroade's friendly advice against dealing with the Soviets, Nasir pointed to domestic reasons (largely the need to maintain the confidence of his army) but also to 'Egypt's desire to negotiate on or deal with, if this should become necessary, the Israeli problem from a position of strength instead of weakness'. Once again, Nasir cited Israel's Gaza raid as having been the crucial turning-point in his decision to turn to the Soviets – a disingenuous claim which was taken at face value by most observers and researchers, who were unaware of a secret Egyptian–Czech arms deal concluded in Cairo in February 1955, *before* Israel's Gaza raid.[16]

The State Department naively persisted for some days in its attempts to use American arms sales for political leverage with Egypt. Even as news of the dramatic Egyptian–Czech deal was being received, Under-Secretary Hoover responded to Byroade's persistent pleas by reaffirming that 'We cannot extend credit or grant of arms to Egypt in [the] absence of clear progress on [the] program outlined in the Sec[retar]y's speech of August 26.'[17] But the news of Nasir's arms deal effectively broke up the Alpha discussions in London, with several dossiers now overtaken by events. British and (especially) American policy-makers found themselves diverted from following up the Dulles statement to disjointed attempts at damage control regarding the Soviet–Egyptian arms agreement.

The prospect of a polarized Middle East, with Soviet-backed Arab states pitted against Western-supported Israel, was a nightmare to strategic planners in Washington, London and Paris. Under the immediate impact of the news of the arms deal, Francis Russell desperately hoped that the US and UK would not be presented with a situation in which they might have to 'support either [the] Arab countries or Israel in complete disregard of the other'. For a few days, he and Shuckburgh looked in vain for some way to prevent Egypt from consummating the arms deal, which 'would lead to a grave threat to the ultimate security of the Suez Canal' and the opening up of other Arab countries to similar Soviet 'penetration'. Russell and Shuckburgh proposed that the US and UK Ambassadors be instructed to make 'vigorous representations' in Cairo – speaking 'perhaps in the name of the President and the Prime Minister' – threatening that the two powers might have to 'review [their] entire policy in regard to Egypt'. The week leading up to Nasir's public announcement of the deal on 27 September was filled with assorted, but unsuccessful, attempts to persuade the Egyptians to back out of the arms agreement.[18] As Evelyn Shuckburgh lamented in his diary, the 'folly and fragility of our Palestine policy' was 'beginning to come home to roost at last.'[19]

British and American officials now recognized that Nasir had injected a new factor which upset all their previous calculations: namely, his intent on first erasing his perceived 'position of weakness' *vis-à-vis* Israel before agreeing to deal with the Jewish state. The Ambassadors in Cairo were instructed to warn the Egyptians that their quest for Soviet arms 'would result only in a great increase of armaments on both sides, without any improvement in Egypt's relative position, and a consequent increase of dangerous tensions in the area.' The Americans and British were also prepared to respond to Nasir's 'balance-of-power' fears by offering to

> assure him that if he is willing to negotiate a settlement which we believe would safeguard Egypt's vital interests, we would be prepared to exert US and United Kingdom influence on behalf of such a settlement. We would be prepared to discuss with him what the terms of such a settlement would be.[20]

From Cairo, Ambassador Byroade urged that Washington's reactions not be planned 'in haste', and pointed out that it was already too late for him to make any of the 'vigorous representations' which State Department officials were recommending. In his opinion, to ask Nasir to hold back on developing his military capability until after making substantial progress on a settlement with Israel was to ask him to put the cart before the horse.[21] Byroade echoed Egyptian spokesmen who stressed Egypt's need to redress the military imbalance in favour of the Arabs. He reported their continued interest in co-operation with the US and portrayed the Soviet arms deal as purely commercial and defensive. Not for the first or last time, Gamal Abd al-Nasir informed the Americans that 'Egypt had no aggressive intentions against Israel whatsoever; Egypt wished merely to strengthen its armed forces.'[22]

Despite all the consternation, stern disapproval and veiled diplomatic threats, the US and the UK were unable to cause Cairo or Moscow to undo their arms deal. The agreement marked an end to the unchallenged exclusive Anglo–American predominance in the Middle East. The deal also cast a heavy shadow over the 'Big Four' disarmament talks in Geneva.[23] The Soviet entry into the region now put into doubt all previous Anglo–American assumptions about stabilizing Arab–Israeli tensions through the United Nations, the Tripartite Declaration of May 1950, or Alpha's proposed Anglo–American security guarantees with individual countries. 'To the chagrin of the United States, the era of tripartite diplomacy had come to an end.'[24]

Britain also felt the new developments provided compelling evidence for strengthening the Baghdad Pact, making US adherence even more desirable than before. But Dulles remained as reluctant as ever to take such a step. Alpha's partners remained at odds over this issue, with Britain and the US holding differing assessments of whether a stronger Northern Tier would lead to better or worse behaviour on the part of Gamal Abd al-Nasir. Faced with reports of Henry Byroade's recommendation to 'go slow on the Northern Tier concept and encourage Egypt to build up a "second tier"', Anthony Eden's handwritten marginal comments in red pencil included the words: 'No. Foolish man.'[25] Within six weeks of the arms deal, a senior official at the FO noted that the 'Soviet intrusion into Middle Eastern affairs' had 'not only increased the danger of war between the Arab States and Israel: it ha[d] also exposed the whole weakness of our position in the Middle East.'[26]

One retrospective critique of the US approach at this time holds that the 'rigid link' Eisenhower and Dulles maintained between their global anti-communism and the quest for regional allies prevented bureaucrats and statesmen alike from showing the required flexibility to revise their Middle East policy even after seeing ample evidence of Egypt's unwillingness to play along. Steven Spiegel has written that:

Instead of plotting an uncooperative leader's overthrow as the Eisenhower administration had done when challenged in Iran and Guatemala, Dulles sent emissaries to protest Nasser's decision and to persuade him to change his mind.[27]

This, as we shall see in this and the following chapters, seems to have been the approach taken by both America and Britain for more than five months after the Czech–Egyptian arms deal. Serious efforts to isolate and topple Nasir were contemplated only in March 1956, under Operation 'Omega' (Chapter XIII, below).

For a brief moment in late September 1955 it appeared as if the crisis in American–Egyptian relations might be averted when Nasir sent signals, through CIA operative Kermit Roosevelt, of his willingness to insert a carefully worded paragraph regarding Egypt's desire to discuss 'concrete steps to reduce Arab–Israeli tensions' into his next scheduled speech. The hope was that such a declaration would have a 'good chance of, at least, "softening [the] blow"' of the Soviet arms deal.[28] Upon learning of this offer, Secretary Dulles looked forward to the prospect of 'an immediate exchange of views' as a follow-up to his 26 August statement, but ruled out Nasir's further suggestion for a high-level meeting between the two at this time, citing the likelihood of adverse public reaction in the US to the announcement of the Soviet arms deal.[29]

As it turned out, Nasir omitted the proposed conciliatory paragraph from his speech at the last moment, owing to his angry reaction to an Associated Press report to the effect that Dulles was despatching Assistant Secretary of State George Allen to Cairo to deliver an 'ultimatum' to the Egyptian leader.[30] 'This', recalls an American official stationed in Cairo, 'was Dulles at his worst ... at his most impulsive.'[31] Despite Allen's professed efforts 'to present United States views with dignity and calmness' and to avoid an 'ultimatum approach', the Assistant Secretary's sudden arrival in Cairo sent American–Egyptian relations into a severe tailspin.[32] These complications added weight to the tendency for some Alpha planners to reconsider, temporarily, a shift away from Egypt to Jordan as the prospective Arab partner for co-operation towards a settlement.[33]

As tension mounted, American officials from the Departments of State and Defense and members of the CIA and National Security Council [NSC] became engrossed in drawing up and discussing plans to 'deter aggression by Israel or Egypt', and also reassessed possible modes of American intervention should full-scale war break out. Reviewing the existing official statement of American Middle East policy (drafted in July 1954), Secretary Dulles was not very happy and called for revisions, which were duly approved after extensive consultations.[34]

The dangers of an imminent Middle East arms race also became clear to all parties. As Sir Ivone Kirkpatrick, Permanent Under-Secretary at the Foreign Office, saw it:

> The weakness of our position stems from the fact that our arms policy has hitherto rested on the illusion that we have a monopoly, and could, by an act of our own volition, control the flow of arms to the Middle Eastern countries.... In consequence of the Russian initiative, the Arab arms ceiling will henceforth be limited only by budgetary considerations.[35]

Predictably, in the United States domestic lobbying intensified for increased American military aid to Israel. Reacting to the latter development, Nasir sought to exert pressure of his own on Washington by warning that aid to Israel was one of the two things that 'would decide the future course of US–Egyptian relations'.

> If it would be our policy [Ambassador Byroade reported Nasir as saying] to strengthen Israel so that Egypt remains in [the] same relative defenseless position *vis-à-vis* her as before, then he could only conclude that we had nothing but hostile intentions toward him and Egypt.[36]

Soon British and American policy-makers learned to their dismay that the USSR was also offering economic and technical aid for the High Aswan Dam and other projects. Following the Czech arms announcement, the British Prime Minister began pressing his American allies to join him in expediting negotiations between Egypt and the International Bank for Reconstruction and Development (IBRD) so as to block the rumoured Russian offer to finance the ambitious dam project at Aswan. 'On our success at excluding the Russians from this contract', Anthony Eden cabled dramatically to Eisenhower, 'may depend the future of Africa.'[37] During the coming months, the Western powers felt their influence over Nasir progressively vanishing as they searched awkwardly for an effective

'Poor Cure for Volcanoes', *The Christian Science Monitor*,
1 November 1955, cartoon by Carmack
© 1955 The Christian Science Monitor

blend of carrots and sticks to keep Nasir from moving completely into the Soviet orbit.[38]

SHARETT'S HAT-IN-HAND DIPLOMACY: PARIS AND GENEVA

One of John Foster Dulles' immediate concerns was that the Czech deal might invite an early Israeli attack before the arms shipments started arriving in Egypt, and that this would 'produce chaos in the Middle East and in effect hand [the] area to [the] Russians on [a] silver platter'.[39] In addition, the Soviet–Egyptian arms deal made even more difficult the task of preparing the Israelis to make concessions under Operation Alpha.[40] As one writer has recently put it, '[f]or many Israelis the countdown to war had begun'.[41]

Israel's first official diplomatic reaction to the news of the arms deal was to ask 'friendly powers [to] use their influence with [the] USSR and [the] Egyptians to cause them [to] desist from implementing [the] agreement'. Failing this, Ambassador Eban warned, 'Israel would be forced [to] request that she be given sufficient arms from [the] West to maintain [the] balance of power.'[42] Despite the fact that Defence Minister David Ben-Gurion was slow to react, the deal soon created 'an atmosphere of national emergency' inside Israel. Shortly before the announcement, Israel had been dealt another provocative blow when Egypt had declared on 11 September that all ships intending to sail through the Gulf of Aqaba had to obtain Egypt's permission at least 72 hours in advance.[43] In late October, Ben-Gurion called upon the IDF's Chief of Staff, Moshe Dayan, to prepare operational plans for the capture of the Gaza Strip and Sinai Peninsula so as to break the blockade of Israel's southernmost port of Eilat.[44]

With this heightened sense of urgency, Israeli spokesmen abroad advanced a series of arguments which:

- sharply questioned the wisdom of Western reliance on the Arabs in general and on Nasir in particular as allies in a global confrontation between East and West;
- pointed out that a serious arms imbalance had favoured the Egyptians even before deliveries of the new and menacing Soviet arms;[45]
- demanded an opportunity to purchase arms to rectify this imbalance; and

- renewed Israel's request for a security treaty, stressing that such a treaty be based not on some future agreement on revised boundaries, but on the *status quo*.

This diplomatic campaign reached its peak during Moshe Sharett's meetings with John Foster Dulles and Harold Macmillan in Paris and Geneva at the end of October 1955.[46] 'While Israel [was] not alone in being threatened by the new situation', Sharett argued, 'Israel alone face[d] the issue of survival.' The Israeli Foreign Minister's handwritten notes in preparation for his second talk with Dulles elaborated the following links between arms deliveries and the quest for a peaceful settlement:

> We desire a settlement with our neighbors and will make no claims at their expense, nor will we ask them to sacrifice their national existence in any way.... There have never been worse conditions for a settlement than those which now prevail, at a time when an aggressive Egypt feels that she is about to have the upper hand. Only if Israel has a sense of assurance on the basic issues of the balance of power and of her own security will she be able to contribute constructively to a settlement. A nervous, fearful Israel will be far more inflexible and obdurate than an Israel at ease on the basic issue of her security.... *You will not get serious negotiations in the Middle East* [Sharett underlined] unless you first solve the basic security problem.

What, he pleaded, was the US 'prepared to do *now* to clarify its stand in favor of Israel's integrity, permanence and immunity from aggression?'[47]

In their separate and measured replies, both Dulles and Macmillan did not dispute the Israeli leader's views on the seriousness of recent Soviet–Egyptian moves, but they did not believe that it would be wise to cut off relations with Nasir and thereby drive him completely into the Soviet camp. Neither did they accept Sharett's estimation that there existed an arms imbalance in the Arabs' favour; nor were they prepared to supply arms to Israel on a scale that would run the risk of an arms race. Rather than fixing its hopes on a security treaty, the two Secretaries argued in their separate meetings with Foreign Minister Sharett that Israel should be concentrating instead on the *concessions* it would be prepared to offer the Arabs. The 'only way to deal with [the] situation', Dulles lectured, was for Israel to work out a settlement with the Arabs. Israel could probably have reached a better settlement last year than this and [could] make a better settlement this year that it probably [could] next. Israel ought seriously [to] consider the extent of [the] sacrifice it [was] willing to make to obtain [a] settlement.[48]

Sharett returned home disappointed at the failure of his 'crisis diplomacy' to elicit commitments for American and British arms in Paris and Geneva. Yet his late-October European trip was not completely wasted, as it did convey the full sense of Israel's alarm to both Western and Soviet leaders and, in practical terms, did advance Israel's quest for weapons with the more sympathetic government of France.[49] During November, Israel continued to press for British and American arms and a security treaty, although in the wake of the heightened Soviet–Egyptian threat Sharett wanted to shift the focus of Israeli lobbying clearly to the former.[50]

At the same time, Ambassador Eban indicated Israel's readiness to open discussions with the Americans regarding refugee compensation, but 'strongly implied Israel would stand adamantly against sizeable repatriation' and 'predicted he would not live to see [any] serious change in Israel's frontiers'.[51] In view of the Soviet armament of Egypt, the Israelis intimated to the State Department that they would not long 'sit here like rabbit[s] waiting for [the] kill', and they intensified their earnest requests for Western arms to 'correct [the] threatened imbalance'.[52]

In Washington, Reuven Shiloah, Gideon Rafael and Abba Eban tried to convince the visiting Evelyn Shuckburgh and George Allen at the State Department that Nasir's recent behaviour had laid to rest the 'naive illusion which "certain people" both in London and Washington were nurturing to their own confusion' – namely that Nasir, 'if given a chance, would work towards a decent settlement with Israel.' Shuckburgh noted that Israel's argument was 'to make the utmost use of this golden opportunity to show that the interests of the West coincide[d] with those of Israel and demand[ed] the suppression of the Egyptians.' But the senior British policy-maker found the Israeli arguments 'wholly unconvincing'.[53] In response to the latest public campaign by Israel's supporters in the US, John Foster Dulles sought President Eisenhower's help in an effort to bolster the line that 'nothing ha[d] so far happened that leads us to revise our policy of being friends both of Israel and [the] Arabs'.[54]

FEARS OF AN ISRAELI PRE-EMPTIVE STRIKE

In addition to rumours of Egypt launching a 'second round' against Israel, there was also much speculation about a possible Israeli 'preventive war' or pre-emptive strike. As Mordechai Bar-On makes clear in his path-breaking study of Israel's defence and foreign policy during these years, the IDF General Staff were unanimously in favour of launching such a war, but were held back by Israel's Defence Minister (and soon-to-be Prime Minister). Both Ben-Gurion and Chief of Staff Dayan contented themselves with preparing for the capture of the Straits of Tiran or an invasion of Sinai, while utilizing stepped-up retaliations in attempts to provoke (or 'prod') Nasir into initiating an all-out war before his armed forces had sufficient time to absorb all their recently acquired Soviet equipment.[55]

The connection to Israel's ongoing reprisals policy is instructive. While the original rationale for swift and heavy retaliations may have been primarily the *deterrence* of future infiltrations, Israeli strategists now saw a new purpose for reprisals. According to analyst Jonathan Shimshoni, there was 'ample evidence that Israeli leaders conceived of reprisals as a tool of brinkmanship, to demonstrate that the results of general war would be unpleasant for Egypt and to create a risk of inadvertent escalation to such a war.'[56] Bar-On, who served as head of the IDF Chief of Staff's Bureau and as General Dayan's private secretary at the time (and who subsequently wrote an archives-based doctoral dissertation on Israel's Sinai campaign), quotes from Dayan's report of a crucial meeting with Ben-Gurion on 23 October 1955:

> The basic solution to Israel's worsening security problems is the overthrow of the Nasir régime.[57] In order to bring down Nasir, we must bring about a decisive and comprehensive contest between the IDF and the Egyptian army. In spite of this, we must rule out, from the start, the idea of a preventive war, since this would mean an aggressive war initiated by Israel. While the downfall of the Nasir régime is indispensable, Israel cannot permit herself to stand against the whole world, which would regard her as an aggressor state in the full sense of the word. Such a situation would undo the full success of the war itself.[58]

Ben-Gurion's clear stand against launching a 'preventive war' did nothing to stifle an intense internal debate over the merits of such a course of action. This Israeli debate, in turn, had its echoes in international diplomatic circles during the late autumn and winter of 1955–56. An Israeli attack on Egypt, Henry Byroade warned from Cairo, 'would be interpreted throughout the area as [the] United States['] reply to [the] Soviet arms deal'.[59] These late-1955 calculations about the prospect of an Israeli pre-emptive strike became an integral part of the 'descent to Suez' that was now fully in motion and would result in the October 1956 war.[60]

Much of the attention of the 'Big Four' during meetings in Paris and Geneva in late October and early November dealt precisely with the need to deter Israel from undertaking such military action, including firm warnings that the Tripartite Declaration would be invoked to counter aggression from any quarter.[61] Even Egyptian officials, in their contacts with American officials, spoke openly of their hopes for '[c]ontinuation of efforts by the United States to prevent Israel from engaging in [a] preventive war against Egypt'. Such hopes were joined to threats that, 'If an Israeli so-called preventive war were to be launched against the Arabs, public opinion in Egypt and all the Arab countries would turn against the West.'[62]

NEW MOVES TO COURT NASIR

By mid-November, Israeli leaders were reported to be 'a bit nonplussed by [the] failure of [the] US G[overnment] to adopt [a] more vigorous policy towards Egypt'.[63] Contrary to Israeli hopes, policymakers in Washington and London were still a long way from giving up on Nasir. Macmillan, Dulles and others believed that Nasir might still – as a token of good faith with the West, and to offset the effect of the Soviet arms deal – be counted on to provide his personal backing for the Johnston plan for the Jordan waters, and perhaps even to cooperate in the search for an overall settlement with Israel.[64] Indeed, during the Arab League council meetings in Cairo in early October, Nasir appears to have taken a 'constructive line' – although he proved not as helpful as in the past. Definitive Arab assent to co-operate in the project remained elusive.[65] The assessments of many State Department and CIA officials, as one analyst has recently summarized them, continued during this period to regard Gamal Abd al-Nasir 'as a sort of errant protégé, who might still be maneuvered into leading the Arabs toward a settlement with Israel and into some kind of loose association with Western defense plans in the Middle East.'[66]

For much of October and November, senior British and American officials could not determine just how deeply the Egyptian leader had become committed to an alliance with the Soviet Union and, as a consequence, how energetically the Western powers should continue to woo him. But the atmosphere for courting Nasir in the aftermath of the Soviet arms deal was hardly promising. Political and military tensions increased steadily as the Western powers continued to contemplate moves that might limit the extent of Soviet 'penetration'. The US, Britain and France sought to control and co-ordinate the flow of arms to Israel and the Arab states, and at the same time avert an Israeli pre-emptive attack. UN officials also requested American help to defuse the mounting tensions between Israel and Egypt in the al-Auja/Nitzana demilitarized zone along the Sinai frontier.[67]

In Jerusalem, a new Cabinet was formed with David Ben-Gurion returning to the Prime Ministership and Moshe Sharett retaining the post of Foreign Minister. In his inaugural speech to the Knesset on 2 November, Ben-Gurion stressed Israel's security predicament in the face of an Egyptian arms build-up and an escalation of bellicose statements by Arab leaders.

> The people of Israel in the Land of Israel [he declared] will not be led like sheep to the slaughter. What Hitler did to six million helpless Jews in the ghettoes of Europe will not be done by any foe of the House of Israel to a community of free Jews rooted in their own land.

At the same time, the Israeli leader continued, '[O]ur aim is peace – but not suicide.... We do not covet a single inch of foreign soil, just as we will not permit anyone to deprive us of a single inch of our territory as long as we live.' In order to 'overcome the dangers inherent in the present unstable situation', Ben-Gurion was 'prepared to meet with the Prime Minister of Egypt and with every other Arab ruler as soon as possible, to achieve a mutual settlement without any prior conditions.' If the other side was 'not yet ready for that', Israel would also be prepared to work for a 'limited settlement' providing for guarantees of the complete implementation of the Armistice Agreements, mutual elimination of all incidents and acts of hostility, boycott and blockade, observance of freedom of the seas, and any further terms agreeable to both sides.[68]

Ben-Gurion's call for peace went hand-in-hand, however, with the implementation of the new IDF strategy of using limited 'reprisal raids' to provoke Nasir into launching an all-out war. Within hours of the Prime Minister's speech, Israeli troops staged a large-scale attack (Operation Volcano) on as-Sabha in the al-Auja DMZ.[69] In

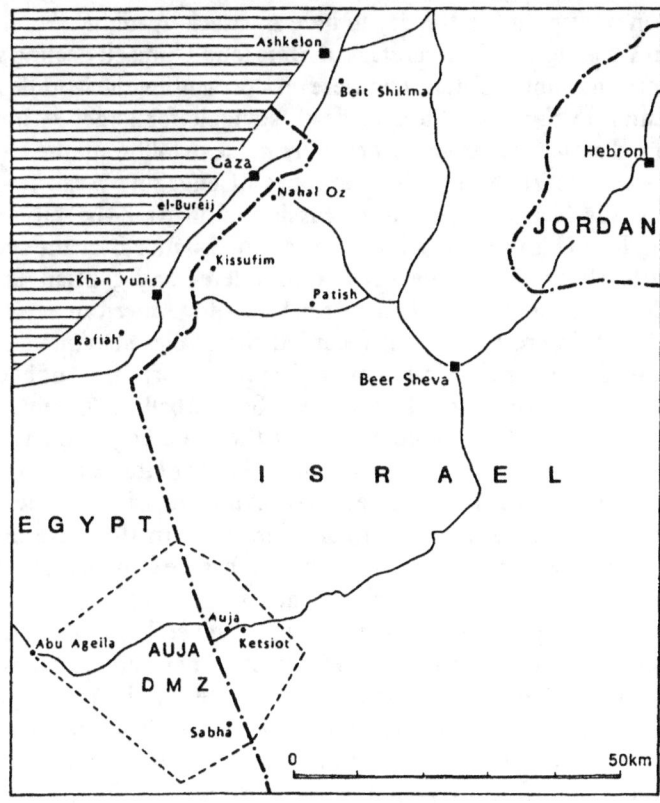

Map: 'Southwestern Israel, Gaza, and Auja, 1949–1956' from Jonathan Shimshoni, *Israel and Conventional Deterrence: Border Warfare from 1953 to 1970*, Ithaca/London: Cornell University Press, 1988

an extra effort to provoke the desired counter-attack, General Dayan planned to hold on to the conquered Egyptian positions, but was overruled by a cautious Ben-Gurion who ordered a return to base. Seventy Egyptian and seven Israeli soldiers were killed, with dozens of wounded and 50 Egyptians taken prisoner – making the battle what one historian has called 'the IDF's most extensive operation since the end of the 1948 War'.[70] But, although the operation proved even more devastating than the Gaza raid and caused tempers to rise in Cairo, Col. Nasir would not be goaded into escalating the border conflict at this time. The Egyptian leader was left bitter and sobered, able only to heap scorn on Ben-Gurion's peace overture as a 'smoke screen put up during the day to hide an attack by night'.[71]

In Washington, the Secretary of State found himself dealing with American Zionist leaders who were now presenting the Middle East situation to him 'as a life-and-death struggle for Israel'.[72] In this charged atmosphere, new efforts were made to follow up the Dulles statement of 26 August in the hopes of engaging Arab leaders (especially Nasir himself) in discussion of an Arab–Israeli settlement. From his vantage point in Cairo, Ambassador Byroade agreed with Washington that the arms deal rendered an Egyptian–Israeli settlement more urgent than ever before – for American as well as for Israeli interests. He still regarded the Dulles statement of 26 August as the 'proper foundation [for] this effort', but, unlike his superiors in Washington, Byroade now felt the ball was firmly in the Israelis' court. He recommended that the State Department convince Tel Aviv that, for the US to make further efforts in favour of a settlement, 'Israel must offer territorial concessions. Otherwise there [was] no hope of Arab consideration.' In the wake of the Soviet–Egyptian arms agreement, he felt that the United States 'had no leverage to achieve Arab acceptance'.[73]

While Dulles and Macmillan conveyed general reminders to the Israelis that concessions would be inevitable, more attention was still being devoted to following up the Dulles statement in Arab capitals. Belated responses to the Secretary's speech continued to trickle in from various Arab quarters. While there was little change in the hostile or indifferent reactions noted earlier, one British envoy felt that 'further efforts should now be made to reawaken Arab interest in the Dulles statement and to try to get some definite reactions out of them'[74] – a suggestion that was soon taken up in Prime Minister Anthony Eden's Guildhall speech (below, Chapter IX).

Partly in response to the Dulles initiative, a number of Arab politicians launched their own trial balloons at this time. Several Lebanese leaders, for example, urged that the Western powers promote – in place of the Dulles proposals – the Lausanne Protocol, which, they claimed, 'had been accepted by both sides' in May 1949.[75] A little research at the Foreign Office led, however, to the conclusion that this advice was 'tantamount to saying that both sides should accept the [1947] UN Partition Resolution as a starting point'. FO officials quickly realized that it was 'extremely unlikely that we could induce the Israelis to agree', and concluded that the Lausanne *démarche* was 'not even a starter'.[76]

Wishing to leave no stone unturned, Shuckburgh none the less proceeded to sound out Tel Aviv on the viability of basing new talks on the 1949 document. Recalling his personal involvement in creating the Protocol as a device 'to break the log jam' at Lausanne, Walter Eytan offered the British Ambassador several reasons why his government would not be keen to revive it in the present circumstances. Among other things, Nicholls reported, the Director-General of the IMFA

> did not believe that any fruitful negotiations could take place with any Arab leader who found it necessary to resort to face-saving devices of this kind. What was needed was rather an Arab leader with sufficient guts to tell his people that, though they all hated the Jews and wished that Israel did not exist, it was time to stop playing the ostrich and come to terms.[77]

Would Abd al-Nasir be the 'prodigy' whom Eytan didn't really believe existed? For his part, the Egyptian leader confused his Western critics by hinting, on at least two separate occasions in October, at his continued willingness to bargain over a possible settlement with Israel. In talks with an Iraqi representative, as well as with 'a sensitive source' (presumably a CIA operative), Nasir engaged in some negotiation overtures of his own, offering 'to agree to no further extensions' of his agreement with the Soviets 'if a settlement of the Israeli problem were worked out on the basis of the UN 1947 resolution'.[78]

Henry Byroade offered his interpretation of the Egyptian bargaining position in a mid-October cable to Washington. Nasir, he argued, would be receptive to reaching a settlement 'if Israel [were] willing to make [a] move in [the] direction [of a] settlement of [the]

Negev question'. The Ambassador felt that the Egyptian leader, along with other Arabs,

> might adhere at least at [the] outset to [the] standard Arab position on [a] Palestine settlement, that is [a] settlement based mainly on [the] fulfillment [of the] 1947 and subsequent United Nations resolutions re borders, refugees, Jerusalem etc.[79]

At the same time, however, Colonel Nasir continued to dispute American claims that Egypt stood to benefit from his endorsement of Secretary Dulles' statement of 26 August. In turning aside such American arguments, Nasir claimed that

- the Negev 'constituted [a] partition of Arab lands and [the] initiative rested with Israel'; and
- the Dulles proposals favoured Israel, 'since [the] only benefit to [the] Arabs might be some minor adjustment of frontiers'.[80]

Still, in late October, both Washington and London continued to believe that the 'best prospects' were 'offered by an approach to Nasser seeking an understanding with him on Middle East problems in general including agreement by him to work towards an Arab–Israel settlement.'[81] Empathizing with the Egyptian leader, a top-level Anglo–American consultation team reasoned that 'the increased sense of independence and strength' which Nasir had now achieved by the arms agreement might 'enable him to move toward a settlement'.[82] The recommended American approach was set out clearly in the following series of *quid pro quos*:

If Nasir would

- 'cooperate to prevent further Soviet economic or military penetration in the area';
- 'exert his full influence in favor of the Jordan Valley plan'; and
- 'work with us towards an Arab–Israeli settlement';

the Americans would, in return,

- 'support Egypt's legitimate aspirations to area leadership';
- 'continue various types of economic assistance including restraint in [US] cotton exports';
- 'assist in financing the High Aswan Dam, and securing an Egyptian–Sudan[ese] agreement on Nile waters'; and
- 'meet reasonable requests for arms in the context of a settlement'.[83]

British policy-makers' assessments at this time dovetailed perfectly with those of the State Department. Evelyn Shuckburgh's nine-page analysis of policy options in the wake of the Soviet–Egyptian arms agreement concluded that the Western powers had little choice but to 'expose the motives behind Soviet offers' and to 'convince Nasser and his supporters – and the remainder of the Arab world – that their interest lies in co-operation with the West.' He proposed eight guidelines regarding arms exports, financial aid and future attempts 'to bring Egypt back onto the rails politically'. As for the Arab–Israeli conflict, Shuckburgh was more certain than ever that a settlement was the only 'honourable way out of our difficulties'.

> However discouraging the prospects may seem, this must continue to be our major and urgent objective; for if we cannot achieve it, some form of abandonment of Israel will become the only alternative to the loss of Middle East oil. ... Some form of the Alpha proposals remains the only possible objective to which we can direct the States concerned.

Ending on a mildly optimistic note, Shuckburgh felt that Nasir might now 'feel better able to contemplate a settlement now that he has restored his standing in the Arab world and can negotiate from a position of greater strength.'[84]

Although he argued that the time was not yet ripe for any new overtures to be made to Nasir,[85] Sir Ivone Kirkpatrick at the Foreign Office proceeded to draw up his own proposal for joint action with the Americans: a 'package deal' to be presented to Nasir at the 'first favourable opportunity' (Document 7).[86] After listing several *quid pro quos* similar to those in Russell's policy paper quoted above, Kirkpatrick ended with a more ominous catalogue of actions to be undertaken in the event of Nasir's rejection of these Anglo–American overtures:

(a) Refuse all economic aid to Egypt.
(b) Cut off all further arms deliveries.
(c) Endeavour to isolate Egypt.
(d) Consider ways and means of bringing down the Régime, and make it plain to Nasser that we have vital interests in the area and will shrink from nothing to protect them from Soviet encroachments.[87]

State Department officials announced that they were 'in substantial agreement' with the points made in Kirkpatrick's minute,[88] which was subsequently incorporated into the broader statement of an agreed Anglo–American position on the Middle East produced by Macmillan, Shuckburgh, Dulles and Russell in Geneva (Document 9).

As was evident in the final portion of Kirkpatrick's original memorandum, the plans for wooing the increasingly independent and defiant Egyptian leader involved some 'sticks', and not only 'carrots'.[89] This approach was similar to Shuckburgh's simple formulation offered a month earlier: 'We must first try to frighten Nasser, then to bribe him, and if neither works, get rid of him.'[90] During October and afterwards, feelers to sound out Nasir were made against a backdrop of speculation about possibilities of undermining or toppling the Egyptian leader. Almost a year before it actually happened, the State Department heard reports that Israel might be planning to 'drive to Suez across Sinai in [an] endeavor to trap Egyptian forces[,] thereby causing Nasser's downfall'.[91] Rumours also abounded about Israel's intention to either test, or militarily break through, Egypt's blockade of the Strait of Tiran.[92] Passing through Geneva *en route* to Belgrade, senior IMFA adviser Gideon Rafael told a member of the American delegation that his government was 'firm in its objective [to] bring about [the] elimination of Nasser' and 'intend[ed] to engage Nasser by sending a warship up [the] Gulf of Aqaba':

> If [the] Egyptians fire[d] on it[, the] IDF w[ould] respond in force[,] claiming Egypt [was the] aggressor and [would] demand [the] assistance of [the] Tripartite Powers under [the] 1950 Declaration.[93]

Dulles and the State Department were opposed to taking any threatening or drastic steps for the time being, although the Secretary did intimate to his British counterpart that there might be '[u]npleasant events which we might instigate' which would 'have the appearance of happening naturally'.[94] For the time being, the Americans recommended that they and their British allies 'refrain from punitive measures' against Nasir for two or three months 'until we see whether he will cooperate in preventing further Soviet penetration in [the] area'.[95] Likewise, Evelyn Shuckburgh could not escape the conclusion that Egypt remained 'the key' and that 'we must make sense of Nasser by some means or other'.[96] The Foreign Ministers of the three Western powers ended their Geneva meetings in agreement with Harold Macmillan that

> [w]hile Nasser undoubtedly [felt] that he ha[d] scored a popular success and [was] in [a] good bargaining position[,] he [was] also probably somewhat alarmed by what ha[d] happened and [the] time may soon come when he will wish [to] return to [a] closer association with [the] West.[97]

In the meantime, informal discussions involving both Nasir and Fawzi in Cairo kept open the door to future collaboration with the Western powers. In late October, Nasir's CIA confidants reported the Egyptian leader's readiness to resume discussions on a Palestine settlement.[98] On 1 November, Ambassador Byroade had what he described as a 'profitable' two-and-a-half hour conversation with Colonel Nasir. Byroade disavowed any US 'punitive feelings toward him' and appealed for Egypt's co-operation in restricting Soviet influence in the Middle East and in promoting a settlement of the Arab–Israeli dispute. The latter, the Ambassador argued, was

> more important to Egypt and [the] area as a whole now than ever before. With his new strength we hoped [Nasir] would adopt [a] statesmanlike approach and be willing [to] discuss such a possibility without delay.

It was impossible, Byroade added, to separate the Aswan High Dam project from the 'state of affairs that would be existent here over [the] next ten years[,] i.e. war or peace[, the] question of [the] necessity for large scale military expenditures on [the] part of Egypt[,] etc.'[99]

According to Byroade's report, the Egyptian leader was now 'more conscious of [the] true nature of our concern and apparently more willing to make more of an effort [to] improve our relations.' This included a willingness to continue, 'on a highly secret basis', discussions regarding the 'specifics of [a] settlement'. The next step would therefore be for the Americans and Nasir to formulate 'some proposition about the frontier', which could then be put to the Israelis. Ambassador Trevelyan also recommended zeroing in on the thorniest issue: Egypt's claim to a substantial Negev land-bridge to Jordan.[100] The British Ambassador, following a wide-ranging discussion on all the major sensitive topics of the day, concluded that Nasir 'still believe[d] his interests to lie with the West, and that we may still be able to do business with him'.[101] Alpha's top planners meeting in Geneva in early November seemed to be presuming the accuracy of such an appraisal when they agreed that '[w]e should not write off Egypt or drive her into Russia's arms'.[102]

CHAPTER IX

Eden's Guildhall Speech, November 1955

GUILDHALL SPEECH: SEEKING A COMPROMISE
BETWEEN 1947 AND THE STATUS QUO

During the very days when Macmillan, Shuckburgh, Dulles and Russell were in Geneva and producing their draft statement of an agreed position on the Middle East (Document 9), officials in London were also weighing the options for moving ahead with Operation Alpha. In early November, the Foreign Office wished to press ahead with

> a new approach to the parties, or another public statement, in the hope of getting the contestants, and particularly the Arabs, to think in terms of settlement, or at least negotiations, rather than war.

In order to get beyond Dulles' statement in a way that would 'make it possible for our Arab friends to support us and difficult for our Arab enemies to attack', G.G. Arthur suggested that his government 'move towards some acknowledgement of the validity of the United Nations resolutions on Palestine' in the form of a public statement endorsing *both* the Arabs' basis of 1947 *and* the Israelis' basis of the present situation as legitimate, 'perfectly tenable positions from which to start a negotiation'.[1] As historian Michael Oren has pointed out, this approach coincided with a formula favoured by Britain's leading ally in the Arab world, Iraq's Nuri Sa'id.[2]

By issuing an official pronouncement as soon as possible, Arthur hoped to create a better chance 'of getting the Arabs to talk seriously'.

The proposed British statement, Arthur realized, would have to be phrased in such a way as to avoid, on the one hand, angering the Israelis and 'precipitat[ing] the war that we must avoid', and, on the other, giving 'a triumph for Colonel Nasser's policy of blackmail'. A statement of this kind, he acknowledged, would be 'a blow to the Israelis' and would meet with American disapproval, but Arthur argued that 'we must face the fact that if we are ever to bring about a Palestine settlement we shall have to be nasty to the Israelis at some stage'. This, Arthur believed, 'was implicit in the Alpha proposals', though he often 'wonder[ed] whether the Americans really faced it'.[3]

Within a few days, Evelyn Shuckburgh arranged for the insertion of several paragraphs on a Middle East settlement into Anthony Eden's scheduled speech at London's Guildhall (Mansion House). The Prime Minister

> would be stating openly for the first time that a solution for the Palestine problem must be found in a compromise between the present *status quo* and the 1947 Resolutions. Although this is well-known to be the fact, it will be a painful thing [Shuckburgh accurately predicted] for the Jews to hear it stated by one of the Great Powers.[4]

Thus, the British Prime Minister would be taking upon himself responsibility for the second public disclosure of the main ideas behind Operation Alpha – 'lift[ing] the veil a little',[5] but still hiding the existence of extensive Anglo–American planning for specific terms of a settlement. Partly because there was barely any time to consult John Foster Dulles (then in Geneva) or the State Department, the Guildhall speech would also become a source of new strains in the Anglo–American partnership.

On 9 November 1955, the Prime Minister prefaced his important remarks dealing with frontiers by referring to the recent flare-ups, the dangers of an imminent arms race leading to war, and the 'tragic problem of the refugees' (Document 8).[6] Regretfully, he declared to the dignitaries assembled at the Guildhall, 'time ha[d] proved no healer' and there had been no progress since the armistice agreements signed six years earlier.

> We must somehow attempt to deal with the root cause of the trouble, and our country has a special responsibility in all this, for we have a long tradition of friendship with the Middle East.

Security guarantees to both sides and financial assistance to resolve the refugee problem were examples of the contributions which Britain and other powers could make, but first the parties ought to arrive at 'accepted arrangements ... about their boundaries'.

Before concluding with an open-ended offer of his personal services, the Prime Minister submitted the following suggestion:

> The position today is that the Arabs on the one side take their stand on the 1947 and other United Nations resolutions. That is where they are. They have said that they would be willing to open discussions with Israel from that basis. The Israelis[,] on the other side, found themselves on the later armistice agreement of 1949, and on the present territories which they occupy.

Eden recognized that there was a wide gap between those two positions; but, he asked, was it 'so wide that no negotiation is possible to bridge it?'

> It is not right, I agree, that United Nations resolutions should be ignored, but equally can it be maintained the United Nations resolutions on Palestine can now be put into operation just as they stand? The stark truth is that if these nations want to win a peace, which is in both their interests and to which we want to help them, they must make some compromises between these two positions.

The Guildhall speech was backed up with an elaborate barrage of diplomatic representations in the Middle East. British embassies and legations were instructed to approach government officials, urging them to ensure that the speech received a favourable reception and also calling upon leaders 'to associate themselves with the Prime Minister's remarks and to accept the idea of a compromise on the basis suggested'. Given Britain's recognition of the UN resolutions, it was now 'the Arabs' chance', the FO argued, 'to show their statesmanship and move towards an honourable settlement'. British envoys were instructed to emphasize that the views of HMG and the US government were 'identical', and that no settlement could be reached 'without the considerable help, both diplomatic and financial, which Her Majesty's Government and the United

States Government are alone able to provide'. In phrases reminiscent of earlier efforts to bring about the 'gradual education' of the Arabs (above, Chapter II), the FO suggested that Arab leaders be told that they had

> missed many chances of negotiating a reasonable settlement, and they ha[d] always lost by doing so. We hope they will respond constructively to the Prime Minister's offer of help and show their willingness to relax the rigidity of their stand on the United Nations resolutions. ... Each side must at least acknowledge the other's starting point.[7]

The Foreign Office was especially hoping that Gamal Abd al-Nasir would be 'willing to talk Palestine' now that the Prime Minister had 'done his best to make this easy for him. He can scarcely complain, as he did after Mr Dulles' statement ..., that this speech contains nothing of advantage for the Arabs'.[8] Instructions to Tel Aviv, correctly anticipating unfavourable reactions to Eden's references to the UN resolutions, asked the British Ambassador to stress that this represented neither a blanket endorsement of those resolutions nor a change in British policy. Jack Nicholls was also asked to point out to the Israelis that the Prime Minister's speech and Mr Dulles' August statement were to be read as 'complementary'. The Foreign Office hoped that Eden's 'plain speaking [would] break the deadlock and that both sides [would] now begin to look for common ground'.[9]

ARAB REACTIONS

Initial reactions in Arab capitals were mixed, but they were interpreted in London as being as favourable as could have been expected.[10] While Lebanese Prime Minister Karamé was willing to concede that the speech's reference to the 1947 resolution 'offered a very small step forward', he resisted British arguments in favour of issuing a public statement, claiming he was 'not convinced of the value of negotiating at all'.[11] Nuri Sa'id hailed Eden's speech as having 'opened a real possibility of reaching ... a settlement', but the Iraqi leader again preferred to wait for an Egyptian lead before saying so publicly. He also stressed the need for strong American endorsement to avert the possibility of Israel 'play[ing] off the United States against the rest' – a theme that was echoed in Jordan and elsewhere.[12]

In Egypt, Foreign Minister Mahmud Fawzi informed the British Ambassador 'confidentially' that his government 'welcomed the statement, and would be prepared to associate themselves with the task of seeking a settlement', but, he added, 'it would be a tactical mistake for the Egyptian press and radio to support the speech' openly. Significantly, Dr Fawzi now indicated that the Bernadotte proposals of 1948 – which suggested that the Negev Desert be given to Arab rule in exchange for Israeli sovereignty over western Galilee – might be a more appealing starting point for negotiations than the November 1947 partition plan.[13] He reiterated that the Arabs would be demanding the Negev, including Beersheba, without 'Jewish corridors through an Arab Negev' or 'Arab corridors through a Jewish Negev'. Fawzi was not, however, willing to negotiate directly with the Israelis, and insisted on secret discussions in London, Washington and Cairo without transforming the contacts into multilateral talks involving other Arab countries.[14]

In a subsequent private talk with Ambassador Trevelyan, Gamal Abd al-Nasir welcomed Eden's speech as 'the first constructive declaration from the British side since the end of the Palestine war'. The Egyptian Premier claimed that he would be arranging for a favourable response from the Egyptian press, which was quick to take propaganda advantage of reports of Israel's rejection of the British proposals. Cairo papers accused Israel of 'looking towards a preventive war, not to forestall an Arab attack but to forestall a just peace'. Nasir also claimed that he had personally praised the speech in talks with Saudi, Syrian and Lebanese leaders. He expressed his willingness to carry the discussions further with Trevelyan and Byroade in ways 'which would not attract attention', but he would definitely not discuss the matter directly with the Israelis.[15] Although Nasir would continue to claim that he feared that any moves towards reconciliation with Israel might open him to public criticism by Nuri Sa'id, the Iraqi leader assured the British at this time that he would not use peace with Israel as a weapon against his Egyptian rival.[16]

THE ISRAELI REACTION

Despite Eden's even-handed presentation of the proposed bridging of the Arab and Israeli positions, Israeli spokesmen were predictably upset by references to the 1947 United Nations partition resolution.

The Israeli Embassy in London issued a statement which sought to place that resolution in the larger context of the events between 1947 and 1950, and concluded that '[b]oth in theory and in practice ... the UN resolutions of 1947 ceased to be valid on the day when the Arabs, having formally rejected them, later proceeded by force to try and prevent their implementation.' The statement referred to Israel's long-standing offer to transform the existing armistice lines into final boundaries in the framework of a peace settlement, making 'such necessary minor adjustments of those boundaries as may be mutually agreed upon in order to facilitate the solution of local problems and to make the "Line" more workable'. The government of Israel, the statement affirmed, 'backed by unanimous public opinion', did 'not admit any claim on the part of the Arabs, whether alone or supported by other Powers, to any of the territory Israel now holds. If the Arab States need anything, it is certainly not land.' Several days later, Ambassador Elath and Evelyn Shuckburgh had an unpleasant encounter on the subject in which both men 'got rather heated'.[17]

From Tel Aviv, the British Ambassador reported that initial reaction to the Guildhall speech was 'at best unenthusiastic', with the local press highlighting Foreign Minister Sharett's remarks in New York that 'it was difficult to consider Britain as an impartial arbiter'. Editorialists began referring to Eden's speech as a 'Middle Eastern Munich' (cf. below, Chapter X). The Director-General of the IMFA was 'struck by the emphasis placed on territorial changes', which, he claimed, could 'only give rise to great anxiety in Israel'. Acting Foreign Minister Golda Myerson (Meir) informed the British Ambassador that

> [t]he Israelis would meet the Arabs at any time, with no conditions on either side, and in the course of negotiations would be prepared to discuss frontier rectifications; but she [*sic*] would not in any circumstances cede territory.[18]

Observing this hardening of opinion in Israel, Ambassador Jack Nicholls became convinced that it would be 'quite unrealistic' for the British and Americans to go further in their talks with Egyptians than the Negev 'triangles' solution worked out by Alpha planners. He also advised London of the need to convince the Israelis of two things before they would agree to start negotiating:

(a) that the Arabs, or at least one of the Arab States, are really prepared to negotiate on a realistic basis; and
(b) that we have not decided in advance to compel them to surrender the whole of the southern Negev.[19]

After a few weeks, Nicholls reported that the Israelis feared the worst and were 'working themselves up into a mood of defiance and desperation'. He elaborated on Israeli fears that the Egyptians, 'with [British] support', intended to 'demand cession of a large part of the Negev'. In setting forth agenda items for talks, he warned, 'Any phrase which might suggest that cession of [Eilat] was in our view open to discussion would effectively put paid to all chance of negotiation.' The Israelis were, in the British Ambassador's view, 'deeply suspicious that, at the appropriate moment, we shall subject them to intolerable pressure to accept an intolerable settlement', and warned of the 'risk that they might think it less dangerous to nip negotiations in the bud than to find themselves in such a situation'. Unless, he concluded, 'we can convince them soon that our intentions are honourable, we cannot be sure that they will not adopt their own methods of sabotaging further discussions.'[20]

The full force of Israel's critical reaction came on 15 November, when Prime Minister Ben-Gurion stated before the Knesset that the Guildhall speech – which he described as a 'proposal to truncate the territory of Israel for the benefit of its neighbours' – would not bring peace nearer but was more 'likely to encourage and intensify Arab aggression and to lessen the likelihood of peace in the Middle East.' The Israeli leader invoked historical and legal arguments against portraying the cession of former Palestinian territory now held by Israel to neighbouring Arab states as a 'compromise'. Rehearsing phrases from his inaugural address (above, pages 166–7) regarding Israelis' determination not to allow anyone to deprive them of 'a single inch of [their] land', Ben-Gurion concluded by repeating his proposal for 'a direct meeting with any of the Arab rulers in order to achieve a mutual settlement, without any prior conditions'. There was

> room for local frontier rectifications, agreeable and beneficial for both sides, carried out as a result of mutual agreement. But the British Prime Minister's proposal for the truncation of the territory of Israel means giving a reward to the aggressors. The

Government of Israel will not conduct any negotiation on this basis.[21]

In private talks with American Ambassador Edward Lawson following his Knesset statement, the Israeli Prime Minister pointed to his country's deteriorating security situation and claimed that Eden's speech had 'greatly strengthened Egypt's intransigence'. Ben-Gurion recalled, for Lawson's benefit, an earlier interview with the *Sunday Times* in which he had said that

> if [the] UK wanted Israel to make concessions of its sovereign area then she must send troops to enforce that wish, in which event Israel would fight. That attitude re[garding] Eden's proposal of territorial concessions held good today.[22]

The Prime Minister's remarks aroused the growing fears, in some Israeli circles, that the UK intended to become actively involved in supporting the Arabs during any forthcoming major warfare.[23]

During his trip to the US, Foreign Minister Sharett also attacked the Eden speech. Although it had 'the semblance of impartiality and equal justice' between the 1947 and 1949 lines, Sharett described the speech as being 'in effect logically fallacious, legally incongruous and morally untenable'.

> The apparent equality of sacrifice is a mere fiction. All the Arabs are invited to give up is a part of a claim which they have staked out as a bargaining counter. Israel, on the other hand, is expected to cede ... an area over which its sovereignty extends today with full United Nations sanction as expressed in the official Security Council endorsement of the Armistice Agreements.

Sharett declared it was 'one of the paradoxes of history' that the Arab states 'should now be clamoring for the revival of the 1947 plan – a plan which they did their utmost to kill' and that Great Britain, 'with its record of non-cooperation' in implementing those UN recommendations, should now 'advocate that plan as one of the starting points in the quest for a new solution'. Privately, he told Secretary Dulles that he regarded Eden's speech 'not only as a blunder but as a disaster'.[24]

Sensing some possible discrepancy between US and British policy and wishing to exploit it, Ben-Gurion met with the American

Ambassador, who reported the Israeli Premier incredulous and 'considerably exercised' at British claims that the Guildhall speech had been fully endorsed by Secretary Dulles.[25] The Israeli leader had accurately hit upon a weak spot, since the US attitude to Eden's speech was indeed ambivalent – even to the point of causing some embarrassment to the British government. In response to the British Prime Minister's request for American backing, Secretary Dulles had demurred. While admitting that it was 'probably good to administer some shock treatment to Israelis about territory', Dulles was glad to see *the British* doing the job. The Secretary of State was 'not sure we [Americans] need to repeat it', and wished to 'preserve our most useful role' by refraining from a public endorsement.[26] Although this attitude necessarily left both the British and the Arabs disappointed, within two weeks Dulles would find himself administering his own 'shock treatment', albeit behind closed doors, to Moshe Sharett (below, Chapter X).

During a NSC meeting following his return from Geneva, the Secretary expressed 'some distaste' for Eden's speech, and seemed especially bitter that he had not been consulted about it long enough in advance. Still, he affirmed, 'no significant cleavage between the US and the UK on Near Eastern policy could be permitted'.[27] Faced with Israeli attempts to drive a wedge between America and Britain over the Guildhall speech, Ambassador Nicholls in Tel Aviv underlined the importance of 'disabus[ing] the Israeli Government of their belief that the Jewish vote in the US will be sufficient to protect them from the necessity of ceding territory'.[28] Despite his own personal reservations, Dulles instructed Ambassador Lawson in Tel Aviv to inform Ben-Gurion that the 'US and UK [saw] alike on [the] imperative need for [an] Arab–Israeli settlement even at [the cost of] some substantial sacrifice by Israel', and that the US 'endorse[d] Eden['s] speech insofar as it support[ed his] speech of August 26'.[29]

MAHMUD FAWZI: PRINCIPLES BEHIND THE EGYPTIAN POSITION

After Eden's Guildhall speech, British and American officials were once again faced with the problem of choosing the right moment to promote Alpha's next steps with Egypt and Israel. In the immediate wake of the speech, London and Washington looked for an opening through low-key ambassadorial contacts in Cairo with Mahmud Fawzi and Gamal Abd al-Nasir. Noting that Nasir was 'presently riding high and would be difficult to reach an agreement with', Foreign Secretary Macmillan was prepared to wait, suggesting that '[A]t the end of a few months he may have sobered down and we might at that time go to him with a package deal.'[30]

In the meantime, Henry Byroade was instructed to attempt to extract from Fawzi 'Egyptian ideas with respect to terms of [a] possible settlement' and, more importantly, a commitment to embark upon a Trieste style of negotiation – using the US and UK as go-betweens with Israel.[31] Likewise, Sir Humphrey Trevelyan received detailed instructions from the Foreign Office regarding possible ways to elicit an Egyptian commitment to begin negotiations that would prove useful in making a subsequent approach to the Israelis. London suggested that there was no need 'to set too fast a pace'.[32]

In a talk with Ambassador Byroade in mid-November, Foreign Minister Fawzi confirmed his interest in continuing secret discussions with the US and UK, but again explicitly ruled out direct talks with Israelis. The two men 'shadow-boxed' around Alpha, each reluctant to be the first to make concrete suggestions for a territorial settlement,[33] but a subsequent informal dinner with Dr Fawzi proved to be a more favourable opportunity to 'clear the ground for serious discussions to start'. During that dinner meeting of 16 November, the Egyptian Foreign Minister was reported to have been, unlike in his previous conversations, 'forthright' and 'obviously speaking with [the] authority [of] Nasser'. In clarifying Egypt's attitude to tactics, Fawzi insisted on continuing secret exchanges with the US and UK ambassadors for the time being. The use of a 'Trieste approach or even direct contact' was not ruled out in later stages, but only when Egypt believed there was a '51 percent chance' of success would it take the lead in trying to involve other Arab states.[34]

Dr Fawzi then outlined the general principles behind the Egyptian position on a settlement of the Arab–Israeli dispute so that the Americans and British would have something with which to approach the Israelis. This approach, he insisted, would have to be made tentatively and evasively; it should not involve stating that *Egypt had agreed* to this or that, but rather, the approach should be that, in view of their conversations in Cairo, the *US and UK felt that Egypt might be willing* to consider a settlement 'along [the] lines [of] certain principles'. Except for an apparent (but minor) tactical retreat on Egypt's previous demand for most of the Negev, the outline resembled earlier expositions offered by the Foreign Minister to the two Ambassadors:

- *Jerusalem*: Egypt was willing to follow the UN consensus, whether on internationalization or a split system for protection of the holy places;
- *refugees*: repatriation inside Israel 'to the extent practicable', followed by resettlement elsewhere with compensation;
- *territory*: the principle that 'actual continuity of Arab sovereign territory should be reestablished'; actual size of 'territory to be transferred' (and possible arrangements for Israel's 'peacetime use' of the port of Eilat) to be negotiated at a later stage; and
- *blockade*: if other items could be worked out, there would be an 'end [to the] state of belligerency and [the] legislative and legal positions based on it', i.e., complete freedom of transit through Suez and an end to blacklisting of third countries trading with Israel.

Both American and British Ambassadors considered Fawzi's approach a very positive one, even if it did not contain a commitment to designate an Egyptian negotiator as the Alpha planners had been hoping. Byroade 'strongly recommended' that Washington and London now 'approach Israel upon [the] basis outlined'. Trevelyan endorsed this recommendation, noting that

> [w]e cannot expect the Egyptians to give away anything more at this stage, and, if we press them more now on the details, their position may harden. Nor can we hope to press them at this stage towards more formal and open negotiations.[35]

In London, policy-makers had reason to believe that the calculations behind the Guildhall speech had borne some useful fruit – despite Harold Macmillan's impression that the Egyptian foreign minister was being 'smooth and false'.[36] Evelyn Shuckburgh found it 'quite exciting' that they now had Nasir and Fawzi 'nibbling strongly at "Alpha"', and Macmillan decided to try to persuade John Foster Dulles that this was 'enough of an opening' for a *démarche* to be taken in Tel Aviv. Even though they felt that, 'ideally', the next step ought to have been trying 'to induce the Egyptians to go a little further and commit themselves definitely to negotiations on the basis of an agenda which included an item on the Negev', Foreign Office officials shared Trevelyan's fears of pushing the Egyptians too hard at this point: 'We shall not be able to move them further until we can show them that the Israelis too are ready to move.'[37]

The State Department also regarded Byroade's report as 'encouraging', but wished confirmation that Fawzi was indeed speaking with Nasir's authority before taking further steps. Byroade and Trevelyan met separately with Nasir in late November, and both were able to confirm that Fawzi had indeed been speaking with the Egyptian Prime Minister's authority. Nasir's views on each point were identical to those conveyed by Dr Fawzi, except that the Prime Minister took a firmer line on the refugees' right of return.[38] The time had come for the Americans to turn to the Israelis.

CHAPTER X

Showdown with Sharett

BUILD-UP TO A CONFRONTATION BETWEEN THE US AND ISRAEL

In the aftermath of the Soviet–Egyptian arms deal, the Western powers saw their influence over Middle Eastern leaders and governments decline sharply. With the entry of the Soviet Union as an active player in the region, Egypt seemed to be on the verge of having 'both arms and the [Aswan] dam',[1] the latter either from a Western consortium or from the Soviet Union. In the regional balance of power, the Israelis felt the improvement of Nasir's bargaining position most acutely. Seen from Tel Aviv, Gamal Abd al-Nasir appeared in mid-November to be 'getting everything he wanted'. He was, a senior IMFA official complained, 'getting his arms from the Soviet Union, the High Aswan Dam from the US and now Eden had come along and offered him slices of Israel's territory.'[2] Reflecting the widespread fears of the Israeli public, Acting Foreign Minister Golda Myerson questioned Nasir's motives and sincerity in claiming to desire a settlement. 'His real aim', she affirmed to the US Chargé d'affaires in Tel Aviv, 'was the destruction of Israel, and a settlement which gave him part of the Negev would be nothing more than a first step in the achievement of this aim.' Myerson went on to express her astonishment that the British could support territorial contiguity between Egypt and Jordan, given new evidence that 'Nasser was already trying to subvert Jordan against Great Britain[... A] land link would simply make his task easier.'[3]

Israeli diplomats also countered with a public and private campaign in the US and at the UN focusing on the question of compensation for Arab refugees (thus de-emphasizing the territorial issue), and underlining Israel's need for 'additional arms and a security guarantee ... as bulwarks against aggression in the absence of a peace settlement.'[4] In a private breakfast conversation with an influential friend of John Foster Dulles, Israeli representatives played upon the theme of Soviet–Western rivalry and

> expressed great concern as to whether Israel was not in effect being punished for its attitude of cooperation with the free nations of the western world, whereas Egypt, which was in effect thumbing its nose at the western world by buying arms from Czechoslovakia and in general cooperating with the Russians and with Nehru on a program of neutralism, was in effect being rewarded for its bad conduct.[5]

Only at the end of November, following several weeks of bitter anti-British press commentary, was Ambassador Nicholls able to report that the atmosphere in Israel was 'less highly-charged' and that it might 'shortly be possible to move towards a more realistic study of the elements of a settlement to which the majority of Israelis aspire'.[6] But the Alpha planners chose Washington – where Foreign Minister Moshe Sharett was visiting – rather than Tel Aviv, for the next step in unfolding their operation. When Sharett requested an appointment for a courtesy call at the State Department, Secretary Dulles began preparing for a crucial showdown, informing British Ambassador Makins that he proposed to tell the Israeli Foreign Minister

- 'that the Israel Government must accept the proposals of the Secretary's August 26th speech more unequivocally than it has';
- 'with respect to territory, it must do more than make a few minor mutual adjustments[;] it must relinquish a section of the Negev to the Arabs to make possible a land connection between Egypt and the rest of the Arab world'; and
- 'the Israel Government must undertake to keep the situation in the area calm. It must not take advantage of little incidents to launch reprisal riots [sic].'

Dulles also planned to reaffirm that there was 'no material difference' between the American and British positions on a settlement, and that 'Israel "must put something more in the pot" to make a settlement possible.' Makins reported to London that the Secretary expected that

> the Israel Foreign Minister would not like what he would hear.... It was, however, very necessary. The Israelis could not expect us to support them in a position which would not only be suicidal for themselves, but threatened to be suicidal for us if we supported them in it.[7]

DULLES' 'BOMBSHELL SURPRISE',[8] 21 NOVEMBER 1955

On the very day of his fateful interview with Secretary Dulles, Foreign Minister Sharett delivered an address to the National Press Club in which he repeated his country's objections to the logic of Eden's speech suggesting 'some golden mean' between the 1947 and 1949 lines. 'It has been said before, but it bears repeating: peace with Israel means peace with Israel as it is, both as to its population and to its area.'[9] The Dulles–Sharett meeting later that day exploded into far more than the courtesy call which the Israeli Foreign Minister had intended. It was, in many ways, the 'day of reckoning' foreseen by the Alpha planners since their first joint meetings in early 1955.

John Foster Dulles began by presenting the Israeli leader with a prepared *aide-mémoire*[10] and bluntly lectured him about the need for Israel 'to make some concession in the Negev which would make possible an area of contact between Egypt and the other Arab states.' The actual area to be conceded for this purpose, he continued, 'would not necessarily be large nor of great value'.[11] In any event, the 'compensation to Israel from effecting a settlement', Dulles argued, 'would outweigh any loss of territory.' While appreciating that Israel should not have to offer concessions in advance of negotiation, the US needed to know that there was 'flexibility' in order to be 'in a position to push things along'.[12]

The ensuing discussion was reported, in diplomatic parlance, as being 'somewhat heated'. Sharett protested about the unfairness of the demand for Egyptian–Jordanian contiguity through an Israeli cession of part of the Negev. There was, he argued,

> nothing vital in that contiguity. There are no roads that go through that part of the country, no railroads, and no traffic.

> ... It is only a national[ist] slogan and for that Israel is expected to cut itself in two.

Sharett did not believe Israel was 'capable of making the concession that the Secretary [had] asked'. He recalled Israel's offers 'to provide communication facilities for the Arabs across Israel[i] territory, following a settlement'. But 'giving up its sovereignty over present Israel territory to meet a whim of Nasir's [was] another matter'.

Francis Russell regarded Sharett's arguments as 'legalistic', and Secretary Dulles remained firm. '[W]e are not talking about a whim', he replied. 'We are talking about the continued existence of Israel.' The Secretary alluded to the 'great stakes' which the West had in the Middle East, and put the Israelis on the spot. The US believed that, despite the risks involved, there was a chance for a settlement – 'whether 50–50 or 1 in 10, no one could say.'

> It cannot, however, be explored without knowing what Israel's position is going to be. If Israel says no then the possibility of a settlement is off and we shall all have to face the consequences.... [A]ny further attempt towards a settlement has to be based on our knowledge that Israel will cooperate.

If 'no' was to be the last word, the Secretary continued, then Israel would be 'putting us all in great peril'. No less than the very 'safety and continued existence of the free world' were at risk, and Dulles spoke ominously of the 'grave choice' which Americans would face about continuing to support an unco-operative Israel. The US had 'to know whether there [was] flexibility in Israel's immediate answer'. The Secretary hoped that Sharett would not give him a negative answer: 'The consequences to everyone concerned', he warned, 'would be most serious.'

Sharett expressed doubts that signs of Israeli flexibility on this issue would be reciprocated by the Egyptians, and invoked the experience of the 1939 White Paper to challenge the Secretary's methods of appeasement in attempting to win Arab support for the Western democracies.[13] If it were a question 'of give and take, of exchanging territory on a small scale on the principle of mutuality, it could be discussed.' But Israel 'could not give up vital points, such as E[i]lat, nor could it agree to something that would result in cutting Israel in two.' The Foreign Minister agreed to Dulles' request for a written reply within the next few days, leaving the Secretary under the 'impression ... that he had made a dent and that it was just possible that the response would provide something to build on.'

The next day Reuven Shiloah called at the State Department to seek clarifications. Shiloah, then serving as a counsellor at the Israeli Embassy in Washington, was a close confidant of both Sharett and Ben-Gurion and also one of the founding fathers of the Mossad, Israel's highly-regarded intelligence service. Russell disclosed to him that 'Egypt had claimed all of the Negev south of Beersheba.' In what turned out to be the last time the Americans would mislead the Israelis on this issue, Dulles' senior Alpha adviser said that the US itself 'had no lines on the map to present. This would have to be worked out by the parties themselves.' Russell did, however, reveal to Shiloah that the various possibilities under consideration were 'cession of a portion of the Negev, a corridor across the Negev under Egyptian sovereignty but with Israeli transit rights, or a cession by Israel of two triangular territories with underpasses at their apexes.'

The Israeli representative replied that these clarifications represented an important novelty for Foreign Minister Sharett, who had been under the impression that corridors for free transit between Egypt and Jordan might have been sufficient. Under the impact of Russell's disclosures, Shiloah was unable to stick to his limited information-gathering mission, and was soon drawn into disputing the wisdom and fairness of the basic American backing for Egypt's claims. The Israeli diplomat drew a parallel with the dismemberment of Czechoslovakia at Munich in 1938, and pointed to the historical irony that it had been the same John Foster Dulles of the US mission to the UN General Assembly who had fought to block the adoption of the late-1948 Bernadotte plan, which would have ceded the Negev to the Arabs.[14]

On the same day that Dulles was administering his 'bombshell surprise' to Moshe Sharett in Washington, Ambassador Jack Nicholls in Tel Aviv wrote a four-page despatch explaining to London the Israeli feelings which lay behind the 'clear and categorical' rejection of the territorial compromise suggested in Eden's Guildhall speech. After outlining some of the Israelis' 'deeply-held convictions' (which, Nicholls stressed, were 'not put forward as debating points'), the Ambassador offered some 'pointers to what should be done and what should not be done as regards Israel in the next few weeks.' Nicholls, who was not generally known for his sympathy towards Israelis, put forth recommendations which nevertheless showed a sensitive understanding of their position:

- The need to convince the Israelis that some Arab leaders 'really are prepared at last to admit that Israel is here to stay and that some kind of settlement must be made' – but without seeming to take Arab assurances 'at their face value, which would merely strengthen [Israeli] suspicions of gullibility, wishful thinking or sinister designs on our part.'
- The need to convince the Israelis 'that we are aiming at a *reasonable* [he underlined] settlement – that is, one which will not make intolerable demands upon them – and that it is not our intention to use pressure or force to impose a solution designed not so much to solve the Arab–Israel problem as to improve Western relations with the Arab States at Israel's expense.'
- A call to do more, through statements and practical friendly gestures, to show both Israel and the Arab states 'that we regard Israel as a permanent feature of the Middle East and not as a tiresome temporary phenomenon.'
- The need to intimate, 'through discreet channels', that 'no major concessions by Israel are contemplated'[15] and that 'our immediate object is to hook Nasser and get him used to the idea of peace talks.'
- The need to get Nasir 'to show certain tangible signs of goodwill, which we could repeat to the Israelis as *prima facie* evidence that he is in earnest over the possibility of negotiation.'[16]

NOT ANOTHER MUNICH: ISRAEL SETS OUT ITS POSITION

While Nicholls' advice was duly noted – but not endorsed or actively followed up – in London, the real focus of activity continued to be American–Israeli contacts in Washington. On 1 December 1955, Francis Russell was notified that an official Israeli response was not yet ready, but that when it came it would be 'in the negative', based on the argument that Anglo–American suggestions for Israeli concessions in the Negev were 'a Munich type of appeasement in the free world's effort to deal with the Soviet menace in the Middle East'.[17] The next day, Eban and Shiloah met with State Department officials and cast doubts on current American optimism regarding Arab intentions and the chances of a peace settlement. In reply to

Francis Russell's urging that Israel test Arab intentions by making 'a serious offer', Eban declared that there was 'a limit to what Israel could do' and expressed the hope that 'the US had not, like Eden, hinted to the Arabs, even in private, that Israel should give up territory'. The Israeli Ambassador again invoked the Munich analogy in rejecting any thought of Israel making territorial concessions, and provided a preview of the reply which Sharett would be bringing to Washington – 'the furthest limits of what Israel could do'.[18]

On 6 December, the Israeli Embassy in Washington provided the State Department with an *aide-mémoire* outlining Israel's approach to a settlement of the conflict with the Arab states (Document 10). The text of the official statement had been worked out in close consultation with IMFA officials and with Prime Minister Ben-Gurion in Jerusalem.[19] In outlining 'its confidential views on the contribution which Israel might make in the context of a peace settlement', the Israeli government made it clear from the outset that 'Israel sees no reason for ceding any of its territory to any of the neighboring Arab States, and cannot see its way to discussing a settlement on such a prejudicial basis.'

The 'general outline of a settlement' proposed by Israel consisted of five paragraphs, the first three of which contained uncompromising clarity in precisely those areas where the Alpha planners had been hoping to find constructive ambiguity. Israel's conditions for peace were presented in careful and cleverly positive diplomatic phrases, stressing Israel's 'readiness' and 'willingness' to:

- meet Egyptian representatives – 'it being clearly understood that the basis for such a meeting would not include the cession of any part of Israel territory to a neighboring state';
- discuss mutual frontier adjustments 'for the benefit of both parties, on the understanding that the integrity and continuity of Israel's territory is not impaired';
- 'contribute substantially to the opening of freer communications between all States of the Near East', including port facilities for Jordan at Haifa and transit arrangements between Egypt and Jordan through Israel – 'it being clearly understood that Israel will not cede territory, whether populated or unpopulated, in the Negev';
- embark upon Dulles' proposals of 26 August for refugee compensation, 'subject to certain reservations';

- co-operate in the Johnston plan for sharing the waters of the Jordan and Yarmuk Rivers.

Pointing to a 'corresponding contribution' which should be forthcoming from the Arab states, Israel expected the latter to be offering freedom for Israeli traffic, access to the Wailing Wall and Mount Scopus in Jordanian-held Jerusalem, and a cessation of the blockade and boycott.

At his one-and-a-half-hour meeting with Dulles on 6 December, Sharett repeated Israel's scepticism regarding a recent surge of optimistic analyses from journalists and political observers in Cairo and in Washington. He also disputed British and American presumptions that it was 'inevitable for Israel to make territorial concessions to Egypt and possibly to others'. Such pressure from the Western powers seemed, to Sharett, to be 'nothing less than a premium [for Nasir] upon doing business with the Kremlin'. Once again, the Israeli leader invoked the 'ghost of Munich'. What Nasir wanted, Sharett warned

> would be ultimately at the expense of Israel's security and ultimate survival. He [was] creating the impression of willingness to talk settlement in order to get the Aswan loan and also to gain time to absorb his new arms and achieve military confidence.[20]

Following the lines of his government's *aide-mémoire*, Sharett emphasized to the Secretary that there was 'no question of Israel agreeing to cede territory'. Even though Israel preferred to approach a settlement through direct negotiation, it was 'not opposed in principle to mediation', as demonstrated in its co-operation with Ambassador Johnston and even as recently suggested in the Guildhall speech. However, Anthony Eden had disqualified himself, since 'a mediator should not take up a position on a question such as the Negev in advance'. Wishing to be 'constructive as well as critical', however, the Israeli Foreign Minister hoped the Arabs would finally agree to the Jordan Valley scheme. Sharett concluded by recalling Nasir's pledges to try to persuade reluctant Arab leaders to co-operate with the Johnston plan and suggested the US wait several months for results which would be a test of Nasir's sincerity.[21]

In his reply, Dulles challenged many of the points raised in Sharett's presentation and expressed his disappointment that the

Israeli *aide-mémoire* did not appear, at first glance, to be 'adequately responsive' to his requests of 21 November. The Secretary of State hoped that Sharett could see the possibility of revising the Negev boundaries without entailing the 'dismemberment of Israel', and yet going beyond a simple right of transit for Egypt. The meeting ended inconclusively, with Sharett asking for some indication of the US answer to Israel's request for arms. On Dulles' suggestion, Russell met afterwards with Shiloah to discuss specific suggestions – including intersecting 'triangles' – for revising the Negev frontier.[22]

Dulles reported the results of his talk with the Israeli Foreign Minister orally to British Ambassador Makins and in writing to Henry Byroade in Cairo. Despite Sharett's explicit rejection of the idea of conceding parts of the Negev, the Secretary focused on the Israeli formulation, 'mutual adjustments', and was left feeling 'that there might be some give in the Israeli position'. Harold Macmillan expressed his admiration for the way in which Dulles had handled Moshe Sharett; he was pleased that the Israelis had 'not been able to bully the State Department as much as they had hoped'.[23] Gratified by what it called Secretary Dulles' 'courageous stand' and 'plain speaking' to Sharett, the British Foreign Office recommended accepting Ambassador Nicholls' advice to 'proceed rather gently with [the Israelis] for the time being'.[24]

A NEW ISRAELI 'PEACE OFFENSIVE'?

Within two weeks the Israeli Embassy in Washington undertook an initiative which attempted to make a virtue out of necessity. It informed 'a group of favoured correspondents' of the contents of the *aide-mémoire* which it had recently submitted to the State Department (Document 10). Subsequently, the press was full of reports about a seven-point 'peace plan' – not a new Israeli policy, but rather the 'pulling together [of] offers of concessions made from time to time in the last three years'.[25] In Israel, the IMFA added to the mystery by declining to comment on the peace plan.[26] While *The Times* of London recognized that the proposals were not new in themselves, what was considered new was 'their formulation as a basis for peace negotiations' at this time.[27] On 22 December, a 63-page booklet, entitled *Peace in the Middle East: A Record of Israel's Peace Offers to Arab States*, was published by the Government Printer in Jerusalem.[28]

In London, the Foreign Office, which was late in receiving information about the Israeli *aide-mémoire* to the State Department, was anything but impressed by the Israeli peace offensive being carried out through the press. Not only was there 'nothing new in the Israeli "plan"', commented G.G. Arthur, there was 'no sign of "compromise": indeed the rejection of refugee repatriation ... [was] blunter than usual.'

> The Israelis know quite well [he continued] that the Arabs will not look at their 'plan,' and the object in putting it forward now is presumably to impress the world with Israeli reasonableness, to offset the proceedings of the Security Council over the Galilee reprisal raid [see below, Chapter XI], and to undermine US attempts to get negotiations going on a basis of territorial compromise.[29]

State Department spokesmen, according to the British Embassy in Washington, were commenting that the Israel peace initiative did not 'represent any advance on previous positions' and confirmed that the document had not been 'presented as a body of proposals intended for submission to the Arabs'.[30]

When Moshe Sharett subsequently referred to these proposals during the course of a major Knesset debate,[31] international comment focused briefly on a 'Sharett peace plan'. Both CIA agent Wilbur Eveland and researcher Mordechai Bar-On have interpreted the widely publicized Israeli peace initiative as partly a preparation for the expected contacts with Egypt through US mediator, Robert Anderson,[32] but, from a reading of the available archival documents, it seems more accurate to conclude that the true purpose of the whole exercise – which was shortly abandoned and forgotten – was a tactical one: namely, 'to present Israel in a favourable light' before the Western powers and to deflect Operation Alpha's pressure for Israeli territorial concessions.[33]

FINESSING US–ISRAELI DIFFERENCES

Following a debriefing session with his advisers, John Foster Dulles consulted the British about his next step in the quest for Israel's co-operation. The American Secretary of State suggested that Reuven Shiloah be informed of the basic ingredients of the Alpha settlement.[34] The Foreign Office raised no objections to disclosing some details of Alpha to Shiloah (especially as he was also a close confidant to Sharett), but advised Russell (a) to make clear that the 'triangles' idea was merely one of several possible ways of reconciling incompatible Egyptian and Israeli claims, and (b) to avoid any mention of British participation in the formulation of the proposals. Both steps, the FO hoped, would minimize the chance of antagonizing the Israelis 'in their present mood' by seeming to present them with a forced or 'prejudged plan'. All that was needed, London reminded the State Department, was an 'Israeli admission that the problem of the Negev may form a part of negotiations for a settlement, and that the Egyptians may be informed accordingly'.[35]

Thus, on 8 December, Francis Russell took another decisive step in the unfolding of Operation Alpha by making Reuven Shiloah the first Israeli (or Arab) to be given a full outline of the Alpha proposals on refugees, Jerusalem, the boycott, terminating the state of belligerency, communications agreements, Jordan Valley waters, border adjustments and territorial guarantees. The proposals, Russell claimed, had evolved as a result of 'intensive consideration' (Russell omitted to mention among which parties) since the spring of 1955.[36] This was an important moment for the Israelis and for Shiloah, whose biographer commented:

> The year 1955 was the year of Israel's deceit by the Americans. Indeed, Shiloah incessantly spoke in his letters of the 'State Department foxes', but now it became clear that Dulles himself stood at the head of those foxes, together with his special assistant on this subject, Francis Russell.[37]

Although he did not wish to 'negotiate' at this time on any of the items, Shiloah commented briefly on the overall fairness of the proposals – with the exception of the Negev. This gave Russell an opportunity to reiterate the State Department's view that a settlement might

> stand or fall over [the] Negev. It should be possible [to] reconcile [the] opposing views of Israel and Egypt without impairing [the] vital interests of either. [The m]ajor question was whether Israel would agree that [the] Negev problem [was] negotiable. [It w]ould be [a] great tragedy if either side stated it [was] not prepared even [to] negotiate on [the] subject.

Drawing upon the results of months of secret American and British conversations with Fawzi and Nasir, Russell was able to state with some authority that the US was 'convinced that if [a] settlement is to be reached it must be worked out with Egypt[,] and Egypt would not consider [a] settlement unless some arrangements [were] made regarding [the] Negev.' Shiloah promised to convey the American position to Sharett, whose visit to North America was nearing its end.

Two days later Reuven Shiloah returned with Sharett's interim reply, pending the Foreign Minister's return to Israel and a full Cabinet discussion. Israel's position on the Negev, he reported, had already been defined during Sharett's 6 December meeting with Secretary Dulles. But Shiloah was authorized to state that Israel was

> ready to enter [into] negotiations without conditions even if it [knew] that the question of the Negev [would] be raised. There [was] nothing tabu on bringing up any issue. However, as now formulated [the State] Dep[artmen]t's proposal on [the] Negev amount[ed] to a precondition.... [The] US should not deceive Egypt into thinking Israel will enter negotiations morally bound to do something regarding [the] Negev.[38]

The State Department pounced upon this formulation as representing enough of an opening to proceed with preparations for negotiation. In Russell's estimation, there was 'sufficient flexibility in the Israel position to warrant pursuing our efforts further at this time'. During the next three weeks, he believed, an attempt should be made for a first meeting between Egyptian and Israeli representatives.[39] In London, a Foreign Office official agreed, finding Sharett's response 'rather more forthcoming that we had expected', and hoping that the Israeli Cabinet would confirm it, thus allowing the Alpha planners 'just enough to enable us to make another approach to the Egyptians'.[40] Only Evelyn Shuckburgh dissented from the hopeful reactions to Sharett's message:

> I do not feel very optimistic about this, coming as it does at the moment of another major Israeli raid [on Lake Kinneret; below, Chapter XI]. I suspect that Ben-Gurion's idea is to keep the Americans in play while he does his best to provoke the Arabs into action which will make a settlement impossible.[41]

Before leaving the United States, Foreign Minister Sharett addressed three crucial issues in a farewell letter to Secretary Dulles. First, he provided a further detailed exposition of the reasons why Israel was 'deeply disturbed' by the State Department's advocacy of creating a land link between Egypt and Jordan through the Negev. He noted that Israel's apprehensions had not been allayed by Russell's explanations of the 'triangles' proposal. Eilat 'would be left hanging at the end of a slender thread, which the Egyptians and the Jordanians would be in a position to snap at any moment from [the] scissor-like position which they would acquire.' Second, despite Israel's willingness to resolve the refugee problem, the Foreign Minister had to 'say in all frankness that [he could not] envisage how an Israel Government ... c[ould] undertake to settle tens of thousands of Arab families in Israel.' And finally, Sharett raised the issue which would soon overshadow and reshape American–Israeli relations: the Foreign Minister was most anxious to receive an affirmative answer to Israel's request to purchase American arms (cf. below, Chapter XI).[42]

The latest tug of war between the US and Israel over the need for the latter to make an advance gesture – this time, on cession of territory in the Negev – remained unresolved for weeks after Sharett's visit. Although the most serious confrontations remained hidden from public view, the American press did report on the Dulles–Sharett encounter of 6 December, stressing the State Department's insistence on greater Israeli flexibility.[43] Behind the scenes, however, the US and Israeli positions remained seriously deadlocked. Israeli representatives lobbied Arthur Dean, an influential friend of the Secretary, in an attempt to convince Dulles to abandon altogether the State Department's call for Israel to give up territory to Egypt.[44] During mid-December meetings in Washington, Russell and Dulles repeatedly made clear their view that without an Israeli concession on the Negev there could be no negotiation with Egypt, while Shiloah and Eban were under orders to reject categorically any idea of Negev triangles.[45]

BETWEEN OPTIMISM AND PESSIMISM

While Dulles, Russell, Sharett and Shiloah were engaged in their Alpha discussions in Washington, British Foreign Secretary Harold Macmillan returned from a visit to Iraq to inaugurate the Baghdad Pact, sounding optimistic for the first time in many months.

> I think there really is a chance now of making some progress towards a settlement. I was impressed by the general Arab view ... in favour of a settlement of some kind.... I believe that they are now ready to accept the fact that they will have to live with an Israel[i] state.

As a result of the Guildhall speech, the Foreign Office felt it had achieved 'an important advance' in that the 'idea of a settlement of some kind [was] gaining currency with the Arabs though their terms [were] still often unrealistic.'[46] The atmosphere in early December was, according to the Foreign Office, 'now more propitious than it has ever been.'[47]

In Cairo, too, the feeling was that 'the iron was now red hot' for peace moves. At the United Nations in New York, a senior Egyptian Foreign Ministry official rejected direct talks with Israel but announced that his country was ready for 'mediation'.[48] Parallel to the State Department's Alpha, an operation code-named 'Chameleon' was reactivated by the CIA during November and December. The plan was to arrange a top-secret meeting between Colonel Nasir and Prime Minister Ben-Gurion, using Ambassador Eric Johnston (with his Jordan waters mission as a 'cover') as mediator.[49]

The increasing prominence of the 'crypto-diplomacy' of CIA officials at this time reflected the declining effectiveness of normal American diplomatic channels, both in Tel Aviv and in Cairo. Some have suggested that John Foster Dulles' disappointment in Byroade's inability to block Nasir's turn to the Soviets led to the Secretary's increasing reliance, from September 1955, on Kermit Roosevelt's Cairo channels.[50] Others have been blunt in their criticism of Henry Byroade's personal weakness for the bottle and his rumoured skirt-chasing, making him largely ineffective in the performance of his professional duties.[51] Some analysts have seen CIA involvement as having been necessary and beneficial, given contemporary Egyptian and Israeli leaders' feelings of greater trust in CIA rather than USSD personnel.[52] Others have been more critical, pointing to the drawbacks and confusions of reliance on these parallel covert channels of communication for delicate questions of peacemaking.[53] Some officials inside the State Department were worried that CIA intelligence activities in the area were getting out of control and becoming 'unrealistic' under the Dulles brothers.[54] In any case, CIA involvement in Middle Eastern peacemaking efforts grew during late 1955 and would subsequently reach its peak in the planning of Operation 'Gamma' (below, Chapters XII–XIII).

During mid-December conversations with Ted Streibert, director of the US Information Agency, Ben-Gurion – still doubting Nasir's motives, and insisting that Israelis were 'deadly afraid' – left his American interlocutors feeling optimistic. The 'not an inch of territory' attitude was replaced by talk of 'mutual minor border adjustments' and 'give and take'. The Israeli Prime Minister, wishing to test Streibert's eloquently stated belief that Nasir truly wanted a settlement, offered to proceed towards a 'peace in stages' with Egypt, beginning with an experimental, unpublicized ceasefire. If it held, it could be followed by mediation, ending eventually with direct talks between Egyptian and Israeli representatives. The State Department, however, not wishing to complicate ongoing discussions with Shiloah (representing Sharett) in Washington, did not take up the invitation to transmit Ben-Gurion's offer to Nasir at this time.[55]

By late December, the British Ambassador in Tel Aviv expressed his view that the Israelis were 'moving steadily towards the idea of a bargain under which they would make territorial concessions somewhere in return for control of the Gaza Strip'.[56] Indeed, the mid-1949 notion that an Egyptian–Israeli settlement might be built around the transfer of Gaza and its Palestinian population to Israeli rule was revived and briefly became one of the few bright spots in the wishful-thinking complex of Alpha planners.[57] At the same time, British journalist and MP Richard Crossman, who was considered both a long-time 'friend of Israel' and a confidant of Nasir, transmitted a message from Cairo to Jerusalem about the Egyptian leader's continued desire for peace and his willingness to engage in secret negotiations, on the Trieste model, based on Eden's Guildhall speech.[58]

This apparent build-up of favourable signals for peace was however, counterbalanced by a series of pessimistic indicators. At a press conference on 28 November, Gamal Abd al-Nasir evaded questions regarding his endorsement of Eden's Guildhall speech, claiming that it did not really contain any specific 'proposals' which required a response. The Egyptian Prime Minister was equally evasive on the subject of Deputy Foreign Minister Khairat Sa'id's reported remarks in New York welcoming mediation, noting that the 'matter did not require negotiation so much as implementation of United Nations resolutions'. Nasir also reaffirmed Egypt's support for the Palestinian cause, and repeated that it was Egyptian policy that the 'Palestine problem concern[ed] all the Arab States and no Arab State ha[d] the right to deal with it alone'. Following Nasir's lead, the Cairo press took a harsher line, criticizing Sir Anthony Eden for asking Arabs to compromise on issues over which there was nothing to compromise.[59]

By mid-December, Ambassador Nicholls in Tel Aviv alerted the Foreign Office to a serious discrepancy which he noticed between Ambassador Trevelyan's reports that Nasir's 'intentions [were] on the whole pacific and that it [was] more likely than not that he would accept a lasting settlement with Israel', on the one hand, and the monthly reports of the British Military Attaché in Cairo, who had written: 'of Egypt's ultimate aggressive intentions there can be little doubt', on the other.[60] From Cairo, Sir Humphrey Trevelyan answered that understandably aggressive attitudes within the army did not necessarily prove that Nasir was 'guilty of bad faith in his professions of willingness to attempt a negotiated settlement'. The British Ambassador believed that

> the dominant motive for the arms purchases was probably, as Nasser said, the incorrect reports that the Israelis could easily beat all the Arab forces together and perhaps also his desire to negotiate from strength.[61]

During November and December, Acting Foreign Minister Golda Myerson indicated both publicly and privately that there was no change in Israel's opposition to major border adjustments or a large-scale return of Arab refugees. During a fund-raising speech in New York City, Myerson heaped scorn on Israel's 'good friends' who were trying to convince her that Nasir, once

> strengthened with MIGs and British Centurion tanks, and the Soviet Stalin tanks, [would find] his heart ... filled with peace and good will to men and women of Israel[;] but in order to serve this peace to Nasser in a very palatable manner, it must be served on a platter of the Negev.

Mocking those same friends who reassured Israel that it was not being asked to give up the whole of the Negev, Myerson continued:

> Poor Nasser! Only a hundred yards of sand he must have in order to make him and especially the people of Egypt happy

and prosperous.... [T]he government and people of Israel have said it in no uncertain terms: Not one grain of sand – not one.... [N]o fancy plans of cutting up the Negev will mean anything to the State of Israel.[62]

Meanwhile, in London, a letter to *The Times* by Israel's Ambassador scandalized Prime Minister Eden with the harshness of its criticism of the Guildhall speech, and led briefly to thoughts of demanding Eliahu Elath's recall by Tel Aviv.[63] By mid-December, long-simmering, but privately expressed, accusations that Britain had its own selfish designs for establishing strategic control of the Negev erupted into front-page press attacks on British motives, causing strains in Anglo–Israeli relations and further undermining Britain's potential role as mediator for Operation Alpha.[64]

Thus, by late 1955, the chances of starting up secret Egyptian–Israeli peace talks in pursuit of Operation Alpha were far from good. The Americans had taken the difficult step of factoring in the Israelis, but serious obstacles still remained. The British still wondered whether the latest Israeli stance – the hard-won fruit of Dulles' toughness – was 'sufficient to justify another approach to the Egyptians'.[65] Against the backdrop of an escalation of threats of war in the Middle East, progress on Alpha was now inextricably linked with the arms race in the region. As we shall see below, Israel would not agree to negotiate without the promise of American arms, while the already-slim chances of Egypt entering into peace talks would be immediately scuttled by any news of a favourable US response to Israel's requests.

CHAPTER XI

Arms and Alpha: The Israeli Connection

HESITATIONS REGARDING ISRAEL'S ARMS REQUESTS

As the year 1955 came to a close, Operation Alpha was once again in a state of uncertainty. In Washington, Francis Russell was concerned that the Israelis

> regarded the present time as very unfavourable from their point of view for negotiating a settlement and might be unable to resist the temptation deliberately to sabotage the whole operation by revealing the Egyptian position and forcing Nasser to disavow it.

These developments, Russell believed, required a quickening of the steps in Operation Alpha.

> It might be best to concentrate, for the time being, on getting Nasser to cover the not very great distance between his present position and what we regard as a basis for a settlement, and then put the maximum pressure on Israel to accept it.[1]

The Americans also feared that Britain's continuing interest in strengthening and expanding the Baghdad Pact might not only annoy the Russians but might also further antagonize Colonel Nasir.[2]

Perhaps the most delicate question affecting the progress of Operation Alpha at this crucial juncture was the American attitude to Israel's repeated requests for arms. The latest request, which had been submitted in the wake of the Soviet–Egyptian arms deal, remained 'under consideration' even during and after the strenuous campaign for a speedy and positive reply that coincided with Foreign Minister Sharett's visit to the United States. Israel's *aide-mémoire* of 6 December, after answering Secretary Dulles' request for an outline of Israel's attitude to a settlement (above, Chapter X), concluded by reminding the US government of the 'prejudicial effects of the increasing preponderance of the Arab States, and especially of Egypt, in armed strength' and by renewing Israel's request for adequate arms 'to reduce this perilous disparity'.[3] On the eve of his departure from the US, Sharett wrote to the Secretary indicating that 'the main preoccupation weighing on [his] mind' was the 'growing weakness and vulnerability' of his country, which was caused by a continuing flow of Soviet arms into Egypt 'while no corresponding increase in defensive strength has yet been made available to Israel'.[4] At the same time, Israel was also stepping up its efforts to acquire Mystère IV-A aircraft from France.[5]

The Israeli arms request, and increasing Arab pressure on the US government to cut back its support for Israel, created a delicate tactical situation in which taking any further steps to advance Operation Alpha would be most difficult.[6] Francis Russell feared that an affirmative American reply to Israel's request would likely spoil what he called 'the present atmosphere among the Arabs', especially since Israeli security fears were being increasingly played up in the American press. Russell recommended further delaying the long-awaited reply to Israel's arms requests, and speculated on ways in which the eventual announcement might be made so as 'to limit the impact on the Arab states'.[7]

LAKE KINNERET RAID

On the night of 11–12 December 1955, Israeli forces attacked Syrian positions on Lake Kinneret (also known as Lake Tiberias, or the Sea of Galilee) ostensibly in retaliation for Syrian gunners firing on Israeli fishing vessels. The attack, labelled by one scholar as 'one of the most daring and brilliant raids ever carried out by the IDF', caused at least 49 Syrian and six Israeli deaths and appeared to US and UN officials (and even to some highly placed Israelis) as grossly out of proportion to the provocation.[8] The widespread impression that the raid had been carefully pre-planned was indeed correct.

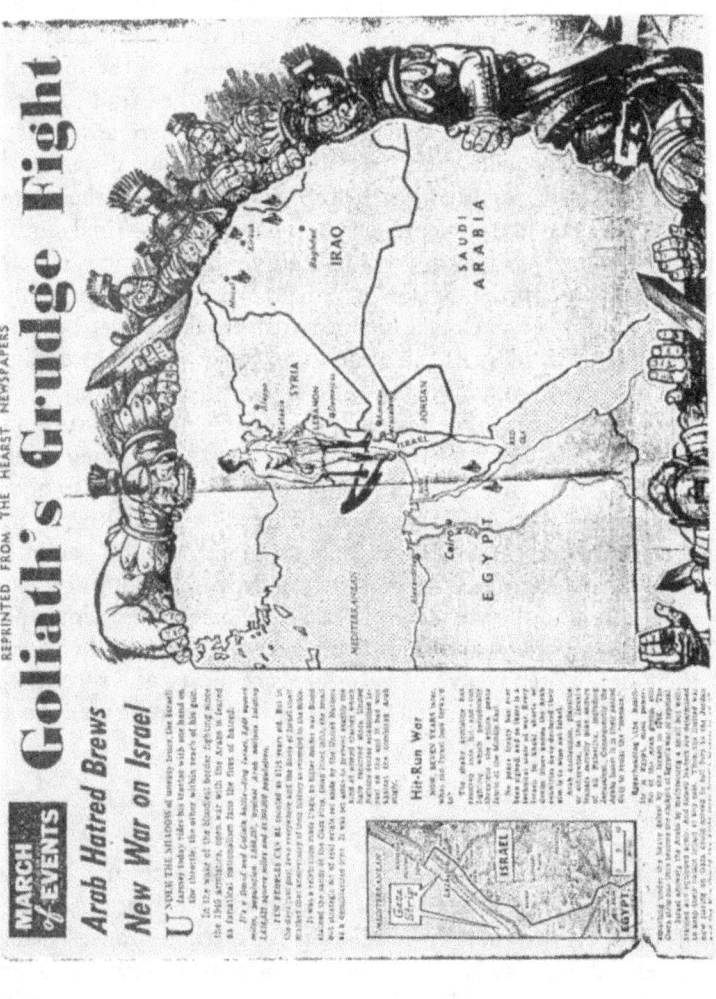

Cartoon and text: 'March of Events: Goliath's Grudge Fight', reprinted from the Hearst Newspapers, [1955]

Mordechai Bar-On's study of archival sources shows that 'Operation Kinneret' (also known as 'Operation Olive Leaves') was another in the series of IDF attempts to provoke Nasir, who had recently concluded a bilateral defence treaty with Syria, into launching an all-out war. Inside the IDF hierarchy, some saw authorization for the raid as a 'compensation' to a disappointed Chief of Staff following cancellation of a daring operation to seize the Straits of Tiran.[9]

Syrian complaints to the UN Security Council opened a series of debates on draft resolutions throughout December and January, leaving Ambassador Eban 'as golden-tongued as ever, but heavy-hearted as never before'.[10] Acting in solidarity with his new Syrian allies, Prime Minister Nasir wrote to UN Secretary-General Dag Hammarskjöld, providing a selected list of Israeli attacks since the 28 February Gaza raid, and warning of the limits of Egyptian patience. The Cairo press played up Nasir's letter as an indication that Egypt was ready to use force if the UN and the Western powers were not capable of restraining Israel. This threat was met by renewed rumours of Israeli preparations for a 'preventive war'.[11]

Unaware of the precise IDF tactic of using such 'retaliations' to provoke Gamal Abd al-Nasir into a massive military campaign, policy-makers in both Washington and London proceeded to speculate on the possible political motives behind the Israeli reprisal. The State Department listed various possibilities, including: 'a desire to counter the view that this is a propitious time for a peace settlement', a show of strength by Israel's 'activists' and the IDF, and a wish to test the new Egyptian–Syrian military alliance.[12] UNTSO chief, General Burns, was not alone in surmising that the 'message' of the raid along the eastern shore of Lake Tiberias was intended more for Cairo than Damascus.[13]

British Foreign Office analyses concentrated on the impact of Israel's military operation on Alpha efforts towards a settlement. 'When the Israelis undertake a large raid against their neighbours', noted Evelyn Shuckburgh, 'it is usually to relieve them from some sort of pressure.' And, he went on, during the preceding six weeks Israel had certainly not been under any serious *military* pressure from its neighbours. The only pressure it had been subjected to had been British and American 'pressure to make territorial compromises with a view to a settlement'. Given Israeli fears of having an intolerable solution imposed on them, the Lake Tiberias raid was seen in the Foreign Office as a carefully orchestrated manoeuvre designed to 'induce Nasser to make some foolish move in aid of his ally Syria' and, generally, 'to provoke the Arabs into action which will make a settlement impossible'.[14] Shuckburgh appears to have been at least half right in his analysis.

In addition to causing such international speculation, Operation Kinneret also left its mark on Israeli domestic politics and foreign policy. The raid had been decided by David Ben-Gurion, acting in his dual capacity of Prime Minister and Minister of Defence, without Cabinet consultation.[15] Following a storm of protest among the various coalition partners, a Cabinet decision demanded that, in future, all reprisal operations be submitted for approval.[16] In response to Abba Eban's privately expressed criticism of the raid's planners for their lack of concern about international repercussions, Ben-Gurion wrote personally to the Ambassador, justifying the need for, and the timing of, the reprisal. While acknowledging the damage done to Israel's international image, the Prime Minister regretted that the killing of Israeli citizens two or three times a week did not attract the same world attention or indignation as the raid had done.[17] The Kinneret raid also rekindled the wider internal debates among Israelis about the alleged interference of IDF officers in setting political priorities, and on the wisdom and effectiveness of the policy of reprisals.[18] Although confident and unapologetic before Israeli and world opinion, Ben-Gurion reportedly confided to one of his commanders that the operation might have been 'excessive' and 'too successful'.[19]

The timing of the Lake Kinneret raid – the eve of Moshe Sharett's return from the US – seriously compromised the Foreign Minister's personal credibility with John Foster Dulles and his role as the leading spokesman for a 'moderate' approach to Arab–Israeli relations. Sharett and Eban both complained bitterly, at the time, that the raid had the effect of undermining Israel's quest for American arms, which they believed was on the verge of receiving a positive response. Eban reported Assistant Secretary George Allen as saying that the US was unable to reach a decision on arms for Israel for a number of reasons, 'prominent among them being the recent incident on the Syrian border'.[20]

In retrospect, it is highly unlikely that the Lake Kinneret raid, in itself, actually *led to* an American decision to hold back expected arms deliveries to Israel. Bar-On has argued, rather convincingly, that during the winter of 1955–56 the US administration consistently

> deluded Israeli diplomats and political leaders into believing there was a serious possibility that Washington would respond to Israel's request for heavy arms. ... All those vague statements by the members of the US administration [were intended] merely to keep Israel from learning that a negative decision had already been taken. The American government's problem was not deciding whether to provide Israel with arms, but rather how to go about hiding the decision not to provide them.[21]

Israel's Kinneret raid thus 'provid[ed] the State Department with a golden opportunity to put off its response' to Sharett's latest request for arms and 'a convenient recess of several weeks'.[22]

Seven days after the raid, a Near East Staff Study inside the State Department argued that

> [p]rovision of military equipment to Israel would not only preclude hopes of obtaining an Arab–Israel settlement, but, particularly on the heels of the Israel attack on Syria, do major damage to the US position in the Middle East.[23]

The British Foreign Office also saw in the reprisal action a good pretext for postponing arms deliveries and the consideration of new requests. Shuckburgh also recommended that a stern admonition be delivered to the Israeli Ambassador. Under-Secretary Sir Ivone Kirkpatrick agreed, noting that the 'practice of constantly barking without biting, or even a little nip, [was] very damaging in the long run'.[24] Although French military circles were upset with Israel for contributing to a dangerous destabilization of Syria, and although some Israelis feared the closing off of the promised source of French arms, the Kinneret raid did not, in the end, have an adverse effect on Israel's ongoing campaign to acquire military supplies from France.[25]

During consultations in Paris in mid-December, Russell and Shuckburgh agreed that it would be best to leave it to the US to maintain its friendly pressure on the Israelis.[26] Anger and criticism over the Lake Tiberias raid were channelled through the UN Security Council, whose resolution of 19 January 1956 unanimously condemned the Israeli action. On this front, Israeli policy-makers were forced to admit a decline of their 'moral power' which 'even a hundred speeches of speakers like Abba Eban could not help'.[27]

ARMS AS CARROTS FOR NEGOTIATIONS

In both public and private pleading, Israeli spokesmen were no different from their Arab counterparts in listing incidents which proved the aggressive intentions of the other side and pointed to the crucial need for 'defensive' weapons.[28] While the Gaza strip might have been perceived by Arabs and by some outside observers as 'a death trap for the Egyptian Army and a concentration camp for a quarter of a million refugees', to the Israelis it was becoming 'a dagger pointed at the heart of Israel'.[29]

The State Department's reasoning during late 1955 and early 1956 was that withholding arms from Israel was the best way both (a) to provide effective pressure on Israel to work for a settlement, and (b) to minimize the chances of Israel launching a pre-emptive war. As Mordechai Bar-On has concluded:

> [s]o long as the Americans considered the Alpha Plan feasible, they were committed not to furnish arms to Israel. ... So long as Israel still believed American arms would be forthcoming, it would refrain from resorting to desperate measures and would not embark on a preventive war or resume work on the Jordan River project.[30]

At the same time, Francis Russell continued to regard 'a concession in the Negev' as 'the touchstone of Israeli sincerity in seeking a settlement', and a mid-December 1955 Near East Staff Study recommended that the US 'should refuse to accept a negative Israeli reply'.[31]

Confirming the Israeli Foreign Minister's worst fears, John Foster Dulles in late December waved the carrot of the expected arms announcement before Sharett in an effort to encourage Israeli co-operation in arranging a meeting with Nasir under the CIA's Operation Chameleon (cf. Chapter X). The implications were clear: 'If the negotiations move[d] sufficiently rapidly, then [the] arms issue will fall into [a] different pattern.'[32] American policy-makers now regarded further steps towards a settlement between Israel and Egypt as their first priority, and treated the Israeli request for arms as a secondary issue and a means to achieving an Israeli–Egyptian breakthrough. While he could understand Israeli fears and the desire to have 'arms in their own hands' as 'the best deterrents', Secretary Dulles tried to argue that 'other deterrents' – and not 'primary reliance upon the capacity of Israel to defend itself by force of arms' – were required in the existing circumstances.³³

Moshe Sharett regarded such advice as 'tantamount to telling a starving person that man does not live by bread alone'.³⁴ Public expressions of Israel's concern for the deterioration of its relative armed strength *vis-à-vis* Egypt only seemed to encourage belligerent rhetoric from Cairo.³⁵ The Israeli Foreign Minister informed Dulles that '[a]ny refusal to respond favorably to our November 16 request for arms would, in our view, constitute a serious danger to Israel's very survival, and to the peace in the Middle East.'³⁶ In amplifying this message, Ambassador Eban linked the proposed negotiations with the arms issue by noting that '[i]t would be an invidious situation for Israel to face negotiations with a steadily weakening military position.' In reply, Secretary Dulles argued that Israel had no hope of winning an arms race against 40 million Arabs supplied by the Soviet Union. For him, the 'critical question' was

> how best to deal with Soviet efforts to exploit the Israel–Arab controversy. The Secretary said he was convinced it could not be met by supplying arms to Israel. The only real way of removing the threat and obtaining security [was] by settling the controversy itself.³⁷

As Dulles would later confide to Robert Anderson, a policy of 'assist[ing] Israel in maintaining military superiority' would only 'drive the Arabs further into the Soviet camp'.³⁸ During the coming months, the Secretary of State would deliberately keep the quantities of arms supplies to Israel 'relatively trivial', frankly admitting his fears that 'the US would imperil what remaining influence it had with the Arab States if it were to become an important supplier of arms to Israel'.³⁹ It should be added that,

> although the secretary of state was well aware that the provision of Soviet arms to Egypt was liable to upset the regional balance of power dangerously, ... he was still convinced that the balance tilted in Israel's favor and that a decision could be put off without seriously endangering Israel's security.⁴⁰

Israel's leading spokesmen were not, of course, as sanguine about their presumed military superiority. Isser Harel, the chief of Israeli intelligence, added his voice to those of politicians and diplomatic representatives in a last-ditch attempt to convince American officials of the need to match Egypt's military potential. In early January, Harel travelled to Washington to meet with CIA Director Allen W. Dulles for what he called a 'fateful conversation' regarding Operation Chameleon. At this moment, Operations Alpha and Chameleon overlapped, embodied in the intimate connection between the Dulles brothers. According to his own account of the meeting, Harel presented Israel's case in far blunter fashion than his political superiors. Without an affirmative American reply to Israel's request for arms, he claimed, there could be no negotiations with Nasir and Israel would be forced into launching a 'preventive war'. Harel provided Allen Dulles with documentary evidence showing that Ben-Gurion – contrary to his own and Moshe Dayan's advice – was definitely *opposed* to such a war for the moment. But, the Mossad chief warned, this situation could not last indefinitely. The report from Harel, who bore the CIA code-name 'Daniel', was duly passed along to Alpha planners in the State Department.[41]

While falling short of explicitly threatening that non-receipt of arms would precipitate an Israeli pre-emptive strike, Prime Minister Ben-Gurion spoke to the American Ambassador in Tel Aviv 'with fire and emotion' of his fears of a possible Egyptian air attack against Israeli cities within the coming six to eight months. Israel had to be prepared to deal militarily with an aggressive Egypt which, he argued, continued to receive arms from both the Soviet Union and the UK.[42] The Prime Minister claimed that Israel, which was 'in mortal danger', was in effect undergoing 'sanctions' in the form of an undeclared 'arms embargo' by the US, the UK and France.[43]

As the Security Council debate over Israel's Lake Tiberias raid was winding up, Foreign Minister Sharett renewed 'with all the earnestness at [his] command, the urgent plea [he had] repeatedly put forward ... in Paris, Geneva and Washington for the supply of arms to Israel', adding that '[o]ur information does indeed point to [Nasir's] intention to launch an offensive with the object of annihilating the State of Israel as soon as he considers himself ready.' While Israelis were 'eager as ever to explore any possibility of a settlement', they could not 'pin all [their] hopes on that extremely problematical chance whilst resigning [them]selves to an imminent and mortal danger'.[44]

Continued delay of an American reply led Sharett to appeal to Ambassador Lawson with the additional argument that to trust Nasir's 'humanitarianism or statesmanship to refrain from attacking

[was] to "tax quite unduly Israel's capacity for wishful thinking"'. Having heard reports of British suggestions made during talks in Washington, Sharett warned against the 'self-delusion' of those who might be hoping that Israel was 'so desperately pressed' that it could be persuaded to make 'far-reaching concessions'. In an effort to make things easier for the US administration, Israel offered to accept a confidential assurance of imminent arms deliveries and to forgo the deterrent effect of a public announcement.[45]

ARMS AND THE ANDERSON MISSION

The issue of arms for Israel became heavily entangled with the shuttle diplomacy undertaken by Robert Anderson between late January and mid-March 1956 (below, Chapter XII). During their first meeting in Jerusalem, David Ben-Gurion repeated to the presidential emissary what Israeli officials had been saying to the American administration for the past three months: 'We are in deadly danger', and the US bore a grave responsibility by maintaining its 'attitude of an embargo against Israel while Egypt receives arms from Russia and the United Kingdom'. The Israeli Prime Minister implied that if the US was not going to assist Israel with jet planes and other weapons, then Anderson 'had come for nothing'.[46] Throughout his talks with the Israelis, Anderson's focus on how to start negotiations with Nasir was shifted by Israeli leaders who underlined that, for them, 'the most important problem at the moment was our [i.e., America's] decision concerning additional arms for Israel'.[47]

During his meetings with Anderson, Ben-Gurion frequently expounded on his fears that the growing arms imbalance between Egypt and Israel was both an irresistible temptation to Nasir to undertake an attack and also a disincentive for pursuing a settlement. 'Nasser as a soldier [in 1948–49] had once been defeated in battle with Israel and would therefore be moved to take revenge if he secured equality or superiority in arms.' The Israeli Prime Minister also regretted the growing 'philosophy' in the US that 'Israel should be sacrificed in order to achieve Arab alliances with the Western powers'.[48] Nobody knew when war might break out, Ben-Gurion argued, and only the US could prevent such a war by placing Israelis 'in [a] situation where they did not fear this flow of arms to Egypt'. Removing the danger of war – 'the most urgent step of all' – would 'increase the chances for peace'. Given Ben-Gurion's doubts about Nasir's intentions, 'the situation of relative strength was the most important element'. The US, he felt, should make it clear to Nasir that Israel could not be eliminated, and also that 'Israel will not attack'.[49]

Among the difficulties which Anderson reported to Washington during his mission was that the Israelis brought 'into each conversation the necessity for arms to offset those received by Egypt'.[50] John Foster Dulles was fully aware that it was impossible to divorce Anderson's mediation from the arms issue, and went so far as to recommend utilizing this chief 'carrot' (being withheld from the Israelis) as a small 'stick' to be brandished in front of Nasir. The Secretary instructed Anderson to inform the Egyptian leader that the American postponement of a reply to Israel's arms request would be maintained 'only so long as I [Dulles] feel confident that Israel will not be attacked by Arab states who are rapidly increasing their armaments'. The withholding of arms by the US had increased America's 'moral responsibility to Israel', and the situation needed to be clarified by actions from Nasir which would demonstrate a sincere interest in a 'peaceful settlement or other firm evidences that Israel [was] not facing Arab aggression'.[51] On 27 January, Anderson dutifully informed the Egyptian leader of the American position.[52]

At the start of the Anderson mission, Secretary Dulles believed that the temporary denial of Israel's arms request would be an effective tool to 'maintain [an] atmosphere conducive to [a] settlement and to induce [Israel] to adopt [a] reasonable position on major issues', but the price for this American holding-back of arms deliveries to Israel would be Nasir's 'agreement in specific terms' on the eight Alpha headings so that 'we can take [the] position with [Israel] that [a] reasonable settlement [was] within reach and urge it to make reasonable concessions'.[53] As the weeks went by with few signs of progress, however, pressure mounted on the US to accede to Israel's arms requests. In mid-February, Prime Minister Ben-Gurion wrote to President Eisenhower, once again warning that the US was 'assuming a very grave moral responsibility' by its 'denial of defensive arms to Israel' against the combination of continued flow of Soviet arms into Egypt, hostile Arab declarations calling for 'Israel's early destruction', and Egyptian provocations along the armistice lines. While pledging his backing for Anderson's mission, Ben-Gurion concluded:

ARMS AND ALPHA: ISRAEL

> Yet even the great might of the US cannot compel Col. Nasser to make peace. It is however within your power, perhaps within your power alone, to prevent a war in the Middle East by affording us adequate defensive means in proper time. It is highly probable that this will also contribute towards peace; no Arab country is ever likely to make peace with a defenceless Israel.[54]

In anticipation of a negative US reply or (what they considered even worse) further delay in receiving a 'yes or no answer', Ben-Gurion and Sharett followed up the Prime Minister's letter with yet another plea addressed to Ambassador Lawson. The American Ambassador reported that he had 'never seen Ben Gurion so emphatic, forceful or so emotionally upset and, on several occasions, so near to tears'. If the US rejected 'this last-minute appeal for [a] favorable reply on arms', Lawson was 'convinced we may have no further opportunity to influence [the] course of events by diplomatic action aimed at Israel alone.' Without Western arms, Lawson predicted a dramatic shift in Israel to a militant new security policy, including partial mobilization, immediate resumption of the Bnot Yaacov water diversion, a serious reprisal attack against Egyptian firing across the border ('which [was] now [a] daily occurrence'), enforcement of transit rights through the Gulf of Aqaba, and possibly even an Israeli overture to obtain Soviet arms.[55]

In Washington, too, Israel's representatives continued to press for an American reply to the arms request. The limited progress achieved by Anderson led Ambassador Eban to argue that there was 'no immediate prospect of concluding [a] settlement even if talks should continue and ... Israel therefore should receive the arms she ha[d] requested from [the] US.'[56] Once again Eban pointed to the danger that the disparity in armed strength would leave Egypt 'unable to resist the impulse to create havoc ... by air attack' on an Israel left 'naked and exposed' with insufficient defensive weapons. Secretary Dulles, while appreciating Israel's frustrations, maintained that the delay in supplying arms to Israel had contributed to an 'up-turn' during the past few months, and that he 'did not feel discouraged by the present [Anderson] talks ... although a quick solution might not be in sight.'

> He [Dulles] was profoundly convinced that Israel had no future if it continued indefinitely as an embattled state

surrounded by hostile forces. Israel had no future without a settlement with its neighbors. He strongly believed that Israel should not jeopardize present prospects for a momentary respite which arms might give.

The Secretary hoped to find 'intermediate steps' (such as radar equipment and anti-aircraft guns) which might strengthen Israel militarily 'without causing an Arab reaction which would bar [the] development of friendly relations'.[57] A number of sources advised the State Department that 'any substantial delivery of arms to Israel during the period of [proposed] negotiations would result in the complete frustration of such negotiations.'[58]

The US State Department, keen to avoid anything that might 'unduly increase public excitement about the problem' of arms, found itself facing a dilemma. 'The tension in Israel will increase as long as they receive no arms. On the other hand, the granting of arms to Israel would seriously lessen the possibility of a settlement at this time.'[59] The Secretary of State was also aware of the domestic political situation which 'made it not easy to resist indefinitely pressures for the supply of arms'. Yet counterbalancing these pressures was the need to remove the Arab perception that US Middle East policy was just part of 'a political game' which yielded to pro-Israeli lobbying in Washington.[60]

Although he was privately of the opinion that 'perhaps we were being too tough with the Israelis', and although he would have liked to send Israel some interceptor aircraft and Nike missiles, the President fell in with the State Department's concern to avoid any statement that might jeopardize Anderson's 'delicate mission'. In his reply to Ben-Gurion's letter, Eisenhower side-stepped the latest reminder about Israel's unanswered arms request, offering the familiar formula that the request was 'being given the most careful consideration in light of the need both to ensure Israel's security and to create a situation which will be most conducive to peace in the area.'[61]

During the third week of February 1956, rumours of the imminent approval of American arms deliveries to Israel 'brought forth an outburst which almost broke up the meeting' between Nasir, Zakaria Muhi al-Din and their CIA confidant. The latter reported that he had never seen the two Egyptians 'so upset about anything', and 'unhesitatingly' predicted that American arms for Israel would not only put an end to the Anderson mission but also 'produce a fearsome reaction and one which will be beyond our power to avert of soften'.[62] This view was amplified by Ambassador Byroade in impassioned personal messages to Hoover and Dulles.[63]

The Israeli interpretation of the psychological effect of arms deliveries on the chances for peace negotiations was just the opposite. In his Washington campaign to extract a reply to Israel's requests for arms, Ambassador Eban argued that the Anderson mission was 'bound to fail if Israel [was] not strengthened. ... *The growing imbalance in arms*', the record of one such conversation underlined, was '*destroying any incentive for Nasser to think of peace*'.[64] A true dilemma faced State Department planners. Although many saw some truth in the Israeli logic (added to which were fears of a desperate Israel launching a pre-emptive attack), when forced to choose between these two competing arguments they decided to hold back on arms for Israel for fear of what they considered the greater evil of completely alienating Nasir and the rest of the Arab world as well.

Gradually, however, the force of Israeli arguments and the continuing escalation of tension in the Middle East began to have some effect on American official thinking. On the eve of Anderson's final visit to the region, State Department planners recognized that

> Israel's apprehensions at the shift in the balance of power in the area as a result of Egypt's absorption of military equipment from the Soviet bloc has [sic] reached a point where it threatens to embark upon preventive action and where the Western powers must consider their moral responsibility for Israel's security in the face of a shift in the balance of power.[65]

This recognition, however, still did not translate into immediate satisfaction of Israeli arms requests. By early March, as we shall see in the following chapter, Israel faced the double disappointment of Nasir's resolute rejection of any high-level meetings and yet another postponement of Washington's decision regarding its request for arms. Again, Prime Minister Ben-Gurion cited America's responsibility to redress the arms imbalance as the only way to deter a possible Egyptian attack. Sharett endorsed Ben-Gurion's analysis, adding that the possibility of Soviet intervention further undermined Israel's position, while Nasir had gained two months of military preparation during Anderson's mission. The Israeli

Foreign Minister now expected accusations from his right-wing political adversaries that he and Ben-Gurion had 'lost precious time of national importance because of the illusion that we believed in'. The lack of a clear American reply to Israel's arms requests had become 'humiliating' and could 'no longer be justified by reference to [Anderson's] mission'.[66]

A BRIEF ASSESSMENT[67]

It is likely, as Isaac Alteras has suggested, that Acting Secretary Herbert Hoover was correct in believing that the real reasons why Israelis were pressing the US had less to do with the actual need for military hardware (supplies were available through European countries), but were rather 'due to their desire to have [the Americans] *morally committed* to furnishing them with arms for their own purposes in dealing with the Arabs'.[68] Once resigned to the disappointing attitude of the United States by the spring of 1956, Israel would continue its arms-procurement activities in earnest, focusing its energies on France and other suppliers.[69]

In his penetrating and original study of Israel's security and foreign policy during 1955–57, Mordechai Bar-On has argued that '[p]olitical influence in the long run cannot be boosted by withholding arms'.[70] Benny Morris has further questioned the wisdom of the Anglo–American approach from the angle of Israeli domestic politics and the 'border wars' with the Arab states:

> Washington and London, happy with Sharett's assumption of the premiership, hoped that he would usher in a period of tranquillity along Israel's borders that would permit them to pursue their anti-Soviet aims untroubled by Israeli–Arab skirmishing. But neither was willing to give Sharett the arms and security guarantees or pact that might have helped him fend off the Activists baying at his heels.[71]

In his study of the collapse of Operation Alpha, Shimon Shamir concluded that, 'instead of providing the Israelis with a sense of security that would allow them greater flexibility', the American attitude during 1955 and 1956 'confronted them with alarming international pressures which only consolidated their determination never to exchange their strategic self-reliance for outside guarantees of any kind'.[72]

From what we have seen in both Chapter VIII and the present chapter, the US State Department failed utterly in its attempts to use arms-sales as a lever with which to win either Egyptian or Israeli co-operation in Operation Alpha. In retrospect, one can easily see the futility of the American tactic of holding out a security treaty or arms deliveries as 'prizes' to be awarded to Israel only *after* reaching a settlement with Egypt. As we have seen, American manipulation of possible sales to Israel did not serve as an effective method of producing a willingness to negotiate – whether as a carrot to induce the Israelis or a stick to threaten the Egyptians. Dangling arms as carrots not only failed to achieve its goal but actually backfired. Non-delivery of significant quantities of heavy US armaments contributed to the desperation inside Israel which helped precipitate the decision to join France (and Britain) in the Suez–Sinai war. At the same time, the ambiguity of American intentions left many Egyptians equally apprehensive, leading them to suspect that the US was nevertheless arming Israel in clandestine or circuitous ways.

CHAPTER XII

Alpha's Last Chance: The Anderson Mission

PREPARING FOR AMERICAN MEDIATION

On the basis of the available documents, the origins of the Anderson mediation mission – a combined CIA–USSD operation – are not entirely clear. Mordechai Bar-On describes the mission as having been 'devised' within the ranks of the CIA, which proceeded to win the close co-operation of the President.[1] Basing himself largely on Miles Copeland's account, Saadia Touval also offers a version of events in which the CIA 'masterminded' this final attempt to start up Egyptian–Israeli negotiations.[2] Michael Oren, on the other hand, presents the mission as a specific response to a message from CIA sources in Cairo, indicating Prime Minister Nasir's renewed interest in discussing a Palestine settlement with the US. Oren (erroneously, in this writer's view) attributes much significance to a CIA message from Cairo on 26 October, calling it 'Nasser's *volte face* on the question of peace' and claiming that his *démarche* 'generated considerable excitement in Washington', where '[t]he Administration moved quickly to exploit the opportunity by launching a new initiative, code-named Gamma'.[3]

While it seems reasonable to suppose that senior USSD officials would have been pleased to learn of any hopeful signal coming from either Cairo or Tel Aviv, it is difficult to view this particular message as being more dramatic than any of its half-dozen predecessors since the start of Operation Alpha. In fact, a closer look at the documents shows that the initiative for the Anderson mission came several days *before* receipt of Nasir's latest message, and from the *State Department* rather than the Central Intelligence Agency. State had already begun considering, prior to 25 October, the selection of a special envoy for a mission to the Arab states and Israel, in particular to Egypt 'for [a] basic talk with Nasser' regarding topics raised in Dulles' 26 August statement as well as the question of the High Aswan Dam.[4] After consultations with CIA director Allen Dulles, Department officials felt 'we should have one more good go-round with [Nasir] in an endeavor to reach an understanding'.[5] Likewise, a review of the available options in early November led the Foreign Office to recommend 'one last determined effort to interest [Nasir] in Alpha, however small our chance of success'.[6]

In mid-December, a Near East Staff Study argued that 'the US national interest demand[ed] a major effort to resolve the Arab–Israel problem in the weeks immediately ahead'. The effect of the Soviet–Egyptian arms deal and Soviet–Western rivalry were prominent in the list of five reasons for taking this position. Other factors justifying active intervention were the fear that the growing feeling of frustration in Israel might lead to a 'preventive war', and the coming election year in the US which would lead to a decrease in 'our maneuverability on the issue' (a round-about phrase meaning politicians' unwillingness to alienate Jewish voters by criticizing Israel). The key to a settlement, the Staff Study concluded, continued to be 'Israel's willingness to negotiate over the question of a land connection between Egypt and the other Arab states'.[7] At the same time as the State Department was clarifying its policy, the British Foreign Office received yet another report that Mahmud Fawzi was still insisting on '"substantial territorial continuity" after ruling out corridors. This', Ambassador Trevelyan felt, 'would appear to rule out triangles too'.[8]

Unlike the previous phases of Operation Alpha, the mediation being planned in late 1955 was a uniquely American initiative undertaken without British involvement and launched after only token consultation with the British Foreign Office.[9] Arthur Dean, George Brownell, Dean Rusk and the President's brother, Milton Eisenhower, were among those considered as candidates for this special mission before Robert B. Anderson, a highly esteemed personal friend of President Eisenhower and former Deputy Secretary of Defense, would finally agree to serve.[10]

Anderson's mission would be Alpha's last chance. For those who had been expressing doubts as to Nasir's reliability, the Egyptian leader's attitude to Anderson – and to Eugene Black, visiting Cairo on behalf of the International Bank for Reconstruction and Development (IBRD) which was interested in financing the Aswan Dam project – would be the test of 'whether the West can, in fact, hope to work with him'.[11] In late December 1955 and early January 1956, the State Department's Operation Alpha and the CIA's Operation Chameleon became closely intertwined as final arrangements were made for Robert Anderson to begin visits to Nasir and Ben-Gurion as part of a 'covert operation'.[12]

During the second week of January 1956, while Robert Anderson was being briefed in preparation for his covert mission, high-level Anglo–American political talks were taking place in Washington. British and American officials met to map out various scenarios in response to an explosive situation in the region, with working papers bearing such titles as: 'What is the importance of Egypt[ian] co-operation to us?', 'How much co-operation can we expect from Colonel Nasser's régime?', 'Possible Courses of Action Designed to Forestall Hostilities in the Palestine Situation', and 'Tripartite Courses of Action in Case of Threat or Outbreak of Israel–Arab Hostilities'.[13] While a naval show of force in the eastern Mediterranean was eventually proposed behind closed doors,[14] public declarations following the meetings stressed Anglo–American concern for 'the tensions which prejudice the stability of the area and carry a potential threat to world peace', and repeated the Western powers' offer to help Israel and the Arabs reach a settlement 'by assisting financially in regard to the refugee problem and by guaranteeing agreed frontiers'.[15]

As before, the British seemed more prepared than their American counterparts to contemplate military action in the region. Several suggestions were made for an enhanced United Nations role in conflict management during this period. Some senior officials also considered the possibility of using a United Nations Security Council resolution as a 'cover' or mandate for military action to be undertaken by the signatories of the Tripartite Declaration.[16] From the Middle East, however, came clear signals that 'anything that seemed ... like a three-Power approach using the United Nations simply as an instrument would ... be quite unacceptable'.[17]

The Washington consultations exposed some of the underlying cracks in the Anglo–American approach to Middle Eastern issues. Evelyn Shuckburgh was disturbed by the pro-Egyptian thrust of American thinking which favoured freezing the current Baghdad

Pact by opposing the accession of any new states, thereby helping Nasir to consolidate his pan-Arab leadership.[18] The British were gravely concerned at the Egyptian leader's vigorous activities aimed at undermining the Baghdad Pact, which was, in the words of one author, 'in effect an anti-Nasser league'.[19] The Nasirist-inspired riots in Jordan in December and January (which had thwarted the Chief of the Imperial General Staff's attempts to have the young King Husain join the pact) were still fresh in the minds of British policy makers. Anthony Eden openly wondered 'how long we could go along with Nasser'.[20]

The British attitude to Nasir was in fact ambivalent. Briefing papers prepared in the Foreign Office for Shuckburgh argued that 'HMG's essential interests in that area can hardly be secured without a reasonable degree of Egyptian co-operation'. After weighing the option of 'work[ing] for Nasser's removal and his replacement by any government that will sever the Russian connexion', one brief concluded that:

> So long as there [was] a reasonable chance that Nasser will help over a Palestine settlement and provided he has not gone too far with the Russians it may be best to persevere with him for the sake of our primary objective. If he fails us over Palestine we should probably be better off with a government of [Wafd] politicians.[21]

Although American advisers were split between those who favoured support of Nuri Sa'id and the Northern Tier (especially in the Department of Defense) and those who were 'Egypt-firsters', the latter orientation was the one which informed official policy.[22] Eisenhower considered the riots in Jordan – 'one of the most severe diplomatic defeats Britain ha[d] taken in many years' – a result of the failure to heed American advice regarding unrealistic British expectations of the Baghdad Pact.[23] Francis Russell defined the first goal of American policy as follows: 'Every feasible effort should be made to bring about an Israel–Arab settlement. To achieve it, we should be prepared to give Egypt assurances of our political support for Arab unity once a settlement is in effect'.[24] On the question of Nuri *versus* Nasir, British and American interests appeared to be pulling in different directions, although several formulations were devised to minimize the differences in approach.[25]

ANDERSON'S MISSION: MANDATE AND EXPECTATIONS

John Foster Dulles believed that the Anderson mission would help the US determine 'whether our whole attitude toward Nasser would have to be changed'.[26] Indeed, differing appraisals as to 'how long we could go along with Nasir' and how far to support him in his quest for pan-Arab leadership would continue to shape American and British approaches to Egypt during the unsettling months that would lead to the Suez crisis later that year.

During the only recorded briefing session for the Anderson mission on 11 January 1956,[27] President Eisenhower and Secretary Dulles gave Robert Anderson an open-ended mandate to work for an Egyptian–Israeli *rapprochement*. The records of that briefing contain no mention of any specific terms of an eventual agreement. Neither was there any reference to the existence of Operation Alpha which had preceded the current peace mission, although Anderson seems to have been informed about Alpha in May of the previous year.[28] Dulles stressed 'the future leadership of the Arab world' as the appropriate 'larger context' in which Anderson should approach Nasir regarding a settlement with Israel. Dulles believed that Nasir

> would be willing to pay a considerable price to get the support of the United States in limiting the Baghdad Pact to its present Arab membership with concentration upon the peril from the North, with Egypt maintaining its hegemony of the Arab countries.

In addition to this, the Secretary suggested two economic inducements to be 'delicately suggested' during Anderson's mission to Cairo: cotton ('where we could either destroy or help Egypt's market') and financing for the High Aswan Dam. Eisenhower concluded the briefing by expressing 'his great personal confidence' in Anderson, leaving the emissary feeling that the President had 'just about [given him] carte blanche'.[29] During the coming weeks, however, Anderson would discover just how limited was the leverage of these incentives to win Nasir's co-operation.

As Touval has pointed out, '[b]oth Egypt and Israel accepted the American initiative out of tactical considerations', each side with its own reservations and apprehensions.[30] Only the most intimate circles of the leadership in Egypt and Israel were alerted to the coming visit of the special presidential emissary, who would be handled exclusively by security personnel and without contacting any American embassies. In Cairo, only Gamal Abd al-Nasir and Colonel Zakaria Muhi al-Din would take part in the first meetings with Anderson; Ali Sabri was one of the few others brought into the small circle. In Israel, only the Prime Minister, Foreign Minister and their closest advisers (Yaacov Herzog, Gideon Rafael and Teddy Kollek) were informed of Anderson's imminent visit. Rafael, then serving as special adviser on Arab affairs, set to work with Foreign Ministry officials on the preparation of extensive background documentation on Israeli–Egyptian relations and on tactical considerations for future negotiations.[31]

When Operation Chameleon failed to result in a meeting between Nasir and Ben-Gurion as had been hoped, the Israelis agreed to the idea of an American intermediary, but differed with the Americans on the nature of the proposed mediation. Looking back, Abba Eban called Operation Gamma 'a far more rational and, at one stage, hopeful project than the ludicrous Alpha'.[32] In accordance with previous Israeli policy, Eban requested that the mediator's task be to 'concentrate on bringing about a direct meeting of the heads of State and not on the substance of the various issues'. In stressing this point, the Israeli Ambassador held up the Rhodes example, pointing out that 'Dr Bunche had always insisted that the parties had to win each other over and not to convince him'.[33]

Secretary Dulles, however, envisaged a broader role for the intermediary: first, 'frank talks' with each of the heads of state; 'then engaging in an effort to get agreement on the various principle [sic] issues'. Arranging a meeting between the two heads of state 'at some feasible time' would 'also' be 'one of his objectives' – but obviously not the priority which Israelis sought.[34] Only after two rounds of unsuccessful 'shuttle diplomacy' would the arranging of a direct high-level meeting become the main goal.

Prior to Anderson's arrival, Nasir had already made his opposition to the idea of any direct meetings with Ben-Gurion clear to his CIA confidant, Kermit Roosevelt. When Roosevelt explained that Ben-Gurion might not be willing 'to make as many concessions to an intermediary as he might be willing to make directly', the Egyptian leader had reluctantly agreed to think it over and leave open the possibility.[35]

Ben-Gurion, for his part, was not expecting much from Anderson's mission, 'even though it was being undertaken in Eisenhower's name'. On the eve of the emissary's departure from the US, the Israeli Prime Minister confided to his diary:

> Nasir is not interested in peace. His political ambitions regarding the Arab (and Muslim) world and his behaviour during the past two years show that he is heading for war with Israel, and he waits only for the day when he is sure of his military superiority.[36]

Senior Israeli officials reflected Ben-Gurion's caution and scepticism. Gideon Rafael informed the American Chargé d'Affaires in Tel Aviv of his view that the mission 'would prove abortive' because Nasir was 'not serious' about peace with Israel but was 'merely playing for time while impressing [the] United States with his reasonableness'. For this reason, the government of Israel would not be 'prepared to disclose its hand to any third party', but would wait until Nasir had taken the 'dramatic step' of dispelling Israelis' distrust by agreeing to meet personally with Ben-Gurion.[37] Rafael, the Americans noted, was reflecting the cynical mood of government circles about the 'many failures in the past to make progress with Nasser through third parties', and was 'personally quite bitter' at the failure of Elmore Jackson's mediation efforts during the previous August.[38] Yaacov Herzog, who headed the US Division at the IMFA, was somewhat less pessimistic, summarizing Ben-Gurion's view that he was 'prepared to conduct [the] earlier stages of any negotiations through an intermediary', but that 'before much progress could be made, direct talks would be necessary'.[39]

FIRST MEETINGS IN CAIRO

On the evenings of 17, 19 and 21 January, Robert Anderson and his CIA escort met secretly with Colonel Nasir at the home of Zakaria Muhi al-Din. According to his detailed 27-paragraph report of the first meeting, Anderson explained that his task was to facilitate a solution through exploration of ideas, rather than 'advocacy' of any particular solution. Nasir began his exposition of Egyptian views about a settlement with Israel by reviewing the recent history of Western efforts to organize regional defence, and his perception of the Baghdad Pact as an effort to isolate Egypt. The Israeli question was presented within the framework of efforts at Arab unity and feelings of insecurity. Public opinion, Nasir felt, was 'at least 60 per cent' opposed to an Egyptian–Israeli settlement.[40]

Anderson seemed pleased to note that Nasir was 'much more concerned with the question of Arab leadership than with the immediate problem of tensions between Egypt and Israel'. Despite the friendly atmosphere of the meeting, participants were 'quite frank' in expressing their views about the difficulties involved. Anderson believed that 'we should be conservative in our hopes for an early resolution of this problem'.[41] If we are to believe two other accounts of the same meeting, however, Anderson's written report of his first encounter with Nasir (as understated as it was) exaggerated both the level of coherence of the discussion and the degree of mutual understanding the two men had achieved.[42]

During his second meeting with Anderson, Nasir again invoked the need to achieve pan-Arab acceptance of an accord with Israel as a reason why a 'quick settlement' would not be possible. The Egyptian leader outlined his position (unchanged from what he had presented in April 1955) on the right of return of Palestinian refugees and on boundaries, the solutions to which had to go 'hand in hand'. While recognizing that a land-link between Egypt and Jordan was a 'psychological' as well as a practical demand, Anderson and Nasir discussed the issue in some detail and even consulted maps. Nasir and Muhi al-Din were reportedly 'visibly shaken' when Anderson and his associates were 'emphatic' in informing them that the line drawn by the Egyptian leader (from Dhahariya to Gaza) would be 'completely unacceptable' to the Israelis.[43]

On this point, there is a discrepancy between the American record of the talk and the retrospective account of Nasir's friend and confidant, Muhammad H. Heikal. In the latter, far more colourful version, Gamal Abd al-Nasir was reported to have been shocked at Anderson's 'ignorance' of the basic geography of the area, and was forced to draw him an explanatory map.[44] Heikal's account of the Egyptian leader's reaction to the American suggestion for intersecting triangles in the Negev has become a minor legend in the folklore of American–Egyptian relations:

> The Americans put an enormous amount of work on the scheme. The United States Army, the CIA, and the State Department produced dozens of detailed engineering drawings for building this overpass in the desert. These drawings

were shown to Nasser who examined them with interest and then destroyed the whole scheme. 'The Arabs', he said, 'will be on the overpass and the Israelis will be on the underpass. Well, all right, suppose an Arab was on the overpass one day and felt the call of nature and it landed on an Israeli car on the underpass. ...What would happen? There would be war'.

Nasser [Heikal continued] always referred to that meeting as the 'pee-pee discussion'. He felt that the Americans were too concerned with superficial and artificial ways of settling problems, and he could not take these gimmicks seriously.[45]

According to the American emissary's report of his second meeting with Nasir, the Egyptian leader indicated that, given the achievement of a settlement on the two main issues (Negev and refugees), other frontier adjustments, the lifting of the Arab blockade and a settlement of the Jerusalem question would not present insurmountable difficulties. Anderson outlined America's views on the urgency of a Palestine settlement, the damage to Egypt of continued insecurity, and the need for Egyptian flexibility to enable the US to continue its co-operation and collaboration with Egypt.[46]

Prior to Anderson's last scheduled meeting with Nasir, an unsuccessful attempt was made to soften Egypt's position on the Negev in a lower-level working session with Colonel Muhi al-Din.[47] During his last evening in Cairo, the American envoy again conveyed to Nasir the importance of 'the operation at hand'. Anderson hoped that he might be able to 'indicate flexibility' in Egypt's position when he met with Israeli leaders the following day. Nasir seemed fatalistic about Egypt's need to prepare to face Israel militarily, and was unmoved by Anderson's arguments about the advantages of a settlement to the social and economic development of his country. He continued to regard the Negev as 'the only real problem in achieving [a] settlement'. While 'some flexibility was possible', Nasir

> insisted that the territorial link between the Arab countries had to reflect not only lines of communication but (A) the establishment of substantial sovereign Arab territory in the Negev and (B) give the impression to the Arabs that they had recovered a substantial part of the territory which they feel was unjustly taken from them.[48]

During this third meeting, Anderson said he anticipated that the Israelis 'would be looking forward to direct negotiations at some point and would probably make more concessions by direct negotiations than through an emissary'. Nasir categorically rejected any direct negotiations with Israel 'in the near future'. 'Should it become known that any Arab leader has opened direct negotiations with Israel', he claimed, 'such [a] leader would have committed political suicide or worse.'

The Egyptian Prime Minister again referred to the need for time in order to prepare the other Arab states and public opinion to accept the idea of a settlement. He also rejected Anderson's suggestion for an exchange of documents signed by both countries, and insisted that, while he was 'willing to make commitments and pledges to [Anderson] as an Emissary on a Top Secret basis', he

> could not exchange any form of agreement directly with Israel and could not allow any of his pledges to be made public. He stated emphatically that if news of the operation at hand should leak, he would immediately deny having had any such conversation.

Faced with Nasir's determination to avoid direct dealings with the Israelis, Anderson suggested instead that Nasir send a letter, 'on a unilateral basis' and without reference to the current talks, to President Eisenhower, offering 'assurances that Egypt would not engage in further hostilities' and setting forth the 'broad principles' of the solutions which Egypt deemed possible regarding boundaries and refugees.[49] A similar letter might then be sought from Israel. Although Heikal claims that Nasir reacted to Anderson's draft proposal with 'astonishment intermixed with anger',[50] the Egyptian leader did agree to this procedure (which Dulles found an 'excellent' suggestion). Ali Sabri was assigned the task of producing a satisfactory draft letter and statement. The result (below, pages 239–41), sent two weeks later, was a considerably watered-down version of the text initially proposed by Anderson.[51]

Participants in the Anglo–American consultations in Washington found Anderson's report of his first talks with Nasir 'on the whole not discouraging'.[52] What concerned Secretary Dulles most, however, was Nasir's reference to the likely need for a period of six months of tranquillity before a proper psychological atmosphere could be created for announcing any settlement. For reasons of both domestic politics and Israeli insecurity, Dulles found this an impossibly long time. 'We would have great difficulty in getting Israel to sit by waiting for 6 months while Egypt absorbs arms. Israelis [have] always contended this would be Egypt's tactic.'[53]

Furthermore, the Secretary doubted the sincerity of Nasir's professed need for such a delay. It was difficult for him to understand 'how Nasser could expect to be in a stronger position ... to engage in negotiations with [the] I[srael] G[overnment]' than he was at the present time:

> His arms strength is increasing rapidly. [The w]est is temporarily denying arms to Israel. He has [the] Aswan Dam within his grasp. He has [the] possibility of acquiring our support for Arab unity and Egyptian leadership in it. Israel has just been censored by Security Council for its policy of retaliatory raids.

With every week and month of waiting without a 'substantial and concrete advance toward a settlement', the chances would increase of Israel 'forcing' some outstanding issue, such as resumption of water-diversion work at Bnot Yaacov (in the continued absence of Arab agreement to the Johnston plan for sharing the Jordan waters)[54] or sending a ship to Eilat in order to test Egypt's shipping blockade of the Gulf of Aqaba.[55] CIA Director Allen Dulles agreed with his brother Foster's assessment, adding that even if Israel didn't 'move to destroy Nasr' during a three- or six-month waiting period, the 'pressures for resumption of arms shipments to Israel will have become so impelling as to be irresistible'.[56]

A debriefing discussion between Nasir and his Cairo CIA confidants several days later revealed that at least a few of the issues discussed with Anderson had not been mutually understood. While he claimed that he was sticking to the 'most tremendous and difficult decision' he had taken in December to 'make peace with Israel', Nasir now said he was 'nervous' about the American stress on achieving a settlement so quickly.

> This problem is seven years old [Nasir was quoted as saying,] and many people have tried to solve it. Mr Anderson seems to think that only three days after his arrival he can get us to agree and arrange an immediate meeting with Ben-Gurion.

He reiterated his belief that a 'tension-reducing period' of many months would be necessary before a settlement could be negotiated. The one bright spot in the report was that the Egyptian leader, in response to some prodding by his CIA confidant, seemed to admit that his stand on the Negev was 'an asking price' rather than an absolute demand.[57]

FIRST MEETINGS IN ISRAEL

On Monday morning, 23 January 1956, Robert Anderson held the first of three secret meetings scheduled for that day in Jerusalem. His presence in Israel coincided with the widely publicized arrival of the UN Secretary-General on his first visit to the area as part of a world tour. The tense frontier situation, especially in the al-Auja area, was Dag Hammarskjöld's main preoccupation during his Middle Eastern stops.[58] During the first meeting with Anderson, a 'most impassioned'[59] David Ben-Gurion dominated the discussions, at which Moshe Sharett, Teddy Kollek, Yaacov Herzog and CIA agent James Angleton were also present. The Israeli Prime Minister began with an historical survey of the Zionist struggle for statehood, emphasizing the spiritual side of that struggle. Ben-Gurion made brief reference to various missed opportunities for peace with Jordan and Egypt, and spoke of the Negev's strategic importance (given Israel's vulnerability along the coastal plain) as well as its potential for economic development and the absorption of immigrants. 'There would never be a real peace', Ben-Gurion declared, if Israel 'had to give up territory which was essential.' According to Anderson's full, 47-paragraph report of the meeting, the Israeli Prime Minister said:

> [E]ven if there was but a one per cent chance, the Israeli Government would do everything to obtain it[,] since it was only through peace that it could perform the [ingathering] task before it. Mr BEN-GURION concluded by stating that nothing would be omitted in order to obtain peace *except* [Anderson underlined] to give up a part of 'this little country'.[60]

Robert Anderson then gave his Israeli listeners a summary of his meetings in Cairo, explaining, as he had done to Nasir, that he was exploring possibilities for negotiation and not advocating any particular solution. From his Cairo talks, the territorial question of the Negev appeared to be the most difficult obstacle to an agreement, while Nasir's insistence on the need to prepare public opinion in the Arab world was a serious consideration affecting the timing of negotiations. In an attempt to move forward, Anderson repeated to Ben-Gurion the suggestion he had made to Nasir for the first step to be parallel declarations addressed by Egypt and Israel to a common destinee, such as US President Eisenhower.

Responding to the emissary's account, the Israeli Prime Minister noted that 'the facts as he knew them were incompatible with what was stated to be NASR's desire for peace'. He speculated that the Egyptian leader's main interest in appearing to co-operate with the Anderson mission was a desire to undermine his rival, Iraq, and the Baghdad Pact. While agreeing with the need to maintain absolute secrecy, Ben-Gurion stated that 'no positive advances could be made without some kind of meeting'. He also disputed Nasir's historical claim to Arab land contiguity across the Negev. Throughout the conversation, the Prime Minister coloured his remarks with disparaging comparisons between Israel's commitment to democracy and human dignity and the Egyptian régime's alleged lack of the same, and to the Soviet Union's designs to dominate Africa through its infiltration of Egypt.

While welcoming the idea of declarations of intent and strict enforcement of the ceasefire to be followed by the start of negotiations, Ben-Gurion was nevertheless worried that this process, which would necessarily be spread over several months, 'might result in a serious illusion to the President and the Secretary of State'. As much as he would like to believe Nasir's professed desire for peace, and while not wishing to call Nasir 'a liar or insincere', Ben-Gurion expressed 'strong reservations regarding the outcome', given the 'terrible temptation' for Nasir to use his military advantage to launch devastating air strikes against Israel's population centres and thereby emerge the unchallenged hero of the Arab world. Even if Nasir maintained the ceasefire and entered into secret discussions, the Israeli Prime Minister felt that his preparations for war would continue and that ultimately Nasir – who was governed by his philosophy of Egyptian leadership of the Arab and Muslim world and by his 'military mentality' – 'would be tempted to believe that Israel could be wiped out'. If Nasir thought he could 'destroy us in six or eight months' time, why', Ben-Gurion asked 'should he make peace[?]'[61] Given this Israeli appraisal of Nasir's psychology and the persisting undeclared Anglo–American arms 'embargo' on Israel, Ben-Gurion informed Anderson that Israel could not rely on the Egyptian leader's assurances given in utmost secrecy to the Americans. Only assurances given publicly, or directly to Israelis, would carry any weight.

Several hours later, Anderson held a private lunch meeting with Foreign Minister Sharett, who stressed Israel's refusal to concede any land for peace and questioned the sincerity of Nasir's motives for demanding contiguity with Jordan. On the refugee issue, however, the Foreign Minister 'saw a ray of hope'.[62] In the late afternoon Anderson and Ben-Gurion resumed where they had left off in their morning session. By his own account of their second meeting, Ben-Gurion elaborated before the American emissary the historical and strategic reasons for maintaining Israeli control of the Negev and its southernmost port of Eilat. He also rehearsed a detailed history of the 1947–49 fighting in order to give Israel's version of Arab responsibility for the creation of the refugee problem and his country's reasons for rejecting the principle of the refugees' 'freedom of choice' to return to Israel.[63]

Anderson's account of the same meeting recorded the Israeli Prime Minister's rejection of the call for 'flexibility', arguing that American expectations when applying this term to the demands of Egypt and to the position of Israel constituted a double standard. On the strategic situation in the Middle East, Ben-Gurion expressed his fears that it was already too late to reverse Soviet penetration, and that well-intentioned American efforts to lure Egypt back into the Western camp were doomed to backfire.[64]

Anderson held two further meetings with Ben-Gurion and Sharett the following day. During the morning session, the Foreign Minister told the emissary that Israel

> attached the most decisive importance to [a] direct meeting at the highest level since this would constitute an earnest or token of good will by Nasser. Otherwise the I[srael] G[overnment] would be suspicious that Nasser will be misleading the President and the Israelis ... into [a] sense of false assurance.

Such a meeting, which would serve to dispel anxiety that Nasir was merely playing for time to absorb his Soviet weapons, would be more than symbolic and could 'clarify and feel out the future courses and possibilities for peace'. Ben-Gurion joined Sharett in welcoming the steps proposed by Anderson, but drew a logical distinction between the pursuit of peace on the one hand, and the prevention of war on the other. With respect to the former, Israel was prepared to wait one, five, or more years in deference to the political difficulties inhibiting Nasir from making peace. In the meantime, efforts at removing the danger of war were 'the most urgent step of all', and these would 'increase the chances for peace'. Verbal assurances alone would not suffice. Anderson concluded his report by underlining Israel's preoccupation with the arms question and a direct Egyptian–Israeli meeting. The tone of the discussions, he felt, was gradually becoming one of 'real determination to make the most of what they call this "decisive effort"'.[65]

Following Sharett's afternoon meeting with Dag Hammarskjöld, Anderson met with the two Israeli leaders again to be briefed on Egypt's and Israel's reactions to the Secretary-General's latest proposals to lessen border tensions. Ben-Gurion again offered the suggestion (made to US Information Agency director Ted Streibert in mid-December) that both sides undertake an undeclared 'experimental' ceasefire for a week or two.[66] In reviewing the possible next steps, the Prime Minister repeated his willingness to discuss refugees and territory directly with the Egyptians. He predicted that, if Nasir could be persuaded to participate personally in direct meetings, 'peace might be attained in ten days'. No outsider, Ben-Gurion argued, not 'even the best and noblest of men', could understand the issues well as he and Nasir did. Israel was willing to send high-level representatives anywhere, even to Cairo if that venue gave Nasir more confidence in exerting control over the talks and the maintenance of secrecy.[67]

The following morning, Sharett and his aides had a final meeting with Anderson. The emissary explained that he wished to avoid confronting Nasir with a deadline to reply about a meeting with the Israelis. Sharett briefed Anderson on the history of secret Egyptian–Israeli contacts, pointing out that the problem should not be viewed as a new one for the Egyptian régime, since Nasir had been giving thought to the matter for several years. Sharett also wanted the emissary to emphasize to the Egyptian Prime Minister that President Eisenhower considered a meeting between Egyptian and Israeli representatives 'urgent'.[68]

In summarizing the Israeli position for the State Department, Anderson listed Israel's

- total 'preoccupation' with holding a direct meeting;
- concern that time was working against the Jewish state;
- emphasis on the need to keep the Negev and rejection of references to 'flexibility' which really meant 'surrender [of] a portion of their territory'; and
- repeated insistence on 'the necessity for arms to offset those received by Egypt'.[69]

RETURN TO CAIRO

As Anderson left Jerusalem and prepared to return to Cairo, via Athens, Secretary Dulles had an opportunity to despatch instructions for the next steps in the mediation effort. Dulles recommended that 'at this stage we should not press Nasser for early direct meetings'.[70] In making this suggestion, the Secretary was basing himself on CIA sources in Cairo which had recently reported that

> we have no arguments which will make sense to the Egyptians as to why [direct contacts] are essential. The holding of secret meetings at this time would seem to be irrelevant to overcoming what Nasr sees as [the] most serious obstacle [to an] ultimate solution [of] this problem, i.e., bringing other Arab States into line behind Nasr's position.... [The m]ere fact that Israelis [were] attaching so much importance to these meetings [was] causing [the] gravest suspicions on [the] part of Nasr'.[71]

The Secretary of State now instructed Anderson to attempt to focus his activities on ascertaining the extent of Egyptian–Israeli agreement on 'the eight or ten principal issues' between them.

At this point Dulles provided the presidential emissary, for the first time, with documentation on the Alpha proposals to serve as a framework for continuing his mediation efforts. He instructed Anderson to obtain 'explicit statements' of Nasir's 'best position' on each of the eight Alpha headings: refugees, territory, Jerusalem, the boycott, the state of belligerency, the Jordan waters plan, communications arrangements and great-power guarantees.[72] Thus, the Americans were again in the position of attempting to cajole the would-be negotiating partners into declaring their 'starting price'.

Anderson, however, soon reported that he found 'little disposition on either side to catalogue items which they will discuss'.

Apart from staking out their general positions on the Negev and on refugees, Egyptian and Israeli leaders were almost completely preoccupied with the issues of *process* on which Anderson had already reported, but were not ready to pronounce themselves definitively on matters of *substance*.[73] Dulles was disappointed that Anderson had not been able to get Nasir to go beyond general statements to the effect that most of the issues would 'work themselves out in [the] event of [an] end of hostilities'. The US really wanted to have Nasir's 'agreement in specific terms' on the eight Alpha headings so that 'we can take [the] position with [Israel] that [a] reasonable settlement [was] within reach and urge it to make reasonable concessions'.[74] Knowledge that 'discussions were going on expeditiously at a high level' would also enable the Americans 'to place the most effective possible deterrents upon the Israelis' regarding potentially destabilizing activities such as the resumption of the Bnot Yaacov water-diversion project.[75]

Anderson's second round of meetings in Cairo on 26 and 27 January began with a report of his visit to Israel, in which he dwelt 'on those aspects which served to humanize the Israelis with whom [he had] talked and to point up their sincere desire to arrive at [a] peaceful settlement'. Although still dubious about Israel's sincerity, the Egyptian leader expressed his willingness to pursue initial steps for reducing tension, and agreed reluctantly to consider reopening 'direct [communication] channels along [the] line previously arranged' through the CIA (presumably a reference to Operation Chameleon).[76] Nasir's hesitations over the latter were attributed largely to his feeling that the Israelis had used those channels in late 1954 and early 1955 'to deceive him' into a false sense of security prior to the Gaza raid.[77]

At their second meeting, Anderson reviewed the understandings reached at their previous meetings and attempted to have Nasir comment specifically on each of the eight Alpha headings. While the Egyptian Prime Minister did venture a few specific ideas (e.g., hints about taking John Blandford's 1951 recommendations as a basis for discussing resettlement of refugees), most of his replies deferred to Zakaria Muhi al-Din, who would consult technical experts and draw up a working paper. Before being able to conclude that progress had been made during the emissary's secret mission, Colonel Nasir said he wanted to study Israeli behaviour during the coming two or three weeks. The Egyptian Prime Minister, who had begun his remarks with assurances of 'his real desires and intentions ... for the attainment of a settlement', ended with a declaration 'that his intentions were not aggressive and his arms were intended only for his self[-]defense'.[78]

In summarizing his latest round of talks, Robert Anderson recommended allowing several weeks for Nasir to work out the details of Egypt's position on the various points on the Alpha list. Dulles replied by underlining the 'greatest urgency' of 'maintaining unbroken momentum in your discussions' and of making an 'all[-]out effort to obtain [the] largest measure of agreement at this time in specific and concrete terms' on the list of eight main issues. In response to Nasir's frequently expressed views on the need to prepare Arab opinion, the Secretary was willing to see an agreement, once reached, 'kept secret as long as necessary'. Francis Russell would be sent from Washington to Athens to meet with Anderson for a more complete briefing.[79]

RETURN TO JERUSALEM

Anderson returned to Israel on the night of 30 January and met with Ben-Gurion, Sharett, Kollek and Herzog the following afternoon. During their four-hour meeting, the emissary updated the Israelis on Nasir's latest thinking regarding the timing, process and (to a lesser extent) the substance of a settlement.[80] While continuing his personal effort to see things through Nasir's eyes and to understand the limitations and fears with which the Egyptian leader worked, Ben-Gurion nevertheless insisted on seeing evidence of Nasir's control of frontier incidents and his consent to enter into direct contacts as proof of his sincerity. As Gideon Rafael would later recall, it would have been 'irresponsible' for Israel's leaders to ignore the possibility that Nasir was merely 'playing for time'. The Egyptian leader 'feigned interest in peace as long as he was not ready for war. ... In the stillness of his nightly talks with the emissary Nasser protested his desire for peace, but all day long his organs of propaganda trumpeted Israel's doom'.[81]

The Israeli Prime Minister suggested, through Robert Anderson, a three-step process:

- quiet along the borders to create a better atmosphere ('If only the shooting at the border would cease, I could then believe'.);[82]

- secret Egyptian–Israeli contacts, aimed at avoiding flare-ups and settling minor issues; followed by
- high-level meetings to discuss the larger issues of a political settlement.

Ben-Gurion hinted that 'he had several constructive ideas to present to NASR which would benefit him greatly without hurting Israel', and again speculated that, if the Egyptian leader would participate personally in high-level meetings, an agreement was possible within ten days of bargaining. The Israeli leader 'stated that he was willing to concede "things that Nasser never dreamed of" but only if he could discuss matters with him personally.... [H]e would never spell out the price he was willing to pay for peace to any third person'.[83] As much as he wanted to act in accordance with his *hopes* about Nasir's peaceful intentions, the Israeli leader needed tangible evidence to contradict the view – espoused by his Mossad chief, Isser Harel, among others – that Nasir had already 'sold his soul to the Soviets'.

While pledging to devote his efforts over the coming months and even years to pursuing the 'great hope' of peace aroused by Anderson's mission, Ben-Gurion also spoke of the simultaneous 'great danger' of Nasir unleashing an attack on Israel. Israel 'could be reasonable', he explained, 'only if the anxiety of war [was] removed'. If his people did not feel secure, he hinted ominously, 'then unreasonable things become reasonable'.[84] The Israeli Prime Minister reiterated that

> the danger of war existed and that therefore the I[srael] G[overnment] must have the minimum number of planes and tanks for defensive purposes. Otherwise, ... it would be impossible for the I[srael] G[overnment] to do what [was] necessary in order to bring about peace.

Underscoring the slippery connection between the acquisition of arms and peace negotiations described in the previous chapter, Ben-Gurion's version of these remarks is even more telling: 'if within four or six weeks we do not get a minimum of planes and tanks we shall not be able to do what is needed for a settlement'.[85]

In his reply, Anderson urged the Israelis to be patient and restrained, thereby allowing negotiations to proceed. On the main issues of refugees and the Negev, he indicated his optimism that the problems were not insoluble so long as both sides adopted an attitude of give-and-take. Anderson followed Dulles' instructions and probed Israeli attitudes towards the Johnston plan, holy places, minor border adjustments, the lifting of restrictions on transit and trade, and great-power guarantees.

INTERLUDE: WASHINGTON, CAIRO, JERUSALEM

For much of the month of February, the parties were stalled in a holding pattern. The Egyptian Prime Minister appeared to be, in the opinion of the UN Secretary-General following his visit to Cairo, 'temporarily suspended between two possible policies, an aggressive one favoured by some of his military subordinates and a possible peace initiative'.[86] In reviewing the progress of his first two rounds of talks, Anderson was left with the following 'vicious circle': Ben-Gurion would not 'spell out the price which Israel will be willing to pay for [a] settlement in the absence of a meeting with Nasr', while the Egyptian Prime Minister had 'stated that it [was] impossible for him to consider a meeting from the standpoint of his own security, the position of his government, and the attitude of the other Arab States'. Both parties had commented only non-committally on the list of Alpha headings.[87]

While Anderson reported various tentative conclusions based on a survey of the available options, Francis Russell went on from Athens to Cairo to consult briefly with the American agents responsible for following up contacts with Ali Sabri and Zakaria Muhi al-Din. From Cairo, Russell reported suggestions for a 'package' of proposals that reflected the 'absolute minimum Nasr could be induced to accept'.[88] Meanwhile, some progress was achieved on the small, practical steps suggested during Anderson's talks. On 4 February, Ali Sabri approved the text of a general statement to be addressed over Nasir's signature to President Eisenhower affirming that Egypt had 'no hostile intentions to any other state and will never be party to an aggressive war'. Despite the 'sense of injustice' evoked by the 'establishment of Israel in Palestine' (which he defined as 'the gravest imaginable challenge to the peaceful preoccupation of the Egyptian and Arab people'), Egypt

> recognize[d] the desirability of seeking to eliminate the tensions between the Arab states and Israel. At the same time

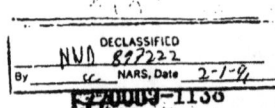

My dear Mr. President,

Thank you for the letter presented to me by your personal representative and the expressions of personal regards contained therein. May I reciprocate your kindness.

Knowing and sharing the World Wide anxiety for the preservation of peace, I wish to address myself to you, whose many declarations on behalf of peace and justice are well known to my countrymen.

Egypt has always declared and has sought every occasion to prove her desire for peace and her determination to develop her resources for the welfare of the Egyptian people. This means that Egypt harbors no hostile intentions toward any other state and will never be party to an aggressive war.

Egypt is a part of the Middle East area; concerned with the stability of the area. Any disturbance in the Middle East necessarily has profound effects on Egyptian ability to pursue a policy of peaceful development. The establishment of Israel in Palestine was the gravest imaginable challenge to the peaceful preoccupation of the Egyptian and Arab people. But, despite the sense of injustice evoked by this development, in the interest of peace Egypt recognizes the desirability of seeking to eliminate the tensions between the Arab States and Israel. At the same time Egypt must affirm its continuing desire to see the fundamental rights and aspirations of the Arab people respected. And can foresee possibilities in this respect which we would earnestly entertain and support.

Sincerely yours,

Jamal Abdel Nasser

PRIME MINISTER

Photocopy of letter: Gamal Abdel Nasser to
President Dwight D. Eisenhower, 6 February 1956, USNA
Source: USNA, RG59, NEA Documents on Projects Alpha, Mask and
Omega, 1945–1957; folder title: 'Alpha-Anderson Talks w/BG
and Nasser'.

THE ANDERSON MISSION   241

> [the letter concluded] Egypt must affirm its continuing desire to see the fundamental rights and aspirations of the Arab people respected and can foresee possibilities in this respect which we would earnestly entertain and support.[89]

More important than his letter to Eisenhower was Nasir's simultaneous authorization of a 'statement of general principles which would provide a satisfactory basis for the resolution of the several points at issue between the Arab states and Israel' (Document 11).[90] The document – consisting of paragraphs on territory, refugees, Jerusalem, the state of belligerency, and the Jordan waters plan – represented one of the clearest definitions to date of the Egyptian leader's bargaining position. The phrasing of the most contentious issue, the Negev, called for 'the establishment of Arab sovereignty over a satisfactorily substantial territory connecting Egypt and Jordan and forming a part of one or the other of those two states'.

Nasir's letter to Eisenhower, his approved 'statement of general principles', and CIA reports of follow-up activities all combine to contradict the version of events given by Nasir's confidant, M.H. Heikal, who claims that the Egyptian leader rejected unacceptable proposals which were drafted by Anderson and cut off all contacts with the Americans.[91] In their meetings with Ali Sabri, American agents in Cairo found him at first 'unusually interested and cooperative' in discussing a timetable for preparing Arab opinion for a settlement, formulating an 'agreed Egypt/US statement of area objectives', and steps to decrease tensions along the Egyptian–Israeli frontier.[92] On 8 February, CIA representatives discussed with Sabri a memorandum on reducing Arab–Israeli tensions, including specific suggestions for establishing mutual confidence through better border control and various propaganda measures. Whereas Ben-Gurion had proposed a three-step process leading to talks, the CIA document envisaged a timetable of *eight* steps culminating in meetings of authorized Egyptian and Israeli representatives, meetings of the chiefs of state and, finally, the announcement of an agreement.[93]

A week later, however, Ali Sabri was reported 'gloomy' and preoccupied with the 'bad situation' due, he claimed, to tensions caused by Western press statements about the dangers of war and tripartite intervention, and by rumours of British efforts to push other Arab states into joining the Baghdad Pact. This mood was no doubt encouraged by the Soviet statement of 14 February which hailed the disintegration of the 'imperialist colonial system' and was critical of the Western powers' intervention in Middle Eastern politics.[94] Although some subsequent meetings were 'businesslike', progress on elaborating the practical steps for tranquillizing the Egyptian–Israeli frontier was slowed by reported Egyptian 'indecision and hesitation', with Sabri expressing some impatience for the return visit of Robert Anderson.[95] While Nasir would have few new details to provide regarding Egypt's terms for a settlement with Israel, the Egyptian leader hoped that Robert Anderson would be prepared on his return to discuss 'broader area policy', mainly his fears about British anti-Egypt collusion with the rulers of Iraq and Jordan.[96] One issue which cast a dark shadow over the imminent return of Robert Anderson in mid-February was the hostile Egyptian reaction to the rumoured approval of American arms deliveries to Israel. As we have seen (above, pages 216–17), Nasir and Zakaria Muhi al-Din were reported to be particularly upset.[97]

By mid-February, the State Department was informed that Ben-Gurion and Sharett were 'advocat[ing] a quick resumption so that momentum [of the Anderson mission should] not be lost'. It was 'urgent', from the Israeli perspective, 'to put the Parties' basic desire for a settlement at this time to an early test'.[98] As arranged, the Israeli Prime Minister forwarded to President Eisenhower a letter which, like Gamal Abd al-Nasir's, conveyed lofty sentiments about his people's commitment to peace. The Prime Minister declared his government's

> full and unqualified readiness to enter forthwith into contact with the head of the Egyptian Government or with such representatives as he may designate, in order to explore possibilities of a settlement or of progress by stages towards an ultimate peace.

But Ben-Gurion felt 'impelled' by 'frankness' to go beyond these noble sentiments to raise 'fateful questions' about Nasir's sincerity and ability to maintain his integrity against Soviet penetration and communist influence. He also used the opportunity of the letter to repeat his warnings that the US was 'assuming a very grave moral responsibility' by its denial of 'defensive arms' to Israel.[99]

Conclusions

CHAPTER XIII

Alpha and Gamma: Post-Scripts and Post-Mortems

'LAST SHOT' AT A MEETING BETWEEN NASIR AND BEN-GURION

By mid-February, Israel's Ambassador in Washington informed the planners behind Alpha and Gamma that his country's 'deeply ingrained' suspicions of Nasir were being 'fully confirmed' by the Egyptian leader's guarded responses to Anderson's approaches. According to Abba Eban, the Israeli view of Nasir contained three elements:

- 'His objective towards Israel [was] not a negotiated peace but dictation and intimidation from a position of military preponderance. In a few months he may feel strong enough to try his hand either in a swift assault or in a grab for a part of the Negev, or both.'
- 'His relationship with the West [was] not affirmative, direct or trustful[,] but rather tactical and extortionist.'
- Even if he were sincere about peace with Israel, Nasir may not have been strong enough, within the RCC leadership, to maintain such a policy in the face of pressures for war with Israel.

For these reasons, Israelis believed that Anderson's next move ought to be to summon the parties to a meeting. 'There would be little value', Eban was reported as saying, 'in further skirmishing about the issues without a direct encounter[,] since this has gone on for six years.'[1]

An unsigned memorandum (possibly by Robert Anderson), dated 10 February, attempted to define the deadlock between Nasir and Ben-Gurion in terms of timing. Nasir's requirement of up to six months 'within which to bring the other Arab states along' clashed with Ben-Gurion's insistence on a high-level meeting with Nasir within a month, so as to give Israelis the assurance that Israel would not be risking an Egyptian attack during this waiting period. 'We think', the memorandum concluded, 'it is more likely that Nasr would eventually agree to such a meeting than that Ben Gurion would renounce it.'[2]

Faced with these two irreconcilable positions, the State Department was forced to take a stand. Perhaps its position on delaying an answer to the Israeli arms request and the disappointment it was causing to Israel helped to tilt the Department's decision on the need for an immediate face-to-face meeting, thus favouring the Israeli position. Nasir continued to express his fears that the Americans were 'pressing a bit too fast on ... specifics' and to argue for allowing more time to create a favourable 'atmosphere' in the region,[3] but Francis Russell now believed that time was running out.

> In Egypt and elsewhere in the Arab world an attitude of cockiness and over-confidence [was] already showing itself and [would] probably soon reach a point where it [would] make it even more difficult than at present for us to obtain cooperation from them in a settlement.[4]

The prestige of the Western powers and the United Nations – and not just Israeli interests – were now involved. Dag Hammarskjöld, recently returned from his tour of the region, agreed with John Foster Dulles that, for the Americans to continue to hold back on supplying arms to Israel, 'we must have something positive from the Arab side', and that the Arabs had to be prevented from thinking that they had the Western powers and the UN 'on the run'.[5]

Thus the State Department decided to instruct Anderson to take one 'last shot' at bringing about 'a direct meeting between Nasser and Ben Gurion (or some other Israel representative)'. Given the repeated strong signals from Cairo that Nasir would not agree to any meetings at this time, Russell was probably being over-optimistic when he estimated the prospects of success at 'less than fifty-fifty'.[6]

For a brief moment, the State Department considered that winning Nasir's co-operation might be easier if Ben-Gurion would agree to allow 'a private Israeli citizen', or perhaps Nahum Goldmann, President of the World Jewish Congress, to meet with Nasir. Dr Goldmann had offered his services as 'a friendly mediator' earlier, after being approached by the Egyptian Military Attaché in London. But Ben-Gurion and Sharett did not wish to introduce any extraneous actors, particularly since (a) Goldmann held unorthodox views on the future disposition of the Negev,[7] and (b) Ben-Gurion had explicitly stated that his own 'bare-fist' approach to negotiation would be more appropriate for dealing with Nasir than Goldmann's accommodating style, which had been effective in dealing with the Americans in 1948 and with the Germans during the reparations negotiations.[8]

Having decided to make this final attempt, Francis Russell immediately began preparing contingency plans for the possible unsuccessful termination of the Anderson mission. These plans included yet another eight-point plan for a settlement – the last of several variations of the original Alpha proposals. The eleventh-hour revision contained two options for the thorny Negev issue: (a) cession of the central Negev to Egypt or Jordan, or (b) internationalization of the southern Negev.[9] Reflecting the mood of pessimism in the State Department, Acting Secretary Herbert Hoover, Jr, on the following day created an *ad hoc* committee which quickly produced policy papers on arms shipments to the Middle East, measures for the 'Prevention of War between the Arab States and Israel', and 'Measures to Minimize Danger of Immediate Hostilities in Arab–Israel Dispute'. All this work was done as background for policy options 'assuming that efforts to find an early solution of the dispute should be unsuccessful'.[10]

Thus, on the eve of Anderson's 'last shot', the position of the US as a neutral mediator consisted of a balancing act between two pro-Egyptian and two pro-Israeli stances. As a logical outgrowth of its approach from the early days of Alpha, the State Department sided with Egypt by being

- ready to go along with Egyptian insistence on 'Arab sovereignty over a satisfactorily substantial territory connecting Egypt and Jordan',[11] perhaps even to the point of abandoning ideas of corridors or triangles as in the original Alpha plan; and

- deferential to Egyptian sensitivities on the question of arms supplies to Israel, prolonging the delay in replying to Israel's repeated requests.

However, it was only during the February break in Anderson's Cairo–Athens–Jerusalem shuttle[12] that the planners of Operation Gamma took the key decision to support Israel on two crucial aspects, namely by

- agreeing with Israel's views on timing: i.e., the need to speed-up a planned meeting, rather than allowing six months for preparing the atmosphere and reducing tensions in the area; and
- siding with Israel on the need to concentrate almost exclusively, at this stage, on arranging a direct high-level meeting.[13]

ANDERSON'S FINAL VISIT

Expectations for the resumption of the Anderson mission were thus simple, although there was little reason to hope for success. Secretary Dulles informed the British that the 'main objective for the time being' was 'to bring about a situation in which talks could be held'.[14] Announcing the resumption of his emissary's mission, President Eisenhower on 27 February signed parallel replies to Ben-Gurion's and Nasir's letters, putting as positive a 'spin' as he could on the situation. To the Israeli Prime Minister, Eisenhower wrote that, while Anderson's 'exploratory conversations' had 'not advanced as far toward a resolution of the issues' as he had hoped, 'a foundation ha[d] been laid on which we may hope to build'.[15] To the Egyptian Prime Minister, President Eisenhower held out several inducements, affirming that 'The present time may offer the best opportunity to work out a settlement which will make it possible for the United States to give increasing assistance in achieving the aspirations of the Arab peoples.' The President added that he had been following with interest reports of the negotiations for the High Aswan Dam project, which 'represent[ed] in finest form the policy of peaceful development for your people of which you wrote'.[16] As William Burns notes, Nasir

> could not have failed to notice the connection Eisenhower was drawing between progress towards an Arab–Israeli settlement and American aid for the Aswan project, with High Dam aid

being offered as an incentive to spur Egyptian concessions on the Palestine issue.[17]

Despite the optimism expressed in the President's letters, the atmosphere to which Robert Anderson returned in early March was even more charged than it had been during his first visit in late January. A Syrian attack on an Israeli police patrol near the Sea of Galilee was followed by the downing of an Israeli plane which had allegedly violated Syrian airspace.[18] On 1 March, Jordan's King Husain abruptly dismissed General John Bagot Glubb as head of the Arab Legion, giving encouragement to nationalist and anti-colonialist elements throughout the region.[19]

During his tour of the Middle East, the motorcade of the new British Foreign Secretary, Selwyn Lloyd, was pelted with stones in Bahrain. Lloyd also met with Colonel Nasir for talks which the Foreign Office regarded as offering but 'one chance in 100' that the Egyptian leader might yet be persuaded to help prevent a 'landslide of Arabs towards Russia and Communism'.[20] For his part, the Foreign Secretary was unable either to allay Nasir's fears regarding expansion of the Baghdad Pact or to reassure himself of the Egyptian leader's pro-West orientation. Lloyd's reports to London contributed to a hardening of Anthony Eden's views. With the deadline for the completion of the evacuation of British bases fast approaching (as negotiated in the Anglo–Egyptian Treaty of 1954), the Prime Minister and some of his ministers were reported 'mad keen to land British troops somewhere', including the possibility of re-occupying the Suez Canal zone 'to show that we are alive and kicking'.[21]

Owing to Lloyd's visit and a scheduled conference with the Syrian and Saudi heads of state, Anderson's secret late-night meetings with Nasir, Zakaria Muhi al-Din and Ali Sabri in Cairo on 4 and 5 March were more difficult to arrange than usual.[22] Given Nasir's preoccupations, Anderson found it impossible to get right to the point of pressing for a top-level meeting with Israeli representatives. As in all their previous meetings, the American envoy found Nasir 'as much preoccupied with the Baghdad Pact as any other single thing'. In accordance with one of his briefing papers on a related issue, Anderson pressed Nasir to honour his commitment to persuade the Arab states to accept the Jordan waters plan worked out by Eric Johnston. To Anderson's disappointment, the Egyptian leader stated firmly that a favourable reply on this issue – and on a settlement with Israel – was 'virtually impossible' before 'the danger of the Baghdad Pact being expanded was removed from his back'.[23]

During a second meeting with Nasir the following evening, Anderson and his CIA handlers were taken aback at what they interpreted as Nasir's introduction of several 'completely new and discouraging' elements into what they considered 'the most disappointing conference since the beginning of the mission'. Referring throughout to 'the Israeli problem' as secondary to his main concerns, Nasir claimed he was 'somewhat confused as to what he regarded as our insistence [on] his meeting with a representative of the Israeli Government prior to the development of agreed plans for wider problems in the area.' The Egyptian leader was concerned, Anderson reported, that this American emphasis was 'simply an effort on our part to please Ben-Gurion and was not really directed toward the solution of his problem'. Nasir therefore affirmed that he was interested in discussing the issues *with the United States*, but flatly refused to meet with any Israeli representative. Apparently referring to Nahum Goldmann, he also rejected any meetings with an 'American citizen of Jewish faith, either under the auspices of the I[srael] G[overnment] or simply in his capacity as a US citizen'.[24]

While a negative reply regarding direct talks had been half-expected by most Alpha planners, Gamal Abd al-Nasir's clear stand against Egypt's taking the lead on a settlement with Israel came as a shock to the Americans as it contradicted all their previous expectations. Nasir now insisted that the initiative for such a task would lie exclusively with the US or the UN, although these initiatives could certainly benefit from secret American–Egyptian understandings. Referring, for at least the fourth time, to the July 1951 assassination of Jordan's King Abdullah for his willingness to consider a peace treaty with Israel, Nasir declared that he would not 'gamble [his] future or that of [his] country in any circumstances similar to the Abdulla incident'. The Egyptian leader's real goal, Anderson concluded, was to maintain indefinitely 'a more effective armistice without a settlement'. The only measures needed to attain this were, in Nasir's view, a mutual withdrawal of forces to create a one kilometre wide buffer along the border and a strengthening of UN peacekeeping machinery.

In analysing Nasir's apparent retreat, Anderson noted that his latest conversations were taking place on the eve of the Egyptian leader's talks with the Syrian and Saudi heads of state. Another novelty was Nasir's emphasis on the Palestinian factor as a reason for his inability to back the Jordan waters scheme. 'I could not openly urge the acceptance of a plan', he said, 'that would destroy the entire case for the refugees.' This led Anderson and his CIA associates to speculate that the Egyptian leader had recently come to fear the 'growing restiveness among the refugees' as a threat to the stability of the Jordanian and Syrian régimes.[25] To the more experienced experts on Egypt at the British Foreign Office, however, this was merely a tactic on Nasir's part:

> [H]e does not wish to see the problem of the Palestinian refugees mitigated, for the reason ... that it is a valuable instrument of discontent on which he can play a tune which appeals to all Arabs, and because the refugees are also a valuable source of Egyptian influence, especially in Jordan.[26]

On both the Johnston plan (on which he had been rather cooperative in the past) and the more difficult question of Israel, Nasir was now 'unwilling to assume the kind of leadership' which might result in 'the loss ... of public popularity and which could incur the danger of increasing differences between Nasr and other Arab leaders'.[27]

In cabling instructions for a possible third and final meeting with Nasir, Acting Secretary Hoover authorized Anderson to allude to President Eisenhower's 'personal keen disappointment' in the 'negative position' adopted by the Egyptian leader. The emissary was told to draw Nasir's attention to the likelihood of a dangerous increase of the risks of war in the area 'in the absence of real prospects for a settlement', and to point out that the '[c]limate for [a] settlement [was] not likely [to] be more favorable in [the] future'.[28] But both parties soon realized that they had no new proposals or information to put forth, and the scheduled third meeting between Anderson and Nasir never took place. As a discouraged Anderson flew to Athens and prepared for his talks in Israel, a fateful change of orientation was about to take place at the State Department.

On the morning of 9 March 1956, Robert Anderson held his last meeting with Israeli officials at the Tel Aviv home of David Ben-Gurion. The emissary reported the results of his two meetings in Cairo and transmitted the US President's letter of 27 February. In response, the Israeli Prime Minister delivered a lengthy and eloquent post-mortem on the emissary's mission, praising Eisenhower's intentions and Anderson's efforts, but concluding that he could not help seeing 'war approaching, inevitably, as in a Greek drama'. Ben-Gurion repeated the now-familiar themes of

- the unrelenting pressures building up on Nasir to start a war with Israel, especially given his growing military advantage and his ambitions to lead a united, anti-colonialist Arab world; and
- America's moral responsibility to redress the arms imbalance.

The Israeli leader saw no harm in Anderson continuing his mediation if that could serve to prevent an outbreak of war, but announced that his 'faith in miracles' was 'melting away'.[29]

FROM 'ALPHA' TO 'OMEGA'

While Robert Anderson was wrapping up his shuttle diplomacy in the Middle East, Thursday, 8 March 1956, was a crucial turning-point in both London's and Washington's attitude to Gamal Abd al-Nasir. In addition to the State Department's receipt of Anderson's disappointing cables, rumours reached Washington of expanded Egyptian arms acquisitions, while the British Embassy in Cairo reported reliable information that Egypt was planning to attack Israel at the end of the current university year (in June).[30] In early March, British policy seemed mired in contradictions: 'Alpha was still officially in play, the Aswan High Dam was to involve Britain in a £5.5 million gift to the Egyptian régime, yet Eden was speaking more and more as if Nasser were the enemy.'[31] Stunned and enraged by King Husain's summary dismissal of General Glubb, the British Prime Minister was (incorrectly) holding the Egyptian leader – whom he dubbed a second Mussolini – responsible; Evelyn Shuckburgh wrote in his diary: 'Today both we and the Americans really gave up hope of Nasser and began to look around for means of destroying him.'[32]

Thus, after almost two years of courting and 'pacifying' Nasir, the Western powers were now intent on 'punishing' the defiant Egyptian leader.[33] The State Department would henceforth be 'proceeding on [the] premise [that] Nasser will not cooperate at present in seeking [an] Arab–Israel settlement and [was] in fact working against [the] West.' The Department began studying 'measures which might be taken against Egypt itself and against

Egyptian influence in [the] area', in an effort to register a 'clear-cut challenge to Soviet–Egyptian ambitions'.[34] While not wishing to alter America's public posture of remaining 'friends with both contestants in that region in order that we can bring them closer together', the President reacted to Nasir's growing 'arrogance' by agreeing with Dulles' suggestion that the US secretly attempt to isolate Egypt by winning over Saudi Arabia and Libya firmly into the Western camp.[35]

Upon his return to Washington, Robert Anderson met with President Eisenhower and Acting Secretary Hoover on 12 March for the final debriefing of his failed mediation mission. While Herbert Hoover noted that no 'definitive course of action' was recommended following the two-hour meeting, American attention in the wake of the unsuccessful mission would be directed towards:

- a tripartite resolution in the UN Security Council;
- efforts 'to effect a split between Saudi Arabia and Egypt'; and
- further letters from Eisenhower to Nasir and Ben-Gurion urging 'the two sides to get together'.[36]

While at first senior State Department officials felt that Anderson should be available 'to resume his talks with both sides at any time that it appeared that anything might result from such a resumption',[37] this proved to be the end of his attempted mediation between Egypt and Israel. Several months later, the State Department would recommend sending Anderson on a secret mission of 'evaluation and appraisal' of Nasir's intentions, but this time there would be no question of discussing an Arab–Israeli settlement – only Washington's concern at the deterioration of Egypt's relations with the Western powers.[38]

In his diary account of the 12 March meeting with Anderson, Eisenhower recorded his frustration with both protagonists. While the Israelis were 'anxious to talk with Egypt', the President found them 'completely adamant in their attitude of making no concessions whatsoever in order to obtain a peace'. But Nasir had 'proved to be a complete stumbling block', and Eisenhower referred to his ambition 'to be acknowledged as the political leader of the Arab world'. In reviewing various options in 'a very sorry situation', Eisenhower considered steps to isolate Egypt as 'our best move', but realized that winning over Saudi Arabia might require painful concessions from his British allies, who were locked in a bitter dispute with the Saudis over the control of Buraimi.[39] The State Department shared the President's and Hoover's apportioning of blame between the two protagonists: 'Both the Israelis and the Egyptians have proved difficult, but the Egyptians have been the main stumbling block in recent weeks.'[40]

On the very day of Anderson's debriefing in Washington, Anthony Eden was considering his own schemes for driving a wedge between King Sa'ud and Abd al-Nasir and was 'quite emphatic that Nasser must be got rid of ... It is either him or us', he told Shuckburgh, 'don't forget that'.[41] Following his tour of Middle Eastern capitals, Foreign Secretary Lloyd was reported to be 'thinking seriously of approaching the US G[overnment] with the proposal that the US–UK abandon the attempt to bring about a voluntary Arab–Israel settlement at this time'.[42] Indeed, after mid-March 1956, Anglo–American attentions, along with those of UNSG Dag Hammarskjöld and his UNTSO Chief, General E.L.M. Burns, were focused increasingly on merely 'preventing war' – with little hope or effort directed at seeking a political settlement to the Arab–Israeli dispute.[43]

By the end of March, the United States also moved from 'Alpha' to 'Omega' – closing the books on the fifteen-month-old Anglo–American plan to foster an Arab–Israeli settlement through Nasir. The new code-named operation was designed to isolate and undermine the Egyptian leader. If 'Alpha' (the hopeful first letter of the Greek alphabet) had been built largely around the use of positive inducements, 'Omega' (the final letter) signified the end of the road and would involve veiled, but very real, threats to harm Egyptian interests. Among the methods to be used were: the suspension of the Aswan Dam financing, arousing Islamic and conservative Saudi opinion against Nasir's revolutionary and destabilizing influences, and economic warfare against Egypt's cotton industry. The possibility of deciding later on 'more drastic action in the event that the above courses of action do not have the desired effect' was not excluded. The 'primary purpose', as Secretary Dulles described it, was 'to let Colonel Nasser realize that he cannot cooperate as he is doing with the Soviet Union and at the same time enjoy most-favored-nation treatment from the United States.' For the time being, the US would try to avoid an 'open break which would throw Nasser irrevocably into a Soviet satellite status' and would try to leave him a bridge back to good relations with the West if he so desire[d]'.[44]

Although the possibility of reviving Alpha approaches would be considered occasionally,[45] the British were also engaged in their own hard-line policy whose aim seemed to waver between actually 'downing' Nasir and keeping him 'guessing'.[46] Parallel to American and British efforts, the Israelis also prepared their own propaganda campaign to discredit Nasir both in Western eyes and among his would-be regional allies, including a weekly English-language compilation of press extracts under the title 'Nasser's Axis'.[47] During his visit to Israel, Foreign Secretary Selwyn Lloyd confided to Moshe Sharett that he too was 'turning over in his mind various possibilities of clipping Nasser's wings'. The Israeli Foreign Minister saw that his country might be 'an indirect beneficiary' of this turn in British thinking, but appreciated that the real preoccupation of the UK was 'not with Israel's plight but with Nasser's threat to [the] remaining British positions of influence in [the] area'.[48] Complementing these Israeli speculations, Evelyn Shuckburgh was indulging in fantasies of his own: 'It *would* be nice', he wrote in mid-March, if the Israelis could attack and defeat Egypt, 'and do it quick before any of us (including the Russians) had time to save Nasser: then we could fall upon them as aggressors.'[49]

Meanwhile, in Cairo, Nasir and his associates were alerted to the fact that the highest echelons of American and British policy-makers were now debating whether to assassinate him, overthrow his régime, or merely 'clip his wings'.[50] The British Ambassador, finding his requests for an interview unanswered, speculated that Colonel Nasir was 'convinced that the British Government [was] hostile to him'.[51] The British and Americans were indeed co-operating in flushing out ideas about what they could 'do' to Egypt to undermine Nasir's growing confidence.[52]

During February and March 1956, a number of developments in the region and in US domestic politics contributed to an erosion of support for financing the proposed dam at Aswan.[53] While the enthusiasm for the project had been, several months earlier, based on the wish to outflank the Russians, the collapse of Operation Alpha caused a rapid disillusionment with a plan which now seemed to be rewarding Nasir without earning his co-operation in return. Egypt's formal recognition of Communist China in mid-May provided a further twist in the spiral of the West's deteriorating relations with Gamal Abd al-Nasir.

After several more weeks of uncertainty, John Foster Dulles finally informed Ambassador Ahmad Hussein on 19 July 1956 of the definitive withdrawal of the Anglo–American offer to finance the High Aswan Dam project.[54] One week later, Gamal Abd al-Nasir retaliated against 'American and British conspiracies against Egypt' by nationalizing the Suez Canal.[55] These last two events are often cited as crucial turning points, setting the stage for the final 'descent to Suez'. Yet, as we have seen, these events were preceded by three earlier developments which made equally important contributions to the advent of the second Arab–Israeli war:

- the final collapse of Operation Alpha;
- the formulation of American and British plans to undermine Nasir; and
- the withdrawal of Western plans to finance the High Aswan Dam.

THE PRINCIPAL PLAYERS: NASIR AND ISRAEL

A number of retrospective studies on the Anderson mission have underlined the historical turning-point that it represented. As one Israeli participant in these events has reflected, '[t]he failure of the Anderson mission removed the last barrier before the brink of war. Ben-Gurion ... prepared the nation for the approaching ordeal.'[56] Historian Shimon Shamir has pointed out that

> when in late March both London and Washington lost their patience with Nasser, the ground was set for Western collaboration with Israel of a kind that would have been unthinkable before the collapse of Alpha.[57]

Similarly, US intelligence agent Wilbur Eveland has suggested that the success of Alpha and the Anderson mission might have averted the process which led to the outbreak of the Sinai–Suez war in late October of that year.[58]

The import of the failure of the Anderson mission was not immediately felt by its leading Egyptian players, who continued to hope for an opportunity to spin out discussions with the US despite all the disappointments. Several weeks after Anderson's last visit to Cairo, Ali Sabri complained of 'Egyptian discouragement with the ... mission' based on Nasir's feeling that he 'was being led into [a] trap' by American efforts 'to get him to make commitments and take positive steps not reciprocated by the Israelis'. Mirroring the Israelis' accusations about Egyptian motives, Sabri believed that the Israelis had not tried to use the Anderson mission 'to arrive at a settlement' but rather as a tool 'to expose Nasr and damage Arab unity'.[59] Sabri's view was partly shared by Henry Byroade, who recalled telling Secretary Dulles at the beginning of Anderson's visit: 'What really scares me is that no matter how this fails, Nasser will get the blame.'[60]

In his own review of the emissary's failed mission, Gamal Abd al-Nasir again listed for Ambassador Byroade the constraints which had prevented him from agreeing to a direct meeting with Israeli representatives. The Egyptian leader regretted that his frankness had resulted in Anderson leaving Cairo so 'discouraged', but disputed the emissary's allegation that he had committed an about-face by declining to present and endorse proposals for a settlement with Israel to the other Arab states. Nasir claimed that he had consistently pledged only to 'do his best' if terms of settlement could be launched by someone else – the US, UK, or the United Nations.[61]

During a mid-March conversation with Byroade, the Egyptian Prime Minister went on explicitly to deny that he was 'playing [a] game of stalling until he gained greater arms for striking purposes'. He was, he claimed, in favour of a settlement 'and would help to [the] extent of his ability but could do no more'. Referring to his letter of 6 February to President Eisenhower (above, pages 239–41), Nasir was equally emphatic about not starting a war with Israel. 'I give to you and to him my word on that issue', he told the American Ambassador, 'not as a politician but as a soldier.' As he saw it, the Anderson mission 'should most certainly not be abandoned' – but two preconditions were required for its success: a reduction of tensions along the borders (mainly through UN efforts), and a reduction of inter-Arab tensions (in other words, by Britain reducing its support for Iraq and the Baghdad Pact).

These preconditions were perfectly consistent with the Egyptian leader's goals and tactics during the entire mediation episode. His main purpose seems to have been to give as little as possible to Anderson, all the while

- keeping up the military pressure on Israel (including holding off arms sales from the US) with the lowest possible cost to himself;

- attempting to repair strained relations with the Western powers;
- keeping open the door to Anglo–American financing of his cherished High Aswan Dam project;

and especially

- using American help to advance his quest for regional leadership and a weakening of the Baghdad Pact.[62]

This reading of Nasir's goals with respect to Anglo–American pressure during Operation Alpha is consistent with the recent scholarly analysis of Arab regional politics of the period by Fawaz Gerges, who concluded:

> Nuri's alliance with the West and his hostility toward the communist camp were motivated largely by regional concerns as was Nasser's opposition to the Baghdad Pact. Iraq's adherence to the Baghdad Pact was perceived in Cairo as a direct challenge to Egyptian leadership of the Arab arena. Egyptian–Iraqi rivalry over the pact should be seen as a struggle for the soul of the Arab world; their international alignments were subordinate and secondary to this objective. ... Far from being pawns in the game of great power politics, local states had tried to maintain and consolidate independence by exploiting the rivalry between the superpowers. Their goals were to escape dependency, gain aid, [sic] and influence.[63]

In his recent assessment of how Alpha fitted into the scheme of Nasir's broader political aims, Mordechai Bar-On has argued that Israel really had no reason to fear being exposed to pressure from the powers for concessions because, as the record clearly shows, the Egyptian leader 'was not even willing to pay even the small price demanded of him by the Alpha Plan' – that is, agreement to direct talks. By 1956 Nasir was 'already deeply involved in his life's work: the unification of the Arab world and the unfettering of Arab dependence on the West'.[64]

In late March, Ali Sabri's CIA confidants reported that, while the Egyptians remained 'adamant' in their opposition to direct negotiations with Israel, they still wished to co-operate with a US intermediary to work out the preliminary steps to an agreement, 'hopeful of [a] settlement in [a] year or two by means and along [the] lines discussed with Anderson, providing no US Government arms [were sold] to Israel.'[65] The continued downward spiral in American–Egyptian relations after March 1956 was occasionally interrupted by rumours of Nasir's interest in resuming talks with Anderson and 'work[ing] out problems ... , forget[ting] mistakes [made by] both sides'.[66] Then, as before, Nasir stood to benefit more by continuing 'the *process* of negotiations' with Anderson than by 'any concrete outcome from them'[67] – even the most favourable solution hypothetically available through his mediation. As Shimon Shamir has perceptively argued:

> In a way, his willingness to discuss Alpha ... was designed to mobilize some goodwill for freezing or neutralizing the Baghdad alliance. His British interlocutors tried to achieve exactly the opposite: to use Alpha to get him to accept the reality of that Western strategic system. These cross-purposes could not be reconciled.[68]

In his evaluation of the Anderson mission, Saadia Touval has noted that both Israeli and Egyptian attitudes were determined by 'their expectations of the side effects and outcomes' of their co-operation with the American mediator.[69] As we have seen, Ben-Gurion had been the first to offer an official post-mortem on the Anderson mission, in the emissary's presence during his final visit on 9 March. The following week, Ambassador Eban told State Department officials that his government felt that the abortive mission had none the less proven 'necessary and desirable', particularly because it had proved the correctness of Israel's assessment that 'peace with Israel [was] not in Nasser's calculations'.[70] Israeli policy-makers, who had suspected all along that 'the mission [had been] used by the Administration to deny Israel arms, and by Nasser to gain the time needed to absorb his Soviet weaponry',[71] could now breathe a collective sigh of relief.

In a personal letter to the American President, David Ben-Gurion praised Eisenhower for his 'noble and imaginative initiative' which, despite its failure, 'may yet bear fruit sometime in the future'. The Israeli Prime Minister took the opportunity to issue a further warning about Soviet penetration of the Arab world and Africa, and launched into another attack on Colonel Nasir, whose refusal 'to sustain his oft-repeated intimations that he was willing to work towards a settlement with Israel' had 'confirm[ed] – I am sorry to say – our presentiment from the outset, that he would merely utilize Mr Anderson's mission to gain time for the absorption of Soviet arms by his army.' With great earnest, Ben-Gurion indicated that 'time [was] running out' and he pressed for America's much-deferred reply to Israel's request for defensive arms and planes, underlining the inadequacy of 'rest[ing] our safety, indeed our very existence, merely on outside intervention' via the Tripartite Declaration or the UN.[72]

The main motives for Israel's cautious co-operation with Anderson's efforts can be found between the lines of Ben-Gurion's letter, namely:

- using the opportunity to demonstrate Nasir's unreasonableness and hostile intentions for the benefit of the American administration;
- demonstrating Israel's own reasonableness; and
- keeping open the door to resume lobbying for the procurement of American arms supplies to restore Israel's declining military power *vis-à-vis* the Arab states.[73]

As Mordechai Bar-On has concluded, the Israeli tactic of insisting on direct talks was expected to produce one of two favourable outcomes:

- if Nasir had agreed, it would have been a giant step towards Arab *de facto* recognition of the Jewish state;
- if Nasir refused, the onus of responsibility for Anderson's failure would fall upon the Egyptian leader and this would remove what Israelis felt was the last remaining obstacle to delivery of US arms.[74]

The major risk, as Sharett had explained to Anderson, was that Ben-Gurion and his entourage would be blamed for pursuing a chimera while leaving Israel defenceless and allowing the continuation of Egyptian build-up for war.[75]

In the end, Ben-Gurion's advisers took special comfort in the knowledge that Washington and London blamed Nasir, rather than the Israeli leadership, for the failure of the emissary's mission.[76] John Foster Dulles had now come to the conclusion that a 'comprehensive settlement' was 'impossible at the present time unless and until Arab hopes *vis-à-vis* Israel are somewhat deflated',[77] while the British Foreign Office also held the Egyptians chiefly to blame.[78]

Israelis would also have been gratified to read internal State Department assessments which were finally starting to give credence to the Israeli reading of Nasir's intentions. For example, a late-March memorandum prepared by the Near East and African Bureau of the State Department reflected some of the worst scenarios that Israelis had been predicting for months: namely, that there existed 'a serious danger that, despite his protestations to the contrary, Nasser in fact plan[ned] to lead the Arab countries in a war of annihilation against Israel as soon as he feels that victory is assured'.[79]

To Israel's continuing disappointment, however, this change of thinking at the State Department did not lead to a generous outpouring of American military assistance. Dulles' 'Omega' proposals included a recommendation to deny export licences for any major military equipment to Israel and the adjoining Arab states 'for a further indefinite period'.[80] Israel's principal supplier of armaments continued to be France, whose shipments increased dramatically during and after the spring of 1956.[81] Neither did Gamal Abd al-Nasir ever get the opportunity to prove the correctness of the State Department prediction that he would 'lead the Arab countries in a war of annihilation against Israel'. What took place instead was a tripartite Anglo–French–Israeli 'collusion' which resulted in an attack *against Egypt* in late October of that year.

An unstable situation of eight years of 'no peace, no war' thus gave way to the second Arab–Israeli war. By the spring of 1956, several years of sustained efforts at Anglo–American diplomacy for resolving the post-1948 Arab–Israeli dispute had run their course. United Nations and great power peacemaking efforts had indeed proven futile.

CHAPTER XIV

Carrots and Sticks: The Limits of Anglo–American Coercive Diplomacy

MILITANT PROTAGONISTS AND INTERNATIONAL OPINION

The Bible has often been cited as the source of some of the principles which have guided the behaviour and attitudes of both (Jewish) Israelis and (Muslim and Christian) Arabs in their twentieth-century political struggle. 'An eye for an eye, a tooth for a tooth' (*Deut.* 19:21), for example, has become a motto justifying a vicious cycle of attacks and retaliations.[1]

In the same vein, Israeli and Arab behaviour has often displayed an unbreakable interconnection between diplomatic manoeuvring on the one hand, and military capability on the other, in ways which recall Thomas Hobbes' admonition made three hundred years earlier:

> And covenants without the sword are but words, and of no strength to secure a man at all. Therefore, notwithstanding the laws of nature (which everyone has then kept when he has the will to keep, when he can do it safely), if there be no power erected, or not great enough for our security, every man will – and may lawfully – rely on his own strength and art for caution against all other men.[2]

These are among the philosophies that have shaped the militant attitudes that lie behind the frequent resort to force by Arabs and Israelis and their apparent lack of respect for international opinion. Numerous resolutions of the United Nations Security Council and the General Assembly since May 1948 have urged a whole range of correctives to end a seemingly endless conflict: repatriation or compensation of Palestinian refugees; avoidance of cross-border attacks; ending of blockades and interference with shipping; and the seeking of a negotiated settlement to the dispute.

Not surprisingly, the United Nations and other would-be peacemakers discovered at an early stage the negligible impact on the protagonists of the moral force of international opinion alone. One student of the UN's peacekeeping efforts has pointed to a 'curious organizational deficiency':

> Despite its endowment (at least theoretically) with devices to punish offenders against the peace, it can offer virtually no incentives to desirable behavior. Beyond announcing its moral and political approval, the rewards it offers are hypothetical ... The most persuasive implements for resolving conflicts in the Eastern Mediterranean may well be force and reward. The UN system can reliably use neither.[3]

Following the practice – rather than the theory – of international behaviour, the parties to the Arab–Israeli conflict have moulded the dictates of the United Nations and world public opinion to the needs of their respective national struggles. Each party has become skilled in scoring points against its adversary by invoking any available means of international pressure, while deflecting the same pressures directed against it with the most eloquent rhetorical and legalistic arguments.

Amidst all their frustrations and setbacks, however, some mediators in the Arab–Israeli conflict did come to believe that there was at least one area where world public opinion, although disappointingly weak, could prove useful to their peacemaking efforts. This was the use of international legitimacy and moral pressure as a 'cover' for national leaders to justify a retreat or a proposed compromise in the eyes of their followers. During his short but intense mediation effort of 1948, Count Folke Bernadotte became a firm believer in the idea that the bitter and defeated leaders of the Arab states, though unable to agree voluntarily to make peace with victorious Israel, might be 'willing to be coerced' by international pressure into doing so.[4]

Similar expectations from both parties seem to have been operating in the back of the minds of some of the key participants in Operation Alpha. At the time of the first disclosures of the plan to the Egyptian Foreign Minister in Cairo, Dr Fawzi had remarked that 'a final settlement ... might have to be *imposed* on the Arab States and Israel, as it was doubtful whether any of them could be brought to accept it otherwise.'[5] In the final weeks before the collapse of the Anderson mission, Francis Russell continued to assume (in accordance with the original premises behind Operation Alpha) that 'neither side [would] be able to bring itself on its own steam to make the necessary concessions for a settlement', but that each might successfully 'justify' such concessions under the moral pressure of external factors.[6] Such an observation would seem, on the surface, a perceptive and reasonable one, but its validity was never properly tested since Operation Alpha never reached the stage of negotiation where fateful decisions might have been made regarding compromises or concessions.

THE CONTEXT: BRITISH AND AMERICAN INTERESTS

In the foregoing chapters we have isolated, for purposes of analysis, one episode of Middle East peacemaking in which two Western powers attempted to induce the local protagonists to take the first steps in what might have become a 'peace process' towards a settlement. In setting out our conclusions, it is important to bring back into focus parts of the broader context in which Operation Alpha unfolded.

In his pioneering study of 'The Collapse of Project Alpha', Shimon Shamir has commented that 'contacts in search for a settlement were always by-products and side-shows of greater dramas'.[7] The two main characteristics of the period we have studied are

- the unravelling of the armistice between Israel and four neighbouring states; and
- the replacement of Anglo–French hegemony in the region by Western–Soviet rivalry, sometimes referred to as the evolving 'Cold War'.[8]

The Cold War was one of the 'greater dramas' of which Alpha was a 'by-product', as were the domestic and regional political agendas of Egypt, Israel, the United States and Great Britain. There is still much to be researched and written about the internal, domestic political constraints that influenced the decision-making options of all the officials who became involved in Alpha. This is especially the case for Gamal Abd al-Nasir, whose moves and motives still require a fuller explanation in relation to Egypt's aspirations to lead a united Arab world, independent and beholden to no outside powers.[9]

In the following pages we shall attempt to situate Operation Alpha mainly within the context of British and American interests. As a CIA agent involved in the operation, Wilbur Crane Eveland felt that the failure of the project was due in part to an absence of sufficient commitment on the part of the *British*, whose other interests in the region – notably, support for Nuri Sa'id and the Baghdad Pact – had taken precedence over the quest for an Israeli–Egyptian peace settlement.[10] Such an assessment of Alpha involving the singling-out of one party as being responsible for a 'missed opportunity' for peace leaves something to be desired. But it does inadvertently touch on a crucial point: namely that, like all efforts by the powers to resolve the Arab–Israeli conflict, this operation was not launched in a void, nor merely for its own sake. Rather, it is best understood in relation to Britain's and America's strategic interests in the area.

One of the clearest definitions of Anglo–American presumptions and aims was contained in the draft 'Proposed Agreed Position ... on Middle East Policy' which was worked out by Shuckburgh and Russell and approved by Macmillan and Dulles during meetings in Geneva in early November 1955 (Document 9). Although it was never put through the final ratification process at the State Department,[11] and although it was formulated in what turned out to be the twilight weeks of Alpha (and the dawn of US-inspired Gamma), this statement provides one of the most authoritative definitions of the strategic thinking of senior British and American policy-makers at this time.

What is noteworthy in this document is that, within its 16 paragraphs, the Arab–Israeli dispute is mentioned explicitly only twice and is, even then, clearly secondary to other aims such as:

> retaining the area within the free world, developing the oil resources, assisting in the economic and social development of the countries concerned, ensuring an adequate defense arrangement for the area as a whole, keeping a reasonable arms balance between Israel and the Arab states. (para.1)

'[W]orking toward a settlement of the Israel–Arab dispute' comes at the end of the above list of objectives, while the conflict is recognized in para. 10 merely as an unwanted obstacle, the cause of

> weaken[ing] Western influence in the Middle East and open[ing] the door to Russia. If we wish to maintain a position of influence with the Arabs we must bring the conflict to an end as soon as possible.

In his concluding assessments of the Anderson mission (and without being aware of the larger Operation Alpha), Saadia Touval has focused on the 'decline of American motivation' to pursue the mediation effort once the US had despaired of Nasir. The American initiative in despatching Robert Anderson had been

> part of a comprehensive effort to limit Soviet influence and test Nasser's claim that he wanted to preserve American friendship. Peace, however desirable, was not a goal on its own merits ... As it became clear that the mediation could not serve the goal of containing or limiting Soviet penetration, the American willingness to exert itself in the search for peace faded away.

The mediation attempting to reach an Egyptian–Israeli agreement, Touval stresses, 'was in part an instrument used in the pursuit of another and more important goal'.[12] Similarly, in his description of 'British planning and the misconceptions of Alpha', Shimon Shamir reminds us that the purpose of an Egyptian–Israeli settlement was to have been 'to strengthen what [Shuckburgh] called Britain's "influence and position in the Arab world" and [to] check Soviet penetration into the area.'[13]

The specific elements that made up America's and Britain's 'influence and position' have varied over the years. For several years after 1948, resumption of the flow of Iraqi oil through the port of Haifa, preservation of their ally Abdullah in his newly expanded kingdom of Jordan, and potential access to the Negev were three identifiable British aims which helped determine the Foreign Office's attitude towards an Arab–Israeli settlement. Between 1951 and 1955, British and American pursuit of an Arab–Israeli settlement was related to a number of overriding strategic interests. Even the local protagonists appreciated that their own goals with respect to the Arab–Israeli dispute were subservient to larger issues such as:

- Western interest in combatting the perceived threat of Soviet 'penetration' through the organization of a Middle East defence network;
- Anglo–Egyptian negotiations for the evacuation of British forces from the Suez Canal zone;[14] and
- Britain's fear of becoming militarily involved against Israeli troops in accordance with the terms of the Anglo–Jordanian Treaty.[15]

While all three have interesting, and often complicated, links with an Arab–Israeli settlement, we shall single out the first of these for our concluding remarks.

The whole Western enterprise of building up Arab countries for regional defence against Soviet 'penetration' could not be divorced from the unresolved Arab–Israeli impasse. Each had direct repercussions on the other, but the interests of the Western powers, the Arabs and the Israelis on this issue pulled in three directions, which did not augur well for either regional stability or an eventual resolution of the Arab–Israeli conflict. In Chapter II we saw the British embark on the 'gradual education' of the Arabs to accept Israel because such a course was deemed a necessary prerequisite to advancing regional defence plans.[16] Three years later, Operation Alpha was based upon similar presumptions and a greater sense of urgency but, from the FO's first forays into 'gradual education' until Dwight Eisenhower's musings following the failure of the Anderson mission (below, page 280), the Western powers were mistaken in presuming that they could convince the Arabs that 'the real frightening danger to them [was] Communism and Russia'; that it was 'imperative to the Arabs as well as to others to have stability in the Middle East'; and that, as a result, the Arabs 'might themselves begin to think more realistically about Israel'.[17]

The reluctance of most Arab states to join a Western-led security alliance severely disappointed Washington and London. In their talks with American and British officials, Arab politicians frequently justified their reluctance to co-operate in defence schemes in the area by pointing to popular feeling against the West's responsibility for the Palestine problem. The Arabs could hardly welcome the prospect of greater Western involvement in, and control over, the region – still less if this Western presence was associated with greater security for Israel based on the *status quo*. As Syrian leader Adnan

Atassi made clear to Sir Geoffrey Furlonge at the Foreign Office in late 1951, he understood perfectly well why an Arab–Israeli peace would have been 'in the interests of the Western Powers'.

> But unfortunately the Arab States could not feel that it was in their interests to sign treaties of peace with Israel. So far as they were concerned, Israel represented the immediate and adjacent menace, whereas Russia was a far distant one.[18]

On his May 1953 trip to the Middle East, John Foster Dulles encountered the same arguments while attempting to enlist Arab support for a pro-Western defence scheme.[19]

The situation looked completely different from the Israeli perspective. Israelis saw the whole process of Western 'wooing' of the Arabs for regional defence alliances as inimical to their basic security interests and adding to their sense of isolation and vulnerability. Israeli officials sought desperately to convince the UK and the US of the dangers of placing all their 'eggs' in Arab 'baskets.' As early as 1950, Ambassador Eliahu Elath presented an argument to the British that would later become a familiar refrain in building an American–Israeli partnership: namely, that

> Israel was the only democratic country in the Middle East and during the war she had shown her ability to fight and would do so again and can therefore play her part not perhaps in halting Russian expansionism but in delaying it.[20]

Unfortunately for Israel, this was not to be the line of reasoning which Britain or America would adopt in their approach to setting up a pro-Western defence system in the Middle East. As the Western powers continued to court Egypt to become the centrepiece of Middle East defence alliances, Israel's representatives in Washington and London expressed resentment at being excluded and registered their fears that Arabs were preparing to launch a 'second round' against the Jewish state.[21]

In the period just prior to the decision to launch Operation Alpha, an announcement about imminent American arms sales to Iraq, as part of an attempt to strengthen Northern Tier defences against Soviet attack, triggered a new cycle of Israel's expressions of concern and requests for quantities of military equipment in order to maintain its relative strength in the region.[22] In the summer of 1954, the US State Department was thus faced with a horse-and-cart policy dilemma: should American co-operation with the Arab states in regional defence matters precede – or be preceded by – an Arab–Israeli settlement?[23] The realization that Western defence plans could not succeed without first resolving at least some components of the Arab–Israeli problem was, as we have shown, one of the logical steps on the way to launching Operation Alpha.[24]

CARROTS AND STICKS: AN INVENTORY

In an earlier study we drew up a list of forms of great-power intervention with their 'client states' in the Middle East.[25] These avenues of intervention are the basic levers of influence – either 'carrots' or 'sticks' – used by outside powers to induce a local client into appropriate behaviour. A leading American theorist has written that successful negotiation requires a 'redistribution of goods (outcomes) so that all parties exchange an unpleasant present for a better future'.

> Parties need to feel better off with the promised new situation, or else there will be no incentive to sign and to hold [to] an agreement. Mediators use carrots and sticks to bring out the perception of the present as unpleasant and the future as promising for all. Both are required: the future must be seen as preferable to the present, and promises as well as pressures are needed. The stick needs to be associated with carrots, so that the promise as well as the pain can be brought out.[26]

In his comprehensive review of the theoretical literature on the subject, Abraham Ben-Zvi similarly notes that coercive diplomacy is almost always ineffective if it is based solely on the threat of sanctions and punishments. To be successful, Ben-Zvi argues, coercive diplomacy must include 'an optimal mixture or equilibrium between threats and conciliation, or between intimidation and accommodation,' and he quotes Alexander L. George: 'What the stick cannot achieve in itself ... can possibly be achieved by combining a carrot with a stick.'[27]

Throughout our examination of Operation Alpha, we have seen how American and British policy-makers were frequently unsuccessful in their attempts to use these levers to influence Arabs or Israelis in the direction of moderation and compromise. In our concluding review of these carrots and sticks, we shall highlight the limited effectiveness of each of these methods of persuasion.

1. Diplomatic representations

This was perhaps the most frequently used form of diplomatic intercourse between the powers and Middle Eastern states, and also the mildest method the patrons had for exerting pressure on the clients. Patron states have offered their friendly advice, or expressed concern or disappointment, about a client's recent (or anticipated) military action or political statement if it was considered provocative to the other side or liable to lead to a breach of the peace. This 'quiet diplomacy' was normally carried out orally in confidential conversations involving embassy staff and Foreign Ministry officials.

This form of third-party intervention required some delicacy, as both the UK and the US had to follow the norm in international relations whereby one sovereign country respects the right of another to hold a different point of view regarding the pursuit of its foreign policy and legitimate self-defence. If the patron was not threatening to impose sanctions, the client state had to decide whether the representations were merely passing or *pro forma* expressions of mild disapproval, or whether there were possible political risks attached to side stepping or ignoring the rebuke. More often than not, the client's behaviour was not significantly altered in response to such gentle forms of persuasion, leaving the patron in a position of having to decide whether the situation warranted turning to other, more forceful, forms of intervention.

2. Diplomatic support or condemnation

During periods when frontier incidents were occurring, with the attendant risks of escalating violence, supportive patrons have backed a client's complaint against another state through diplomatic representations made in 'enemy' capitals, in consultation with other powers, or at the United Nations. Such support sometimes took the form of endorsing a decision or recommendation of the UN peacekeepers, making speeches, and sponsoring resolutions at the United Nations, or the threat or use of its veto in the Security Council. Conversely, a critical patron could show its displeasure with a client's behaviour by holding back from offering diplomatic support or – the most extreme sign of rebuke – by participating in a UN condemnation of its own client.

Two prominent examples of Western support for a UNSC condemnation during the period under study were both directed against Israel following 'reprisal' raids: the Qibya incident (October 1953), and the attack on Syrian positions along the Sea of Galilee (December 1955). Israel, on the other hand, remained frustrated in its attempts to enlist Great Power support for a Security Council resolution censuring Egypt for its failure to comply with the September 1951 resolution calling for freedom of navigation through the Suez Canal.[28]

3. Offer or withhold financial aid

Patron states have also resorted to economic sanctions when lesser measures proved incapable of modifying a client state's behaviour. Following the logic of 'he who pays the piper calls the tune', patrons have attempted to discourage 'bad' behaviour by withholding, or delaying, financial assistance being sought by the client, or by rewarding 'good' or co-operative behaviour by promising or making such aid available.

Between 1948 and 1956 there were several examples of US attempts to use 'dollar diplomacy' in the search for an Arab–Israeli settlement. One of the earliest instances was the suspension of loan payments to Israel during the later stages of the 1949 Lausanne conference, a move which did not have the desired result of extracting a more generous Israeli offer to repatriate Palestinian refugees.[29] One of the few cases of the effective use of this lever was the threatened cut-off of financial aid in 1953, which did result in Israel suspending its water-diversion plans of the upper Jordan River near Bnot Yaacov for several years.[30]

If the former was an unsuccessful example of the use of financial aid in pursuit of conflict *resolution*, the latter was an application of the same lever for conflict *management*. The success of the US in causing the suspension of Israel's water-diversion became a minor legend in its time, frequently invoked by Arab spokesmen arguing the case for stronger American pressure on Israel on other contentious issues.[31] Faced with a deteriorating situation along the Israeli–Jordanian border in mid-1954, the American Ambassador in Amman called upon his country to intervene more forcefully to back up UN admonitions. He pointed to the Bnot Yaacov case as an illustration of the effectiveness – and difficulty – of Tripartite teeth for UNTSO's decisions. Perhaps nothing so dramatic as the suspension of aid could be found for all of the 'major' cases. Nevertheless, it is imperative to bring such pressures as will compel respect for the decisions.[32]

Using economic aid as an instrument of Middle East peacemaking was not without its complications, and these were noted in the State Department as early as 1952 (see below, pages 283, 286). At the height of their promotion of Operation Alpha, the senior British partners expressed their concern that less experienced American diplomats might have been putting their economic inducements forward too clumsily, running the risks of making it impossible for the destined client to accept so-called 'bribery' in exchange for adopting a co-operative attitude on the question of Israel.[33] The episode involving the biggest stakes was the attempt to link Anglo–American backing for the Aswan Dam project with Egyptian co-operation in Operation Alpha. We shall examine below (pages 283–7) why that attempt proved a dismal failure.

4. *Offer, delay or withhold military aid*

In the case of arms procurement, the patron–client relationship becomes a more clearly defined one of 'supplier' and 'recipient', but the conditions under which the former can exert influence over the latter (to the extent of modifying the recipient's policies) have always been difficult to pinpoint or predict with any degree of certainty.[34] Although complicated by the fears of promoting an arms race in the volatile Middle East, 'the temptation to use the export licence procedure to attempt fine steering of pressures and penalties' proved irresistible to the powers between 1949 and 1956.[35]

Even though the scale of arms supplies was relatively modest in the early 1950s, both the British and American patrons sought to reward 'good' behaviour or to punish 'bad' or unco-operative behaviour by offering, delaying, or withholding military equipment. A corollary to this was the question of possible 'security guarantees' by one or both of the powers, to reassure anxious local clients – as the Tripartite Declaration of May 1950 (Document 1) was supposed to, but did not, do[36] – that no state could violate with impunity the sovereign boundaries of its neighbours. One of the key Alpha proposals

– intended as an inducement to both Egypt and Israel – was to have been an Anglo–American guarantee of the new frontiers to be agreed upon in peace negotiations, superseding the ineffective Tripartite Declaration. But, as we have seen, the parties were not tempted by this (or other proposed terms) to get beyond the stage of manoeuvring and prenegotiation. In a final section of our conclusions (below, pages 283–6), we shall discuss the limitations on the political uses of arms aid in further detail.

5. Offering good offices to the parties

From time to time, one of the Western powers has felt that the risks of allowing a specific dispute to fester unresolved were serious enough to warrant an attempt to invite the parties to consider proposals for settling their differences. This has usually produced an offer of good offices to facilitate direct or indirect meetings between representatives of the parties in conflict. The offer normally included the services of a senior US, UK or UN official as chairman, and a specific, restricted agenda. Sometimes good offices have been offered for the purpose of conflict management, as in the case of UN and UK attempts to defuse tension by proposing discussions to consider a revision of the Israeli–Jordanian GAA during 1953 and 1954.[37] At other times good offices have been linked to hopes for an overall political settlement, as in the case of US good offices offered to Egypt and Israel to discuss the disposition of the Gaza strip in mid-1949.[38]

In most cases, Israel welcomed such offers, although invariably with reservations regarding the format or contents of the proposed discussions. Israelis hoped that good offices might lead to face-to-face meetings between themselves and Arab representatives. Arab spokesmen, on the other hand, have generally spurned such offers on the grounds that they were opposed in principle to steps implying diplomatic recognition of the Jewish state.[39]

6. Conciliation

Going beyond good offices, conciliation implies a sustained commitment to help the parties resolve a wider range of issues in dispute. The powers have usually left it to the United Nations and the Palestine Conciliation Commission to perform these functions. With strong behind-the-scenes US involvement, the PCC held numerous, but separate, meetings with Arabs and with Israelis at Lausanne in 1949 (a five-month-long conference), Geneva in 1950, and Paris in 1951 – all in a fruitless effort to assist the parties to resolve their differences.

7. Mediation

As the term was generally understood during the period under discussion, mediation was a form of involvement in conflict resolution that went beyond conciliation in that the third party was not restricted to receiving and transmitting proposals originating from the principal protagonists. The mediators themselves were expected to propose peace plans to the parties, as in the case of Count Folke Bernadotte (June and September 1948), the PCC Paris Conference of autumn 1951 (but *not* the Lausanne Conference of 1949), and Eric Johnston's mediation in the quest for an agreement for sharing the Jordan waters.

Although the Anderson mission which brought Operation Alpha to its demise is normally considered a good case-study of mediation,[40] a closer look at Alpha as a whole shows it to be a rather unusual form of that genre. In the first place, the existence of the would-be mediators' peace proposals was kept secret from the parties (and, initially, even from Robert Anderson) who were encouraged to believe that the powers would limit their involvement to narrowing the differences between the two sides (merely 'conciliation'). Alpha further departed from the classic mediation model in that Anglo–American collaboration also extended to secret lists of inducements and pressures which the powers were prepared to use on the parties. Hence, we have preferred to use the label 'coercive diplomacy' to describe Operation Alpha – the nearest thing to an 'imposed' settlement.

ANGLO–AMERICAN CO-OPERATION

Despite an overall convergence of ideas, British and American interests in, and approaches to, the Middle East were not always in complete harmony and, as we have seen, they occasionally pulled in different directions. Perhaps the most serious differences for the success of Alpha occurred with regard to the relative levels of support offered by Britain and the US for Nuri Sa'id and his rival

Gamal Abd al-Nasir. America's position against active participation in the Baghdad Pact was a recurring source of strain in Anglo–American relations. Shuckburgh, Macmillan and Eden had to accept, and work around, this American reluctance which was a necessary ingredient enabling the US to maintain a minimum level of goodwill with (and potential influence over) Egypt.

In late February 1956, both Dwight D. Eisenhower and John Foster Dulles appreciated that their British allies were 'disposed to take a stronger line' against Nasir than the Americans were. US policy-makers realized that Britain 'felt the menace' of Nasir's defiance and Soviet influence

> much more sharply than we did, fearing anything which would result in an impairment of their relations with the Arab states, oil from which was so important to Western Europe. To [the US] ... oil from the Arab states was not of paramount importance. American companies had great investments in the area, but if they should be lost it would be most unfortunate but not catastrophic.[41]

Yet, despite these differences and some British difficulties in dealing with the American Secretary of State on a personal level,[42] there was a high level of compatibility and co-operation between the UK and the US leading up to, and during, Operation Alpha. In his memoirs, Abba Eban wrote: 'The Dulles-Eden relationship was abrasive, and the diminution of Israel's territory was almost their only common purpose.'[43] In a less simplistic and partisan manner, Shimon Shamir has referred to a 'remarkable congruence' of outlook between Sir Anthony Eden and John Foster Dulles, both of whom 'regarded the Arab–Israeli conflict as a principal obstacle to the fulfilment of their [wider strategic] objectives' of maintaining Western influence in, and excluding Soviet influence from, the Middle East.[44]

This overriding sense of common purpose may also help to explain why the powers found it so difficult to take 'no' for an answer when confronted – as they were on half a dozen occasions – with clear indications that the Egyptians and the Israelis would not co-operate by playing the roles assigned to them under Operation Alpha. Faced with recurring signs of the project's imminent collapse, one is struck by the persistence of its American and British promoters, ever ready to pounce upon the slightest ambiguity and declare it enough of an opening to proceed, however shakily, to some future stage of Alpha. This Anglo–American persistence is indeed remarkable when one recalls the abundant evidence illustrating Nasir's and Fawzi's tough terms and conditions regarding the disposition of the Israeli-held Negev Desert, the unmistakable Israeli insistence on not ceding parts of the Negev (and especially not the port of Eilat), and the extreme unpopularity, throughout the Arab world, of the policy of seeking a settlement with Israel.

This Anglo–American persistence seems to have been based largely on a combination of desperation and wishful thinking. The latter was periodically fanned by ambiguous signals received from parties in the region, who no doubt felt it prudent to avoid disappointing, in too categorical terms, the expectations of the powers.[45] As Keith Kyle has noted, most of the Alpha activity from February to December 1955 was centred on the Egyptians, who

> were skilful at keeping Alpha in play. Mahmoud Fawzi, a diplomat of the old order, subtle, allusive, (rather oriental ...), would give the impression that much progress was possible. Nasser would then often pull back, plead bad timing but still keep the door open. They were both ... liable to reopen the subject themselves whenever a tilt towards the West seemed expedient.[46]

Finally, there were bureaucratic factors which help to explain the longevity of a peace effort which seems, with hindsight, to have been doomed to collapse so early and often. The enormous investment of time and energy in the preparation and co-ordination of this ambitious joint operation generated its own momentum which no doubt contributed to decisions to sustain, rather than drop, Alpha at each of its crucial turning points.

AMERICAN AND BRITISH PRESUMPTIONS

In his analysis of the Alpha episode, Mordechai Bar-On has singled out three mistaken premises entertained by the planners:

- that Israel was the main obstacle to consolidating Britain's weakening position in the region;
- that it was possible to convince Nasir to acquiesce in the existence of Israel; and
- that it was possible to get Israel to make substantial concessions.[47]

Bar-On, like others, found it easy to cast doubt on the realism of the powers' starting assumptions by singling out the territorial aspect. In referring to one of their early joint working papers, the Israeli researcher has mocked the Alpha planners' preoccupation with detail:

> Today, some forty years later, the meticulous delineation of the exact borders between Arab Kalkilya and Jewish Kfar Saba in Shuckburgh and Russell's plan and the detailed calculations of financial restitution for the refugees seem pathetic. The naïve belief that the important questions were whether to transfer 5,000 acres from one side to the other or whether it was enough to transfer only 4,375 acres, as against the total lack of any chance whatsoever of bringing the two sides to any dialogue on a fundamental conclusion to the conflict, makes the Alpha Plan document seem more than slightly ridiculous.[48]

Given the evidence we have seen that the powers did indeed focus on getting the parties to meet – at least as much as they did on working out the details of various hypothetical proposals, Bar-On's judgment seems somewhat harsh and unfair.

Recent critiques of Alpha are, however, more well founded when they focus on the Anglo–American willingness to back Egyptian claims to part of the Negev Desert. The intersecting triangles proposal, which seemed so ingenious to Dulles, Macmillan, Russell and Shuckburgh at the time, appears, with hindsight, fantasy-like and an obvious non-starter. Yet, in pursuing their Negev proposals, the planners of Operation Alpha managed to maintain a remarkable blind spot regarding the build-up of evidence that Egypt's and Israel's stances on this issue would prove utterly irreconcilable. Given the frequency of Egyptian statements about the unacceptability of corridors or triangles, British and American policy-makers were equally unrealistic in thinking, during the last months of Alpha, that there would be anything to be gained by attempting to finesse the issue and have the parties meet with an ambiguously-worded agenda. The fact that an Alpha breakthrough was nevertheless built around pressuring the Israelis into ceding part of the Negev is, for some analysts, glaring evidence of one of the most unachievable expectations of Alpha's planners.[49]

But, apart from the Negev issue, were American and British officials proceeding from such a faulty or misguided understanding of the nature of the conflict and the deeply-ingrained attitudes of the protagonists? The opening of the archives allows researchers to draw their own conclusions as to whether the Anglo–American planners of Alpha had been basing their hopes for peace on a sufficiently accurate appreciation of the parties' stances. Shimon Shamir's analysis, for example, highlights evidence which suggests a number of erroneous or 'problematic' perceptions.[50]

Yet there is also evidence which points in the other direction. The voluminous correspondence on Alpha is sprinkled with insightful and sober assessments, not merely wishful thinking or dream-like misreadings of Middle Eastern realities of the time.[51] Neither the senior British nor the junior American partners enjoyed a monopoly over analyses which proved to be perceptive. The American Ambassador in Tel Aviv, for example, was under no illusions. 'We find ourselves', Edward B. Lawson wrote in mid-1955,

> with the task of obtaining an agreement between two parties,
> (a) one of which stands as the winner of the war between them and is militarily capable of winning another war, but who desires peace virtually on the basis of the status quo;
> (b) one, the loser in the war who is determined to await the opportunity to drive the winner into the sea, and one who does not seek peace or recognize the existence of the other party.[52]

The head of the BMEO, Sir John Sterndale-Bennett, one of the strongest behind-the-scenes sceptics with regard to Alpha, was also keenly aware of the psychological obstacles when he wrote:

> The fact that the proposed settlement may offer in our view an honest and reasonable basis of agreement ... is beside the point when you are dealing with so emotional a question and with two parties each of which labours under a deep sense of injustice and frustration.[53]

Some senior British statesmen, it is true, rivalled Arab leaders in their exaggerated appraisals of America's ability to influence Israel. '[I]t must be recalled', wrote Harold Macmillan in a mid-July 1955 memorandum to the Cabinet, 'that Israel is in effect at the mercy of the United States if the latter should wish to put pressure on her.'[54] But counterbalancing those who may have naïvely expected to be successful at pressuring Israel into making territorial concessions in the Negev, there were other British and American policy-makers who were more realistic and better able to empathize with the

Israelis' predicament. In late November 1955, for example, the British Ambassador in Tel Aviv – whose earlier anti-Israel and anti-Semitic 'gems' have been quoted by both Shimon Shamir and Keith Kyle[55] – gave an excellent and not unsympathetic appreciation of Israeli thinking, which he summarized for London in point form:

(a) that any indication of Arab willingness to talk peace should be regarded with deep suspicion;
(b) that the Western powers, if they place credence in such indications, are at best being extremely gullible or at worst have sinister reasons of their own for pretending to believe them;
(c) that there is no sort of obligation on Israel to offer any concession to the Arabs in order to make them do what they ought to do anyway, ...;
(d) that in any case ... it would be a tactical error to show any willingness to compromise, since any sign of willingness on their part to discuss changes in the *status quo* would be the first step on a slippery slope which might lead to destruction.[56]

Earlier, Jack Nicholls had argued repeatedly for his government to take steps which would reassure Israelis 'by going as far as we possibly can to satisfy the gnawing sense of insecurity which, however imaginary – and it is of course by no means entirely so – poisons all Israel's policies.'[57]

By contrast, both the British and the Americans proved less accurate in their assessments of the position of Egypt's leader, Gamal Abd al-Nasir. A study of the documents reveals that the Western powers seriously misread Egyptian attitudes in the larger conflict between East and West in which the implementation of Operation Alpha was entangled. Nasir emerged from the April 1955 Bandung Conference as the leader of the non-aligned nations of the world. 'In a single stroke', wrote Michael Oren, Nasir 'managed to associate neutralism and opposition to both Israel and the Northern Tier [Baghdad Pact] and, in the process, to establish Egypt's leadership of the neutralist movement in the Middle East.'[58] For Mordechai Bar-On, Alpha had already 'missed the boat' by the time Nasir set out for the Bandung Conference:

> The dramatic change in Nasir's self-image and his perception of Egypt's place in the world robbed the Alpha Plan of its very minuscule chance of being implemented. Nasser's evolution

into the charismatic and acknowledged leader of Arab nationalism was well on its way, but it would take the British and the Americans a full year to assess correctly the profound transformation which had taken place in the Middle East.

Bar-On further takes the British and Americans to task for having tied themselves, during this period, 'to a plan lacking any hope of success', a policy which prevented them from adopting 'the flexibility needed to prevent, or at least slow down, the snowballing negative processes in the region'.[59]

Other scholars have underscored the British misreading of the Egyptians during this period. The 'outstanding feature of [the] British perception of the Arab side', in Shimon Shamir's view, 'was its low awareness of the authenticity, intensity and autonomy of the Arab anti-Western posture.' The Foreign Office seemed 'oblivious' to the fact that Nasir – 'as a good representative of his generation' and 'faithful to the historic role of national liberator that he was willing and expected to play' – rejected above all the 'perpetuation of Western regional hegemony through a system of military bases and alliances'. Shamir found it 'remarkable how long the British planners persevered in their belief that Nasser's pan-Arabism could somehow be reconciled with a Western-controlled regional strategic system.'[60]

Surprisingly, perhaps, American policy-makers – who were supposedly 'more attuned to the anti-colonial mood in the Arab world'[61] – were equally guilty of underestimating the force and genuineness of Arab nationalism in the cold-war context. Concluding his diary entry of that fateful day, 8 March 1956, President Eisenhower wrote:

> I am certain of one thing. If Egypt finds herself thus isolated from the rest of the Arab world, and with no ally in sight except Soviet Russia, she would quickly get sick of that prospect and would join us in the search for a just and decent peace in that region.[62]

This view is one which some have criticized as typical of the Eisenhower–Dulles team's ideological rigidity and insufficient 'awareness of the independent strength of Egyptian and Arab nationalism and the necessity to analyze such dynamic forces independent[ly] of a concern for suspected Soviet-communist subversion'.[63] It was precisely this sort of faulty and wishful thinking that paved the road to the larger Suez crisis which culminated in the next Arab–Israeli war.

THE LIMITS OF COERCIVE DIPLOMACY

While, in retrospect, the positions taken by Shuckburgh, Russell, Dulles and Eden in pursuing Operation Alpha proved to be misguided and fruitless, it would be an oversimplification to portray British and American attitudes as totally naïve and unrealistic. Despite all their careful preparations designed to stage-manage the course of Operation Alpha, the Anglo–American planners were faced with four sets of interrelated developments which proved to be truly beyond their control:

- the inability of UNTSO peacekeeping machinery (even with the backing of the tripartite powers) to prevent the continuing build-up of tension and violence along the Gaza and al-Auja frontiers;
- the accompanying insecurity of the Israeli and Egyptian régimes, and their increasingly desperate race to arm themselves;
- inter-Arab tensions, especially between the newer, anti-Western pan-Arab nationalism headed by Nasir's Egypt and the 'old-guard' under Iraq's Nuri Sa'id, who attempted to assert regional leadership via the pro-Western Baghdad Pact; and
- the emergence of the Soviet Union as ally and supporter of the Arab cause against Western domination and as an alternative supplier of arms.

Despite the apparent naïveté which seemed to propel Alpha planners to ignore or sidestep repeated setbacks and obstacles, there were within the ranks of the British and American foreign services a number of experienced officers who contributed sober assessments of their countries' truly limited ability to influence the Egyptians and the Israelis in the pursuit of a settlement. Some British diplomats were quick to recognize the growing *rapprochement* between Nasir and the Soviets as an important factor contributing to the decline of their own influence. A month prior to the announcement of the Czech arms deal, Sir John Sterndale-Bennett was prophetic when discussing the 'calculated risk' involved in pursuing Operation Alpha. 'What we are being asked to do', he wrote, 'is to participate in a pure gamble with our whole Middle Eastern policy and our whole position in the Middle East – at a time moreover when Soviet Russia is particularly well-placed to profit.'⁶⁴

Advice to London from Ambassador Nicholls in Tel Aviv often included additional perceptive comments, in one case on the problematic British role in transmitting proposals from one party to the other. Nicholls warned the Foreign Office not to 'delude ourselves that it is open to us to act as a mere post office'.

> It ... seems to me essential that we should not put forward to the Israelis, with our explicit or implicit endorsement, any Arab demands which we would not be prepared in the last resort to support with every form of pressure open to us.

Nicholls added his voice to those of other policy-makers and advisers who were concerned that a clumsily presented peace plan might actually increase the chances of war:

> What we *cannot* [he underlined] afford to do is to transmit, without a specific disclaimer, a complete set of proposals so far from anything that the Israelis could accept that they would regard the hazards of war as a lesser danger to their hopes of survival than negotiation on such a basis.⁶⁵

On the whole, Washington seems to have been more sanguine than the British regarding Alpha's chances of success. Yet, even the State Department was frequently confronted by evidence of the limitations of its ability to affect Arab behaviour. For many, the main obstacle to US influence over the Arabs was the latter's perception that the United States was incorrigibly biased in favour of Israel.⁶⁶ In a Washington conversation during the final days of the Anderson mission, John Foster Dulles drew an interesting connection between Israeli behaviour and America's ability to influence the Arabs. 'Israel', the Secretary lectured Ambassador Eban, 'should be constantly concentrating on the question of how to get into a peaceful relationship with the Arab states'. The United States had, he said, 'a great many pressures and influences it can bring to bear on the Arabs if Israel [did] not force us to throw them away'.

> We have many arrows in our quiver, a great deal more than the Israel Government does, but we are in danger of getting in a position where we cannot use them. The oil and cotton markets as well as other economic relations give us opportunities to

exert influence. But when the Jews put on mass meetings in this country they create a situation where the Arabs feel it is not safe for them to rely on the United States.[67]

During the course of Operation Alpha, as with earlier episodes seeking concessions from Israel or gradually 'educating' the Arabs to accept Israel, both the UK and the US were confronted more often by disappointments than by successes. In a perceptive late-1952 internal State Department memorandum entitled, 'An American Policy for Arab–Israeli Peace',' Donald Bergus was already keenly aware of the limits of American influence over both Israel and the Arab states. With regard to the former, he noted that 'American Jewry would not stand idly by if the Department tried to force major concessions down Israel's throat – concessions which Israel claimed menaced her very existence.'

> We are also in the curious position [he went on] of being unable to threaten the complete withdrawal of American aid, should American–Israeli negotiations take a turn for the worse. We are only too well aware that in the desperation which would follow withdrawal of American support, the Israelis might attempt further military adventures in the neighbouring Arab states.[68]

American ability to influence the Arab states was, of course, even more tenuous, given the indelible impression in Arab minds that the US was unwilling or unable to criticize Israel and incapable of understanding Arab grievances.

'ARMS AND THE DAM'[69]

For a final indication of the limits of Anglo–American coercive diplomacy, let us take a closer look at the two main levers of influence which the powers considered using: the carrots and sticks of military assistance and financial aid. In Chapters VIII and XI we saw how futile were American attempts to use the promise of arms sales to obtain either an Egyptian willingness to open discussions on a settlement with Israel or an Israeli commitment to consider territorial concessions. The Byroade-Dulles disagreement over the link between arms aid and a favourable response to the Secretary's statement of 26 August 1955 (above, pages 153–4) was but one indication of the problematic nature of the relationship. A similar disappointment for the Western powers had occurred several weeks earlier, when the British Prime Minister and Foreign Secretary were lobbying their American counterparts to provide Centurion tanks to Iraq (above, page 135). In Eden's telegraphic appeal to Eisenhower for American aid for the Centurions, the following paragraph was, significantly, *deleted* at the last moment:

> When Nuri is informed of the intention to make the Alpha statements, he could be told that delivery of the tanks will depend on the manner in which his Government receives these statements.[70]

Both Evelyn Shuckburgh and Michael Wright, Britain's Ambassador to Baghdad, warned that any *overt* attempts to link Nuri Sa'id's co-operation in Alpha with delivery of the tanks or American adhesion to the Baghdad Pact might backfire and be used against Nuri and Anglo–American interests.[71] Shuckburgh feared that a too-obvious linkage 'would force the Iraqi Prime Minister into a position in which he would have to refuse the tanks or lay himself open to a charge of selling [out] Arab rights in Palestine'.[72] Yet, even the Foreign Office was not immune to occasional wishful thinking and misreading the impact of arms-sales on Arab political behaviour.[73]

The Czech arms deal of September 1955 signalled the Soviet Union's breaking of Anglo–Franco–American hegemony in the Middle East. 'So long as we [were] supplying the arms', wrote Sir Ivone Kirkpatrick in mid-October 1955, 'we retain[ed] some measure of control, either by delaying or stopping deliveries or by withholding spare parts and ammunition.'[74] The loss of the Western powers' monopoly was one of several factors which contributed to the failure of the attempted use of Anglo–American arms sales as a means of controlling the political behaviour of Arabs and Israelis. Not only did the manipulations of prospective weapons sales fail to win Egyptian and Israeli co-operation in Operation Alpha, but – as we have argued above (pages 218–19) – the withholding of requested armaments may well have been counterproductive, increasing the levels of frustration and insecurity of the would-be recipients and contributing, in the end, to the outbreak of war in late 1956.

There were many political and psychological obstacles which almost nullified the powers' ability to use arms aid to foster peace between Arabs and Israelis. One was the behaviour of the implacable and embattled client-states, summed up in the adage: 'When I am weak, how can I compromise? When I am strong, why should I compromise?'[75] The perception of which party was the weaker and which the stronger has always affected the motivation of the adversaries to negotiate or to consider concessions.

One vivid illustration of the applicability of this maxim to Operation Alpha was the Western powers' expectation that Gamal Abd al-Nasir, once his perceived military disadvantage was corrected by Soviet arms, might feel confident enough and 'farsighted enough to see in this situation an opportunity to extricate himself from the state of permanent conflict with Israel by giving the lead to the Arabs in making a peace settlement.' But as a disappointed Francis Russell confessed in late April 1956, 'nothing came of these hopes'.

> [O]n the contrary [he was quoted as saying], Nasser has become dangerously over-confident of his military strength and political power to an extent that makes us think the preservation of peace in the Middle East would be helped if the Israelis acquired some defensive arms.[76]

Two major 'revisionist' studies of Israel's security and foreign policy in the period under study have recently raised a further consideration about the supposed ability of arms suppliers to influence the policies of intended recipients. Both Benny Morris and Mordechai Bar-On have touched on a paradox by contrasting the results of the United States' *withholding* of requested arms from Israel with France's *willingness* to supply the Jewish state during 1955 and 1956. In concluding his study of Arab infiltration and Israeli retaliation, Benny Morris has raised the possibility that 'the IDF's convincing performance in the reprisals of 1954-6 probably helped persuade France of Israel's military worth', while Sharett's period of 'restraint' did not produce any 'major increase in Western aid or arms sales to Israel, and no Western security guarantees or pacts'.[77] Bar-On has likewise suggested that the axiomatic assumption of the IMFA – according to which 'Israel had to "behave itself" and avoid an activist defense policy' in order to receive armaments – was simply erroneous with regard to Britain and the US, while the opposite proved to be the case with France:

> [E]xhibiting the IDF's fighting ability and Israel's willingness to follow an active security policy had confirmed the French in their conclusion that Israel could be useful in France's North African campaign. The French gave Israel arms not for it to avoid fighting for its interests, but to allow it to become an active military factor in the service of those security needs that the French estimated were congruent with their own.[78]

* * *

In his memorandum 'An American Policy for Arab–Israeli Peace' (discussed above), Donald Bergus wished to refute the 'feeling in the [State] Department that peace can be hastened by attaching conditions to US economic aid to the area'.

> The idea of requiring an Arab State to make some kind of peaceful gesture towards Israel (or vice versa) before receiving economic aid from the US simply will not work. The Arabs are fully capable of behaviour such as Mosadeq's in Iran and would refuse economic aid in such circumstances no matter how desperately they needed it.[79]

On the other side of the coin, potential Arab recipients of US economic assistance had already attempted to attach their own 'strings' or conditions to such aid. In mid-1952, for example, the Syrian leader, Adib Shishakli, was reportedly 'stalling on the aid agreements until US–Syrian relations [were] strengthened by a US "gesture" persuading Israel to comply with UN resolutions and [by] an offer of more economic and technical aid'.[80]

Bergus's late-1952 analysis proved to be equally valid during the years 1955 and 1956. Among the proposals for Operation Alpha, the main inducement for winning Egyptian co-operation was to have been financial assistance for the construction of the High Dam at Aswan. The logic which Francis Russell suggested for linking this key carrot with a settlement with Israel was that Egypt could 'only have security and the domestic and foreign economic resources for the construction of the dam if there [was] a relaxation of tensions that would flow from a settlement'.[81]

But, as in the case of military supplies, the Western powers discovered their powerlessness to manipulate this particular lever in pursuit of Operation Alpha. After October 1955, British and

American plans had to take into account the existence of a competing Russian offer to build the dam, a factor which gave additional bargaining leverage to Egyptian negotiators who were attempting to obtain the most favourable possible terms with the IBRD. The Russian offer became more and more tempting to the Egyptians as their representatives encountered delays and obstacles in their negotiations for the anticipated $1.3 billion, ten-year project.[82]

During and after late November 1955, American officials quietly offered to use their influence to help speed up and finalize the protracted Egyptian negotiations with the IBRD as a carrot to induce Egyptian co-operation in Alpha. 'It was clear', Francis Russell told British Ambassador Makins, 'that Egypt could not afford both the Dam and an arms race, and this would have to be brought out.' Yet Russell himself recognized the limitations of making his point 'too' obvious: 'it might be fatal to suggest to Nasser that acceptance of a settlement [with Israel] were a condition of Western assistance for the Dam.'[83]

Indeed, what had once been considered the main incentive with which to win Egyptian co-operation in Operation Alpha seemed to disintegrate when put to the test. During the last months of 1955, any American hints given to the Egyptian leadership of a link between US financial aid for the dam and a settlement of the Egyptian–Israeli dispute had to be kept subtle and discreet. In briefing Robert Anderson for his mission to Cairo, the Secretary referred to aid for the Aswan Dam as an incentive which 'could probably not be openly negotiated, but could be delicately suggested.'[84] Yet, despite this careful briefing, Mohamed H. Heikal claims that Nasir was 'taken aback' by the 'blunt and crude manner' in which the presidential envoy presented 'the relation between financing of the High Dam and reconciliation with Israel'.[85] This account is consistent with other evidence suggesting that Anderson's skills as a mediator were somewhat wanting.[86]

From an Egyptian point of view, any American hint that a settlement with the Israelis would be linked to assistance for the dam was considered heavy-handed pressure and an unacceptable use of 'political strings'.[87] Thus, rather than providing an ideal economic carrot, the linkage between Alpha and Aswan proved incapable of creating the desired Egyptian flexibility on the Israel issue. By early February 1956, Eisenhower, Hoover, and Dulles began to realize 'that there was little chance that financial backing for the Aswan project would produce enough political leverage to pressure the Nasser régime into a negotiated settlement of the Arab–Israeli conflict'.[88]

* * *

Just as the United Nations and the Western powers had proved incapable of employing sufficient leverage to cajole or coerce the reluctant protagonists to move from four limited and unstable armistice agreements to more durable peace treaties between 1948 and 1954, so too did the concerted Anglo–American exercise in secret diplomacy fail in its more modest goal of achieving an Egyptian–Israeli settlement during 1955 and 1956. The terms of agreement so carefully worked out in Washington and London contained some elements which both of the main protagonists, each for its own reasons, found highly undesirable.

The reasons for the failure of Operation Alpha, however, lie beyond the mere attractiveness or unattractiveness of the various proposals for a settlement. A full understanding of the collapse of the operation must take into account the international and regional context of Western–Soviet rivalry, and the motives and fears of the main protagonists, Egypt and Israel. Timing was also a determinant which proved perhaps even more important than the proposed terms of agreement. We need only recall the highly unpropitious coincidence of the launching of Alpha with the signing of the Baghdad Pact, Israel's raid on Gaza and Nasir's neutralist leadership efforts during and after the Bandung Conference. Further steps in the promotion of Operation Alpha coincided with the Soviet–Egyptian arms deal and the Arab League's final failure to endorse the Johnston plan for the development of the Jordan waters.[89]

Although it may be fashionable in some circles to paint an unflattering picture of the 'selfish' motives of the Western 'imperialist' powers who had no real interest in an Arab–Israeli peace, six men – Eden, Macmillan, Shuckburgh, Eisenhower, Dulles and Russell – were heavily committed to the success of Operation Alpha and worked to salvage it from collapse on more than one occasion. For the sake of manoeuvring Egypt and Israel into negotiations towards a settlement, Britain and America were prepared to mobilize all the political, economic and military inducements at their disposal.

As we have seen, these Anglo–American plans failed mainly because the available inducements were less effective than British and American policy-makers imagined them to be. Some might wish to conclude, rather, that these inducements were potent in themselves, but were incompetently manipulated at crucial moments. Whatever the truth in this latter claim, the end result was the same: the Western powers were simply unable to budge the parties from their irreconcilable stances, or even to advance beyond the stage of prenegotiation.

In retrospect, the failure of Alpha may be seen as a combination of

- an underestimation of the determination and the capability of the client states to withstand this exercise in coercive diplomacy; and
- a corresponding overestimation by the Western powers of the potency of the carrots and sticks with which they had hoped to manipulate Israel and Egypt towards a settlement.

With the failure of Alpha and Gamma in March 1956, the powers abandoned the ambitious quest for peace (conflict resolution) and reverted to the no less difficult task of avoiding war (conflict management). While the Foreign Office and the State Department concentrated quietly on outmanoeuvring and subverting Nasir during and after April 1956, the UN and its Secretary-General became the forum and focus of all overt activity in the quest for preventing open warfare between Egypt and Israel. The eruption of the Suez–Sinai War several months later was, however, a product of the dangerous dynamic that had been operating in the Arab–Israeli conflict since 1949: namely, that simply concentrating on conflict management (or, 'nibbling at the edges'), without taking risks in the search for a resolution of the core issues of the conflict, was itself an inherently unstable and unsatisfying exercise.

Documents

Document 1: Tripartite Declaration, 25 May 1950

The Governments of the United Kingdom, France, and the United States, having had occasion during the recent Foreign Ministers meeting in London to review certain questions affecting the peace and stability of the Arab states and of Israel, and particularly that of the supply of arms and war material to these states, have resolved to make the following statements:

1. The three Governments recognize that the Arab states and Israel all need to maintain a certain level of armed forces for the purposes of assuring their internal security and their legitimate self-defence and to permit them to play their part in the defense of the area as a whole. All applications for arms or war material for these countries will be considered in the light of these principles. In this connection the three Governments wish to recall and reaffirm the terms of the statements made by their representatives on the Security Council on August 4, 1949, in which they declared their opposition to the development of an arms race between the Arab states and Israel.

2. The three Governments declare that assurances have been received from all the states in question, to which they permit arms to be supplied from their countries, that the purchasing state does not intend to undertake any act of aggression against any other state to which they permit arms to be supplied in the future.

3. The three Governments take this opportunity of declaring their deep interest in and their desire to promote the establishment and maintenance of peace and stability in the area and their unalterable opposition to the use of force or threat of force between any of the states in the area. The three Governments, should they find that any of these states was preparing to violate frontiers or armistice lines, would, consistent with their obligations as members of the United Nations, immediately take action, both within and outside the United Nations, to prevent such violation.

Source: Hurewitz, *Diplomacy*, II: 308f.

Document 2: Tentative Conditions for an Arab–Israel Settlement, 29 July 1952

1. GENERAL
The Arab States to undertake to end the state of war with Israel and to rescind all measures taken in virtue thereof. The Arab States and Israel to undertake to exchange diplomatic representatives and in other ways to encourage the establishment of normal political and economic relations with one another.

TERRITORIAL PROVISIONS
2. (a) Rectification of the Israel–Jordan frontier in such a way as to reunite lands with villages to which they belonged.
   (b) Israel to surrender (against compensation) all claims to Mount Scopus, which will be handed over to Jordan.
   (c) Recognition by all Arab States of Israel's and Jordan's sovereignty over their respective sectors in Jerusalem, and a promise of support in the United Nations for a resolution giving such recognition, against guarantees to preserve international rights and interests there.
   (d) Adjustments to the line of demarcation in Jerusalem to establish a logical common frontier.
   (e) Israel sovereignty over the Huleh area to be acknowledged.
   (f) Syria to be given the Ein Gev area, access to Lake Tiberias and, consequently, a say in the disposal of Jordan waters.
   (g) Jordan to have the El Hamma salient, unless she is prepared to waive her claim in favour of Syria.
   (h) The United Nations to guarantee the frontier as established in the foregoing paragraphs and to request the signatories of the Tripartite statement, who accept the duty to see that this guarantee is implemented. In consequence of this guarantee, the frontiers to be placed within six months under exclusively police control; and Israel and the Arab States to give an undertaking to this effect.
   (i) The United Nations to undertake to make available a sum sufficient to dispose of resettlement problems in Jerusalem, including a grant for the re-building elsewhere of the Hebrew University and Hospital on Mount Scopus, compensation to owners of property deprived of its use, reconstruction of damaged areas and the establishment of frontier posts facilitating movement.

ETHNOGRAPHIC PROVISIONS
3. (a) Agreement on the principle that Arab refugees should not return to Israel, but should be compensated for the loss of all their property, movable as well as immovable.
   (b) The Arab countries to collaborate with the United Nations in the resettlement of all Arab refugees on Arab soil.
   (c) Israel to offer to buy out, on a generous scale of compensation, Arabs still resident in Israel, and the Arab States to encourage and help them to settle outside Israel, which would thus become homogeneous.

(d) Lifting of anti-Jewish and anti-Arab legislation and discriminatory practices in the Arab States and Israel respectively, and freedom for minorities to emigrate if they so desire.

MISCELLANEOUS
4. (a) The United Nations to establish a board of technicians to report on the allocation of the waters of the Jordan and its tributaries. Israel and the Arab States to undertake to accept and implement the findings of such a report upon their ratification by the General Assembly. A permanent technical mission to be established to supervise execution.
(b) Israel to establish a free port at Haifa; and Israel and Jordan might establish a free zone and possibly a free port in the Aqaba–Elath area, with free transit rights across Israel and Jordan territory between Saudi Arabia and Egypt.
(c) Jordan to grant free access to Jewish Holy Places in the Jordan sector of Jerusalem.

Source: Enclosure in Ross (FO) to Burrows (UKEmb Washington), 29 July 1952, PRO FO371/98258 E1056/83.

Document 3: Possible Terms of Settlement, 2 December 1953

The lines which a Palestine settlement might theoretically take were discussed tentatively some months ago between the Foreign Office and the State Department, who were in general agreement. These tentative provisions, which have been somewhat revised by the Levant Department in the light of later developments, are listed below. They might in some cases be facilitated by the rescission of relevant UN resolutions. [...]

(a) The Arab States and Israel should end the state of war, rescind all discriminatory legislation, and establish normal political, diplomatic and economic relations with one another.
(b) Rectification of the Israel–Jordan Armistice line in such a way as to re-unite lands with villages to which they belonged.
(c) Israel to surrender (against compensation) all claims to the Mount Scopus area of Jerusalem (at present a UN enclave in Jordan territory). The area would be handed over to Jordan and its important Jewish institutions transferred elsewhere (see also (h) below).
(d) Adjustments to the line of demarcation in Jerusalem, and recognition of Israel's and Jordan's sovereignty over their respective sectors.
(e) Israel and Jordan to guarantee free access to Christian, Moslem and Jewish Holy Places for all, including each other's nationals; and to agree to a system of UN control of the Holy Places.
(f) Other territorial adjustments designed mainly to render politically acceptable a scheme for joint use of the Jordan and Yarmuk waters on the lines of the TVA [Tennessee Valley Authority] scheme recently commissioned by UNRWA, which both sides should agree to carry out under UN auspices (see also (j) below). The suggested adjustments are as follows:

- (i) Israel sovereignty over the Huleh area to be acknowledged.
- (ii) Syria to be given the Ein Gev area, access to Lake Tiberias and consequently a say in the disposal of the waters of the River Jordan.
- (iii) Jordan to have the El Hamma salient unless she is prepared to waive her claim in favour of Syria.
- (iv) Israel to have the demilitarised Banyas zone (on the Syrian frontier); this would bring under Israel control the dam on the head waters of the River Banyas which is proposed in the TVA scheme.
- (v) Jordan to have a triangle south of Lake Tiberias which would be bounded on the west by the River Jordan, on the south by the River Yarmuk and on the east by a line at the southern end of the Ein Gev zone (to be agreed with Syria), so as to leave in Jordan the proposed line of the diversion canal taking the flood waters into Lake Tiberias. This proposal takes account of the TVA scheme and avoids Israel control of the in-flow and out-flow between Lake Tiberias and the East Ghor (Jordan) irrigation scheme.

(g) The UN or the signatories of the Tripartite Declaration, to guarantee the frontiers resulting from (b), (c), (d) and (f) above, which should be placed within six months under exclusively police control.

(h) The United Nations to make available a sum sufficient to dispose of resettlement problems in Jerusalem (including a grant for the rebuilding elsewhere of the Hebrew University and Hospital on Mount Scopus), compensation to owners of property deprived of its use, reconstruction of damaged areas, and the establishment of frontier posts facilitating movement.

(i) Agreement on the principle that Arab refugees should not return to Israel but should be compensated for the loss of all their property (...). The Arab countries to collaborate with UNRWA in the resettlement of all Arab refugees on Arab soil.

(j) The United Nations to undertake to finance through UNRWA the TVA scheme (which should eventually settle some 200,000 refugees) and to provide a technical mission to supervise its execution.

(k) The United Nations to guarantee the continued payment through UNRWA of relief funds until the refugees are resettled, and to give sympathetic consideration to financing further resettlement schemes which might later be evolved, e.g. in Syria and Iraq.

(l) It might be useful, as an insurance against future trouble between Israel and Jordan, if the former were to establish a free port at Haifa. Similarly,

(m) Israel and Jordan might establish a free zone and possibly a free port in the Aqaba–Elath area, with free transit across Israel and Jordan territory between Egypt and Saudi Arabia.

Source: Extract from R. Allen memorandum, 'Settlement of the Palestine Problem', 2 December 1953, PRO FO371/104770 ER1078/3.

Document 4: C.A.E. Shuckburgh, the Elements of a Settlement, 15 December 1954

The following are some preliminary thoughts on the elements of which a possible settlement might consist. Careful Anglo–American discussion will be necessary before any final conclusions can be reached.

(a) Territorial. – Some significant territorial concession by Israel is essential. They certainly will not go back to the 1947 frontiers, which is the present Arab demand. No-one can ma[k]e them do so. But something might be found from amongst the following suggestions:–

   (i) From the Egyptian point of view, it seems that the most valuable concession would be the grant of direct access between Egypt and Jordan on the Gulf of Aqaba. This means the cession to Jordan of a part of the Negev south of Beersheba. It has psychological importance since it would end 'the partition of the Arab world', and it would facilitate the settling of refugees from Gaza. It might conceivably be balanced by the cession of the Gaza strip to Israel. (Egypt is willing to give this territory up – but to Jordan, not to Israel.)

   (ii) The surrender to Jordan of an area in Galilee, into which refugees might be returned for resettlement. This might possibly be offset by the surrender to Israel of some 'desert' territory, perhaps south of Hebron.

   (iii) Frontier rectifications designed to restore agricultural land to the Jordanian border villages.

   (iv) Final adjudication to Syria and Jordan of the 'demilitarised zones'.

   (v) Alteration of the frontier on Lake Tiberias so as to give Syria access to the Lake. (This might be a contribution to a settlement of the Jordan Waters problem (see paragraph (d) below).)

   (vi) Jerusalem. A very complicated issue for which there are many conflicting solutions, all of them beset with difficulty. Internationalisation or neutralisation should still be our aim.

(b) Refugees. –

   (i) *Repatriation.* – Israel will not accept the principle of the right to return, upon which the Arabs are now insisting. She might, however, find ways and means of re-admitting a certain number through enlarging the existing categories (relatives of Arabs already in Israel) who are allowed to return. She would insist on their becoming Israeli citizens. Needless to say, a cession of territory would greatly alleviate this problem.

   (ii) *Compensation.* – Israel has already accepted the principle of compensation for Arab property in Israel. The Egyptians (unlike the other Arab States) say that they do not mind from whose pocket the money comes, and that they do not insist upon a degree of compensation which would 'cripple' Israel. Compensation will need clear definition and assessment and Israel would require loans if she were to pay. But she will not pay so long as the blockade continues. The Arab countries in return must relax restrictions on employment of refugees and movement across the frontiers. Every effort must be made to provide employment and attract refugee labour into Syria and Iraq.

(c) *Economic.* – The principal Israeli requirement is the lifting of the blockade (*i.e.* Suez Canal restrictions, blacklisting of neutral firms, ships, etc., trading with Israel[,] and other aspects of economic warfare). This is essential to any settlement. Israel would be ready to make a free port at Haifa and access thereto for Jordan trade. It may *not* be necessary, at any rate to begin with, for the Arabs to remove restrictions on their own trade with Israel. Mr Sharett told me he considered this to be their own affair. They may well wish before doing so to make sure that they can protect themselves against economic exploitation by Israel. It may be necessary, in order to reassure the Arabs against this danger, for the Powers to secure additional investment for development in Arab countries.

(d) *Jordan Waters.* – I doubt if it will be possible to achieve a settlement without including some provision to guarantee the fair distribution of the Jordan Waters. This is a major source of suspicion on the Arab side in view of Israeli water projects and of the fact that Lake Tiberias, which is the main reservoir, lies entirely under Israeli control. It will be necessary to induce the Israelis to accept effective international control of any water distribution that is agreed upon. H.M. Government and the U.S. Government should call upon Mr Eric Johnston to make specific proposals to us, strictly in confidence, in the light of Arab and Israeli reactions to his earlier approach. If we find that an over-all plan for the Jordan Waters is not a practical possibility, we should at once turn our attention to individual projects and endeavour to bring about a bargain on a more limited scale.

(e) *Political.* – Any proposals will need to be reinforced by the strongest possible British and U.S. political support. I do not recommend re-issue or elaboration of the Tripartite Declaration. In the first place, French participation is a weakness; second, the unilateral and 'olympian' use of declarations is not best calculated to inspire confidence. A better system would be to arrange separate arrangements guaranteeing the frontiers on both sides. This means extending to Syria and the Lebanon (? and Egypt) guarantees of the kind now enjoyed by Jordan, but if possible on an Anglo–U.S. basis. It means also giving Israel parallel guarantees. Some machinery for enforcement will probably be required. (If the Arab States join a defence organisation with the Western Powers there will be a strong demand in Israel for the right to make some similar arrangements. This will have to be a second stage.)

Source: Annex to Shuckburgh, 'Notes on Arab–Israel Dispute', 15 December 1954, PRO FO371/111095 VR1079/10G, incorporating handwritten corrections.

Document 5: Points of Agreement in [Anglo–American] London Discussions of Arab–Israel Settlement, 10 March 1955

I. GENERAL
A. While initiating the project at present is complicated by the still unfinished Johnston negotiations, the ferment in the Arab world created by the Turk–Iraq [Baghdad] Pact which may be increased by UK adherence to the Pact and by the new Israel attack on Gaza, it is probable that the current year is as favorable a time as is likely to arise in the foreseeable future for an attempt to achieve a settlement in the dispute between the Arab states and Israel.
B. An attempt at an overall settlement will allow us to present a balanced set of proposals which might permit us to dispose of some problems such as boundaries which are resistant to solution in isolation. Indeed, Egyptian Prime Minister Nasser recently stated to Sir Anthony Eden that no solution was to be found in partial settlements.
C. The method which offers the best chance of success and involves the least risk is that the United States and United Kingdom Governments should work out the general terms of a reasonable settlement and then by separate discussion with the parties concerned, and if possible through direct talks between them, attempt to get them to agree to the settlement or to an agreed variation of it.
D. Success of the Johnston Mission would be most helpful in creating a favorable atmosphere for Alpha, but the Alpha inducements, particularly the security guarantee, should not be extended to secure acceptance of the Unified Development Plan alone.
E. The present proposals have been worked out on an ad referendum basis.

II. METHOD AND TIMING OF THE APPROACH TO THE PARTIES
A. The first approach should be made to Egypt, difficult as this may appear at the moment. ... [Material omitted from the published version; access restricted at the USNA.]
B. Two alternatives with respect to the precise timing of the approach to Egypt are foreseen. [Omitted here: material dealing with impact of Baghdad Pact negotiations and 'Gaza incident'.] The advice of the two ambassadors in Cairo should be sought regarding which course is preferable.
C. Other possibilities [regarding timing, omitted here].
D. In either event consideration should be given to parallel letters to Sharett from Mr Dulles and Sir Anthony Eden covering the following points:
    1. Because of the overriding need which must concern all of us, including Israel, we intend to continue our policy of strengthening the Middle East against outside aggression by working out agreements based on the northern tier approach. Because of the state of Arab feeling toward Israel, not improved since the Gaza raid, it is not possible to consider associating Israel with these area defense arrangements at this time. The first essential is to get these arrangements into shape. When this has been achieved and when the state of Israel's relations with the Arab states permits, we would be prepared to consider discussions with Israel about its role in area defense.

DOCUMENTS   297

>   2. Israel's security problem is receiving our active consideration, but
>   we are not disposed to assume obligations with respect to the security
>   of a border which is continuously marked by border raids and military
>   actions. Therefore, we are giving consideration to steps that could be
>   taken to produce a genuine reduction of tension as a prelude to a security
>   undertaking.
>   3. The Israel Government's Gaza raid has obviously set back for some
>   time the possibility of success in this effort.
>   4. But we intend to press forward with it, and, in view of Israel's need
>   for a security guarantee, we entertain the hope that we may receive more
>   cooperation in the future than we have had in the past in our efforts to
>   reduce tensions.

E. [Omitted paragraph on suggestions for preparing Ambassador Byroade to broach the matter further in forthcoming meetings with Nasir.]
F. In revealing the proposal to the parties we would not be too specific at first and would not present the plan as a whole. The purpose would be to develop the proposal gradually so that the solution should appear to emerge from the discussions with the parties rather than to have been worked out fully by the UK and US Governments in advance.
G. We should inform the French and the Turks in very general terms of out intentions to make some approaches as soon as we are satisfied from contacts with Nasser that progress can be made and thenceforth we should keep both governments informed in a very general way of our discussions with the parties.
H. The UK would outline our intentions to Jordan after headway had been made with Nasser and immediately before the approach to Israel. This is necessary because of the special treaty relationship between the UK and Jordan.
I. We should inform Iraq of our intentions at about the time we inform Israel in order to ensure that she did not make it difficult for Egypt to cooperate by accusing her of following a pro-Israel policy. We should seek an assurance that Iraq would accept whatever Israel's Arab neighbors accept and if necessary we should relay that assurance to Egypt. The Iraqis themselves need not be involved in the negotiations or the settlement.
J. After steps G, H and I above, which we contemplate should not take more than two or three days, the plan would be discussed with Israel. We would indicate that Nasser was prepared to consider a settlement and that from discussions with him we had reached the conclusion that we were justified in putting forward as a basis for discussion a set of ideas which we consider offers prospect of progress toward a settlement. We would state that if Israel is ready to pursue discussions on this basis, we were prepared to continue our efforts. If it should be necessary, we would make clear to Israel the effects of a refusal on her part to cooperate, mentioning particularly that under such circumstances we would be unable to extend the security guarantee she has requested, and that she would have to bear the onus for failure of our efforts toward peace.
K. Mr Johnston should continue his efforts to secure Israel acceptance of a Unified Development Plan but Alpha need not be delayed until after a possible trip by Johnston to the area in April or May. If Mr Johnston is unsuccessful the Unified Development Plan should be incorporated as one of the elements in Alpha.

III. INDUCEMENTS AND PSYCHOLOGICAL FACTORS

A. The terms of the settlement itself will contain inducements to the parties, but these will probably be insufficient to overcome the Arabs' resistance to any settlement and Israel's reluctance to make the concessions required of her. Outside inducements will therefore be necessary: e.g., military and economic aid, and security guarantees.

B. Since no Arab state is likely to participate in a settlement unless it knows that Egypt is sympathetic, Egyptian cooperation is of first importance in any attempt at a settlement. We shall therefore need to offer inducements to Egypt. However, we could not acquiesce in Nasser's attitude towards the Turk–Iraq Pact as an inducement to him to move towards a Palestine settlement. The following are the main possibilities:

1. The prestige implied in the fact that we have chosen to consult Nasser first.
2. The suggestion that if Egypt will take the lead in solving this problem it will generally strengthen her position as an influential power and enable her to obtain the advantages of cooperation with the West. The solution of the Palestine problem will eliminate a major impediment to such cooperation.
3. Military assistance, the extent and conditions of which will in any case depend on the state of the relations between Israel and the Arab states.
4. Prospects of support for Colonel Nasser's domestic plans for the future of Egypt.
5. Specific offers of economic aid, for example, on the High Aswan Dam project.
6. The offer of a security guarantee.
7. Elimination of the possibility of constant clashes with Israel.

C. Inducements to Israel include:

1. A security guarantee.
2. Elimination of factors creating tension between Israel and her neighbors.
3. Removal of Suez Canal restrictions. Termination of the secondary boycott.
4. Continued US–UK interest in Israel's economic future.
[5.] ... [Material omitted from the published version; access restricted at the USNA.]
6. Military assistance.
7. Brighter prospects for Israel's association in area defense arrangements.

IV. ELEMENTS OF A SETTLEMENT

A. *Territorial Adjustments*

1. Israel must make concessions. The Arabs will not reconcile themselves to reaching a settlement with an Israel with the present boundaries. However, we cannot expect large transfers of territory. The changes proposed should be such that in presenting them to Israel they can be made to appear as 'frontier adjustments' which Sharett has stated Israel would be prepared to make. From

the Arab point of view they will reunite village lands. They will be designed to produce a frontier which could last with a minimum of friction.
2. No change is proposed in the border between Israel and Lebanon; it should continue to follow the old international boundary.
[3.] ... [Material omitted from the published version; access restricted at the USNA.]
4. The Jordan frontier should be adjusted so that Arab villages on the Jordan side recover a portion of their former lands from which they were separated by the demarcation line, certain Arab villages lying at the border are placed within Jordan and a more rational border is established. All modifications would be in favor of Jordan with the exception of the Latrun salient which would be relinquished to Israel to permit restoration of the old Tel Aviv–Jerusalem Road and eliminate an awkward salient. Israel would give up small areas, generally not containing Israeli settlements, along most of the present line. ... [Material omitted from the published version; access restricted at the USNA.] The changes suggested would not affect Israel adversely either militarily or economically and the total area would amount to about __ square miles. ... [Material omitted from the published version; access restricted at the USNA.]
[5.] ... [Material omitted from the published version; access restricted at the USNA.]
[6.] ... [Material omitted from the published version; access restricted at the USNA.]
7. Israel would cede to Egypt and Jordan two small triangles of territory in the southern Negev based respectively on the Egyptian–Israel[i] and Jordan[ian]–Israel[i] frontiers with their apexes meeting on the present or proposed road to Elath. The purpose would be to permit a land connection between Egypt and the rest of the Arab world. International supervision would be provided at the intersection.
8. Appendix 1 [not reproduced] describes the changes in detail.

B. Refugees

1. To prove acceptable to the Arabs the proposals must contain provision for repatriation of Arab refugees and the payment of compensation. In practice only a small number of refugees probably wish to return to Israel and in general it would not be desirable to increase too greatly Israel's Arab population.
2. Israel would be asked to repatriate as Israel citizens up to 75,000 refugees over a five-year period. This could be done through a non-renewable quota system providing for the admittance of 15,000 yearly with priority given to refugees from the Gaza strip. Persons readmitted would be settled by the Government of Israel in the same manner as new Jewish immigrants and UNRWA would provide financial assistance to this end.
3. The eventual resettlement of all refugees depends upon the general economic development of the area as well as upon specific UNRWA projects and freedom of the refugees to move in order to take employment. In the long run the best prospects are provided by the economic development program under way in Iraq. A very rough forecast of resettlement possibilities is as follows: Syria, 80,000; Lebanon, 40,000; Iraq, 60,000 (initial increment); Jordan Valley including the Unified Development Plan 200,000; Sinai Project,

70,000; Israel, 50,000 (it is very doubtful that the full 75,000 would want to return); total, 500,000.

4. Compensation.

a. Both the Arabs and Israel will advance large claims and counter-claims which will prove almost impossible to evaluate. These will include: on the part of Israel claims for abandoned Jewish property in Jordan, war damage and Jewish property sequestered in the Arab states; on the part of the Arabs, movable property, tenants' rights and loss of use and rents on property. The most practical approach is first to negotiate with Israel a fixed figure which will represent the net amount to be paid by Israel for compensation after all claims and counter-claims have been taken into account. The suggested figure is £100,000,000. This is the PCC estimate, which is understood to be conservative, of Arab immovable property abandoned in areas of Palestine now held by Israel.

b. It is important for psychological reasons with respect to the Arabs as well as to minimize the financial burden on the US and UK that Israel[i] contributions to compensation be as large as possible but it [is] recognized that unassisted she is unable to finance such a large sum. In view of the time which will be consumed in determining individual claims, the difficulty of providing funds and the low economic [absorptive] capacity of the area[,] payments should be made over a ten-year period. Of the total Israel and world Jewry combined should pay 30 per cent and 70 per cent would have to be provided by the world community, primarily the US and UK, in the form of loans to Israel. Israel should accept responsibility for repayment and servicing of the loans.

c. The funds available for compensation should be distributed through a quasi-judicial process to persons who are able to establish title to real property. [details omitted]

d. A special UN agency should be established to administer the program: UNRWA would make the actual payments.

e. [details omitted]

f. [details and reference to Appendix 2 omitted]

C. Jerusalem

1. The US and UK would inform the parties that they were prepared to sponsor a UN resolution on the lines of the Swedish proposal of 1950 on the supervision of an access to the Holy Places. ... [Material omitted from the published version; access restricted at the USNA.][1]

1. In a subsequent memorandum ('Next Steps to Advance Alpha Settlement', 2 June 1955, USNA NEA Lot 59, D518, Box 32), Francis Russell discussed the Jerusalem question as follows: 'In the context of a settlement we would be willing to support Jordan in obtaining sovereignty over Old Jerusalem and Mt Scopus', but the latter words are underlined and bear a handwritten question mark. Following talks at the FO in London in July, the paragraph on Jerusalem read (telegraphically) as follows: 'Only practicable solution is Israeli and Jordan sovereignty de jure in their respective parts of the city, but first we would try get through UN resolution providing for functional internationalization of Holy Places along line of Swedish 1950 draft. In view close UN interest in Jerusalem we cannot reveal our ideas at this stage.' Russell (London) to USSD, 12 July 1955, USNA 684A.86/7-1255. Cf. censored versions of these two documents in *FRUS 1955-1957*, XIV, 212 and 289.

2. Israel would be informed that following agreement upon a settlement and pending the adoption of such a resolution, the US and UK Ambassadors would start to call at the Israeli Foreign Office in Jerusalem. ... [Material omitted from the published version, access restricted at the USNA.]
3. Government House would become the seat of the international authority charged with the supervision of the Holy Places and possibly other UN agencies.
4. Jerusalem would be demilitarized along the lines of plans which are being discussed by the Consuls-General of Britain, France and the USA.
5. If France is willing to support the present plan she should be invited to participate in the negotiations on Jerusalem and to use her influence with the Vatican. If she does not favor the plan she should not be included and other means of influencing the Vatican and the Catholic States should be sought.
6. No approach should be made to the Vatican at this time.

D. *Communications arrangements*
1. Israel to offer Jordan free port facilities at Haifa and free access to the port.
2. Mutual overflight rights for civil aircraft of the parties.
3. Israel to permit the restoration or construction of telecommunications facilities between the Arab states across her territory.
4. Some mixed or UN authority to be established to hear complaints on the infringements of communications rights.

E. *The Boycott*
1. The Arab states would:
   a. remove restrictions on transiting the Suez Canal, including those on Israel[i] vessels,
   b. cease the 'secondary boycott', defined as attempts to prevent trade between Israel and non-Arab countries, including termination of all pressure on non-Arab forms trading with Israel,
   c. abolish the Arab League Boycott offices; repeal all legislation based on the existence of a state of belligerency.
2. The Arab states would not be pressed to engage in direct trade with Israel.

V. THE FORM OF A SETTLEMENT AND GUARANTEES TO THE PARTIES

A. While treaties of peace between Israel and the Arab states remain our ultimate objective, the state of Arab public opinion does not make it feasible to insist upon such treaties as an immediate objective. We should endeavor to bring about to the maximum extent possible permanent arrangements which would provide the substance, if not the form, of peace. It should be our objective to obtain the termination of the state of belligerency between the countries both to remove the basis for the Suez Canal blockade and the secondary boycott and to justify to the US and UK public and law makers the security guarantees and substantial financial contributions required. The termination of belligerency could be provided for by inserting in the preamble of the revised Armistice Agreements the phrase 'recognizing that the state of war (or belligerency) between them has come to an end, the parties, etc.'

B. Instruments of Settlement

1. Permanent frontiers should be established by re-negotiation of the Armistice Agreements. These contain provisions for modification by consent of both parties. The UNTSO should continue to supervise the boundaries as long as necessary. The new frontiers should be noted in any guarantee decided upon.
2. The whole settlement need not be covered in a single document. Different means should be used for the different components, possibly as follows:

    a. *Territorial.* The Territorial settlement to be embodied in a revision of the Armistice Agreements (see above).

    b. *Jordan Waters.* A separate agreement would be made between the parties on the development of the Jordan Valley and the operation of the unified scheme.

    c. *Refugees.* A UN resolution should be passed incorporating the provisions of repatriation, resettlement and compensation previously agreed to and calling upon Israel and the Arab states to comply. The resolution could also provide for the creation of a new agency to handle the mechanics of compensation. Israel and the several Arab states could indicate their intentions to comply by separate letters to the Secretary General.

    d. *Jerusalem.* Arrangements for Jerusalem and the Holy Places would be the subject of a UN resolution.

    e. *Communications.* Free ports and transit arrangements would be the subject of direct agreements between the parties.

    f. *The Blockade.* The Arab states would dissolve the Arab League Boycott office and repeal domestic legislation based on or presupposing a state of war. This would remove the legal basis for restriction on Suez Canal traffic and the boycott. We would if necessary make it clear to the Arabs that we were not insisting on removal of prohibitions on direct trade with Israel provided these were not based on legislation claiming the existence of a state of belligerency.

C. Security Guarantees

1. It will be necessary for the US and UK and possibly Turkey and France to guarantee the frontiers to be established between Israel and the Arab states against alteration by force. This could be accomplished by separate treaties between the guaranteeing powers and Israel and the Arab states. The operative clause might read: 'The parties to the present treaty will jointly or separately take appropriate measures for the maintenance or restoration of the agreed boundaries.'
2. The Guarantee would not cover other aspects of the settlement; nor would it come into operation in the case of frontier incidents not involving the occupation of territory. Such incidents, however, if they constituted 'any threat of an attack by armed force' would bring into operation the commitment of the parties to consult together. The guarantors might inform the Arab states and Israel that they are prepared to discuss the means of implementing the guarantee.
3. The participating powers might offer one treaty to Israel embodying the guarantee and a separate similar treaty to each Arab state. Should the Arab states be unwilling to sign treaties with the Western Powers, a unilateral guarantee by the Western Powers might be extended to them and the offer of a treaty left open.

4. In the proposed Treaty with Jordan a special article might be included stating that rights and obligations under the Anglo–Jordan[ian] Treaty are not affected.
5. Draft treaties are attached [not reproduced].

VI. THE ROLES OF FRANCE, TURKEY, AND THE UNITED NATIONS

1. France should not be included in the planning or negotiations but should be informed of the proposals prior to the approach to Israel. In order to avoid offending her she would not be informed of the project as a complete plan worked out by the US and UK, but its various components would be revealed gradually to her as they are unfolded to the parties. If France were prepared to cooperate, she might be included in the negotiations on Jerusalem. (See IV.C.) The participation of France as a guaranteeing power would be considered in the light of the reaction of the guaranteed states and the general situation at the time.
2. Turkey would not be included in the planning or in the negotiations but would be informed at the same time and in the same manner as France. The question of Turkey's participation in the guarantee would be considered in the light of the reaction of the guaranteed states and the general situation at the time.
3. The UN would be involved in the machinery of a settlement, for example, in supervision of the frontier, and UN resolutions would probably be required, for example, in connection with Jerusalem and the refugees. The UN should not be informed of the project until negotiations with the parties are well advanced.
4. The possibility should be borne in mind that Pakistan might play a useful part in including [*sic*? 'inducing'] the Arab states to accept the proposals.

VII. COST OF THE OPERATION

A. As inducements to a resolution of the Arab–Israel problem, it is anticipated that it would be necessary for the United States and the United Kingdom to provide assistance in addition to present and already projected commitments (development assistance, UNRWA relief and rehabilitation, and the unified development of the Jordan Valley). Such new assistance might include:
    1. US–UK participation in the financing of compensation by Israel to the Palestine refugees.
    2. Economic inducements such as substantial grant aid for the High Aswan Dam, etc.
    3. Military aid to the cooperating countries.

Source: *FRUS 1955–1957*, XIV, 98–107 (D48). This document is a revised version of an earlier one, dated 2 Feb. 1955, reproduced (with similar deletions) in ibid, 35–42.

Document 6: Proposals by Secretary of State Dulles for a Settlement in the Arab–Israel Zone, 26 August 1955

One of the first things I did as Secretary of State was to go to the Middle East. I wanted to see for myself that area so rich in culture and religious tradition, yet now so torn by strife and bitterness. So, in the spring of 1953, I visited Egypt, Israel, Jordan, Syria, Lebanon, Iraq and Saudi Arabia. Upon my return I spoke of the impressions gathered on that trip and of the hopes which I held as a result of talks with leaders and people there.

Some of those hopes have become realities. At that time the Suez Base was a center of controversy and of potential strife. Now, as a result of patient effort, in a spirit of conciliation, the problem of the Suez Base has been successfully resolved.

Another problem which was then concerning many of the leaders in the Middle East was that of the security of the area. It was clear that effective defense depended upon collective measures and that such measures, to be dependable, needed to be a natural drawing together of those who felt a sense of common destiny in the face of what could be a common danger. Here, too, there has been some encouraging progress.

A third problem which called for attention was the need for water to irrigate land. I mentioned in my report the possibility that the rivers flowing through the Jordan Valley might be used to make this valley a source of livelihood rather than dispute. Since then Ambassador Eric Johnston has held talks with the governments of countries through which the River Jordan runs. They have shown an encouraging willingness to accept the principle of coordinated arrangements for the use of the waters. Plans for the development of the valley are well advanced. Ambassador Johnston is on his fourth visit to the countries concerned in an effort to eliminate the small margins of difference which still exist.

A beginning has been made, as you see, in doing away with the obstacles that stand in the way of the aspirations of the Middle Eastern peoples. It is my hope – and that is the hope of which I would now speak – that the time has come when it is useful to think in terms of further steps toward stability, tranquillity, and progress in the Middle East.

THE ARAB–ISRAELI PROBLEM
What are the principal remaining problems? They are those which were unresolved by the armistices of 1949 which ended the fighting between Israelis and Arabs. Before taking up these problems specifically, I would first pay high tribute to what the United Nations has done to preserve tranquillity and to serve humanity in the area. Despite these indispensable efforts, three problems remain that conspicuously require to be solved.

The first is the tragic plight of the 900,000 refugees who formerly lived in the territory that is now occupied by Israel.

The second is the pall of fear that hangs over the Arab and Israel[i] people alike. The Arab countries fear that Israel will seek by violent means to expand at their expense. The Israelis fear that the Arabs will gradually marshal superior forces to be used to drive them into the sea, and they suffer from the economic measures now taken against them.

The third is the lack of fixed permanent boundaries between Israel and its Arab neighbors.

There are other important problems. But if these three principal problems could be dealt with, then the way would be paved for the solution of others.

These three problems seem capable of solution, and surely there is need.

Border clashes take an almost weekly toll of human lives and inflame an already dangerous mood of hatred. The sufferings of the Arab refugees are drawn out almost beyond the point of endurance. The fears which are at work, on each side, lead to a heavy burden of armament, which constitutes a serious drag on economic and social progress. Responsible leaders are finding it hard to turn their full attention and energies to the positive task of creating conditions of healthy growth.

Serious as the present situation is, there is a danger that, unless it improves, it will get worse. One ill leads to another, and cause and effect are hard to sort out. The atmosphere, if it worsens, could becloud clear judgments, making appear attractive what would in fact be reckless.

Both sides suffer greatly from the present situation, and both are anxious for what they would regard as a just an equitable solution. But neither has been able to find that way.

This may be a situation where mutual friends could serve the common good. This is particularly true since the area may not, itself, possess all of the ingredients needed for the full and early building of a condition of security and well-being.

The United States, as a friend of both Israelis and Arabs, has given the situation deep and anxious thought and has come to certain conclusions, the expression of which may help men of good will within the area to fresh constructive efforts. I speak in this matter with the authority of President Eisenhower.

PROPOSED LOAN TO ISRAEL
To end the plight of the 900,000 refugees requires that these uprooted people should, through resettlement and – to such an extent as may be feasible – repatriation, be enabled to resume a life of dignity and self-respect. To this end there is need to create more arable land where refugees can find permanent homes and gain their own livelihood through their own work. Fortunately, there are practical projects for water development which can make this possible.

All this requires money.

Compensation is due from Israel to the refugees. However, it may be that Israel cannot, unaided, now make adequate compensation. If so, there might be an international loan to enable Israel to pay the compensation which is due and which would enable many of the refugees to find for themselves a better way of life.

President Eisenhower would recommend substantial participation by the United States in such a loan for such a purpose. Also he would recommend that the United States contribute to the realization of water development and irrigation projects which would, directly or indirectly, facilitate the resettlement of the refugees.

These projects would, of course, do much more than aid in the resettlement of refugees. They would enable the people throughout the area to enjoy a better life. Furthermore, a solution to the refugee problem would help in eliminating the problem of recurring incidents which have plagued and embittered the settlements on both sides of the borders.

COLLECTIVE SECURITY MEASURES
The second problem which I mentioned is that of fear. The nature of this fear is such that it is hardly within the capacity of the countries of the area, acting alone, to replace the fear with a sense of security. There, as in many other areas, security can be assured only by collective measures which commit decisive power to the deterring of aggression.

President Eisenhower has authorized me to say that, given a solution to the other related problems, he would recommend that the United States join in formal treaty engagements to prevent war or thwart any effort by either side to alter by force the boundaries between Israel and its Arab neighbors. I hope that other countries will be willing to join in such a security guaranty, and that it would be sponsored by the United Nations.

By such collective security measures the area could be relieved of the acute fears which both sides now profess. The families located near the boundaries could relax from the strain of feeling that violent death may suddenly strike them; the peoples of the area whose standards of living are already too low would no longer have to carry the burden of what threatens to become an armaments race if indeed it does not become a war; the political leadership of the area could devote itself to constructive tasks.

PROBLEM OF BOUNDARIES
If there is to be a guaranty of borders, it would be normal that there should be prior agreement upon what the borders are. That is the third major problem. The existing lines separating Israel and the Arab States were fixed by the armistice agreements of 1949. They were not designed to be permanent frontiers in every respect; in part, at least, they reflected the status of the fighting at the moment.

The task of drawing permanent boundaries is admittedly one of difficulty. There is no single and sure guide, for each of two conflicting claims may seem to have merit. The difficulty is increased by the fact that even territory which is barren has acquired a sentimental significance. Surely the over-all advantages of the measures here outlined would outweigh vastly any net disadvantages of the adjustments needed to convert armistice lines of danger into boundary lines of safety. In spite of conflicting claims and sentiments, I believe it is possible to find a way of reconciling the vital interests of all the parties. The United States would be willing to help the search for a solution if the parties to the dispute should desire.

If agreement can be reached on these basic problems of refugees, fear, and boundaries, it should prove possible to find solutions for other questions, largely economic, which presently fan the flames of hostility and resentment.

It should also be possible to reach agreement on the status of Jerusalem. The United States would give its support to a United Nations review of the problem.

I have not attempted to enumerate all the issues on which it would be desirable to have a settlement; nor have I tried to outline in detail the form which a settlement of any of the elements might take. I have tried to show that possibilities exist for an immeasurable improvement and that the possibilities do not require any nation taking action which would be against its interests, whether those interests be measured in terms of material strength or in terms of national prestige and honor. I have also, I trust, made clear that the Government of the United States is disposed to enlarge those possibilities by contributions of its own, if this be desired by those concerned.

Both sides in this strife have a noble past, a heritage of rich contributions to civilization; both have fostered progress in science and the arts. Each side is predominantly representative of one of the world's great religions. Both sides desire to achieve a good life for their people and to share, and contribute to, the advancements of this century.

At a time when a great effort is being made to ease the tension which has long prevailed between the Soviet and Western worlds, can we not hope that a similar spirit should prevail in the Middle East? That is our plea. The spirit of conciliation and of the good neighbor brings rich rewards to the people and to the nations. If doing that involves some burdens, they are burdens which the United States would share, just as we would share the satisfaction which would result to all peoples if happiness, contentment, and good will could drive hatred and misery away from peoples whom we hold in high respect and honor.

Source: Department of State Bulletin, no. 33, 5 Sept. 1955, 378–80; reproduced in Hurewitz, Diplomacy, II: 395–8.

Document 7: Sir Ivone Kirkpatrick Minute: The Middle East, 30 October 1955

...

EGYPT

Egypt constitutes the most difficult problem. We should not write her off or drive her irrevocably into Russia's arms. On the other hand it would be a mistake to give the impression that blackmail pays.

An attempt should be made to detach Egypt from Russia. But it would be a mistake to make representations to Nasser at this stage. If he were to reject them, relations with Egypt would be exacerbated. If he complied, we should not be ready with measures to reward him and relations would once more deteriorate.

Moreover reports from Cairo describe Nasser as being intoxicated with the popularity which defiance of the West has brought him. The moment does not seem propitious.

Finally, an approach to Nasser now would be regarded in Turkey, Iraq and elsewhere as appeasement. It would be better to fortify the Northern Tier before undertaking any move in Cairo.

Nevertheless the United Kingdom and United States Governments should begin now to concert a package deal which should be put to Nasser at the first favourable opportunity after the necessary preparatory work has been done. The following would be the elements of the package deal.

A. Nasser would undertake:–

(a) To turn away from Russia on completion of the present arms deal, which would be a once and for all commercial transaction.

(b) To limit his arms purchases thereafter to an expenditure which the Egyptian economy can bear, having regard to the regime's commitments in social welfare.

(c) To agree to open negotiations with Israel for a settlement on Alpha lines.

B. The Western powers would undertake:–

(a) To license the sale of weapons to Egypt within the limits defined in A (b).

(b) To bring concerted and strong pressure on Israel to agree to a just settlement.

(c) To finance the immense cost of the High Dam.

(d) To use such influence as they have in Iraq and the Sudan to put Egyptian relations with these countries on a sound footing.

These terms would be negotiable, but if Nasser rejects collaboration with the West on these lines we should:–

(a) Refuse all economic aid to Egypt.

(b) Cut off all further arms deliveries.

(c) Endeavour to isolate Egypt.

(d) [1]Consider ways and means of bringing down the Regime, and make it plain to Nasser that we have vital interests in the area and will shrink from nothing to protect them from Soviet encroachments.

Source: PRO FO371/115469 V1023/19G.

---

1. Item (d) does not appear in (or was excised, without ellipsis, from) the published version of the telegraphic and abridged text in *FRUS 1955–1957*, XIV, 709 (D384)

Document 8: Anthony Eden's Guildhall (Mansion House) Speech, 9 November 1955

... Between Israel and Egypt lies an area of dangerous tension. During the past seven years we have been trying to bring about some kind of settlement – successive governments in this country and our allies in that part of the world – and to prevent competition in armaments there. We have not been entirely unsuccessful. Despite frontier incidents from time to time – some more serious than others – there has been no war since 1948. The level of arms has been kept comparatively low, and this applies especially to more modern weapons. There's been some kind of a balance, though naturally each side cries loudly that it is less favoured than the other.

... I had hopes, real hopes, that many peoples in these lands were beginning to see that a way to peace must somehow be found in all their interests. We have been working for a long time past without publicity to promote such a result. In this connection the reception given to Mr Dulles' proposals last August was by no means discouraging. It should be followed up, but now – now into this delicate situation the Soviet Government have decided to inject a new element of danger and to deliver weapons of war, tanks, aeroplanes, even submarines, to one side only. It is fantastic to pretend that this deliberate act of policy was an innocent commercial transaction. Of course, ... it is no such thing. It is a move to gain popularity at the expense of the restraint shown by the West, and by this means it is intended to make it easier for Communism to penetrate the Arab world. Its consequences should be clear for all to see. Many proud states, some of which have not long enjoyed independence and national identity, will be threatened with submergence in the Communist Empire if they fall victims to these tactics. For our part, we find it impossible to reconcile this Soviet action with protestations that they wish to end the cold war in the new spirit of Geneva. The authors of these actions must have known well enough in advance what the effect of the sudden arrival of these large quantities of arms must be. It has brought a sharp increase of tension with very dangerous possibilities, particularly between Egypt and Israel. And yet, when nations face each other in hostility, it's not much use just blaming them for getting arms wherever they can. It is not with the recipients but with the suppliers that the main responsibility must lie.

BRITISH AIMS

Now, ... what is our immediate task? It is to prevent the outbreak of war. ... [References to hostilities in the al-Auja DMZ and to efforts of UNTSO under General Burns.]

... I have never known a situation where it was clearer that neither party had anything whatever to hope for in the long term from any military conflict. ... [More references to hostilities in the al-Auja DMZ and to recent talks with General Burns.] It will be a great gain if the risk of frontier incidents can be reduced. It will be a greater gain if the tragic problem of the refugees can be dealt with. I much regret that the hard work which Mr Johnston of the United States has devoted to preparing irrigation schemes has not yet been accepted by those concerned. It should be, for it is in the interests of all, Israeli and Arab alike; and we are ready to help here also, as we have done with the Arab refugees. But, ... beneath the volcanic crust of these smouldering dangers lies a deeper peril [still]: the hostility between Israel and her Arab neighbours is unreconciled. Here time has proven no healer. There is no progress to report to you since the armistice agreement six years ago. If it were not for these harsh and enduring sentiments, the countries of the Middle East could give all their efforts to their economic and social plans. They could concentrate on building up happy and prosperous societies in their lands. As I have said, we have tried for a long time past to find common ground for some kind of settlement. I think that the time has come now when the acute dangers of the situation command us to try again. We must somehow attempt to deal with the root cause of the trouble, and our country has a special responsibility in all this, for we have a long tradition of friendship with the Middle East. I believe that it should be possible to find common ground between the two positions. There is, after all, one interest which both parties ought to share. Neither Israel nor her Arab neighbours can want to see their differences turned to the advantage of anyone else: and there is somebody else quite ready to receive the advantage.

Now Sir, from that starting point, can we not look once again at the proposals which the United States Government and we ourselves have advocated? We have only one desire in this – if our Arab and Israeli friends would only believe us – to help to find a means of living which will enable the peoples concerned to dwell side by side in peace.

FRONTIER PROBLEMS
Let us give one instance. If there could be accepted arrangements between them about their boundaries, we, Her Majesty's Government, and, I believe, the United States Government and perhaps other powers also, would be prepared to give a formal guarantee to both sides; and that might bring real confidence and security at last. Our countries would also offer substantial help, financial and other, over this tragic problem of the refugees.

All this we will do. But can we not now move even a little further than this? And I think the Guildhall is the right place to make this suggestion. The position today is that the Arabs on the one side take their stand on the 1947 and other United Nations resolutions. That is where they are. They have said that they would be willing to open discussions with Israel from that basis. The Israelis[,] on the other side, found themselves on the later armistice agreement of 1949, and on the present territories which they occupy. Now, ... between those two positions there is, of course, a wide [gap. But is it] so wide that no negotiation is possible to bridge it? It is not right, I agree, that United Nations resolutions should be ignored, but equally can it be maintained the United Nations resolutions on Palestine can now be put into operation just as they stand? The stark truth is that if these nations want to win a peace, which is in both their interests and to which we want to help them, they must make some compromise between these two positions.

OFFER OF SERVICES
... I am convinced that it is possible to work this out. And if we could do so it would bring relief and happiness to millions, and the sooner the better. If we

fail to do so, none can tell what the consequences will be. I want to say tonight, ... that Her Majesty's Government, and I personally, are available to render any service in this cause. If there is anything – anything – that we can do to help we would gladly do it for the sake of peace.

Source: BBC Overseas Service transcription reproduced in Hurewitz, *Diplomacy*, II: 413–15. Prepared text in PRO FO371/115880 VR1076/335G. Ellipses are mainly rhetorical references to 'My Lord Mayor' of London, etc.

Document 9: Draft of Proposed Agreed Position Between US and UK on Middle East Policy, 9 November 1955

'Mr Russell took me in to see Mr Dulles this morning and the latter read through the document. The amendments shown in ink [here in *italics*; paras. 9, 15 and 16] were made at Mr Dulles's suggestion. He said he would want further time to study the paper if it were to become an agreed document and instructed Mr Russell to telegraph it to Washington for comment. [These comments, transmitted on 14 Nov., are given in subsequent footnotes.] I said that on our side too there was no commitment. Mr Russell and I agreed that we would try to reach final agreement on this paper when he visited London next week.'[1]

THE MIDDLE EAST

The Premises

1. Our policy in the Middle East has been directed towards retaining the area within the free world, developing the oil resources, assisting in the economic and social development of the countries concerned, ensuring an adequate defense arrangement for the area as a whole, keeping a reasonable arms balance between Israel and the Arab states, and working toward a settlement of the Israel–Arab dispute.
2. The Russians have now elected to open a new cold war front in the Middle East. Our recent exchanges show that they are not to be moved from this policy.
3. In consequence we must be prepared to settle down to a long contest. This means that a consistent long term policy must be devised. There is no short cut.
4. This Western policy must be based upon the need to have most of the inhabitants of this large area with the West and upon their willingness to let the West have easy access to their oil fields.
5. The obligations of the Western Powers to Israel under the 1950 Declaration [Document 1, above] must be fulfilled. But Israel must be made to understand that the West cannot afford to estrange the Moslems. Otherwise the Arab states will fall away, come under Russian domination; and it will then be impossible for the West effectively to protect Israel.[2]

1. Shuckburgh to Kirkpatrick, 10 Nov. 1955, PRO FO371/115469 V1023/23G.
2. State Department suggested adding the words: 'and Arab states'. Hoover to Dulles (Geneva), 14 Nov. 1955, *FRUS 1955-1957*, XIV, 746 (D407).

6. In the coming contest with Russia the West enjoys certain solid advantages. There is no reason to be stampeded into panic measures; or to give the Russians and the Arabs the impression that we have lost confidence in our ability to protect our interests.

7. Egypt is the largest of the Arab states and no Western policy in the Middle East which is actively opposed by Egypt will be entirely satisfactory. An effort should be made to prevent Egypt falling completely under Russian domination. Only if this is seen to have failed should we have recourse to a policy of isolating Egypt.

8. Meanwhile the Northern Tier[3] can constitute a focus of Western influence. It must be sustained and strengthened. We must demonstrate that association with the West pays.

9. We must try to influence the smaller Arab states against association with Egypt or Saudi Arabia for purposes hostile to our policies.

10. Finally, we must recognize that it is the Israel–Arab conflict[4] which has weakened Western influence in the Middle East and opened the door to Russia. If we wish to maintain a position of influence with the Arabs we must bring the conflict to an end as soon as possible. This means strong pressure on Israel and also *on the Arab states*. [*modified from:* 'on those Arab states on which we still have influence'.]

Future Policy

11. General. We must continue to make plain to the people of the Middle East our policy of equal friendship and desire to assist in the development of the area. We must avoid being pushed by the Russians into a position of opposition to Arab interests. We must not start a competition with the Soviet Union to arm the countries of the area.

12. The Soviet Union. We should make no further attempt to plead with the Russians to abandon their present offers to the Middle East countries, although we should continue to make it plain to the world that we regard this as incompatible with the Soviet pretense to desire reduction of tension. We should resist any effort by the Soviet Union to claim as of right to participate in decisions regarding Middle East affairs. Means should be found of assuring the Soviets that it is not the purpose of the Baghdad Pact to provide the Western Powers with strategic air bases in countries contiguous to the Soviet Union. This must be considered in the light of the British position in Iraq. Subject to this, we should continue our efforts to build up a defensive system in the area while keeping open the possibility, when our position is stronger, of working out some *modus vivendi* with the Soviet Union.

13. Israel. Under present conditions the US and the UK should not grant a special security guarantee to Israel. Such a guarantee will continue to be offered to Israel in the context of a settlement of the Palestine question. This policy might have to be reviewed if it should develop that Egypt was working closely

---

3. State Department suggested adding the words: 'backed up by other states of [the] N[ear] E[ast].' *Loc. cit.*

4. State Department comments at this point that 'Western influence has also been weakened by [the] slow pace of economic and political development in the Arab world.' *Loc. cit.*

with the Soviet bloc and there was no chance of bringing about a reversal of this trend. In such an event the US might adhere to the Northern Tier and grant a guarantee to Israel at the same time.

Israel should be urged in her own interests to try to reach a settlement with the Arab states. If she is to survive, she cannot afford to pursue a policy which estranges the Arabs from the West. This will involve a willingness to agree upon some compromise between the United Nations resolutions of 1947 and the present armistice frontiers.[5]

14. Armament supplies. We should try to arrange a coordinated policy of arms supplies to Middle East countries on the part of the Tripartite Powers, Italy, and perhaps other NATO Powers. Machinery to this effect should be worked out in Washington at an ambassadorial level between the three Powers. Consideration should be given to the question of associating Italy in this study.

Our guiding principle is that we should not seem to be moving in to supply Israel with arms on a large scale to offset those supplied by the Iron Curtain [countries]. The Western Powers have in the past supplied arms to both sides under the principles of the 1950 Declaration and this should continue to guide our arms shipments to the area. With respect to Israel,[6] arms shipments by any one of the Western Powers should take into account shipments to Israel either made or contemplated by other Powers, and should reflect the security afforded to Israel under the 1950 Declaration. It should be our purpose not to allow a substantial increase in the striking power of the Israeli armed forces, although some increase in their defensive equipment should be contemplated.

15. Egypt. We should not write off Egypt or drive her into Russia's arms. There are indications that Nasser does not desire to be identified with the Soviet bloc. It is probable that he envisages a neutralist policy in which the Arab world, with Egypt at its head, would be in a strong bargaining position. His present attitude to the West has been affected (a) by the Israel question and (b) by his opposition to the development of the Baghdad Pact. We should not make an immediate approach to Nasser on either of these two issues. He is intoxicated by his present popularity and this is clearly not a propitious moment. *However, we should not of course reject any overture Nasser might make.*[7] We should hope that the next few months will show whether he is ready to mend his fences with the West and avoid further involvement with the Soviet bloc. We should assist him in this period by refraining from any punitive measures, and keeping contact with him over such matters as the Aswan Dam, the Sudan, and other subjects of common interest. The object would be to reach a point at which Egypt would be willing in effect to turn away from Russia as a source of arms, to limit arms purchases to her economic capacity, to give

5. State Department comments generally on this section regarding the implications of the Tripartite Declaration, the prospect of US adhesion to the Baghdad Pact, and the existence of other 'possibilities for agreement' other than the two mentioned ('unduly restrictive'). *Loc. cit.*
6. Presumably, State Department suggested adding the words: 'and Arab states' at this point. *Loc. cit.*
7. State Department generally endorses idea of letting Egypt take the initiative, especially since Nasir 'continues to appear very interested in economic development [of] his country'. *Loc. cit.*

support to the Jordan Waters Plan, and to agree to open negotiations for a settlement with Israel. In such a case we would offer to supply Egypt with her reasonable arms requirements, assist in the financing of the High Dam, bring influence on Israel to agree to a just settlement, and help Egypt to play a role of leadership in the Arab world. An opportunity might be made at the November 20 meeting at Baghdad to make it plain that behind the defense of the free countries of the area provided by the Baghdad Pact it is our object to foster cooperation among the Arab powers for constructive purposes, and that this need not be confined to members of the Pact. Egyptian leadership in such an effort is not excluded.[8]

If all this fails and Egypt is clearly lost to Western influence, we should have to consider policies which would minimize the harm which she could do to Western interests.

16. Northern Tier. It is the intention of the United States to maintain [*deleted:* 'a high level'] liaison with the Baghdad Pact Council and to give material support to its members. *The scope of the material support which the US will give to the Baghdad Pact members will depend on further studies by the US Government. These will take account of the sensitivity of the Soviet Union to Western military relations with Iran.* Her Majesty's Government as a member of the Pact will seek to establish effective machinery for cooperation among the members in the interest of common security. It is the intention of both the US and the UK to give full public support to the Pact as evidence of Arab cooperation with the free world. Advantage might be taken of the forthcoming Baghdad meeting to announce the creation of machinery (with appropriate United States participation) to consider and satisfy the arms requirements of the countries concerned.

Source: PRO FO371/115469 V1023/23G (typed copy with revisions in pen). Cf. text in *FRUS 1955–1957*, XIV, 728–32 (D396), which incorporates these revisions, with slight stylistic alterations.

---

8. State Department comments: 'We should start devising [a] formula whereby Nasser while remaining outside [the] Baghdad [P]act is able in some way to associate himself with it.' *Loc. cit.*

Document 10: Aide-Mémoire from the Israeli Embassy, Washington, to the Department of State, 6 December 1955

The Government of Israel has always upheld the necessity of a settlement with the neighboring Arab States.
2. It notes that the Secretary of State, in his Aide-Mémoire of November 21, advocates an 'approach which involves concessions by Arab states as well as Israel'. While the Israel Government believes that the legitimate interests of Israel and the Arab States are reconcilable as they stand, it holds that if concessions are to be made they must be based on equality and reciprocity. The Aide-Mémoire of November 21, however, discusses a territorial concession by Israel, without indicating the need for any specific territorial concession to be made by any Arab State.
3. If the Arab States prevent violence from their side of the demarcation line, Israel will maintain complete calm on its side. Israel's policy is, also, to avoid reaction to provocation, except when such abstention imperils the security of its population or the integrity of its territory. The assistance of the United States would be welcomed in securing the cessation of 'commando' raids and other violent actions now being carried out against Israel on various fronts, principally on Egypt's responsibility.
4. Israel's only intentions in the Gulf of Aqaba are those of free passage in conformity with its elementary rights under international law. If Egypt does not use force to impede passage in the Gulf, there is no reason to anticipate the use of force by Israel to ensure it. Moreover, if negotiations with Egypt prove feasible, Israel will abstain from any action in the Gulf likely to prejudice them.
5. The Government of Israel was interested to hear the view expressed by the Secretary of State on November 21, that there is now a chance of a settlement. Unfortunately, this impression is not borne out by the current acts and statements of Arab Governments. Encroachments continue into Israel, on the Egyptian, Syrian and Jordanian fronts. There is still no certainty of Arab acceptance of Ambassador Johnston's plan, which may well serve as a test of Arab sincerity. Arms from Soviet sources continue to flow into Egypt. In these circumstances, it is likely that the Egyptian regime is merely attempting to give an illusory impression of peaceful intent, in order to gain time for strengthening its forces in preparation for intimidation or aggression when the time is ripe. At any rate, the Government of Israel is unaware of any concrete evidence which would disprove this analysis of Egyptian intentions.
6. Nevertheless, in order to assist the Secretary in his exploration, the Government of Israel submits its confidential views on the contribution which Israel might make in the context of a peace settlement. The settlement to which Israel aspires is one which would benefit both parties, by inaugurating an era of development and social progress; by enabling a reduction of defence expenditures; and by initiating processes of political, economic and cultural co-operation. Israel does not advance a claim to any of the territory held by Arab States under the General Armistice Agreements. On the other hand, Israel sees no reason for ceding any of its territory to any of the neighboring Arab States, and cannot see its way to discussing a settlement on such a prejudicial basis.

7. The following is the general outline of a settlement which Israel would envisage:

(i) The Government of Israel is ready to authorize a meeting at any appropriate level between its representatives and those of the Government of Egypt, to discuss progress towards a settlement, it being clearly understood that the basis for such a meeting would not include the cession of any part of Israel['s] territory to a neighboring state.

(ii) Israel is prepared to discuss mutual adjustments of the armistice frontier for the benefit of both parties, on the understanding that the integrity and continuity of Israel's territory is not impaired.

(iii) Israel would be willing, in the context of a peace settlement, to contribute substantially to the opening of freer communications between all the States of the Near East, so as to enhance the economic strength and commercial enterprise of the region, and promote political and cultural understanding. These measures, which would in each case be effected without change of the existing territorial jurisdiction, might include on Israel's part:

(a) Provision for communication by air and railway between Egypt and Lebanon;

(b) Port facilities in Haifa for the Kingdom of Jordan, including transit rights by road to and from the Port;

(c) A transit arrangement to be agreed to by Israel for communication between Egypt and the Kingdom of Jordan, it being clearly understood that Israel will not cede territory, whether populated or unpopulated, in the Negev.

(iv) The Government of Israel recalls that it had already conveyed its affirmative attitude, subject to certain reservations, to the proposal on refugee compensation contained in Secretary Dulles' speech of August 26, 1955.

(v) The United States is also aware of Israel's readiness to cooperate in an agreed plan for the coordinated use of the Jordan and Yarmuk Rivers, as elaborated by Ambassador Johnston. The Government of Israel would welcome information on the attitude of the Arab Governments to this project.

8. The subjects proposed above for discussion and action represent a significant contribution by Israel to the establishment of peace with the Arab States. These States would, of course, have to make a corresponding contribution in order to ensure fair conditions for a peaceful settlement on the basis of mutuality. Thus, freedom of transit for Arab traffic between Egypt and Lebanon would entail corresponding freedom for Israeli traffic northwards over Lebanon and southward over Egypt. Similarly, if the Kingdom of Jordan is to have free access to and from Haifa and port facilities therein, it should agree to restore free access to the Wailing Wall, the Mount of Olives and Mount Scopus. Similarly, there should be a broad element of mutuality in any territorial adjustments agreed upon in accordance with Paragraph 2. Egypt should abstain from blockades and practices of maritime interception. Indeed, this duty is incumbent upon her under the Armistice Agreement, whether or not a settlement is achieved. In the context of a settlement such as that discussed

here, all Governments should undertake to abstain from pressure and intimidation against governments or agencies wishing to trade with any state in the Middle East.

9. In discussing the prospect of a peaceful settlement, the Government of Israel cannot ignore the prejudicial effects of the increasing preponderance of the Arab States, and especially of Egypt, in armed strength. Unless prompt steps are taken to reduce this perilous disparity, by providing Israel with additional arms for self-defence, such as would be matched in quality and effectiveness to the arms now obtained in Egypt, there will be an inevitable aggravation of Arab intransigence and of Israel's apprehensions. In such circumstances the Israel Government finds it difficult to conceive any hopeful discussion of progress towards peace.

Source: FRUS 1955–1957, XIV, 823–5 (D436).

Document 11: Statement of General Principles which would Provide a Satisfactory Basis for the Resolution of the Several Points at Issue between the Arab States and Israel, Authorized by Gamal Abd al-Nasir, 4 February 1956

I. TERRITORIAL
A. The establishment of Arab sovereignty over a satisfactorily substantial territory connecting Egypt and Jordan and forming a part of one or the other of those two states.
B. The establishment of permanent boundaries by means of alterations of the Armistice Demarcation Lines for such purposes as:
   1. Restoring to Arab border villages adjoining farmlands and groves formerly tilled by the inhabitants of those villages,
   2. Improvement of communications,
   3. Improvement of access to water supplies, and
   4. The general rationalization of boundaries.

II. REFUGEES
A. Arab refugees from Palestine to be provided a choice between repatriation and compensation for loss of real property.
B. Phasing of the return to assume all rights and obligations of Israeli citizens.
C. Refugees granted repatriation to assume all rights and obligations of Israeli citizens.
D. Refugees electing resettlement and compensation to be moved from the refugee camps and resettled as rapidly as possible.
E. Assistance to be provided by the International Community, probably under UN auspices, for the reestablishment of all refugees.

III. JERUSALEM
Formulation of solutions of the problems of territorial division and supervision of the Holy Places which are acceptable to the world community.

IV. STATE OF BELLIGERENCY AND ECONOMIC RESTRICTIONS DERIVING THEREFROM

A. The parties to recognize formally the termination of the state of belligerency.

B. Following the termination of this state of belligerency:

    1. Lifting of the secondary boycott – that is, discontinuance of all measures taken by the Arab states to prevent trade with Israel by non[-]Arab countries and non[-]Arab firms, and

    2. Removal of all restrictions on shipping, other than normal maritime regulations.

V. UNIFIED DEVELOPMENT OF THE JORDAN VALLEY

The states affected to agree to the proposals for the unified development of the Jordan Valley developed in discussions with Ambassador Eric Johnston.[1]

Source: Text in 'Message (No. 74, from Cairo) to Robert B. Anderson, at Washington', 4 February 1956, *FRUS 1955–1957*, XV, 139–40 (D75).

---

1. The unsigned message continues: 'Nasr asked that Mr Anderson be told that he did not regard the question of the development of the Jordan Valley waters as an integral part of a settlement, but that he was willing to reaffirm his approval and support of the Johnston plan.'

Notes

INTRODUCTION

1. Although many historians designate 14 May 1948 as the start of the first Arab–Israeli war, Itamar Rabinovich argues that this inter-state war was preceded by a *de facto* civil war which had broken out in Mandatory Palestine on the morrow of the 29 November 1947 UN vote which recommended partition. See his 'Seven Wars and One Peace Treaty', in *The Arab–Israeli Conflict: Perspectives*, 2nd ed., ed. Alvin Z. Rubinstein (New York: Harper Collins, 1991), 34–58.
2. A detailed examination of these five episodes is given in the author's *Futile Diplomacy*, Vol. 3: *The United Nations, the Great Powers, and Middle East Peacemaking, 1948–1954* (London: Frank Cass, 1997), cited hereafter as *FD3*.
3. I am grateful to Professor Shimon Shamir for suggesting this terminology. The concept is also used by Abraham Ben-Zvi in his recent study, *The United States and Israel: The Limits of the Special Relationship* (New York: Columbia University Press, 1993).
4. On the concept of prenegotiation, see, e.g., Janice Gross Stein, ed., *Getting to the Table: The Processes of International Prenegotiation* (Baltimore/London: Johns Hopkins University Press, 1989); Jay Rothman, 'Developing Pre-Negotiation Theory and Practice' (Project on Pre-Negotiation Update), Hebrew University of Jerusalem: Leonard Davis Institute, Policy Studies #29, May 1989; special issue of the *Jerusalem Journal of International Relations*, XIII:1 (March 1991).
5. Evelyn Shuckburgh, *Descent to Suez: Diaries 1951–56*, selected for publication by John Charmley (London: Weidenfeld & Nicolson, 1986).
6. For a discussion of the appropriate and inappropriate applications of the term 'collusion', see Mordechai Bar-On, *The Gates of Gaza: Israel's Road to Suez and Back, 1955–1957* (New York: St Martin's Press, 1994), 243f.
7. See, e.g., *Diplomacy in the Near & Middle East: A Documentary Record: 1914–1956*, Vol. 2, ed. J.C. Hurewitz, (Octagon Reprint, 1972), documents 109 and 113; Fred J. Khouri, *The Arab–Israeli Dilemma*, 3rd ed. (Syracuse: Syracuse University Press, 1985), 301f.; Saadia Touval, *The Peace Brokers: Mediators in the Arab–Israeli Conflict, 1948–1979*, (Princeton: Princeton University Press, 1982), 110–14, 122f. The latter work (p.110) makes passing reference to Francis Russell 'collaborating with British officials'.
8. Abba Eban, *An Autobiography* (New York: Random House, 1977), 184. Cf. Eban's second autobiography, *Personal Witness: Israel Through My Eyes* (New York: G.P. Putnam's Sons, 1992), 245f.
9. David Ben-Gurion, 'ha-Mum ha-Sodi Im Nasser' (The Secret Negotiations with Nasser), *Maariv (Weekly Supplement)*, 2, 9, 16 and 23 July 1971; *My Talks with Arab Leaders* (Jerusalem: Keter/New York: Third Press, 1972), Chs 47–53.

10. Mohamed Heikal, *The Cairo Documents: The Inside Story of Nasser and his Relationship with World Leaders, Rebels, and Statesmen* (Garden City, NY: Doubleday, 1973), 55f. Cf. Heikal's later, more detailed, accounts of the episode in *Milaffat as-Suways: Harb al-Thalathin Sana (The Suez Files: The Thirty Years War)* (Cairo: 1986), 388–94, 780–3 (D117, D118) and *Cutting the Lion's Tail: Suez Through Egyptian Eyes* (London: Corgi, 1988), 105–8, 249–52.
11. Yaacov Herzog, *A People that Dwells Alone: Speeches and Writings of Yaacov Herzog* ed. Misha Louvish (London: Weidenfeld & Nicolson, 1975), 237–42; reproduced in *Israel in the Middle East: Documents and Readings on Society, Politics and Foreign Relations, 1948–Present*, eds. Itamar Rabinovich and Jehuda Reinharz (New York/Oxford: Oxford University Press, 1984), 105–9.
12. Moshe Sharett, *Yoman Ishi (Personal Diary, 1953–1957)*, 8 vols., ed. Yaacov Sharett, Tel Aviv: Sifriyat Maariv, 1978; Teddy Kollek (with his son, Amos Kollek), *For Jerusalem: A Life by Teddy Kollek* (New York: Random House, 1978), 114–16.
13. Touval, *Peace Brokers*, Ch. 5.
14. Wilbur Crane Eveland, *Ropes of Sand: America's Failure in the Middle East* (New York: W.W. Norton, 1980).
15. See, in this regard, the two highly-subjective presentations by Miles Copeland: *The Game of Nations: The Amorality of Power Politics* (New York: College Notes & Texts, 1969), and *The Game Player: Confessions of the CIA's Original Political Operative* (London: Aurum, 1989).
16. Touval, *Peace Brokers*, 123, 130. Touval's observation, with regard to Israeli attitudes, is validated by many passing references in Sharett's *Yoman Ishi* and by numerous reports in ISA files from Israeli envoys in Washington, especially Reuven Shiloah and Yaacov Shimoni.
17. Shuckburgh, *Descent*. Israel's Ambassador to London at the time, whose suspicions were strong but who was effectively kept in the dark about Alpha, has written his own account which reveals little beyond what already appears in Shuckburgh's diaries. See Eliahu Elath, *Me'ever le-Arafel ha-Yamim: Pirqei Zikhronot (Through the Mists of Time: Reminiscences)* (Jerusalem: Yad Ben-Zvi, 1989), 54–75.
18. United States, Department of State, *Foreign Relations of the United States: 1955–1957*, Vol. XIV: Arab–Israeli Dispute, 1955, ed. Carl N. Raether (Washington: 1989), hereafter: *FRUS 1955–1957*, XIV; *Foreign Relations of the United States: 1955–1957*, Vol. XV: Arab–Israeli Dispute, 1 January – 26 July 1956, ed. Carl N. Raether (Washington: 1989), hereafter: *FRUS 1955–1957*, XV.
19. Shimon Shamir, 'The Collapse of Project Alpha', in *Suez 1956: The Crisis and its Consequences*, eds Wm. Roger Louis and Roger Owen (Oxford: Clarendon Press, 1989), 73–100.
20. W. Scott Lucas, *Divided We Stand: Britain, the US and the Suez Crisis*, London: Hodder & Stoughton, 1991. Unfortunately, I had not seen this study early enough to integrate many of its findings and insights into the manuscript of the present volume.
21. Both dissertations have now been published: Michael B. Oren, *Origins of the Second Arab–Israel War: Egypt, Israel and the Great Powers: 1952–56* (London: Frank Cass, 1992), Ch. 5; Mordechai Bar-On, *Sha'arei Aza: Mediniut ha-Bitahon ve-ha-Hutz shel Medinat Yisrael: 1955–1957 (The Gates of Gaza: Israel's Defense and Foreign Policy)*, (Tel Aviv: Am Oved, 1992), Chs 7–8 (also in the English translation, *The Gates of Gaza*).
22. *Futile Diplomacy*, Vol. 1: *Early Arab–Zionist Negotiation Attempts, 1913–1931*, (London: Frank Cass, 1983) hereafter *FD1*; *Futile Diplomacy*, Vol. 2: *Arab–Zionist Negotiations and the End of the Mandate* (London: Frank Cass, 1986) hereafter *FD2*.

23. For a discussion on coping with the relative lack of Arabic primary sources, see Caplan, *FD3*, xxii–xxiv.
24. Edward Hallett Carr, *What Is History?* (New York: Random House (Vintage), 1961), 15, 26f.

CHAPTER 1

1. On the Anglo–American Committee of Inquiry and other pre-1948 illustrations of Anglo–American co-operation, see: Allen H. Podet, *The Success and Failure of the Anglo–American Committee of Inquiry, 1945–46: Last Chance in Palestine* (Lewiston NY: E. Mellen, 1986); Miriam Joyce Haron, *Palestine and the Anglo–American Connection, 1945–1950*, (New York: Peter Lang, 1986); Martin Jones, *Failure in Palestine: British and U.S. Policy after the Second World War* (London/New York: Mansell, 1986); Richard Crossman, *Palestine Mission: A Personal Record* (New York/London; Harper, 1947); Bartley C. Crum, *Behind the Silken Curtain: A Personal Account of Anglo-American Diplomacy in Palestine and the Middle East* (New York: Simon & Schuster, 1947); United States, Department of State, *Foreign Relations of the United States: Diplomatic Papers: 1947*, Vol. V (Washington: United States Government Printing Office, 1971), 485f., 652–67.
2. Nathan A. Pelcovits, *The Long Armistice: UN Peacekeeping and the Arab–Israeli Conflict, 1948–1960*, foreword by Samuel W. Lewis (Boulder/San Francisco/Oxford: Westview Press, 1993), 24f.
3. Deborah J. Gerner, 'Missed Opportunities and Roads Not Taken: The Eisenhower Administration and the Palestinians', in *U.S. Policy on Palestine from Wilson to Clinton*, ed. Michael W. Suleiman (Normal IL: AAUG Press, 1995), 105.
4. For a detailed discussion of the entrenchment of these irreconcilable positions between 1948 and 1954, see Caplan, *FD3*.
5. Copeland, *The Game Player*, 198. Cf. the views of Jefferson Caffery, the American Ambassador in Cairo during the Anglo–Egyptian treaty negotiations, quoted in Keith Kyle, *Suez* (New York: St Martin's Press, 1991), 49.
6. Sir John Bagot Glubb, *A Soldier with the Arabs* (London: Hodder & Stoughton, 1957), 327.
7. See, e.g., Jessup to Marshall, 6 Aug. 1948, United States, Department of State, *Foreign Relations of the United States: Diplomatic Papers: 1948*, Vol. V, Pt. 2, (Washington: United States Government Printing Office, 1976), 1291 (hereafter: *FRUS 1948* V/2); Marshall to Douglas, 12 Aug. 1948, ibid., 1304.
8. Several scholars have written extensively on Israeli–Jordanian negotiations: Joseph Nevo, *Abdallah ve-Arviyei Eretz-Israel (Abdullah and the Arabs of Palestine)* (Tel Aviv: Shiloah Institute, 1975), Chs 3–4; Avraham Sela, *Mi-Maga'im le-Masa u-Matan: Yihasei ha-Sokhnut ha-Yehudit u-Medinat Yisrael 'im ha-Melekh Abdallah, 1946–1950 (From Contacts to Negotiations: Relations Between the Jewish Agency and the State of Israel with King Abdullah)* (Tel Aviv: Shiloah Institute, 1985), Chs 6–11; Uri Bar-Joseph, *The Best of Enemies: Israel and Jordan in the War of 1948* (London: Frank Cass, 1987); Avi Shlaim, *Collusion Across the Jordan* (Oxford University Press, 1988), Chs 9–19; Mary Wilson, *King Abdullah, Britain and the Making of Jordan* (Cambridge/New York/etc: Cambridge University Press, 1987), Chs 10–11; Itamar Rabinovich, *The Road Not Taken: Early Arab–Israeli Negotiations* (New York/Oxford: Oxford University Press, 1991), Ch. 4; A. Sela, 'Transjordan, Israel and the 1948 War: Myth, Historiography and Reality', *Middle Eastern Studies* 28:4 (Oct. 1992), 623–88.

   On Israeli–Syrian contacts, see: Avi Shlaim, 'Husni Za'im and the Plan to Resettle Palestinian Refugees in Syria', *Journal of Palestine Studies* 15:4 (Summer

1986), 68–80; Aryeh Shalev, *Shituf Pe'ula be-tzel Imut: Mishtar Shevitat ha-Nesheq Yisrael-Suriya, 1949–1955 (Co-operation under the Shadow of Conflict: The Israeli-Syrian Armistice Regime)* (Tel Aviv: Ma'arachot, 1989), and the English edition: *The Israel-Syria Armistice Regime, 1949–1955* (Boulder: Westview Press and Jerusalem: The Jerusalem Post (Jaffee Center for Strategic Studies, Study No. 21), 1993); Rabinovich, *Road Not Taken*, Ch. 3.

On early Israeli–Egyptian contacts, see Rabinovich, *Road Not Taken*, Ch. 5.

9. Furlonge minute, 30 March 1950, PRO FO371/82198 EE10111/1G. Cf. correspondence between Chapman-Andrews (Cairo) and Wright (FO), 24 March–29 April 1950, *loc. cit.* /1G, /8G, /10G and FO141/1395 1033/3/50G. For Egyptian feelers from another quarter, see also: Caffery to Acheson, 25 April 1950 (desp.880), USNA RG84 E/C/TSG Box 4/DF320.

10. See, e.g., Furlonge minute, 3 Jan. 1950, PRO FO371/82177 EE1015/2; Millar (Washington) to FO, 6 Feb. 1950 (tgm.471), FO371/82177 E1015/19; Chapman-Andrews (Cairo) to Wright, 24 March 1950 (desp.1033/2/50G), FO371/82198 EE10111/1G; Acheson to USEmb UK, 4 Jan. 1950 (tgm.28), USNA 684A.85/1-450; Comay to Eliash, 9 Feb. 1950, ISA 130.02/2593/12; McDonald to Murphy, 7 March 1950, USNA 684A.85/3-750; Kirkbride to FO, 8 March 1950 (tgm.101), PRO FO371/82178 EE1015/39; material in PRO FO371/82179 file EE1015, papers /86, /90, /101, /106, /107; Davies, note of talk with Elath, 15 Sept. 1950, FO371/82529 ER1054/47; Helm to FO, 22 Feb. 1951 (tgm.64), FO371/91364 EE1041/11; United States, Department of State, *Foreign Relations of the United States: 1950*, Vol. V (Washington: 1978), 665f., 698–702, 721f., 735, 781–3, 789f., 798, 803f., 864, 925, 976f. (hereafter: *FRUS 1950* V); Israel State Archives, *Documents on the Foreign Policy of Israel*, Vol. 5 (1950), ed. Yehoshua Freundlich (Jerusalem: 1988), 182f., 399, 564f. (hereafter: *ID5*); Barry Rubin, *The Arab States and the Palestine Conflict* (Syracuse: Syracuse University Press, 1981), 210; Shlaim, *Collusion*, 579; Rabinovich, *Road Not Taken*, 141–3.

11. A. David Fritzlan, who was stationed in Amman during the period, recounts his talks with Samir Rifa'i and records his regret that the State Department had refrained from intervening, not wishing to press Israel to make the talks succeed. See his oral history interview, Georgetown University Library, 29 May and 15 June 1990, pp. 33–5. Yet Edward Warren Holmes, who was stationed in the Embassy in Tel Aviv during the same period, believed that both embassies in Tel Aviv and Amman were working to encourage an Israeli–Jordanian agreement. Oral history interview, Georgetown University Library (date and page 1 missing), 24, 34.

12. Furlonge minute, Israel–Jordan Negotiations, 22 Aug. 1950, PRO FO371/82179 EE1015/88. See also: Kirkbride to FO, 6 March 1950 (tgm.99), FO371/82715 ET1051/18; Furlonge minute, Israel–Jordan Negotiations, 6 March 1950, *loc. cit.*; Furlonge minute, Israel Government's complaints against H.M. Government, 3 April 1950, FO371/82568 ER1193/29; Keeley to USSD, 7 April 1950 (desp.207), USNA 684A.85/4-750; Furlonge to Chadwick, 30 Aug. 1950, PRO FO371/82179 EE1015/90; *FRUS 1950* V, 787–9, 804, 942, 969; Shlaim, *Collusion*, 567; C. Ernest Dawn, 'Pan-Arabism and the Failure of Israeli–Jordanian Peace Negotiations, 1950', in *Islam and its Cultural Divergence: Studies in Honor of Gustave E. von Grunebaum*, ed., Girdhari L. Tikku, ed. (Urbana/Chicago/London: University of Illinois Press, 1971), 27–51; Mordechai Gazit, 'The Israel–Jordan Peace Negotiations (1949–51): King Abdallah's Lonely Effort', *Journal of Contemporary History* 23 (1988), 419f.

13. See, e.g., Douglas (London) to Marshall, 2 Aug. 1948, *FRUS 1948*, V/2, 1266-71.

14. Cf. Caplan, *FD3*, Ch. II, and below, Ch. IV (n.28).

15. See, e.g., FO to UKEmb Washington, 1 Feb. 1949 (tgm.1272), PRO FO371/75336 E1369/1016/31. Cf. Caplan, *FD3*, Ch. III.
16. Troutbeck to FO, 4 Jan. 1949 (tgm.5), PRO FO371/75334 E156/1016/31G; Wm. Roger Louis, *The British Empire in the Middle East, 1945–1951: Arab Nationalism, The United States, and Postwar Imperialism* (Oxford: Clarendon Press, 1984), 566.
17. Lovett to USEmb UK, 13 Jan. 1949, United States, Department of State, *Foreign Relations of the United States: Diplomatic Papers: 1949*, Vol. VI (Washington: 1977), 658 (hereafter: *FRUS 1949*, VI); UKEmb Washington to USSD, *Aide-mémoire*: Palestine (18 Jan. 1949), ibid., 675f.
18. Lovett, memorandum of conversation (Franks, Bromley, Satterthwaite, Wilkins, McClintock), 5 Jan. 1949, *FRUS 1949*, VI, 611; Lovett to USEmb UK, 13 Jan. 1949, ibid., 659f.
19. Sargent minute for Bevin, 17 Jan. 1949, PRO FO371/75336 E1273/1016/31G.
20. FO to UKEmb Washington, 10 Aug. 1951 (tgm.3530), PRO FO371/91365 EE1071/10. See also: FO to UKEmb Amman, etc., 11 Aug. 1951 (tgm.332), *loc. cit.*; Furlonge to Burrows, 30 Aug. 1951, FO371/91365 EE1071/14; Oliver brief, Palestine Conciliation Commission Conference to be held in Paris on the 10th September 1951, 7 Sept. 1951, FO371/91365 EE1071/30.
21. Minute on Hayter to FO, 14 Aug. 1951 (tgm.459 Saving), FO371/91365 EE1071/11. Cf. Bowker, note (14 Aug.) of talk with Crouy-Chanel, 13 Aug. 1951, FO371/91365 EE1071/16.
22. Furlonge minute, Arab/Israel Relations, 14 Aug. 1951, FO371/91368 EE1072/21.
23. Furlonge to Burrows, 30 Aug. 1951, FO371/91365 EE1071/14.
24. For a detailed examination of the 1951 Paris Conference, see Caplan, *FD3*, Chs IX–X.
25. For a discussion of the 1952 direct-negotiations resolution, see Caplan, *FD3*, Ch. XI.
26. Furlonge to Bowker, 24 Dec. 1952 (desp.10706/100) PRO FO371/104753 ER1071/2.
27. Troutbeck (Baghdad) to Bowker, 2 Jan. 1953 (desp.1461/1/1953), PRO FO371/104753 ER1071/4. Cf. Pelham (Jedda) to Bowker, 24 Jan. 1953 (desp. 1072/10/53), PRO FO371/104753 ER1071/11; Roger Louis, 'Britain at the Crossroads in Palestine 1952–1954', *Jerusalem Journal of International Relations* 12:3 (Sept. 1990), 71–3.
28. Furlonge to Allen, 18 Nov. 1953 (desp.1075/63/53), PRO FO371/104757 ER1071/106; Louis, 'Britain at the Crossroads', 78f. On the Article XII episode, see Caplan, *FD3*, Ch. XII.

CHAPTER II

1. Helm to Wright, 7 Oct. 1950 (desp.1034/182/50), PRO FO371/82179 EE1015/106. Cf. Strang to Rapp, 5 Feb. 1951, FO371/91364 EE1041/9; Helm, note of talk with Shiloah, 22 June 1951, PRO FO371/91364 EE1041/37; Helm to Bowker, 23 June 1951 (desp.1105/303/51), PRO FO371/91368 EE1072/14; Shlaim, *Collusion*, 579, 603. For one of several critiques of Helm's views, see Troutbeck to Morrison, 25 July 1951 (desp.131, 1063/10/51), PRO FO371/91368 EE1072/19.
2. Oliver minute, Israel–Arab Relations: Prospects of a Peace Settlement, 9 July 1951, PRO FO371/91368 EE1072/20.
3. Wardrop minute, 'The Effect of Arab–Israel Relations on the Defence of the Middle East', 8 Aug. 1951, PRO FO371/91368 EE1072/21. Quotations in this and the following paragraph are from this minute.

4. Furlonge minute, Arab/Israeli Relations, 14 Aug. 1951, PRO FO371/91368 EE1072/21.
5. Bowker to Beeley (Baghdad) *et al.*, 24 Aug. 1951, PRO FO371/91368 EE1072/21. Quotations in this and the following paragraph are taken from this despatch.
6. Bowker to Chadwick, 24 Aug. 1951, PRO FO371/91368 EE1072/21.
7. Furlonge to Burrows, 31 Aug. 1951, PRO FO371/91368 EE1072/21; Troutbeck to Bowker, 11 Oct. 1951 (desp.1063/21/51), FO371/91368 EE1072/32.
8. Stevenson to Bowker, 14 Sept. 1951 (desp.10710/27/51), FO371/91368 EE1072/25.
9. Montagu–Pollock to Bowker, 18 Sept. 1951 (desp.10706/7/51), PRO FO371/91368 EE1072/26. For other replies from the field, see: Kirkbride to Bowker, 1 Sept. 1951 (desp.S107/9/21/51), PRO FO371/91368 EE1072/23; Troutbeck to Bowker, 5 Oct. 1951 (desp.1063/19/51), FO371/91368 EE1072/28.
10. Troutbeck to Bowker, 11 Oct. 1951 (desp.1063/21/51), FO371/91368 EE1072/32.
11. Oliver minute, 26 Sept. 1951, PRO FO371/91368 EE1072/25.
12. Wardrop minute, Arab–Israel Relations, 27 Oct. 1951, FO371/91368 EE1072/34.
13. See, e.g., Dana Adams Schmidt, 'Israel–Arab Peace Is Believed Closer – West's Envoys More Hopeful Than at Any Time Since War', *New York Times*, 16 Nov. 1952, 1, 14 (dateline Jerusalem, 15 Nov.). For comments on the accuracy and motives of Schmidt's reporting, see: Sasson (Rome) to Shiloah, 23 Nov. 1952, ISA 130.02/2410/9/I; Chadwick (Tel Aviv) to Wardrop, 8 Dec. 1952 (desp.10320/71/52), PRO FO371/98479 EE1073/101.
14. Davis to USSD, 23 Oct. 1952, United States, Department of State, *Foreign Relations of the United States: 1952–1954*, Vol. IX, eds Paul Claussen, Joan M. Lee & Carl N. Raether (Washington 1986), 1037–9 (D505) (hereafter: *FRUS 1952–1954*, IX/1).
15. Caffery to USSD, 20 Nov. 1952 (desp.975), USNA 611.80/11-2052 (reporting *Al-Ahram*, 19 Nov.); Donohue, *Before Suez*, 199f.
16. Byroade to Near East Chiefs of Missions, 22 Nov. 1952 (tgm.586), USNA 611.80/11-2252.
17. 'U.S. Foreign Policy in the Middle East', address to Chicago Council on Foreign Relations, 5 Dec. 1952, *Department of State Bulletin*, 15 Dec. 1952, Vol. 27/Pt. 2, 932 (hereafter: *DSB*).
18. Dulles radio broadcast, Report on Trip to the Middle East, 1 June 1953, in Hurewitz, *Diplomacy* II: 342. For a detailed account and assessment of Dulles' three-week trip to the Middle East, see: *FRUS 1952–1954*, IX/1, 1–166; Donohue, *Before Suez*, 200–74; Isaac Alteras, *Eisenhower and Israel: US–Israeli Relations, 1953–1960* (Gainsville, etc.: University Press of Florida, 1993), Ch. 3.
19. Quoted in Donohue, *Before Suez*, 257.
20. See, e.g., the expectations of Elizabeth Monroe, 'The Arab–Israel Frontier'. Address at Chatham House, 16 June 1953, *International Affairs*, Vol. 29, 448.
21. Byroade remarks, memorandum of conversation (Eban, Goitein, Waller), 9 June 1953, *FRUS 1952–1954*, IX/1, 1235 (D622).
22. Russell–Comay talk (22 June), reported in Russell to USSD, 23 June 1953, *FRUS 1952–1954*, IX/1, 1248 (D630). Cf. Donohue, *Before Suez*, 270; Dulles' earlier remarks to Ben-Gurion, quoted in ibid., 209f. and also discussed in Ben-Zvi, *The United States and Israel*, 33f.
23. Al-Yafi talk with Chapman-Andrews, reported in Chapman-Andrews to Eden, 13 Jan. 1954 (desp.7, 1071/18/1/54), PRO FO371/111069 VR1072/8. Quotations in this and the following paragraph are taken from this despatch.
24. Bowker to Chadwick, 24 Aug. 1951, PRO FO371/91368 EE1072/21.
25. Chapman-Andrews to Bowker, 5 Sept. 1951 (desp.10722/5/51), FO371/91368 EE1072/24.

26. Gardener to Eden, 5 Jan. 1954 (desp.3, 10601/1/54), PRO FO371/111069 VR1072/6.
27. See, e.g., Oliver minute, Israel–Arab Relations: Prospects of a Peace Settlement, 9 July 1951, PRO FO371/91368 EE1072/20; Wardrop minute, The Effect of Arab–Israel Relations on the Defence of the Middle East, 8 Aug. 1951, FO371/91368 EE1072/21; Evans (Tel Aviv) to Eden, 30 March 1954 (desp.65, 1031/18/54), FO371/111069 VR1072/34; Eytan–Russell talk, reported in Eytan to IsrEmb Washington, 31 March 1954 (tgm.IW248/297), ISA 130.16/2948/6; Tripp note of talk with Gazit, 29 July 1954, PRO FO371/111073 VR1072/162. For a critique of this approach to Arab–Israeli peacemaking, see Caplan, *FD3*, Ch. XIII.
28. See Caplan, *FD3*, *passim*.
29. Eban to Fischer, 14 Nov. 1951, Israel State Archives, *Documents on the Foreign Policy of Israel* Vol. 6 (1951), ed. Yemima Rosenthal (Jerusalem: 1991), 788–90 (D487) (hereafter: *ID6*). Cf. Eban–McGhee talk, 12 Oct., reported in Eban to Eytan, 15 Oct. 1951, *ID6*, 706 (D431).
30. USSD Position Paper: The Palestine Question, 12 Oct. 1951, *FRUS 1951*, V, 894.
31. See, e.g., Donohue, *Before Suez*, 195; Alteras, *Eisenhower and Israel*, 42, 80f, 86–8.
32. Palmer to Acheson, 7 June 1951, United States, Department of State, *Foreign Relations of the United States: 1951*, Vol. V (Washington: 1982), 705 (hereafter: *FRUS 1951*, V). See, also: Acheson to Palmer, 19 June 1951, ibid., 725; Comay to Lourie, 7 June 1951, *ID6*, 366f. (D214); Eliav memorandum of talks with Ludlow and Burns, 30 Nov. 1951, ISA 130.15/2566/11; Fritzlan report, Conversations with Israeli Officials, encl. in Furlonge to Ross, 16 Oct. 1952 (desp.10706/62), PRO FO371/98479 EE1073/83; Kidron to Rafael, 27 May 1954, ISA 130.16/2948/6.
33. Waller, memorandum of conversation (Byroade, Sharett, Eban), 8 April 1953, *FRUS 1952–1954*, IX/1, 1164–70 (D592); Alteras, *Eisenhower and Israel*, 44f. Cf. other US–Israeli meetings at that time, discussed in ibid., 46–8.
34. Rafael–Russell talk, 16 April, reported in Rafael to Eban, 20 April 1954 (tgm.338/467), ISA 130.16/2948/6.
35. NSC Statement of Policy: United States Objectives and Policies with Respect to the Near East, 23 July 1954, *FRUS 1952–1954*, IX/1, 534f.

CHAPTER III

1. Text in: *Israel's Foreign Relations: Selected Documents 1947–1974*, ed. Meron Medzini (Jerusalem: Ministry of Foreign Affairs, 1976), 213; Hurewitz, *Diplomacy* II: 308f.; *ID5*, 342.
2. Acheson talk with US Congressmen, 28 March 1950, *FRUS 1950*, V, 127.
3. Rockwell, memorandum of conversation (Hare, Burrows, Greenhill), 6 April 1950, *FRUS 1950*, V, 847. Cf. George McGhee, *Envoy to the Middle World: Adventures in Diplomacy* (New York: Harper & Row, 1983), 207.
3a. McGhee, *Envoy*, 208f.
4. Kopper, Policy Statement: Near East, 3rd revision, 28 Dec. 1950, *FRUS 1950*, V, 278.
5. E.g., 'None of the three Governments (was) by this statement giving any undertaking of any character towards any Government except the other two parties to the statement.' Furlonge minute, Proposed Anglo–American Statement on the Middle East, 5 May 1950, FO371/81910 E1023/89; Shlomo Slonim, 'Origins of the 1950 Tripartite Declaration on the Middle East', *Middle Eastern Studies* 23 (1987), 144.
6. E.g., '... and we mean what we say.' McGhee–Rockwell–Elath–Keren talk, reported in Elath to USDiv, 25 May 1950, *ID5*, 345 (D250).

7. See, e.g., McGhee, *Envoy*, 211f.; Ben-Gurion, Knesset statement, 31 May 1950, Hurewitz, *Diplomacy* II: 309. For other reactions of Arabs and Israelis, see Caplan, *FD3*, Ch. VIII.
8. Webb to Lay, Second Progress Report on NSC 47/2, 13 September 1950, *FRUS 1950* V, 1003; Department of State Policy Statement: Israel, 2 Feb. 1951, *FRUS 1951* V, 575; McGhee to Eban, 10 Aug. 1951, *ID6*, 539f. (D319) Cf. *FRUS 1950*, V, 1048; *FRUS 1951*, V, 65, 139–41, 577; McGhee, *Envoy*, 211f.
9. Kyle, *Suez*, 36. Cf. Oren, *Origins*, 77f.
10. Details in *ID5*, 535–40, 545–7, 551, 553–5; *FRUS 1950*, V, 1013–7, 1027f.; Furlonge to Chadwick, 16 Sept. 1950, PRO FO371/82179 EE1015/90; FO to UKEmb Tel Aviv, 21 Sept. 1950 (tgm.672), FO371/82529 ER1054/49; minutes of meeting between UK and US representatives, London, 22 Sept. 1950, FO371/81922 E10213/11; Stevenson to FO, 23 Sept. 1950 (tgm.690), FO371/82198 EE10111/21.
11. UNSC Resolutions 92 and 93, 8 and 18 May 1951, *United Nations Resolutions on Palestine and the Arab–Israeli Conflict, Vol. I: 1947–1974*, ed. George J. Tomeh (Washington: Institute for Palestine Studies, 1975), 133f. For background, see: *FRUS 1951*, V, 626, 629, 634f., 673f., 679f., 684f., 690–9; *ID6*, 226f., 297f., 310–18, 320–9, 335–9, 341f., 352–4, 358, 363f., 380f., 397f.; Helm to FO, 9 April 1951 (tgm.122), PRO FO371/91368 EE1072/6; Stevenson (Cairo) to FO, 16 April 1951 (tgm.294), FO371/91368 EE1072/6; Cannon (Damascus) to USSD, 21 May 1951 (desp.514), USNA RG84 E/C/TSG Box 5/DF350.
12. On the Qibya raid and its far-reaching political implications, see Caplan, *FD3*, Chs XI and XII; Donald Neff, *Warriors at Suez: Eisenhower Takes America into the Middle East* (New York: The Linden Press/Simon & Schuster, 1981 (Brattleboro VT: Amana Books, 1988)), 48–53; Benny Morris, *Israel's Border Wars, 1949–1956: Arab Infiltration, Israeli Retaliation, and the Countdown to the Suez War* (Oxford: Clarendon Press, 1993), Ch. 8; Robert B. Satloff, *From Abdullah to Hussein: Jordan in Transition* (New York/Oxford: Oxford University Press, 1994), 81–5.
13. See, e.g., Acheson to USEmb Cairo, 6 Jan. 1951 (airgr.253), USNA 684A.00/1-651; Crocker (Baghdad) to USSD, 23 Jan. 1951 (desp.735), 684A.00/1-2351; Caffery (Cairo) to USSD, 7 Feb. 1951 (desp.1882), 684A.00/2-751.
14. See French Embassy, London to FO, Note Verbale, 11 June 1951, PRO FO371/91368 EE1072/11; Helm to Bowker, 23 June 1951 (desp.1105/303/51), FO371/91368 EE1072/14; Furlonge minute, 30 June 1951, FO371/91368 EE1072/15; FO to UKEmb Washington, 6 July 1951 (tgm.3291 Saving), FO371/91368 EE1072/11. At the same time, the French offered their good offices to Syria and Israel, a move of which the latter were extremely guarded. See, e.g., Shiloah–Helm conversation, 22 June 1951, FO371/91364 EE1041/37; *ID6*, 373f., 387, 392–4, 401–4, 427f.
15. For one of many examples of the former see memorandum of conversation (Zayn ad-Din, Gross, Ross, Maffitt), 5 July 1951, *FRUS 1951*, V, 746f. For one of many expressions of the latter attitude, see Shiloah–Helm conversation, 22 June 1951, PRO FO371/91364 EE1041/37.
16. See, e.g., Cannon (Damascus) to USSD, 21 May 1951 (desp.514), USNA RG84 E/C/TSG Box 5/DF350; Comay to Elath, 24 June 1951, *ID6*, 402 (D236); Chapman-Andrews (Beirut) to Bowker, 5 Sept. 1951 (desp.10722/5/51), PRO FO371/91368 EE1072/24; Troutbeck to Bowker, 5 Oct. 1951 (desp.1063/19/51), FO371/91368 EE1072/28; meeting of HM diplomatic representatives, 23 June 1952, FO371/98258 E1056/83.
17. For some of the pertinent literature on the border disputes and peacekeeping efforts in accordance with the GAAs, see: J.B. Glubb, 'Violence on the Jordan–Israel Border: A Jordanian View', *Foreign Affairs* 32:4 (July 1954), 552–62; Moshe

Dayan, 'Israel's Border and Security Problems' *Foreign Affairs* 33:2 (Jan. 1955), 250–67; E.H. Hutchison, *Violent Truce: A Military Observer Looks at the Arab–Israeli Conflict, 1951–1955* (New York: Devin-Adair, 1956); E.L.M. Burns, *Between Arab and Israeli* (New York: Ivan Obolensky, 1963); Fred J. Khouri, 'Friction and Conflict on the Israel–Syrian Front', *Middle East Journal* 17:1–2 (Winter–Spring 1963), 14–34; Earl Berger, *The Covenant and the Sword: Arab–Israeli Relations, 1948–56* (Toronto: University of Toronto Press, 1965); Fred J. Khouri, 'The Policy of Retaliation in Arab–Israeli Relations', *Middle East Journal* 20:4 (Autumn 1966), 435–55; Natanel Lorch, *One Long War: Arab versus Jew Since 1920* (New York: Herzl Press, 1976), Ch. 3.

Two important recent books, based on newly available archival sources, are: Pelcovits, *The Long Armistice*, and Morris, *Israel's Border Wars*.

18. For some Israeli evaluations of the effectiveness of the reprisal policy during the early 1950s, see: Sharett, *Yoman Ishi*, IV: 1025 (28 May 1955), transl. in Rabinovich and Reinharz, *Israel in the Middle East*, 97; Eytan remarks, quoted in Nicholls to Rose, 19 Dec. 1955 (desp.10310/109/55), PRO FO371/115911 VR1092/483. For some social science analyses of reprisal and deterrence, see: Khouri, 'Policy of Retaliation', *op. cit.*; Barry M. Blechman, 'The Impact of Israel's Reprisals on Behavior of the Bordering Arab Nations Directed at Israel', *Journal of Conflict Resolution* 16:2 (June 1972), 155–81; Jonathan Shimshoni, *Israel and Conventional Deterrence: Border Warfare from 1953 to 1970*, Ithaca/London: Cornell University Press, 1988; Morris, *Israel's Border Wars*, 183–262.
19. Morris, *Israel's Border Wars*, 426.
20. In mid-1950, the US State Department instructed UNTSO chief, Gen. William Riley, discreetly 'to approach the Governments concerned and suggest that the inclusion of political representatives from each Government on the Armistice Commission might be useful'. Franks to FO, 30 Aug. 1950 (tgm.556 Saving), PRO FO371/82196 EE10110/47.
21. For some of the primary documentation on this episode, see: *FRUS 1951*, V, 739f., 742f., 752f., 757, 785; *ID6*, 193f., 372–4, 377f., 491, 496, 513, 532; Shalev, *Shituf Pe'ula*, 215–18 and *Israel–Syria Armistice Regime*, 132–5. For other evidence of IJMAC and ISMAC being seen as a potentially 'political' body at this time, see: Kirkbride to FO, 5 July 1950 (tgm.245), PRO FO371/82178 EE1015/69; Jones, memorandum of conversation with Kollek, 2 Aug. 1951, *FRUS 1951*, V, 814.
22. For a detailed discussion of the Article XII episode, see Caplan, *FD3*, Ch. XII.
23. Geren (Amman) to USSD, 10 May 1954, *FRUS 1952–1954*, IX/1, 1553 (D820).
24. See, e.g., Evans (Tel Aviv) to Eden, 30 March 1954 (desp.65, 1031/18/54), PRO FO371/111069 VR1072/34; Evans to FO, 14 April 1954 (tgm.114), FO371/111070 VR1072/55; Allen, Brief to Eden for NATO meeting and Geneva Conference, 20 April 1954, PRO FO371/111070 VR1072/62; Falla, minute, Anglo–Jordan Treaty, 26 April 1954, FO371/111101 VR1091/72; Evans to Allen, 27 April 1954 (desp.1031/59/54) FO371/111071; UKEmb Amman, *Aide-mémoire*, 29 April 1954 (presented to Fawzi al-Mulqi), FO816/190; IMFA, 'Anglo–Jordanian Treaty' (Information for Israel Legations, No. 873), 30 April 1954, ISA 43/gimmel-5570/4120; Morris, *Israel's Border Wars*, 263–5, 294–312.
25. Allen memorandum, Settlement of the Palestine Problem, 2 Dec. 1953, PRO FO371/104770 ER1078/3. Quotations in this and the following paragraph are taken from this memorandum and from Allen's minute of 3 Dec. (see previous note).
26. Allen, Brief to Eden for NATO meeting and Geneva Conference, 20 April 1954, PRO FO371/111070 VR1072/62 and other correspondence and papers in ibid., /59, /67, /71; FO371/111071 VR1072/73, /76, /91; FO371/111072 VR1072/140.; *FRUS 1952–1954*, IX/1, 1529f., 1554. In late August, France again declined when Britain sought to organize tripartite representations urging the Israelis to

avoid military manoeuvres near the Jordanian frontier. See: Jebb to FO, 31 August 1954 (tgm.340 Saving), FO371/111105 VR1091/183; same to same, 4 September 1954, FO371/111105 VR1091/193.

27. FO to UKEmb Washington, 12 April 1954 (tgm.1567), PRO FO371/111070 VR1072/56; Dulles (London) to Smith, 13 April 1954, *FRUS 1952–1954*, IX/1, 1513f. (D794). On the successful Anglo–American mediation over the Trieste conflict, see: Dwight D. Eisenhower, *Mandate for Change, 1953–1956 (The White House Years)*, (Garden City NY: Doubleday, 1963), 409–19; Anthony Eden *Full Circle: The Memoirs of the Rt. Hon. Sir Anthony Eden* (London: Cassell, 1960), Ch. VIII; Kyle, *Suez*, 56.

28. Conference Conclusions on the Danger of Arab–Israeli Tensions and Recommended Line of US Action, Istanbul, 14 May 1954, *FRUS 1952–1954*, IX/1, 1561–4 (D824).

29. NSC 5428, United States Objectives and Policies With Respect to the Near East, 23 July 1954, *FRUS 1952–1954*, IX/1, 525–36 (D219).

30. E.g., memorandum of conversation (Jernegan, Hart, Burdett, Beeley), 22 April 1954, USNA 684A.85/4-2254. For a minor exception, see Eden marginal note on Furlonge to FO, 23 April 1954 (tgm.213), PRO FO371/111070 VR1072/67.

31. For the US circular telegram sent to Middle East capitals, 15 April 1954, see *FRUS 1952–1954*, IX/1, 1515f (D796). For the suggestions cabled back (13–14 April) to London by British missions, see PRO FO371/111070 VR1072/49 (Damascus), /54 (Amman) and /57 (Tel Aviv); Levant Dept. minute. Suggested practical measures to improve frontier control on Israel's borders, 20 April 1954, FO371/111070 VR1072/56. For the suggestions cabled back (16–18 April) to Washington by their American counterparts, see *FRUS 1952–1954*, IX/1, 1516–28 (Docs.797, 799–805).

32. Chapman-Andrews to FO, 14 April 1954 (tgm.226), PRO FO371/111070 VR1072/58. The FO reply to Chapman-Andrews summarized the thinking that had considered, but abandoned, the option of the powers trying to promote a comprehensive Middle East settlement. Falla to Chapman-Andrews, 7 May 1954, FO371/111070 VR1072/58.

33. Evans to FO, 13 April 1954 (tgm.111), PRO FO371/111070 VR1072/51. See also: Evans to Eden, 30 March 1954 (desp.65, 1031/18/54), FO371/111069 VR1072/34; Evans to Allen, 27 April 1954 (desp.1031/59/54) FO371/111071 VR1072/74.

34. Hare to USSD, 18 April 1954, *FRUS 1952–1954*, IX/1, 1525 (D802).

35. Moose to USSD, 19 April 1954, *FRUS 1952–1954*, IX/1, 1527 (D804).

36. Tyler to USSD, 17 April 1954, *FRUS 1952–1954*, IX/1, 1519 (D799).

37. The latter reference is to a disputed Israeli water-diversion project, begun in mid-1953, in the Israel–Syria demilitarized zone. For details, see: Caplan, *FD3*, 220–1, 225–6, Ch. XV.

38. Russell to USSD, 17 April 1954, *FRUS 1952–1954*, IX/1, 1520–2 (D800).

39. 'Facing Realities in the Arab–Israeli Dispute', address to American Council for Judaism, Philadelphia, 1 May 1954, *DSB*, 10 May 1954, 710.

40. Allen, Brief to Eden for NATO meeting and Geneva Conference, 20 April 1954, PRO FO371/111070 VR1072/62. This attitude was later reiterated, with specific scenarios 'if and when the Israelis show signs of adopting an aggressive policy' towards Jordan, in FO Brief for Washington Talks, 22 June 1954, FO371/111072 VR1072/131.

41. See: Beeley to Falla, 29 April 1954, PRO FO371/111071 VR1072/75; Smith to Certain Diplomatic and Consular Offices, 28 April 1954, *FRUS 1952–1954*, IX/1, 1532f. (D811); Lloyd to Eden (Geneva), 5 May 1954 (tgms.213 and 214), PRO FO371/111071 VR1072/76. Replies from American postings can be found in *FRUS 1952–1954*, IX/1, 1539f., 1548–53 (Docs. 814, 818–20).

42. Views of Gen. Glubb, reported in Duke (Amman) to FO, 19 May 1954 (tgm.264), PRO FO371/111071 VR1072/85.
43. The French would have preferred simultaneous approaches to Jordan and Israel, while both the Americans and the French indicated that the UK representative in the UNSC ought to be assigned a more central role. See: Lloyd to Eden (Geneva), 5 May 1954 (tgm.213), PRO FO371/111071 VR1072/76; Butterworth (London) to USSD, 7 May 1954, *FRUS 1952–1954*, IX/1, 1547f. (D817); Dulles to Byroade (Istanbul), 11 May 1954, ibid., 1553f. (D821); Dulles to USEmb France, 15 May 1954, ibid., 1565f. (D826) Falla, Minute (Israel–Jordan, 19 May) of conversation with de Beaumarchais, 18 May 1954, PRO FO371/111071 VR1072/91; Dulles to USEmb Israel, 27 May 1954, *FRUS 1952–1954*, IX/1, 1567 (D828).
44. Hammarskjöld memorandum, Israel–Jordan Situation, 3 July 1954, enclosed in Crosthwaite to Falla, 8 July 1954, PRO FO371/111073 VR1072/152.
45. UKEmb Amman, *Aide-mémoire* to Jordan Government: Possible Practical measures for reducing frontier incidents, 22 May 1954, FO371/111072 VR1072/99.
46. Duke to FO, 22 May 1954 (tgm.270), PRO FO371/111071 VR1072/89. Cf. *FRUS 1952–1954*, IX/1, 1566 (esp. n.4); Duke to Falla, 24 May 1954 (desp.1072/79/54), PRO FO371/111072 VR1072/100; Byroade, Memorandum of Conversation with Eban, Shiloah, 8 June 1954, *FRUS 1952–1954*, IX/1, 1574 (D831); Caplan, *FD3*, Ch. XII; Satloff, *From Abdullah to Hussein*, 91.
47. Jordan MFA, *Aide-mémoire*, 14 June 1954, PRO FO371/111072 VR1072/132; Aldrich (London) to USSD, 14 June 1954, *FRUS 1952–1954*, IX/1, 1576 (D832); Dulles to USEmb UK, 15 June 1954, ibid., 1577 (D833); Satloff, *From Abdullah to Hussein*, loc. cit.
48. Rafael–Russell talk, 16 April, reported in Rafael to Eban, 20 April 1954 (tgm. 338/467), ISA 130.16/2948/6; Rafael, note (31 May) of talk with Hammarskjöld (Geneva), 27 May 1954, 130.16/2947/12/a.
49. See, e.g., Dorsey, memorandum of conversation (Eban, Shiloah, Sherman, Byroade), 17 June 1954, *FRUS 1952–1954*, IX/1, 1581f. (D835).
50. Russell to Sharett, *Aide-mémoire*, 19 June 1954, *FRUS 1952–1954*, IX/1, 1583f. (D836). The British followed Russell's *démarche* by submitting their own *aide-mémoire* to Dr Eytan at the IMFA. See Evans to FO, 20 June 1954 (tgm.169), PRO FO371/111072 VR1072/120.
51. Evans to FO, 20 June 1954 (tgms.170 and 171), FO371/111072 VR1072/121 and /122; Evans to Falla, 22 June 1954 (desp.1031/230/54) FO371/111072 VR1072/136; Sharett and Rafael remarks, IMFA Consultation, 24 June 1954, ISA 130.02/2410/9/I.
52. See, e.g., Wikeley (Jerusalem) to Falla, 20 July 1954 (desp.1062/419), PRO FO371/111104 VR1091/160.
53. FO Brief for Washington Talks, 22 June 1954, FO371/111072 VR1072/131.
54. IMFA Consultation, 24 June 1954, ISA 130.02/2410/9/I.
55. Note (29 July) transmitted in Russell to USSD, 30 July 1954, *FRUS 1952–1954*, IX/1, 1594–6 (D846). Quotations in this and the following paragraph are from this note. Cf. Evans to FO, 30 July 1954 (tgm.213), PRO FO371/111073 VR1072/158.
56. Russell to USSD, 3 August 1954, *FRUS 1952–1954*, IX/1, 1598 (D848). Cf. same to same, 10 August 1954, ibid., 1608f. (D858).
57. Evans to Shuckburgh, 3 August 1954 (desp.1031/269/54), PRO FO371/111073 VR1072/166; same to Falla, 10 August 1954 (desp.1031/273/54), FO371/111073 VR1072/172.
58. Duke to Falla, 4 Sept. 1954 (desp.1072/118/54), PRO FO371/111074 VR1072/189.

59. Falla minute, Israel–Jordan Relations, 25 August 1954, FO371/111073 VR1072/178. For an earlier table of responses from Israel and Jordan to the 11 proposals, see Falla to Crossthwaite, 19 August 1954, FO371/111073 VR1072/166.
60. Brewis to Richmond, 16 July 1954, PRO FO371/111073 VR1072/151.
61. See: Duke to Shuckburgh, 10 August 1954 (desp.1063/14/54), FO371/111073 VR1072/175; Evans to Shuckburgh, 31 August 1954 (desp.1033/362/54), FO371/111074 VR1072/181.
62. NSC 5428, United States Objectives and Policies With Respect to the Near East, 23 July 1954, *FRUS 1952–1954*, IX/1, 533 (D219). Cf. ibid., 1602, 1649; Bailey (Washington) to Brewis, 9 Sept. 1954 (desp.1071/721/54), PRO FO371/111105 VR1091/206.
63. Material on this episode is found in *FRUS 1952–1954*, IX/1, 1603, 1606–8, 1610–12, 1616f., 1622, 1630f.; Duke note of talk with Mallory, 20 August 1954, PRO FO816/191; note of Lavon–Burns talk, 26 August 1954, ISA 130.16/2947/12/a. For accounts of the operations of Israel–Jordan LCAs in earlier years, see Morris, *Israel's Border Wars*, 74–9, 209f.
64. See, e.g., Bailey (Washington) to Brewis, 4 Sept. 1954 (desp.1071/75/54), PRO FO371/111074 VR1072/186; Dorsey to Jernegan, 20 Sept. 1954, *FRUS 1952–1954*, IX/1, 1656f. (D895); Smith to USEmb Israel (etc), 21 Sept. 1954, ibid., 1657 (D896).
65. Russell (Tel Aviv) to USSD, 23 Sept. 1954, *FRUS 1952–1954*, IX/1, 1658f. (D897); Mallory (Amman) to USSD, 24 Sept. 1954, ibid., 1659f. (D898).
66. Falla minute, Arab–Israel Relations, 23 Sept. 1954, FO371/111074 VR1072/208; FO to UKEmbs Washington, etc. 27 Sept. 1954 (tgm.4868), *loc. cit.*
67. Makins (Washington) to FO, 28 Sept. 1954 (tgm.465 Saving), FO371/111075 VR1072/222. On the announced unblocking of accounts, see: Israel Government statement, 27 Sept. 1954, quoted in Israel Ministry for Foreign Affairs, *Peace in the Middle East: A Record of Israel's Peace Offers to Arab States* (Jerusalem: n.d. (Dec. 1955)), 52; H. Gilroy, 'Israel Frees Cash of Arab Refugees', *New York Times*, 28 Sept. 1954; Don Peretz, *Israel and the Palestine Arabs* (Washington: Middle East Institute, 1958), 236f.
68. Falla to Reilly, 28 Oct. 1954, FO371/111075 VR1072/233.
69. See, e.g., *ID6*, 584–7, 695f., 705, 731; Israel State Archives, *Documents on the Foreign Policy of Israel*, Vol. 7 (1952), ed. Yehoshua Freundlich (Jerusalem: 1992), 26f., 48f., 77, 80f., 100f., 150f., 178f., 186f., 240f., 284., 316f., 377f., 387–91, 421, 473–6, 545, 640, 661f., 674f., 716 (hereafter: *ID7*); Oren, *Origins*, 39–48.
70. Caccia, note of Eden–Dulles talk, 2 Oct. 1954, PRO FO371/111075 VR1072/223. Cf. Rumbolt note on same, 2 Oct. 1954, *loc. cit.* /228; Dulles (London) to USSD, 2 Oct. 1954, *FRUS 1952–1954*, IX/1, 1662 (D901).
71. FO to Nutting, 5 Oct. 1954 (tgm.1679), PRO FO371/111075 VR1072/222. Cf. Nutting to FO, 8 Oct., 1954 (tgm.1466), *loc. cit.* /229; Bergus, memorandum of conversation (Dulles, Hoover, Eban, Shiloah, Byroade), 8 Oct. 1954, *FRUS 1952–1954*, IX/1, 1668 (D905). On the *Bat Galim* incident, see: *FRUS 1952–1954*, IX/1, 1660f. (n.2), 1663–7, 1672–4, 1700–4, 1714f., 1726f., 1731f.; Berger, *Covenant*, 162 (and Ch. 11, generally, on the blockade against Israeli shipping).
72. Falla to Murray, 26 Nov. 1954 (desp.297), PRO FO371/111076 VR1072/271.
73. Caffery to USSD, 7 Oct. 1954, *FRUS 1952–1954*, IX/1, 1666f. (D904).
74. Bergus, memorandum of conversation (Dulles, Hoover, Eban, Shiloah, Byroade), 8 Oct. 1954, *FRUS 1952–1954*, IX/1, 1669 (D905).
75. E.g., Dulles to USMis UN, 4 Nov. 1954, *FRUS 1952–1954*, IX/1, 1680f. (D913); Dulles to USEmb Egypt, 13 Nov. 1954, ibid., 1693 (D919). For a discussion of international law aspects of this controversy, see the essays by Johnson, Huang,

Gross and Khadduri in *The Arab–Israeli Conflict*, ed. John Norton Moore (Princeton: Princeton University Press, 1974) I: 820–912.
76. For details, see: Easterman and Barou to Sharett, 30 Nov. 1954, ISA 130.09/2453/21; Orbach to Sharett, 2 Feb. 1955, ISA 130.09/2453/21/b; Maurice Orbach, 'The Orbach File', 3 parts, *New Outlook* (Oct. 1974), 8–23 (Nov.–Dec. 1974), 8–21, and (Jan. 1975), 12–20; Eliav report, Talks and Contacts to Examine the Chances of a Settlement between Israel and Egypt, 1949–1955, 18 Jan. 1956, ISA 130.02/2454/2; Michael Bar-Zohar, *Ben-Gurion: A Biography*, transl. Peretz Kidron (New York: Delacorte, 1978), 209–16; Michael M. Laskier, 'From War to War: The Jews of Egypt from 1948 to 1970', *Studies in Zionism* 7:1 (Spring 1986), 129–31; Shamir, 'Collapse', 74, 77; Michael Oren, 'Secret Egypt–Israel Peace Initiatives Prior to the Suez Campaign', *Middle Eastern Studies* 26:3 (July 1990), 355f.; Oren, *Origins*, 105–8; Shabtai Teveth, *Ben-Gurion's Spy: The Story of the Political Scandal that Shaped Modern Israel* (New York: Columbia University Press, 1996).
77. Sharett interview (J. Fromm), *U.S. News & World Report*, 17 Sept. 1954, 66; Rafael Peace Broadcast (Israel's Arabic Radio Service), 25 Sept. 1954, text in PRO FO371/111075 VR1072/227; 'Israel's Offer to the Arabs: 3-Point Scheme to Ease Tension', *Manchester Guardian*, 27 Sept. 1954; 'Israel Appeals to Arabs for a Peace Agreement,' *New York Times*, 29 Sept. 1954; Moore to Falla, 5 Oct. 1954 (desp. 10301/300/54), FO371/111075 VR1072/227; IMFA, *Peace in the Middle East: A Record* ... 51f.
78. Elath–Shuckburgh talk (19 Oct.), reported in Eden to Moore, 21 Oct. 1954 (desp.206), FO371/111075 VR1072/239; Shuckburgh, *Descent*, 240 (27 Oct. 1954); Falla(?), minute, Israel–Jordan Relations: Port Facilities at Haifa, 13 Nov. 1954, FO371/111076 VR1072/258.
79. Richmond to Falla, 1 Nov. 1954 (desp.1072/155/54), FO371/111076 VR1072/258.
80. Falla(?), minute, Israel–Jordan Relations: Port Facilities at Haifa, 13 Nov. 1954, FO371/111076 VR1072/258. Although no evidence has yet been found to ascertain whether this was as a *result* of British intervention, the Israel Embassy in London requested and received in mid-December an estimate of economic losses to Jordan as a result of lack of access to Haifa. See Yaari to Gazit, 15 Dec. 1954, ISA 130.02/2593/12.
81. See, e.g., Jernegan, memorandum of conversation (Eban, Shiloah, Hoover, Murphy), 17 Dec. 1954, *FRUS 1952–1954*, IX/1, 1722 (D935).
82. Jebb (Paris) to FO, 31 Aug. 1954 (tgm.340 Saving), PRO FO371/111105 VR1091/183; same to same, 4 Sept. 1954, FO371/111105 VR1091/193; Scott (Washington) to FO, 7 Sept. 1954 (tgm.1965), PRO FO371/111105 VR1091/194; Jebb to FO, 15 Sept. 1954 (tgm.638), FO371/111105 VR1091/207; Smith to USEmb Israel (etc.), 21 Sept. 1954, *FRUS 1952–1954*, IX/1, 1657 (D896); Mallory (Amman) to USSD, 24 Sept. 1954, *FRUS 1952–1954*, IX/1, 1659f. (D898).
  For expressions of Arab concern about an imminent Israeli attack, see FO371/111105 VR1091/180–2 and /184–195.
83. Duke to Eden, 27 July 1954 (desp.1033/179/54), PRO FO371/111073 VR1072/159; Duke to Shuckburgh, 10 Aug. 1954 (desp.1063/14/54), FO371/111073 VR1072/175; same to same, 27 Aug. 1954 (desp.1063/18/54), FO371/111105 VR1091/190; Duke to FO, 1 Sept. 1954 (tgm.442), FO371/111073 VR1072/180; same to same, 2 Sept. 1954 (tgm.446), FO371/111105 VR1091/189.
84. Duke to Eden, 27 July 1954 (desp.1033/179/54), PRO FO371/111073 VR1072/159; Falla to Duke, 19 Aug. 1954, FO371/111073 VR1072/159; Duke to FO, 1 Sept. 1954 (tgm.442), FO371/111073 VR1072/180.

85. Wilson to Falla, 28 August 1954 (desp.1075/13), PRO FO371/111073 VR1072/179. For a similar contemporary analysis from Tel Aviv, see Evans to Shuckburgh, 31 August 1954 (desp.1033/362/54), FO371/111074 VR1072/181.
86. Interview (J. Fromm), *U.S. News & World Report*, 17 Sept. 1954, 68.
87. Caffery to USSD, 7 Oct. 1954, *FRUS 1952-1954*, IX/1, 1667 (D904).
88. Dulles to Certain Diplomatic Missions, 21 Aug. 1954, *FRUS 1952-1954*, IX/1, 1619f. (D867).
89. Evans to Eden, 3 Aug. 1954 (desp.137, 1051/12/54), PRO FO371/111073 VR1072/164. See also: Shuckburgh, *Descent*, 238 (11 Oct. 1954); Moore (Tel Aviv) to Eden, 19 Oct. 1954 (desp.187, 1031/308/54), PRO FO371/111075 VR1072/240; Richmond (Amman) to Eden, 8 Nov. 1954 (desp.165, 1072/160/54), PRO FO371/111076 VR1072/267; Nicholls to Eden, 9 Nov. 1954 (desp.199, 1031/334/54), ibid., /256; Uri Bialer, *Between East and West: Israel's Foreign Policy Orientation, 1948-1956* (Cambridge/New York: Cambridge University Press (LSE Monograph Series), 1990), 263.
90. Smith to Certain Diplomatic Missions, 1 Sept. 1954, *FRUS 1952-1954*, IX/1, 1639-41 (D881), discussed below, 80.
91. Mallory (Amman) to USSD, 3 Sept. 1954, *FRUS 1952-1954*, IX/1, 1643 (D884); Caffery (Cairo) to USSD, 3 Sept. 1954, in ibid., 1643 n.3; Dillon (Paris) to USSD, 4 Sept. 1954, ibid., 1648 (D889).
    On British concern about Israel's reprisal policy at this time, see Falla minute, and FO to Tel Aviv (tgm.553), 14 Sept. 1954, PRO FO371/111105 VR1091/209.
92. Ireland to USSD, 3 Sept. 1954, *FRUS 1952-1954*, IX/1, 1645f. (D886). Cf. Strong (Damascus) to USSD, 4 Sept. 1954, ibid., 1646f. (D887).
93. Wadsworth (Jidda) to Byroade, 6 Sept. 1954, *FRUS 1952-1954*, IX/1, 1650f. (D891). Cf. Hare to USSD, 4 Sept. 1954, ibid., 1647f. (D888).

CHAPTER IV

1. For an analytical discussion of the issue of the 'ripeness' of a conflict for resolution, see Richard N. Haass, *Conflicts Unending: The United States and Regional Disputes*, New Haven/London: Yale University Press, 1990.
2. Oliver minute, Arab–Israel Relations, 20 Oct. 1951, PRO FO371/91368 EE1072/34.
3. Oliver minute, *loc. cit.*
4. Wardrop minute, Arab–Israel Relations, 27 Oct. 1951, FO371/91368 EE1072/34.
5. Bowker minute, 11 Oct. 1951, FO371/91368 EE1072/30. Cf. Furlonge note (11 Oct.) of talk with Adnan al-Atassi, 8 Oct. 1951, *loc. cit.*
6. Minute (initials undecipherable), 29 Oct. 1952, PRO FO371/98479 EE1073/86.
7. Pullar minute, 28 Oct. 1952, *loc. cit.*
8. Furlonge to Allen, 18 Nov. 1953 (desp.1075/63/53), PRO FO371/104757 ER1071/106. Quotations in this and the following paragraph are taken from this despatch. Cf. Louis, 'Britain at the Crossroads', 78f.
9. Troutbeck to Allen, 8 Dec. 1953 (desp.1079/324/53), PRO FO371/104757 ER1071/121. Cf. Gardener to Allen, 25 Nov. 1953 (desp.10601/352/53), PRO FO371/104757 ER1071/124; Louis, 'Britain at the Crossroads', 71.
10. Evans to Eden, 8 Dec. 1953 (desp.260, 1031/49/53), PRO FO371/104757 ER 1071/117; quotations in the following paragraphs are taken from this despatch. Cf. Louis, 'Britain at the Crossroads', 62, 64, 66f. The impact of British and American policy on the 'activist-vs-moderate' split within Israel was also a concern of Evans' successor, Jack Nicholls. See below, Ch. V, and Morris, *Israel's Border Wars*, 266.

11. Furlonge to Allen, 30 Dec. 1953 (desp.1052/12/53), PRO FO371/111069 VR1072/5. Cf. Troutbeck to Eden, 28 Dec. 1953 (desp.213, 1079/383/53), PRO FO371/111069 VR1072/1; Louis, 'Britain at the Crossroads', 74.
12. Gardener to Eden, 5 Jan. 1954 (desp.3, 10601/1/54), PRO FO371/111069 VR1072/6.
13. Baker minute, Arab–Israel Relations, 18 Jan. 1954, PRO FO371/111069 VR1072/9.
14. Evans to Eden, 30 March 1954 (desp.65, 1031/18/54), FO371/111069 VR1072/34.
15. Nicholls to Shuckburgh, 8 March 1955 (desp.1041/6/55), FO371/115825 VR1051/8G.
16. Allen memorandum, Settlement of the Palestine Problem, 2 Dec. 1953; Allen minute, Palestine Problem, 3 Dec. 1953, PRO FO371/104770 ER1078/3. Quotations in this and the following paragraphs are taken from these documents.
17. Dodds-Parker to Gaitskell, 26 Jan. 1954, FO371/111068 VR1071/13.
18. For a detailed examination of the Article XII affair, see Caplan, *FD3*, Ch. XII.
19. Falla memorandum, Arab–Israel Relations, 2 Feb. 1954, FO371/111069 VR1072/14.
20. Baker minute, 12 Feb. 1954, FO371/104757 ER1071/117.
21. Tripp minute, 23 March 1954, FO371/111069 VR1072/16.
22. For details, see Caplan, *FD3*, Chs IX–X and Documents 11–13.
23. On the Johnston mission, see: Don Peretz, 'Development of the Jordan Valley Waters', *Middle East Journal* 9:4 (Autumn 1955), 397–412; Yoram Nimrod, *Mei Meriva: ha-Mahloqet al Mei ha-Yarden (Angry Waters: The Dispute over the Jordan Waters)*, (Givat Haviva: Center for Arabic and Afro-Asian Studies, 1966), 40–67; Samir N. Saliba, *The Jordan River Dispute* (The Hague: Martinus Nijhoff, 1968), Ch. 6; Michael Brecher, *Decisions in Israel's Foreign Policy* (New Haven: Yale University Press, 1975), 194–206; Mordechai Gazit, 'Mediation and Mediators', *Jerusalem Journal of International Relations* 5:4 (1981), 92–4; Alteras, *Eisenhower and Israel*, 118–25; Miriam R. Lowi, *Water and Power: The Politics of a Scarce Resource in the Jordan River Basin* (New York/Cambridge: Cambridge University Press, 1993), Ch. 4.
24. For expressions of Anglo–American differences regarding the Johnston mission, see: Allen minute, Palestine Problem, 3 Dec. 1953, PRO FO371/104770 ER1078/3; Falla minute, 7 Dec. 1953, FO371/104757 ER1071/114; Beeley to Shuckburgh, 29 Dec. 1954, FO371/115864 VR1076/2G; Shuckburgh, *Descent*, 245.
25. Douglas to Marshall, 3 tgms., 27 Aug. 1948, *FRUS 1948*, V/2, 1354–9. On the Bernadotte mediation, see: Count Folke Bernadotte, *To Jerusalem*, transl. from Swedish by Joan Bullman, London: Hodder & Stoughton, 1951; Sune O. Persson, *Mediation and Assassination: Count Bernadotte's Mission to Palestine in 1948*, London: Ithaca Press, 1979; Joseph Heller, 'Failure of a Mission: Bernadotte and Palestine, 1948', *Journal of Contemporary History* 14 (1979), 515–34; Mordechai Gazit, 'American and British Diplomacy and the Bernadotte Mission', *Historical Journal* 29:3 (1986), 677–96; Amitzur Ilan, *Bernadotte in Palestine: A Study in Contemporary Humanitarian Knight-Errantry*, New York: St Martin's Press, 1989; Caplan, *FD3*, Ch. II.
26. See, e.g., Ilan, *Bernadotte*, 186–91.
27. For the text of the Proposals, see Caplan, *FD3*, Document 2.
28. Wright, Brief for (Bevin) conversation with M. Schuman, 10 Jan. 1949, PRO FO371/75051 E937/1023/65G. Cf. Michael Oren, 'The Diplomatic Struggle for the Negev, 1946–1956', *Studies in Zionism* 10:2 (Autumn 1989), 199–212.
29. See, e.g.: *FRUS 1948*, V/2, 1415–18, 1421f., 1426, 1433–7, 1459f., 1463–5; PRO FO371/68588 files E12362, E12423, E12426 and E12436/4/31; FO371/68589

files E12460, E12504 and E12505/4/31; FO371/68591, files E13284 and E13345/4/31; Israel State Archives, *Documents on the Foreign Policy of Israel* Vol. 1 (14 May – 30 September 1948), ed. Yehoshua Freundlich (Jerusalem: 1981), 624 (hereafter: *ID1*).

30. For Bunche's personal diplomacy on behalf of the Bernadotte proposals, see: Israel State Archives, *Documents on the Foreign Policy of Israel* Vol. 2 (October 1948 – April 1949), ed. Yehoshua Freundlich (Jerusalem: 1984), 53f. (hereafter: *ID2*); 'Dr Bunche Discusses Palestine', *Al-Ahram*, 12 Oct. 1948, 1,2; Bunche talks with Khashaba, Fawzi, Riad as-Sulh, Daoud, and Ammoun, (Oct.–Nov.), UNA DAG-13/3.2.0 Box 2 (file: Paris Conference: Notes from Conversations); CBS radio interview, 17 Oct. 1948, UN Press Release P/Pal/35, RJB Box 101 folder 14 (Pal: Misc Memoranda 1948).
31. *FRUS 1948*, V/2, 1512–18, 1610–13, 1628f.; Sargent minute, 18 Nov. 1948, PRO FO371/68598 E15000/4/31.
32. For the text of resolution 194, see: Tomeh, *United Nations Resolutions* I: 15–17; Caplan, *FD3*, Document 4. Cf. ibid., 57–8.
33. Ethridge to Acheson, 28 Feb. 1949, *FRUS 1949*, VI, 780f. Cf. Griffis to Acheson, 13 Feb. 1949, *FRUS 1949*, VI, 747f. For early examples of PCC meetings with British diplomats, see: Campbell to FO, 16 Feb. 1949 (tgm.36 Saving), PRO FO371/75347 E2291/1017/31; Mack to FO, 21 Feb. 1949 (tgm.164), PRO FO371/75347 E2416/1017/31. The latter reported his view that the American members of the Commission were overrating British influence over the Arabs.
34. Acheson to Ethridge (Jerusalem), 25 February 1949 (tgm.111), USNA 501.BB Pal/2-2549; *FRUS 1949*, VI, 772 n.1; Acheson to Griffis, 25 Feb. 1949, ibid., 771f.
35. Acheson, memorandum of conversation with Bevin *et al.*, 2 April 1949, *FRUS 1949*, VI, 51. Cf. Satterthwaite to McGhee, 5 April 1949, ibid. 897f.
36. Acheson (Paris) to Webb, 31 May 1949, *FRUS 1949*, VI, 1077f.
37. Bevin to Troutbeck, 20 May 1949 (desp.154), PRO FO371/75054 E3518/1026/65. This important despatch also contains an outline of British 'objectives', some of the 'obstacles' to their achievement, and some suggestions for overcoming these obstacles. For another outline of British attitudes, as given to Israel's representative in London, see: M. Kidron, note (29 June) of talk with Beith, 28 June 1949, Israel State Archives, *Documents on the Foreign Policy of Israel* Vol. 4 (May – December 1949), ed. Yemima Rosenthal (Jerusalem: 1986), 185 (D110) (hereafter: *ID4*).
38. PRO FO371/75350 E8393/1017/31, reproduced in Caplan, *FD3*, Document 7. Cf. Benny Morris, *The Birth of the Palestinian Refugee Problem, 1947–1949*, (Cambridge/New York: Cambridge University Press, 1987), 272f. One researcher mistakenly refers to this document, signed by Bevin on 11 July, as the 'result' – rather than the starting-point – of 'close, high-level British–US consultations regarding the shape of the much hoped-for settlement'. Varda Shiffer, 'The 1949 Israeli Offer to Repatriate 100,000 Palestinian Refugees', *Middle East Focus* 9:2 (Fall 1986), 14, 18.
39. Millar (Washington) to FO, 14 July 1949 (tgm.3572), PRO FO371/75350 E8636/1017/31; FO to UKEmb Washington, 23 July 1949 (tgm.7309), FO371/75350 E8789/1017/31; Acheson to USEmb UK, 1 Aug. 1949, *FRUS 1949*, VI, 1275; Douglas to Acheson, 4 Aug. 1949, ibid., 1285.
40. Acheson to USEmb UK, 7 Aug. 1949, *FRUS 1949*, VI, 1289.
41. (Final?) revised text in FO to UKEmb Paris, 8 Aug. 1949 (tgm.2176), PRO FO371/75351 E9411/1017/31; reprinted in *FRUS 1949*, VI, 1345f. and Ilan Pappé, *Britain and the Arab–Israeli Conflict, 1948–51* (London: Macmillan Press/St Antony's College, 1988), 215f. For reactions, see PRO FO371/75351, files E9908, E10201, E10056, E10699 and E10800/1017/31.

42. See, e.g., FO to UKEmb Damascus, 28 July 1949 (tgm.525), PRO FO371/75350 E9048/1017/31; UKEmb Washington to USSD, memorandum, 1 Sept. 1949, *FRUS 1949*, VI, 1343; Burrows, brief for Bevin talks with Turkish Minister for Foreign Affairs, Paris, 1 Nov. 1949, FO371/75067 E13727/1052/65; Pappé, *Britain*, 122, 187.
43. E.g., McGhee to Webb, 7 Oct. 1949 ('Proposed Plan for Development and Coordination of US Near East Policies and Coordination with the UK'), *FRUS 1949*, VI, 165f. Cf. McGhee to Wright, 24 Oct. 1949, ibid., 54f.; Agreed Conclusions of the Conference of Near Eastern Chiefs of Mission Held at Istanbul, 26–29 Nov. 1949, ibid., 172; McGhee, *Envoy*, 80f.
44. Statement by the United States and the United Kingdom Groups: Discussion on a Palestine Settlement, 14 Nov. 1949, *FRUS 1949*, VI, 64f. Cf. McGhee, *Envoy*, 55f. For documentation and accounts of the November 1949 Anglo–American consultations in Washington, see: *FRUS 1949*, VI, 56–89; McGhee, *Envoy*, 53–8.
45. Rapp to Eden, 28 May 1952 (desp.15; 101/38/1), FO371/98476 EE1073/28; Rapp to Ross, 2 June 1952 (desp.101/38/1), *loc. cit.*; Louis, 'Britain at the Crossroads', 68.
46. Foreign Office: Conference of Her Majesty's Representatives in the Middle East, minutes of meeting of 23 June 1952, PRO FO371/98258 E1056/83.
47. Ross to Burrows, 29 July 1952, PRO FO371/98258 E1056/83. Quotations in this and the following paragraph are taken from this despatch.
48. See, e.g., the exchange between PM Winston Churchill and William Strang at the FO, 17 and 19 Nov. 1952, PRO FO371/98485 EE1081/9. In late 1949, senior British officials recognized the 'strategic disadvantages of having no common land frontier between Jordan and Egypt', but made no mention of the desirability of trying to persuade Israel to consider a land corridor. Chapman-Andrews, note of conversation with Bevin, Troutbeck *et al.*, Fayed, 30 Dec. 1949, PRO FO141/1401 1072/1/50G.
49. Rapp to Ross, 1 Nov. 1952 (desp.222/6), PRO FO371/98479 EE1073/90.
50. Bowker to Rapp, 21 Nov. 1952, PRO FO371/98479 EE1073/90. Quotations in this and the following paragraph are taken from this despatch.
51. Bergus memorandum, An American Policy for Arab–Israeli Peace, 2 Dec. 1952, USNA 684A.86/12-1852. Cf. Byroade to Chiefs of Mission, 22 Nov. 1952, 611.80/11-2252, quoted above, 19.
52. Allen memorandum, Settlement of the Palestine Problem, 2 Dec. 1953, PRO FO371/104770 ER1078/3.
53. Conference Conclusions on the Danger of Arab–Israeli Tensions and Recommended Line of US Action, Istanbul, 14 May 1954, *FRUS 1952–1954*, IX/1, 1561–4 (D824).
54. NSC 5428, United States Objectives and Policies With Respect to the Near East, 23 July 1954, *FRUS 1952–1954*, IX/1, 525–36 (D219). In making this last point, the paper added: 'While reminding the Arabs that peace is the ultimate objective, exercise caution lest stress on this goal prevent Arab acceptance of the necessary intermediate steps.'
55. Both were fully prepared, however, to utilize UN legitimacy and UN agencies eventually to 'complement' the 'peace process' they would be initiating. Cf. Leon Gordenker, 'The United Nations as a Third Party in Arab–Israeli Conflicts', *Jerusalem Journal of International Relations* 10:1 (March 1988), 67–71.
56. Alteras, *Eisenhower and Israel*, 55–7, 81 and Ch. 4 *passim*; Ben-Zvi, *The United States and Israel*, 32–7.

CHAPTER V

1. Arab Ambassadors' *Aide-mémoire*, 17 Sept. 1954; FO to UKEmb Amman, 21 Sept. 1954 (tgms.678 and 679), PRO FO371/111074 VR1072/202; Lloyd, note of talk with Nuri Sa'id, 20 Sept. 1954, ibid. /203. Cf. 'British Reply to Arabs – Seeking Peace on Israel Borders', *The Times*, 22 Sept. 1954.
2. Falla, Brief for Eden interview with Israeli Ambassador Eliahu Elath, 22 Sept. 1954, FO371/111074 VR1072/207; Eden–Elath conversation, reported in Eden to Evans, 22 Sept. 1954 (desp.180), and Israel Govt. *Aide-Mémoire* (EE 368/21257), 22 Sept. 1954, ibid. /209.
3. See, e.g., Oren, *Origins*, 49f. For earlier expressions of Israeli fears, see Waller, memorandum of conversation (Byroade, Sharett, Eban), 8 April 1953, *FRUS 1952–1954*, IX/1, 1164–6 (D592); Alteras, *Eisenhower and Israel*, 44.
4. Eden–Elath conversation, reported in Eden to Evans, 22 Sept. 1954 (desp.180), FO371/111074 VR1072/209. Cf. Sharett press conference, 24 Sept., reported in Evans to Eden, 30 Sept., 1954 (desp.171, 1031/294/54), FO371/111075 VR1072/218.
5. Nassuh Babil, *Ayyam*, 23 Sept. 1954, transl. extract in FO371/111075 VR1072/216. Cf. UKEmb Damascus to Levant Dept. FO, 25 Sept. 1954 (desp.10601/96/54), *loc. cit.*
6. Damascus press report, 24 Sept. 1954, Eng. transl. in PRO FO371/111075 VR1072/216; Beirut radio report, 24 Sept. 1954, Heb. transl. in ISA 130.02/2410/10. For other Arab reactions, see: UKEmb Beirut to Levant Dept., 5 Oct. 1954 (desp.1076/3/11/54), FO371/111075 VR1072/233. An Israeli summary of Arab reactions, dated 27 Sept. 1954, found them 'angry' and showing 'no softening of the Arab stance on the Palestine question'. Only the Lebanese Foreign Minister offered his 'personal' views of the conditions upon which talks with Israel might be possible. ISA 130.02/2410/10.
7. Caccia, note of Eden–Dulles talk, 2 Oct. 1954, PRO FO371/111075 VR1072/223. Cf. Rumbolt note on same, 2 Oct. 1954, ibid. /228; Dulles (London) to USSD, 2 Oct. 1954, *FRUS 1952–1954*, IX/1, 1662 (D901).
8. Dulles to Certain Diplomatic and Consular Offices, 22 Nov. 1954, *FRUS 1952–1954*, IX/1, 1698 (D922). Cf. ibid., 1560.
9. Shuckburgh, *Descent*, 238 (11 Oct. 1954). Emphasis in original.
10. See, e.g., Dulles to Eban, 18 Oct. 1954, *FRUS 1952–1954*, IX/1, 1675 (D909).
11. Richmond (Amman) to Eden, 8 Nov. 1954 (desp.165, 1072/160/54), PRO FO371/111076 VR1072/267.
12. Garvey (for Murray) (Cairo) to Eden, 25 Oct. 1954 (desp.202, 1072/79/54), PRO FO371/111076 VR1072/242. Quotations in this and the following paragraphs are taken from this despatch.
13. Internal FO minutes on this despatch noted the inconsistency of Nasir's argument, given that the UN partition resolution of 1947 accorded most of the Negev *to Israel*, thereby preventing such territorial contiguity between Egypt and Jordan.
14. Tripp minute, 1 Nov. 1954, PRO FO371/111076 VR1072/242.
15. E.g., Nusrat overture, cited above, page 7; Stevenson to FO, 16 April 1951 (tgm.294), PRO FO371/91368 EE1072/6; *JTA Daily News Bltn.*, 15 Sept. 1954 ('Egyptian Premier Wants Israel to Give Up the Negev').
16. Tripp minute, 1 Nov. 1954, PRO FO371/111076 VR1072/242.
17. Nicholls to Falla, 16 Nov. 1954 (desp.10320/43/54), PRO FO371/111076 VR1072/270. This researcher has found no signals at this time that Israel was interested in making such an 'offer'. For an earlier Israeli proposal to allow King Abdullah a corridor to the Mediterranean (with no reference to any land-bridge to Egypt), see summary of Israel–Jordan agreement, 13 Dec. 1949, *ID4*, 716

(editorial note); Shlaim, *Collusion*, 528–30; Rabinovich, *Road Not Taken*, 122–30; Bruce Maddy-Weitzman, *The Crystallization of the Arab State System, 1945–1954* (Syracuse: Syracuse University Press, 1993), 130. For Ben-Gurion's opposition to the idea, see his talk with Arthur Henderson, 1 Oct. 1950, *ID5*, 564 (D399).

18. Falla to Murray, 26 Nov. 1954 (desp.297), PRO FO371/111076 VR1072/271.
19. On the frontier situation, see, e.g., Shimshoni, *Israel and Conventional Deterrence*, 76–9; Oren, *Origins*, 23; Morris, *Israel's Border Wars*, 312–16. For Israeli surveys of Arab intentions, see: 'Arab declarations against peace with Israel' (Nov. 1954), ISA 130.02/2410/10; Research Division, IMFA, Special Survey #224 (Threats of a Second Round), 14 Nov. 1954, ISA 130.16/2593/23; Rony E. Gabbay, *A Political Study of the Arab–Jewish Conflict: The Arab Refugee Problem (A Case Study)* (Genève: Librairie E. Droz (Paris: Librairie Minard), 1959), 425 n.49; Sharett, Knesset speech, 15 Nov. 1954, CZA A245/76.

    For individual press reports, see: 'King of Jordan Bars Talks or Peace with Israelis', *New York Times*, 1 Nov. 1954; Faris al-Khouri speech to Syrian parliament, *Al-Hayat*, 5 Nov. 1954, 3 (also quoted in Gabbay, *Political Study*, 425 and Ben-Gurion, *Israel: A Personal History*, 440); 'King Saud's Statement on Palestine, the Arab Maghrib and Foreign Policy on the occasion of the first anniversary of his accession to the throne', reported in *Filastin*, 13 Nov. 1954 (1, 6) and *The Egyptian Gazette*, 15 Nov. 1954.

    For American reports and comments, see *FRUS 1952–1954*, IX/1, 1679f., 1682, 1692, 1712, 1720–4. For British reports and comments, see: PRO FO371/111107 VR1091/251 and /268; FO371/111076 VR1072/256.

20. Nicholls–Sharett talk (4 Nov.), reported in Nicholls to Falla, 5 Nov. 1954 (desp. 1031/328/543), PRO FO371/111107 VR1091/251; same to Shuckburgh, 14 Dec. 1954 (desp.1031/362/54), ibid. /268.
21. For an interesting discussion of the internal split between activism and restraint as exemplified in Foreign Minister Moshe Sharett and IDF Chief of Staff Moshe Dayan, see Avner Yaniv, *Deterrence without the Bomb: The Politics of Israeli Strategy* (Lexington/Toronto: D.C. Heath, 1987), 64–8. Yaniv presents Ben-Gurion as 'torn between the world of Dayan and the world of Sharett' (ibid., 68–71). Cf. Bar-On, *Gates of Gaza*, 215–17.

    For the more common dichotomy drawn between Ben-Gurion's unabashed activism and Sharett's restraint and diplomatic subtlety, see Caplan, *FD3*, 12–13 and sources cited there.

22. Nutting, note (20 Nov.) of conversation with Eban and Comay, 19 Nov. 1954, PRO FO371/111107 VR1091/259.
23. Eden to Elath, 19 Oct. 1954, reproduced in *Documents on International Affairs, 1954*, Denise Folliot, ed. (London/New York/Toronto: Oxford University Press (under the auspices of the Royal Institute of International Affairs), 1957), 247f. Cf. ibid., 254–7; Ben-Gurion, *Israel: A Personal History*, 440.
24. Nicholls to Shuckburgh, 7 Dec. 1954, PRO FO371/115865 VR1076/19G. Cf. a similar appraisal of Israeli fears and the need for Great Power reassurances by Nicholls' predecessor. Evans to Eden, 3 Aug. 1954 (desp.137, 1051/12/54), FO371/111073 VR1072/164.
25. Nicholls to Shuckburgh, 8 March 1955 (desp.1041/6/55), FO371/115825 VR1051/8G.
26. Mordechai Gazit, 'Israeli Military Procurement from the United States', in *Dynamics of Dependence: US–Israeli Relations*, ed. Gabriel Sheffer (Boulder and London: Westview Press, 1987), 83. Gazit points out that '[b]y 1961, the sum total of US military aid to Israel was $0.9 million, compared with $137.1 million worth of arms supplied to the four Arab states that had participated in the 1948–1949 war against Israel'. *Op. cit.*, 89.

27. For details, see Donohue, *Before Suez*, Ch. VIII; Bialer, *Between East and West*, 262–4; Alteras, *Eisenhower and Israel*, 108f., 335 (n.66); below, 268–9.
28. Smith to Certain Diplomatic Missions, 1 Sept. 1954, *FRUS 1952–1954*, IX/1, 1639–41 (D881). Cf. Alteras, *Eisenhower and Israel*, 113–16.
29. Mallory (Amman) to USSD, 3 Sept. 1954, *FRUS 1952–1954*, IX/1, 1643 (D884); Caffery (Cairo) to USSD, 3 Sept. 1954, in ibid., 1643 n.3; Dillon (Paris) to USSD, 4 Sept. 1954, ibid., 1648 (D889).
  On British concern about Israel's reprisal policy at this time, see Falla minute, and FO to Tel Aviv (tgm.553), 14 Sept. 1954, PRO FO371/111105 VR1091/209.
30. Russell to USSD, 3 Sept. 1954, *FRUS 1952–1954*, IX/1, 1644 (D885). On Israel's proposals for American measures of reassurance, see Shiloah to Herzog, 21 Oct. 1954, ISA RS/4373/17; Bergus, memoranda of conversations (Dulles, Hoover, Eban, Shiloah, Byroade), 15 Sept. and 8 Oct. 1954, ibid., 1652–4 (D893) and 1667–9 (D905). Following the latter meeting, Eban wrote to express his grave concern about the draft statement, which he considered a 'most serious setback and disappointment'. Eban to Dulles, 8 Oct. 1954, ibid., 1669–72 (D906).
31. Bergus, memorandum of conversation (De Laboulaye, Jernegan, Dixon, Kitchen), 21 Dec. 1954, USNA 780.00/12-2154. Cf. Allen views at Alpha meeting, 21 Jan. 1955, 10h00, USNA NEA Lot 59, D518, Box 28.
32. Cf. Kyle, *Suez*, 56. The choice of this starting point for the unfolding of Operation Alpha differs from that of Michael Oren, who claims that '[j]oint Anglo–American planning for an Egypt–Israel settlement began in April 1953'. *Origins*, 111.
33. FO to UKEmb Washington, 4 Nov. 1954 (tgm.5512), PRO FO371/111095 VR1079/1; Merchant, memorandum of conversation (Dulles, Makins, Scott), 5 Nov. 1954, *FRUS 1952–1954*, IX/1, 1683f.; UKEmb Washington *aide-mémoire* to USSD, Israel and the Arab States, 5 Nov. 1954, ibid., 1684f. (D915).
34. *FRUS 1952–1954*, IX/1, 1683. On Dulles' domestic political battles at this time, see Donohue, *Before Suez*, Ch. VIII, and below, Ch. XIV.
35. Makins to FO, 5 Nov. 1954 (tgm.2380), PRO FO371/111095 VR1079/2G.
36. USSD to UKEmb Washington, *aide-mémoire*, 17 Nov. 1954, *FRUS 1952–1954*, IX/1, 1693f. (D920). Cf. conversation with Kermit Roosevelt, reported in Shimoni to USDiv IMFA, 18 Nov. 1954, ISA 130.20/2475/3/II; William J. Burns, *Economic Aid and American Policy toward Egypt, 1955–1981* (Albany: State University of New York Press, 1985), 18f., 22f.
37. Dulles to Certain Diplomatic and Consular Offices, 22 Nov. 1954, *FRUS 1952–1954*, IX/1, 1695–1700 (D922). Quotations in this and the following paragraph are taken from this despatch.
38. Wadsworth (Jidda) to USSD, 10 Dec. 1954, *FRUS 1952–1954*, IX/1, 1710–14 (D929); Caffery (Cairo) to USSD, 11 Dec. 1954, ibid., 1715–17 (D931); Moose (Damascus) to USSD, 13 Dec. 1954 (desp.227), USNA 684A.86/12-1354 (summary in *FRUS 1952–1954*, IX/1, 1718 (D932); Mallory (Amman) to USSD, 23 Dec. 1954, ibid., 1734–8 (D942); Gallman (Baghdad) to USSD, 4 Jan. 1955 (desp.296), USNA 684A.86/1-455; same to same, *FRUS 1955–1957*, XIV, 2f. (D2); White (Tel Aviv) to USSD, 7 Jan. 1955 (desp.413), 684A.86/1-755 (short version in *FRUS 1955–1957*, XIV, 5–7 (D4); Meyer (Beirut) to USSD, 10 Jan. 1955 (desp.385), 684A.86/1-1055.
39. Ogburn to Jernegan, 16 Dec. 1954, USNA NEA Lot 59, D518, Box 28.
40. E.g., Arab–Israeli–Settlement, 9 Dec. 1954, *FRUS 1952–1954*, IX/1, 1708–10 (D928); Burdett, draft instruction to Cairo, 16 Dec. 1954, USNA NEA Lot 59, D518, Box 28; Ogburn to Jernegan, memorandum: Possibilities of an Arab–Israel Settlement, 16 Dec., 1954, *loc. cit.*
41. Apart from Shuckburgh's final report (discussed below), there is little documentary material open to researchers in the PRO describing Shuckburgh's

six-week tour of Middle Eastern capitals. One of the few available contemporary documents is Nicholls to Shuckburgh, 7 Dec. 1954, FO371/115865 VR1076/19G. See also: Sterndale-Bennett, The Arab Israel Imbroglio, 22 Nov. 1954, and Tripp's detailed critique, 7 Dec. 1954, PRO FO371/111076 VR1072/276.

This period was also excluded from Shuckburgh's published diaries (see *Descent*, 242), but Keith Kyle has consulted the unpublished diaries, on the basis of which he has provided some additional insight into Shuckburgh's impressions of Gamal Abd al-Nasir and Nuri Sa'id (see *Suez*, 56–8).

42. Notes on Arab–Israel Dispute, 15 Dec. 1954, PRO FO371/111095 VR1079/10G. For a similar positive British view of Nasir's leadership and personality, see Strachey to Sharett, 17 Dec. 1954, ISA 130.02/2403/12/a.
43. Rafael talk with Shuckburgh and Nicholls, 25 Nov., reported in Rafael to Eytan, 6 Dec. 1954, ISA 130.02/2403/12/a. Cf. Sharett's remarks to visiting American Congressmen and Ambassador George Allen, 7 Dec. 1954, encl. in White to USSD, 13 Dec. 1954 (desp.356), WNRC RG84 E/C/TSG Box 8/DF320 Arab–Israel.
44. Eytan to Elath, 29 Nov. 1954, ISA 130.02/2410/10.
45. ISA correspondence, 27 Dec. 1954 and 27 Jan. 1955, cited in Alteras, *Eisenhower and Israel*, 129.
46. Notes on Arab–Israel Dispute, 15 Dec. 1954, FO371/111095 VR1079/10G. Except where otherwise indicated, quotations in this sub-chapter are taken from this document. Cf. Shamir, 'Collapse', 81; Bar-On, *Gates of Gaza*, 84f.
47. Cf. Shuckburgh, Russell and Dulles remarks, 27 Jan. 1955, *FRUS 1955–1957*, XIV, 32; Russell memorandum, 18 May 1955, ibid., 201.
48. Notes on Arab–Israel Dispute, annex: The Elements of a Settlement, 15 Dec. 1954, FO371/111095 VR1079/10G. Cf. Shamir, 'Collapse', 81.
49. E.g., Shuckburgh to Makins (Washington), 17 Dec. 1954, PRO FO371/111095 VR1079/10G; Sterndale-Bennett to Shuckburgh, 21 Dec. 1954, *loc. cit.*; Shuckburgh to Stevenson (also to Nicholls, Richmond, Sterndale-Bennett), 30 Dec. 1954, *loc. cit.*

    For comments from the field, see: Stevenson (Cairo) to Shuckburgh, 11 Jan. 1955 (tgm. 45), FO371/115864 VR1076/4G; Nicholls (Tel Aviv) to Shuckburgh, 11 Jan. 1955, ibid./13G; Sterndale-Bennett (BMEO, Nicosia) to Shuckburgh, 20 Jan. 1955 (desp. 10752/7/4G), ibid./8G; Brewis to Shuckburgh, 26 Jan. 1955, FO371/115469 V1023/1.
50. Memorandum of conversation (Shuckburgh, Butterworth, Wilson), 15 Dec. 1954, WNRC RG84 E/C/TSG Box 8/DF320 Arab–Israel; Eden (Paris) to FO, 16 Dec. 1954 (tgm.814), PRO FO371/111095 VR1079/9G; Shuckburgh, *Descent*, 242f (16 Dec. 1954); memorandum of conversation (Shuckburgh, Allen, Butterworth, Wilson), 20 Dec. 1954, WNRC RG84 E/C/TSG Box 8/DF320 Arab–Israel.
51. Dulles (Paris) to Hoover, 17 Dec. 1954, *FRUS 1952–1954*, IX/1, 1719f. (D934); Jernegan, memorandum of conversation with Beeley, 17 Dec. 1954, ibid., 1724f. (D936); Russell to Butterworth, 21 Dec. 1954, ibid., 1732 (D941).
52. *FRUS 1952–1954*, IX/1, 1730–2.
53. See, e.g., Shiloah's 'fishing expedition' mentioned in Russell to Shuckburgh, 21 Dec. 1954, *FRUS 1952–1954*, IX/1, 1733f. (D941), esp. n.1; Gazit talk with Tripp at the British FO (20 Dec.), in Gazit to Elath, 22 Dec. 1954, ISA 130.02/2403/12/a; Shuckburgh to Russell, 7 Jan. 1955, *FRUS 1955–1957*, XIV, 4 (D3); Dulles–Eban conversation, reported in Dulles to USEmb Israel, 19 Jan. 1955 (tgm.406), USNA 684A.86/1-1955.
54. Russell to Shuckburgh, 21 Dec. 1954, *FRUS 1952–1954*, IX/1, 1733 (D941).
55. Shuckburgh to Kirkpatrick, 3 Jan. 1955, PRO FO371/115864 VR1076/1G; same to Russell, 7 Jan. 1955, *FRUS 1955–1957*, XIV, 3f. (D3); Wilson–Shuckburgh

talk (7 Jan.), reported in Brewis to Beeley, 11 Jan. 1955 PRO FO371/115864 VR1076/3G. Cf. Beeley to Shuckburgh, 29 Dec. 1954, FO371/115864 VR1076/2G.
56. Russell, 'Agenda for Discussions', 6 Jan. 1955, fwd. Beeley to Shuckburgh, 7 Jan. 1955, PRO FO371/115864 VR1076/5G. Russell's draft agenda contained six items: basic approach; inducements to parties to co-operate; elements of a settlement; measures for guaranteeing security of co-operating states; roles of various states and bodies; and timing and integration of various steps.
57. Revised agenda, enclosed in Shuckburgh to Beeley, 12 Jan. 1955, FO371/115864 VR1076/5G. On 15 Jan., Beeley wrote to inform Shuckburgh that Russell agreed entirely with the revised agenda. *Loc. cit.*
58. NEA memorandum, Suggested Main Points of Approach Toward Israel–Arab Settlement, 14 Jan. 1955, *FRUS 1955–1957*, XIV, 9–19 (D6).
59. Alpha meeting, 21 Jan. 1955, 10h00, USNA NEA, Lot 59, D518, Box 28.
60. Cf. Memorandum of conversation: Unified Development of the Jordan Valley, 21 Jan. 1955, *FRUS 1955–1957*, XIV, 21–3 (D8). Johnston was systematically kept in the dark about Operation Alpha until late June ostensibly out of concern for the success of the delicate Jordan Valley negotiations. See: Allen to Hoover, 23 Feb. 1955 (memo: Mr Eric Johnston and Operation Alpha), USNA NEA Lot 59, D518, Box 29; *FRUS 1955–1957*, XIV, 114, 251f.; Russell to Dulles and Hoover, 10 June 1955, NEA Lot 59, D518, Box 29.
61. Alpha meeting, 22 Jan. 1955, 10h00, USNA NEA Lot 59, D518, Box 28. See also Shuckburgh, *Descent*, 246f. (22 Jan. 1954).
62. Shuckburgh to Kirkpatrick, 22 Jan. 1955, PRO FO371/115864 VR1076/9G; Shuckburgh, *Descent*, 246f.
63. Alpha meetings, 26 Jan. 1955, 10h00 and 15h00, USNA NEA Lot 59, D518, Box 28.
64. *FRUS 1955–1957*, XIV, 36.
65. *FRUS 1955–1957*, XIV, 24; Byroade remarks, Alpha meeting, 1 Feb. 1955, USNA NEA Lot 59, D518, Box 28.
66. Burdett draft instruction to Cairo, Approach to Egypt on Over-all Arab–Israel Settlement, 16 Dec. 1954, USNA NEA Lot 59, D518, Box 28.
67. Memorandum of conversation: Report on Discussion with the British on Alpha, 27 Jan. 1955, *FRUS 1955–1957*, XIV, 24–8 (D9); memorandum of conversation: Operation Alpha, 27 Jan. 1954, ibid., 28–32 (D10).
68. *FRUS 1955–1957*, XIV, 25, 38. See the speculative map produced by Michael Oren, *Origins*, 120. After several extensive readings of the Alpha material in the files open to researchers at the British Public Record Office and the US National Archives during 1990–92, this reviewer was unable to find any map actually produced by the Alpha planners.
69. Macmillan memorandum to Cabinet, Palestine Settlement (CP55/35), 11 June 1955, PRO CAB129/75. Cf. Harold Macmillan, *Tides of Fortune, 1945–1955* (New York: Harper & Row, 1969), 631; Eban, *Autobiography*, 194; Oren, 'Diplomatic Struggle', 211; Bar-On, *Gates of Gaza*, 86f.
70. Shuckburgh to Nicholls, 2 Dec. 1955, FO371/115883 VR1076/435G. Cf. Oren, *Origins*, 114.
71. Alpha meeting, 26 Jan. 1955, 10h00, USNA NEA Lot 59, D518, Box 28. Cf. *FRUS 1955–1957*, XIV, 30.
72. Shuckburgh (Washington) to Kirkpatrick, 2 Feb. 1955 (tgm.311), PRO FO371/115864 VR1076/10G. Cf. *FRUS 1955–1957*, XIV, 26, 30, 36.
73. Dulles would advance this argument frequently in expressing his impatience for a clear commitment from Nasir. See, e.g., Eden–Dulles talk, reported in Eden (Bangkok) to FO, 23 Feb. 1955 (tgm.147), FO371/115866 VR1076/31G.

74. Cf. Shuckburgh, *Descent*, 247 (27 Jan. 1955); Makins, note (29 Jan.) of conversation with Dulles, 28 Jan. 1955, PRO FO371/115865 VR1076/20G; Shuckburgh (Washington) to Kirkpatrick, 2 Feb. 1955 (tgm.311), PRO FO371/115864 VR1076/10G.
75. Alpha meeting, 1 Feb. 1955, USNA NEA Lot 59, D518, Box 28. On the question of reassurances to Sharett, see: memorandum of conversation (Dulles, Hare, Jernegan, Russell, Hart), 11 Feb. 1955, *FRUS 1955–1957*, XIV, 49–51 (D18); Dulles to Sharett, in Dulles to USEmb Israel, 14 Feb. 1955, ibid., 55f. (D22); Lawson to USSD, 17 Feb. 1955, ibid., 63–5 (D25).
76. Hare and Shuckburgh remarks, *FRUS 1955–1957*, XIV, 27, 26 (27 Jan.); Byroade remarks, Alpha meeting, 1 Feb. 1955, USNA NEA Lot 59, D518, Box 28. Cf. Byroade to USSD, 14 April 1955, *FRUS 1955–1957* XIV, 153 (74).
77. Shuckburgh (Washington) to Kirkpatrick, 2 Feb. 1955 (tgm.311), PRO FO371/115864 VR1076/10G.
78. Russell to Hoover, Points of Agreement in Discussion on Arab–Israel Settlement, 2 Feb. 1955, *FRUS 1955–1957*, XIV, 41 (D13). Cf. ibid., 45; Shuckburgh (Washington) to Kirkpatrick, 2 Feb. 1955 (tgm.311), PRO FO371/115864 VR1076/10G.
79. Russell remarks, Alpha meeting, 1 Feb. 1955, USNA NEA Lot 59, D518, Box 28.
80. Jernegan to Hoover, 14 Jan. 1955, *FRUS 1955–1957*, XIV, 7–9 (D5).
81. SD drafts dated 17 and 18 Feb. 1955, in PRO FO371/115865 VR1076/25G and FO371/115866 VR1076/35G. Cf. *FRUS 1955–1957*, XIV, 39 (n.4), 41 (n.7), 46f., 51; draft treaty (UK–US–Israel Security Agreement), 29 April 1955, USNA NEA Lot 59, D518, Box 29.

    Israeli compensation of Palestinian refugees was estimated to cost £100 million, of which the £50 million would be made available 'by gift or loan from the United States Government', £5 million from the French or other governments, and £15 million from the UK, along with other arrangements to help Israel finance the remaining £30 million. See R.A. Butler, Palestine Settlement: Memorandum by the Chancellor of the Exchequer (CP55/36), 14 June 1955, PRO PREM11/945.
82. Six Alpha papers, 26 Feb. 1955, PRO FO371/115866 VR1076/34G; cf. Shamir, 'Collapse', 81f.
83. Dulles to Lawson and White, 9 Feb. 1955, *FRUS 1955–1957*, XIV, 47 (D16); Lawson to USSD, 14 Feb. 1955, ibid., 56–8 (D23); Lawson to USSD, 21 Feb. 1955 (tgm.704), USNA NEA Lot 59, D518, Box 32.

CHAPTER VI

1. Points of Agreement, 2 Feb. 1955, *FRUS 1955–1957*, XIV, 35 (D13). Cf. Oren, *Origins*, 114, where the author erroneously asserts that it was Harold Macmillan who was Secretary of State.
2. Shuckburgh to Stevenson, 15 Feb. 1955, PRO FO371/115865 VR1076/22G.
3. Shuckburgh, Brief for the Secretary of State's Visit to Cairo: Prospects for a Settlement of the Arab/Israel Dispute, 15 Feb. 1955, FO371/115865 VR1076/22G; fwd. Wilson to USSD, *FRUS 1955–1957*, XIV, 59–62 (D24).
4. See, e.g., Kyle, *Suez*, 60f., and the sources cited there.
5. Stevenson to Shuckburgh, 22 Feb. 1955 (tgm.278), PRO FO371/115866 VR1076/28G.
6. Eden–Dulles talk, reported in Eden (Bangkok) to FO, 23 Feb. 1955 (tgm.147), FO371/115866 VR1076/31G.
7. Dulles (Bangkok) to USSD, two tgms., 24 Feb. 1955, *FRUS 1955–1957*, XIV, 70–2 (D29, D30).

8. Hare remarks, Alpha meeting, 1 Feb. 1955, USNA NEA Lot 59, D518, Box 28. Cf. Byroade to USSD, 14 April 1955, *FRUS 1955–1957*, XIV, 151f. (D74).
9. For the text of the Pact (24 Feb. 1955), see Hurewitz, *Diplomacy*, II: 390f. On the general background of this regional rivalry, see, e.g., Maddy-Weitzman, *The Crystallization of the Arab State System, 1945–1954, passim*; Kyle, *Suez*, 56–60; Fawaz Gerges, *The Superpowers and the Middle East: Regional and International Politics* (Boulder/San Francisco/Oxford: Westview Press, 1994), 25–30.
10. Stevenson to Shuckburgh, 16 March 1955, PRO FO371/115866 VR1076/45G. Cf. interviews with Anwar Sadat (27 Feb.) and Abd ar-Rahman Azzam (6 March 1955), Slade-Baker diaries, MEC; *Al-Gumhuriyya*, 31 March 1955 (A. Sadat), summary enclosed Allen to Russell, 1 April 1955, USNA NEA Lot 59, D518, Box 29; communiqués and joint statements of inter-Arab talks (2–19 March 1955), in Noble Frankland, ed., *Documents on International Affairs, 1955* (London/New York/Toronto: Oxford University Press (under the auspices of the Royal Institute of International Affairs), 1958), 326f.; Copeland, *Game of Nations*, 209f.; Burns, *Economic Aid*, 24f. For brief academic assessments of the inter-Arab context at this time, see: Malcolm H. Kerr, *The Arab Cold War: Gamal Abd al-Nasir and His Rivals, 1958–1970*, 3rd ed. (London Oxford/New York: Oxford University Press, 1971), 1–5; Geoffrey Aronson, *From Sideshow to Center Stage: US Policy Toward Egypt, 1946–1956* (Boulder, CO: Lynne Rienner, 1986), 107–11; Oren, *Origins*, 68–71, 118, 121.
11. Anderson remarks, meeting with Ben-Gurion *et al.* (Jerusalem), 16h30, 31 Jan. 1956, USNA NEA Lot 59, D518, Box 34.
12. For details, see: *FRUS 1955–1957*, XIV, 73–8, 80–3, 86–9, 92f.; E.L.M. Burns, *Between Arab and Israeli*, 17–21; Ariel Sharon, with David Chanoff, *Warrior: The Autobiography of Ariel Sharon* (New York: Simon & Schuster, 1989), 102–9; Shimshoni, *Israel and Conventional Deterrence*, 79–81; Kyle, *Suez*, 62f.; Morris, *Israel's Border Wars*, 324–7.
13. Moshe Dayan refers in his memoirs to an 'intelligence failure' which led to a bigger battle than expected. Moshe Dayan, *Avnei Derekh: Autobiografia (Stepping Stones: An Autobiography)*, (Jerusalem: Edanim (with Dvir, Tel Aviv), 1976), 142. Cf. Sharon, *loc. cit.*; Bar-Zohar, *Ben-Gurion*, 218; Shabtai Teveth, *Moshe Dayan: The Soldier, the Man, the Legend* (Boston: Houghton Mifflin, 1973), 241f.; Morris, *Israel's Border Wars*, 326.
14. Heikal, *Cutting the Lion's Tail*, 79. See also: ibid., 79–81; Nasir interview with K. Love ('Nasser Says US Knew Arms Plan'), *New York Times*, 6 Oct. 1955, 4; Wm. Burns, *Economic Aid*, 26, 227 (quoting Saleh Salem); Kyle, *Suez*, 64f.; Gerges, *The Superpowers and the Middle East*, 32f.
15. Ehud Yaari, *Mitsrayim ve-ha-Fidayyin, 1953–1956 (Egypt and the Fedayeen)*, (Givat Haviva: Center for Arabic and Afro–Asian Studies, 1975), 18–20 (transl. in Rabinovich and Reinharz, eds, *Israel in the Middle East*, 78–80); Morris, *Israel's Border Wars*, 85, 91, 337–49, 427. Cf. below, Ch. VII.
16. Burns–Nasir talk, reported in Byroade to USSD, 1 June 1955 (tgm.1827), USNA 674.84A/6-155. Cf. *FRUS 1955–1957*, XIV, 238; Crossman–Nasir talk, 27 Dec. 1955, reported in Lawson to USSD, 13 Jan. 1956 (tgm.703), USNA NEA Lot 59, D518, Box 33; Elmore Jackson, *Middle East Mission: The Story of a Major Bid for Peace in the Time of Nasser and Ben-Gurion* (New York/London: W.W. Norton, 1983), 41; E.L.M. Burns, *Between Arab and Israeli*, 18; Herzog, *A People*, 240; Morris, *Israel's Border Wars*, 328f.

    For details of the secret contacts (mainly through Israeli and Egyptian embassies in Paris), see: Oren, 'Secret Egypt–Israel Peace Initiatives', 353f.; Oren, *Origins*, 99–104; Muhsin Muhammad, 'Al-Ittisal bayna Misr wa-Isra'il l-is-Salam Bad'at fi Ughustus 1952!' (Contacts for Peace between Egypt and Israel Began in August

1952!), *Akhbar al-Yaum*, 9 Nov. 1985, 16.
17. See, e.g., Sharett, *Yoman Ishi* III: 903 (6 April), 909 (9 April 1955); Herzog–Hirschmann talk, reported in Y. Herzog to Eban, 11 July 1955, ISA 130.20/2477/19; Crossman–Nasir talk, 27 Dec. 1955, reported in Lawson to USSD, 13 Jan. 1956 (tgm.703), USNA NEA Lot 59, D518, Box 33; K. Roosevelt message to Harel, in Isser Harel, *Bitahon ve-Democratia (Security and Democracy)*, (Tel Aviv: Edanim/Yediot Aharonot, 1989), 393.
    For Sharett's views on Nasir's reasoning, see Sharett's draft message to Nasir (not sent), (30 Aug.) 1955, Jackson, *Middle East Mission*, 113–15.
18. Anderson minutes, meeting (Jerusalem), 16h30, 31 Jan. 1956, USNA NEA Lot 59, D518, Box 34. Cf. Ben-Gurion, *My Talks*, 297f., 301, 306; Oren, *Origins*, 109.
19. Kyle, *Suez*, 62.
20. Morris, *Israel's Border Wars*, 334. Cf. Shimshoni, *Israel and Conventional Deterrence*, 111.
21. Oren, *Origins*, 70; Alteras, *Eisenhower and Israel*, 140f.
22. Shimshoni, *Israel and Conventional Deterrence*, 112 (emphasis added).
23. See, e.g., IMFA ResDiv, Special Survey #187: Arab Threats of a Second Round (Oct. 1953–Jan. 1954), 29 Jan. 1954, ISA 130.20/2477/21/aleph; Survey of Arabic Press #217, 9 May 1954, *loc. cit.*; Kohn to Sharett, 16 June 1954, encl. 'The Arab War Against Israel', 43/gimmel-5570/4120; Special Survey #224: Threats for a Second Round (15 Aug.–10 Nov. 1954), 14 Nov. 1954, 130.16/2593/23; Special Survey #238/samakh: Arab Threats of a Second Round (Feb.–May 1955), 6 June 1955, 43/gimmel-5570/4120; Special Survey #240/samakh: Arab Threats of a Second Round (end May/mid-June 1955), 26 June 1955, 43/gimmel-5570/4120; Special Survey: Arab Threats of a Second Round (22 Aug.–15 Oct. 1955), 6 Nov. 1955, 43/gimmel-5569/4115; Egyptian Threats of a Second Round (21 May–16 Dec. 1955), *loc. cit.* Cf. Bar-Zohar, *Ben-Gurion*, 218f.; Bar-On, *Gates of Gaza*, 23f.; Morris, *Israel's Border Wars*, 9–13.
24. On this score, Ben-Gurion was forcefully backed up by the chief of Israeli intelligence. See Harel, *Bitahon*, 389–400 *passim*.
25. CIA Director Allen Dulles, NSC, 239th meeting, 3 March 1955, extract in *FRUS 1955–1957*, XIV, 82.
26. Byroade to Allen, 27 March 1955, *FRUS 1955–1957*, XIV, 122 (D58). Cf. Wm. Burns, *Economic Aid*, 26.
27. Copeland, *Game Player*, 199.
28. See Bar-On, *Gates of Gaza*, Ch. 4; below, Ch. VIII.
29. Morris, *Israel's Border Wars*, 330.
30. Byroade to USSD, 4 March 1955, *FRUS 1955–1957*, XIV, 82 (D39).
31. Morris, *Israel's Border Wars*, 330; UNTSO Report (UN Doc. S/3373), 17 March 1955; Eban statement to UNSC, 23 March 1955, in Medzini, *Israel's Foreign Relations*, 321–5; UNSC resolutions 106 and 107, 29 and 30 March 1955, *United Nations Resolutions*, I: 136f.
32. Hart to Allen, brief for conversation with Eban, 14 March 1955, USNA NEA Lot 59, D518, Box 29. On the Qibya raid and its political aftermath, see Caplan, *FD3*, Ch. XII.
33. On UN, Tripartite and Anglo–American consultations during this period, see: *FRUS 1955–1957*, XIV, 216–22, 242–54, 269f., 351–3; Lawson to USSD, 10 June 1955 (tgm.1047), USNA 674.84A/6-1055.
34. Shuckburgh, *Descent*, 252 (7 March 1954); Shuckburgh to Kirkpatrick, 8 March 1954, PRO FO371/115866 VR1076/36G; Russell to USSD, 9 March 1954, *FRUS 1955–1957*, XIV, 90–2; Russell (London) to Byroade, 10 March 1955, USNA NEA Lot 59, D518, Box 29.

35. Points of Agreement in London Discussions of Arab–Israel Settlement, 10 March 1955, *FRUS 1955–1957*, XIV, 98–107 (D48).
36. Shuckburgh remarks, Alpha meeting with Secretary of State, 9 March 1955, FO371/115866 VR1076/41G. Cf. Byroade remarks, *FRUS 1955–1957*, XIV, 121f.; Oren, *Origins*, 115.
37. See, e.g., Dean to Dulles, 11 March 1955, USNA NEA Lot 59, D518, Box 29; Shiloah to Y. Herzog, 13 March 1955. ISA RS/4374/22; Hart to Allen, brief for conversation with Eban, 14 March 1955, USNA NEA Lot 59, D518, Box 29; Bialer, *Between East and West*, 265–9; Alteras, *Eisenhower and Israel*, 127f. For the origins of Israel's quest of such a bilateral treaty or guarantee, see: Donohue, *Before Suez*, 208, 280, 380f.; Bialer, *op. cit.*, 263–5.
38. Shuckburgh to Kirkpatrick, 8 March 1954, PRO FO371/115866 VR1076/36G. Cf. Alpha meeting with Secretary of State, 9 March 1955, ibid. /41G; Shuckburgh minute, 23 March 1955, ibid. /44G; *FRUS 1955–1957*, XIV, 91, 93f.
39. Record of a Meeting, British Foreign Office, London, 10 March 1955, *FRUS 1955–1957*, XIV, 97 (D47).
40. Eden remarks, Alpha meeting with Secretary of State, 9 March 1955, FO371/115866 VR1076/41G; Aldrich to USSD, 10 March 1955, *FRUS 1955–1957*, XIV, 93f. (D46); Shuckburgh to Stevenson, 11 March 1955, PRO FO371/115866 VR1076/41G.
41. Shuckburgh to Kirkpatrick, 10 March 1955, PRO FO371/115866 VR1076/41G; Shuckburgh to Stevenson, 11 March 1955, *loc. cit.*; cf. Aldrich to USSD, 1 April 1955, *FRUS 1955–1957*, XIV, 129 (D61).
42. Stevenson to Shuckburgh, 16 March 1955, PRO FO371/115866 VR1076/45G.
43. Stevenson to FO, 21 March 1955 (tgm.412), PRO FO371/115866 VR1076/44G; Byroade to USSD, two tgms. dated 21 March 1955, *FRUS 1955–1957*, XIV, 116f. (D53, D54). Cf. Russell to Allen and Jernegan, 14 March 1955 (with handwritten note from Jernegan to Allen), 14 March 1955, USNA NEA Lot 59, D518, Box 29; memorandum of conversation (Hoover, Murphy, Russell), 17 March 1955, *FRUS 1955–1957*, XIV, 113f. (D51); Makins to FO, 17 March 1955 (tgm.600), PRO FO371/115866 VR1076/43G; Hoover to USEmb Egypt, 19 March 1955, *FRUS 1955–1957*, XIV, 114f. (D52).
44. Russell, draft memorandum, Effects of Northern Tier Pact on ALPHA Strategy, 23 March 1955, USNA NEA Lot 59, D518, Box 29. Cf. Shuckburgh minute, 23 March 1955, PRO FO371/115866 VR1076/44G; Aldrich to USSD, 1 April 1955, *FRUS 1955–1957*, XIV, 128f. (D61).
45. Memorandum of conversation (Dulles, Allen, Jernegan, Russell), 24 March 1955, *FRUS 1955–1957*, XIV, 118f. (D55).
46. Russell memorandum, 28 March 1955, USNA NEA Lot 59, D518, Box 29.
47. Dulles to USEmb Egypt, 31 March 1955, *FRUS 1955–1957*, XIV, 127f. (D60). On American hopes to side-step such complications in Anglo–American relations, see: ibid., 129, 146f.
48. See, e.g., Burns, *Between Arab and Israeli*, 75–82; Berger, *Covenant*, 185–7; Shimshoni, *Israel and Conventional Deterrence*, 82–4; Morris, *Israel's Border Wars*, 334–7.
49. See, e.g., *FRUS 1955–1957*, XIV, 221 n.4, 242 n.4, 245, 257f.; Makins to FO, 7 April 1955 (tgms.794, 795), PRO PREM11/945; Oren, *Origins*, 130–2; Morris, *Israel's Border Wars*, 332–4; Kyle, *Suez*, 66.
50. See, e.g., FO to UKEmb Cairo, 6 April 1955 (tgm.812), PRO FO371/115867 VR1076/57G; *FRUS 1955–1957*, XIV, 157f., 208, 221; Stevenson to FO, 19 May 1955 (tgm.640), PRO FO371/115869 VR1076/96G.
51. On Burns' efforts and American assistance (as 'post office'), see: *FRUS 1955–1957*, XIV, 142–5, 148, 157f., 163–5, 167f., 182–4, 186f.; Burns, *Between*

Arab and Israeli, 70f. On Sharett's proposal for high-level meetings, see: ibid., 135–8, 142–5, 148, 157f., 163–5, 167f., 190f., 195, 208; Sharett, *Yoman Ishi* III: 899–912 and IV: 913–49 (4–20 April 1955), *passim*; Y. Herzog to Sharett, 14 April 1955, ISA 130.20/2477/19; Hart to Jernegan, 26 April 1955, USNA NEA Lot 59, D518, Box 29.

52. Dulles to USEmb Egypt, 16 April 1955, *FRUS 1955–1957*, XIV, 161 (D80).
53. Salah Gohar's views, reported in Byroade to USSD, 7 May 1955 (tgm.1671), USNA 674.84A/5-755. Cf. *Al-Akhbar*, 29 June 1955, extract in IMFA, The Arab Struggle Against Peace, No.3, ISA 130.02/2410/10; Cole (Jerusalem) to USSD, 25 May 1955 (tgm.331), USNA 674.84A/5-2555; same to same, 30 June 1955, *FRUS 1955–1957*, XIV, 267f.
54. Byroade to USSD, 10 May 1955, *FRUS 1955–1957*, XIV, 183 (D93). Cf. ibid., 187, 190, 193.
55. Burns, *Between Arab and Israeli*, 64.
56. See, e.g., Lawson to USSD, 16 May 1955 (tgm.966), USNA 674.84A/5-1655; cf. *FRUS 1955–1957*, XIV, 190 n.2.
57. Stevenson to FO, 19 May 1955 (tgm.640), PRO FO371/115869 VR1076/96G; Byroade to USSD, 20 May 1955, *FRUS 1955–1957*, XIV, 192 (D101); same to same, 20 May 1955 (tgm.1749), USNA 674.84A/5-2055 (cf. *FRUS 1955–1957*, XIV, 190 n.3). Cf. ibid., 191–7.
58. These were for (a) a mutual pull-back of troops half a kilometre from each side of the Gaza frontier, and (b) a meeting between Egyptian and Israeli military personnel at a lower level than originally envisaged. See: Burns account of talk with Nasir, reported in Byroade to USSD, 1 June 1955 (tgm.1827), USNA 674.84A/6-155; Hammarskjöld press conference, 2 June 1955, reproduced in *Public Papers of the Secretaries-General of the United Nations: Vol. II Dag Hammarskjöld, 1953–1956*, eds Andrew W. Cordier & Wilder Foote, (New York/London: Columbia University Press, 1972), 496–8 (hereafter: *PPSG* II); Burns, Notes (2 June) for Use in Interview with Israel Ministry of Foreign Affairs, reporting my interview with Egyptian Prime Minister, 1 June 1955, UNA DAG-13/3.4.0 Box 96 (file: EIMAC Conversations – 1955); *FRUS 1955–1957*, XIV, 220 n.3, 226–30, 234f., 236f. 240f.; Byroade to USSD, 10 June 1955 (tgm.1889), USNA 674.84A/6-1055.
59. Lawson to USSD, 10 June 1955 (tgm.1047), USNA 674.84A/6-1055. Cf. *FRUS 1955–1957*, XIV, 259f., 267f.
60. Stevenson–Nasir talk (5 June), reported in Byroade to USSD, 6 June 1955, *FRUS 1955–1957*, XIV, 221f. (D116).
61. Byroade–Nasir talk, reported in Byroade to USSD, 9 June 1955, *FRUS 1955–1957*, XIV, 236f. (D122). Cf. Nasir speech at Fayum, 6 July 1955, quoted in IMFA, 'The Arab Struggle Against Peace', No. 3, ISA 130.02/2410/10; K. Love, 'Mideast Peace a Little Closer', *New York Times*, 10 July 1955 (dateline Cairo, 9 July).
62. Lawson to USSD, 10 June 1955 (tgm.1047), USNA 674.84A/6-1055.
63. Memorandum of conversation (Byroade–Fawzi), 26 March 1955, *FRUS 1955–1957*, XIV, 122–5 (D58). Cf. Stevenson to Shuckburgh, 1 April 1955, PRO FO371/115867 VR1076/51G; K. Love, 'Mideast Peace a Little Closer', *New York Times*, 10 July 1955 (dateline Cairo, 9 July).
64. Stevenson to Shuckburgh, 1 April 1955, PRO FO371/115867 VR1076/51G; Cf. Byroade to Dulles, 3 April 1955, *FRUS 1955–1957*, XIV, 130 (D62); Byroade to Allen, 27 March 1955, ibid., 120–2 (D58); Shuckburgh remarks, quoted in ibid., 133 n.6.
65. Byroade to Dulles, 3 April 1955, *FRUS 1955–1957*, XIV, 130–3 (D62). Quotations in this and the following paragraph are taken from this despatch.

66. Fawzi offered a summary of his talk with Byroade in a subsequent meeting with the British Ambassador. See Stevenson to Shuckburgh, 3 April 1955 (tgm.465), PRO FO371/115867 VR1076/52G.
67. Byroade to USSD, 5 April 1955 (tgm.1480), USNA 774.00/4-555; same to same, 5 April 1955, *FRUS 1955–1957*, XIV, 141 (D67). Cf. Stevenson to FO, 6 April 1955 (tgm.487), PRO FO371/115867 VR1076/57G. For a brief account of the meeting as given by Nasir to an associate one month later, see Muhammad Tawil, *Lu'bat al-Umam wa-'Abd an-Nasir (The Game of Nations and Abd an-Nasir)*, (Cairo: 1986), 420.
68. Byroade to USSD, 5 April 1955, *FRUS 1955–1957*, XIV, 141 (D67); Stevenson to FO, 6 April 1955 (tgm.487), PRO FO371/115867 VR1076/57G. The British Treasury was, however, taken aback by the unexpected disclosure occurring before adequate consideration could be given to Britain's financial commitments under Alpha. See, e.g., Butler to Macmillan, 7 May 1955, PREM11/945.
69. FO to UKEmb Cairo, 6 April 1955 (tgm.812), PRO FO371/115867 VR1076/57G; Allen to Byroade, 11 April 1955, USNA NEA Lot 59, D518, Box 29.
70. Shuckburgh, *Descent*, 254 (5 April 1955); *FRUS 1955–1957*, XIV, 141 n.4; FO to Cairo, 6 April 1955 (tgm.812), PRO FO371/115867 VR1076/57G.
71. Stevenson to FO, 7 April 1955 (tgm.497), PRO FO371/115867 VR1076/59G. Cf. Byroade to USSD, 14 April 1955, *FRUS 1955–1957*, XIV, 152f. (74); Stevenson to FO, 14 April 1955 (tgm.525), PRO FO371/115867 VR1076/60G; Shamir, 'Collapse', 82f.; Oren, 'Diplomatic Struggle', 212.
72. Kyle, *Suez*, 71.
73. Allen, memorandum of conversation (Fawzi, Dulles), 24 June 1955, *FRUS 1955–1957*, XIV, 264f. (D138). Cf. ibid., 283; Dorsey, memorandum of conversation (Fawzi, Dulles), 7 July 1955, USNA 684A.86A/7-755.
74. Shuckburgh minute, Palestine Settlement (for meeting of British Ambassadors), 3 Jan. 1956, PRO FO371/121708 VR1071/4G. Shuckburgh attributed the one-third figure to remarks made privately by Dulles.
75. See Butler–Macmillan correspondence for May 1955 in PRO PREM11/945; Butler, Palestine Settlement: Memorandum by the Chancellor of the Exchequer (CP55/36), 14 June 1955, *loc. cit.*; extract of Cabinet Conclusions (CM55/15), 16 June 1955, *loc. cit.*; other correspondence for May 1955 in FO371/115868 VR1076/82. For continuing British consideration of various problems connected to compensation proposals, see Rose to Bailey, 31 Jan. 1956, FO371/121708 VR1071/25G.
76. Byroade to USSD, 14 April 1955, *FRUS 1955–1957*, XIV, 152f. (74); three tgms. from Stevenson to FO, 14 April 1955 (tgms.525, 526, 527), PRO FO371/115867 VR1076/60G. Cf. Macmillan memorandum to Cabinet, Palestine Settlement, 11 June 1955 (CP55/35), PRO CAB129/75; Bar-On, *Gates of Gaza*, 90.
77. See, e.g., Alteras, *Eisenhower and Israel*, 59, 63f., 66, 74; Burdett, memorandum of conversation (Byroade, Eban, Dayan, Shiloah), 16 July 1954, *FRUS 1952–1954*, IX/1, 1589f. (D842).
78. See Oren's map, *Origins*, 120.
79. FO to UKEmb Washington, 4 May 1955 (tgm.2110), FO371/115867 VR1076/74G. Cf. Russell to MacArthur, 5 May 1955, *FRUS 1955–1957*, XIV, 176f. (D89); Shuckburgh brief for Macmillan Paris meeting, 6 May 1955, FO371/115869 VR1076/93G; Macmillan memorandum to Cabinet, Palestine Settlement, 11 June 1955 (CP55/35), PRO CAB129/75; Shamir, 'Collapse', 87. See also the interesting, but conjectural, map produced in Oren, *Origins*, 120.
80. FO to UKEmb Washington, 4 May 1955 (tgm.2110), FO371/115867 VR1076/74G.
81. Shuckburgh to Kirkpatrick, 4 May 1955, PRO FO371/115867 VR1076/74G. Cf.

Shuckburgh, *Descent*, 264 (26 June 1955).
82. Russell to Byroade, 29 April 1955, *FRUS 1955–1957*, XIV, 167 (D84).
83. Dulles (Paris) to Hoover, 12 May 1955, *FRUS 1955–1957*, XIV, 185 (D95). Cf. Macmillan's version: 'In view of Jewish pressure on the United States Government it would be psychologically difficult for them to sell the proposal.' Record of conversation (Macmillan–Dulles), Paris, 12 May 1955, PRO FO371/115870 VR1076/110G.
 John Foster Dulles had, in fact, been aware of Israel's position on the Negev, along with the importance of not alienating US Jewry, back in early 1953. See, e.g., Alteras, *Eisenhower and Israel*, 64, 66, 68–70.
84. Makins to FO, 3 May 1955 (tgm.1038), FO371/115867 VR1076/74G; Dulles to USEmb Egypt, 3 May 1955, *FRUS 1955–1957*, XIV, 169 (D86); Russell to MacArthur, 5 May 1955, ibid., 176f. (D89). Cf. Nicholls' reservations about the Negev triangles, in Nicholls to Shuckburgh, 4 May 1955, PRO FO371/115868 VR1076/89G.
85. Shuckburgh to Kirkpatrick, 4 May 1955, PRO FO371/115867 VR1076/74G.
86. Shuckburgh to Duke (*et al.*), 15 April 1955 ('Top Secret & Personal'), PRO FO371/115867 VR1076/63G; Allen to Chiefs of Mission, 15 April 1955, USNA NEA Lot 59, D518, Box 29. Cf. Shuckburgh to UKEmb Washington, 14 April 1955 (tgm.1677), PRO FO371/115867 VR1076/53G; *FRUS 1955–1957*, XIV, 156f., 162, 166f., 175f.; Shuckburgh, *Descent*, 256–8 (18, 25 and 28 April 1955); Shuckburgh to Nicholls, 28 April 1955, PRO FO371/115867 VR1076/75G; same to Kirkpatrick, 4 May 1955, PRO FO371/115867 VR1076/74G.
87. Lawson to USSD, 4 March 1955, *FRUS 1955–1957*, XIV, 88f. (D42). For the Ambassador's analysis of Israel's international, regional and domestic motives for the Gaza raid, see same to same, 4 March 1955, ibid., 86–8 (D41).
88. Bialer, *Between East and West*, 260–71. Cf. Yaniv, *Deterrence without the Bomb*, 53f.
89. Extract of minutes, in Shuckburgh to Kirkpatrick, 8 March 1955, PRO FO371/115866 VR1076/36G; Russell remarks, Alpha meeting with Secretary of State, 9 March 1955, FO371/115866 VR1076/41G. Cf. *FRUS 1955–1957*, XIV, 91.
90. Sharett to Dulles, in Lawson to USSD, 12 April 1955, *FRUS 1955–1957*, XIV, 150 (D73). See also: Bialer, *Between East and West*, 266–71; Alteras, *Eisenhower*, 127f.
91. Lawson to USSD, 5 April 1955, *FRUS 1955–1957*, XIV, 135–40 (D65, D66); 'Israel Asks Coexistence', *New York Times*, 12 April 1955 (dateline Jerusalem, 11 April); Sharett, *Yoman Ishi* IV: 927–30 (12 April 1955); 'Israel Offers Six-Point Program to Arabs – Answers Bandung', *JTA Daily News Bltn.*, 25 April 1955 (dateline UN, 24 April); Bialer, *Between East and West*, 270f.
92. Sharett to Dulles, in Lawson to USSD, 12 April 1955, *FRUS 1955–1957*, XIV, 149–51 (D73).
93. Memorandum of conversation (Dulles, Allen, Eban, Shimoni), 13 April 1955, USNA NEA Lot 59, D518, Box 29; Dulles to USEmb Israel, 14 April 1955, *FRUS 1955–1957*, XIV, 153f. (D75). Coincidentally, on the same day in London, Ambassador Elath was received by Evelyn Shuckburgh, who wrote disparagingly of Israel's campaign for a treaty guarantee 'of their present conquests, so that they shall not have to make any concessions'. Shuckburgh, *Descent*, 255 (13 April 1955).
94. Bergus, memorandum of conversation (Allen, Eban, Shimoni), 14 April 1955, USNA NEA Lot 59, D518, Box 29.
95. Shuckburgh, *Descent*, 256 (16 April 1955).
96. Dulles to USEmb Egypt (etc.), 19 April 1955, *FRUS 1955–1957*, XIV, 162 (D81). From Cairo, Ambassador Byroade hoped that the Dulles–Eban talk would 'help stay their hand for a time'. Byroade to USSD, 15 April 1955, ibid., 155 (D76).

97. Dulles to Sharett, 16 April 1955, *FRUS 1955–1957*, XIV, 159f. (D79).
98. Notes of Meeting at Sharett's home, 19 April 1955, ISA RS/4374/22.
99. Brief for discussion with Attlee, 20 April 1955, PRO FO371/115867 VR1076/70G.
100. Draft treaty, 29 April 1955, USNA NEA Lot 59, D518, Box 29. Cf. *FRUS 1955–1957*, XIV, 176.
101. Sharett to Dulles, 4 May 1955, in Lawson to USSD, 5 May 1955, *FRUS 1955–1957*, XIV, 170–4 (D87). Quotations in this and the following paragraphs are taken from this letter. Cf. Oren, *Origins*, 115.
102. Cf. Caplan, *FD3*, Chs. VI–VII, IX–X. The point was emphasized again by Israeli spokesmen during the first months of the Eisenhower administration. See Alteras, *Eisenhower and Israel*, 46, 48.
103. Cf. expressions of this position in the early months of the Eisenhower administration, discussed in Alteras, *Eisenhower and Israel*, 45–7.
104. Following the Israeli elections, Sharett presented Ambassador Lawson with a similar outline of his country's attitude to US approaches to resolve the Arab–Israel dispute. See Lawson to USSD, 16 Aug. 1955 (tgm.118), USNA 684A. 86/8-1655 (cf. *FRUS 1955–1957*, XIV, 391 n.4.).
105. Sharett to UKEmb Tel Aviv, 5 May 1955, encl. in Nicholls to Macmillan, 10 May 1955 (desp.62, 1031/63G), PRO FO371/115868 VR1076/86G. Cf. Nicholls to FO, 6 May 1955 (tgm.151), FO371/115868 VR1076/79G; Schneerson to Elath, 11 May 1955, ISA 130.02/2593/21/b.
106. Arthur minutes, 10 and 16 May 1955, PRO FO371/115868 VR1076/79G and 86G; Shuckburgh to Nicholls, 21 May 1955, FO371/115868 VR1076/86G.
107. Shuckburgh to Caccia, 7 May 1955, PRO FO371/115869 VR1076/93G.
108. Shuckburgh to Caccia, 7 May 1955, PRO FO371/115869 VR1076/93G. Cf. Shuckburgh brief for Macmillan, 6 May 1955, *loc. cit.*; Shuckburgh minute, 17 May 1955, FO371/115868 VR1076/86G; *Descent*, 259 (23 May 1955); Nicholls to Shuckburgh, 25 June 1955, FO371/115871 VR1076/123G.
109. Dulles (Paris) to Hoover, 12 May 1955, *FRUS 1955–1957*, XIV, 185 (D95). Cf. record of conversation (Macmillan–Dulles), Paris, 12 May 1955, PRO FO371/115870 VR1076/110G; memorandum of conversation (Dulles, Macmillan, Russell, Shuckburgh), Paris, 14 July 1955, *FRUS 1955–1957*, XIV, 295–8 (D158).
110. Shuckburgh to Nicholls, 21 May 1955, FO371/115868 VR1076/86G.
111. Schneerson to Elath, 11 May 1955, ISA 130.02/2593/21/b. Cf. extract from Elath interview in the London *Jewish Chronicle*, 3 June 1955, reproduced in Arthur minute, 4 June 1955, PRO FO371/115870 VR1076/110G.
112. Shuckburgh–Elath talk, 2 June 1955, copy given by Bailey to Russell (6 June), USNA NEA Lot 59, D518, Box 29; also reported in FO to UKEmb Tel Aviv, 4 June 1955 (tgm.324), PRO FO371/115870 VR1076/110G. Cf. Comay talk with Pearson and Ford (Ottawa), 7 June 1955, ISA 130.02/2410/10; Nicholls to Shuckburgh, 25 June 1955, PRO FO371/115871 VR1076/123G.
113. Bergus, memorandum of conversation (Eban, Shiloah, Allen), 10 May 1955, *FRUS 1955–1957*, XIV, 180–2 (D92).
114. Bergus, memorandum of conversation (Eban, Shiloah, Allen), 8 June 1955, USNA NEA Lot 59, D518, Box 29. Quotations in this and the following paragraph are taken from this memorandum. Cf. *FRUS 1955–1957*, XIV, 231.
115. See, e.g., Allen, memorandum of conversation with Eban, 23 June 1955, USNA NEA Lot 59, D518, Box 29.

CHAPTER VII

1. See, e.g., *FRUS 1955–1957*, XIV, 179, 200–5, 280; Hart to Allen and Jernegan, 24 May 1955, USNA NEA Lot 59, D518, Box 29; PRO FO371/115869 VR1076/100G, /107G; FO371/115870 VR1076/114G; FO371/115871 VR1076/126G, /132G; FO371/115872 VR1076/146G; Macmillan memorandum to Cabinet, Palestine Settlement, CP55/35, 11 June 1955, PRO CAB129/75.
2. (Unsigned) report of talk with Lewis Jones, n.d. (? early July 1955), Tawil, *Lu'bat*, 410. Cf. Ben-Gurion electoral campaign speech at Beersheba, 9 July 1955, cited in Burns, *Between Arab and Israeli*, 82.
3. 'Israel's Sharett on the Arabs: "Rabid Nonsense"' – 'Egypt's Nasser on the Jews: "Sheer Defiance"', *Newsweek*, 23 May 1955, 2–3.
4. Stevenson to FO, 19 May 1955 (tgm.640), PRO FO371/115869 VR1076/96G.
5. See, e.g., Byroade to USSD, 5 and 16 May 1955, *FRUS 1955–1957*, XIV, 178, 188 (D90, D97); Stevenson to FO, 10 May 1955 (tgm.609), PRO FO371/115868 VR1076/85G; Shuckburgh to Macmillan, 13 June 1955, FO371/115870 VR1076/115G.
6. Byroade to USSD, 30 May 1955 (tgm.1806), USNA 684A.86/5-3055. Cf. Stevenson to FO, 30 May 1955 (tgm.687), PRO FO371/115869 VR1076/103G. On the continuing Gaza tensions, see: *FRUS 1955–1957*, XIV, 280–2, 299f., 318f., 347f., 364f.; K. Love, 'Mideast Peace a Little Closer', *New York Times*, 10 July 1955 (dateline Cairo, 9 July); Cole–Reedman talk, reported in Cole to USSD, 16 Aug. 1955, USNA 674.84A/8-1655; Michael B. Oren, 'Escalation to Suez: The Egypt–Israel Border War, 1949–56', *Journal of Contemporary History* 24 (1989), 359f.
7. See, e.g., Tawil, *Lu'bat*, 420f.; *FRUS 1955–1957*, XIV, 188 n.2, 189, 192; Copeland, *Game of Nations*, 188f.; Dorsey, memorandum of conversation (Fawzi, Dulles), 7 July 1955, USNA 684A.86A/7-755; Aronson, *From Sideshow to Center Stage*, 125–8; Barry Rubin, *Secrets of State: The State Department and the Struggle Over US Foreign Policy* (Oxford/New York: Oxford University Press, 1985), 89; Bar-On, *Gates of Gaza*, 89f.
8. Dulles (Paris) to Hoover, 12 May 1955, *FRUS 1955–1957*, XIV, 185 (D95); record of conversation (Macmillan–Dulles), Paris, 12 May 1955, PRO FO371/115870 VR1076/110G; Macmillan memorandum to Cabinet, Palestine Settlement, CP55/35, 11 June 1955, CAB129/75; Makins to FO, 13 May 1955 (tgm.1113), FO371/115868 VR1076/91G; Shuckburgh to Makins, 16 May 1955 (tgm.2344), *loc. cit.*; Stevenson to FO, 10 May 1955 (tgm.609), PRO FO371/115868 VR1076/85G.
9. Beginning in June, increasing attention would be given to Egypt's attempts to organize financing for the High Aswan Dam project. See: *FRUS 1955–1957*, XIV, 238f., 255f., 261–3, 270–6, 304–6, 327f., 332–4, 337f., 355–8, 371f., 377; Tuhami memorandum, 15 June 1955, in Tawil, *Lu'bat*, 416–19; Shuckburgh, *Descent*, 261f. (17 June 1955); Sabri to Byroade, 30 June 1955, in Tawil, *Lu'bat*, 413–15; (Tuhami?) to Nasir (late June 1955), in ibid., 411f.; Dorsey to Wilkins, 15 July 1955, USNA NEA Lot 59, D518, Box 29; Ali Mahir interview, 6 June 1955, Slade–Baker Diaries, Vol. V, 828, MEC; Mahmud Fawzi interview, 9 June 1955, *loc. cit.*, 836.
10. Russell to Dulles, 24 May 1955, *FRUS 1955–1957*, XIV, 206 (D107). Cf. ibid., 199–205, 207f., 210–14, 231–3.
11. Macmillan memorandum to Cabinet, Palestine Settlement, CP55/35, 11 June 1955, PRO CAB129/75.
12. Russell to Dulles, 2 June 1955, *FRUS 1955–1957*, XIV, 210f. (D110). Cf. Dulles to Byroade, 8 June 1955 (draft tgm.), USNA NEA Lot 59, D518, Box 29.

13. Shuckburgh to Makins, 2 June 1955 (tgm.2609), PRO FO371/115869 VR1076/105G. Cf. Duke (Amman) to Shuckburgh, 19 July 1955, encl. report on Local Conditions, fwd. Rose to Bailey (for Russell), 2 Aug. 1955, FO371/115873 VR1076/153G.
14. Byroade to USSD, 9 June 1955 (tgm.1878), USNA 684A.86/6-955. Cf. Stevenson to FO, three tgms. 4, 9 and 10 June 1955 (tgms.707, 727, 731), PRO FO371/115869 VR1076/109G, /112G and /113G; Shuckburgh to Macmillan, 13 June 1955, FO371/115870 VR1076/115G.
15. Shuckburgh to Kirkpatrick, 8 July 1955, PRO FO371/115871 VR1076/131G. Cf. Dulles to Byroade, 9 July 1955, *FRUS 1955–1957*, XIV, 282f. (D150).
16. For an authoritative summary of 1954–1955 Soviet–Egyptian 'prenegotiation' manoeuvres with a view to an arms deal, see Ginat, *The Soviet Union and Egypt*, 206–9.
17. See, e.g., *FRUS 1955–1957*, XIV, 338f., 353f., 361f.; Wilbur Crane Eveland, *Ropes of Sand: America's Failure in the Middle East* (New York: W.W.Norton, 1980), 101; Peter L. Hahn, *The United States, Great Britain, and Egypt, 1945–1956: Strategy and Diplomacy in the Early Cold War* (Chapel Hill/London: University of North Carolina Press, 1991), 184–6; Gerges, *The Superpowers and the Middle East*, 34f. Cf below, Ch. VIII.
18. Cf. Oren, *Origins*, 115; Bar-On, *Gates of Gaza*, 90f.
19. Makins to FO, 1 June 1955 (tgm.1262), PRO FO371/115869 VR1076/106G. For Byroade's warnings against such Israeli tactics, see: Byroade to USSD, 15 April 1955, *FRUS 1955–1957*, XIV, 155f. (D76). Cf. ibid., 200.
20. See, e.g., Allen to Dulles, 26 April 1955, USNA NEA Lot 59, D518, Box 29; Russell to Byroade, 29 April 1955, *FRUS 1955–1957*, XIV, 166 (D84).
21. E.g., Sharett, *Yoman Ishi* III: 908 (8 April) and IV: 931 (13 April 1955); Sharett remarks, meeting at Minister's home, 19 April 1955, ISA RS/4374/22; Shuckburgh, *Descent*, 259 (1 May 1955); Nicholls to Macmillan, 10 May 1955 (desp.62, 1031/63G), PRO FO371/115868 VR1076/86G; Information Dept IMFA, Outline of Proposals to Settle the Israel–Arab Conflict (Information for Israel Missions Abroad #1031), 7 June 1955, ISA 130.20/2477/21/b.
22. *The Times*, 3 May 1955, clipping in PRO FO371/115868 VR1076/78G.
23. Russell to Allen and Jernegan, 3 May 1955, USNA NEA Lot 59, D518, Box 29.
24. White–Kollek talk, reported in White to Lawson, 18 May 1955, encl. in Lawson to Russell, 20 May 1955, USNA NEA Lot 59, D518, Box 29. After examining the evidence, Russell still believed it was conceivable that the Israelis had pieced together information based on 'solid guesswork', rather than a serious breach of secrecy. Russell to Lawson, 10 June 1955, *loc. cit.*
25. Sharett, *Yoman Ishi* IV: 1024f. (28 May 1955); Eng. transl. in Rabinovich and Reinharz, eds, *Israel in the Middle East*, 95f.; Jacob Tsur, *Prélude à Suez: Journal d'une ambassade 1953–1956* (Paris: Presses de la Cité, 1968), 218f.
26. William C. Burdett, oral history interview, Georgetown University Library, 16 December 1988, 6. Another US foreign service official, stationed in Haifa, shared this belief that Israeli intelligence had penetrated US consulates and embassies abroad. See Wilbur P. Chase, oral history interview, Georgetown University Library, 24 July 1990, 30f.
27. Makins to FO, 27 May 1955 (tgm.1218), PRO FO371/115869 VR1076/101G.
28. Makins to FO, 28 May 1955 (tgm.1231), FO371/115869 VR1076/102G.
29. Hoover to USEmb Jordan (etc.), 28 May 1955, *FRUS 1955–1957*, XIV, 209f. (D109).
30. Makins to FO, 28 May 1955 (tgm.1231), FO371/115869 VR1076/102G.
31. *FRUS 1955–1957*, XIV, 210 n.3. Lawson also doubted whether such a statement would indeed prove damaging to the ultimate success of Alpha.

32. Heath (Beirut) to USSD, 30 May 1955 (tgm.1252), USNA 684A.86/5-3055; Mallory (Amman) to USSD, 31 May 1955 (tgm.424), 684A.86/5-3155. Cf. Russell to Dulles and Hoover, 10 June 1955, NEA Lot 59, D518, Box 29; *FRUS 1955–1957*, XIV, 210 n.3.
33. Byroade to USSD, 30 May 1955 (tgm.1806), USNA 684A.86/5-3055; Stevenson to FO, 30 May 1955 (tgm.687), PRO FO371/115869 VR1076/103G.
34. Aldrich to USSD, 30 May 1955 (tgm.5222), USNA 684A.86/5-3055.
35. FO to Makins, 31 May 1955 (tgm.2573), PRO FO371/115869 VR1076/102G.
36. Makins to FO, 1 June 1955 (tgm.1262), PRO FO371/115869 VR1076/106G.
37. Dulles to Hoover, 6 June 1955, *FRUS 1955–1957*, XIV, 222–6 (D117); Russell to Dulles, 15 June 1955, USNA NEA Lot 59, D518, Box 2 (cf. *FRUS 1955–1957*, XIV, 233 n.9); Dulles draft (18 June), sent to FO, 23 June 1955, PRO FO371/115870 VR1076/121G; Dulles to Hoover, 28 June 1955, USNA NEA Lot 59 D518 Box 29; Macmillan memorandum to Cabinet, Palestine Settlement (CP55/75), 13 July 1955, PRO PREM11/945; Dulles draft (15 July), enclosed in Russell to Certain American Ambassadors, 22 July 1955, *FRUS 1955–1957*, XIV, 314–18 (D169); Macmillan memorandum to Cabinet, Palestine (CP55/87), 22 July 1955, Annex 1, PREM11/945.
38. See, e.g., Byroade to Dulles, 3 July 1955, *FRUS 1955–1957*, XIV, 277 (D146); same to same, 11 July 1955, ibid., 286 (D152); Lawson to USSD, 8 July 1955 (tgm.15), USNA 684A.86A/7-855; Wright (Baghdad) to Shuckburgh, 14 July 1955 (tgm.636A), PRO FO371/115871 VR1076/130G; Lawson to Jernegan, 14 July 1955, USNA NEA Lot 59, D518, Box 29; Duke to Shuckburgh, 19 July 1955, PRO FO371/115873 VR1076/153G; Allen to Dulles, 9 Aug. 1955, *FRUS 1955–1957*, XIV, 343 (D185).
39. Burns, memorandum of conversation (Dulles, Hoover, Allen, Hare, Russell), 8 June 1955, *FRUS 1955–1957*, XIV, 232f. (D120).
40. Macmillan memorandum to Cabinet, Palestine Settlement (CP55/75), 13 July 1955, PRO PREM11/945.
41. Burns, memorandum of conversation (Dulles, Hoover, Allen, Hare, Russell), 8 June 1955, *FRUS 1955–1957*, XIV, 232f. (D120).
42. Record of conversation (Dulles, Macmillan *et al.*), 16 June 1955, PRO FO371/115870 VR1076/116G. Cf. Macmillan to Eden, 16 June 1955 (UKUN tgm.477), PREM11/945; Hoover to USEmb Egypt, 20 June 1955, *FRUS 1955–1957*, XIV, 248f. (D128).
43. Shuckburgh to Macmillan, 13 June 1955, PRO FO371/115870 VR1076/115G. See also: Shuckburgh, *Descent*, 260 (10 June 1955); FO to UKEmb Washington, 4 July 1955 (tgm.3101), FO371/115870 VR1076/121G; Arthur minute, 4 July 1955, FO371/115871 VR1076/123G.
44. Shuckburgh, *Descent*, 266f. (7 July 1955); Russell to USSD, 8 July 1955, *FRUS 1955–1957*, XIV, 279f. (D148).
45. Cf. Eden's remark about the need to help Dulles resist Israeli pressures for a security treaty with the US: 'American elections last too long'. Eden to Macmillan, 20 June 1955 (tgm.9), PRO PREM11/945.
46. Nutting to Macmillan, 11 July 1955, PRO FO371/115871 VR1076/131G.
47. Draft Cabinet Paper, 16 July 1955, PRO FO371/115871 VR1076/134G; Macmillan, *Tides of Fortune*, 633f.
48. Arthur minute, 4 July 1955, PRO FO371/115871 VR1076/123G; Shuckburgh to Kirkpatrick, 8 July 1955, ibid./131G; FO to UKEmb Washington, 12 July 1955 (tgm.3238), ibid./125G; Rose to Duke, 12 Aug. 1955, FO371/115873 VR1076/159G; Rose to Sterndale-Bennett, 15 Aug. 1955, FO371/115872 VR1076/150G.
49. Troxel to Russell, 5 July 1955, *FRUS 1955–1957*, XIV, 278f. (D147); same to same, 7 July 1955, USNA NEA Lot 59, D518, Box 29. See also: *FRUS 1955–1957*,

XIV, 291–3, 306f., 322, 331, 334f.; Burdett to Allen, 15 July 1955, USNA NEA Lot 59, D518, Box 29; Dorsey to Wilkins, 15 July 1955, *loc. cit.*; Gallagher to FO, 5 Aug. 1955 (tgm.290), PRO FO371/115873 VR1076/164G.
50. The first change was from 15 to 25 August, and later (tentatively) to 28 September. See: Burdett, memorandum of conversation (Johnston, Dulles, Allen), 11 July 1955, *FRUS 1955–1957*, XIV, 284f. (D151); Russell memorandum, 12 Aug. 1955, ibid., 349 (D190); Wilkins to Allen, 15 Aug. 1955, USNA NEA Lot 59, D518, Box 29.
51. Dulles–Johnston telephone conversation, 18 Aug. 1955, *FRUS 1955–1957*, XIV, 363f. (D198). Cf. ibid., 369.
52. See, e.g., *FRUS 1955–1957*, XIV, 279f., 287–90, 294, 298f., 329, 341–3, 349f.; material in PRO files FO371/115870 VR1076/121G, FO371/115871 VR1076/131G, /134G; FO371/115872 VR1076/147G, /150G; FO371/115873 VR1076/157G, /158G, /167G, /168G, /175G; Lawson to Jernegan, 14 July 1955, USNA NEA Lot 59, D518, Box 29; Burdett to Allen, 15 July 1955, *loc. cit.*; Allen to Hoover, 19 July 1955, *loc. cit.*; Russell memorandum, Suggested Steps Prior to and Following Secretary's Statement, 12 Aug. 1955, *loc. cit.*
53. See Draft British Statement, [15] July 1955, in PRO FO371/115872 VR1076/144G. Cf. material in files FO371/115872 VR1076/147G, FO371/115873 VR1076/158G and /167G; *FRUS 1955–1957*, XIV, 335f.
54. Russell to Certain American Ambassadors, 22 July 1955, *FRUS 1955–1957*, XIV, 310–18 (D169). Shuckburgh's letter (presumably almost identical) has been withheld from the British archives 'under Section 3(4)'. See PRO FO371/115872 VR1076/140G.
55. Duke (Amman) to FO, 25 July 1955 (tgm.288), FO371/115872 VR1076/148G. See also telegraphic replies from Murray (Cairo), Duke (Amman), Nicholls (Tel Aviv), Beaumont (Baghdad), Chapman-Andrews (Beirut), Sterndale-Bennett (BMEO, Nicosia) and Gallagher (Damascus) in FO371/115872 VR1076/150G; further correspondence in FO371/115873 VR1076/159G, /164G, /165G, /167G and /168G. For a summary of American replies, see Allen to Dulles, 9 Aug. 1955, *FRUS 1955–1957*, XIV, 341–3 (D185).
56. Nicholls to Shuckburgh, 1 Aug. 1955, PRO FO371/115873 VR1076/165G; Lawson to Jernegan, 14 July 1955, USNA NEA Lot 59, D518, Box 29.
57. Dulles to Byroade, 9 July 1955, *FRUS 1955–1957*, XIV, 283 (D150).
58. See, e.g., Byroade–Hussein talk (14 Aug.), reported in Byroade to USSD, 15 Aug. 1955, *FRUS 1955–1957*, XIV, 355–8 (D194); Byroade dinner with Egyptian leaders (16 Aug.), reported in Byroade to USSD, 17 Aug. 1955, ibid., 360–2 (D196).
59. 'Fawzi said "Don't quote me, but if we can get a solution to Negev we might be willing [to] take a position that there should be no return of refugees and that Arabs now residing [in] Israel should even have evacuation facilitated".' *FRUS 1955–1957*, XIV, 359.
60. Talks with Hussein (14 Aug.) and Fawzi (16 Aug.), reported in Byroade to USSD, 17 Aug. 1955, *FRUS 1955–1957*, XIV, 358–60 (D195).
61. Byroade to USSD, 17 Aug. 1955, *FRUS 1955–1957*, XIV, 362 (D196); Dulles to Macmillan, 19 Aug. 1955, *FRUS 1955–1957*, XIV, 366–8 (D201). Cf. Makins to FO, 18 Aug. 1955 (tgm.1931), PRO FO371/115873 VR1076/176; Dulles to Eisenhower, 19 Aug. 1955, ibid., 368f. (D202); Cabell (CIA) to Dulles, 25 Aug. 1955, ibid., 395f. (D221); Bar-On, *Gates of Gaza*, 91.
62. Extract from Cabinet Minutes (CM55/23), 14 July 1955, PRO PREM11/945; Macmillan memorandum to Cabinet, Palestine (CP55/87), 22 July 1955, *loc. cit.*
63. Macmillan to Dulles, [20] Aug. 1955, *FRUS 1955–1957*, XIV, 370f. (D203); Russell, memorandum of conversation with Dulles, 20 Aug. 1955, ibid., 373f.

(D205). For Eden's angry reaction to 'Mr Dulles's latest antics', see David Carlton, *Anthony Eden: A Biography* (London: Allen Lane, 1981), 382; Graham to Macmillan, 25 Aug. 1955, PRO FO371/115875 VR1076/200G.
64. These disagreements did not, as Michael Oren has claimed (*Origins*, 116), drive 'a permanent wedge between the US and Britain on the question of peace'.
65. Dulles tgms., dated 20 Aug. 1955, in *FRUS 1955–1957*, XIV, 375–80 (D206–D209); two tgms. from Dulles to USEmb Israel (etc.), 24 Aug. 1955, ibid., 384–6 (D213, D214).
66. FO tgms. to UKEmb Amman, etc., 22 Aug. 1955, PRO FO371/115874 VR1076/181G.
67. Macmillan to UKEmb Baghdad, 22 Aug. 1955 (tgm.1155), PRO FO371/115874 VR1076/181G.
68. Wilkins, memorandum of conversation (Eban, Shiloah, Allen), 25 Aug. 1955, USNA NEA Lot 59, D518, Box 30. Cf. Dulles to Lodge, 24 Aug. 1955, USNA NEA Lot 59, D518, Box 29; Wilkins to Allen, 24 Aug. 1955, *loc. cit.*; *FRUS 1955–1957*, XIV, 383, 394.
69. Sterndale-Bennett to Shuckburgh, 19 Aug. 1955, PRO FO371/115874 VR1076/196G. Cf. Shuckburgh to Brownjohn, 22 Aug. 1955, FO371/115874 VR1076/187G; FO to Amman, 22 Aug. 1955 (tgm.523), FO371/115874 VR1076/181G.
70. See material in PRO files FO371/115871 VR1076/125G, /127G, /130G, /131G, /134G; FO371/115873 VR1076/169G; Macmillan memorandum to Cabinet, Palestine Settlement (CP55/75), 13 July 1955, PRO PREM11/945; extract from Cabinet Minutes (CM55/23), 14 July 1955, *loc. cit.*; Macmillan memorandum to Cabinet, Palestine (CP55/87), 22 July 1955, *loc. cit.*; extract of Cabinet Minutes (CM55/27), 28 July 1955, *loc. cit.*; *FRUS 1955–1957*, XIV, 287, 295–8, 301f., 320–2, 345; Shuckburgh, *Descent*, 269f.; Macmillan, *Tides of Fortune*, 632f.
71. Dulles, memorandum of conversation with Eisenhower, 5 Aug. 1955, *FRUS 1955–1957*, XIV, 339f.; ibid., 340f., 351; Rose minute, Alpha, 9 Aug. 1955, PRO FO371/115873 VR1076/169G; Dulles to Makins, 16 Aug. 1955, reprinted as Appendix B of Macmillan memorandum for Cabinet, Note on Mr Dulles' Statement on Palestine (CP55/127), 20 Sept. 1955, PREM11/945. Cf. Eden to Eisenhower, 23 July 1955, PREM11/945; extract of Cabinet Minutes (CM55/27), 28 July 1955, *loc. cit.*
72. Stark to Kirkpatrick, 19 Aug. 1955, PRO FO371/115874 VR1076/185G; Kirkpatrick to Macmillan, 20 Aug. 1955, PREM11/945; Macmillan to UKEmb Washington, 20 Aug. 1955 (tgm.3759), FO371/115873 VR1076/177G. A month later, Macmillan's report to the Cabinet made it appear as though the two UK conditions (assurance of ultimate US adhesion to the Baghdad Pact and delivery of tanks to Iraq) 'ha[d] been fulfilled', even if only partially. Macmillan memorandum for Cabinet, Note on Mr Dulles' Statement on Palestine (CP55/127), 20 Sept. 1955, PREM11/945.
73. Dulles to Macmillan, 25 Aug. 1955, *FRUS 1955–1957*, XIV, 393 (D219).
74. Two telegrams from Byroade to USSD, 24 Aug. 1955, *FRUS 1955–1957*, XIV, 387–9 (D215, D216). For British Ambassadors' reports of the moderate views expressed by Nuri Sa'id and Nasir on the eve of the Dulles statement, see: Wright to FO, 24 Aug. 1955 (tgm.711), and Trevelyan to FO, 24 Aug. 1955 (tgm.1112), both in PRO FO371/115874 VR1076/186G.
75. Byroade to Dulles, 22 Aug. 1955, *FRUS 1955–1957*, XIV, 381f. (D210); Dulles to USEmb Egypt, 23 Aug. 1955, ibid., 382f. (D211).
76. Nicholls to Shuckburgh, 23 Aug. 1955, PRO FO371/115875 VR1076/198G.
77. Nicholls–Sharett talk (24 Aug.), reported in Nicholls to FO, 25 Aug. 1955 (tgm. 284), FO371/115874 VR1076/186G; Lawson to USSD, 25 Aug. 1955, *FRUS 1955–1957*, XIV, 391f. (D218).

78. Byroade to USSD, 24 Aug. 1955, *FRUS 1955–1957*, XIV, 390f. (D217); Trevelyan–Nasir talk, reported in Trevelyan to FO, 24 Aug. 1955 (tgm.1112), PRO FO371/115874 VR1076/186G; Burns, *Between Arab and Israeli*, 83; Morris, *Israel's Border Wars*, 91, 336f.
79. Russell, memorandum of conversation with Morris, 25 Aug. 1955, *FRUS 1955–1957*, XIV, 397 (D222).
80. Byroade to Allen, 26 Aug. 1955, USNA 684A.86/8-2755; same to same, (27) Aug. 1955, *loc. cit.*; Byroade to USSD, 27 Aug. 1955 (tgm.316), 674.84A/8-2755. Cf. *FRUS 1955–1957*, XIV, 398, 404, 406 n.4.
81. See, e.g., IDF Gaza frontier situation reports (hourly entries), 30–31 Aug. 1955, ISA 43/gimmel-5571/4132; Hoover to Dulles (Geneva), 7 Nov. 1955 (tgm. TOSEC186), USNA NEA Lot 59, D518, Box 31; Lawson to USSD, 12 Nov. 1955, *FRUS 1955–1957*, XIV, 739 (D403); Dulles to USEmb Egypt, 23 Nov. 1955, ibid., 804 (D426); Ben-Gurion, *My Talks*, 272f., 289; Oren, 'Escalation', 360; Burns, *Between Arab and Israeli*, 58, 84, 86, 89, 124f.; Yaari, *Mitsrayim*, 18–20 (transl. in Rabinovich and Reinharz, eds, *Israel in the Middle East*, 78–80); Shimshoni, *Israel and Conventional Deterrence*, 84f.; Bar-On, *Gates of Gaza*, 11; Morris, *Israel's Border Wars*, 91, 337–49, 352–4.
82. Yaari, *Mitsrayim, loc. cit.*; Morris, *Israel's Border Wars*, 46–9, 84–90, 271f., 338–49.
83. E.g., 'We will not be duped by the calls for peace after Israel's savage attack on 28 February.' Nasir speech, 9 July 1955, in Gamal Abd al-Nasir, *Filastin (Palestine)*, (Cairo: (1965)), 17; Byroade to USSD, 1 Sept. 1955, *FRUS 1955–1957*, XIV, 438 (D251); Burns, *Between Arab and Israeli*, 79; Morris, *Israel's Border Wars*, 272f. n.36.
84. Radi Abdallah to Chief of Staff, Arab Legion, 5 Sept. 1955, quoted in Morris, *Israel's Border Wars*, 35, 347.
85. See, e.g., *FRUS 1955–1957*, XIV, 400f., 406f., 412–16, 421f., 424f., 427–30, 437–9, 441f., 446f., 456; draft tgm. to USEmb Israel, [?26] Aug. 1955, USNA NEA Lot 59, D518, Box 30; Burns, *Between Arab and Israeli*, 87–91; Oren, 'Escalation', 360f.; Bar-On, *Gates of Gaza*, 11; Morris, *Israel's Border Wars*, 345–51.
86. See, e.g., Jackson, *Middle East Mission*, 40–56, 113–15; *FRUS 1955–1957*, XIV, 431f, 439–41, 447, 456, 463, 470; Gideon Rafael, *Destination Peace: Three Decades of Israeli Foreign Policy: A Personal Memoir* (New York: Stein & Day, 1981), 43f.; Dayan, *Avnei Derekh*, 151.
87. Lawson[?] to USSD, 27 Aug, 1955, quoted in *FRUS 1955–1957*, XV, 270 n.7; Sharett, *Yoman Ishi* IV: 1153, 1165f., 1172–5. During September, Israeli officials began to suspect that Egyptians were at least partly responsible for terrorist attacks occurring in the *north* of the country.
88. Shimshoni, *Israel and Conventional Deterrence*, 85–7; Oren, *Origins*, 28f.; Morris, *Israel's Border Wars*, 345–54.
89. Macmillan statement, 27 Aug. 1955, PRO FO371/115875 VR1076/197G; text reproduced in Muhammad Khalil, *The Arab States and the Arab League: A Documentary Record, V. II International Affairs* (Beirut: Khayats, 1962), 641 (D293). Cf. *FRUS 1955–1957*, XIV, 407f. For the preparation of practical steps in support of the Dulles initiative, see, e.g., Arthur memorandum, The Financing of Compensation, 17 Sept. 1955, PRO FO371/115877 VR1076/256G.
90. FO to Bonn (etc.), 26 Aug. 1955 (tgm.691, etc.), PRO FO371/115875 VR1076/203G.
91. E.g., Hoover to USEmb Israel, 14 Sept. 1955, *FRUS 1955–1957*, XIV, 466 (D273); Arthur minute, 15 Sept. 1955, PRO FO371/115878 VR1076/292G; Lawson–Sharett talk, reported in Lawson to USSD, 21 Sept. 1955, *FRUS 1955–1957*, XIV, 498f. (D294); Meyerson–Nicholls talk (15 Nov.), reported in Nicholls to FO, 16 Nov. 1955 (tgm.473), PRO FO371/115881 VR1076/381.

92. T.J. Hamilton, 'UN Weighs the Danger of a Middle East War', *New York Times*, 6 Nov. 1955, E3.
93. Two Macmillan memoranda to Cabinet, Palestine Settlement (CP55/75), 13 July 1955, and Palestine (CP55/87), 22 July 1955, PRO PREM11/945. By issuing their own statement on the day following Dulles' speech, the British also hoped to reserve for themselves the option of 'mak[ing] new suggestions or interpretations to meet the points of friction that emerged as the most sensitive'.
94. Byroade to USSD, 27 Aug. 1955, *FRUS 1955–1957*, XIV, 402 (D226). Cf. Trevelyan (Cairo) to FO, 27 Aug. 1955 (tgm.1136), PRO FO371/115874 VR1076/186G; [CIA] memo, Views submitted by our station in Cairo in reference to Deptel 442 of September 5, (12 Sept. 1955), USNA NEA Lot 59, D518, Box 30.
95. Communication with Byroade, quoted in Burns, *Economic Aid*, 52f. For an assortment of Israeli and other Arab reactions to the Dulles statement, see: *FRUS 1955–1957*, XIV, 405, 408–10, 414, 417–20, 422f.; USNA NEA Lot 59, D518, Boxes 30, 32; PRO FO371/115875 VR1076/204, /209; FO371/115876 VR1076/230G, /237; FO371/115877 VR1076/245, /254G; Heikal, *Cutting the Lion's Tail*, 88; Eveland, *Ropes of Sand*, 129.
96. 'NFC' (PMO) to Hancock (FO), 1 Sept. 1955, PRO PREM11/945.
97. Geren to USSD, 28 Aug. 1955, *FRUS 1955–1957*, XIV, 410 (D232).
98. 'Dulles and Johnston Projects are Twins', *Al-Bilad as-Saudiyya*, no. 1948, 18 Sept., transl. encl. in Jenkins (Jidda) to USSD, 4 Oct. 1955 (desp.40), USNA NEA Lot 59, D518, Box 30. See also: *FRUS 1955–1957*, XIV, 410f., 426f., 442f.; Troxel (Amman) to Bergus, 30 Aug. 1955, USNA 684A.85322/8-3055; Geren to USSD, 30 Aug. 1955 (tgm.99), *loc. cit.*; Duke to FO, 31 Aug. 1955 (tgm.349), PRO FO371/115876 VR1076/236; Geren to USSD, 1 Sept. 1955 (tgm.104), USNA NEA Lot 59, D518, Box 32; Geren to USSD, 13 Sept. 1955 (desp.89), NEA Lot 59, D518, Box 30.
99. Johnston (Cairo) to USSD, 16 Sept. 1955, *FRUS 1955–1957*, XIV, 473f. (D278); same (London) to same, 22 Sept. 1955, ibid., 501f. (D296).
100. Adam Garfinkle, *Deep and Wide: Water, War and Negotiations in the Jordan Valley, 1916–1993*, (draft MS, June 1993), Ch. 4.
101. Dulles to USEmb Egypt (etc.), 30 Aug. 1955, *FRUS 1955–1957*, XIV, 420 (D238). Cf. ibid., 439; Shuckburgh, *Descent*, 275 (30 Aug. 1955); Allen remarks, conversation with Charles Malik, 30 Aug. 1955, USNA NEA Lot 59, D518, Box 30; FO to Amman (etc.), 31 Aug. 1955 (tgm.563 etc.), PRO FO371/115876 VR1076/218G; Shuckburgh minute, 5 Sept. 1955, FO371/115877 VR1076/267G; Burns, *Economic Aid*, 52.

The British Foreign Secretary reported to Cabinet in mid-September that the Arab states and Israel had 'received the statement as well as we could possibly have expected'. Macmillan memorandum for Cabinet, Note on Mr Dulles' Statement on Palestine (CP55/127), 20 Sept. 1955, PREM11/945.
102. See reports in USNA 684A.86/9-1055; NEA Lot 59, D518, Boxes 30, 32; PRO FO371/115877 VR1076/280; FO371/115878 VR1076/284, /287, /289; *FRUS 1955–1957*, XIV, 454f.; Israeli monitoring reports summarized in Bar-On, *Gates of Gaza*, 92. For Jewish and Israeli reactions, see below, 143–4.
103. Article in *Al-Jihad*, quoted in Geren to USSD, 27 Sept. 1955 (desp.109), NEA Lot 59, D518, Box 30.
104. UKEmb Damascus to Levant Dept., FO, 10 Sept. 1955 (desp.10601/148/55), FO371/115878 VR1076/289.
105. Wadsworth (Jidda) to USSD, 6 Sept. 1955 (tgm.102), USNA NEA Lot 59, D518, Box 32. See also *Al-Bilad as-Saudiyya*, no. 1947, 16 Sept., transl. encl. in Jenkins (Jidda) to USSD, 4 Oct. 1955 (desp.40), NEA Lot 59, D518, Box 30.
106. Eilts to USSD, 10 Sept. 1955 (desp.169), USNA 684A.86/9-1055. Cf. hostile

comments in *Al-Akhbar*, quoted in Gallman to USSD, 6 Sept. 1955 (tgm.215), USNA NEA Lot 59, D518, Box 32.
107. Haikal–Shuckburgh talk (29 Aug.), reported in Rose to Duke, 2 Sept. 1955, PRO FO371/115876 VR1076/237. See also: Heath to USSD, 3 Sept. 1955 (tgm.224), NEA Lot 59 D518 Box 32.
108. Bergus, memorandum of conversation (Eban, Shiloah, Allen), 6 Sept. 1955, *FRUS 1955–1957*, XIV, 451–3 (D264); Eban, *Personal Witness*, 244f. For accounts of Ambassador Elath's similar discussion with Foreign Secretary Macmillan in London, see ibid., 474f.; Macmillan to Nicholls, 15 Sept. 1955 (desp.174), PRO FO371/115878 VR1076/294G.
109. Blaustein to Dulles, 3 Sept. 1955, USNA NEA Lot 59, D518, Box 30; Sharett to Shiloah, 5 Sept. 1955 (tgm.51/174), ISA 130.02/2446/3; Bergus, memorandum of conversation (Bernstein, Miller, Segal, Kenen, Jernegan), 12 Sept. 1955, USNA NEA Lot 59, D518, Box 30; Sharett press release, 9 Sept. 1955, ISA 130.02/2446/3; 'Positive Features in Dulles' Plan – PM Sharett Gives Interview to UP', *Jerusalem Post*, 11 Sept. 1955; Max Freedman (Washington), 'Israel Wants Frontier Guarantee Now – Appeal to America Not to Await Revision', *Manchester Guardian*, 13 Sept. 1955; 'Policy on Dulles' Plan – Territorial "Adjustments" but no "Cession"', *Jewish Observer and Middle East Review*, 16 Sept. 1955, 5f.
110. Sharett to Eban, 29 Aug. 1955 (tgm.), ISA 130.02/2455/4, quoted in Bialer, *Between East and West*, 271. For expressions of Sharett's and Ben-Gurion's concern, see: Bar-On, *Gates of Gaza*, 92; Oren, *Origins*, 116; Alteras, *Eisenhower and Israel*, 133f.
111. E.g., Hoover to USEmb Israel, 14 Sept. 1955, *FRUS 1955–1957*, XIV, 467 (D273); Arthur minute, 19 Sept. 1955, PRO FO371/115879 VR1076/314G.
112. Lawson to USSD, 10 Sept. 1955, *FRUS 1955–1957*, XIV, 457–61 (D267). For another version of Lawson's report, see Westlake (Tel Aviv) to FO, 9 Sept. 1955 (tgm.331), PRO FO371/115878 VR1076/283G. No diary entries of Moshe Sharett have been found for the period 25 Aug. to 10 Sept. See Sharett, *Yoman Ishi*, IV: 1148. See also Lawson to USSD, 21 Sept. 1955, *FRUS 1955–1957*, XIV, 498f. (D294); Touval, *Peace Brokers*, 117f.
113. 'In the case of such decisive problems as territory and population, the setting forth in advance of concrete terms by a third party may lead to fatal results and should at all costs be avoided.' Cf. above, 116–17.
114. Shiloah to Y. Herzog, 22 Sept. 1955, ISA RS/4374/22.
115. Geren to USSD, 13 Sept. 1955 (desp.89), USNA NEA Lot 59, D518, Box 30 (emphasis in original). Cf. same to same, 27 Sept. 1955 (desp.109), *loc. cit.*
116. Rabinovich, *Road Not Taken*, 82.
117. Wright to FO, 27 Aug. 1955 (tgm.720), PRO FO371/115875 VR1076/210. Cf. *FRUS 1955–1957*, XIV, 420f., 454; FO to UKemb Washington, 31 Aug. 1955 (tgm.4014), PRO FO371/115876 VR1076/218G.
118. Byroade to USSD, 27 Aug. 1955, *FRUS 1955–1957*, XIV, 403 (D226). Cf. ibid., 417, 423; Trevelyan to FO, 29 Aug. 1955 (tgm.1147), PRO FO371/115876 VR1076/219; same to same, 30 Aug. 1955 (tgm.1163), FO371/115876 VR1076/224; Edgar (Alexandria) to USSD, 17 Sept. 1955 (desp.42), USNA NEA Lot 59, D518, Box 30.
119. Allen's remarks in conversation with Charles Malik, 30 Aug. 1955, USNA NEA Lot 59, D518, Box 30. See also: Russell–Jernegan conversation, 29 Aug. 1955, *loc. cit.*; Nicholls to FO, 29 Aug. 1955 (tgm.295), PRO FO371/115876 VR1076/219; FO to Amman (etc.), 31 Aug. 1955 (tgm.563 etc.), FO371/115876 VR1076/218G; FO to UKemb Washington, 31 Aug. 1955 (tgm.4014), *loc. cit.*; Shuckburgh minute, 5 Sept. 1955, FO371/115877 VR1076/267G; *FRUS 1955–1957*, XIV, 419–22, 432–5.

120. Byroade to USSD, 11 Sept. 1955, *FRUS 1955–1957*, XIV, 461 (D268); Trevelyan to Shuckburgh, 12 Sept. 1955 (desp.10313/102/55G), FO371/115878 VR1076/297G; Byroade–Fawzi talk (13 Sept.), reported in Byroade to USSD, 14 Sept. 1955, *FRUS 1955–1957*, XIV, 468 (D274); Trevelyan to FO, 14 Sept. 1955 (tgm. 1258), PRO FO371/115878 VR1076/288G; Macmillan memorandum for Cabinet, Note on Mr Dulles' Statement on Palestine (CP55/127), 20 Sept. 1955, PREM11/945.
121. E.g., Trevelyan–Fawzi talk, reported in Trevelyan, 1 Sept. 1955 (tgm.1193), PRO FO371/115876 VR1076/244G; Shuckburgh to Trevelyan, 3 Sept. 1955 (tgm. 1891), *loc. cit.*
122. Trevelyan to FO, 3 Sept. 1955 (tgm.1210), PRO FO371/115876 VR1076/244G.
123. FO to UKEmb Washington, 13 Sept. 1955 (tgm.4184), PRO FO371/115878 VR1076/283G; Scott (Washington) to FO, 14 Sept. 1955 (tgm.2166), FO371/115878 VR1076/292; same to same, 15 Sept. 1955 (tgm.2195), FO371/115878 VR1076/295G.
124. See, e.g., *FRUS 1955–1957*, XIV, 448f., 476–8, 496f., 515f., 535f., 834f., 840f., 893f.; Trevelyan to Shuckburgh, 12 Sept. 1955 (desp.10313/102/55G), FO371/115878 VR1076/297G.; K. Love, 'Israel and Arabs Expect No Peace – Problem of Restoring Truce Overshadows for Present the Dulles Proposals', *New York Times*, 4 Sept. 1955; Morris, *Israel's Border Wars*, 355–8.
125. Trevelyan to FO, 11 Sept. 1955 (tgm.1238), PRO FO371/115878 VR1076/282G; same to Shuckburgh, 12 Sept. 1955 (desp.10313/102/55G), ibid. /297G.
126. Trevelyan–Fawzi talk (13 Sept.), reported in Trevelyan to FO, 13 and 14 Sept. 1955 (tgms.1256 and 1258), PRO FO371/115878 VR1076/288G; Byroade–Fawzi talk (13 Sept.), reported in Byroade to USSD, 14 and 16 Sept. 1955, *FRUS 1955–1957*, XIV, 468f. (D274) and 475f. (D280); Macmillan memorandum for Cabinet: Note on Mr Dulles' Statement on Palestine (CP55/127), 20 Sept. 1955, PREM11/945.
127. Arthur minute, 19 Sept. 1955, PRO FO371/115879 VR1076/314G; Shuckburgh minute (for Macmillan), 21 Sept. 1955, ibid. /310G.
128. Minutes of meetings of UK–US representatives, Foreign Office, 20 Sept. 1955, *FRUS 1955–1957*, XIV, 485–91 (D288). Quotations in this and the following paragraphs are taken from these minutes.
129. Hoover to USEmb Israel, 14 Sept. 1955, *FRUS 1955–1957*, XIV, 466f. (D273); same to USEmb Egypt, 15 Sept. 1955, ibid., 472f. (D277); ibid., 485.
130. Nasir–Trevelyan talk, reported in Trevelyan to FO, 20 Sept. 1955 (tgms.1286 and 1287), PRO FO371/115879 VR1076/306G; *FRUS 1955–1957*, XIV, 493.
131. Arthur minute, 4 Oct. 1955, on Stewart to Rose, 28 Sept. 1955 (desp.1063/69/55), PRO FO371/115879 VR1076/318G. Cf. Hooper to Rose, 28 Oct. 1955 (desp. 1071/144/55), *loc. cit.*
132. Minutes of meeting of representatives of the UK and US, Foreign Office, 21 Sept. 1955, *FRUS 1955–1957*, XIV, 493–5 (D291).
133. Minutes of meeting of representatives of the UK and US, Foreign Office, 21 Sept. 1955, *FRUS 1955–1957*, XIV, 493–5 (D291); Shuckburgh minute (for Macmillan), 21 Sept. 1955, PRO FO371/115879 VR1076/310G; Agenda (21 Sept. 1955), FO371/115879 VR1076/316G.
134. Shuckburgh, *Descent*, 278f. (22 Sept. 1955). For first American reactions to the news, see Hoover to Dulles (New York), 19 Sept. 1955, *FRUS 1955–1957*, XIV, 481 (D284). Cf. Byroade to USSD, 21 Aug. 1955, ibid., 492f. (D290).

CHAPTER VIII

1. Ginat argues that, in fact, two deals (involving not only the Soviet Union and Czechoslovakia, but also Poland) lay behind the dramatic September 1955 public announcement. *The Soviet Union and Egypt*, 206–10, 215f.
2. For a broad discussion, see Gerges, *The Superpowers and the Middle East*, 35–40.
3. Burns, *Economic Aid*, 35; cf. ibid., 13–19, 33–5; Kyle, *Suez*, 72; Gerges, *The Superpowers and the Middle East*, 31–5.
4. Ibid., 23f. Cf. Aronson, *From Sideshow to Center Stage*, 101–6, 114f., 128f.
5. See, e.g., Dorsey to Wilkins, 15 July 1955, USNA NEA Lot 59, D518, Box 29; *FRUS 1955–1957*, XIV, 237–40, 255f., 261–3, 270–4, 304–6, 332f., 337–9; Tawil, *Lu'bat*, Chs 7–8 and 410f., 413f., 416; Byroade's retrospective account, in Byroade to USSD, 16 June 1956, *FRUS 1955–1957*, XV, 731f. (D399); Burns, *Economic Aid*, 28–31; Aronson, *From Sideshow to Center Stage*, 129–38; Kyle, *Suez*, 72f.; Ginat, *The Soviet Union and Egypt*, 217.
6. See, e.g., Uri Ra'anan, 'Soviet Arms Transfers and the Problem of Political Leverage', in *Arms Transfers to the Third World: The Military Buildup in Less Industrial Countries*, eds Uri Ra'anan, Robert L. Pfaltzgraff, Jr., and Geoffrey Kemp (Boulder: Westview Press, 1978), 133–5; Gerges, *The Superpowers and the Middle East*, 31f.
7. Byroade to Dulles, 22 Aug. 1955, *FRUS 1955–1957*, XIV, 381 (D210). Cf. Kyle, *Suez*, 73f.
8. Dulles to USEmb Egypt, 23 Aug. 1955, *FRUS 1955–1957*, XIV, 382 (D211); Aronson, *From Sideshow to Center Stage*, 101f.
9. On 10 August 1955, Nasir received an invitation to visit the USSR in the spring of 1956. Ginat, *The Soviet Union and Egypt*, 214.
10. Byroade to Hoover, 20 Sept. 1955, *FRUS 1955–1957*, XIV, 484 (D287); same to USSD, 30 Aug. 1955 (tgm.345), in ibid., 436 n.2; same to same, 11 Sept. 1955, ibid., 462 (D268); (CIA) note, 12 Sept. 1955 ('our station in Cairo'), USNA NEA Lot 59, D518, Box 30; Alteras, *Eisenhower and Israel*, 137–9. For an interesting account of Byroade's attitude to Nasir, see Copeland, *Game of Nations*, 151–6.
11. Hoover to USEmb Egypt, 15 Sept. 1955, *FRUS 1955–1957*, XIV, 471 (D276). Cf. ibid., 482, 525. Parker T. Hart, who was deputy chief of mission in Cairo from August 1955 to March 1958, recalled the curt reply from the SD as being: 'Military aid to Egypt only if they agree on a peace with Israel.' Parker T. Hart, oral history interview, Georgetown University Library, 27 January 1989, 58.
12. Hoover to Dulles (New York), 19 Sept. 1955, *FRUS 1955–1957*, XIV, 481. Cf. Byroade to USSD, 21 Aug. 1955, ibid., 492f. (D290); Kyle, *Suez*, 74.
13. Yaniv, *Deterrence without the Bomb*, 33; Bar-On, *Gates of Gaza*, 16–18. Slightly different US intelligence estimates are cited by Ginat, *The Soviet Union and Egypt*, 215. On Soviet arms supplies to Egypt during 1955 and 1956, see also: ibid., 209–19; Jon D. Glassman, *Arms for the Arabs: The Soviet Union and War in the Middle East* (Baltimore/London: Johns Hopkins University Press, 1975), Ch. 2.
14. Shuckburgh minute (for Macmillan), 21 Sept. 1955, PRO FO371/115879 VR1076/310G; Arthur minute, Inducements to Egypt, 19 Sept. 1955, FO371/115879 VR1076/314G.
15. L. Carl Brown, *International Politics and the Middle East: Old Rules, Dangerous Game* (Princeton: Princeton University Press, 1984), 236.
16. Byroade to USSD, 21 Sept. 1955, *FRUS 1955–1957*, XIV, 497f. (D293). Cf. ibid., 538, 540, 571, 609; Nasir speech to cadets at the Military College, 2 Oct. 1955, reproduced in Nasir, *Filastin*, 19; K. Love, 'Nasser Says US Knew Arms Plan', *New York Times*, 6 Oct. 1955, 1; Kyle, *Suez*, 73; Gerges, *The Superpowers and the Middle East*, 34f.

The Czech–Egyptian deal of February 1955 is documented in Ginat, *The Soviet Union and Egypt*, 210.
17. Hoover to USEmb Egypt, 20 Sept. 1955, *FRUS 1955–1957*, XIV, 491 (D289). Cf. Byroade to Hoover, 20 Sept. 1955, ibid., 484 (D287); Dulles proposed message to Nasir, in Dulles (New York) to Hoover, 27 Sept. 1955, ibid., 525 (D314).
18. Russell (London) to USSD, 22 Sept. 1955, *FRUS 1955–1957*, XIV, 504f. (D299). Cf. memorandum of conversation (Macmillan, Dulles, Shuckburgh, Russell, *et al.*), New York, 26 Sept. 1955, *FRUS 1955–1957*, XIV, 516–19 (D310); Dulles oral message to Nasir, quoted in Dulles (New York) to Hoover, 27 Sept. 1955, ibid., 525 (D314); Burns, *Economic Aid*, 31; Kyle, *Suez*, 81 (discussing Eden's proposed late-October 'letter of reproach' to Nasir); Gerges, *The Superpowers and the Middle East*, 35f.
19. Shuckburgh, *Descent*, 278f. (22 and 23 Sept. 1955). Cf. minute, 22 Sept. 1955, PRO FO371/113674 JE1194/151G; Arthur to Morris, 26 Sept. 1955, PRO FO371/115879 VR1076/309G; Macmillan, *Tides of Fortune*, 635f.; Kyle, *Suez*, 74f.
20. Russell (London) to USSD, 22 Sept. 1955, *FRUS 1955–1957*, XIV, 504f. (D299). Cf. the letter which Dulles proposed sending to Nasir following consultations with Macmillan, in Dulles (New York) to Hoover, 27 Sept. 1955, *FRUS 1955–1957*, XIV, 526f. (D315).
21. Byroade to USSD, 23 Sept. 1955, *FRUS 1955–1957*, XIV, 508f. (D302).
22. Nasir message to Dulles, conveyed by Ambassador Ahmad Hussein, memorandum of conversation (Dulles, Hussein, Allen, Wilkins), 17 Oct. 1955, *FRUS 1955–1957*, XIV, 604, 607 (D341). Cf. ibid., 608f.; Nasir interview with K. Love ('Nasser Says US Knew Arms Plan'), *New York Times*, 6 Oct. 1955, .1; Heikal, *Cutting the Lion's Tail*, 93f.; Gerges, *The Superpowers and the Middle East*, 36.
23. See, e.g., *FRUS 1955–1957*, XIV, 516–9, 529–32, 542–9; Macmillan, *Tides of Fortune*, 635–50.
24. Alteras, *Eisenhower and Israel*, 141.
25. Scott (Washington) to FO, 15 Sept. 1955 (tgm.537), PRO PREM11/945; similar comments on Trevelyan to FO, 2 Nov. 1955 (tgm.1609), FO371/115469 V1023/20. Cf. Macmillan–Dulles talk, reported in Macmillan (Paris) to FO, 26 Oct. 1955 (tgm.419 Saving), PRO FO371/115469 V1023/14G; Trevelyan to FO, 5 Nov. 1955 (tgm.1641), FO371/115880 VR1076/330G; Shuckburgh–Russell conversation, 8 Nov. 1955, FO371/115469 V1023/24; Russell, memorandum of conversation (Dulles, Macmillan, *et al.*), Geneva, 9 Nov. 1955, *FRUS 1955–1957*, XIV, 722 (D391); Macmillan–Dulles talk (10 Nov.), reported in Dulles to USSD, 11 Nov. 1955 (tgm.SECTO247), USNA NEA Lot 59 D518, Box 31; *FRUS 1955–1957*, XIV, 542–9, 553–60, 576f., 606, 636–8, 680, 692f., 705–10, 741f., 797; Rubin, *Arab States*, 277f.; Shamir, 'Collapse', 88 n.36 and 95 n.60; Oren, *Origins*, 118.
26. Arthur minute, Palestine Settlement, 4 Nov. 1955, PRO FO371/115880 VR1076/331G.
27. Steven L. Spiegel, *The Other Arab–Israeli Conflict: Making America's Middle East Policy, from Truman to Reagan* (Chicago/London: University of Chicago Press, 1985), 66. Cf. Aronson, *From Sideshow to Center Stage*, 144.
28. Hoover to USMis UN, 27 Sept. 1955, 520f. (D311). See also ibid., 521–3; Copeland, *Game of Nations*, 157–9; Copeland, 'Nasser's secret diplomacy with Israel', *The Times*, 24 June 1971, 14; Kyle, *Suez*, 75.
29. Dulles oral message to Nasir, quoted in Dulles (New York) to Hoover, 27 Sept. 1955, *FRUS 1955–1957*, XIV, 525f. (D314); cf. Heikal, *Milaffat*, 774. For the official Tass statement on the deal (1 Oct.), see Yaacov Ro'i, *From Encroachment to Involvement: A Documentary Study of Soviet Policy in the Middle East, 1945–1973*

(New York/Toronto: John Wiley & Sons, 1974), 143–6. The official Soviet announcement was preceded by a *British* Foreign Office news release (27 Sept.). See Kyle, *Suez*, 75f.

30. The text of Dulles' letter to Nasir is given in *FRUS 1955–1957*, XIV, 527f. (D315). See also: Dulles (New York) telephone conversations with SD officials, 28 Sept. 1955, *FRUS 1955–1957*, XIV, 533–5 (D318, D319); Copeland, *Game of Nations*, 161–7; Heikal, *Cairo Documents*, 54f.; Copeland, *Game Player*, 200; Burns, *Economic Aid*, 32; Ginat, *The Soviet Union and Egypt*, 220.
31. Parker T. Hart, oral history interview, Georgetown University Library, 27 January 1989, 59f.
32. Allen–Byroade–Nasir talks, reported in Allen (Cairo) to USSD, 1 and 3 Oct. 1955, *FRUS 1955–1957*, XIV, 537–40 (D321) and 551f. (D325). Cf. Makins to FO, 11 Oct. 1955 (tgm.2444), PRO FO371/115469 V1023/10; Wilkins, memorandum of conversation (Dulles, Hussein, Allen), 17 Oct. 1955 , ibid., 604–7 (D341); Byroade to USSD, 18 Oct. 1955, ibid., 608–12 (D342); Copeland, *Game of Nations*, 165–9; Heikal, *Cutting the Lion's Tail*, 93–6; Ahmad Hussein talk with Dulles, reported in Hussein to Deputy MFA, 18 Oct. 1955, Heikal, *Milaffat*, 774–6 (D113); Hussein–Roosevelt talk, reported in same to same, 22 Oct. 1955, ibid., 778f. (D115); Kyle, *Suez*, 77; Aronson, *From Sideshow to Center Stage*, 142f.
33. See, e.g., Turton memorandum, The Arab/Israel Dispute, 29 Sept. 1955, PRO FO371/115880 VR1076/321; Shuckburgh minute, 5 Oct. 1955, FO371/115879 VR1076/318G; Macmillan–Sharett meeting, Geneva, 31 Oct., reported in Macmillan (Geneva) to FO, 1 Nov. 1955 (tgm.64), PRO FO371/115537 V1076/5. Cf. Arthur's negative conclusion in his minute, Palestine Settlement, 4 Nov. 1955, FO371/115880 VR1076/331G; Michael B. Oren, 'A Winter of Discontent: Britain's Crisis in Jordan, December 1955 – March 1956', *International Journal of Middle East Studies* 22:2 (May 1990), 175.
34. NSC, 260th meeting, 6 Oct. 1955, *FRUS 1955–1957*, XIV, 555 (D326). See also: *FRUS 1955–1957*, XIV, 577–86, 588, 592–603, 614–30, 639–41, 649f., 661–8, 750–72; Mathews memorandum, Measures to Deter Aggression by Israel or Egypt, 8 Oct. 1955, USNA NEA Lot 59, D518, Box 34; Dixon to Russell, 10 Oct. 1955 (incl. List of Major Weapons, 18 July 1955), NEA Lot 59, D518, Box 31; Bonesteel memorandum for NSC, Factors Bearing on Current Problems in the Middle East, 10 Oct. 1955, NEA Lot 59, D518, Box 34; Burdett memorandum, Political and Economic Measures to be taken against an Aggressor in the Arab–Israeli Controversy, 12 Oct. 1955, NEA Lot 59, D518, Box 34; Ogburn memorandum to Bowie, Consequences of Alternative US Responses to the Soviet–Egypt Arms Deal, 21 Oct. 1955, NEA Lot 59, D518, Box 30.
35. Kirkpatrick, minute on Shuckburgh memorandum ('Policy in the Middle East'), 15 Oct. 1955, PRO FO371/115480 V1054/5G.
36. Nasir remarks, quoted in Byroade to USSD, 27 Sept. 1955 (tgm.576), USNA 774.56/9–2755. Cf. Nasir's speech to graduating class at Military Academy, 2 Oct. 1955, in Khalil, *The Arab States*, II: 642f. (D295) and in Nasir, *Filastin*, 21f.; Nasir interview with K. Love ('Nasser Says US Knew Arms Plan'), *New York Times*, 6 Oct. 1955, 4; K. Love and H. Gilroy, 'Danger of War: As Egypt and Israel See It – Both Disavow Intention to Attack But Both also Look to Arms', ibid., 23 Oct. 1955 (dateline Cairo & Jerusalem); *Al-Gumhuriyya* editorial, cited in Trevelyan to FO, 11 Nov. 1955 (tgm.1699), PRO FO371/115881 VR1076/347; Trevelyan–Nasir talk, in Trevelyan to FO, 12 Nov. 1955 (tgm.1708), PRO FO371/115881 VR1076/350G; Nasir interview with NBC Cairo correspondent, as reported in *Akhbar al-Yaum*, 12 Nov. 1955, cited in Trevelyan to FO, 14 Nov. 1955 (tgm.231 Saving), FO371/115849 VR1072/300; Kennett Love, *Suez: The Twice-Fought War* (New York/Toronto: McGraw-Hill, 1969), 113f.; Aronson, *From Sideshow*

to *Center Stage*, 144–6; Kyle, *Suez*, 76f.
37. Quoted in Kyle, *Suez*, 83f. Cf. Aronson, *From Sideshow to Center Stage*, 155–7.
38. See, e.g., Kyle, *Suez*, 82–5; Aronson, *From Sideshow to Center Stage*, 144; below, Ch. XIII.
39. Byroade to USSD, 9 Oct. 1955 (tgm.694), quoted in *FRUS 1955–1957*, XIV, 609 n.4; see also ibid., 502, 509, 525.
40. In addition to relevant primary sources cited in other notes to this Chapter, see Kyle, *Suez*, 76–80, for a good summary of both the Anglo–American and Israeli reactions to the Soviet–Egyptian arms deal.
41. Kyle, *Suez*, 78.
42. Eban remarks, conversation with Allen, reported in Hoover to USEmb Israel, 27 Sept. 1055, *FRUS 1955–1957*, XIV, 529 (D316).
43. *FRUS 1955–1957*, XIV, 791 n.5; Shuckburgh, *Descent*, 279; Sharett, *Yoman Ishi*, IV: 1166, 1180f., 1183, 1185f., 1191; Kyle, *Suez*, 79; Bar-On, *Gates of Gaza*, 13; Alteras, *Eisenhower and Israel*, 158.
44. Bar-On, *Gates of Gaza*, Ch. 4. Cf. Sharett, *Yoman Ishi*, IV: 1185–1216 *passim*; Oren, *Origins*, 132–5; Kyle, *Suez*, 79f.; Morris, *Israel's Border Wars*, 274, 277–82.
45. On the Arabs' quantitative advantage in armaments, see: Bar-On, *Gates of Gaza*, 16–9; Kyle, *Suez*, 75f., 78, 578 n.44.
46. There are several archival records of Sharett's four meetings with Dulles and Macmillan:
   1. Dulles–Sharett meeting, Paris, 26 Oct. 1955, in (a) *FRUS 1955–1957*, XIV, 657–9 (D359), and (b) USNA NEA Lot 59, D518, Box 31;
   2. Macmillan–Sharett meeting, Paris, 26 Oct. 1955, in (a) PRO FO371/115537 V1076/4, and (b) CZA A245/74/I;
   3. Dulles–Sharett meeting, Geneva, 30 Oct. 1955, in (a) *FRUS 1955–1957*, XIV, 683f. (D371), (b) USNA NEA Lot 59, D518, Box 31, and (c) CZA A245/74/I;
   4. Macmillan–Sharett meeting, Geneva, 31 Oct. 1955, in Macmillan (Geneva) to FO, 1 Nov. 1955 (tgm.64), PRO FO371/115537 V1076/5.

   For other accounts, see: Tsur, *Prélude*, 256–68; Sharett, *Yoman Ishi* V: 1251–60, 1275; Bialer, *Between East and West*, 272f.; Kyle, *Suez*, 79; Bar-On, *Gates of Gaza*, Ch. 3; Alteras, *Eisenhower and Israel*, 142–5.
47. Sharett, handwritten notes ('A few comments on the Secretary's observations last Wednesday'), (Geneva, 30 Oct. 1955), CZA A245/74/I. Cf. Russell, memorandum of conversation (Dulles–Sharett *et al.*), Geneva, 30 Oct. 1955, USNA NEA Lot 59, D518, Box 31.
48. Dulles–Sharett meeting, Paris, 26 Oct. 1955, *FRUS 1955–1957*, XIV, 659 (D359).
49. Bar-On, *Gates of Gaza*, Ch. 3. On the quest for French arms supplies, see ibid., 48–53; Tsur, *Prélude*, *passim*; Kyle, *Suez*, 79; Zach Levey, 'Israel's Pursuit of French Arms, 1952–1958', *Studies in Zionism* 14:2 (Autumn 1993), 194f.
50. See, e.g., Sharett, *Yoman Ishi*, IV: 1180 (30 Sept. 1955).
51. Allen–Eban talk (7 Nov.), reported in Hoover to Dulles (Geneva), 8 Nov. 1955, *FRUS 1955–1957*, XIV, 718f. (D390). Cf. Russell, memorandum of conversation (Dulles, Macmillan, *et al.*), Geneva, 9 Nov. 1955, *FRUS 1955–1957*, XIV, 722 (D391); Macmillan–Dulles talk (10 Nov.), reported in Dulles to USSD, 11 Nov. 1955 (tgm.SECTO247), USNA NEA Lot 59, D518, Box 31.
52. Dulles–Eban talk (30 Sept.), reported in Dulles to USEmb Jordan, 2 Oct. 1955, *FRUS 1955–1957*, XIV, 540f. (D322). Cf. ibid., 546, 591, 773–6, 784f.; Kyle, *Suez*, 78.
53. Shuckburgh, *Descent*, 286 (2 Oct. 1955). See also Eban's and Rafael's 'catalogue' of evidence against Nasir's reliability, memorandum of conversation, 11 Oct. 1955, *FRUS 1955–1957*, XIV, 571–5 (D333).
54. Dulles (Geneva) to Hoover, 8 Nov. 1955, *FRUS 1955–1957*, XIV, 717f. (D389).

Cf. ibid., 720, 790; Shuckburgh–Russell conversation, 8 Nov. 1955, FO371/115469 V1023/24; two unsigned and undated memoranda, 'Suggested Steps in Light of Sharett's Coming Trip to the US' and 'Suggested 7-Point Statement by the President', USNA NEA Lot 59, D518 Box 31.
55. Bar-On, *Gates of Gaza*, 3–6, 37–55; Morris, *Israel's Border Wars*, 278–82. Cf. Copeland's characterization of Israel's February 1955 Gaza raid as 'the prod'. Above, 100; Copeland, *Game Player*, 199.
56. Shimshoni, *Israel and Conventional Deterrence*, 109.
57. Cf. 'The only thing we can gain from the war … is Nasser's overthrow.' Ben-Gurion at meeting with Dayan, 5 April 1956, quoted in Bar-On, *Gates of Gaza*, 317.
58. Bar-On, *Sha'arei Aza*, 61 (transl. from the Heb. edition). For some reason, a different paragraph from the Chief-of-Staff Diary of 23 Oct. 1955 is given in the English version (*Gates of Gaza*, 45). See also Kyle, *Suez*, 80; Morris, *Israel's Border Wars*, 279f.
59. Byroade to USSD, 18 Oct. 1955, *FRUS 1955–1957*, XIV, 611 (D342). Cf. ibid., 735.
60. For various American, British and Israeli discussions on the likelihood of a 'preventive' war during the fall of 1955, see: *FRUS 1955–1957*, XIV, 561f., 578–81, 590f., 593f., 609f., 622, 638; Shuckburgh, *Descent*, 293 (26 Oct. 1955); Sharett, *Yoman Ishi*, IV: 1182 (1 Oct.) and 1186 (3 Oct. 1955); Meinertzhagen memorandum, 2 Oct. 1955, in ISA 130.16/2593/23; Bonesteel memorandum for NSC, Factors Bearing on Current Problems in the Middle East, 10 Oct. 1955, NEA Lot 59, D518, Box 34; Heikal, *Milaffat*, 775f. (D113); H.W. Baldwin, 'Thin Mideast War Cloud', *New York Times*, 7 Nov. 1955; Reuters, 'Israel Scents Attack', *Christian Science Monitor*, 15 Nov. 1955.
61. Sharett–Macmillan conversation, Paris, 26 Oct. 1955, PRO FO371/115537 V1076/4; Dulles (Geneva) to USSD, 13 Nov. 1955 (tgm.SECTO283), USNA NEA Lot 59, D518, Box 31; *FRUS 1955–1957*, XIV, 657–9, 689. For examples of warnings to Israel, see, FO to UKEmb Tel Aviv, 9 Nov. 1955 (tgm.771), FO371/115880 VR1076/335G; Russell, memorandum of conversation (Dulles, Macmillan, Margerie *et al*.), Geneva, 12 Nov. 1955, USNA NEA Lot 59, D518, Box 31; *FRUS 1955–1957*, XIV, 742; Kyle, *Suez*, 79; Bar-On, *Gates of Gaza*, 27f., 50f.
62. Ahmad Hussein report (18 Oct.) of talk with Dulles, 17 Oct. 1955, in Heikal, *Milaffat*, 775 (D113); Wilkins, memorandum of conversation (Dulles, Hussein, Allen), 17 Oct. 1955, *FRUS 1955–1957*, XIV, 606 (D341). Cf. Macmillan conversation with Prime Minister of Pakistan, 3 Nov. 1955, PRO FO371/115881 VR1076/363.
63. Lawson to USSD, 12 Nov. 1955, *FRUS 1955–1957*, XIV, 739 (D403).
64. E.g., Macmillan and Dulles remarks, memorandum of conversation, 3 Oct. 1955, *FRUS 1955–1957*, XIV, 542–9 (D323); Consensus of Meeting with respect to Policy to be Followed as a result of the Egypt–Soviet Arms Deal as discussed by the British Foreign Secretary and the US Secretary of State, 3 Oct. 1955, USNA NEA Lot 59, D518, Box 30; Rubin, *Arab States*, 277f.; Burns, *Economic Aid*, 37f.
65. Conversation between Dulles, Allen and Ambassador Ahmad Hussein, 17 Oct. 1955, in (a) *FRUS 1955–1957*, XIV, 606 (D341), and (b) Heikal, *Milaffat*, 774 (D113). On Johnston's intensive attempts to rally Arab and Israeli support for his project at this time, see: Dudgeon (Amman) to Rose, 6 Oct. 1955 (desp.1077/87/55G), PRO FO371/115880 VR1076/322; *FRUS 1955–1957*, XIV, 564–8, 586f., 589f.; Oren, *Origins*, 116f. Nasir's overall support for the Johnston mission prior to October 1955 is stressed and analysed in Garfinkle, *Deep and Wide*, Ch. 4.
66. Burns, *Economic Aid*, 38.
67. See, e.g., Russell, memorandum of conversation (Dulles, Macmillan, Margerie *et*

al.), Geneva, 12 Nov. 1955, USNA NEA Lot 59, D518, Box 31; *FRUS 1955–1957*, XIV, 563f., 676f., 687f., 690f., 712, 739–42, 748f., 752, 768, 774f., 791f., 804, 812; Sharett, *Yoman Ishi*, IV: 1156–63, 1171f, 1175, 1180; Shuckburgh, *Descent*, 293, 296–8; Moshe Dayan, *Diary of the Sinai Campaign* (New York: Harper & Row, 1966), 13f.; Burns, *Between Arab and Israeli*, 92–8; *Observer*, 6 Nov. 1955, 1 (several articles); 'Peace in Mideast Pressed by West – 3 Powers Agree Settlement Between Israel and Arabs Is Imperative Now', *New York Times*, 14 Nov. 1955 (dateline Geneva 13 Nov.); Love, *Suez*, 309; Morris, *Israel's Border Wars*, 358–60.

68. Ben-Gurion, Knesset speech, 2 Nov. 1955, quoted in Ben-Gurion, *Israel: A Personal History*, 448f. See also: H.B. Ellis, 'Ben-Gurion Offers Truce Bid', *Christian Science Monitor*, 2 Nov. 1955; H. Gilroy, 'Ben Gurion Offers to Meet Arab Chiefs to Settle Crisis', *New York Times*, 3 Nov. 1955; 'Israel Asks Peace Talks with Arabs', *New York Herald Tribune*, 3 Nov. 1955 (AP).
69. Cf. Map of 'Recent Incidents' reproduced above, page 137.
70. Bar-On, *Gates of Gaza*, 49f.; Morris, *Israel's Border Wars*, 280, 359f. Cf. *FRUS 1955–1957*, XIV, 697–74, 712, 804–7; Oren, *Origins*, 32f.
71. 'Nasser Ridicules Ben-Gurion Plea', *New York Times*, 4 Nov. 1955 (dateline Cairo 3 Nov.). Cf. Nasir interview with NBC Cairo correspondent, as reported in *Akhbar al-Yaum*, 12 Nov. 1955, cited in Trevelyan to FO, 14 Nov. 1955 (tgm.231 Saving), FO371/115849 VR1072/300; Morris, *Israel's Border Wars*, 370.
72. NSC, 264th meeting, 3 Nov. 1955, *FRUS 1955–1957*, XIV, 698 (D380)
73. Byroade to USSD, 18 Oct. 1955, *FRUS 1955–1957*, XIV, 610 (D342)
74. Duke (Amman) to Shuckburgh, 20 Oct. 1955 (desp.1077/92/55G), PRO FO371/115880 VR1076/326G. Cf. Arthur minute, Palestine Settlement, 4 Nov. 1955, FO371/115880 VR1076/331G; Shuckburgh to Duke, 14 Nov. 1955, FO371/115880 VR1076/326G.
75. Scott (Beirut) to FO, 3 Oct. 1955 (tgm.731), PRO FO371/115880 VR1076/320; Emmerson (Beirut) to USSD, 17 Oct. 1955 (tgm.441), USNA NEA Lot 59, D518, Box 30; same to same, 17 Nov. 1955 (tgm.559), *loc. cit.* Box 31. See also: Hooper (Baghdad) to Rose, 28 Oct. 1955 (desp.1071/144/55), PRO FO371/115879 VR1076/318G; Macmillan conversation with Prime Minister of Pakistan, 3 Nov. 1955, FO371/115881 VR1076/363; 'Syrian (i.e., Ahmad Shuqayri) Insists on Repatriation as Key to Problem of Palestine', *New York Herald Tribune*, 19 Oct. 1955. On the significance of the agreement contained in the Lausanne Protocol, see: Neil Caplan, *The Lausanne Conference, 1949: A Case Study in Middle East Peacemaking*, (Tel Aviv University: Moshe Dayan Center for Middle Eastern and African Studies (Occasional Paper No.113), 1993), Ch. 5, and *FD3*, 81–8, 108–9, 122–5.
76. Arthur minute, Palestine Settlement, 5 Oct. 1955, PRO FO371/115880 VR1076/320; Shuckburgh to Nicholls, 20 Oct. 1955, PRO FO371/115880 VR1076/323.
77. Nicholls to Shuckburgh, 31 Oct. 1955 (desp.1031/107/55), PRO FO371/115880 VR1076/329.
78. Nuri Sa'id's account of Nasir–Bashayan talk, reported in Gallman to USSD, 7 Oct. 1955 (tgm.325), USNA 774.56/10–755; Hoover to Russell (Geneva), 28 Oct. 1955 (tgm.1037), USNA NEA Lot 59, D518, Box 34; *FRUS 1955–1957*, XIV, 674. Both reports were duly conveyed to Secretary Dulles.
79. Byroade to USSD, 18 Oct. 1955, *FRUS 1955–1957*, XIV, 611 (D342).
80. Allen–Byroade–Nasir talk, reported in Allen (Cairo) to USSD, 3 Oct. 1955, *FRUS 1955–1957*, XIV, 552 (D325). Cf. ibid., 606f., 674.
81. Burdett, Arab–Israel Settlement: Position Paper (for tripartite foreign ministers' meeting), 20 Oct. 1955, USNA NEA Lot 59, D518, Box 31. For a critique of the realism of such an approach, see Shamir, 'Collapse', 90.

82. Consensus of Meeting with respect to Policy to be Followed as a result of the Egypt–Soviet Arms Deal as discussed by the British Foreign Secretary and the US Secretary of State, 3 Oct. 1955, USNA NEA Lot 59, D518, Box 30. Cf. NIE, The Outlook for Egyptian Stability and Foreign Policy, 15 Nov. 1955, *FRUS 1955–1957*, XIV, 768 (D411); O.M. Marashian, 'Peace Talk Echoes in Mideast', *Christian Science Monitor*, 29 Nov. 1955 (dateline Cairo).
83. Burdett, Soviet Bloc Arms Offers – Position Towards Near East States: Position Paper (for tripartite Foreign Ministers' meeting), 20 Oct. 1955, USNA NEA Lot 59, D518, Box 31. For similar American lists of incentives and desiderata, see: Burdett's more detailed memorandum, Soviet–Egyptian Arms Sale: Steps to be Followed in Egypt, 5 Oct. 1955, NEA Lot 59, D518, Box 30; Hoover to Dulles, 29 Oct. 1955, *FRUS 1955–1957*, XIV, 678 (D368). For British interest in proceeding with Anglo–American financing of the Aswan Dam project, see Kyle, *Suez*, 77.
84. Shuckburgh memorandum, Policy in the Middle East, 14 Oct. 1955, PRO FO371/115480 V1054/5G. Cf. Kyle, *Suez*, 74, quoting an earlier memorandum where Shuckburgh speculated that the 'very high price' of keeping Egypt 'on our side ... may well include having to abandon Israel'.
85. Cf. '[Nasir's] present attitude to the West has been affected (a) by the Israel question and (b) by his opposition to the development of the Baghdad Pact. We should not make an immediate approach to Nasser on either of these two issues. He is intoxicated by his present popularity and this is clearly not a propitious moment.' 'Draft of Proposed Agreed Position between US and UK on Middle East Policy', 9 November 1955 (Document 9, para. 15).
86. Kirkpatrick minute, The Middle East, 30 Oct. 1955, PRO FO371/115469 V1023/19G.
87. Interestingly, item (d) does not appear in (or was excised, without ellipsis, from) the telegraphic and abridged text of Kirkpatrick's minute given in *FRUS 1955–1957*, XIV, 707–10 (D384).
88. See, e.g., *FRUS 1955–1957*, XIV, 713–16, 728–32, 746; Shuckburgh, *Descent*, 298 (8 Nov. 1955); Shuckburgh to Kirkpatrick, 10 Nov. 1955, PRO FO371/115469 V1023/23G. Kirkpatrick had presented merely his 'personal thoughts', noting originally that they had no 'authority' behind them. Palliser (Geneva) to Shuckburgh, 31 Oct. 1955, PRO FO371/115469 V1023/19G.
89. The bluntness and explicit character of Sir Ivone's list of sanctions quoted above was rendered innocuous in the final Anglo–American draft by the phrase: 'If all this fails and Egypt is clearly lost to Western influence, we should have to consider policies which would minimize the harm which he could do to Western interests.'
90. Shuckburgh, *Descent*, 281 (26 Sept. 1955). For American and British consideration of steps to undermine Nasir at this time, see: Macmillan–Dulles (*et al.*) conversation, Washington, 3 Oct. 1955, *FRUS 1955–1957*, XIV, 543f. (D323); Consensus of Meeting..., 3 Oct. 1955, ibid., 561f. (D327); Burdett memorandum, Soviet–Egyptian Arms Sale: Steps to be Followed in Egypt (5 Oct.) and draft tgm. from Secretary of State to USEmb Cairo, 6 Oct. 1955, NEA Lot 59, D518, Box 30; Shamir, 'Collapse', 88; Kyle, *Suez*, 75f. (quoting Harold Caccia).
91. USSD to USEmb Egypt, 11 Nov. 1955 (tgm.340), quoted in *FRUS 1955–1957*, XIV, 735 n.2. Cf. Byroade to USSD, 12 Nov. 1955, ibid., 734f. (D400); Kyle, *Suez*, 80. For evidence of Israeli desires to undermine or topple the Nasir régime at this time, see, e.g.: Sharett, *Yoman Ishi* IV: 1190f. (5 Oct. 1955); *FRUS 1955–1957*, XIV, 727; Dulles (Geneva) to USSD, 15 Nov. 1955 (tgm.SECTO297), USNA NEA Lot 59, D518, Box 31.
92. See, e.g., Dulles (Geneva) to USSD, 15 Nov. 1955 (tgm.SECTO297), USNA NEA Lot 59, D518, Box 31. Cf. Dayan, *Diary of the Sinai Campaign*, 11f.; *FRUS*

1955–1957, XIV, 474, 768, 791, 793, 802, 829, 831; Macmillan–Elath talk, in Macmillan to Nicholls, 15 Sept. 1955 (desp.174), PRO FO371/115878 VR1076/294G.
93. Dulles (Geneva) to USSD, 15 Nov. 1955 (tgm.SECTO297), USNA NEA Lot 59, D518, Box 31. Commenting on this information, Secretary Dulles wondered whether the SD might 'consider whether we should discreetly suggest to Nasser (that) he not fall into [the] trap if [the] I[srael] G[overnment] should attempt it. Conceivably he might be persuaded that in view of [the] political strength he has achieved from arms acquisitions, he could afford [to] terminate [the] Aqaba blockade.'
94. Macmillan–Dulles (*et al.*) conversation, Washington, 3 Oct. 1955, *FRUS 1955–1957*, XIV, 543 (D323); Kyle, *Suez*, 77f.
95. Memorandum for the Secretary, Items for Discussion with Macmillan on Middle East, 25 Oct. 1955, USNA NEA Lot 59, D518, Box 31; cf. Burns, *Economic Aid*, 38.
96. Shuckburgh, *Descent*, 295 (30 Oct. 1955).
97. Dulles (Geneva) to USSD, 13 Nov. 1955, *FRUS 1955–1957*, XIV, 741 (D404); Russell, memorandum of conversation (Dulles, Macmillan, Margerie *et al.*), Geneva, 12 Nov. 1955, USNA NEA Lot 59, D518, Box 31.
98. Hoover to Russell, 28 Oct. 1955 (reporting information dated 26 Oct., 'received from Cairo, from a sensitive source'), *FRUS 1955–1957*, XIV, 645 and USNA NEA Lot 59, D518, Box 34 ; Oren, *Origins*, 121. In early November, American newsman Michael Chinigo of the Hearst chain transmitted another veiled peace feeler from Nasir to Ben-Gurion. Chinigo to Kollek, 11 Nov. 1955, ISA 43/gimmel–5571/4132.
99. Byroade to Dulles (Geneva), 2 Nov. 1955, *FRUS 1955–1957*, XIV, 693–6 (D379); same to same, 9 Nov. 1955, ibid., 724f. (D392). Quotations in this and the following paragraph are taken from these despatches.
100. Trevelyan to FO, 2 Nov. 1955 (tgm.1609), PRO FO371/115469 V1023/20; same to same, 5 Nov. 1955 (tgm.1641), FO371/115880 VR1076/330G.
101. Trevelyan to FO, 4 Nov. 1955 (tgm.1625), PRO PREM11/945. The issues discussed were: the Anglo–Saudi dispute over Buraimi, a Palestine settlement, accession of new members to the Baghdad Pact, 'Soviet penetration' and 'the Western position in the Middle East', and financing for the Aswan Dam project.
102. 'Draft of Proposed Agreed Position between US and UK on Middle East Policy', 9 November 1955 (Document 9, para. 15).

CHAPTER IX

1. Arthur minute, Palestine Settlement, 4 Nov. 1955, FO371/115880 VR1076/331G. Cf. Shuckburgh, *Descent*, 296f. (4 Nov. 1955).
2. Oren, *Origins*, 110, 118; cf. Michael B. Oren, 'Nuri al-Sa'id and the Question of Arab–Israel Peace, 1953–1957', *Asian and African Studies* 24:3 (November 1990), 267–82. This notion was also evident in Shuckburgh's formulation in paragraph 13 of the Anglo–American draft (Document 9).
3. Arthur minute, Palestine Settlement, 4 Nov. 1955, FO371/115880 VR1076/331G.
4. Shuckburgh minute, 7 Nov. 1955, PRO FO371/115880 VR1076/334G. Cf. Shuckburgh–Russell conversation, 8 Nov. 1955, FO371/115469 V1023/24; Russell, memorandum of conversation (Dulles, Macmillan, *et al.*), Geneva, 9 Nov. 1955, *FRUS 1955–1957*, XIV, 720 (D391).
5. Kyle, *Suez*, 81.

6. Guildhall (Mansion House) speech, 9 Nov. 1955, Hurewitz, *Diplomacy* II: 413–15 (D113).
7. FO to UKEmb Amman (etc.), 9 Nov. 1955 (tgms.740 and 742), and FO to Baghdad, 9 Nov. 1955 (tgm.1550), PRO FO371/115880 VR1076/335G.
8. FO to UKEmb Cairo, 9 Nov. 1955 (tgm.2587), PRO FO371/115880 VR1076/335G; Arthur minute, 9 Nov. 1955, FO371/115880 VR1076/330G.
9. FO to UKEmb Tel Aviv, 9 Nov. 1955 (tgm.771), PRO FO371/115880 VR1076/335G. Cf. Nicholls' proposed approach in Nicholls to FO, 11 Nov. 1955 (tgm.457), FO371/115880 VR1076/343.
10. Optimism was fostered by newspaper correspondents like Robert Stephens, who reported that 'Arab States (were) giving more serious consideration to Sir Anthony Eden's speech than to any previous Western initiative for a settlement of the Arab–Israeli conflict.' 'Nasser's Condition for Peace', *The Observer*, 13 Nov. 1955, 1.
11. Scott (Beirut) to FO, 11 Nov. 1955 (tgm.853), PRO FO371/115880 VR1076/342. Cf. Shuckburgh, *Descent*, 302 (20 Nov. 1955). Nasir later accused the US Information Agency of manipulating the sections of the Lebanese press against his positive reactions to the Guildhall speech. *FRUS 1955–1957*, XV, 33.
12. Talk with Nuri Sa'id, reported in Wright to FO, 15 Nov. 1955 (tgm.917), FO371/115881 VR1076/370. Cf. Aldrich to Dulles (Geneva) and Hoover, 11 Nov. 1955, *FRUS 1955–1957*, XIV, 733 (D398); Shuckburgh, *Descent*, 300 (15 Nov. 1955); Emmerson to USSD, 17 Nov. 1055 (tgm.559), USNA NEA Lot 59, D518, Box 31; Duke to Macmillan, 21 Nov. 1955 (desp.1077/122/55G – no.92), FO371/115883 VR1076/437. For other Arab reactions and FO assessments see: PRO FO371/115881 VR1076/369G, /381; FO371/115882 VR1076/392, /393, /395, /400G; FO371/115885 VR1076/467, /479, /483; FO371/115887 VR1076/509G; Shuckburgh, *Descent*, 301 (16 Nov. 1955); 'Jordanian Comment on Israel', *New York Herald Tribune*, 21 Nov. 1955 (Reuters, dateline Amman, 20 Nov.); O.M. Marashian, 'Peace Talk Echoes in Mideast', *Christian Science Monitor*, 29 Nov. 1955 (dateline Cairo); Love, *Suez*, 306; Neff, *Warriors at Suez*, 115f.
13. Cf. Heikal, *Milaffat*, 388; 'Nasser's Condition for Peace' (interview with Robert Stephens), *The Observer*, 13 Nov. 1955, 1. For the text of the Bernadotte proposals, see Caplan, *FD3*, Document 1.
14. Trevelyan to FO, 10 Nov. 1955, full text in *FRUS 1955–1957*, XIV, 737f. (D402). Cf. Arthur minute, Alpha, 14 Nov. 1955, PRO FO371/115881 VR1076/369G.
15. Trevelyan–Nasir talk, in Trevelyan to FO, 12 Nov. 1955 (tgm.1708), PRO FO371/115881 VR1076/350G; cf. Bar-On, *Gates of Gaza*, 94f. For Egyptian press reactions, see: FO371/115881 VR1076/351 and /371; FO371/115882 VR1076/400G; Love, *Suez*, 307.
16. On British efforts to defuse friction between Nasir and Nuri on this issue see: Arthur minute, Alpha, 14 Nov. 1955, PRO FO371/115881 VR1076/369G; Wright–Nuri talk, reported in Wright (Baghdad) to FO, 15 Nov. 1955 (tgm.917), FO371/115881 VR1076/370; Trevelyan–Fawzi–Byroade talk (16 Nov.), reported in Trevelyan to FO, 17 Nov. 1955 (tgm.1745), FO371/115882 VR1076/391G; Macmillan (Baghdad) to Eden, 23 Nov. 1955 (tgm.956), FO371/115883 VR1076/436; Shuckburgh, *Descent*, 304f. (23 Nov. 1955); Macmillan message to Nasir, in FO to UKEmb Cairo, 25 Nov. 1955 (tgm.2800), FO371/115883 VR1076/436; Wright–Nuri talk, reported in Wright to FO, 25 Nov. 1955 (tgm.964), FO371/115884 VR1076/446; Wright–Nuri talk (2 Dec.), reported in Wright to FO, 5 Dec. 1955 (tgm.994), FO371/115885 VR1076/481.

These British efforts to keep Nuri from criticizing Nasir did not remain secret from the Israelis. See, e.g., Ben-Gurion remarks in his talk with Anderson, 23 Jan. 1956, USNA NEA Lot 59, D518, Box 34.

17. IsrEmb London, Statement, 10 Nov. 1955, ISA 130.02/2403/12/b; Shuckburgh, *Descent*, 301 (15 Nov. 1955).
18. Myerson–Nicholls talk (15 Nov.), reported in Nicholls to FO, 16 Nov. 1955 (tgm.473), PRO FO371/115881 VR1076/381 (marginal exclamation marks by an official at the FO highlighted the internal inconsistency in this sentence); Nicholls to FO, 11 Nov. 1955 (tgm.459), FO371/115881 VR1076/355; same to same, 11 and 14 Nov. 1955 (tgms.460 and 470), FO371/115880 VR1076/344; same to same, 14 Nov. 1955 (tgm.471), FO371/115881 VR1076/367; editorials in *Davar* and *Ha-Boqer*, 17 Nov. 1955, transl. in FO371/115883 VR1076/427; Nicholls to Macmillan, 28 Nov. 1955 (desp.150–1034/55/55), FO371/115885 VR1076/468; D. Cook, 'Israel Angry at Eden Plan – Indignation Mounts over Idea of Ceding Any Land', *New York Herald Tribune*, 14 Nov. 1955 (dateline Jerusalem, 13 Nov.); *FRUS 1955–1957*, XIV, 744, 775; Bar-On, *Gates of Gaza*, 95.
19. Nicholls to Shuckburgh, 12 Nov. 1955 (desp.1041/39/55), PRO FO371/115882 VR1076/400G; same to FO, 11 Nov. 1955 (tgm.455), FO371/115880 VR1076/332G; same to same, 14 Nov. 1955 (tgm.466), FO371/115881 VR1076/360.
20. Nicholls to FO, 21 Nov. 1955 (tgm.487), PRO FO371/115883 VR1076/420G. Cf. H. Gilroy, 'Israelis Suspect Britain is Seeking a Negev Corridor', *New York Times*, 18 Dec. 1955, 1, 2 (dateline Jerusalem, 17 Dec.).
21. Ben-Gurion, Knesset statement, 15 Nov. 1955, transl. in FO371/115881 VR1076/383. Cf. Ben-Gurion, *Israel: A Personal History*, 453f.; H. Gilroy, 'Ben-Gurion Says New Eden Offer Benefits Arabs', *New York Times*, 26 Nov. 1955, 1.
22. Lawson–Ben-Gurion talk (16 Nov.), in Lawson to USSD, 17 Nov. 1955, *FRUS 1955–1957*, XIV, 784–6 (D417). Cf. Bar-On, *Gates of Gaza*, 90.
23. See, e.g., Bar-On, *Gates of Gaza*, 42f., 51.
24. Sharett address to National Press Club, Washington, 21 Nov. 1955, text in *Israel Digest* VI:47, 25 Nov. 1955, 3, copy in CZA A245/50; Russell, memorandum of conversation (Dulles, Allen, Sharett, Eban, Shiloah), 6 Dec. 1955, *FRUS 1955–1957*, XIV, 828 (D437).
25. *FRUS 1955–1957*, XIV, 785. Cf. F. Ofner, 'Eden's Offer Unrealistic Say Israelis', *The Observer*, 13 Nov. 1955, 1; Bar-On, *Gates of Gaza*, 96.
26. Dulles (Geneva) to USSD, 12 Nov. 1955 (tgm.SECTO260), quoted in *FRUS 1955–1957*, XIV, 733 n.4. Cf. Aldrich to Dulles (Geneva) and Hoover, 11 Nov. 1955, ibid., 733 (D398); same to same, 16 Nov. 1955, ibid., 776f. (D414); Nicholls to FO, 16 Nov. 1955 (tgm.473), PRO FO371/115881 VR1076/381; Makins to FO, 20 Nov. 1955 (tgm.2829), FO371/115883 VR1076/419G; Rose minute, Alpha, 24 Nov. 1955, FO371/115884 VR1076/447G; Stevens to Hood, 7 Nov. 1958, FO371/134298 VR10710/1; Oren, *Origins*, 119.
27. Dulles remarks, NSC 267th meeting, 21 Nov. 1955, quoted in *FRUS 1955–1957*, XIV, 797 (D422). Cf. 'US Hopes Mount on Mideast Peace', *New York Times*, 30 Nov. 1955, 1, 16 (dateline Washington, 29 Nov.); Shamir, 'Collapse', 93 n.54.
28. Nicholls to Shuckburgh, 21 Nov. 1955, PRO FO371/115883 VR1076/433G. Cf. *FRUS 1955–1957*, XIV, 791.
29. Dulles (Geneva) to Lawson, 16 Nov. 1955, *FRUS 1955–1957*, XIV, 772f. (D412). Cf. ibid., 789, 791; Nicholls to FO, 22 Nov. 1955 (tgm.488), PRO FO371/115883 VR1076/426; Elath–Eden talk (23 Nov.), reported in FO to UKEmb Washington, 24 Nov. 1955 (tgm.5563), FO371/115883 VR1076/444G, and in Elath, *Me'ever le-Arafel*, 72f.
30. Russell, memorandum of conversation (Dulles, Macmillan, *et al.*), Geneva, 9 Nov. 1955, *FRUS 1955–1957*, XIV, 723 (D391). Cf. ibid., 725; Dulles to USSD, 11 Nov. 1955 (tgm.SECTO247), USNA NEA Lot 59, D518, Box 31.
31. Dulles (Geneva) to USSD, 11 Nov. 1955, *FRUS 1955–1957*, XIV, 732 (D397); Hoover to Dulles (Geneva), 12 Nov. 1955, ibid., 736 (D401).

32. FO to Macmillan (Geneva), 14 Nov. 1955 (tgms.482, 483), PRO FO371/115881 VR1076/369G; Arthur minute, Alpha, 14 Nov. 1955, PRO FO371/115881 VR1076/369G; Dulles (Geneva) to USSD, 11 Nov. 1955, *FRUS 1955–1957*, XIV, 732 (D397); Hancock (Geneva) to Shuckburgh, 14 Nov. 1955 (tgm.173), PRO, FO371/115881 VR1076/359G; Macmillan (Geneva) to FO, 15 Nov. 1955 (tgm. 197), FO371/115881 VR1076/374G.
33. Byroade–Fawzi talk (14 Nov.), quoted in Byroade to USSD, 15 Nov. 1955, *FRUS 1955–1957*, XIV, 749f. (D410).
34. Byroade–Trevelyan–Fawzi talk (16 Nov.), reported in Byroade to USSD, 17 Nov. 1955, *FRUS 1955–1957*, XIV, 781–3 (D416). Quotations in this and the following paragraphs are taken from this report. Cf. Arthur minute, Alpha, 14 Nov. 1955, PRO FO371/115881 VR1076/369G.
35. Trevelyan to FO, 17 Nov. 1955 (tgms.1745, 1746), FO371/115882 VR1076/391G. Trevelyan's account of the talk with Fawzi was only slightly less 'up-beat' than Byroade's.
36. Quoted in Kyle, *Suez*, 82.
37. Arthur minute (Shuckburgh marginal note), Alpha, 18 Nov. 1955, FO371/115882 VR1076/391G; Shuckburgh, *Descent*, 301 (18 Nov. 1955): Macmillan to Dulles, 19 Nov. 1955, quoted in *FRUS 1955–1957*, XIV, 783 n.3.; FO to UKEmb Washington, 19 Nov. 1955 (tgm.5480), FO371/115882 VR1076/391G.
38. Rountree and Russell to Dulles, 18 Nov. 1955, encl. draft tgm. to USEmb Cairo, USNA NEA Lot 59, D518, Box 31; Byroade to USSD, 27 Nov. 1955, *FRUS 1955–1957*, XIV, 807f. (D428); Trevelyan to FO, 28 Nov. 1955 (tgm.1813), PRO FO371/115884 VR1076/456G.

CHAPTER X

1. Kyle, *Suez*, 73, and Ch. 4 *passim*.
2. Y. Herzog, reported in White to USSD, 19 Nov. 1955, *FRUS 1955–1957*, XIV, 789 (D419). Cf. Murphy, memorandum of conversation with Shiloah, 22 Nov. 1955, USNA NEA Lot 59, D518 Box 31; Sharett remarks to Dulles, 6 Dec. 1955, *FRUS 1955–1957*, XIV, 827 (D437).
3. Myerson remarks to US chargé d'affaires, Tel Aviv (7 Dec.), quoted in Arthur minute, Israel/Egyptian Relations, 9 Dec. 1955, PRO FO371/115887 VR1076/508G. Cf. White to USSD, 8 Dec. 1955, *FRUS 1955–1957*, XIV, 838f. (D444); Shamir, 'Collapse', 88.
4. Sharett address to National Press Club, Washington, 21 Nov. 1955, text in *Israel Digest* VI:47, 25 Nov. 1955, 2f., copy in CZA A245/50; Eban, statement to Special Political Committee, UNGA, 18 Nov. 1955, in Medzini, *Israel's Foreign Relations*, 407f., 410f.; Bergus, memorandum of conversation (Russell, Shiloah), 22 Nov. 1955, USNA NEA Lot 59, D518, Box 31. During late 1955 and early 1956, a Foreign Office task force continued its own study of the compensation and resettlement questions as an element in Operation Alpha. See PRO FO371/115884 VR1076/461G; FO371/121708 VR1071/25G.
5. Arthur Dean, memorandum of conversation with Eban and Shiloah, 9 Dec. 1955, USNA NEA Lot 59, D518 , Box 31.
6. Nicholls to Macmillan, 28 Nov. 1955 (desp.150, 1034/55/55), FO371/115885 VR1076/468.
7. Russell, memorandum of conversation (Dulles, Makins, Hoover, Morris), 20 Nov. 1955, *FRUS 1955–1957*, XIV, 790–2 (D420); Makins to FO, 20 Nov. 1955 (tgm. 2829), PRO FO371/115883 VR1076/419G. For the FO's more elegantly worded suggestions for how the powers ought to approach the Israelis, see FO to UKEmb

Washington, 19 Nov. 1955 (tgm.5480), FO371/115882 VR1076/391G.
8. *'Afta'a mefutsetset'*. Sharett, *Yoman Ishi* V: 1297 (21 Nov. 1955). Cf. *FRUS 1955–1957*, XIV, 811.
9. Sharett address to National Press Club, Washington, 21 Nov. 1955, text in *Israel Digest* VI:47, 25 Nov. 1955, 2f., copy in CZA A245/50.
10. Dulles *aide-mémoire* to Sharett (21 Nov.), text reported in Dulles to USEmbs Egypt, Israel, 22 Nov. 1955, *FRUS 1955–1957*, XIV, 802f. (D424). Cf. Bar-On, *Gates of Gaza*, 95f.
11. Later Shuckburgh remarked that 'Mr Dulles had said privately that he believe[d] these [concessions] might have to amount to one third of the total area' of the Negev. See: Shuckburgh minute, Palestine Settlement, 3 Jan. 1956, PRO FO371/121708 VR1071/14G; Rose brief, Palestine Settlement, 7 Jan. 1956, PRO FO371/121724 VR1073/63G.
12. The reconstruction of the meeting of 21 November is based on: Russell, memorandum of conversation (Dulles, Hoover, Allen, Sharett, Eban), 21 Nov. 1955, *FRUS 1955–1957*, XIV, 793–6 (D421); Russell account of Dulles–Sharett meeting, reported in Makins to FO, 21 Nov. 1955 (tgm.2839), PRO FO371/115883 VR1076/421G. Quotations in this and the following paragraphs are taken from these sources. Cf. Bar-On, *Sha'arei Aza*, 122; Alteras, *Eisenhower and Israel*, 148f.
13. On the 1939 White Paper, see: Rubin, *Arab States*, Ch. 8; Caplan, *FD2*, Ch. 5.
14. Bergus, memorandum of conversation (Russell, Shiloah), 22 Nov. 1955, USNA NEA Lot 59, D518, Box 31. Cf. Eban remarks, 13 Dec. 1955, *FRUS 1955–1957*, XIV, 857 (D454); Eban, *Personal Witness*, 178; Donohue, *Before Suez*, Chs II–III; Alteras, *Eisenhower and Israel*, 56; Haggai Eshed, *Mossad Shel Ish Ehad: Reuven Shiloah, Avi ha-Modiyin ha-Yisraeli (One Man Mossad: Reuven Shiloah, the Father of Israeli Intelligence)*, Jerusalem: Edanim, 1988.
15. Here a marginal notation by a FO official reads: 'But they are!' Cf. Shuckburgh to Nicholls, 2 Dec. 1955, FO371/115883 VR1076/435G.
16. Nicholls to Shuckburgh, 21 Nov. 1955, PRO FO371/115883 VR1076/434G. Nicholls conveyed similar advice in his telegram to FO, 2 Dec. 1955 (tgm.508), and Shuckburgh explained FO reservations in his reply of 20 Dec. 1955, both in PRO FO371/115885 VR1076/475G.
17. Russell–Shiloah talk, reported in Russell to Dulles and Hoover, 1 Dec. 1955, USNA NEA Lot 59, D518, Box 31. Cf. Alteras, *Eisenhower and Israel*, 153.
18. Bergus, memorandum of conversation (Eban, Shiloah, Allen, Russell), 2 Dec. 1955, USNA NEA Lot 59, D518, Box 31.
19. IsrEmb Washington to USSD, *aide-mémoire*, 6 Dec. 1955, *FRUS 1955–1957*, XIV, 823–5 (D436). Quotations in this and the following paragraph are taken from this *aide-mémoire*. Cf. Bar-On, *Gates of Gaza*, 96f., 105 and *Sha'arei Aza*, 454 n.42.
20. Russell, memorandum of conversation (Dulles, Allen, Sharett, Eban, Shiloah), 6 Dec. 1955, *FRUS 1955–1957*, XIV, 826–32 (D437). Quotations in this and the following paragraphs are taken from this source. Cf. ibid., 833; Makins to FO, 7 Dec. 1955 (tgm.2991), PRO FO371/115886 VR1076/490G; Allen and Russell to Dulles (briefing for meeting with Sharett), 5 Dec. 1955, USNA NEA Lot 59, D518, Box 31; 'Sharett Gloomy on Mideast Peace', *New York Times*, 7 Dec. 1955, 1, 10.
21. On the hopes attached to using Nasir's influence in favour of Arab acceptance of the Johnston plan, see: Nasir–Trevelyan talk, reported in Trevelyan to FO, 20 Sept. 1955 (tgm.1286), PRO FO371/115879 VR1076/306G; Johnston (Cairo) to Dulles, 25 Sept. 1955, *FRUS 1955–1957* XIV, 513 (D306); ibid., 521, 565–8, 586f., 606, 876f.; Trevelyan–Fawzi talk, reported in Trevelyan to FO, 17 Nov. 1955 (tgm.1745), FO371/115882 VR1076/391G; *FRUS 1955–1957*, XV, 285.

22. *FRUS 1955–1957*, XIV, 826–32; Makins to FO, 7 Dec. 1955 (tgm.2991), PRO FO371/115886 VR1076/490G; Sharett, *Yoman Ishi*, V: 1305 (6 Dec. 1955).
23. Macmillan to Dulles, in FO to UKEmb Washington, 25 Nov. 1955 (tgm.5599), FO371/115469 V1023/26G; Macmillan note (8 Dec.) of talk with Sieff, 7 Dec. 1955, FO371/115886 VR1076/501G; MacArthur, memorandum of conversation (Dulles, Makins, Merchant), 6 Dec. 1955, *FRUS 1955–1957*, XIV, 832–4 (D438); Dulles to Byroade, 6 Dec. 1955, ibid., 835f. (D440); Makins to FO, 6 Dec. 1955 (tgm.2983), PRO FO371/115885 VR1076/485G; same to same, 7 Dec. 1955 (tgm.2994), FO371/115886 VR1076/491G.
24. Rose minute, Alpha, 25 Nov. 1955, PRO FO371/115884 VR1076/447G; Arthur minute, Alpha, 5 Dec. 1955, FO371/115885 VR1076/475G. Cf. FO to UKEmb Washington, 26 Nov. 1955 (tgm.5621), FO371/115884 VR1076/447G; Shuckburgh to Nicholls, 2 Dec. 1955, FO371/115883 VR1076/435G; Shuckburgh to Nicholls, 20 Dec. 1955, FO371/115885 VR1076/475G.
25. D.A. Schmidt, 'Israel Restates Her Peace Offers – Recapitulates 7-Point Plan of Concessions on Urging of State Department', *New York Times*, 20 Dec. 1955 (dateline Washington, 19 Dec.). Cf. 'Efforts to Peace – Reported Plan by Israel', *Manchester Guardian*, 20 Dec. 1955 (dateline Washington, 19 Dec.); Morris to Hadow, 29 Dec. 1955 (desp.1042/627/55), PRO FO371/121708 VR1071/3; Sharett, *Yoman Ishi* V: 1306 (8 Dec. 1955); Eveland, *Ropes of Sand*, 155–7.
26. Nicholls to FO, 20 Dec. 1955 (tgms.538), PRO FO371/115887 VR1076/525G; same to same, 21 Dec. 1955 (tgm.544), *loc. cit.* /527G.
27. 'Israel Plan for Middle East Settlement', *The Times*, 21 Dec. 1955 (dateline Jerusalem, 20 Dec.). Cf. 'Peace Plan – Washington Reports an Israel Offer', *Jewish Observer and Middle East Review*, 23 Dec. 1955, 5.
28. 'Israel, in White Paper, Compiles Peace Offer', *New York Herald Tribune*, 22 Dec. 1955 (AP 21 Dec.).
29. Arthur minute, 23 Dec. 1955, PRO FO371/115887 VR1076/527G.
30. Morris to Hadow, 29 Dec. 1955 (desp.1042/627/55), FO371/121708 VR1071/3.
31. Extract of speech, 2 Jan. 1956, in PRO FO371/121709 VR1071/48.
32. Eveland, *Ropes of Sand*, 157; Bar-On, *Gates of Gaza*, 105f.
33. Cf. Bar-On, *loc. cit.*; Shamir, 'Collapse', 100.
34. Makins to FO, 7 Dec. 1955 (tgm.2994), FO371/115886 VR1076/491G; Shuckburgh, *Descent*, 309 (8 Dec. 1955).
35. FO to UKEmb Washington, 8 Dec. 1955 (tgm.5828), FO371/115886 VR1076/491G.
36. Russell–Shiloah talk (8 Dec.), as reported in Dulles to USEmb Egypt (etc.), 10 Dec. 1955, *FRUS 1955–1957*, XIV, 841–3 (D446). Except where otherwise noted, quotations in this and the following paragraph are taken from this report.
37. Eshed, *Mossad*, 205. For discussions of Shiloah's report of this meeting, see: ibid., 204–6; Bar-On, *Gates of Gaza*, 97. For another report of Shiloah's reaction to the Negev triangles suggestion, see Dean, memorandum of conversation with Eban and Shiloah, 9 Dec. 1955, USNA NEA Lot 59, D518, Box 31.
38. Shiloah–Russell talk, reported in Dulles to USEmb Egypt (etc.), 10 Dec. 1955, *FRUS 1955–1957*, XIV, 843f. (D447).
39. Russell to Dulles, 10 Dec. 1955, USNA NEA Lot 59, D518, Box 31.
40. Arthur minute, Alpha, 13 Dec. 1955, PRO FO371/115887 VR1076/522G.
41. Shuckburgh minute, 13 Dec. 1955, *loc. cit.*
42. Sharett to Dulles, 12 Dec. 1955, *FRUS 1955–1957*, XIV, 844–8 (D448). Cf. Alteras, *Eisenhower and Israel*, 153. Adam Garfinkle (*Deep and Wide*, Ch. 4) refers to 'Sharett's brilliant and moving letter to Dulles' as 'surely one of the greatest masterpieces of Israeli diplomacy despite its failure to penetrate Dulles' mind.'
43. 'Sharett Gloomy on Mideast Peace', *New York Times*, 7 Dec. 1955, 1, 10; Tait, in

New York Herald Tribune, 8 Dec., quoted in Makins to FO, 8 Dec. 1955 (tgm.709 Saving), PRO FO371/115886 VR1076/503; Nicholls to FO, 8 Dec. 1955 (tgm.517), FO371/115886 VR1076/498; Sharett, *Yoman Ishi* V: 1305f. (8 Dec. 1955).
44. Dean, memorandum of conversation with Eban and Shiloah, 9 Dec. 1955, USNA NEA Lot 59, D518, Box 31.
45. Eban tgms. to IMFA, 17 and 20 Dec. 1955, quoted in Bar-On, *Gates of Gaza*, 97 and *Sha'arei Aza*, 123.
46. Macmillan to Dulles, in FO to UKEmb Washington, 25 Nov. 1955 (tgm.5599), FO371/115469 V1023/26G; *FRUS 1955–1957*, XIV, 820 n.2; Macmillan, *Tides of Fortune*, 654f.
47. Message to Nehru, in Commonwealth Relations Office to UK High Commissioner, India, 7 Dec. 1955 (tgm.2708), FO371/115886 VR1076/496.
48. 'Egypt Ready for Mediation – "We Are Seeking Peace"', *Manchester Guardian*, 26 Nov. 1955 (dateline United Nations, NY); 'Cairo Bars Talks with Egypt [*sic*]', *New York Times*, 26 Nov. 1955 (dateline United Nations, NY, 25 Nov.), 2; Trevelyan–Fawzi talk (24 Nov.), reported in Trevelyan to FO, 26 Nov. 1955 (tgm.1793), PRO FO371/115884 VR1076/448G; Love, *Suez*, 306.
49. For various fragments of evidence relating to Operation Chameleon, see: Trevelyan–Fawzi talk (24 Nov.), reported in Trevelyan to FO, 26 Nov. 1955 (tgm.1793), PRO FO371/115884 VR1076/448G; Sharett, *Yoman Ishi*, V: 1305, 1316, 1320; Harel, *Bitahon*, 394–7 (where the operation is code-named 'Mirage'); [CIA] message re: venue for talks with Johnston, ca.19 Dec. 1955, USNA NEA Lot 59, D518, Box 33; *FRUS 1955–1957*, XIV, 890; Touval, *Peace Brokers*, 116f.; Oren, *Origins*, 122.
50. Aronson, *From Sideshow to Center Stage*, 142. Cf. Copeland's suggestion that George Allen's visit to Cairo (above, 158) was undertaken primarily to 'check on Byroade's sanity' or 'to slip in quietly to substitute for a deranged Byroade'. *Game of Nations*, 165, 167.
51. James Cortada, who was stationed at the Cairo Embassy between 1955 and 1959, makes such allegations in his oral history interview, Georgetown University Library, 1 September 1992, 25f.
52. Touval, *Peace Brokers*, 123, 130; cf. above, xx.
53. Eveland, *Ropes of Sand*, 155, 157, 159–61; Shamir, 'Collapse', 95–8.
54. 'We were actively intervening – in ham-handed ways in some cases – all over the landscape.' Harrison M. Symmes, oral history interview, Georgetown University Library, 25 February 1989, 35f.
55. Streibert–Ben-Gurion talks (14–15 Dec.), reported in White to USSD, 16 Dec. 1955, *FRUS 1955–1957* XIV, 871–3 (D462), and in Nicholls to FO, 19 Dec. 1955 (desp.1076/128/55), PRO FO371/115887 VR1076/531G. Cf. *FRUS 1955–1957*, XIV, 884; Ben-Gurion interview with Agence France Presse, 25 Dec., discussed in Nicholls to Shuckburgh, 29 Dec. 1955 (desp.10320/702/55), PRO FO371/121722 VR1073/7.
56. Nicholls to Shuckburgh, 29 Dec. 1955 (desp.10320/702/55), PRO FO371/121722 VR1073/7.
57. For other signals picked up by the American and British Ambassadors in Tel Aviv, indicating that there was a good chance of winning Israeli co-operation by offering Gaza as a *quid pro quo* in future territorial bargaining, see: Nicholls to FO, 2 Dec. 1955 (tgm.509), FO371/115885 VR1076/474; Arthur minute, 5 Dec. 1955, *loc. cit.*; Shuckburgh–Russell talk, Paris, 15 Dec. 1955, FO371/115887 VR1076/524G; Nicholls to FO, 19 Dec. 1955 (desp.1076/128/55), FO371/115887 VR1076/531G; White to USSD, 24 Dec. 1955 (tgm.643), USNA 684A.86/12-2455 (section excised from *FRUS 1955–1957*, XIV, 887); ibid., 885; Rose

brief, Palestine Settlement, 7 Jan. 1956, PRO FO371/121724 VR1073/63G; Sharett views, discussed in Shuckburgh to Nicholls, 25 Feb. 1956, FO371/121709 VR1071/31G.

On the 1949 attempts to start up Israeli–Egyptian negotiations over the Gaza Strip, see: Caplan, *The Lausanne Conference, 1949*, 61–9, 78–86.

58. Crossman–Nasir talk (27 Dec. 1955), reported in Crossman to Sharett, 6 Jan. 1956, summarized in Lawson to USSD, 13 Jan. 1956 (tgm.703), USNA NEA Lot 59, D518, Box 33. Cf. Rafael to Sharett, 18 Jan. 1956, ISA 130.02/2454/2.
59. Trevelyan to FO, 30 Nov. 1955 (tgm.254 Saving), PRO FO371/115884 VR1076/462A; same to same, 28 Nov. 1955 (tgm.1813), FO371/115884 VR1076/456G; same to same, 29 Nov. 1955 (tgm.1820), FO371/115884 VR1076/462; O.M. Marashian, 'Peace Talk Echoes in Mideast', *Christian Science Monitor*, 29 Nov. 1955 (dateline Cairo); F. Abaza, 'The Compromise', *Al-Musawwar*, 1 Dec. 1955, transl. in PRO FO371/115886 VR1076/489; 'Nasser's Israel Policy – Eden's "Recognition" of Arab Rights', *Jewish Observer and Middle East Review*, 2 Dec. 1955, 6
60. Nicholls to Rose, 14 Dec. 1955 (desp.10320/681/55), PRO FO371/115911 VR1092/482; cf. Rose to Nicholls, 1 Feb. 1956, *loc. cit.* Interestingly, during the same period the American Chargé in Tel Aviv was also expressing doubts about Nasir's ultimate intentions. White to USSD, 21 Dec. 1955, *FRUS 1955–1957*, XIV, 880 (D465).
61. Trevelyan to Watson, 10 Feb. 1956 (desp.1072/44/56G), PRO FO371/121724 VR1073/72G.
62. Extract of Myerson speech, 18 Dec. 1955, quoted in Morris to Hadow, 6 Jan. 1956 (desp.1081/1/8/56), PRO FO371/121708 VR1071/10; Nicholls to FO, 19 Dec. 1955 (tgm.537), FO371/115887 VR1076/522G; E. Downton, 'Israel Rejects "Major" Border Adjustments', *Daily Telegraph*, 29 Nov. 1955; Arthur minute, Israel/Egyptian Relations, 9 Dec. 1955, FO371/115887 VR1076/508G; *FRUS 1955–1957*, XIV, 838f., 880f.
63. Millard to Rae, 2 Dec. 1955, PRO FO371/115886 VR1076/493; Shuckburgh, *Descent*, 307 (2 Dec. 1955).
64. H. Gilroy, 'Britain Assures Israel on Negev', *New York Times*, 12 Dec. 1955, 10 (dateline Jerusalem, 11 Dec.); H. Gilroy, 'Israelis Suspect Britain is Seeking a Negev Corridor', *New York Times*, 18 Dec. 1955, 1, 2 (dateline Jerusalem, 17 Dec.); Morris to Hadow, 21 Dec. 1955 (desp.1031/7/38/55), PRO FO371/115887 VR1076/530G; Nicholls–Sharett talk, reported in Nicholls to FO, 30 Dec. 1955 (tgm.557), FO371/115887 VR1076/531G.

Some attributed this accusation directly to Ben-Gurion's own 'obsessive belief' and 'delusions' about British ambitions for Negev air bases dating back to his meeting with Ernest Bevin in February 1947. See, e.g., Nicholls to Shuckburgh, 19 Dec. 1955 (desp.1031/157/55), FO371/115887 VR1076/531G; same to FO, 22 Dec. 1955 (tgm.545), FO371/115887 VR1076/529G; FO to UKEmb Tel Aviv, 30 Dec. 1955 (tgm.961), *loc. cit.*; Rose to Nicholls, 26 Jan. 1956, FO371/121708 VR1071/23; *FRUS 1955–1957*, XIV, 881; Dayan, *Avnei Derekh*, 174f.; Eshed, *Mossad*, 202; Kyle, *Suez*, 80.
65. Shuckburgh minute, Palestine Settlement (for meeting of British Ambassadors), 3 Jan. 1956, PRO FO371/121708 VR1071/4G.

CHAPTER XI

1. Makins–Russell talk, reported in Makins to FO, 28 Nov. 1955 (tgm.2896), PRO FO371/115884 VR1076/455G. For a similar, but less certain, British appraisal, see Shuckburgh minute, Palestine Settlement (for meeting of British Ambassadors), 3 Jan. 1956, PRO FO371/121708 VR1071/4G.
2. On complications surrounding the Baghdad Pact, see Shuckburgh, *Descent*, 298 (8 Nov. 1955); Dulles to Macmillan, 5 Dec. 1955, *FRUS 1955–1957*, XIV, 820f. (D434).
3. IsrEmb Washington to USSD, *aide-mémoire*, 6 Dec. 1955, *FRUS 1955–1957*, XIV, 823–5 (D436). Cf. Bar-On, *Gates of Gaza*, 142.
4. Sharett to Dulles, 12 Dec. 1955, *FRUS 1955–1957*, XIV, 844–8 (D448).
5. See, e.g., Ben-Gurion to Billotte, 9(8?) Dec. 1955, BGA; *FRUS 1955–1957*, XIV, 880, 884f., 892; ibid. XV, 5f., 10–12, 79f., 84, 126f., 137f., 146f., 173, 181, 221f., 240, 269, 292f., 301f., 310, 339f., 370; Tsur, *Prélude, passim*; Shimon Peres, *David's Sling: The Arming of Israel* (London: Weidenfeld & Nicolson, 1970), 38–65 (extract in Rabinovich and Reinharz, eds, *Israel in the Middle East*, 84–92; Sylvia Crosbie, *A Tacit Alliance: France and Israel from Suez to the Six Day War*, (Princeton: Princeton University Press, 1974), 56–63; Matti Golan, *The Road to Peace: A Biography of Shimon Peres*, transl. Akiva Ron (New York: Warner Books, 1989), 31–6; Glassman, *Arms*, 9–12; Levey, 'Israel's Pursuit', 194f.; Bar-On, *Gates of Gaza*, 156–62.
6. See, e.g., *FRUS 1955–1957*, XIV, 821f., 837, 848f., 851f., 868; Wilkins, memorandum of conversation (Dulles, Arab Ambassadors), 12 Dec. 1955, USNA 611.86A/12-1255.
7. Russell to Dulles, 10 Dec. 1955, USNA NEA Lot 59, D518, Box 31; Makins–Russell talk, reported in Makins to FO, 28 Nov. 1955 (tgm.2896), PRO FO371/115884 VR1076/455G. Cf. White to USSD, 30 Nov. 1955 (tgm.559), USNA 784A.5/11-3055; H. Gilroy, 'Israel Sees Smokescreen', *New York Times*, 30 Nov. 1955, 16 (dateline Jerusalem, 29 Nov.).
8. The quotation is from Bar-On, *Gates of Gaza*, 57. Other reports place Syrian deaths at 50, 54 or 73 (see sources in note 9).
9. Bar-On, *Gates of Gaza*, Ch. 5. On the raid and reactions to it, see: *FRUS 1955–1957*, XIV, 852–60, 866–8; 'Israelis Capture Syrian Positions in Galilee Fight', *New York Times*, 12 Dec. 1956, 1, 10; Tsur, *Prélude*, 286–8, 290f., 296f.; Eban, *Autobiography*, 198f.; Rafael, *Destination Peace*, 47f.; Sharon, *Warrior*, 123–7; Kyle, *Suez*, 80; Alteras, *Eisenhower and Israel*, 154, 161; Morris, *Israel's Border Wars*, 364–9.
10. Rafael, *Destination Peace*, 48. Cf. Eban speeches to UNSC, 16 and 22 Dec. 1955, Medzini, *Israel's Foreign Relations*, 325–34; Ben-Gurion, *Israel: A Personal History*, 455–7.
11. Nasir to Hammarskjöld, 15 Dec., text in Trevelyan to FO, 17 Dec. 1955 (tgm. 1938), PRO FO371/115911 VR1092/464; Trevelyan to FO, 17 Dec. 1955 (tgm. 1940), PRO FO371/115911 VR1092/465; 'West Sees Israel Tempted to Fight – Diplomats Fear a Decision to Test Cairo Warning May Precipitate New War', *New York Times*, 17 Dec. 1955 (dateline Cairo 16 Dec.); Ben-Gurion, Address to General Staff, 16 Dec. 1955, transl. in USNA NEA Lot 59, D518, Box 33; 'Ben-Gurion: "We Will Not Be Defeated"', *Jewish Observer and Middle East Review*, 23 Dec. 1955, 5; *FRUS 1955–1957*, XIV, 879f., 883; ibid. XV, 103; Love, *Suez*, 114–6, 308; Neff, *Warriors at Suez*, 119f.; Bar-On, *Gates of Gaza*, 65.
12. Bergus, NEA Staff Study, 19 Dec. 1955, USNA NEA Lot 59, D518, Box 33. Bar-On suggests that only the third of these formed part of the IDF rationale for the attack. Bar-On, *Gates of Gaza*, 64.

13. Cole–Burns talk, reported in Cole (Jerusalem) to USSD, 14 Dec. 1955, USNA 674.84A/12–1455 (cf. excised version, *FRUS 1955–1957*, XIV, 859f. (D456)); Wikeley–Burns talk, reported in Wikeley (Jerusalem) to FO, 14 Dec. 1955 (tgm. 467), PRO FO371/115849 VR1072/319; Burns, *Between Arab and Israeli*, 107f.; Neff, *Warriors at Suez*, 120.
14. Shuckburgh note, 13 Dec. 1955, PRO FO371/115887 VR1076/522G; Shuckburgh note, 14 Dec. 1955, FO371/115911 VR1092/468. Cf. Copeland's interpretation of the Gaza raid as an earlier example of 'the Prod', or provocation, tactic. *Game Player*, 199.
15. Sharett wrote mockingly in his diary: 'Ben-Gurion the Defense Minister consulted with Ben-Gurion the (Acting – during Sharett's absence in America) Foreign Minister and received the green light from Ben-Gurion the Prime Minister.' *Yoman Ishi*, V: 1310 (16 Dec. 1955), quoted in Morris, *Israel's Border Wars*, 365.
16. Bar-On, *Gates of Gaza*, 62f.
17. Ben-Gurion to Eban, 19 Dec. 1955 (draft), BGA. Cf. Sharett, *Yoman Ishi*, V: 1314 (25 Dec. 1955); *Autobiography*, 198f.; Ben-Gurion, *Israel: A Personal History*, 454f., 460; *FRUS 1955–1957*, XIV, 882f.; Morris, *Israel's Border Wars*, 367f.
18. Nicholls–Eytan talk (18 Dec.), reported in Nicholls to Rose, 19 Dec. 1955 (desp.10310/109/55), PRO FO371/115911 VR1092/483. Cf. *FRUS 1955–1957*, XIV, 882f.; ibid. XV, 6, 19; Bar-On, *Gates of Gaza*, 59–61.
19. Sharon, *Warrior*, 126f. Cf. Bar-On, *Sha'arei Aza*, 78 and 437 n.15; Morris, *Israel's Border Wars*, 366, 368.
20. Conversation of 13 Dec., reported in Eban to IMFA, 29 Dec. 1955, ISA 130.02/2456/3, quoted in Alteras, *Eisenhower and Israel*, 154; same to same, 13 Dec. 1955 (tgm.589/235), 130.02/2455/8, quoted in Bar-On, *Gates of Gaza*, 352 n.19. Cf. Alteras, *Eisenhower and Israel*, 161; Tsur, *Prélude*, 289; Sharett, *Yoman Ishi*, V: 1314f. (25 Dec. 1955); Eban, *Autobiography*, 198f.; Rafael, *Destination Peace*, 47f.; Eshed, *Mossad*, 208; 'Sharett Back in Israel', *New York Times*, 20 Dec. 1955 (dateline Lydda, 19 Dec.); *FRUS 1955–1957*, XIV, 882f.; Nicholls to Shuckburgh, 29 Dec. 1955 (desp.10320/702/55), PRO FO371/121722 VR1073/7; Herzog, *A People that Dwells Alone*, 241; Bar-On, *Gates of Gaza*, 58f., 61; Morris, *Israel's Border Wars*, 368.
21. Bar-On, *Gates of Gaza*, 139–41. Cf. Gazit, 'Israeli Military Procurement', 91.
22. Bar-On, *Gates of Gaza*, 142; Bergus, memorandum of conversation (Eban, Allen, Meroz), 13 Dec. 1955, *FRUS 1955–1957*, XIV, 856f. (D454); Dulles to Sharett, 29 Dec. 1955, ibid., 889 (D471).
23. Bergus, NEA Staff Study, 19 Dec. 1955, USNA NEA Lot 59, D518, Box 33.
24. Shuckburgh note, 13 Dec. 1955, PRO FO371/115887 VR1076/522G; Kirkpatrick note, 14 Dec. 1955, FO371/115911 VR1092/468; Shuckburgh minute, 14 Dec. 1955, *loc. cit.*; Shuckburgh to Nicholls, 20 Dec. 1955, FO371/115885 VR1076/475G; Elath–Lloyd talk, reported in Lloyd to Nicholls, 19 Jan. 1956 (desp.14), FO371/121722 VR1073/18; Eshed, *Mossad*, 208.
25 Bar-On, *Gates of Gaza*, 65f., 159f.; Levey, 'Israel's Pursuit', 195f.; Morris, *Israel's Border Wars*, 368.
26. Shuckburgh note (16 Dec.) of talk with Russell, Paris, 15 Dec. 1955, PRO FO371/115887 VR1076/524G; Bergus, NEA Staff Study, 19 Dec. 1955, USNA NEA Lot 59, D518, Box 33.
27. Eytan lecture, Tel Aviv Commercial and Industrial Club, 27 Jan. 1956, reported in *Ha-Boqer*, 29 Jan. 1956, transl. in PRO FO371/121724 VR1073/52. For the text of UNSC resolution 111 (1956), see *United Nations Resolutions*, I: 137f.; cf. Ben-Gurion, *Israel: A Personal History*, 457.
28. See, e.g., Ben-Gurion's Knesset speech, 2 Jan. 1956, Ben-Gurion, *Israel: A*

Personal History, 458–65; Ben-Gurion, *My Talks*, 271–4; Rafael, *Destination Peace*, 48. Cf. Yussef Haykal statement, 4 Jan. 1956, PRO FO371/121708 VR1071/9.
29. UN official Alex Ladas, quoted in Neff, *Warriors at Suez*, 120.
30. Bar-On, *Gates of Gaza*, 140.
31. Shuckburgh note (16 Dec.) of talk with Russell, Paris, 15 Dec. 1955, PRO FO371/115887 VR1076/524G; Bergus, NEA Staff Study, 19 Dec. 1955, USNA NEA Lot 59, D518, Box 33.
32. Message to Sharett, 23 Dec. 1955, quoted in *FRUS 1955–1957*, XIV, 890 n.2. Cf. Sharett, *Yoman Ishi*, V: 1306 (8 Dec. 1955); Touval, *Peace Brokers*, 123.
33. Memorandum of conversation (Dulles, Allen, Eban, Shiloah), 25 Jan. 1956, *FRUS 1955–1957*, XV, 74–6 (D38).
34. Sharett to Dulles, 16 Jan. 1956, *FRUS 1955–1957*, XV, 26f. (D19); cf. Alteras, *Eisenhower and Israel*, 174.
35. E.g., Ben-Gurion and Sharett Knesset speeches, 2 Jan. 1956 and the immediate reactions of Radio Cairo and *Sawt al-Arab*. See: Ben-Gurion, *Israel: A Personal History*, 458–68; Daily Summary of Arabic Broadcasts #1857, 3 Jan. 1956, ISA 43/gimmel-5570/4120; monitoring report of *Sawt al-Arab*, 3 Jan. 1956, 43/gimmel-5569/4115.
36. Sharett message to Dulles, 30 Dec. 1955, quoted in *FRUS 1955–1957*, XIV, 890 n.3.
37. Russell, memorandum of conversation (Dulles, Eban, Shiloah), 30 Dec. 1955, *FRUS 1955–1957*, XIV, 891 (D472).
38. Dulles to Anderson, 28 Jan. 1956, *FRUS 1955–1957*, XV, 91f. (D47).
39. Merchant, memorandum of conversation (Dulles, Pearson, Heeney), 28 March 1956, *FRUS 1955–1957*, XV, 426 (D227).
40. Bar-On, *Gates of Gaza*, 140. In late February 1956, the British Foreign Secretary was likewise 'on record as saying he considers there is still a rough balance, even though this may be altered in the near future'. Shuckburgh to Jebb, 29 Feb. 1956, PRO FO371/121755 VR1075/17.

   For earlier American assessments of Israel's overall military superiority in the region, see Byroade to Dulles, 3 June 1954, *FRUS 1952–1954*, IX/1, 1572 (D830); Dulles remarks to Eban, reported in Dulles to USEmb Israel, 4 Aug. 1954, ibid., 1601 D851); Dulles remarks to Sharett, Oct. 1955, quoted in Alteras, *Eisenhower and Israel*, 143.
41. Harel, *Bitahon*, 395f.; Ben-Gurion, address to General Staff, 16 Dec. 1955, transmitted by Harel to Allen Dulles, 11 Jan. 1956, USNA NEA Lot 59, D518, Box 33; Ben-Gurion diary, 16 Jan. 1956, BGA; *FRUS 1955–1957*, XIV, 883f. Cf. ibid. XV, 13f., 255f.; Lawson-Goldmann talk, 28 Jan. 1956, encl. in Lawson to USSD, 1 Feb. 1956 (desp.477), USNA NEA Lot 59, D518, Box 33; Nicholls to FO, 7 Mar. 1956 (tgm.99), PRO FO371/121725 VR1073/92; same to same, 19 March 1956 (tgm.4 Saving), FO371/121725 VR1073/111; Ben-Gurion, *My Talks*, 316.
42. In fact, British anger over Nasir's campaign against the Baghdad Pact resulted in withholding of delivery of some 60 Centurion tanks purchased from the UK following the signing of the Suez agreement. See Burns, *Economic Aid*, 30.
43. Lawson's talk with Ben-Gurion and Sharett (9 Jan.), reported in Lawson to USSD, 10 Jan. 1956, *FRUS 1955–1957*, XV, 16–9 (D13). See also Elath–Lloyd talk, reported in Lloyd to Nicholls, 19 Jan. 1956 (desp.14), PRO FO371/121722 VR1073/18.
44. Sharett to Dulles, 16 Jan. 1956, *FRUS 1955–1957*, XV, 26f. (D19). Cf. Bar-On, *Gates of Gaza*, 143.
45. Lawson–Sharett talk (24 Jan.), reported in Lawson to Dulles, 24 Jan. 1956, *FRUS 1955–1957*, XV, 72–4 (D37). Cf. memorandum of conversation (Dulles, Allen,

Eban, Shiloah), 25 Jan. 1956, ibid., 74–6 (D38).
46. Anderson's minutes of meeting with Ben-Gurion, *et al.*, 09h15, 23 Jan. 1956, USNA NEA Lot 59, D518, Box 34.
47. Sharett remarks, quoted in Anderson to USSD, 24 Jan. 1956, *FRUS 1955–1957*, XV, 59 (D31).
48. Anderson to USSD, 24 Jan. 1956, *FRUS 1955–1957*, XV, 65 (D33).
49. Meeting of 11h00, 24 Jan. 1956, in Anderson to USSD, 25 Jan. 1956, *FRUS 1955–1957*, XV, 70 (D35); also minutes in USNA NEA Lot 59, D518, Box 34. Cf. Ben-Gurion, *My Talks*, 292.
50. Anderson to USSD, 27 Jan. 1956, *FRUS 1955–1957*, XV, 81 (D41).
51. Dulles to Anderson, 26 Jan. 1956, *FRUS 1955–1957*, XV, 77 (D39).
52. Meeting of 27 Jan., reported in Anderson to USSD, 28 Jan. 1956, *FRUS 1955–1957*, XV, 88–91 (D46).
53. Dulles to Anderson, 27 Jan. 1956, *FRUS 1955–1957*, XV, 82f. (D42).
54. Ben-Gurion to Eisenhower, 14 Feb. 1956, *FRUS 1955–1957*, XV, 185–7 (D103); also in Ben-Gurion, *My Talks*, 309–11. Cf. Neff, *Warriors at Suez*, 168; Rafael, *Destination Peace*, 51.
55. Lawson to USSD, 29 Feb. 1956, *FRUS 1955–1957*, XV, 257–60 (D140); same to same, 1 Mar. 1956, ibid., 269–72 (D147); Heikal, *Milaffat*, 787; Kyle, *Suez*, 98.
56. Russell, memorandum of conversation with Eban and Shiloah, 9 Feb. 1956, *FRUS 1955–1957*, XV, 158f. (D86).
57. Wilkins, memorandum of conversation (Dulles, Eban, Shiloah), 10 Feb. 1956, *FRUS 1955–1957*, XV, 163–6 (D90).
58. Unsigned draft memorandum (probably by Robert Anderson), Peace in the Middle East, 10 Feb. 1956, USNA NEA Lot 59, D518, Box 33; A. Dulles to Hoover, 20 Feb. 1956, *FRUS 1955–1957*, XV, 193f. (D106); SNIE: Critical Aspects of the Arab–Israel Situation, 28 Feb. 1956, ibid., 249f. (D137); Neff, *Warriors at Suez*, 168.
59. Russell to Dulles, 20 Feb. 1956, *FRUS 1955–1957*, XV, 189 (D105); Russell, memorandum of conversation (Eban, Shiloah, Hoover, Murphy), 20 Feb. 1956, ibid., 184 (D103).
60. Rountree, memorandum of conversation (Dulles, Hammarskjöld, Wilcox), 29 Feb. 1956, USNA NEA Lot 59, D518, Box 33. Cf. *FRUS 1955–1957*, XV, 275f., 278, 280, 282; Kyle, *Suez*, 98. For American–Jewish and party pressure on Dulles at this time, see Bar-On, *Gates of Gaza*, 144–6.
61. Eisenhower to Ben-Gurion, 27 Feb. 1956, *FRUS 1955–1957*, XV, 242 (D132); Hoover telephone conversation with Eisenhower (29 Feb.), reported in Hoover to Dulles, 1 Mar. 1956, ibid., 260f. (D141). Cf. ibid., 277–9; Ben-Gurion, *My Talks*, 314f.; Rafael, *Destination Peace*, 51; Neff, *Warriors at Suez*, 168f.; Shamir, 'Collapse', 94.
62. Talk with Nasir and Zakaria Muhi al-Din (21 Feb.), reported in Cairo CIA message to Washington, 22 Feb. 1956, *FRUS 1955–1957*, XV, 203f. (D111). Cf. Cairo CIA to A. Dulles, 22 Feb. 1956, ibid., 209 (D114); Aronson, *From Sideshow to Center Stage*, 171.
63. Byroade to Hoover, 22 Feb. 1956, *FRUS 1955–1957*, XV, 207–9 (D113); Byroade to Dulles, 23 Feb. 1956, ibid., 210–12 (D115). Cf. Trevelyan to FO, 22 Feb. 1956 (tgms.344, 345), PRO FO371/121724 VR1073/69, /69A; Byroade to USSD, 24 Feb. 1956, *FRUS 1955–1957*, XV, 236 (D127).
64. Unsigned *aide-mémoire*, conversation with Eban, 15 Feb. 1956, USNA NEA Lot 59, D518, Box 33. See also Russell, memorandum of conversation (Eban, Shiloah, Hoover, Murphy), 20 Feb. 1956, *FRUS 1955–1957*, XV, 183 (D103).
65. Russell to Dulles, 23 Feb. 1956, *FRUS 1955–1957*, XV, 213–21 (D116); cf. Shamir, 'Collapse', 94.

66. Meeting of 9 March 1956, Ben-Gurion, *My Talks*, 312–25; Anderson's report of the meeting in *FRUS 1955–1957*, XV, 333–6 (D181); Rafael, *Destination Peace*, 51f.
67. See also 283–9, below.
68. Hoover to Dulles (memorandum of conversation with Eisenhower), 16 March 1956, *FRUS 1955–1957*, XV, 371 (D200) (emphasis added, N.C.); Alteras, *Eisenhower and Israel*, 176f., 184. Bar-On (*Gates of Gaza*, 138f.) lists four reasons why 'the main thrust of (Israeli) political efforts (for arms procurement) was directed at the US government'.
69. See, e.g., Peres, *David's Sling*, 38, 60–65, 87f.; Michael Oren, 'Canada, the Great Powers and the Middle Eastern Arms Race, 1950–1956', *International History Review* 12 (1990), 291–9; Crosbie, *Tacit Alliance*, 63–78; Golan, *The Road to Peace*, 36; Bar-On, *Gates of Gaza*, Chs. 10–11; Alteras, *Eisenhower and Israel*, 176–8, 184; Levey, 'Israel's Pursuit', 196–204.
70. Bar-On, *Gates of Gaza*, 174.
71. Morris, *Israel's Border Wars*, 426.
72. Shamir, 'Collapse', 86.

CHAPTER XII

1. Bar-On, *Gates of Gaza*, 97, 99, 104f. Bar-On's original Hebrew '*halkha ve-nirqema ... yozma ameriqanit hadasha*' (*Sha'arei Aza*, 123) should be translated: 'a new American initiative was being *devised* (lit., embroidered)', but the phrasing has been understated in the English version (*Gates of Gaza*, 97) as '... were *formulating* a new American initiative'.
2. Touval, *Peace Brokers*, 123f.; Miles Copeland, 'Nasser's Secret Diplomacy with Israel', *The Times*, 24 June 1971, 14.
3. Oren, *Origins*, 121f. Cf. Hoover to Russell, 28 Oct. 1955 (reporting information dated 26 Oct., 'received from Cairo, from a sensitive source'), *FRUS 1955–1957*, XIV, 645 and USNA NEA Lot 59, D518, Box 34. Lucas (*Divided We Stand*, 78, 87f.) refers to the Anderson mission as Operation 'Beta', rather than Gamma.
4. Hoover to Dulles (Paris), 25 Oct. 1955 (tgm.TEDUL12), USNA 684A.86/10-2555 (cf. *FRUS 1955–1957*, XIV, 675 n.2); Hoover to Dulles (Geneva), 29 Oct. 1955, *FRUS 1955–1957*, XIV, 674f. (D366); Aronson, *From Sideshow to Center Stage*, 157f.
5. Hoover to Dulles (Geneva), 29 Oct. 1955, *FRUS 1955–1957*, XIV, 677–9 (D368); A. Dulles to J.F. Dulles, 29 Oct. 1955, ibid., 679f. (D369).
6. Arthur minute, Palestine Settlement, 4 Nov. 1955, FO371/115880 VR1076/331G.
7. Bergus, NEA Staff Study, 19 Dec., fwd. Allen to Hoover, 20 Dec. 1955, USNA NEA Lot 59, D518, Box 33. On continuing concern over the possibility of a preemptive Israeli attack on Egypt, see Ahmad Hussein report of talk with Kermit Roosevelt, 22 Oct. 1955, in Heikal, *Milaffat*, 778 (D115); ibid., 785, 787.
8. Trevelyan to FO, 31 Dec. 1955 (tgm.2031), PRO FO371/121708 VR1071/1G. Cf. Shamir, 'Collapse', 82f.
9. See, e.g., Shuckburgh, *Descent*, 320, 323, 338; *FRUS 1955–1957*, XV, 223f.; Burns, *Economic Aid*, 63; Shamir, 'Collapse', 98; Bar-On, *Sha'arei Aza*, 454 n.38.
10. Hoover–Eisenhower conversation, 9 Nov. 1955, *FRUS 1955–1957*, XIV, 725 (D393). Cf. ibid., 810; ibid. XV, 23; Hoover to Dulles (Paris), 25 Oct. 1955 (tgm. TEDUL12), USNA 684A.86/10-2555; Neff, *Warriors at Suez*, 130; Eisenhower diary (11 Jan.1956), quoted in Burns, *Economic Aid*, 59; Muhammad Abd el-Wahab Sayed-Ahmed, *Nasser and American Foreign Policy, 1952–1956* (London: LAAM, 1989), 188.

11. Hoover to Russell (Athens), 1 Feb. 1956, *FRUS 1955–1957*, XV, 121 (D63).
12. *FRUS 1955–1957*, XIV, 888f.; ibid. XV, 9f., 15f., 20–4; Harel, *Bitahon*, 395; Rose brief, Palestine Settlement, 7 Jan. 1956, PRO FO371/121724 VR1073/63G; Ben-Gurion, *My Talks*, 275; Neff, *Warriors at Suez*, 130–5; Sayed-Ahmed, *Nasser*, 115; Burns, *Economic Aid*, 59; Shamir, 'Collapse', 98; Oren, *Origins*, 121–5.
13. For some of the British documentation on the Washington meetings and their follow-up, see: PRO FO371/118861 JE1053/1G; FO371/121724 VR1073/56G, /63G; FO371/121725 VR1073/82G; Shuckburgh, *Descent*, 320f. For similar American documentation, see: USNA NEA Lot 59, D518, Boxes 32 and 33; *FRUS 1955–1957*, XV, 101–12, 121, 125f., 131, 187–9, 399.
14. On the Tripartite Declaration and plans for joint action, see documentation in PRO FO371/121708 VR1071/22G; FO371/121722 VR1073/18; FO371/121723 VR1073/45G, /46; FO371/121725 VR1073/94; *FRUS 1955–1957*, XV, 102f., 263–5, 293; Shuckburgh, *Descent*, 346 (13 Mar. 1956).
15. Anglo–American Discussions: Text of Joint Statement, 1 Feb. 1956, *DSB*, 13 Feb. 1956, 233.
16. For documentation, see: PRO FO371/121708 VR1071/22G; FO371/121723 VR1073/29; FO371/121724 VR1073/53G, /55, /63G; USNA NEA Lot 59, D518, Box 33; *FRUS 1955–1957*, XV, 110f., 121, 293f., 307–9, 370f., 381f.; Shuckburgh, *Descent*, 328f. (30 Jan. 1956).
17. Talk with Hammarskjöld, 8 Feb., reported in Gore Booth to FO, 9 Feb. 1956 (tgm.71), PRO FO371/121724 VR1073/55; Ali Sabri, quoted in Cairo (CIA) message to Washington, 8 Feb. 1956, *FRUS 1955–1957*, XV, 158 (D85); Heikal, *Milaffat*, 399, 786.
18. Shuckburgh (Washington) to Kirkpatrick, 14 Jan. 1956, extract in PRO FO371/121708 VR1071/19G. Cf. *FRUS 1955–1957*, XV, 37–41; Shamir, 'Collapse', 94.
19. Kyle, *Suez*, 90.
20. Memorandum of conversation (Dulles, Hoover, Eden, Lloyd, *et al.*), White House, 30 Jan. 1956, *FRUS 1955–1957*, XV, 107 (D54). Cf. Shuckburgh, *Descent*, 327–9 (29–30 Jan. 1956). On Gen. Sir Gerald Templer's visit and the subsequent rioting in Jordan, see: Glubb, *A Soldier*, 395–400; Eden, *Full Circle*, 343f.; Oren, 'Winter of Discontent', 176–8; Burns, *Economic Aid*, 63f.; Kyle, *Suez*, 89–92; Satloff, *From Abdullah to Hussein*, 116–25.
21. [?Rose], Brief for Mr Shuckburgh for Official Talks with the Americans, 7 Jan. 1956, PRO FO371/118861 JE1053/1.
22. See, e.g., Spiegel, *The Other Arab–Israeli Conflict*, 60f., 64f.; Aronson, *From Sideshow to Center Stage*, 116–19, 163f.
23. Eisenhower diary, 10 Jan. 1956, quoted in Kyle, *Suez*, 91.
24. Russell, talking brief, US–UK Interests and Objectives in Middle East, in Light of Threat Posed by Current Soviet Strategy in the Area, 11 Jan. 1956, USNA NEA Lot 59, D518, Box 32.
25. Shuckburgh memorandum, 'The Interests of the UK and US in the Middle East', 19 Jan. 1956, PRO FO371/121270 V1075/5G. The two powers were clearly in agreement 'that the dispute between the Arab States and Israel constitute[d] the greatest of all the dangers to the Middle East', but were also in definite disagreement over the nature of Saudi Arabia's 'aims and the importance of the Saudi threat'.
26. Neff, *Warriors at Suez*, 153; Burns, *Economic Aid*, 64f.; Aronson, *From Sideshow to Center Stage*, 164f.; Kyle, *Suez*, 96.
27. All the available primary sources suggest that Anderson did *not* begin his mission in December 1955, as suggested by Touval (*Peace Brokers*, 123) and Heikal (*Cutting the Lion's Tail*, 105), but in January 1956.

28. White House meeting (Eisenhower, Hoover, Dillon, Anderson), 5 May 1955, discussed in Alteras, *Eisenhower and Israel*, 130.
29. Dulles, memorandum of conversation (Eisenhower, Anderson), 11 Jan. 1956, *FRUS 1955–1957*, XV, 20–2 (D14). Cf. Eisenhower diary, 11 Jan. 1956, ibid., 23; Burns, *Economic Aid*, 60f.; Neff, *Warriors at Suez*, 130–4; Sayed-Ahmed, *Nasser*, 118; Touval, *Peace Brokers*, 123, 131.
30. Touval, *Peace Brokers*, 123.
31. See, in particular, four memoranda prepared by senior IMFA official Pinhas Eliav on 18 and 19 Jan. 1956, in ISA 130.02/2454/2: Nasir's Claims and Tactics in the area of Foreign Policy; Talks and Contacts to Examine the Chances of a Settlement between Israel and Egypt, 1949–1955; Proposals for Conducting the First Phase; Summary and Lessons of the Contacts and Negotiations with Egypt, 1949–1955. Cf. Rafael, *Destination Peace*, 49. Eliav was not informed by his superior of the reasons for these research papers (conversation with author, June 1993).
32. Eban, *Personal Witness*, 246.
33. Russell, memorandum of conversation (Dulles, Eban, Shiloah), 30 Dec. 1955, *FRUS 1955–1957*, XIV, 890 (D472).
34. *Loc. cit.* Cf. Bar-On's assessment (*Gates of Gaza*, 97) that Operation Chameleon/Gamma was, from the start, aimed primarily at getting the parties to meet.
35. Anderson to USSD, 21 Jan. 1956, *FRUS 1955–1957*, XV, 47 (D26).
36. Ben-Gurion diary, 15 Jan. 1956, BGA. Cf. Alteras, *Eisenhower and Israel*, 166f.
37. Rafael–White talk (4 Jan.), reported in Lawson to USSD, 5 Jan. 1956, *FRUS 1955–1957*, XV, 12f. (D8).
38. Herzog–White talk (15 Jan.), reported in Lawson to USSD, 16 Jan. 1956, *FRUS 1955–1957*, XV, 28 (D20).
39. Herzog–White talk (15 Jan.), reported in Lawson to USSD, 16 Jan. 1956, *FRUS 1955–1957*, XV, 28 (D20).
40. Meeting of 17 Jan., reported in Anderson to USSD, 19 Jan. 1956, *FRUS 1955–1957*, XV, 28–36 (D21).
41. *FRUS 1955–1957*, XV, 34f.
42. Kermit Roosevelt (who was present at the meeting) quoted in Neff, *Warriors at Suez*, 135f. and in Burns, *Economic Aid*, 61f.; Muhammad H. Heikal (who was not present, but who was Nasir's friend and confidant) in *Milaffat*, 388 and *Cutting the Lion's Tail*, 105f. Cf. Kyle, *Suez*, 97 ('From the outset Anderson and Nasser never truly communicated ... .')
43. Meeting of 19 Jan., reported in Anderson to USSD, 21 Jan. 1956, *FRUS 1955–1957*, XV, 43–7 (D26).
44. Heikal, *Cutting the Lion's Tail*, 106.
45. Heikal, *Cairo Documents*, 56. Cf. Heikal, *Qissat as-Suways*, 101, quoted in Rashad Kamil, *Abd al-Nasir fi Tel Abib: al-Qissa al-Kamila li-Mashari' at-Tafawud ma' Israil (Abd al-Nasir in Tel Aviv: The Complete Story of Plans for Negotiating with Israel)* (Cairo: 1991), 80; Burns, *Economic Aid*, 62.
46. Meeting of 19 Jan., reported in Anderson to USSD, 21 Jan. 1956, *FRUS 1955–1957*, XV, 43–7 (D26).
47. Meeting of 21 Jan. 1956, discussed in *FRUS 1955–1957*, XV, 46f., n.5.
48. Meeting of 21 Jan., reported in Anderson to USSD, 22 Jan. 1956, *FRUS 1955–1957*, XV, 47–50 (D27). Quotations in this and the following paragraph are taken from this report.
49. *FRUS 1955–1957*, XV, 49.
50. Heikal, *Milaffat*, 392; Kamil, *Abd al-Nasir fi Tel Abib*, 82.
51. See: *FRUS 1955–1957*, XV, 51, 56–8, 67, 90, 119; Ben-Gurion, *My Talks*, 298; Heikal, *Cutting the Lion's Tail*, 107, 249–51.
52. Shuckburgh, *Descent*, 323 (20 Jan. 1956).

53. Dulles to Anderson, 19 Jan. 1956, *FRUS 1955–1957*, XV, 36f. (D22). Cf. ibid., 35f., 51, 67; Kyle, *Suez*, 97 ('The main trouble was that they were working to completely different timetables.').
54. On the resumption of Johnston's activities in pursuit of Arab agreement on the plan during February and March 1956, see: *FRUS 1955–1957*, XV, 140f., 151f., 161f., 169, 179f., 182, 220f., 224f., 234f., 244–6, 254f., 272f., 286f., 289, 295f., 311, 332, 338f., 347f., 401f., 429f.; Troxel memorandum, 29 Feb. 1956, USNA NEA Lot 59, D518, Box 33; Levant Dept. FO, briefs for Lloyd tour of Middle East, 25 Feb. 1956, PRO FO371/121725 VR1073/94.
55. Dulles to Anderson, 27 Jan. 1956, *FRUS 1955–1957*, XV, 82f. (D42); same to same, 28 Jan. 1956, ibid., 91f. (D47). On the growing concern about Israeli–Arab and specifically Israeli–Syrian tensions on the proposed resumption of water-diversion work, see: unsigned memorandum, Tripartite Courses of Action in Case of Threat or Outbreak of Israel–Arab Hostilities, 14 Feb. 1956, USNA NEA Lot 59, D518, Box 33; *FRUS 1955–1957*, XV, 8, 18f., 24f., 85f., 90, 95, 112f., 118f., 123f., 176–8, 226f.; Ben-Gurion, *My Talks*, 301f., 307, 316f.(n).
56. Message from A. Dulles, 29 Jan. 1956, *FRUS 1955–1957*, XV, 93 (D48); cf. Kyle, *Suez*, 97.
57. [CIA] message to Washington, 24 Jan. 1956, reporting talk with Nasir (22 Jan.), *FRUS 1955–1957* XV, 60–3 (D32). Cf. ibid., 80, 144; Kyle, *Suez*, 97.
58. On Dag Hammarskjöld's visit, Gen. Burns' efforts, and a further mediation attempt by a British MP at this time, see documentation in: PRO FO371/121709 VR1071/35; FO371/121722 files VR1073/9, /10, /11, /12; FO371/121724 VR1073/55; Wilkins–Morris conversation, 14 Feb. 1956, USNA NEA Lot 59, D518, Box 33; Hammarskjöld press conference, 27 Feb. 1956, *PPSG* II:692–4; Rountree, memorandum of conversation (Dulles, Wilcox, Hammarskjöld), 29 Feb. 1956, USNA NEA Lot 59, D518, Box 33; *FRUS 1955–1957*, XV, 7–9, 42f., 69, 132f., 237–9, 281–3. For other accounts, see: Burns, *Between Arab and Israeli*, Ch. 10; Ben-Gurion, *My Talks*, 287–9; Ben-Gurion, *Israel: A Personal History*, 474; Love, *Suez*, 119; Brian Urquhart, *Hammarskjöld* (New York/etc: Harper & Row, 1984), 137.
59. *FRUS 1955–1957*, XV, 56.
60. Anderson's minutes of meeting with Ben-Gurion, *et al.*, 09h15, 23 Jan. 1956, USNA NEA Lot 59, D518, Box 34. This is the most detailed of several available accounts. Quotations in this and the following paragraphs are taken from these minutes, except where otherwise noted. A shorter (18-paragraph) version of these minutes is given in *FRUS 1955–1957*, XV, 51–6 (D29). Ben-Gurion's version is reproduced in *My Talks*, 274–83.
61. Ben-Gurion, *My Talks*, 283.
62. Anderson to USSD, 24 Jan. 1956, *FRUS 1955–1957*, XV, 58f. (D31). On secret contacts between Israelis and representatives of a Palestinian refugee committee at this time, see: summary of consultation, 12 Jan. 1956, ISA 130.02/2445/2; Sharett, *Yoman Ishi*, V: 1330 (12 Jan.) and 1334f. (18 Jan. 1956). Cf. Arab Refugee Committee, petition to UNSG, 23 Jan. 1956, UNA DAG-1/2.1.4 Box 14 (File: UNCCP 1951–58).
63. Meeting between Ben-Gurion, Kollek and emissary, 17h00, 23 Jan. 1956; Ben-Gurion, *My Talks*, 283–6.
64. Anderson to USSD, 24 Jan. 1956, *FRUS 1955–1957*, XV, 63–6 (D33).
65. Meeting of 11h00, 24 Jan. 1956, (a) reported in Anderson to USSD, 25 Jan. 1956, *FRUS 1955–1957*, XV, 68–70 (D35); (b) minutes in USNA NEA Lot 59, D518, Box 34. Cf. Ben-Gurion's version, erroneously identified as an *afternoon* meeting, in *My Talks*, 290–3; Anderson to USSD, 27 Jan. 1956, *FRUS 1955–1957*, XV, 81 (D41).

NOTES TO PAGES 230–41   381

66. Cf. above, 201; Lawson–Goldmann talk, 28 Jan. 1956, encl. in Lawson to USSD, 1 Feb. 1956 (desp.477), USNA NEA Lot 59, D518, Box 33.
67. Meeting at 20h30 at Sharett's home, 24 Jan. 1956, reported in (a) *My Talks*, 287–90 (erroneously identified as 'morning' meeting); (b) Anderson's minutes, USNA NEA Lot 59, D518, Box 34.
68. Meeting at Sharett's home, 09h30, 25 Jan. 1956, reported in (a) *My Talks*, 293–5; (b) Anderson's minutes, USNA NEA Lot 59, D518, Box 34.
69. Anderson to USSD, 27 Jan. 1956, *FRUS 1955–1957*, XV, 81 (D41).
70. Dulles to Anderson, 24 Jan. 1956, *FRUS 1955–1957*, XV, 66f. (D34); same to same, 25 Jan. 1956, ibid., 71 (D36); same to same, 26 Jan. 1956, ibid., 77–9. (D39).
71. Message No.30 from Cairo (CIA) to Anderson, 26 Jan. 1956, quoted in *FRUS 1955–1957*, XV, 77 n.2.
72. Dulles to Anderson, 24 Jan. 1956, *FRUS 1955–1957*, XV, 66f. (D34)
73. Anderson to USSD, 27 Jan. 1956, *FRUS 1955–1957*, XV, 80–2 (D41).
74. Dulles to Anderson, 27 Jan. 1956, *FRUS 1955–1957*, XV, 82f. (D42).
75. Dulles to Anderson, 28 Jan. 1956, *FRUS 1955–1957*, XV, 92 (D47). For a similar appraisal, see message from A. Dulles, 29 Jan. 1956, ibid., 93f. (D48).
76. Meeting of 26 Jan., reported in Anderson to USSD, 28 Jan. 1956, *FRUS 1955–1957*, XV, 86–8 (D45).
77. Anderson minutes, meeting (Jerusalem), 16h30 31 Jan. 1956, USNA NEA Lot 59, D518, Box 34; Heikal, *Milaffat*, 389f.; Ben-Gurion, *My Talks*, 297f., 300. Cf. Eliav report, Promises and Comments on the Cairo Trials, fwd. Rafael to Sharett, Feb. 1956, ISA 130.02/2454/2.
78. Meeting of 27 Jan., reported in Anderson to USSD, 28 Jan. 1956, *FRUS 1955–1957*, XV, 88–91 (D46).
79. Anderson (Athens) to Dulles, 29 Jan. 1956, *FRUS 1955–1957*, XV, 95 (D49); Dulles to Anderson, 30 Jan. 1956, discussed in Editorial Note, ibid., 101 (D53).
80. Anderson minutes, meeting (Jerusalem), 16h30, 31 Jan. 1956, USNA NEA Lot 59, D518, Box 34. Except where otherwise indicated, quotations in this and the following paragraphs are taken from this 49-paragraph document. For two other accounts of this meeting, see (a) Anderson to USSD, 1 Feb. 1956, *FRUS 1955–1957*, XV, 122–4 (D64); (b) Ben-Gurion, *My Talks*, 296–308.
81. Rafael, *Destination Peace*, 51. Cf. Nasir's assurance given to the Americans that he was ordering a reduction of Egyptian propaganda against Israel. *FRUS 1955–1957*, XV, 67 n.4.
82. *FRUS 1955–1957*, XV, 123.
83. *Loc. cit.*
84. *FRUS 1955–1957*, XV, 123f.; Ben-Gurion, *My Talks*, 303f., 307.
85. *My Talks*, 304.
86. Talk with Hammarskjöld, 8 Feb., reported in Gore Booth to FO, 9 Feb. 1956 (tgm. 71), FO371/121724 VR1073/55; Rountree, memorandum of conversation (Dulles, Hammarskjöld, Wilcox), 29 Feb. 1956, USNA NEA Lot 59, D518, Box 33.
87. Anderson to USSD, 3 Feb. 1956, *FRUS 1955–1957*, XV, 133–5 (D72).
88. Russell (Cairo) to Dulles, 5 Feb. 1956, *FRUS 1955–1957*, XV, 143–5 (D78).
89. Nasser to Eisenhower, 6 Feb. 1956, USNA NEA Lot 59, D518, Box 33; text also in Cairo (CIA) message to Anderson, 4 Feb. 1956, *FRUS 1955–1957*, XV, 138f. (D75); Arabic translation given in Heikal, *Milaffat*, 780f. (D117). Cf. ibid., 391, 393; Burns, *Economic Aid*, 71.
90. Text in Cairo (CIA) message to Anderson, 4 Feb. 1956, *FRUS 1955–1957*, XV, 139f. (D75); also in Heikal, *Cutting the Lion's Tail*, 251f. Cf. Heikal, *Milaffat*, 392 and the Arabic translation given on 782f. (D118). On Ali Sabri's instructions, the statement was forwarded to Anderson rather than sent as an attachment to the

letter to President Eisenhower.
91. Heikal, *Milaffat*, 391–3. Cf. Kamil, *Abd al-Nasir fi Tel Abib*, 82.
92. Cairo [CIA] message to Washington, 7 [=6] Feb. 1956, *FRUS 1955–1957*, XV, 147f. (D80).
93. [CIA, Cairo] memorandum to Washington: The Problem of Tension between the Arab States and Israel: Obstacle to Settlement, 8 Feb. 1956, *FRUS 1955–1957*, XV, 152–6 (D84); meeting with Ali Sabri, reported in Cairo (CIA) message to Washington, 8 Feb. 1956, ibid., 157f. (D85).
94. Khrushchev statement to 20th Party Congress, 14 Feb. 1956, Ro'i, *From Encroachment*, 154–61 (D41). Cf. Shuckburgh, *Descent*, 333f. (12 Feb. 1956); Palestine Problem (brief for Lloyd tour of Middle East), 25 Feb. 1956, PRO FO371/121725 VR1073/94.
95. Meetings with Ali Sabri, 15 and 20 Feb., reported in Cairo [CIA] messages to Washington, 16 and 20 Feb. 1956, *FRUS 1955–1957*, XV, 173f. (D96) and 195f. (D107); text of agreed working document for second Anderson visit, in Cairo [CIA] message to Washington, 21 Feb. 1956, ibid., 198–202 (D109).
96. Byroade–Nasir talk (18 Feb.), reported in Byroade to USSD, 21 Feb. 1956, *FRUS 1955–1957*, XV, 197f. (D108). Cf. ibid., 202 n.3, 205f.
97. Talk with Nasir and Muhi al-Din (21 Feb.), reported in Cairo [CIA] message to Washington, 22 Feb. 1956, *FRUS 1955–1957*, XV, 207 (D112).
98. Unsigned *aide-mémoire*, conversation with Eban, 15 Feb. 1956, USNA NEA Lot 59, D518, Box 33.
99. Ben-Gurion to Eisenhower, 14 Feb. 1956, *FRUS 1955–1957*, XV, 185–7 (D103); also in Ben-Gurion, *My Talks*, 309–11. Cf. Neff, *Warriors at Suez*, 168; Rafael, *Destination Peace*, 51.

CHAPTER XIII

1. Unsigned *aide-mémoire*, conversation with Eban, 15 Feb. 1956, USNA NEA Lot 59, D518, Box 33. Eban advanced the same arguments in a talk with Acting Secretary Hoover several days later. See Russell, memorandum of conversation (Eban, Shiloah, Hoover, Murphy), 20 Feb. 1956, *FRUS 1955–1957*, XV, 183 (D103).
2. Unsigned draft memorandum, Peace in the Middle East, 10 Feb. 1956, USNA NEA Lot 59, D518, Box 33. Cf. Neff, *Warriors at Suez*, 168.
3. Byroade–Nasir talk (18 Feb.), reported in Byroade to USSD, 21 Feb. 1956, *FRUS 1955–1957*, XV, 196f. (D108). Cf. Cairo (CIA) message to Washington, no. 86, quoted in ibid., 203 n.5.
4. Russell to Dulles, 20 Feb. 1956, *FRUS 1955–1957*, XV, 189–93 (D105). Cf. Bar-On, *Gates of Gaza*, 108f.
5. Rountree, memorandum of conversation (Dulles, Hammarskjöld, Wilcox), 29 Feb. 1956, USNA NEA Lot 59, D518, Box 33.
6. Russell to Dulles, 20 Feb. 1956, *FRUS 1955–1957*, XV, 189 (D105). Cf. talk with Nasir and Muhi al-Din (21 Feb.), reported in Cairo (CIA) message to Washington, 22 Feb. 1956, ibid., 207 (D112).
7. Goldmann favoured the idea of an 'international condominium' over the Negev. IMFA Director-General Walter Eytan took special pains to denounce the idea. See: Lawson–Goldmann talk, 28 Jan. 1956, in Lawson to USSD, 1 Feb. 1956 (desp.477), USNA NEA Lot 59, D518, Box 33; Eytan lecture, Tel Aviv Commercial and Industrial Club, 27 Jan. 1956, reported in *Ha-Boqer*, 29 Jan. 1956, transl. in PRO FO371/121724 VR1073/52; Eytan speech, 'Israel Will On No Account Renounce Eilat', *Omer*, 1 Feb. 1956, *loc. cit.*; Shuckburgh to Nicholls, 25 Feb. 1956, FO371/121709 VR1071/31G.

8. See: Goldmann–Lawson talk (28 Jan.), reported in Lawson to USSD, 1 Feb. 1956 (desp.477), USNA NEA Lot 59, D518, Box 33; Russell, memorandum of conversation with Goldmann, 15 Feb. 1956, *loc. cit.*; Russell–Anderson talk, 17 Feb. 1956, *loc. cit.*; Goldmann to Ben-Gurion, 17 Feb. 1956, CZA Z6/1111; Sharett, *Yoman Ishi* V: 1362 (19 Feb. 1956); Russell, memorandum of telephone conversation with Goldmann, 21 Feb. 1956, USNA NEA Lot 59, D518, Box 33; Reading–Goldmann talk (21 March), reported in Reading to Lloyd, 22 March 1956, PRO FO371/121726 VR1073/126G; *FRUS 1955–1957*, XV, 298, 300.
9. Russell to Dulles, 20 Feb. 1956, *FRUS 1955–1957*, XV, 189–93 (D105).
10. Russell to Dulles, 23 Feb. 1956 (enclosing papers), *FRUS 1955–1957*, XV, 213–21 (D116). Francis Russell served as chairman of the committee.
11. Statement authorized by Nasir, 4 Feb. 1956 (Document 10).
12. This conclusion is based on the detailed reconstruction of events between December 1955 and March 1956 based largely on recently-released USNA documents, and would seem to contradict Touval's presentation which suggests that it had been hints of Nasir's prior agreement to a high-level meeting with Israelis in late 1955 which had helped to launch the Anderson mission, and that the Egyptian leader subsequently reneged on this 'agreement'. (See Touval, *Peace Brokers*, 124, 127, 128, 133.) At best, Nasir's CIA confidants had conveyed to Washington only the *hope* that they might convince Nasir to meet with the Israelis at some point, but that he persistently refused to agree to suggestions for direct meetings.
13. The analysis of the documentary evidence offered above makes it puzzling to read Michael Oren's remarks that, during February, '[r]esponsibility for the stalemate, in the Administration's opinion, fell on Israel because of its demands for direct talks and arms and its opposition to territorial concessions.' Oren, *Origins*, 124.
14. Russell, memorandum of conversation (Dulles, Makins), 23 Feb. 1956, *FRUS 1955–1957*, XV, 223 (D118).
15. Eisenhower to Ben-Gurion, 27 Feb. 1956, *FRUS 1955–1957*, XV, 242 (D132); Hoover telephone conversation with Eisenhower (29 Feb.), reported in Hoover to Dulles, 1 Mar. 1956, ibid., 260f. (D141). Cf. ibid., 277–9; Ben-Gurion, *My Talks*, 314f.; Rafael, *Destination Peace*, 51; Neff, *Warriors at Suez*, 168f.
16. Eisenhower to Nasir, 27 Feb. 1956, *FRUS 1955–1957*, XV, 243 (D133).
17. Burns, *Economic Aid*, 71.
18. For details of these incidents, see *FRUS 1955–1957*, XV, 290–3, 300f., 318f., 329 n.3.
19. On this pivotal episode, see, e.g.: Glubb, *A Soldier*, Ch. XXVI; Eden, *Full Circle*, 347–53; Anthony Nutting, *No End of a Lesson: The Story of Suez* (London: Constable, 1967), 17, 27, 29; Shuckburgh, *Descent*, 340, 343f. (1, 5 March 1956); *FRUS 1955–1957*, XV, 289; David Carlton, *Britain and the Suez Crisis* (Oxford/New York: Basil Blackwell, 1988), 28–30; Kyle, *Suez*, 93–6.
20. Shuckburgh, *Descent*, 338, 341f. (25 Feb., 3 March 1956); Nutting, *No End*, 28. FO briefs (25 Feb.) for Lloyd's tour are in PRO FO371/121725 VR1073/94.
21. Shuckburgh, *Descent*, 341f., 344 (3, 5 March 1956). For reports of Lloyd's talks with Nasir, see: Aldrich (London) to USSD, 2 March 1956 (tgm.3683), USNA 641.74/3–256; Burrows (Bahrain) to FO, 2 March 1956 (tgm.157), PRO FO371/121709 VR1071/34; Byroade to USSD, 4 March 1956, *FRUS 1955–1957*, XV, 287–9 (D157); Aldrich to USSD, 7 March 1956, ibid., 323f. (D175); Kyle, *Suez*, 93f.
22. *FRUS 1955–1957*, XV, 262f., 273–5, 277. On the Egyptian–Syrian–Saudi consultations of 6–11 March, see joint communiqué, 12 March, transl. text in Byroade to USSD, 13 March 1956 (tgm.1827), USNA 684A.86/3–1356; *FRUS 1955–1957*, XV, 262 n.4.

23. Meeting with Nasir, Zakaria Muhi al-Din and Ali Sabri (4 March), reported in Anderson to Dulles (Karachi), 4 March 1956 (message no. 106), USNA NEA Lot 59, D518, Box 34. Cf. the fuller version reported in same to same, 5 March 1956, *FRUS 1955–1957* XV, 295–300 (D162); ibid., 285f., 295.

    For British pressures on Eisenhower to join the Baghdad Pact and to cease the 'appeasement' of Nasir at this time, see: *FRUS 1955–1957*, XV, 293, 294 n.7, 299 n.6; Shuckburgh, *Descent*, 342f. (4 March 1956).
24. Meeting with Nasir, Zakaria Muhi al-Din and Ali Sabri, 5 March, reported in Anderson to Dulles (Karachi), 6 March 1956, *FRUS 1955–1957*, XV, 302–7 (D164); same to same, 6 March 1956, ibid., 310–14 (D168). Quotations in this and the following paragraphs are taken from these sources.
25. Cf. Ben-Gurion, *My Talks*, 314; Oren, *Origins*, 124. Selwyn Lloyd also was impressed at this time by Nasir's newly heightened concern for the refugee factor. See Burrows (Bahrain) to FO, 2 March 1956 (tgm.157), PRO FO371/121709 VR1071/34; Aldrich (London) to USSD, 7 March 1956, *FRUS 1955–1957*, XV, 323 (D175).
26. Watson memorandum, Egyptian Attitude towards a Possible Solution of the Palestine Refugee Problem, 11 July 1957, PRO FO371/128115 VR1072/55.
27. See also Anderson (Athens) to Hoover, 7 March 1956, *FRUS 1955–1957*, XV, 320–2 (D173); Byroade–Nasir talk (13 March), reported in Byroade to USSD, 14 March 1956, ibid., 360f. (D195).
28. Hoover to Anderson, 6 March 1956, *FRUS 1955–1957*, XV, 309f. (D167).
29. Ben-Gurion, *My Talks*, 312–25. Cf. Anderson's report of the meeting in *FRUS 1955–1957*, XV, 333–6 (D181); Rafael, *Destination Peace*, 51f. Mossad Chief Harel reports a private talk with Anderson prior to the meeting with Ben-Gurion and Sharett, during which the same topics were covered. Harel, *Bitahon*, 398.
30. Trevelyan to Shuckburgh, 8 March 1956, PRO FO371/121726 VR1073/118G. Cf. *FRUS 1955–1957*, XV, 350, 373, 375, 379, 389–92, 571; FO to Washington, 26 March 1956 (tgm.1745), FO371/121726 VR1073/127G; Makins to FO, 28 March 1956 (tgm.801), FO371/121726 VR1073/128G; Burns, *Economic Aid*, 72.
31. Kyle, *Suez*, 93.
32. Shuckburgh, *Descent*, 345 (8 March 1956). Cf. *FRUS 1955–1957*, XV, 366, 384; Burns, *Economic Aid*, 66; Hahn, *The United States*, 201; Kyle, *Suez*, 94–6.
33. Cf. Burns, *Economic Aid*, Chs 2–3; Hahn, *The United States*, 186–206; Kyle, *Suez*, 85 and Ch. 5.
34. Dulles (Karachi) to Hoover, 8 March 1956, *FRUS 1955–1957*, XV, 325f. (D176); Hoover to Dulles, 8 March 1956, quoted in ibid., 326 n. 2. Cf. NSC, 279th meeting, 8 March 1956, ibid., 329 (D178).
35. Eisenhower diary, 8 March 1956, ibid., 326f. (D177); cf. Burns, *Economic Aid*, 73–5.
36. Anderson–Eisenhower conversation, reported in Hoover to Dulles, 12 March 1956, *FRUS 1955–1957*, XV, 341 (D186).
37. Hoover remarks, in conversation with Eban et al., 15 March 1956, *FRUS 1955–1957*, XV, 369 (D199). Cf. ibid., 397.
38. See, e.g., Rountree and Burdett memoranda to Dulles, 23 May 1956, *FRUS 1955–1957*, XV, 658–67 (D360); Rountree to Hoover, 26 May 1956, ibid., 676f. (D368); ibid., 702. Plans for this trip seem to have been interrupted and dropped following Nasir's nationalization of the Suez Canal. In January 1957, President Eisenhower would again consider sending Anderson on a secret mission to Cairo. See United States, Department of State, *Foreign Relations of the United States: 1955–1957*, Vol. XVII: Arab–Israeli Dispute, 1957, ed. Nina J. Noring, (Washington: 1990), 40.
39. Eisenhower diary (13 March), conversation with Hoover and Anderson, 12 March 1956, *FRUS 1955–1957*, XV, 342f. (D187). Cf. ibid., 390, 417, 422, 425, 440f.,

464, 468f., 506; Neff, *Warriors at Suez*, 197f.; Burns, *Economic Aid*, 72; Carlton, *Anthony Eden*, 404f.; Heikal, *Milaffat*, 787; Aronson, *From Sideshow to Center Stage*, 167; Kyle, *Suez*, 99. On the Buraimi dispute, see ibid., 69f., 100.
40. Wilkins memorandum, 14 March 1956, *FRUS 1955–1957* XV, 352 (D192). Cf. ibid., 384, 407, 429–31; Hood (Washington) to Stevens (FO), 10 Dec. 1958 (desp. 10430/91/58G), PRO FO371/134298 VR10710/6G. For Keith Kyle's retrospective apportioning of blame between the two parties, see *Suez*, 98f.
41. Shuckburgh, *Descent*, 346 (12 March 1956). Cf. Nutting, *No End*, 18, 34f.; Kyle, *Suez*, 96, 99.
42. Nicholls–Lawson talk, reported in Lawson to USSD, 16 March 1956, *FRUS 1955–1957*, XV, 376 (D202).
43. On Hammarskjöld's forays into 'preventive diplomacy' during 1956, see: Nicholls to FO, 19 March 1956 (tgm.4 Saving), PRO FO371/121725 VR1073/111; Lawson to USSD, 20 March 1956, *FRUS 1955–1957*, XV, 380 (D205); ibid., 399; Burns, *Between Arab and Israeli*, 139–76; Leon Gordenker, *The U.N. Secretary-General and the Maintenance of Peace*, (New York/London: Columbia University Press, 1967), 185–97; Rosenne, 'Israel and the United Nations', 26f.; Urquhart, *Hammarskjöld*, Ch. 6; Neff, *Warriors*, 221–4; Bar-On, *Gates of Gaza*, Ch. 9; Pelcovits, *Long Armistice*, 109–17; Kyle, *Suez*, 106–9; Morris, *Israel's Border Wars*, 376f.
44. Dulles memorandum to Eisenhower, 28 March 1956, *FRUS 1955–1957*, XV, 419–21 (D223). On the shift in American policy away from Nasir during March and April, see: *FRUS 1955–1957*, XV, 352–7, 371, 387f., 405, 409–25, 431f.; Wilkins memorandum, Measures which this country might take to curtail Egypt's Exports of Cotton, 22 March 1956, USNA NEA Lot 59, D518, Box 39; Burns, *Economic Aid*, 66f., 76–80; Eveland, *Ropes of Sand*, 169f., 180, 192; Aronson, *From Sideshow to Center Stage*, 166–8; Shamir, 'Collapse', 99; Lucas, *Divided We Stand*, 110–14; Kyle, *Suez*, 99–101.
45. E.g., memorandum of conversation (Macmillan, Dulles, Aldrich, Murphy), London, 1 Aug. 1956, United States, Department of State, *Foreign Relations of the United States: 1955–1957*, Vol. XVI: Suez Crisis: July 26 – December 31, 1956, ed. Nina J. Noring, (Washington: 1990), 108f. (D46); Shamir, 'Collapse', 84.
46. On the British re-evaluation of their attitude towards Nasir at this time, see: Shuckburgh, *Descent*, 346, 348 (13, 16 March 1956); *FRUS 1955–1957*, XV, 384–7, 389–92; Shuckburgh to HM Representatives at Beirut, Baghdad, etc., 28 May 1956, PRO FO371/118862 JE1053/37G; Shamir, 'Collapse', 83 n.25; *Ropes of Sand*, 169f.; Burns, *Economic Aid*, 79f.; Aronson, *From Sideshow to Center Stage*, 168f.; Lucas, *Divided We Stand*, Chs 7, 9, 10; Kyle, *Suez*, 99, 101–3.
47. Copies of 'Nasser's Axis' can be found in ISA 43/gimmel-5571/4132; other memoranda and correspondence, esp. by Eliav and Ben-Horin, March–April 1956, in 130.20/2477/19; Divon to Sharett, 12 March 1956 ('Proposed Plan of Action required by the worsening of our situation in the Middle East'), 43/gimmel-5571/4132; Kollek (New York) to Divon, 12 April 1956, *loc. cit.*
48. Sharett–Lawson talk, reported in Lawson to USSD, 16 March 1956 (tgm.959), USNA NEA Lot 59, D518, Box 34. Cf. *FRUS 1955–1957*, XV, 375.
49. Shuckburgh, *Descent*, 348 (15 March 1956).
50. Heikal, *Milaffat*, 395–8, 404–6 (chapter entitled: 'The Race for Murder'), 791 (D124); Kyle, *Suez*, 99.
51. Trevelyan to Watson, 11 April 1956 (desp.1042/31/56), PRO FO371/118862 JE1053/24; same to same, 8 May, 1956, *loc. cit.* /31G.
52. See, e.g., *FRUS 1955–1957*, XV, 419; Watson to Shuckburgh, 11 April 1956, PRO FO371/118862 JE1053/19G; Watson to Trevelyan, 15 May, 1956, *loc. cit.* /31G; Shuckburgh to HM Representatives at Beirut, Baghdad etc., 28 May 1956, *loc.*

cit. /37G; Lucas, *Divided We Stand*, 99, 101f., 106f., 110–13.
53. See, e.g., Burns, *Economic Aid*, 63–7; Spiegel, *The Other Arab–Israeli Conflict*, 69.
54. See, e.g., *FRUS 1955–1957*, XV, 866–74; Burns, *Economic Aid*, 80–100; Spiegel, *The Other Arab–Israeli Conflict*, 69–71; Aronson, *From Sideshow to Center Stage*, 170–9; Lucas, *Divided We Stand*, Ch. 11.
55. Byroade report of Nasir speech, 26 July 1956, *FRUS 1955–1957*, XV, 906–8 (D511).
56. Rafael, *Destination Peace*, 53. Cf. Kollek, *For Jerusalem*, 116.
57. Shamir, 'Collapse', 100.
58. Eveland, *Ropes of Sand*, 161 n.
59. Cairo [CIA] message to Washington, 21 March 1956, *FRUS 1955–1957*, XV, 392f. (D211).
60. Quoted in Burns, *Economic Aid*, 59. Cf. ibid., 235 n. 92.
61. Byroade–Nasir talk (13 March), reported in Byroade to Dulles, 14 March 1956, *FRUS 1955–1957*, XV, 348–51 (D191). Quotations in this and the following paragraph are taken from this report. Cf. Trevelyan to Shuckburgh, 15 March 1956 (desp.1072/96/56G), PRO FO371/121726 VR1073/119G; *FRUS 1955–1957*, XV, 392–4; Love, *Suez*, 119.
62. For a slightly different summation of Egyptian motives for co-operating with America in general and Anderson in particular, see Touval, *Peace Brokers*, 119f., 131f.
63. Gerges, *The Superpowers and the Middle East*, 30.
64. Bar-On, *Gates of Gaza*, 113. Cf. Touval, *Peace Brokers*, 131; Gerges, *The Superpowers and the Middle East*, 39f.
65. Cairo [CIA] message to Washington, 21 March 1956, *FRUS 1955–1957*, XV, 392–4 (D211).
66. See, e.g., Cairo [CIA] message to Washington, 18 April 1956, *FRUS 1955–1957*, XV, 547 (D289); Byroade–Fawzi–Hussein talk (10 July), reported in Byroade to USSD, 11 July 1956, ibid., 807f. (D440).
67. Shamir, 'Collapse', 87f.
68. Shamir, 'Collapse', 90; cf. ibid., 80.
69. Touval, *Peace Brokers*, 132.
70. Russell, memorandum of conversation (Hoover, Murphy, Eban, Shiloah), 15 March 1956, *FRUS 1955–1957*, XV, 367 (D199). Cf. ibid., 406; Ben-Gurion, *My Talks*, 325;
71. Oren, *Origins*, 123.
72. Ben-Gurion to Eisenhower, 16 March 1956, *FRUS 1955–1957*, XV, 372–4 (D201); Rafael, *Destination Peace*, 52.
73. For a slightly different summation of Israeli motives for co-operating with Anderson, see Touval, *Peace Brokers*, 120f., 129, 131–3.
74. Bar-On, *Gates of Gaza*, 110.
75. Above, 217–18; Bar-On, *Gates of Gaza*, 110.
76. Rafael, *Destination Peace*, 51; Herzog, *A People*, 238; Bar-On, *Gates of Gaza*, 109–12.
77. Dulles to Lodge, 31 March 1956, quoted in Shamir, 'Collapse', 98f.
78. In a retrospective look at Alpha shortly after Israel's invasion of Sinai, a senior official at the Foreign Office concluded that the attempts had failed 'chiefly because the Egyptians could never be brought to the point of committing themselves to a path leading towards a settlement'. P.H. Laurence minute, Palestine Settlement, 9 Nov. 1956, PRO FO371/121711 VR1071/127G.
79. NEA memorandum, United States Policy in the Near East, 28 March 1956, *FRUS 1955–1957* XV, 410 (D222). Although certainly not 'soft' in their assessments of Nasir, most British officials were slower to reach such clear-cut conclusions about

Egypt's aggressive intentions towards Israel. See: Rose to Nicholls, 1 Feb. 1956, PRO FO371/115911 VR1092/482; Trevelyan to Watson, 10 Feb. 1956 (desp. 1072/44/56G), PRO FO371/121724 VR1073/72G.
80. *FRUS 1955–1957*, XV, 420. Excluded from this prohibition were Iraq and Saudi Arabia, which were not 'adjoining' to Israel.
81. See, e.g., Bar-On, *Gates of Gaza*, Chs 10–11.

CHAPTER XIV

1. Cf. Morris, *Israel's Border Wars*, 173f. For a popular discussion of Biblical and Quranic inspirations and justifications of Israeli and Arab attitudes, see David K. Shipler, *Arab and Jew: Wounded Spirits in a Promised Land* (New York: Times Books, 1986), Ch. 4.
2. Thomas Hobbes, *Leviathan* (1651), Pt. II Ch. 17 (Indianapolis/New York: Bobbs-Merrill (Library of Liberal Arts), 1958), 139. Cf. Berger, *The Covenant and the Sword*.
3. Gordenker, 'The United Nations as a Third Party', 65.
4. For a discussion, see Caplan, *FD3*, 23, 33. For expectations of similar Arab and Israeli behaviour during the 1991–1992 Madrid and Washington talks, see I. William Zartman, 'The Negotiation Process in the Middle East', in *The Arab–Israeli Search for Peace*, ed. Steven L. Spiegel (Boulder & London: Lynne Reinner, 1992), 65; Galia Golan, 'Arab–Israeli Peace Negotiations: An Israeli View', in ibid., 46.
5. Stevenson to Shuckburgh, 3 April 1955 (tgm.465), PRO FO371/115867 VR1076/52G (emphasis orig.).
6. Russell to Dulles, 20 Feb. 1956, *FRUS 1955–1957*, XV, 191 (D105).
7. Shamir, 'Collapse', 75.
8. '[T]he evolving cold war interjected into the Middle East a superpower race for Arab favor. From this point of view it was no accident that the polarizing global conflict coincided with the gradual collapse of the Israeli–Arab armistice regime.' Yaniv, *Deterrence without the Bomb*, 29.
9. The aspect and its connection to the failure of Alpha is stressed, e.g., by Bar-On, *Gates of Gaza*, 112f. For general background on Nasir's role in Arab politics, see: Wilton Wynn, *Nasser of Egypt: The Search for Dignity* (Cambridge, MA: Arlington Books, 1959), Ch. 8; Charles D. Cremeans, *The Arabs and the World: Nasser's Arab Nationalist Policy* (New York/London: Praeger (Council on Foreign Relations), 1963); Kerr, *The Arab Cold War*; Anthony Nutting, *Nasser* (London: Constable, 1972), Ch. 5; Tawfig Y. Hasou, *The Struggle for the Arab World: Egypt's Nasser and the Arab League*, (London/Boston: KPI, 1985).
10. Eveland, *Ropes of Sand*, 161 n.
11. Shuckburgh to Makins, 25 Nov. 1955, PRO FO371/115469 V1023/23G; Makins to Shuckburgh, 9 Dec. 1955 (desp.1042/602/55G), *loc. cit.*
12. Touval, *Peace Brokers*, 133.
13. Shamir, 'Collapse', 84, 75. Cf. Shuckburgh, *Descent*, 264 (26 June 1955); Oren, *Origins*, 110.
14. See, e.g., *ID7*, 146–8; *FRUS 1952–1954*, IX/1, 1590, 1599–601, 1605; Keren memorandum on Israel and [the Plan to relocate British troops from the Canal Zone to] Gaza, late Feb. 1953 (and subsequent responses, 12–13 March 1953), ISA 43/gimmel-5566/4056; Caffery to USSD, 3 Aug. 1954 (tgm.154), USNA 641.74/8354; *JTA Daily News Bulletin*, 5 Aug. 1954 (dateline London, 4 Aug.); memorandum of conversation (Jernegan, Hart, Rifai), 11 Aug. 1954, USNA 641.74/8354; Ben-Gurion, *Israel: A Personal History*, 438f.; Hahn, *The United States*,

171–9; Oren, *Origins*, 49–55, 111f.; Maddy-Weitzman, *Crystallization*, 167.
15. See, e.g., Oliver minute, Effect of Israel–Jordan Disputes on our Relations with Jordan, 23 Jan. 1951, PRO FO371/82716 ET1053/3G; Evans (Tel Aviv) to Eden, 30 March 1954 (desp.65 – 1031/18/54), FO371/111069 VR1072/34; Evans to FO, 14 April 1954 (tgm.114), FO371/111070 VR1072/55; Allen, Brief to Eden for NATO meeting and Geneva Conference, 20 April 1954, FO371/111070 VR1072/62; Falla, minute, Anglo–Jordan Treaty, 26 April 1954, FO371/111101 VR1091/72; UKEmb Amman, *aide-mémoire*, 29 April 1954 (presented to Fawzi al-Mulqi), FO816/190; FO Brief for Washington Talks: Arab–Israel Situation, 22 June 1954, FO371/111072 VR1072/131.
16. See, esp., Wardrop minute, The Effect of Arab Israel Relations on the Defence of the Middle East, 8 Aug. 1951, PRO FO371/91368 EE1072/21.
17. Views of US Ambassador to Iraq, as reported in Troutbeck (Baghdad) to Bowker, 11 Oct. 1951 (desp.1063/21/51), PRO FO371/91368 EE1072/32. Cf. Copeland's sarcastic reflections of a November 1954 visit to Cairo with the assignment 'to explain to President [*sic*] Nasser how, despite indications to the contrary, his real enemy was the USSR not Israel'. *The Game Player*, 214.
18. Furlonge note (11 Oct.) of talk with Adnan al-Atassi, 8 Oct. 1951, PRO FO371/91368 EE1072/30. Cf. Clark to USSD, 19 Nov. 1951 (desp.270), enclosing note of talk with Faris al-Khoury (1 Nov.), USNA 783.00/11-1951.
19. Donohue, *Before Suez*, 225f.; Alteras, *Eisenhower and Israel*, 58f., 73, 77; Edward Fouracres (of the British Embassy in Amman), quoted in Kyle, *Suez*, 91. For a discussion of Arab reactions to the consecutive Western proposals for a 'Middle East Command' and a 'Middle East Defense Organization', see Maddy-Weitzman, *Crystallization*, 150–5.
20. Davies, note of talk with Elath, 15 Sept. 1950, PRO FO371/82529 ER1054/47. For further evidence of efforts to get Britain and the US to regard Israel as a 'strategic asset' during 1950–1952, see *ID5*, 711f., 723; *ID6*, 30–4, 683; *ID7*, 731; Ben-Gurion diary, 27 Jan. 1951, in *Maariv*, 8 Oct. 1982, p.21; M.J. Sieff memorandum (to Younger), Stability in the Middle East, 27 Aug. 1951, PRO FO371/91716 ER1053/19.
21. *ID6*, 687, 694–6, 701f., 708–11, 712f., 719f., 731, 738f., 742; *FRUS 1951*, V, 241–3; P.R. Oliver minute, 'Arab-Israel Relations', 20 Oct. 1951, PRO FO371/91368 EE1072/34; Morris, *Israel's Border Wars*, 9–13.
22. For details, see: *FRUS 1952–1954*, IX/1, 525–36, 1538f. 1555f. 1560–3, 1589, 1592f., 1596, 1621–3, 1631f.; Byroade address, 'Facing Realities in the Arab–Israeli Dispute' (1 May 1954), *DSB*, 10 May 1954, 708f.; Sharett speeches to Knesset, 10 May and 30 Aug. 1954, texts in PRO FO371/111071 VR1072/94 and CZA A245/35/III; *New York Times*, 2 May 1954; *Manchester Guardian*, 10 May 1954; Avner remarks to Davies, reported in Davies to Eden, 30 July 1954, PRO FO371/111073 VR1072/167; 'US to Arm Egypt – Israel and Arabs Urged to Make Concessions', *JTA Daily News Bulletin*, 29 July 1954 (dateline Washington 28 July); *Jerusalem Post* editorial, 29 Aug. 1954; Donohue, *Before Suez*, Ch. VIII.
23. Dulles to Certain Diplomatic Missions, 21 Aug. 1954, *FRUS 1952–1954*, IX/1, 1619f. (D867) and various replies, ibid., 1622–4, 1826–9, 1834f.; Russell to USSD, 30 Aug. 1954, ibid., 1635f. (D879).
24. Cf. Donohue, *Before Suez*, 381f.; Bar-On, *Gates of Gaza*, 83.
25. Caplan, *FD3*, 9–10, 13, 15–16. For one of many applications of the terminology of international relations between 'patron' and 'client' states, see Yaacov Bar-Siman-Tov, *Israel, the Superpowers, and the War in the Middle East* (New York/Westport/London: Praeger, 1987).
26. I. William Zartman, 'The Negotiation Process in the Middle East', in *The Arab–Israeli Search for Peace*, ed. Steven L. Spiegel (Boulder & London: Lynne

Reinner, 1992), 65.
27. Ben-Zvi, *The United States and Israel*, 3–5.
28. For the relevant UNSC resolutions, see *United Nations Resolutions*, I: 134–8. Cf. Caplan, *FD3*, Ch. XII; above, 42–4. For a discussion which suggests the limited usefulness of condemnations by the UN, see William W. Orbach, *To Keep the Peace: The United Nations Condemnatory Resolution* (Lexington: University Press of Kentucky, 1977).
29. See Caplan, *Lausanne Conference*, 94f.
30. See, e.g., Stephen Green, *Taking Sides: America's Secret Relations with a Militant Israel* (New York: Morrow, 1984), Ch. 4 ('The 1953 Aid Cutoff: A Parable for Our Times'); Yaacov Bar-Siman-Tov, 'The Limits of Economic Sanctions: The American–Israeli Case of 1953', *Journal of Contemporary History* 23 (1988), 425–43; Ben-Zvi, *The United States and Israel*, 35–48; Caplan, *FD3*, Ch. XI, 221.
31. See, e.g., Nuri Sa'id's remarks in conversation with Dulles, 10 Dec. 1957, *FRUS 1955–1957*, XVII, 849.
32. Geren (Amman) to USSD, 10 May 1954, *FRUS 1952–1954*, IX/1, 1553 (D820).
33. Byroade to USSD, 30 May 1955 (tgm.1806), USNA 684A.86/5-3055; Stevenson to FO, 30 May 1955 (tgm.687), PRO FO371/115869 VR1076/103G; Shuckburgh to Macmillan, 13 June 1955, FO371/115870 VR1076/115G.
34. See, e.g., William B. Quandt, 'Influence through Arms Supply: The US Experience in the Middle East', *Arms Transfers to the Third World: The Military Buildup in Less Industrial Countries*, eds Uri Ra'anan, Robert L. Pfaltzgraff, Jr, and Geoffrey Kemp (Boulder: Westview Press, 1978), 121–3, 129. The Soviets faced the same difficulties in translating arms transfers into immediate political benefits. See Ra'anan, 'Soviet Arms Transfers and the Problem of Political Leverage', *op. cit.*, 138f.
35. Kyle, *Suez*, 72.
36. Above, 27–31; Bar-On, *Gates of Gaza*, 144.
37. Cf. Caplan, *FD3*, Ch. XII; above, 32–41.
38. Cf. Caplan, *Lausanne Conference*, 65–9, 78–86.
39. E.g., Selwyn Lloyd's offer of September 1954, discussed above, 73–5.
40. See, e.g., Touval, *Peace Brokers*, Ch. 5.
41. Rountree, memorandum of conversation (Dulles, Hammarskjöld, Wilcox), 29 Feb. 1956, USNA NEA Lot 59, D518, Box 33.
42. See, e.g., Alteras, *Eisenhower and Israel*, 328.
43. Eban, *Personal Witness*, 245.
44. Shamir, 'Collapse', 92f.
45. 'To gain the confidence and goodwill that would facilitate the granting of [their] requests' for arms or economic assistance, Israel and Egypt 'tended to respond positively to propositions which they definitely considered non-starters', Shamir, 'Collapse', 100.
46. Kyle, *Suez*, 72.
47. Bar-On, *Gates of Gaza*, 87–90. For another excellent analysis of the expectations and misconceptions of Britain and the US during Operation Alpha, see Shamir, 'Collapse', 84–99.
48. Bar-On, *Gates of Gaza*, 89.
49. This point is made strongly by Shamir ('Collapse', 85f.), Bar-On (*Gates of Gaza*, 89, 97, 112), and Kyle (*Suez*, 71). But Michael Oren claims – less convincingly – that '[i]nsofar as Israel had previously agreed to concede part of the Negev in exchange for Gaza, it was logical to assume that, with the proper inducements, it would yield even more of the desert.' *Origins*, 111. Even at the height of discussing the proposal to annex Gaza in 1949, Israel was never prepared to concede more than minor rectifications of the Sinai–Negev border. Israeli leaders quickly

50. Shamir, 'Collapse', 89–92.
51. For examples of perceptive analysis and recommendations six months prior to the start of Alpha, see: Russell (Tel Aviv) to USSD, 17 April 1954, *FRUS 1952–1954*, IX/1, 1521 (D800); Allen, Brief to Eden for NATO meeting and Geneva Conference, 20 April 1954, PRO FO371/111070 VR1072/62; Glubb to Richmond, Attempted Appreciation of the Situation Regarding Peace Between Israel and Jordan, 2 May 1954, FO816/190.
52. Lawson to Jernegan, 14 July 1955, USNA NEA Lot 59, D518, Box 29.
53. Sterndale–Bennett to Shuckburgh, 19 Aug. 1955, PRO FO371/115874 VR1076/196G.
54. Macmillan memorandum to Cabinet, Palestine Settlement (CP55/75), 13 July 1955, PRO PREM11/945.
55. 'The centre of infection in the region is Israel and I believe that we must treat the Israelis as a sick people. [etc.]' Nicholls to Shuckburgh, 8 March 1955, PRO FO371/115825 VR1051/8G. Cf. extracts quoted in Shamir, 'Collapse', 91f. and (more extensively) in Kyle, *Suez*, 67.
56. Nicholls to Shuckburgh, 21 Nov. 1955, PRO FO371/115883 VR1076/434G. Nicholls conveyed similar advice in a subsequent telegram (Nicholls to FO, 2 Dec. 1955 (tgm.508)), but Shuckburgh was not convinced by these reports and explained FO counter-arguments and reservations in his reply of 20 Dec. 1955, both in FO371/115885 VR1076/475G.
57. Nicholls to Shuckburgh, 8 March 1955, PRO FO371/115825 VR1051/8G.
58. Oren, *Origins*, 71.
59. Bar-On, *Gates of Gaza*, 89f.
60. Shamir, 'Collapse', 89f.
61. Shamir, 'Collapse', 94.
62. Eisenhower diary, 8 March 1956, *FRUS 1955–1957*, XV, 327 (D177); cf. Burns, *Economic Aid*, 73–5; Aronson, *From Sideshow to Center Stage*, 166.
63. Aronson, *From Sideshow to Center Stage*, 147–8. Cf. Spiegel, *The Other Arab–Israeli Conflict*, 66.
64. Sterndale-Bennett to Shuckburgh, 19 Aug. 1955, PRO FO371/115874 VR1076/196G.
65. Nicholls to Shuckburgh, 21 Nov. 1955, PRO FO371/115883 VR1076/434G. Emphasis in original.
66. For some early examples of this line of thinking, see: Charles Malik (February 1950) remarks, discussed in Caplan, *FD3*, 135–6; Clark note (2 Nov.) of talk with Faris al-Khouri, 1 Nov. 1951, USNA 783.00/11-1951; UK Consul-General, Jerusalem, to EnDept FO, 20 Aug. 1951 (desp.1073/4/51), PRO FO371/91365 EE1071/24 (talk with James Barco, US member of the PCC); Byroade–Eban talk, 22 Sept. 1952, *FRUS 1952–1954*, IX/1, 1005 (D491); Raymond Hare's reports from Beirut in August 1954, *FRUS 1952–1954*, IX/1, 1618f., 1622–4.
67. Russell, memorandum of conversation (Dulles, Hoover, Allen, Eban, Shiloah), 2 March 1956, *FRUS 1955–1957*, XV, 280 (D151). Cf. Kyle, *Suez*, 98.
68. Bergus memorandum, An American Policy for Arab–Israeli Peace, 2 Dec. 1952, USNA 684A.86/12-1852.
69. Cf. Kyle, *Suez*, Ch. 5.
70. FO to UKEmb Washington, 19 July 1955 (tgm.3339); compare copies in FO371/115871 VR1076/134G and PREM11/945.
71. Wright to Shuckburgh, 20 July 1955 (tgm.647), PRO FO371/115871 VR1076/136G. Cf. Macmillan to UKEmb Washington, 29 July 1955 (tgm.3117 Saving),

FO371/115872 VR1076/147G.
72. Shuckburgh, brief for Cabinet meeting (26 July), 25 July 1955, PRO FO371/115872 VR1076/147G.
73. See, e.g., Levant Dept. FO, briefs for Secretary of State's Tour of Middle East, 25 Feb. 1956, PRO FO371/121725 VR1073/94.
74. Kirkpatrick, minute on Shuckburgh memorandum ('Policy in the Middle East'), 15 Oct. 1955, PRO FO371/115480 V1054/5G.
75. Quoted in Thomas L. Friedman, *From Beirut to Jerusalem* (New York: Doubleday Anchor Ed., 1990), 194.
76. Bailey (Washington) to Rose, 4 May 1956 (desp.11916/35/56), PRO FO371/121709 VR1071/50.
77. Morris, *Israel's Border Wars*, 422, 424.
78. Bar-On, *Gates of Gaza*, 174.
79. Bergus memorandum, An American Policy for Arab–Israeli Peace, 2 Dec. 1952, USNA 684A.86/12-1852.
80. Funkhouser to Kopper, 26 May 1952, USNA 783.00/5-2652.
81. Russell memorandum, Suggested Approach by Ambassador Byroade to Colonel Nasser, n.d. (?Nov. 1955), USNA NEA Lot 59, D518, Box 31. Cf. Macmillan remarks, conversation with Dulles, Geneva, 9 Nov. 1955, *FRUS 1955–1957*, XIV, 723 (D391).
82. For some of Nasir's concerns, see Nasir–Byroade talk, reported in Byroade to Hoover, 1 Jan. 1956, *FRUS 1955–1957*, XV, 1–3 (D1). Cf. ibid., 97; Aronson, *From Sideshow to Center Stage*, 158–62.
83. Makins-Russell talk, reported in Makins to FO, 28 Nov. 1955 (tgm.2896), PRO FO371/115884 VR1076/455G. Cf. Dulles–Macmillan talk, reported in Dulles (Paris) to USSD, 17 Dec. 1955, *FRUS 1955–1957*, XIV, 877 (D464); Burns, *Economic Aid*, 53f.
84. Memorandum of conversation, White House (Eisenhower, Anderson, Dulles), 11 Jan. 1956, *FRUS 1955–1957*, XV, 20. Cf. Burns, *Economic Aid*, 53.
85. Heikal, *Milaffat*, 388.
86. E.g., 'Honest Bob (Anderson) was not the brightest of our professional VIPs ... Anderson could speak with the fervour of a born-again Christian, but he could be counted upon to make no sense at all in talking to persons of alien cultures.' Copeland, *Game Player*, 207f. See also: Neff, *Warriors at Suez*, 156; Kamel, *Abd al-Nasir fi Tel Abib*, 81.
87. See, e.g., *New York Times*, 12 Dec. 1955, quoted in Love, *Suez*, 307f., and Burns, *Economic Aid*, 54.
88. Burns, *Economic Aid*, 58f.
89. The latter point is made by Oren, *Origins*, 116f.
90. On the other aspects of this timing, cf. above, Ch. VI and Bar-On, quoted on 279–80.

Bibliography

PRIMARY SOURCES

Archival documents

CZA   Central Zionist Archives, Jerusalem, Israel
series: A245 Moshe Sharett papers
Z6 Nahum Goldmann papers

ISA   Israel State Archives, Jerusalem, Israel
series: RG43 Prime Minister's Office
RG93 Ministry of Foreign Affairs: Missions Abroad
RG130 Ministry of Foreign Affairs: Head Office
RS Reuven Shiloah papers

MEC   Private Papers Collection, Middle East Centre, St Antony's College, Oxford

PRO   Public Record Office, Kew, UK
series: CAB Cabinet Records
FO141 UK Embassy, Cairo
FO371 Foreign Office, general correspondence
FO816 UK Embassy, Amman
PREM11 Prime Minister's papers

RJB   Ralph J. Bunche Papers, Collection 2051, Department of Special Collections, University Library, University of California, Los Angeles CA

UNA   United Nations Archive, New York
series: DAG-1
DAG-13

USNA   United States National Archives, Washington DC
series: 501.BB/Palestine
NEA Lot 59, D518
various decimal series

WNRC   Washington National Records Center, Suitland MD
series: RG84 US Missions Abroad
E/C/G = Egypt/Cairo/General Correspondence
E/C/TSG = Egypt/Cairo/Top Secret General Correspondence

Oral history

Oral history interviews, Foreign Affairs Oral History Collection, Georgetown University Library:
William C. Burdett, 16 December 1988.
Wilbur P. Chase, 24 July 1990.
James Cortada, 1 September 1992.
A. David Fritzlan, 29 May and 15 June 1990.
Parker T. Hart, 27 January 1989.
Edward Warren Holmes, [date and p. 1 missing from transcript].
Harrison M. Symmes, 25 February 1989.

Government documents

Israel Ministry for Foreign Affairs, *Peace in the Middle East: A Record of Israel's Peace Offers to Arab States*, Jerusalem: n.d. [Dec. 1955].

Israel State Archives, *Documents on the Foreign Policy of Israel*
- Vol. 1 (14 May – 30 September 1948), ed. Yehoshua Freundlich, Jerusalem: 1981.
- Vol. 2 (October 1948 – April 1949), ed. Yehoshua Freundlich, Jerusalem: 1984.
- Vol. 4 (May – December 1949), ed. Yemima Rosenthal, Jerusalem: 1986.
- Vol. 5 (1950), ed. Yehoshua Freundlich, Jerusalem: 1988.
- Vol. 6 (1951), ed. Yemima Rosenthal, Jerusalem: 1991.
- Vol. 7 (1952), ed. Yehoshua Freundlich, Jerusalem: 1992.

Israel's Foreign Relations: Selected Documents 1947–1974, 2 Vols., ed. Meron Medzini, Jerusalem: Ministry of Foreign Affairs, 1976.

United States, Department of State, *Department of State Bulletin* (Washington).

United States, Department of State, *Foreign Relations of the United States: Diplomatic Papers* (United States Government Printing Office)
- 1947, Vol. V, Washington: 1971.
- 1948, Vol. V, pt.2, Washington: 1976.
- 1949, Vol. VI, Washington: 1977.
- 1950, Vol. V, Washington: 1978.
- 1951, Vol. V, Washington: 1982.
- 1952–54, Vol. IX, eds. Paul Claussen, Joan M. Lee & Carl N. Raether, Washington: 1986.
- 1955–57, Vol. XIV: Arab–Israeli Dispute, 1955, ed. Carl N. Raether, Washington: 1989.
- 1955–57, Vol. XV: Arab–Israeli Dispute, January 1 – July 26, 1956, ed. Carl N. Raether, Washington: 1989.
- 1955–57, Vol. XVI: Suez Crisis: July 26 – December 31, 1956, ed. Nina J. Noring, Washington: 1990.
- 1955–57, Vol. XVII: Arab–Israeli Dispute, 1957, ed. Nina J. Noring, Washington: 1990.

United Nations documents

Public Papers of the Secretaries-General of the United Nations: Vol. II Dag Hammarskjöld, 1953–1956, eds. Andrew W. Cordier & Wilder Foote, New York/London: Columbia University Press, 1972.

United Nations Resolutions on Palestine and the Arab–Israeli Conflict, Vol. I: 1947–1974, ed. George J. Tomeh, Washington: Institute for Palestine Studies, 1975.

Other primary documentary sources

Abd al-Nasir, Gamal, *Filastin (Palestine*; collected speeches), Cairo: 1965.

Ben-Gurion, David, 'ha-Mum ha-Sodi im Nasser' (The Secret Negotiations with Nasser), *Maariv (Weekly Supplement)*, 2 July 1971, pp. 9–10, 22; 9 July 1971, pp. 11–12; 16 July 1971, pp. 11, 20; 23 July 1971, pp. 14, 22.

Diplomacy in the Near & Middle East: A Documentary Record: 1914–1956, Vol. 2, ed. J.C. Hurewitz, Octagon Reprint, 1972.

Documents on International Affairs, 1954, ed. Denise Folliot (London/New York/Toronto: Oxford University Press (under the auspices of the Royal Institute of International Affairs), 1957).

Documents on International Affairs, 1955, ed. Noble Frankland (London/New York/Toronto: Oxford University Press (under the auspices of the Royal Institute of International Affairs), 1958).

Herzog, Yaacov, *A People that Dwells Alone: Speeches and Writings of Yaacov Herzog*, ed. Misha Louvish (London: Weidenfeld & Nicolson, 1975).

Khalil, Muhammad, *The Arab States and the Arab League: A Documentary Record, Vol. II: International Affairs* (Beirut: Khayats, 1962).

Orbach, Maurice, 'The Orbach File: First Visit to Cairo', *New Outlook* (Oct. 1974), 8–23; 'The Orbach File (part two): Second Visit to Cairo', *New Outlook* (Nov.–Dec. 1974), 8–21; 'The Orbach File (part three): Third Visit to Cairo', *New Outlook* (Jan. 1975), 12–20.

Rabinovich, Itamar, and Jehuda Reinharz, eds, *Israel in the Middle East: Documents and Readings on Society, Politics and Foreign Relations, 1948–Present* (New York/Oxford: Oxford University Press, 1984).

Ro'i, Yaacov, *From Encroachment to Involvement: A Documentary Study of Soviet Policy in the Middle East, 1945–1973* (New York/Toronto: John Wiley & Sons (A Halsted Press Book, for the Shiloah Center, Tel Aviv University), 1974).

Sharett, Moshe, *Yoman Ishi (Personal Diary, 1953–1957)*, 8 Vols., Tel Aviv: Sifriyat Maariv, 1978.

Shuckburgh, Evelyn, *Descent to Suez: Diaries 1951–56*, selected for publication by John Charmley (London: Weidenfeld & Nicolson, 1986).

The Arab–Israeli Conflict, 3 Vols., ed. John Norton Moore (Princeton: Princeton University Press, 1974).

Tsur, Jacob, *Prélude à Suez: Journal d'une ambassade 1953–1956* (Paris: Presses de la Cité, 1968).

Press

Moshe Dayan Center, Tel Aviv University: Press Archives and Documentation Center; Schwadran Newspaper Clipping Collection.

Articles cited:

Al-Ahram (Cairo), 12 Oct. 1948

Christian Science Monitor, 1955: 2, 15, 29 Nov.

Daily Telegraph (London), 29 Nov. 1955

Egyptian Gazette, 15 Nov. 1954

Filastin (Jerusalem), 13 Nov. 1954

Al-Hayat (Beirut), 5 Nov. 1954

Jerusalem Post, 29 Aug. 1954, 11 Sept. 1955

Jewish Observer and Middle East Review (London), 1955: 16 Sept./2, 23 Dec.

Manchester Guardian, 1954: 10 May, 27 Sept.
  1955: 13 Sept./26 Nov./20 Dec.

New York Herald Tribune, 1955: 19 Oct./3, 14, 21 Nov./8, 22 Dec.

New York Times, 1952: 16 Nov.
  1954: 2 May/28–29 Sept./1 Nov.
  1955: 12 April/10 July/4 Sept./6, 23 Oct./3–4, 6–7, 26, 30 Nov./7, 12, 17–18, 20 Dec.

Newsweek, 23 May 1955

The Observer (London), 6, 13 Nov. 1955

The Times (London), 22 Sept. 1954/21 Dec. 1955/24 June 1971

U.S. News & World Report, 17 Sept. 1954

AUTOBIOGRAPHICAL SOURCES

Ben-Gurion, David, *Israel: A Personal History*, trs. Nechemia Meyers & Uzy Nystar (New York: Funk & Wagnalls, 1971 (Tel Aviv: Sabra Books (nd)).

Ben-Gurion, David, *My Talks with Arab Leaders*, transl. from Heb. by Misha Louvish and Aryeh Rubinstein, ed. M. Louvish (Jerusalem: Keter (New York: Third Press), 1972).

Bernadotte, Count Folke, *To Jerusalem*, transl. from Swedish by Joan Bullman (London: Hodder & Stoughton, 1951).

Burns, E.L.M., *Between Arab and Israeli* (New York: Ivan Obolensky, 1963 (Toronto: Clark, Irwin, 1962)).

Copeland, Miles, *The Game of Nations: The Amorality of Power Politics* (New York: College Notes & Texts, 1969).

Copeland, Miles, *The Game Player: Confessions of the CIA's Original Political Operative* (London: Aurum, 1989).

Crossman, Richard, *Palestine Mission: A Personal Record* (New York/London; Harper, 1947).

Crum, Bartley C., *Behind the Silken Curtain: A Personal Account of Anglo–American Diplomacy in Palestine and the Middle East* (New York: Simon & Schuster, 1947).

Dayan, Moshe, *Avnei Derekh: Autobiografia (Stepping Stones: An Autobiography)* (Jerusalem: Edanim (with Dvir, Tel Aviv), 1976).

Dayan, Moshe, *Diary of the Sinai Campaign* (New York: Harper & Row, 1966).

Eban, Abba, *An Autobiography* (New York: Random House, 1977).

Eban, Abba, *Personal Witness: Israel Through My Eyes* (New York: G.P. Putnam's Sons, 1992).

Eden, Anthony, *Full Circle: The Memoirs of the Rt. Hon. Sir Anthony Eden* (London: Cassell, 1960).

Eisenhower, Dwight D., *Mandate for Change, 1953–1956 (The White House Years)* (Garden City NY: Doubleday (London: Heinemann), 1963).

Elath, Eliahu, *Me'ever le-Arafel ha-Yamim: Pirqei Zikhronot (Through the Mists of Time: Reminiscences)* (Jerusalem: Yad Ben-Zvi, 1989).

Eveland, Wilbur Crane, *Ropes of Sand: America's Failure in the Middle East* (New York: W.W.Norton, 1980).

Glubb, Sir John Bagot, *A Soldier with the Arabs* (London: Hodder & Stoughton, 1957).

Harel, Isser, *Bitahon ve-Democratia (Security and Democracy)* (Tel Aviv: Edanim/Yediot Aharonot, 1989).

Jackson, Elmore, *Middle East Mission: The Story of a Major Bid for Peace in the Time of Nasser and Ben-Gurion* (New York/London: W.W. Norton, 1983).

Macmillan, Harold, *Tides of Fortune, 1945–1955* (New York: Harper & Row, 1969).

McGhee, George, *Envoy to the Middle World: Adventures in Diplomacy*, fwd. Dean Rusk (New York: Harper & Row, 1983).

Nutting, Anthony, *No End of a Lesson: The Story of Suez* (London: Constable, 1967).

Peres, Shimon, *David's Sling: The Arming of Israel* (London: Weidenfeld & Nicolson, 1970).

Rafael, Gideon, *Destination Peace: Three Decades of Israeli Foreign Policy: A Personal Memoir* (New York: Stein & Day, 1981).

Sharon, Ariel, with David Chanoff, *Warrior: The Autobiography of Ariel Sharon* (New York: Simon & Schuster, 1989).

SECONDARY SOURCES

Books, dissertations and monographs

Alteras, Isaac, *Eisenhower and Israel: U.S.–Israeli Relations, 1953–1960* (Gainsville: University Press of Florida, 1993).

Aronson, Geoffrey, *From Sideshow to Center Stage: U.S. Policy Toward Egypt, 1946–1956* (Boulder, CO: Lynne Rienner, 1986).

Bar-Joseph, Uri, *The Best of Enemies: Israel and Transjordan in the War of 1948* (London: Frank Cass, 1987).

Bar-On, Mordechai, *The Gates of Gaza: Israel's Road to Suez and Back, 1955–1957*, transl. Ruth Rossing (New York: St Martin's Press, 1994).

Bar-On, Mordechai, *Sha'arei Aza: Mediniut ha-Bitahon ve-ha-Hutz shel Medinat Yisrael: 1955–1957 (The Gates of Gaza: Israel's Defense and Foreign Policy)* (Tel Aviv: Am Oved, 1992).

Bar-Siman-Tov, Yaacov, *Israel, the Superpowers, and the War in the Middle East* (New York/Westport/London: Praeger, 1987).

Bar-Zohar, Michael, *Ben-Gurion: A Biography*, transl. Peretz Kidron (New York: Delacorte (London: Weidenfeld & Nicolson), 1978).

Ben-Zvi, Abraham, *The United States and Israel: The Limits of the Special Relationship* (New York: Columbia University Press, 1993).

Berger, Earl. *The Covenant and the Sword: Arab–Israeli Relations, 1948–56* (Toronto: University of Toronto Press (London: Routledge & Kegan Paul), 1965).

Bialer, Uri, *Between East and West: Israel's Foreign Policy Orientation, 1948–1956* (Cambridge/New York: Cambridge University Press (LSE Monograph Series), 1990).

Brecher, Michael, *Decisions in Israel's Foreign Policy* (New Haven: Yale University Press, 1975).

Brown, L. Carl, *International Politics and the Middle East: Old Rules, Dangerous Game* (Princeton: Princeton University Press, 1984).

Burns, William J., *Economic Aid and American Policy toward Egypt, 1955–1981*, fwd. H. F. Eilts (Albany: State University of New York Press, 1985).

Caplan, Neil, *Futile Diplomacy*, Vol. 1: *Early Arab–Zionist Negotiation Attempts, 1913–1931* (London: Frank Cass, 1983); Vol. 2: *Arab–Zionist Negotiations and the End of the Mandate* (London: Frank Cass, 1986); Vol. 3: *The United Nations, the Great Powers and Middle East Peacemaking, 1948–1954*, (London: Frank Cass, 1997).

Caplan, Neil, *The Lausanne Conference, 1949: A Case Study in Middle East Peacemaking* (Tel Aviv University: Moshe Dayan Center for Middle Eastern and African Studies (Occasional Paper No. 113), 1993).

Carlton, David, *Anthony Eden: A Biography* (London: Allen Lane, 1981).

Carlton, David, *Britain and the Suez Crisis* (Oxford/New York: Basil Blackwell, 1988).

Carr, Edward Hallett, *What Is History?* (New York: Random House (Vintage), 1961).

Cremeans, Charles D., *The Arabs and the World: Nasser's Arab Nationalist Policy* (New York/London: Praeger (Council on Foreign Relations), 1963).

Crosbie, Sylvia Kowitt, *A Tacit Alliance: France and Israel from Suez to the Six Day War* (Princeton: Princeton University Press, 1974).

Donohue, James T., *Before Suez: John Foster Dulles and the Arab–Israeli Conflict, 1940–1954*, New Brunswick, NJ: Ph.D. dissertation, Rutgers, The State University of New Jersey, 1989.

Eshed, Haggai, *Mossad Shel Ish Ehad: Reuven Shiloah, Avi ha-Modiyin ha-Yisraeli (One Man Mossad: Reuven Shiloah, the Father of Israeli Intelligence)*, Jerusalem: Edanim, 1988.

Friedman, Thomas L., *From Beirut to Jerusalem* (New York: Doubleday Anchor Ed., 1990).

Gabbay, Rony E., *A Political Study of the Arab–Jewish Conflict: The Arab Refugee Problem (A Case Study)* (Genève: Librairie E. Droz (Paris: Librairie Minard), 1959).

Garfinkle, Adam, *Deep and Wide: Water, War and Negotiations in the Jordan Valley, 1916–1993*, draft ms., June 1993.

Gerges, Fawaz A., *The Superpowers and the Middle East: Regional and International Politics, 1955–1967*, fwd. William Quandt, Boulder/San Francisco/Oxford: Westview Press, 1994.

Ginat, Rami, *The Soviet Union and Egypt, 1945–1955* (London: Frank Cass, 1993).

Glassman, Jon D., *Arms for the Arabs: The Soviet Union and War in the Middle East* (Baltimore/London: Johns Hopkins University Press, 1975).

Golan, Matti, *The Road to Peace: A Biography of Shimon Peres*, transl. Akiva Ron (New York: Warner Books, 1989).

Gordenker, Leon, *The U.N. Secretary-General and the Maintenance of Peace* (New York/London: Columbia University Press, 1967).

Green, Stephen, *Taking Sides: America's Secret Relations with a Militant Israel* (New York: Morrow, 1984).

Haass, Richard N., *Conflicts Unending: The United States and Regional Disputes* (New Haven/London: Yale University Press, 1990).

Hahn, Peter L., *The United States, Great Britain, and Egypt, 1945–1956: Strategy and Diplomacy in the Early Cold War* (Chapel Hill/London: University of North Carolina Press, 1991).

Haron, Miriam Joyce, *Palestine and the Anglo–American Connection, 1945–1950* (New York: Peter Lang, 1986).

Hasou, Tawfig Y., *The Struggle for the Arab World: Egypt's Nasser and the Arab League* (London/Boston: KPI, 1985).

Heikal, Mohamed, *The Cairo Documents: The Inside Story of Nasser and his Relationship with World Leaders, Rebels, and Statesmen*, intro. Edward R.F. Sheehan (Garden City, NY: Doubleday, 1973).

Heikal, Mohamed H., *Cutting the Lion's Tail: Suez Through Egyptian Eyes* (London: Corgi, 1988).

Heikal, Muhammad Hassanein, *Milaffat as-Suways: Harb al-Thalathin Sana (The Suez Files: The Thirty Years War)*, Cairo: 1986.

Hobbes, Thomas, *Leviathan* (1651) (Indianapolis/New York: Bobbs-Merrill (Library of Liberal Arts), 1958).

Hutchison, E.H., *Violent Truce: A Military Observer Looks at the Arab–Israeli Conflict, 1951–1955* (New York: Devin-Adair, 1956).

Ilan, Amitzur, *Bernadotte in Palestine: A Study in Contemporary Humanitarian Knight-Errantry* (New York: St Martin's Press, 1989).

Jones, Martin, *Failure in Palestine: British and U.S. Policy after the Second World War* (London/New York: Mansell, 1986).

Kamil, Rashad, *Abd an-Nasir fi Tel Abib: al-Qissa al-Kamila li-Mashari' at-Tafawud ma' Israil (Abd al-Nasir in Tel Aviv: The Complete Story of Plans for Negotiating with Israel)*, Cairo: 1991.

Kerr, Malcolm H., *The Arab Cold War: Gamal Abd al-Nasir and His Rivals, 1958–1970*, 3rd ed. (London/Oxford/New York: Oxford University Press, 1971).

Khouri, Fred J., *The Arab–Israeli Dilemma*, 3rd ed. (Syracuse: Syracuse University Press, 1985).

Kyle, Keith, *Suez* (New York: St Martin's Press, 1991).

Lorch, Netanel, *One Long War: Arab versus Jew Since 1920* (New York: Herzl Press, 1976).

Louis, Wm. Roger, *The British Empire in the Middle East, 1945–1951: Arab Nationalism, The United States, and Postwar Imperialism* (Oxford: Clarendon Press, 1984).

Love, Kennett, *Suez: The Twice-Fought War* (New York/Toronto: McGraw-Hill, 1969).

Lowi, Miriam R., *Water and Power: The Politics of a Scarce Resource in the Jordan River Basin* (New York/Cambridge: Cambridge University Press, 1993).

Lucas, W. Scott, *Divided We Stand: Britain, the US and the Suez Crisis*, London: Hodder & Stoughton, 1991.

Maddy-Weitzman, Bruce, *The Crystallization of the Arab State System, 1945–1954* (Syracuse: Syracuse University Press, 1993).

Morris, Benny, *The Birth of the Palestinian Refugee Problem, 1947–1949* (Cambridge/New York: Cambridge University Press, 1987).

Morris, Benny, *Israel's Border Wars, 1949–1956: Arab Infiltration, Israeli Retaliation, and the Countdown to the Suez War* (Oxford: Clarendon Press, 1993).

Neff, Donald, *Warriors at Suez: Eisenhower Takes America into the Middle East*, New York: The Linden Press/Simon & Schuster, 1981 (Brattleboro VT: Amana Books, 1988).

Nevo, Joseph, *Abdallah ve-Arviyei Eretz-Israel (Abdallah and the Arabs of Palestine)*, Tel Aviv: Shiloah Institute for Middle Eastern and African Studies, 1975.

Nimrod, Yoram, *Mei Meriva: ha-Mahloqet al Mei ha-Yarden (Angry Waters: The Dispute over the Jordan Waters)*, Givat Haviva: Center for Arabic and Afro–Asian Studies, 1966.

Nutting, Anthony, *Nasser* (London: Constable, 1972).

Orbach, William W., *To Keep the Peace: The United Nations Condemnatory Resolution* (Lexington: University Press of Kentucky, 1977).

Oren, Michael B., *Origins of the Second Arab–Israel War: Egypt, Israel and the Great Powers: 1952–56* (London: Frank Cass, 1992).

Pappé, Ilan, *Britain and the Arab–Israeli Conflict, 1948–51* (London: Macmillan Press/St Antony's College, 1988).

Pelcovits, Nathan A., *The Long Armistice: UN Peacekeeping and the Arab–Israeli Conflict, 1948–1960*, foreword by Samuel W. Lewis; (Boulder/San Francisco/Oxford: Westview Press, 1993).

Peretz, Don, *Israel and the Palestine Arabs* (Washington: Middle East Institute, 1958).

Persson, Sune O., *Mediation & Assassination: Count Bernadotte's Mission to Palestine in 1948* (London: Ithaca Press, 1979).

Podet, Allen H, *The Success and Failure of the Anglo–American Committee of Inquiry, 1945–46: Last Chance in Palestine* (Lewiston NY: E. Mellen, 1986).

Ra'anan, Uri, Robert L. Pfaltzgraff, Jr, and Geoffrey Kemp, eds, *Arms Transfers to the Third World: The Military Buildup in Less Industrial Countries* (Boulder: Westview Press, 1978).

Rabinovich, Itamar, *The Road Not Taken: Early Arab–Israeli Negotiations* (New York/Oxford: Oxford University Press, 1991).

Rubin, Barry, *The Arab States and the Palestine Conflict* (Syracuse: Syracuse University Press, 1981).

Rubin, Barry, *Secrets of State: The State Department and the Struggle Over U.S. Foreign Policy* (Oxford/New York: Oxford University Press, 1985).

Saliba, Samir N., *The Jordan River Dispute* (The Hague: Martinus Nijhoff, 1968).

Satloff, Robert B., *From Abdullah to Hussein: Jordan in Transition* (New York/Oxford: Oxford University Press, 1994).

Sayed-Ahmed, Muhammad Abd el-Wahab, *Nasser and American Foreign Policy, 1952–1956* (London: LAAM, 1989).

Sela, Avraham, *Mi-Maga'im le-Masa u-Matan: Yihasei ha-Sokhnut ha-Yehudit u-Medinat Yisrael 'im ha-Melekh Abdallah, 1946–1950 (From Contacts to Negotiations: Relations Between the Jewish Agency and the State of Israel with King Abdullah)* (Tel Aviv: Shiloah Institute for Middle Eastern and African Studies, 1985).

Shalev, Aryeh, *The Israel–Syria Armistice Regime, 1949–1955* (Boulder: Westview Press and Jerusalem: The Jerusalem Post (Jaffee Center for Strategic Studies, Study No. 21), 1993).

Shalev, Aryeh, *Shituf Pe'ula be-tzel Imut: Mishtar Shevitat ha-Nesheq Yisrael–Suriya, 1949–1955 (Co-operation under the Shadow of Conflict: The Israeli–Syrian Armistice Regime)*, Tel Aviv: Ma'arachot, 1989.

Sheffer, Gabriel, ed., *Dynamics of Dependence: US–Israeli Relations* (Boulder and London: Westview Press, 1987).

Shimshoni, Jonathan, *Israel and Conventional Deterrence: Border Warfare from 1953 to 1970* (Ithaca/London: Cornell University Press, 1988).

Shipler, David K., *Arab and Jew: Wounded Spirits in a Promised Land* (New York: Times Books, 1986).

Shlaim, Avi, *Collusion Across the Jordan: King Abdullah, the Zionist Movement, and the Partition of Palestine* (Oxford: Clarendon Press, 1988).

Spiegel, Steven L., ed., *The Arab–Israeli Search for Peace*, Boulder and London: Lynne Reinner, 1992.

Spiegel, Steven L., *The Other Arab–Israeli Conflict: Making America's Middle East Policy, from Truman to Reagan* (Chicago/London: University of Chicago Press, 1985).

Stein, Janice Gross, ed., *Getting to the Table: The Processes of International Prenegotiation* (Baltimore/London: Johns Hopkins University Press, 1989).

Suleiman, Michael W., ed., *U.S. Policy on Palestine from Wilson to Clinton*, (Normal IL: Association of Arab-American University Graduates, Inc., 1995).

Tawil, Muhammad, *Lu'bat al-Umam wa-'Abd an-Nasir (The Game of Nations and Abd al-Nasir)*, Cairo: 1986.

Teveth, Shabtai, *Ben-Gurion's Spy: The Story of the Political Scandal that Shaped Modern Israel* (New York: Columbia University Press, 1996).

Teveth, Shabtai, *Moshe Dayan: The Soldier, the Man, the Legend*, transl. from Heb. by Leah and David Zinder (Boston: Houghton Mifflin, 1973).

Touval, Saadia, *The Peace Brokers: Mediators in the Arab–Israeli Conflict, 1948–1979* (Princeton: Princeton University Press, 1982).

Urquhart, Brian, *Hammarskjöld* (New York/etc: Harper & Row, 1984).

Wilson, Mary, *King Abdullah, Britain and the Making of Jordan* (Cambridge/New York/etc: Cambridge University Press, 1987).

Wynn, Wilton, *Nasser of Egypt: The Search for Dignity* (Cambridge, MA: Arlington Books, 1959).

Yaari, Ehud, *Mitsrayim ve-ha-Fidayyin, 1953–1956 (Egypt and the Fedayeen)*, Givat Haviva: Center for Arabic and Afro–Asian Studies, 1975.

Yaniv, Avner, *Deterrence without the Bomb: The Politics of Israeli Strategy* (Lexington/Toronto: D.C. Heath, 1987).

Articles

Bar-Siman-Tov, Yaacov, 'The Limits of Economic Sanctions: The American–Israeli Case of 1953', *Journal of Contemporary History* 23 (1988), 425–43.

Blechman, Barry M., 'The Impact of Israel's Reprisals on Behavior of the Bordering Arab Nations Directed at Israel', *Journal of Conflict Resolution* 16:2 (June 1972), 155–81.

Dayan, Moshe, 'Israel's Border and Security Problems' *Foreign Affairs* 33:2 (Jan. 1955), 250–67.

Dawn, C. Ernest, 'Pan-Arabism and the Failure of Israeli–Jordanian Peace Negotiations, 1950', in *Islam and its Cultural Divergence: Studies in Honor of Gustave E. von Grunebaum*, ed. Girdhari L. Tikku (Urbana/Chicago/London: University of Illinois Press, 1971), 27–51.

Gazit, Mordechai, 'The Israel–Jordan Peace Negotiations (1949–51): King Abdallah's Lonely Effort', *Journal of Contemporary History* Vol. 23 (1988), 409–24.

Gazit, Mordechai, 'Israeli Military Procurement from the United States', in *Dynamics of Dependence: US–Israeli Relations*, ed. Gabriel Sheffer (Boulder and London: Westview Press, 1987), 83–124.

Gazit, Mordechai, 'Mediation and Mediators', *Jerusalem Journal of International Relations* 5:4 (1981), 80–104.

Gazit, Mordechai, 'American and British Diplomacy and the Bernadotte Mission', *Historical Journal* 29:3 (1986), 677–96.

Gerner, Deborah J., 'Missed Opportunities and Roads Not Taken: The Eisenhower Administration and the Palestinians', in *U.S. Policy on Palestine from Wilson to Clinton*, ed. Michael W. Suleiman (Normal IL: AAUG Press, 1995), 81–112.

Golan, Galia, 'Arab–Israeli Peace Negotiations: An Israeli View', in *The Arab–Israeli Search for Peace*, ed. Steven L. Spiegel (Boulder and London: Lynne Reinner, 1992), 37–47.

Glubb, J. B., 'Violence on the Jordan–Israel Border: A Jordanian View', *Foreign Affairs* 32:4 (July 1954), 552–62.

Gordenker, Leon, 'The United Nations as a Third Party in Arab–Israeli Conflicts', *Jerusalem Journal of International Relations* 10:1 (March 1988), 60–76.

Heller, Joseph, 'Failure of a Mission: Bernadotte and Palestine, 1948', *Journal of Contemporary History* 14 (1979), 515–34.

Jerusalem Journal of International Relations, XIII:1 (March 1991), special issue devoted to prenegotiation.

Khouri, Fred J., 'Friction and Conflict on the Israel–Syrian Front', *Middle East Journal* 17:1–2 (Winter–Spring 1963), 14–34.

Khouri, Fred J., 'The Policy of Retaliation in Arab–Israeli Relations', *Middle East Journal* 20:4 (Autumn 1966), 435–55.

Laskier, Michael M., 'From War to War: The Jews of Egypt from 1948 to 1970', *Studies in Zionism* 7:1 (Spring 1986), 111–47.

Levey, Zach, 'Israel's Pursuit of French Arms, 1952–1958', *Studies in Zionism* 14:2 (Autumn 1993), 183–210.

Louis, Roger, 'Britain at the Crossroads in Palestine, 1952–1954', *Jerusalem Journal of International Relations* 12:3 (Sept. 1990), 59–82.

Monroe, Elizabeth, 'The Arab–Israel Frontier', *International Affairs* 29 (Oct. 1953), 437–48.

Muhammad, Muhsin, 'al-Ittisal bayna Misr wa-Isra'il l-is-Salam Bad'at fi Ughustus 1952!' (Contacts for Peace between Egypt and Israel Began in August 1952!), *Akhbar al-Yaum*, 9.11.1985, 16.

Oren, Michael, 'Canada, the Great Powers and the Middle Eastern Arms Race, 1950–1956', *International History Review* 12 (1990), 280–300.

Oren, Michael, 'The Diplomatic Struggle for the Negev, 1946–1956', *Studies in Zionism* 10:2 (Autumn 1989), 197–215.

Oren, Michael B., 'Escalation to Suez: The Egypt–Israel Border War, 1949–56', *Journal of Contemporary History* 24 (1989), 347–72.

Oren, Michael B., 'Nuri al-Sa'id and the Question of Arab–Israel Peace, 1953–1957', *Asian and African Studies* 24:3 (November 1990), 267–82.

Oren, Michael, 'Secret Egypt–Israel Peace Initiatives Prior to the Suez Campaign', *Middle Eastern Studies* 26:3 (July 1990), 351–70.

Oren, Michael B., 'A Winter of Discontent: Britain's Crisis in Jordan, December 1955 – March 1956', *International Journal of Middle East Studies* 22:2 (May 1990), 171–84.

Peretz, Don, 'Development of the Jordan Valley Waters', *Middle East Journal* 9:4 (Autumn 1955), 397–412.

Quandt, William B., 'Influence through Arms Supply: The US Experience in the Middle East', *Arms Transfers to the Third World: The Military Buildup in Less Industrial Countries*, eds Uri Ra'anan, Robert L. Pfaltzgraff, Jr, and Geoffrey Kemp (Boulder: Westview Press, 1978), 121–30.

Ra'anan, Uri, 'Soviet Arms Transfers and the Problem of Political Leverage', in *Arms Transfers to the Third World: The Military Buildup in Less Industrial Countries*, eds Uri Ra'anan, Robert L. Pfaltzgraff, Jr, and Geoffrey Kemp (Boulder: Westview Press, 1978), 131–56.

Rabinovich, Itamar, 'Seven Wars and One Peace Treaty', in *The Arab–Israeli Conflict: Perspectives*, 2nd ed., ed. Alvin Z. Rubinstein (New York: Harper Collins, 1991), 34–58.

Rothman, Jay, 'Developing Pre-Negotiation Theory and Practice' (Project on Pre-Negotiation Update), Hebrew University of Jerusalem: Leonard Davis Institute, Policy Studies 29, May 1989.

Sela, Avraham, 'Transjordan, Israel and the 1948 War: Myth, Historiography and Reality', *Middle Eastern Studies* 28:4 (October 1992), 623–88.

Shamir, Shimon, 'The Collapse of Project Alpha', in *Suez 1956: The Crisis and its Consequences*, eds Wm. Roger Louis and Roger Owen, (Oxford: Clarendon Press, 1989), 73–100.

Shiffer, Varda, 'The 1949 Israeli Offer to Repatriate 100,000 Palestinian Refugees', *Middle East Focus* 9:2 (Fall 1986), 13–18.

Shlaim, Avi, 'Husni Za'im and the Plan to Resettle Palestinian Refugees in Syria', *Journal of Palestine Studies* 15:4 (no. 60) (Summer 1986), 68–80.

Slonim, Shlomo, 'Origins of the 1950 Tripartite Declaration on the Middle East', *Middle Eastern Studies* 23 (1987), 135–49.

Zartman, I. William, 'The Negotiation Process in the Middle East', in *The Arab–Israeli Search for Peace*, ed. Steven L. Spiegel (Boulder and London: Lynne Reinner, 1992), 63–70.

Index

Abd al-Nasir, Gamal xviii–xx, 42, 76–7, 84, 92–3, 95–104, 106–11, 114, 117–18, 123–9, 132, 134–6, 138, 140–1, 146–50, 152–76, 78–80, 184–7, 190, 192, 194, 198, 200–2, 204, 207–8, 210, 212–17, 220–42, 245–61, 265–6, 274–6, 279–81, 285, 287–9, 296–8, 307–8, 313, 317, 339–40, 343, 353–4, 358, 362, 364–6, 369, 372, 375, 381–4, 387–8
Abdullah bin Husain, King of Transjordan (1947–49) and of Jordan (1949–51) 8, 250, 266, 336
Abul-Huda, Tawfiq 37
Acheson, Dean 23, 61–2
Africa 159, 232, 259
Al-Ahram (Cairo daily) 19
Al-Akhbar (Cairo daily) 355–6
Alexandria 17
Allen, George V. 89, 114, 119, 134, 143, 158, 163, 208, 371
Allen, Roger 33, 55–6, 66, 292–3
Alteras, Isaac 68, 218, 377
American Council for Foreign Relations 133, 138
American Council for Judaism 36
Amman 8, 12, 32, 37, 40, 44–5, 52, 54, 75, 127–8, 134, 145, 271, 322
Anderson, Robert xviii–xx, 99, 196, 211, 213–18, 220–42, 245–54, 256–60, 264, 266–7, 274, 282, 287, 318, 378, 384, 386, 391
Angleton, James 231
Anglo-American Committee of Inquiry (1945–46) 3
Anglo-Egyptian Accord on British withdrawal from Suez bases 42, 74–6, 78, 112, 249, 267, 304
Anglo-Egyptian Treaty 74
Anglo-Jordanian Treaty 11, 267, 295, 297, 303

Ankara 62
Aqaba 7, 60, 64, 88, 90, 161, 172, 215, 230, 292–4, 315, 365
Arab blockade, economic boycott of Israel 38, 44, 67, 85, 94, 119, 145, 161, 167, 172, 185, 194, 197, 228, 230, 235, 263, 294–5, 298, 301–2, 316, 318
Arab League (League of Arab States) 38, 44, 46, 74–5, 146, 150, 165, 288, 301–2
Arab Legion 45, 249
Arab–Israeli war of 1948 xvi, xviii, xxi, 23, 27, 149, 168, 179, 213, 309
Arab–Israeli war of 1956 xvi, xxi–xxii, 96–7, 99, 165, 219, 224, 256, 280, 289, 386
Arab–Israeli war of 1973 xv
arms, armaments 19, 28–9, 36, 40–1, 43, 47, 55, 61, 77, 79–81, 84, 87, 98–100, 107, 112–13, 125–6, 135, 143–4, 149, 151–74, 176, 187–8, 194–5, 199, 202–19 *passim*, 221, 230, 233–5, 237–8, 242, 246–7, 252, 257–60, 265, 268, 272, 281, 283–8, 290, 305–6, 308–9, 311, 313–15, 317, 337, 350, 361, 365, 375, 377, 387, 389
armistice agreements *see* General Armistice Agreements
Aronson, Geoffrey 280
Arthur, G.G. 117, 175–6, 196
Associated Press (AP) 158
Aswan, High Dam 92, 124, 128, 132–3, 154, 159, 170, 173, 187, 194, 221–2, 224, 230, 248, 252, 254–7, 272, 283–9, 298, 303, 313, 349, 365
Atassi, Adnan 267–8
Athens 235, 237, 239, 248, 251
Attlee, Clement 115
al-Auja 60, 137, 147, 166–7, 231, 281, 309
Azazmeh tribe 29

Baghdad 18, 53–4, 143, 146, 284, 314
Baghdad Pact 97–101, 103–4, 124, 135, 152, 157, 199–200, 204, 223–4, 227, 232, 241, 249, 257–9, 265, 274, 279, 281, 288, 296, 312–14, 353, 364–5, 375, 384
Bahrain 249
Baker, Geoffrey H. 54
Bandung, conference of non-aligned nations (1955) 103, 106, 108–10, 113–14, 124, 152, 279, 288
Bangkok 97
Banyas 293
Barco, James 24–5
Bar-On, Mordechai xx, 164, 168, 196, 207–10, 218, 220, 258, 260, 276–7, 279, 285, 377
Bat Galim 42
Beersheba 60, 110, 147–8, 179, 191, 294
Beirut 21–2, 34, 84, 127–8
Belgrade 172
Ben-Gurion, David xviii–xix, 32, 53, 86, 95, 98, 100, 105–6, 112, 123, 138, 143, 161, 164–8, 181–3, 191, 193, 198, 200–2, 208, 212–18, 222, 225–6, 230–4, 237–9, 241–2, 245–8, 250–1, 253, 256, 259–60, 337, 362, 365–6, 372, 374, 384
Ben-Zvi, Abraham 269
Bergus, Donald 283, 286
Bernadotte, Count Folke xvi, 9, 23, 58–60, 263
Bernadotte Plan, Proposals (September 1948) 3, 9, 59–60, 64, 179, 191, 274
Bevin, Ernest 10, 60–1, 372
Bialer, Uri 112
al-Bilad as-Saudiyya (Saudi newspaper) 141–2
Black, Eugene 222
Blandford, John 236
Bnot Yaacov (Banat Yaqub) Bridge, water diversion project 35, 215, 230, 236, 271, 380
Bowker, R.J. 16–17, 22, 65
British Middle East Office (BMEO) 58, 63, 278
Brown, L. Carl 155
Brownell, George 221
Bunche, Dr Ralph S. (Acting UN Mediator) xvi, 9, 23, 60, 83, 119, 225
Buraimi 253, 365
Burdett, William 127
Burns, General E.L.M. 104–6, 136, 138, 207, 254, 309

Burns, William J. 152, 165–6, 248
Burrows, Sir Bernard A. 64, 292
Byroade, Henry 19, 25, 36, 43, 48, 89, 96, 100–3, 106–9, 111, 124–5, 127–8, 130, 133, 135–6, 140–1, 153, 155–7, 159, 165, 168–9, 173, 179, 184–6, 195, 200, 217, 256–7, 283, 297, 346–7, 371

Caffery, Jefferson 42–3, 321
Cairo xx, 7, 40, 42–3, 77–8, 92, 96, 98, 104–5, 110, 124–5, 127–8, 133–6, 138, 146, 152, 155–8, 165, 168, 173, 179, 184, 194–5, 200–2, 207, 211, 220, 222, 224–6, 228, 230–1, 234–7, 239, 241–2, 246, 248–9, 251–2, 255–8, 264, 287, 296, 307, 318, 358, 371, 388
Cairo Documents, The (Heikal) xix
Carr, E.H. xxi
Central Intelligence Agency (CIA) xviii, xx, 5, 100, 158, 165, 169, 173, 196, 200–1, 210, 212, 216, 220–2, 225–7, 230–1, 235–6, 241, 249–50, 258, 265, 320, 383
Chadwick, J.E. 17, 22
Chameleon, Operation 200, 210, 212, 222, 225, 236
Chapman-Andrews, Edwin Arthur 20–2, 34
Chase, Wilbur P. 350
China 255
Chinigo, Michael 365
Churchill, Sir Winston 6
coercive diplomacy xvii, xix, 67, 69, 82, 262, 269, 274, 280–3, 289
Cold War xvii, 4, 30, 46, 68, 80, 87–8, 157–8, 187–8, 190, 192, 194, 221, 223, 232–3, 238, 249, 255, 258, 264, 267, 280, 309, 311–14, 387
communism 60, 80, 86–8, 108, 157, 242, 249, 255, 258, 267, 280, 309
conciliation 5, 9, 117, 269, 273–4
confidence-building measures 41–5, 99, 241–2
conflict management 3, 5, 24, 27–48, 53, 104–6, 222, 271, 273, 289
conflict resolution 3, 27, 32, 41, 48–69, 271, 273, 289
Copeland, Miles 100, 220, 371, 374, 388, 391
Cortada, James 371
Crocker, Edward 18
Crossman, Richard 201
crypto-diplomacy xx, 200–1

INDEX

Cyprus 102, 111
Czechoslovakia 151–2, 155, 158–61, 188, 191, 281, 284, 358

Damascus 18, 22, 35, 53–4, 74, 134, 142, 207
Davis, Monnett B. 19
Dayan, General Moshe xx, 105, 161, 164, 168, 207, 212, 337, 342
Dead Sea 60
Dean, Arthur 157, 199, 221
defence, regional schemes xvii, 15–16, 26, 30, 47, 55, 65, 80, 82, 84, 103–4, 112–13, 153, 155, 165–6, 226–7, 267–9, 280, 290, 295–6, 298, 304, 311–12, 314; *see also* Northern Tier
Deuteronomy 262
Dhahariya 227
Dodds-Parker, A.D. 56
Donohue, James T.
Duke, Charles 37, 40, 45, 168
Dulles, Allen W. xx, 200, 212, 221, 230
Dulles, John Foster xviii–xx, 20, 33, 38, 42, 68, 75, 79, 81, 89, 92–4, 97, 103–4, 110–18, 123–50 *passim*, 153, 155, 157–63, 165, 168–70, 172, 175–6, 178, 182–3, 185, 188–91, 193–201, 203, 205, 208, 210–12, 214–15, 217, 224–5, 229–30, 235–7, 239, 246, 248, 253–6, 260–1, 265, 268, 274–5, 277, 280, 282–3, 287–8, 296, 346–7, 353, 365, 369–70; speech of August 1955 xix, 123–50 *passim*, 153–5, 158, 168, 170, 175, 178, 221, 283, 304–7, 309, 311, 316, 355

East Ghor irrigation scheme 292
Eban, Aubrey (Abba) xix, 23–4, 43, 113–14, 116, 119, 126, 134, 143–4, 161, 163, 192–3, 199, 207–9, 211, 215, 217, 225, 245, 259, 275, 282, 338, 361
economic sanctions 38, 40, 56, 65–6, 82, 101, 269–72
Eden, Sir Anthony xviii–xix, 33, 42, 53, 74–5, 78, 81–2, 89, 92, 95–7, 102, 111–12, 133, 135, 141, 156–7, 159, 187, 193–4, 202–3, 223, 249, 252, 254, 274–5, 280, 283, 288, 296, 351, 353; speech of November 1955 (Guildhall speech) xix, 168, 175–86, 189, 191, 194, 200–1, 203, 309–11, 366

Eilat 64, 90, 93, 110–11, 123, 144, 161, 181, 185, 190, 199, 230, 233, 275, 292–3, 299
Ein Gev 291, 293
Eisenhower, Dwight D. xviii–xix, 19, 58, 68, 79, 124, 129, 133, 156–9, 163, 214, 216, 221, 223–4, 226, 229, 232, 234, 239–42, 248, 251, 253, 257, 259, 267, 274, 280, 283, 287–8, 305–6, 348, 381–2, 384
Eisenhower, Milton 221
Elath (Epstein), Eliahu 74, 78, 118–19, 180, 203, 268, 320, 347
Eliav, Pinhas 379
Elijah 144
Ethridge, Mark 23, 61
Evans, Sir Francis E. 34, 39–40, 53–5
Eveland, Wilbur Crane xx, 196, 256, 265
Eytan, Dr Walter 85, 169, 209, 382

Falla, Paul S. 78
Fawzi, Dr Mahmud 30, 76–7, 106–10, 132–3, 135, 147–9, 173, 179, 183–6, 198, 221, 264, 275–6, 346, 352
fidayyin (commandos) 99–100, 136, 138, 306, 315
Fischer, Maurice 24
Foreign Relations of the United States (FRUS) xx
Foreign Office (UK) xix, 5, 7–12, 15–18, 21–4, 28, 31, 33–4, 36–8, 40–1, 44–5, 49–52, 54–67, 69, 74–5, 77–8, 81, 94–5, 103, 107, 109, 111, 117–19, 123, 126–8, 131, 134–5, 139, 141–2, 147, 150, 157, 159, 169, 171, 175, 177–8, 184, 186, 195–8, 200, 202, 207, 209, 221, 223, 249, 251, 260, 266, 268, 280–1, 284, 289, 292, 301, 368; Eight-Point Plan (1949) 11, 61–3; Levant Department 292
France xviii, 11, 17, 27–8, 30, 33, 41–2, 45, 55–6, 62, 91, 134, 163, 166, 205, 209, 212, 218–19, 261, 285, 290, 295, 297, 301–3, 326–9
Fritzlan, A. David 322
Furlonge, Sir Geoffrey 7, 11–12, 16, 52–5, 268, 325

Galilee 59, 179, 196, 205, 249, 270, 294
Gamma, Operation xviii, 201, 220, 225, 245, 248, 265, 289
Gardener, John 22–3, 54–5
Garfinkle, Adam 141–2, 370

Gaza 41, 60, 76, 78, 88, 95, 97–102, 104–7, 110, 123–5, 136–8, 147, 161, 201, 210, 227, 279, 281, 294, 299, 345, 371–2, 389; Israeli raid on (February 1955) 97–102, 104, 112, 114, 149, 152, 155, 168, 207, 236, 288, 296–7, 342, 347, 374
Gazit, Mordechai 8, 337
General Armistice Agreements (GAAs) xvi, 12, 27–8, 30–2, 36, 38–40, 46–7, 82–3, 98, 119, 139, 145, 167, 176–7, 180, 182, 214, 250, 264, 273, 288, 290, 292, 301–2, 304, 306, 310, 313, 315–17, 387; Article VIII 38; Article XII 12, 32, 37–9, 56, 74, 101, 105
Geneva 157, 161–3, 165, 172–6, 183, 212, 265, 273, 309
Geren, Paul F. 32, 145
Gerges, Fawaz 258
Germany 23, 247
Ginat, Rami 358
Glubb, General Sir John Bagot 6, 36, 249, 252
Goldmann, Nahum 246–7, 250, 382
good offices 56, 73–5, 78, 128, 272–3, 326
Gordenker, Leon 263
Guildhall speech *see* Eden

Haifa 22, 41, 44–5, 51, 59, 62, 64, 85, 88, 142, 145, 193, 266, 292–3, 295, 301, 316, 331
el–Hamma 291, 293
Hammarskjöld, Dag 37, 207, 231, 234, 246, 254
Hare, Raymond 34–5, 90
Harel, Isser 211–12, 238, 384
Hart, Parker T. 158, 358
Hebrew University and Hospital 291
Hebron 294
Heikal, Mohamed H. xix, 98, 227, 229, 241, 287
Helm, Sir Alexander Knox 15
Herzog, Yaacov xix, 225–6, 231, 237
Hitler, Adolf 166
Hobbes, Thomas 262
Holmes, Edward Warren 322
Hoover, Herbert J., Jr. 91–2, 153–5, 217–18, 247, 251, 253, 287
Huleh 291, 293
Husain, King of Jordan 78, 223, 249, 252
Hussein, Ahmad 132–3, 146, 165, 255

immigration to Israel 35, 123, 138, 141, 231
International Bank for Reconstruction and Development (IBRD) 159, 222, 286–7
intifada xv
Iran 158, 286, 314
Iraq 22, 52, 59, 62, 66, 73, 78–81, 97–8, 103–4, 112, 135, 143, 146, 169, 175, 178–9, 199, 232, 242, 257–8, 266, 268, 281, 283–4, 293–4, 296–9, 304, 307–8, 312, 353, 387
Ireland, Philip W. 47
Israel: relations and negotiations with Jordan, Lebanon, Syria *see* Jordan, Lebanon, Syria
Israel Defence Forces (IDF) 60, 98–100, 154, 161, 164, 167–8, 172, 205–8, 285
Israel Ministry of Foreign Affairs (IMFA) 38–9, 66, 84–5, 100, 115, 118, 169, 172, 180, 187, 193, 195, 226, 285, 379
Istanbul 33
Italy 3, 313

Jackson, Elmore 138, 226
Jaffa 142
Jernegan, John 80–1, 90
Jerusalem xix, xxi, 35, 46, 56, 59, 61, 73, 104, 139, 144, 147, 166, 170, 185, 193–5, 197, 201, 213, 228, 231, 235, 237, 239, 241–2, 248, 291–4, 299–303, 306, 317
Jerusalem Post 38
Jidda 48
Johnston, Eric 52, 58, 90, 131, 141, 200, 295, 304, 340; mission (plans for shared use of the Jordan waters) 56, 58, 66, 81, 89–92, 107, 114, 117, 128, 131–2, 141, 150, 165, 194, 200, 230, 235, 239, 241, 249, 251, 274, 288, 296–7, 302–4, 309–10, 313–16, 318, 340, 362, 369
Jones, Lewis 123
Jordan, Hashemite Kingdom xviii–xix, 33, 36, 62, 75–6, 78, 86–8, 103–4, 107, 109, 124–5, 133, 136, 141, 144–6, 150, 158, 174, 178, 187, 189, 191, 193, 199, 223, 227, 233, 242, 247, 250–1, 266, 294, 297, 304, 317, 335–6; relations and negotiations with Israel xvi, 7–8, 12–13, 23, 29–34, 37–41, 44–6, 51, 64, 82, 93, 95, 141–2, 231, 250, 273, 291, 295, 297, 300–1, 315–16, 327–8, 331
Jordan River 52, 56, 58, 66, 89–90, 117, 128, 139, 165, 170, 194, 197, 200, 210,

INDEX

230, 235, 241, 249, 271, 274, 288, 292–3, 302–3, 313–14 *see also* Johnston, Eric, mission

Kalkilya 276
Karamé, Rashid 178
Kfar Saba 276
al–Khalidi, Dr Husain Fakhri 142
Khan Yunis 137–8
al–Khouri, Faris 78
Kinneret, Lake (Sea of Galilee) 198, 205–9, 212, 270
Kirkbride, Sir Alec 8
Kirkpatrick, Sir Ivone 159, 171–2, 209, 284, 307–8, 364
Kissufim 105
Knesset 166, 181–2, 196
Kollek, Amos xix
Kollek, Teddy xix, 127, 225, 231, 237
Kyle, Keith 109, 161, 223, 252, 272, 276, 278, 339, 364, 380

Ladas, Alex 210
Latrun 299
Laurence, P.H. 386
Lausanne, conference (1949) at xvi, 11, 23, 58, 61, 271, 273–4
Lausanne Protocol 169, 363
Lavon, Pinhas 100; 'Lavon affair' 43–4
Lawson, Edward B. 112, 127–8, 132, 136, 144, 149, 182–3, 212, 215, 278, 348, 350
League of Arab States *see* Arab League
Lebanon 20, 104, 125, 169, 178–9, 295, 304, 316, 366; relations and negotiations with Israel 31, 58, 299
Lloyd, Selwyn 55–6, 73–4, 78, 249, 254–5, 375
local commanders' agreements (LCAs) 35, 40
London xvii–xviii, xxi, 7–9, 14, 17, 20, 31, 33–4, 36, 42, 56–7, 59–60, 62, 65, 73, 75, 77, 79, 81, 84, 86, 89, 95, 101–3, 109–12, 114–15, 118, 125–30, 133–5, 141, 147–51, 153–5, 163, 165, 170, 175–6, 178–80, 183–5, 189, 191–2, 195–8, 203, 207, 218, 247, 249, 252, 256, 260, 267–8, 278, 281, 288, 290, 296–303, 311, 347
Lovett, Robert 10
Lucas, W. Scott xx

Macmillan, Harold 111, 117–18, 129–33, 135, 140, 162, 165, 168, 172–3, 175, 184–5, 195, 199–200, 265, 274, 277–8,
288, 347, 353, 355
Madrid xv, 387
Makins, Sir Roger 42, 81, 127–8, 135, 188–9, 195, 287
Malta 111
Mansion House *see* Eden, speech of November 1955
McGhee, George 28–9, 62–3
mediation xviii, 5, 9, 24, 39–40, 58, 75, 78, 81, 91, 117–18, 138, 194, 200–1, 214, 220–6, 235, 252–3, 257, 259, 263, 266, 273–4
Mefalsim 136–7
Middle East Command 388
Middle East Defence Organization 20, 388
military balance, Arab–Israeli 35–6, 43, 47, 112, 116, 156–7, 161–3, 187, 202, 211, 213–14, 217, 252, 260–1, 265, 268, 284–5, 309, 311, 313, 375
Mixed Armistice Commissions (MACs) 31–2, 35–6
Montagu-Pollock, William H. 18
Moose, James S., Jr. 35
Morris, Benny 99, 101, 218, 285
Morrison–Grady talks (1946) 3
Moscow 153–4, 157
Mosadeq, Mohammed 286
Mossad 191, 212, 238
Mount of Olives 316
Mount Scopus 51, 95, 194, 291–3, 316
Muhi al-Din, Colonel Zakaria 216, 225–8, 236, 239, 242, 249
Munich 180, 191–4
Mussolini 252
Myerson (Meir), Golda 180, 187, 202–3

Naharayyim 29
Nahhalin 106
Nasser *see* Abd al-Nasir
National Security Council *see* United States, National Security Council
Nazareth 142
Negev xviii–xix, 7, 59–60, 62, 64, 76–8, 90, 92–3, 95, 97, 108–11, 123, 126, 132–3, 139, 141, 144, 147–50, 169–70, 174, 179–81, 185–9, 191–5, 197–9, 202–3, 210, 227–8, 231–3, 235–6, 238, 241, 245, 247, 266, 275, 277–8, 294, 299, 316, 336, 346–7, 352, 369–70, 372, 382, 389
Nehru, Jawaharlal 188
New York 30, 37, 56, 129, 133, 138, 147, 180, 200–2

Newsweek (magazine) 123
Nicholls, Jack 55, 77–9, 85, 117–18, 132, 135, 169, 178, 180–1, 183, 188, 191–2, 195, 202, 278–9, 281–2, 347, 372
Nile River 170
Nitzana 147, 166
Nobel Prize 119
North Atlantic Treaty Organization (NATO) 118, 313
Northern Tier Defence Scheme 98, 103–4, 157, 223, 268, 279, 307, 312–14
Nusrat, Mustafa 7
Nutting, Anthony 42, 76–8, 130–1

oil xv, 4, 21–2, 57, 59, 62, 67, 87, 171, 265–6, 275, 282, 311
Olive Leaves, Operation 207
Oliver, Peter R. 15, 18, 50–1
Omega, Operation xviii, 158, 252–6, 261
Oren, Michael xx, 175, 220, 259, 279, 338, 341, 353, 383, 389
Ottawa 103
Oslo xv

Pakistan 303
Palestine 3, 62, 68–9, 74, 142–3, 239, 284, 300
Palestine, Arab refugees *see* refugees
Palestinian–Israeli relations and negotiations xv, 380
Palmer, Ely 23, 58
Paris 61–2, 89, 110, 118, 127, 155, 161–5, 209, 212, 342
Paris, conference (1951) at xvi, 11–12, 23–4, 57–8, 273–4
patron–client relationships 269–72, 284, 288–9
Peace in the Middle East: A Record of Israel's Peace Offers to Arab States (1955) 195
Persian Gulf 87
Poland 358
Porter, Paul A. 23
prenegotiation xviii, 72, 82, 272, 289, 350
press, Arabic 12, 100, 135, 142–3, 146, 179, 202, 207, 237, 366
press, Israeli 42, 180, 188, 203
preventive diplomacy 385
'preventive war' 40, 47, 53–5, 164–6, 179, 207, 210, 212, 217, 221, 377
Public Record Office (PRO) 340, 352

Qibya 30, 32, 101, 106, 270

Quai d'Orsay 37
quiet diplomacy 270

Rabinovich, Itamar 146, 319
Rafael, Gideon 84–5, 163, 172, 207, 225–6, 237, 256, 361
Rapp, Sir Thomas 63–5
Rifa'i, Samir 322
refugees, Palestinian-Arab xvii, 5, 14, 16, 22–5, 35, 43, 46, 54, 59, 61–2, 64, 66, 68–9, 73–6, 85, 87–8, 92–3, 95, 107, 110, 112, 114, 117, 119, 127, 133, 136, 138–40, 142–3, 145, 147–8, 163, 170, 176–7, 185–6, 188, 193, 196–7, 199, 202, 210, 222, 227–9, 233–6, 238, 241, 250–1, 263, 271, 276, 291, 293–4, 299, 302–6, 309–10, 316–17, 341, 368, 380
reprisal raids xv, 4, 24–5, 30–2, 35, 40, 45–7, 105–6, 113, 123, 138, 164, 167, 188, 196, 205, 207–9, 215, 230, 270, 285, 297, 306
revisionist historians xx, 99, 285
Revolutionary Command Council, Egypt (RCC) 76, 91, 98, 245
Rhodes, negotiations at xvi, 9–10, 59, 83, 114, 225
Richmond, J.C.B. 44, 75
Riley, General William E. 327
Roosevelt, Kermit (Kim) 158, 200, 225
Ross, Archibald D.M. 64, 292
round table conference proposals 33, 55–6
Rusk, Dean 221
Russell, Francis H. xvii, xix, 20, 25, 35–7, 39, 80, 84, 89–91, 94–5, 101–4, 110–12, 115, 124–6, 129–30, 132–3, 135, 147–50, 155–6, 171–2, 175, 190–3, 195, 197–9, 204–5, 209–10, 223, 237, 239, 246–7, 264–5, 276–7, 280, 285–8, 300n, 311, 319, 350

al-Sabha 137, 167–8
Sabri, Ali 225, 229, 239, 241–2, 249, 256, 258, 381–2
Sa'id, Khairat 201
Sa'id, Nuri 73, 98, 135, 146, 150, 175, 178–9, 223, 265, 274, 281, 284, 339, 353, 366
Salem, Major Salah 76
Sargent, Sir Orme 10
Sa'ud ibn Abd al-Aziz, King of Saudi Arabia 78, 254
Saudi Arabia 64, 78, 179, 249–50, 253–4, 292–3, 304, 312, 365, 378, 387

INDEX

Schmidt, Dana Adams 324
Schneerson, 118
security guarantee, treaty 55, 92–3, 102–3, 107, 111–16, 118–20, 125, 127, 129–31, 142–4, 162–3, 188, 218–19, 272, 285, 295–8, 301–3, 306, 310, 312, 344, 351
Shamir, Shimon xx, 218, 256, 259, 264, 266, 275, 277–8, 280, 319
Sharett (Shertok), Moshe xix, 46, 53, 78–9, 86, 94–5, 99, 102, 105, 111–13, 115–19, 124, 127, 132, 134–6, 138, 143–5, 149, 161–3, 166, 180, 182–3, 187–201 *passim*, 205, 208–13, 215, 217–18, 231, 233–4, 237, 242, 247, 255, 260, 285, 295–6, 298, 320, 337, 341, 343, 348, 370, 374, 384
Sharett, Yaacov xix
Shertok *see* Sharett
Shiffer, Varda 334
Shiloah, Reuven 145, 163, 191–2, 195–9, 201, 320, 370
Shimoni, Yaacov 320
Shimshoni, Jonathan 99, 164, 167
Shishakli, Adib 286
Shuckburgh, Evelyn xvii, xx, 44, 75, 81, 84–91, 93–4, 96, 101–3, 107, 109–12, 114–15, 117–18, 124–5, 130, 132, 148–50, 156, 163, 169, 171–2, 175–6, 180, 185, 198, 207–9, 223, 252, 254–6, 265–6, 274, 276–7, 280, 284, 288, 294–5, 338–9, 346–7, 364–5, 369, 390
Shuqayri, Ahmad 74–5, 363
shuttle diplomacy 58, 105–6, 138, 213, 225, 248, 252
Sinai Peninsula 142, 147, 161, 164, 166, 172, 299–300, 386, 389
Smith, General Walter Bedell 47, 80
South Carolina 129
Spiegel, Steven 157–8
State Department *see* United States, Department of State
Stephens, Robert 366
Sterndale-Bennett, Sir John 278, 281
Stevenson, Sir Ralph 17–18, 96–7, 102–3, 107, 109, 124–5, 128, 130
Streibert, Ted 201, 234
Sudan 308, 313
Suez Canal 22, 41–2, 74, 76, 94, 117, 156, 172, 185, 224, 249, 255–6, 267, 270, 295, 298, 301–2, 384
Suez crisis *see* Arab–Israeli war of 1956
Sunday Times (London) 182
Sweden 300

Symes, Harrison M. 371
Syria 23, 58, 78, 104, 136, 145, 179, 207–8, 250–1, 267–8, 294–5, 299, 304;
  relations and negotiations with Israel 7, 29–32, 35, 54, 58, 64, 205, 208–9, 249, 270, 286, 291, 293–4, 315, 326, 380

Tel Aviv 7–8, 15, 17, 19–20, 22–3, 25, 34–5, 39–40, 45, 53, 79–80, 91, 95, 104–6, 112–13, 117–19, 127–8, 132, 134–5, 138, 148, 168–9, 178, 180, 183, 185, 187–8, 191, 200–3, 212, 220, 226, 251, 278, 281, 299, 322
Tel Aviv University 20
Templer, General Sir Gerald 223
Tennessee Valley Authority (TVA) 292–3
terrorism xv, 32, 136, 354
Times, The (London daily) 126, 195, 203
Tiberias, Lake 205, 207, 209, 212, 291, 293–5; *see also* Galilee, Kinneret
Tiran Straits 164, 172, 207
Touval, Saadia xix, 220, 224–5, 259, 266, 320, 383
Transjordan 59
Trevelyan, Sir Humphrey 147, 149–50, 173–4, 179, 184–6, 202, 221, 368
Trieste dispute, model for negotiations 33, 75, 78, 81–2, 90–1, 140, 184, 201
Tripartite Declaration (1950) 11, 27–31, 35, 37, 41, 54, 80, 89, 91, 101, 157, 165, 172, 222, 260, 272, 290–1, 293, 295, 311, 313
Tripp, J.P. 77
Troutbeck, Sir John 18, 54–5
Truman, Harry S. 10, 19, 23
Turkey 11, 97, 103, 296–8, 302–3, 307

Unified Development Plan (for Jordan waters) *see* Johnston, Eric, mission
Union of Soviet Socialist Republics (USSR) xvii, 4, 15, 18, 20, 25, 28, 30, 33, 66, 68, 79–80, 98–101, 125–6, 132–3, 143, 151–8, 161–73, 187–8, 192, 194, 200, 205, 211–15, 217–18, 221, 232–3, 238, 242, 252, 254, 259, 264, 266–8, 274–5, 280–1, 284–5, 288, 307–9, 312, 314–15, 350, 358, 365, 388–9
United Nations Charter 38
United Nations Conciliation Commission for Palestine (PCC) xvi, 9, 11, 23–5, 57–9, 61–2, 116, 273, 300;
  Comprehensive Pattern of Proposals (1951) 57–8

United Nations General Assembly
(UNGA) 9, 12, 34–5, 59–60, 64, 170,
175, 177–8, 191, 201, 263, 292; UNGA
Resolution 194 (11 December 1948)
20, 60, 75
United Nations Partition Plan, Resolution
(November 1947) 5, 51, 73, 78, 110,
117, 142, 169, 175–80, 182, 189, 294,
310, 313, 336
United Nations Relief and Works Agency
(UNRWA) 292–3, 299–300, 303
United Nations Secretary-General (UNSG
see also Hammarskjöld, Dag) xvi, 12,
37–9, 56, 134, 207, 231, 234, 239, 254,
289, 302
United Nations Security Council (UNSC)
9, 30, 43, 56, 101, 182, 196, 207, 209,
212, 222, 230, 253, 262, 270, 290;
UNSC Resolutions: (September 1951)
42–3; (November 1953) 30; (March
1955) 101; (January 1956) 196, 209,
230
United Nations Special Committee on
Palestine (1947) 3
United Nations Truce Supervisory
Organization (UNTSO) 24, 31–2, 36,
46, 88, 104–5, 138, 207, 254, 271, 281,
302, 309
United States: Congress 75, 81, 91, 93–4;
Department of State xviii–xx, 3, 5, 10,
17–20, 24–5, 28–31, 33–7, 40–1, 43,
47–9, 51, 58–9, 61–2, 64–7, 69, 80–3,
90, 92–3, 95–6, 101, 107–9, 111,
114–15, 118–19, 123–9, 142–3, 149,
152–6, 163, 165, 168, 171–2, 176, 186,
188, 191–3, 195–201, 207, 209–10, 212,
216–17, 219, 221–2, 234, 242, 246–7,
251–3, 259–61, 265, 268, 271, 282–3,
289, 292, 307, 315, 322, 358;

Information Agency (USIA) 201, 234,
366; National Archives (USNA) 296,
298–301, 340; National Security
Council (NSC) 33–4, 67, 158–9, 183;
Near East Affairs (Department of
State) 83, 209–10, 221, 260 ; Senate
115
US News & World Report 46
Uvda, Operation 60

Vatican 301
Volcano, Operation 167–8

Wadsworth, James 48
Wafd party 223
Wardrop, J.C. 15–16, 50–1
Washington xvii–xix, xxi, 7–9, 11, 14, 20,
23–5, 31, 34, 36, 38, 42, 51–2, 57,
59–62, 64–6, 75, 81, 83, 89–96, 103,
113, 125, 127, 131–2, 134–5, 145–6,
153, 155–6, 159, 163, 165, 168–70,
179, 183, 185, 188, 191–6, 199, 201,
204, 207, 209, 212–18, 220, 222, 229,
237, 239–40, 245, 252–4, 256, 260,
267–8, 282, 288, 292, 311, 313, 315,
320
West Bank of Jordan River 45, 59
White Paper (1939) 190
White, Ivan 127, 372
Wilson, Bill 46
World Jewish Congress 247
Wright, Michael 60, 284

al-Yafi, Abdullah 20–1
Yaniv, Avner 337
Yarmuk River 62, 194, 292–3, 316
Yugoslavia 33

Zartman, I. William 269

For Product Safety Concerns and Information please contact our EU
representative GPSR@taylorandfrancis.com
Taylor & Francis Verlag GmbH, Kaufingerstraße 24, 80331 München, Germany